D0463632

JOHN GAMBLE KIRKWOOD
COLLECTED WORKS

Theory of Solutions

Documents on Modern Physics

Edited by

ELLIOTT W. MONTROLL, Institute of Defense Analyses

GEORGE H. VINEYARD, Brookhaven National Laboratory

MAURICE LÉVY, Université de Paris

A. ABRAGAM, L'Effet Mössbauer
H. BACRY, Lectures on Group Theory
K. G. BUDDEN, Lectures on Magnetoionic Theory
J. W. CHAMBERLAIN, Motion of Charged Particles in the Earth's Magnetic Field
S. CHAPMAN, Solar Plasma and Geomagnetism and Aurora
H. CHIU, Neutrino Astrophysics
A. H. COTTRELL, Theory of Crystal Dislocations
R. H. DALITZ, The Quark Model for Elementary Particles
BRYCE S. DEWITT, Dynamical Theory of Groups and Fields
R. H. DICKE, The Theoretical Significance of Experimental Relativity
M. GOURDIN, Laws of Symmetry Theorem of T.C.P.
D. HESTENES, Space-Time Algebras
JOHN G. KIRKWOOD, Selected Topics in Statistical Mechanics
JOHN G. KIRKWOOD, Macromolecules
JOHN G. KIRKWOOD, Theory of Liquids
JOHN G. KIRKWOOD, Theory of Solutions
JOHN G. KIRKWOOD, Proteins
JOHN G. KIRKWOOD, Quantum Statistics and Cooperative Phenomena
JOHN G. KIRKWOOD, Shock and Detonation Waves
JOHN G. KIRKWOOD, Dielectrics—Intermolecular Forces—Optical Rotation
V. KOURGANOFF, Stellar Nuclear Reactions and Internal Structure
ROBERT LATTÈS, Methods of Resolutions of Some Boundary Problems in Mathematical Physics
P. H. E. MEIJER, Quantum Statistical Mechanics
A. B. PIPPARD, The Dynamics of Conduction Electrons
H. REEVES, Stellar Evolution and Nucleosynthesis
L. SCHWARTZ, Applications of Distributions to the Theory of Elementary Particles in Quantum Mechanics
M. TINKHAM, Superconductivity
H. VAN REGEMORTER and O. BELY, Les Collisions Atome-Electron

JOHN GAMBLE KIRKWOOD
1907 – 1959

JOHN GAMBLE KIRKWOOD
COLLECTED WORKS

General Editor

IRWIN OPPENHEIM

Professor of Chemistry
Massachusetts Institute of Technology

Theory of Solutions

Edited by

Z. W. SALSBURG

Department of Chemistry
Rice University
Houston, Texas

GORDON AND BREACH

Science Publishers

New York · London · Paris

Copyright © 1968 by Gordon and Breach, Science Publishers, Inc.
150 Fifth Avenue, New York, N.Y. 10011

Library of Congress Catalog Card Number 65–16161

Editorial Office for Great Britain:
Gordon and Breach, Science Publishers, Ltd.
8 Bloomsbury Way, London, W.C.1

Editorial Office for France:
Gordon and Breach
7—9 rue Emile Dubois, Paris 14

Distribution en France par:
Dunod Editeur
92 rue Bonaparte, Paris 6

Distributed in Canada by:
The Ryerson Press
299 Queen Street West, Toronto 2B, Ontario

PRINTED IN ENGLAND BY W. S. COWELL LTD, IPSWICH

Documents on Modern Physics

Seventy years ago when the fraternity of physicists was smaller than the audience at a weekly physics colloquium in a major university a J. Willard Gibbs could, after ten years of thought, summarize his ideas on a subject in a few monumental papers or in a classic treatise. His competition did not intimidate him into a muddled correspondence with his favorite editor nor did it occur to his colleagues that their own progress was retarded by his leisurely publication schedule.

Today the dramatic phase of a new branch of physics spans less than a decade and subsides before the definitive treatise is published. Moreover modern physics is an extremely interconnected discipline and the busy practitioner of one of its branches must be kept aware of break-throughs in other areas. An expository literature which is clear and timely is needed to relieve him of the burden of wading through tentative and hastily written papers scattered in many journals.

To this end we have undertaken the editing of a new series, entitled *Documents on Modern Physics*, which will make available selected reviews, lecture notes, conference proceedings, and important collections of papers in branches of physics of special current interest. Complete coverage of a field will not be a primary aim. Rather, we will emphasize readability, speed of publication, and importance to students and research workers. The books will appear in low-cost paper-covered editions, as well as in cloth covers. The scope will be broad, the style informal.

From time to time, older branches of physics come alive again, and forgotten writings acquire relevance to recent developments. We expect to make a number of such works available by including them in this series along with new works.

ELLIOTT MONTROLL
GEORGE H. VINEYARD
MAURICE LÉVY

The Publishers wish to express their gratitude to the following organizations for permission to quote and reprint material from the journals and books mentioned:

The American Institute of Physics for: *Journal of Chemical Physics*, Vol. 3, "Statistical Mechanics of Fluid Mixtures," pp. 300–313 (1935).

Journal of Chemical Physics, Vol. 2, "Theory of Solutions of Molecules Containing Widely Separated Charges with Special Application to Zwitterions," pp. 351–361 (1934).

Journal of Chemical Physics, Vol. 2, "On the Theory of Strong Electrolyte Solutions," pp. 767–781 (1934).

Journal of Chemical Physics, Vol. 6, "The Electrostatic Influence of Substituents on the Dissociation Constants of Organic Acids. I," pp. 506–512 (1938).

Journal of Chemical Physics, Vol. 6, "The Electrostatic Influence of Substituents on the Dissociation Constants of Organic Acids. II," pp. 513–517 (1938).

Journal of Chemical Physics, Vol. 18, "Light Scattering Arising from Composition Fluctuations in Multi-Component Systems," pp. 54–57 (1950).

Journal of Chemical Physics, Vol. 19, "The Statistical Mechanical Theory of Solutions. I," pp. 774–777 (1951).

Journal of Chemical Physics, Vol. 20, "The Free Volume Theory of Multi-Component Fluid Mixtures," pp. 1538-43 (1952).

Journal of Chemical Physics, Vol. 26, "Theory of Multi-Component Fluid Mixtures. I. Statistical Order–Disorder Analysis in Multi-Component Fluid Mixtures," pp. 1533–41 (1957).

Journal of Chemical Physics, Vol. 27, "Theory of Multi-Component Fluid Mixtures. II. A Corresponding States Treatment," pp. 505–514 (1957).

Journal of Chemical Physics, Vol. 32, "Theory of the Heat of Transport of Electrolyte Solutions," pp. 857–866 (1959).

Journal of Chemical Physics, Vol. 33, "Theory of the Diffuse Double Layer," pp. 1282–90 (1960)

The American Chemical Society for: *Chemical Reviews*, Vol. 19, "Statistical Mechanics of Liquid Solutions," pp. 275–307 (1936).

Chemical Reviews, Vol. 24, "Theoretical Studies upon Dipolar Ions," pp. 233–251 (1939).

Journal of Physical Chemistry, Vol. 43, "Order and Disorder in Liquid Solutions," pp. 97–107 (1939).

Journal of Physical Chemistry, Vol. 58, "The Statistical Mechanical Basis of the Debye–Hückel Theory of Strong Electrolytes," pp. 591–596 (1954).

Annual Reviews of Physical Chemistry, Vol. 2, "Solutions of Nonelectrolytes," pp. 51–56 (1951).

Physikalische Zeitschrift, 33. Jahrg., "Das Verhalten von Zwitterionen und von mehrwertigen Ionen mit weit entfernten Ladungen in Electrolytlosungen Heft 7," pp. 297–300 (1932).

Journal of Polymer Science, Vol. 9, "The Radial Distribution Functions of Electrically Charged Macromolecules," pp. 519–524 (1952).

Preface to the Kirkwood Papers

The following pages contain a reprinting of all the articles published by John Gamble Kirkwood and some of his reports to government agencies. Kirkwood's scientific work covered a wide variety of fields and for this reason it seemed suitable to publish his collected works in two formats. The first consists of a series of eight paper-back volumes each of which presents all of Kirkwood's work on a restricted topic. The papers in each of these volumes are, in general, arranged chronologically. The second format consists of two hard-cover volumes in which all of his work is arranged chronologically. The hard-cover volumes contain all of the papers in the paper-back volumes in addition to several miscellaneous papers which do not appear in any of the paper-back volumes.

Each of the paper-back volumes has been edited by a distinguished scientist who has been closely associated with that portion of Kirkwood's work covered in the particular volume. These editors have written introductions for the various volumes reviewing Kirkwood's work and placing it in historical perspective. These introductions also appear in the hard-cover volumes. Since all of the papers have been reset in type for these volumes, it has been possible to incorporate into them addenda and corrigenda that have appeared in the literature as well as those that have been supplied by co-authors of the various papers and by the editors. It has been the responsibility of the individual editors to incorporate this material and to proof-read the final manuscripts.

The contents and editors of the individual paper-back volumes are:

Dielectrics; Intermolecular Forces; Optical Rotation
Edited by R. B. Cole
Solution Theory: Non-Electrolytes and Electrolytes
Edited by J. C. Poirier and Z. W. Salsburg
Quantum Statistics; Cooperative Phenomena
Edited by F. H. Stillinger
Shock and Detonation Waves Edited by W. W. Wood
Liquid Theory Edited by B. J. Alder
Proteins Edited by G. Scatchard
Transport Processes Edited by R. W. Zwanzig
Macromolecules Edited by P. L. Auer

A bibliography of Kirkwood's work is given in the hard-cover volumes.

Acknowledgments are due to the co-authors of many of the papers for supplying corrigenda and to the editors of the individual volumes without whom this work could not have been published. A special acknowledgment has to be made to Platonia K. Kirkwood for her help and advice in the preparation of this work.

IRWIN OPPENHEIM
Cambridge, Massachusetts

Contents

Introduction to the "Non-Electrolyte Solution Theory" Section of the "Collected Papers of John Gamble Kirkwood"

by Zevi W. Salsburg, *William Marsh Rice University, Houston, Texas*

I. HISTORICAL COMMENTS

The contributions to solution theory covered in these papers fall into five fairly well defined historical and logical groups.

(A) 1934–1938: The Development of the Molecular Distribution Function Theories of Fluid Mixtures.

This development is given in papers 7 and 19 of this series. The first of these articles is by far the most significant for it represents the first introduction of the general method of using molecular distribution functions in the statistical mechanical theory of fluids. This study led to the Kirkwood Integral Equation for the radial distribution function in liquids. In addition, the well-known Kirkwood superposition approximation was introduced in paper number 7.

The approach to the statistical mechanical theory of fluids introduced at this point has been used by many workers in the field and still occupies a central position in current statistical mechanical theories.

Similar developments were presented later by M. Born and H. S. Green[1] and by J. E. Mayer[2] and are basically equivalent to the theory of Kirkwood.

Concurrently but independently of Kirkwood, J. Yvon[3] in France developed the molecular distribution function theory of fluids which differed from Kirkwood's only in certain details. Because of its relative inaccessibility, the work of Yvon was overlooked by Kirkwood and his co-workers until about 1948.

In both papers 7 and 19 only the qualitative aspects of Kirkwood's theory for non-electrolyte solutions are discussed. Most of the emphasis of these papers is on the theory of electrolyte solutions. It is important to note that the application of this theory to solutions depends upon obtaining the chemical potential which in turn requires the general distribution function as a function of the coupling parameter λ.

(B) 1938–1940: Lattice Theories of Non-Electrolyte Solutions.

Paper 25 represents the application of Kirkwood's work on order-disorder theory in solids to the lattice model of liquid solutions, and should

[1] M. Born and H. S. Green, *Proc. Roy. Soc.* **A188**, 10 (1946).
[2] J. E. Mayer, *J. Chem. Phys.* **15**, 187 (1947).
[3] Y. Yvon, Actualites Scientifiques et Industrielles (Hermann et cie, Paris, 1935), p. 203.

be read in conjunction with the article on the moment expansion method.[4] This study can be considered as a detailed analysis of the lattice models proposed by Hildebrand, Scatchard, Guggenheim and Rushbrooke.[5] It was instrumental in showing that the local order effect in regular solution theory was relatively small and was not a major problem in solution theory.

(C) 1950–1952: Fluctuation Theories of Multi-Component Systems.

This work, carried out with the collaboration of R. J. Goldberg and F. P. Buff, represents one of the most significant contributions to the theory of solutions. The development is contained in papers 71 and 84 with some additional features in paper 81, a review article.

The study of the molecular theory of light scattering (Paper 71) led to the investigation of composition fluctuations in multi-component systems. Kirkwood and Buff then formulated a general theory of solutions based on this study in which the thermodynamic properties of mixtures could be expressed in terms of the radial distribution functions. This theory complemented the earlier papers by Kirkwood (numbers 7 and 19) and formed a more satisfactory method of using the molecular distribution functions.

The Kirkwood-Buff theory stands with the earlier work of McMillan and Mayer[6] as a completely general technique for both classical and quantum mechanical multi-component systems.

While Kirkwood's first theory as represented in paper number 7 required the use of a coupling parameter to discuss the properties of solutions in terms of molecular distribution functions the Kirkwood-Buff formulation expresses these properties directly in terms of the usual distribution functions.

(D) 1952–1957: Free Volume and Corresponding States Theories of Solutions.

In his earlier paper on lattice theories of solutions (number 25) Professor Kirkwood suggested that the extension of this theory to the cell model was of much greater significance in solution theory than more elaborate treatments of the order-disorder problem. Papers number (100) and (114) were a result of carrying out this suggestion.

The work in these articles parallels and is essentially equivalent to the earlier studies published by Prigogine and his co-workers.[7] Although the theory is developed from the point of view of the Kirkwood integral equation for the cell model[8] most of the effort centers about the order-disorder analysis involving the occupational configurations of the cells.

It was later realized that the solution of the order-disorder problem encountered above was not restricted to the cell model but could be extended to an arbitrary configuration of molecules. This extension was carried out in paper number 142 and resulted in general relations between the properties of a fluid mixture and a fictitious pure fluid.

---

[4] J. G. Kirkwood, *J. Chem. Phys.* **6**, 70 (1938).

[5] e. g., See E. A. Guggenheim, "Mixtures" (Oxford, London, 1952).

[6] W. G. McMillan and J. E. Mayer, *J. Chem. Phys.* **13**, 276 (1945).

[7] e.g., See I. Prigogine, A. Bellemans and V. Mathot, *The Molecular Theory of Solutions* (Interscience Publishers, Inc., New York, 1957).

[8] One should first study the article, J. G. Kirkwood, *J. Chem. Phys.* **18**, 380 (1950).

II. SOME RECENT EXTENSIONS OF KIRKWOOD'S WORK

By introducing various simplifying approximations this general theory could be treated by means of a corresponding states technique which is given in paper number 143. This application was similar to the concurrent developments reported by Prigogine, Scott and others.[9]

The influence of the papers in this section on the recent development of the theory of solutions has been very extensive and it would be difficult to make an exhaustive survey of these developments. However, given below are some very direct extensions which will be of interest to the reader.

(A) Distribution Functions for Fluid Mixtures.

The calculation of the radial distribution function for pure fluids has proved to be so difficult and challenging a problem that the theory has hardly progressed beyond the treatment of simple pure fluids. Moreover, the general theory for mixtures outlined in Kirkwood's 1935 paper (Paper number 7) has to date never been applied.

One isolated calculation has been carried out by B. J. Alder[10] on the numerical solution of the Born and Green integral equations for binary mixtures of rigid spheres using the Kirkwood superposition approximation. The densities studied in this investigation were relatively low with no indication of phase transitions.

Undoubtedly with the use of modern computing machines there will be further studies of the molecular distribution functions for mixtures. However, we are still a long way from realizing the type of calculation anticipated by Kirkwood in his classical article.

The superposition approximation introduced in this early work has received extensive investigation for pure fluids but its usefulness for solution theory (which was part of Kirkwood's original suggestion) has only received a preliminary study.[11]

(B) Lattice Theories of Non-Electrolyte Solutions.

While Kirkwood's work in the analysis of order-disorder problems has been extended by others[12] there have been no further studies of solutions based on this theory. This is understandable in view of the conclusions reached in paper number 25. The natural extension of Kirkwood's ideas are to be found in the later cell theories of solutions.

(C) Fluctuation Theories of Multi-Component Systems.

Following the basic paper by Kirkwood and Buff (Paper number 84) this work was continued by Buff and Brout[13] with the result that all the thermodynamic functions encountered in solution theory can be expressed in terms of the lower-order molecular distribution functions.

This formulation, which in many ways is the most satisfying and promising approach to solution theory yet given, must wait for a satisfactory procedure for obtaining the molecular distribution functions before it can be fully utilized. However, it does provide a convenient

---

[9] e.g., See R. L. Scott, *J. Chem. Phys.* **25**, 193 (1956) for a review.
[10] B. J. Alder, *J. Chem. Phys.* **23**, 263 (1955).
[11] F. P. Buff and R. Brout, *J. Chem. Phys.* **33**, 1417 (1960).
[12] e.g., F. E. J. Kruseman Aretz and E. G. D. Cohen, *Physica*, **26**, 967, 981 (1960).
[13] F. P. Buff and R. Brout, *J. Chem. Phys.* **23**, 458 (1955).

starting point for the development of systematic approximations. This has been demonstrated by Buff and Schindler[14] in one particular application, and it is unfortunate that more investigators have not taken advantage of this formulation.

(D) Free Volume and Corresponding States Theories of Solutions.

Very little effort has gone into the extended use of the free volume theory of liquids in calculating solution properties. A general formulation, similar to Kirkwood's treatment of pure liquids,[15] has been given for mixtures by Richardson and Brinkley.[16] However, the procedures by which the cell theories of pure liquids can be extended to mixtures can usually be adapted to any treatment of a pure fluid. Thus most of the recent effort has been on formulations which enable one to use the experimental properties of pure liquids.

---

[14] F. P. Buff and F. M. Schindler, *J. Chem. Phys.* **29**, 1075 (1958).
[15] J. G. Kirkwood, *J. Chem. Phys.* **18**, 380 (1950).
[16] J. M. Richardson and S. R. Brinkley, Jr., *J. Chem. Phys.* **33**, 1467 (1960).

Statistical Mechanics of Fluid Mixtures*

JOHN G. KIRKWOOD, *Department of Chemistry, Cornell University*

(Received March 1, 1935)

Expressions for the chemical potentials of the components of gas mixtures and liquid solutions are obtained in terms of relatively simple integrals in the configuration spaces of molecular pairs. The molecular pair distribution functions appearing in these integrals are investigated in some detail, in their dependence upon the composition and density of the fluid. The equation of state of a real gas mixture is discussed, and an approximate molecular pair distribution function, typical of dense fluids, is calculated. Applications of the method to the theory of solutions will be the subject of a later article.

I.

Although statistical mechanics has met with considerable success in the interpretation of the properties of rarefied gases as well as those of crystalline solids, serious practical difficulties have retarded its application to dense gases and to liquids. In the present article, we shall describe a statistical treatment of fluid mixtures, which is formally applicable both to real gases and to liquids. It has the advantage of yielding expressions which lend themselves more readily than the usual statistical formulas, to approximations suitable for condensed systems. While we make no pretension to a resolution of the difficulties presented by the liquid state, the more serious of which resist more than a superficial treatment, we believe that the method to be described throws interesting light upon the problem, and that it may prove useful in opening up new lines of attack, particularly in the field of liquid solutions.

We must first ask whether classical statistical mechanics is competent to describe the dependence of the thermodynamic functions of fluids upon intermolecular forces. At ordinary temperatures, there is good reason to believe that the classical approximation is adequate for most gases and liquids consisting of chemically saturated molecules. When certain conditions involving the molecular masses, moments of inertia, and the intermolecular forces are satisfied, the partition function of a system of molecules is closely approximated by the product of a function of the temperature alone, and the Gibbs phase integral in the phase space associated with the low frequency translational and rotational motion of the molecules.[1] The validity of the assumptions involved in this approximation is of course more questionable for liquids than for gases, particularly when there is strong coupling between the rotational motion of neighboring molecules as in polar liquids. We shall provisionally assume the adequacy of the classical approximation, remembering that our results are applicable only when this is true.

---

* The material of Section V of this article was presented at the eighty-ninth meeting of the American Chemical Society held in New York City during the week of April 22, 1935.

[1] E. Wigner, *Phys. Rev.* **40**, 749 (1932); Uhlenbeck and Gropper, *Phys. Rev.* **41**, 79 (1932); J. G. Kirkwood, *Phys. Rev.* **44**, 31 (1933); *J. Chem. Phys.* **1**, 597 (1933).

When the potential of the intermolecular force is of special form, for example a sum of terms depending upon the relative coordinates of molecular pairs, the explicit use of unwieldy integrals in a many dimensional phase space may be avoided. We shall show how the statistical formulas for certain important thermodynamic functions of a fluid mixture may be recast in terms of comparatively simple integrals in the configuration space associated with the relative motion of a molecular pair. The molecular pair distribution functions, which appear in these integrals are, to be sure, formally defined as ratios of many dimensional phase integrals. However, by certain transformations, they may be expressed in a form which leads to reasonable approximations both in condensed and rarefied systems. The approximation for rarefied systems leads to a novel approach to the problem of the equation of state of a real gas, while the approximation for condensed system promises to be of use in the theory of liquid solutions. On the other hand, the approximate distribution functions which have thus far been obtained do not appear to be sufficiently exact for the calculation of the equations of state of liquids.

The method of the present treatment is based upon the same principle as the charging processes employed in the theory of electrolyte solutions. As Onsager has clearly pointed out, parameters which appear in the potential of the intermolecular forces have essentially the same status as the parameters of external force,[2] which determine the mechanical interaction between a thermodynamic system and its surroundings, and may be manipulated in the same manner. The application of this principle is by no means restricted to intermolecular forces of the Coulomb type, in the potential of which ionic charges enter as natural parameters. Arbitrary parameters may be introduced into the potential of intermolecular force in any system of molecules, by means of which the coupling between the molecules may be continuously varied in any convenient manner. This device allows one to express the chemical potential of any component of a fluid mixture in a particularly simple form. It also proves to be very useful in investigating the dependence of molecular pair distribution functions upon the composition and density of the fluid.

II.

The following analysis is formally applicable to all homogeneous fluids, whether real gas mixtures or liquid solutions. Differences arise only in the method of approximating distribution functions. We therefore consider a homogeneous fluid of ν substances, in thermodynamic equilibrium. By suitably restricting the ranges of composition and pressure so as to exclude coexistent phases containing any of its components, we may suppose that the fluid completely fills a vessel of volume v, which confines the motion of the system to a finite region of configuration space.[3] We denote the absolute

[2] L. Onsager, *Chem. Rev.* **13**, 73 (1933); J. W. Gibbs, *Elementary Principles in Statistical Mechanics*, *Collected Works II*, Chap. VII (Longmans).

[3] We postulate the absence of coexistent phases containing any of the components of the fluid, since we wish to represent the system by a petit ensemble, each example of which contains the same number of molecules. Actually this is a trivial restriction, for Gibbs has shown that although an open system is represented by a grand ensemble, its equilibrium properties do not differ sensibly from those of a closed system represented by a petit ensemble, each example of which is made up of the average number of molecules of a system of the grand ensemble. In case coexistent phases exist, we simply regard v as the volume of the homogeneous part in which we are interested.

temperature by T, the numbers of molecules of the several components by $N_1, \cdots, N_\nu$, and the total number of molecules of all species, $\sum_{s=1}^{\nu} N_s$, by N. According to classical statistical mechanics, we represent the system by a canonically distributed petit ensemble, and obtain the usual expression for the Helmholtz free energy, F_N.

$$e^{-\beta F_N} = \left[\prod_{s=1}^{\nu} \frac{f_s(T)^{N_s}}{N_s!}\right] Z_N$$

$$Z_N = \int \cdots \int e^{-\beta V_N} d\omega_1 \cdots d\omega_N, \tag{1}$$

where β is equal to $1/kT$ and $d\omega_i$ is a differential element of the configuration space associated with the low frequency rotational and translational degrees of freedom of the molecule i. The integration in the sub-space of each molecule is extended over a region bounded by the volume of the vessel containing the fluid. In general

$$\int d\omega_i = \sigma_i v \tag{2}$$

where σ_i is equal to 4π for diatomic molecules which have only two low frequency rotational degrees of freedom and to $8\pi^2$ for polyatomic molecules which in general have three. The potential of the intermolecular forces, V_N, is a function of the configuration coordinates of all N molecules. The functions $f_s(T)$, depending upon the temperature alone, are products of certain momentum integrals associated with the low frequency degrees of freedom of a molecule of type s and the partition function associated with its high frequency vibrational degrees of freedom. For our present purposes we do not need to characterize these functions more closely.

The chemical potential per molecule of a component i of the fluid is thermodynamically defined by the relation

$$\mu_i = (\partial F/\partial N_i)_{T,\, v,\, N_1 \cdots N_{\nu-1}}. \tag{3}$$

It is statistically defined by Gibbs[4] in terms of the grand ensemble. For our purposes, it is more convenient to define μ_i in terms of the petit ensemble upon which Eq. (1) is based. This may be done in a very simple manner. We first observe that the treatment of N as a continuous variable in the thermodynamic definition (3) is simply a convenient mathematical device. A physical definition of chemical potential requires the use of finite differences, ΔF and ΔN_i, in the ratio $\Delta F/\Delta N_i$. For values of ΔN_i which do not sensibly affect the composition of the fluid, this ratio will not differ sensibly from the derivative on the right-hand side of Eq. (3). We are therefore justified in defining μ_i as the change in free energy produced by the subtraction or addition of a single molecule of type i from the macroscopic system, while maintaining the temperature, volume and the numbers of molecules of the other species constant.

$$\mu_i = F(N_1, \cdots, N_i, \cdots N_\nu, T, v) - F(N_1, \cdots, N_i - 1, \cdots N_\nu, T, v). \tag{4}$$

[4] J. W. Gibbs, *Elementary Principles in Statistical Mechanics, Collected Works II*, p. 187, Longmans.

The fact that the removal of a single molecule is scarcely a physically realizable process does not alter the value of the definition (4) when used in conjunction with the petit ensemble, each system of which is supposed to comprise exactly the same number of molecules.

From Eqs. (1) and (4), we obtain the following expression for μ_i:

$$\mu_i = -kT \log\left[\frac{f_i(T)}{N_i} \frac{Z(N_1, \cdots, N_i, \cdots N_\nu, T, v)}{Z(N_1, \cdots, N_i - 1, \cdots N_\nu, T, v)}\right]. \tag{5}$$

Further simplification depends upon the form of the potential of the intermolecular forces, V_N. We shall treat here only systems, for which V_N may be expressed as a sum of terms V_{kl}, each depending only upon the relative coordinates of a molecular pair (kl).[5]

$$V_N = \sum_{k<l} V_{kl}. \tag{6}$$

We now define a fictitious potential of the following type

$$V_N(\lambda_1, \cdots \lambda_N) = \sum_{k<l} \lambda_k \lambda_l V_{kl}, \tag{7}$$

where $\lambda_1 \cdots \lambda_N$ are arbitrary parameters. By varying these parameters between zero and unity, we can continuously vary the coupling between the N molecules from zero to its full value. In particular, we notice that when a value unity is assigned to each of the N parameters λ, we have

$$V_N(1, \cdots, 1) = V_N, \tag{8}$$

where V_N is given by Eq. (6) and represents the actual coupling between the molecules. If, on the other hand, a value unity is assigned to $N - 1$ of the parameters λ and a value zero to a single λ_i, we have

$$V_N(1, \cdots, 0, \cdots 1) = V_{N-1}, \tag{9}$$

where V_{N-1} is the potential in a system of $N - 1$ molecules formed by the

---

[5] It is to be remarked that the potential of Eq. (6) in no way excludes the simultaneous interaction of groups of more than two molecules. It simply states that in such a group, the mutual potential energy of any pair is independent of the presence of the other molecules. For example the electrostatic energy of a system of point charges is of this type. London has shown that the potential of the attractive van der Waals forces between chemically saturated molecules satisfies the requirements of Eq. (6). [F. London, *Zeits. f. physik. Chemie* **11**, 222 (1930).]

No such clear cut statement can be made regarding the repulsive forces, which operate at small distances, determining the effective collision diameters of molecules. However, it is plausible to assume that the potentials of these forces are approximately additive, and even if they are not exactly so, it is only necessary for our purposes that their narrow range of action is not sensibly displaced. In general, we should expect terms depending upon the relative coordinates of three or more molecules to be important only if the total intermolecular field is strong enough to produce a large perturbation in the electronic structure of a molecule in the fluid. Theoretical considerations suggest that not only in gases but also in liquids, this is not the case. Empirical arguments against any appreciable distortion of the electronic structure of molecules in most liquids are furnished by spectroscopic and optical evidence. For example, the molecular refractivity of most liquids is substantially the same as that of their vapor.

There are to be sure some types of intermolecular potential which do not satisfy Eq. (6), for example those of chemical forces of the homeopolar type. Another example is furnished by the energy of polarization of a molecule by a group of ions.

removal of a single molecule i. Corresponding to $V_N(\lambda_1, \cdots \lambda_N)$, we define a phase integral,

$$Z_N(\lambda_1, \cdots \lambda_N) = \int \cdots \int e^{-\beta V_N(\lambda_1 \cdots \lambda_N)} d\omega_1 \cdots d\omega_N. \tag{10}$$

When each of the parameters, λ, is assigned the value unity, we have the following identity:

$$Z_N(1, \cdots 1) = Z(N_1, \cdots, N_i, \cdots N_\nu). \tag{11}$$

When $N - 1$ of the parameters λ are equal to unity, while a single λ_i corresponding, let us say, to a molecule of type i is equal to zero, we may write

$$Z_N(1, \cdots, 0, \cdots 1) = \int \cdots \int e^{-\beta V_{N-1}} d\omega_1 \cdots d\omega_N. \tag{12}$$

Now since V_{N-1} contains no terms depending upon the coordinates of the molecule i, the integration over its configuration space in Eq. (12) may be carried out immediately. Performing this integration and making use of Eqs. (1) and (2), we obtain

$$Z_N(1, \cdots, 0, \cdots 1) = \sigma_i v Z(N_1, \cdots, N_i - 1, \cdots N_\nu). \tag{13}$$

From Eqs. (11) and (13) we may write

$$\frac{Z(N_1, \cdots, N_i, \cdots N_\nu)}{Z(N_1, \cdots, N_i - 1, \cdots N_\nu)} = \sigma_i v \frac{Z_N(1, \cdots, 1, \cdots 1)}{Z_N(1, \cdots, 0, \cdots 1)}. \tag{14}$$

Further we have the identity,

$$\log \frac{Z_N(1, \cdots, 1, \cdots 1)}{Z_N(1, \cdots, 0, \cdots 1)} = \int_0^1 \frac{\partial \log Z_N(\lambda_i)}{\partial \lambda_i} d\lambda_i \,. \tag{15}$$

To simplify notation, we write $Z_N(\lambda_i)$ for $Z_N(1, \cdots, \lambda_i, \cdots 1)$. In the future this convention will be adopted for all functions of the parameters λ, only those differing from unity being explicitly indicated. Returning to Eq. (10), we observe that

$$Z_N(\lambda_i) = \int \cdots \int e^{-\beta [V_{N-1} + \lambda_i V_i]} d\omega_1 \cdots d\omega_N,$$

$$V_i = \sum_{k=1}^{N} V_{ik}. \tag{16}$$

Differentiation of (16) with respect to λ_i yields

$$\partial \log Z_N(\lambda_i)/\partial \lambda_i = -\beta \overline{V_i(\lambda_i)},$$

$$\overline{V_i(\lambda_i)} = \frac{\int \cdots \int V_i e^{-\beta [V_{N-1} + \lambda_i V_i]} d\omega_1 \cdots d\omega_N}{\int \cdots \int e^{-\beta [V_{N-1} + \lambda_i V_i]} d\omega_1 \cdots d\omega_N}. \tag{17}$$

Combining Eqs. (5), (14), (15) and (17), we obtain for the chemical potential:

$$\begin{aligned} \mu_i &= kT \log N_i/v + \int_0^1 \overline{V_i(\lambda_i)} d\lambda_i + \varphi_i(T), \\ \varphi_i(T) &= -kT \log \sigma_i f_i(T). \end{aligned} \tag{18}$$

The mean potential energy $\overline{V_i(\lambda_i)}$ can be expressed as follows:

$$\begin{aligned} \overline{V_i(\lambda_i)} &= \sum_{k=1}^{N} \overline{V_{ik}(\lambda_i)}, \\ \overline{V_{ik}(\lambda_i)} &= \frac{\int \cdots \int V_{ik} e^{-\beta[V_{N-1}+\lambda_i V_i]} d\omega_1 \cdots d\omega_N}{\int \cdots \int e^{-\beta[V_{N-1}+\lambda_i V_i]} d\omega_1 \cdots d\omega_N}. \end{aligned} \tag{19}$$

Since V_{ik} depends only on the coordinates of the molecules i and k, we may write,

$$\overline{V_{ik}(\lambda_i)} = \frac{1}{\sigma_i \sigma_k v^2} \int \int V_{ik} e^{-\beta W_i^k(\lambda_i)} d\omega_i d\omega_k\,, \tag{20a}$$

$$e^{-\beta W_i^k(\lambda_i)} = \frac{\sigma_i \sigma_k v^2 \int \cdots \int e^{-\beta[V_{N-1}+\lambda_i V_i]} d\omega_1 \cdots d\omega_{N-2}}{\int \cdots \int e^{-\beta[V_{N-1}+\lambda_i V_i]} d\omega_1 \cdots d\omega_N}. \tag{20b}$$

The function $W_i^k(\lambda_i)$, as we shall presently show, is the potential of the mean force acting between the molecules i and k. At present we merely observe that in the absence of external fields of force $W_i^k(\lambda_i)$ can depend only upon the relative coordinate of the molecule pair i and k, except in a region of negligible volume near the surface of the fluid.

We may therefore refer the position of the center of gravity and the orientation of the molecule k to a coordinate system fixed in molecule i. Both V_{ik} and $W_i^k(\lambda_i)$ will depend upon these relative coordinates alone. Moreover, the Jacobian of this transformation is unity. If we then integrate over the configuration space of molecule i, the expression for $\overline{V_{ik}(\lambda_i)}$, Eq. (20) becomes:

$$\overline{V_{ik}(\lambda_i)} = (1/\sigma_k v) \int V_{ik} e^{-\beta W_i^k(\lambda_i)} d\omega_k, \tag{21}$$

where $d\omega_k$ is understood to refer to the coordinates of molecule k relative to a system of axes fixed in molecule i. Introducing Eq. (21) into Eq. (18), and remembering that $\overline{V_{ik}(\lambda_i)}$ is the same function for all molecules k of the same type, we may write:

$$\begin{aligned} \mu_i &= kT \left\{ \log N_i/v + \sum_{k=1}^{\nu} \frac{N_k}{v} \int_0^1 B_{ik}(\lambda_i) d\lambda_i \right\} + \varphi_i(T), \\ B_{ik}(\lambda_i) &= (1/\sigma_k kT) \int V_{ik} e^{-\beta W_i^k(\lambda_i)} d\omega_k, \end{aligned} \tag{22}$$

where the summation extends over all molecular types k present in the fluid, and the function B_{ik} refers to a single pair of molecules of types i and k, respectively. Each B_{ik} is a function of temperature, volume and composition, since $W_i^k(\lambda_i)$ is a function of all of these variables. The notation $W_i^k(\lambda_i)$ means of course that all the parameters λ have the value unity except λ_i corresponding to a *single* molecule of type *i*.

The mean energy $\bar{E}$ of the fluid may be expressed quite simply, if we assume classical equipartition with respect to the low frequency rotational and translational degrees of freedom

$$\bar{E} = E_0(T) + \bar{V}_N, \tag{23}$$

where $\bar{V}_N$ is the mean potential energy associated with the intermolecular forces and $E_0(T)$, a function of the temperature alone, is sum of the internal energies of the molecules and their mean translational and rotational kinetic energies. Writing V_N in the form of Eq. (6), and remembering that V_{ik} depends only on the relative coordinates of molecules k and i, we may write*

$$\bar{V}_N = \sum_{i<k} \bar{V}_{ik} = \tfrac{1}{2}\sum_{i,k=1}^{\nu} (N_i N_k/v)\bar{V}_{ik},$$

$$\bar{V}_{ik} = (1/\sigma_k v) \int V_{ik} e^{-\beta W_i^k(1)} d\omega_k. \tag{24}$$

We note that W_i^k appearing in Eq. (24) is $W_i^k(1)$, the value of $W_i^k(\lambda_i)$ when molecule i has its full coupling with the other molecules of the system. Finally we may write,

$$\bar{E} = E_0(T) + \tfrac{1}{2}kT \sum_{i,k=1}^{\nu} (N_i N_k/v) B_{ik}. \tag{25}$$

The quantity B_{ik} in Eq. (25) is equal to $B_{ik}(1)$ of Eq. (22) when λ_i is unity. $E_0(T)$ may be explicitly calculated if the internal partition functions of the molecules are known. We shall not be interested in this point here.

III.

The use of Eqs. (22) and (25) for purposes of calculation depends upon an investigation of the functions $W_i^k(\lambda_i)$ which determine the probability distribution of the pair of molecules i and k relative to each other. It may readily be shown that $W_i^k(\lambda_i)$ is the potential of the mean force acting between the molecules i and k, averaged over all configurations of the remaining $N - 2$ molecules of the system. The force acting at the center of gravity of molecule i for a fixed configuration of the other molecules, is

$$F_i(\lambda_i) = -\nabla_i V_N(\lambda_i), \tag{26}$$

where ∇_i is the gradient operator associated with the coordinates of the center of gravity of molecule i. If we take a mean value with the pair of molecules i and k held fixed, we obtain

$$\overline{F_i(\lambda_i)}^{ik} = -\frac{\int \cdots \int \nabla_i V_N(\lambda_i) e^{-\beta V_N(\lambda_i)} d\omega_1 \cdots d\omega_{N-2}}{\int \cdots \int e^{-\beta V_N(\lambda_i)} d\omega_1 \cdots d\omega_{N-2}}. \tag{27}$$

---

* Eq. (24) has been given by Hildebrand and Wood, *J. Chem. Phys.* **1**, 817 (1933).

Differentiation of both sides of Eq. (20b), which defines $W_i^k(\lambda_i)$ and comparison with Eq. (27) yields

$$\overline{^{ik}F_i(\lambda_i)} = -\nabla_i W_i^k(\lambda_i). \tag{28}$$

The function $W_i^k(\lambda_i)$ is therefore the potential of the mean force acting at the center of gravity of molecule i when k is held fixed at some point in its vicinity. Similarly, it may be shown that $W_i^k(\lambda_i)$ is the potential of the mean generalized forces associated with the relative orientation of i and k. If the relative orientation is specified by the Eulerian angles ϑ, φ and ψ, the mean torque tending to produce rotation through the angle ϑ is $-\partial W_i^k(\lambda_i)/\partial\vartheta$. These relations have been used by Einstein, Schmoluchowski and others,[6] who showed that the simple Boltzmann distribution is valid provided the potential of the mean force is employed in the exponential factor.

It is interesting to remark that the potential $W_i^k(1)$, corresponding to full coupling between molecule i and the other molecules, is susceptible of experimental determination, at least in its dependence on the relative coordinates of the molecular centers of gravity. According to the theory of x-ray scattering by liquids, developed by Prins and Debye,[7] the angular distribution of intensity of the scattered radiation is a sum of mean values of functions depending only upon the relative coordinates of pairs of molecules. Mean values of such functions are determined by the probability distribution function $e^{-\beta W_i^k}$ in a system in thermodynamic equilibrium. By a Fourier integral inversion of the theoretical scattering formula, $(e^{-\beta W_i^k} - 1)$ may be computed from the observed intensity measured as a function of the scattering angle. By Eq. (25), we see that a knowledge of $W_i^k(1)$ suffices for the calculation of the mean energy of the fluid from the potentials V_{ik}. However, it does not suffice for the calculations of chemical potentials or the Gibbs free energy, ζ, which is equal to $\sum_{i=1}^{\nu} N_i\mu_i$. For the latter purpose we must know $W_i^k(\lambda_i)$ for all values of λ_i between zero and unity. This information is not furnished by x-ray scattering experiments. Thus, while they yield valuable information concerning the statistical structure of liquids, they do not provide sufficient data for the calculation of entropy and free energy.

We must consequently depend upon theoretical information about the potentials of mean force $W_i^k(\lambda_i)$. Since the many dimensional phase integrals of Eq. (20b), which defines $W_i^k(\lambda_i)$, are inconvenient to handle, we follow an indirect method of attack, leading to reasonable approximations both for condensed and rarefied systems. Logarithmic differentiation of both sides of Eq. (20b) yields

$$\partial W_i^k(\lambda_i)/\partial\lambda_i = \overline{^{ik}V_i(\lambda_i)} - \overline{V_i(\lambda_i)}, \tag{29}$$

where

$$\overline{^{ik}V_i(\lambda_i)} = \frac{\int\cdots\int V_i e^{-\beta[V_{N-1}+\lambda_i V_i]}d\omega_1\cdots d\omega_{N-2}}{\int\cdots\int e^{-\beta[V_{N-1}+\lambda_i V_i]}d\omega_1\cdots d\omega_{N-2}}, \tag{30}$$

$\overline{^{ik}V_i(\lambda_i)}$ is the mean value of V_i for a fixed configuration of the molecular pair i and k, while $\overline{V_i(\lambda_i)}$ is the mean value of the same function taken over all

[6] For a discussion of this point, see L. Onsager, *Chem. Rev.* **13**, 73 (1933).

[7] Zernicke and Prins, *Zeits. f. Physik.* **41**, 184 (1927); Debye and Mencke, *Physik. Zeits.* **31**, 797 (1930).

configurations of all molecules of the system. By Eq. (10), we may write

$$\overline{{}^{ik}V_i(\lambda_i)} = V_{ik} + \sum_{\substack{s=1\\ \neq k}}^{N} \overline{{}^{ik}V_{is}(\lambda_i)}, \tag{31}$$

since the term V_{ik} is constant for fixed configurations of molecules i and k and is unaffected by a mean value operation in which these are held fixed. Because V_{is} depends only on the relative coordinates of i and s, we have

$$\overline{{}^{ik}V_{is}(\lambda_i)} = (1/\sigma_s v) \int V_{is} e^{-\beta W_{ik}{}^s(\lambda_i)} d\omega_s, \tag{32a}$$

$$e^{-\beta W_{ik}{}^s(\lambda_i)} = \frac{\sigma_s v \int \cdots \int e^{-\beta[V_{N-1}+\lambda_i V_i]} d\omega_1 \cdots d\omega_{N-3}}{\int \cdots \int e^{-\beta[V_{N-1}+\lambda_i V_i]} d\omega_1 \cdots d\omega_{N-2}}, \tag{32b}$$

where the integration in the numerator of (32b) is to extend over the coordinates of all molecules except i, k and s and in the denominator over all but those of i and k. It will be seen at once that $W_{ik}{}^s(\lambda_i)$ is the potential of the mean force acting upon molecule s, averaged over the configurations of all molecules except i, k and s. We note that $W_{ik}{}^s(\lambda_i)$ is not invariant under a permutation of upper and lower indices, although $W_i{}^k(\lambda_i)$ is. It is possible to define a potential of mean force which is symmetric in the coordinates of i, k and s, differing from $W_{ik}{}^s(\lambda_i)$ by a term independent of the coordinates of s, but the latter form is not the most convenient for the present purposes. The second term of Eq. (29) is the sum $\sum_{s-1}^{N} \overline{V_{is}(\lambda_i)}$, each member of which is given by an expression of the form (21). Moreover, each of the mean values ${}^{ik}\overline{V}_{is}$ and $\overline{V}_{is}$ are identical molecules of the same type s, so that we may write,

$$\partial W_i{}^k(\lambda_i)/\partial \lambda_i = V_{ik} + \sum_{s=1}^{\nu} \frac{N_s}{v} \frac{1}{\sigma_s} \int V_{is}[e^{-\beta W_{ik}{}^s(\lambda_i)} - e^{-\beta W_i{}^s(\lambda_i)}] d\omega_s, \tag{33}$$

where the sum is extended over all types s. Each of the integrals refers to a single group of three molecules, i, k, and a single molecule of type s. Properly a term, $(v\sigma_k)^{-1}\int V_{ik'} e^{-\beta W^{k'}{}_{ik}(\lambda_i)} d\omega_{k'}$, where k' is a single molecule of the same type as k, should be omitted from the sum in Eq. (33). Since, however, this term bears a ratio of the order of $1/N_k$ to terms retained, it can be ignored altogether. This is not true of V_{ik}, which is of dominant importance when k is situated in the immediate neighborhood of i.

Before integrating Eq. (33) we shall find it convenient to investigate the behavior of $W_i{}^k(\lambda_i)$ in the neighborhood of $\lambda_i = 0$. First we note that $W_i{}^k(0)$ must be independent of the coordinates of i, since the mean force on i vanishes when λ_i is equal to zero. Moreover, it must also be independent of the coordinates of k except in the surface region, since the mean force on k must also vanish when λ_i is equal to zero. From these facts we conclude that $W_i{}^k(0)$ must be a constant. Making use of Eq. (20b), we write

$$e^{-\beta W_i{}^k(0)} = \frac{\sigma_i \sigma_k v^2 \int \cdots \int e^{-\beta V_{N-1}} d\omega_1 \cdots d\omega_{N-2}}{\int \cdots \int e^{-\beta V_{N-1}} d\omega_1 \cdots d\omega_N}. \tag{34}$$

Now the integral in the denominator of (34) is obviously independent of the coordinate of i and k, since it includes integrations over these coordinates.

Since $W_i^k(0)$ is independent of the coordinates of i and k, we must conclude that the integral in the numerator is also independent of them. The factor $\sigma_i\sigma_k v^2$ may therefore be written as an integration over the configuration spaces of molecules i and k,

$$\sigma_i\sigma_k v^2 \int \cdots \int e^{-\beta V_{N-1}} d\omega_1 \cdots d\omega_{N-2} = \int \cdots \int e^{-\beta V_{N-1}} d\omega_1 \cdots d\omega_N. \tag{35}$$

From Eqs. (34) and (35) we conclude that $e^{-\beta W_i^k(0)}$ has the value unity and that $W_i^k(0)$ vanishes. Bearing this fact in mind, we integrate Eq. (33) between zero and λ_i with the result:

$$W_i^k(\lambda_i) = \lambda_i V_{ik} + \sum_{s=1}^{v}(N_s/v)(1/\sigma_s)\int_0^{\lambda_i}\int V_{is}[e^{-\beta W_{ik}^s(\lambda_i)} - e^{-\beta W_i^s(\lambda_i)}]d\omega_s d\lambda_i. \tag{36}$$

From Eq. (36), we observe that $W_i^k(\lambda_i)$ approaches $\lambda_i V_{ik}$ as the densities of the several components of the fluid approach zero. This approximation is also obtained by neglecting the influence of the fixed molecule k on the distribution of a third molecule s in the vicinity of molecule i, that is by ignoring the difference between $W_{ik}^s(\lambda_i)$ and $W_i^s(\lambda_i)$. In the theory of the equation of state of a rarefied gas, this is essentially the approximation which is made. To obtain a more accurate expression for $W_i^k(\lambda_i)$ we must know something about the potential $W_{ik}^s(\lambda_i)$ involving the group of three molecules i, k and s. Proceeding from Eq. (32b), which defines $W_{ik}^s(\lambda_i)$, we obtain by differentiation with respect to λ_i

$$\partial W_{ik}^s(\lambda_i)/\partial\lambda_i = \lambda_i V_{is} + \sum_{l=1}^{v}(N_l/v\sigma_l)\int V_{il}[e^{-\beta W_{iks}^l(\lambda_i)} - e^{-\beta W_{ik}^l(\lambda_i)}]d\omega_l, \tag{37}$$

$$e^{-\beta W_{iks}^l(\lambda i)} = \frac{\sigma_l v \int \cdots \int e^{-\beta[V_{N-1}+\lambda_i V_i]} d\omega_1 \cdots d\omega_{N-4}}{\int \cdots \int e^{-\beta[V_{N-1}+\lambda_i V_i]} d\omega_1 \cdots d\omega_{N-3}}.$$

Examination of (32b) shows at once that $W_{ik}^s(0)$ is merely W_k^s in a system containing $N_i - 1$ molecules of type i. It is apparent that this function can differ from W_k^s in the original system only by a quantity of completely negligible order, $O(1/N_i)$. Thus when Eq. (37) is integrated with respect to λ_i, there is obtained

$$W_{ik}^s(\lambda_i) =$$

$$W_k^s + \lambda_i V_{is} + \sum_{l=1}^{v}(N_l/v\sigma_l)\int_0^{\lambda_i}\int V_{il}[e^{-\beta W_{iks}^l(\lambda_i)} - e^{-\beta W_{ik}^l(\lambda_i)}]d\omega_l d\lambda_i. \tag{38}$$

This equation is entirely analogous to Eq. (36). Since W_k^s is given by an equation of the form of (36), a first approximation to $W_{ik}^s(\lambda_i)$ is evidently $V_{ks} + \lambda_i V_i$. Similarly a first approximation to $W_i^s(\lambda_i)$ is $\lambda_i V_{is}$. If these approximations are employed in the integrals of Eq. (36), we obtain a second approximation to $W_i^k(\lambda_i)$, namely

$$W_i^k(\lambda_i) = \lambda_i V_{ik} - kT\sum_{s=1}^{v}(N_s/v)(1/\sigma_s)\int (e^{-\beta\lambda_i V_{is}} - 1)(e^{-\beta V_{ks}} - 1)d\omega_s. \tag{39}$$

We should expect this approximation to be adequate in gases of moderate density. The method of successive approximation employed to obtain Eq. (39), can of course be extended without great difficulty, by transforming the potentials $W_{iks}{}^{l}(\lambda_i)$, involving groups of four molecules, in exactly the same manner as $W_i{}^k(\lambda_i)$ and $W_{ik}{}^s(\lambda_i)$. Presumably any desired degree of approximation could be attained in this fashion, but the expressions become very cumbersome. It should also be remarked that the method of approximation just outlined can only be employed when no long range forces, such as the Coulomb forces, act between the molecules, for in such cases the integral of Eq. (39) diverges. It converges whenever the individual potentials decrease asymptotically at least as rapidly as $r_{ik}{}^{-4}$.

For an exact calculation of $W_i{}^k(\lambda_i)$, it would be necessary to solve a set of $N - 1$ simultaneous integral equations of the type of Eqs. (36) and (38), involving potentials $W^s{}_{ik\cdots l}$, in which the number of fixed molecules i, k, $\cdots l$, ranges from one to $N - 1$. Moreover, when the number of fixed molecules becomes comparable with the total number of molecules, N, the equations become more complicated than (36) and (38), due to growth of terms, which are of zero order in the latter equations. Since this is not a practicable procedure, we must resort to some means of approximation. Eq. (39) represents a possible method of approximation in which $W_i{}^k(\lambda_i)$ is developed in powers of the densities of the components of the fluid. However, we should like to find an approximation more suitable in condensed systems than Eq. (39) is likely to be. An obvious and simple approximation may be obtained by assuming superposition in the potentials of mean force,

$$W_{ik}{}^s(\lambda_i) = W_k{}^s + W_i{}^s(\lambda_i). \tag{40}$$

Although the additivity expressed in Eq. (40) holds for the direct action of i and k on s through the terms $V_{ks} + \lambda_i V_{is}$, it cannot hold exactly for their indirect action upon s through their effect on the distribution of the remaining $N - 3$ molecules. The magnitude of this discrepancy will be discussed later. If we introduce the approximation (40) into Eq. (36), we obtain the following integral equation:

$$W_i{}^k(\lambda_i) = \lambda_i V_{ik} + \sum_{s=1}^{\nu} (N_s/v)(1/\sigma_s) \int_0^{\lambda_i} \int V_{is} e^{-\beta W_i{}^s(\lambda_i)} [e^{-\beta W_k{}^s(1)} - 1] d\omega_s d\lambda_i. \tag{41}$$

The potentials $W_i{}^k(\lambda_i)$ will have the same form for any pair of molecules of the same type. From the ν types of molecules present in the fluid, $\nu(\nu + 1)/2$ types of molecular pairs can be formed. There will, therefore, be $\nu(\nu + 1)/2$ types of functions $W_i{}^k(\lambda_i)$, each satisfying an equation like (41). Simultaneous solution of these integral equations will yield values of the functions $W_i{}^k(\lambda_i)$ consistent with the approximation expressed in Eq. (40). Of course for a pure fluid, having only one component, only one integral equation has to be solved.

$$W(q_{12}, \lambda) = \lambda V(q_{12}) + (N\rho/M\sigma) \int_0^{\lambda} \int V(q_{13}) e^{-\beta W(q_{13}, \lambda)} [e^{-\beta W(q_{23}, 1)} - 1] d\omega_3 d\lambda, \tag{42}$$

where q_{12}, q_{13} and q_{23} are the relative coordinates of a set of three molecules, N is Avogadro's number, M the molecular weight of the substance, and ρ its density. We note that the approximation (39) is obtainable from Eq. (41) as the first step in its solution by successive substitution. In general, it will not be feasible to seek analytic solutions of Eqs. (41) or (42). However, by graphical or mechanical quadrature, it should be possible to determine self-consistent functions satisfying these equations. We remark that this process provides a theoretical means of calculating the x-ray scattering curves of liquids, since they are determined by $W_i{}^k(1)$. In some cases the potentials of intermolecular force can be calculated from atomic structure. Although this can be done in relatively few cases, quantum mechanics prescribes an approximate functional form for the V_{ik}. With this functional form, the numerical values of V_{ik} may be deduced from the temperature dependence of the second virial coefficient of the substance in the gaseous state.

While Eq. (40) represents an approximation which is intuitively attractive, it is of course not exact. Although a numerical estimate of the error involved is difficult, we can say something quite definite about the nature of the approximation. To facilitate discussion, we shall introduce the symbol $\epsilon_{ik}{}^s$ to denote the deviation from additivity

$$\epsilon_{ik}{}^s = W_{ik}{}^s(\lambda_i) - [W_k{}^s + W_i{}^s(\lambda_i)]. \tag{43}$$

It is possible to express $\epsilon_{ik}{}^s$ in terms of a third order fluctuation in the potential energy of molecule i. Without entering into the details of the calculation, we state the following result.

$$\epsilon_{ik}{}^s = \beta^2 \int_0^{\lambda_i}\int_0^1\int_0^1 \overline{(V_l - \overline{V_i}^{iks})(V_k - \overline{V_k}^{iks})(V_s - \overline{V_s}^{iks})}^{iks} d\lambda_k d\lambda_s d\lambda_i, \tag{44}$$

where the fluctuation is understood to be a function of the variables λ_i, λ_k, λ_s, mean values being taken with the distribution function $e^{-\beta V_N(\lambda i,\, \lambda k,\, \lambda s)}$. A more useful expression for $\epsilon_{ik}{}^s$ is obtained simply by subtracting the equation for $W_i{}^s(\lambda_i)$ corresponding to (36) from Eq. (38). The result is,

$$\begin{aligned}\epsilon_{ik}{}^s = \sum_{l=1}^{\nu}(N_l/v\sigma_l)\int_0^{\lambda_i}\int V_{il}\{e^{-\beta W_{iks}{}^l(\lambda_i)} \\ + e^{-\beta W_i{}^l(\lambda_i)} - e^{-\beta W_{ik}{}^l(\lambda_i)} - e^{-\beta W_{is}{}^l(\lambda_i)}\}d\omega_l d\lambda_i.\end{aligned} \tag{45}$$

An exact calculation of $\epsilon_{ik}{}^s$ from Eq. (45) is of course impossible without a knowledge of the potential $W_{iks}{}^l(\lambda_i)$. However, we should expect to obtain at least a rough estimate of $\epsilon_{ik}{}^s$ by using the additivity approximation for the potentials $W_{iks}{}^l(\lambda_i)$, $W_{ik}{}^l(\lambda_i)$, and $W_{is}{}^l(\lambda_i)$. Introduction of this approximation yields

$$\epsilon_{ik}{}^s = \sum_{l=1}^{\nu}(N_l/v\sigma_l)\int_0^{\lambda_i}\int V_{il}e^{-\beta W_i{}^l(\lambda_i)}(e^{-\beta W_k{}^l} - 1)(e^{-\beta W_s{}^l} - 1)d\omega_l d\lambda_i. \tag{46}$$

If we rely on Eq. (46) for the order of magnitude of $\epsilon_{ik}{}^s$, we see that the integrand will be very small except for configurations of molecules such that $W_k{}^l$ and $W_s{}^l$ are simultaneously large. If s and k are situated at some distance from each other so that their spheres of influence on the distribution of a third molecule l, do not overlap appreciably, $\epsilon_{ik}{}^s$ will be small. Returning to Eq. (36) we remark that for the calculation of $W_i{}^k(\lambda_i)$, it is only necessary to know $W_{ik}{}^s(\lambda_i)$ accurately in a region in the vicinity of molecule i, where V_{is} is sensibly different from zero. If the molecules i and k are separated by an appreciable distance, s will be distant from k in the greater part of this region, and we may conclude that $\epsilon_{ik}{}^s$ is small. Thus we may expect Eq. (41) to provide a good approximation to $W_i{}^k(\lambda_i)$ at least when the molecules i and k are separated by an appreciable distance, and that $W_i{}^k(\lambda_i)$ will approach the solution of Eq. (41) asymptotically as the distance between i and k is increased. This point is of some importance in the case of long range intermolecular forces, such as those between electrolyte ions. At small distances between i and k the dominant term in $W_i{}^k(\lambda_i)$ becomes V_{ik}, and although the terms depending on the density may still be large, it is not necessary to know them with such great accuracy. Once solutions of Eq. (41) have been obtained, they may be used in Eq. (46) to obtain a rough estimate of $\epsilon_{ik}{}^s$. If this turns out to be small, the solutions of Eq. (41) can be accepted with some degree of assurance as reasonable approximations to the potentials $W_i{}^k(\lambda_i)$. It would be desirable to have a more rigid criterion for judging the adequacy of these approximations, but unfortunately this cannot be obtained without introducing distribution functions involving larger and larger groups of fixed molecules. Unless some approximation such as superposition is introduced at some early stage in this sequence of distribution functions, we are driven back to the many dimensional phase integrals with which we started.

Having obtained approximate expressions for $W_i{}^k(\lambda_i)$ by solution of Eqs. (41), we can calculate the chemical potential of any component of the fluid by means of Eq. (22), as well as the total energy of the fluid by Eq. (25). From the chemical potentials, we may obtain the Gibbs free energy, ζ, of the system.

$$\begin{aligned} \zeta = E + pv - TS &= \sum_{i=1}^{\nu} N_i \mu_i \\ &= kT \left\{ \sum_{i=1}^{\nu} N_i \log N_i/v + \sum_{i,k=1}^{\nu} \frac{N_i N_k}{v} \int_0^1 B_{ik}(\lambda_i) d\lambda_i \right\} + \sum_{i=1}^{\nu} N_i \varphi_i(T). \end{aligned} \tag{47}$$

In principle one can obtain the compressibility, κ, of the fluid by means of the thermodynamic formula,

$$1/\kappa = -v(\partial p/\partial v)_T = -(\partial \zeta/\partial v)_{T,\, N_1, \cdots N_\nu}. \tag{48}$$

However the $B_{ik}(\lambda_i)$ depend upon v through the $W_i{}^k(\lambda_i)$. Even though Eq. (41) may provide good approximations to the $W_i{}^k(\lambda_i)$, it is by no means certain that the derivatives of these solutions with respect to v will be good approximations to $\partial W_i{}^k(\lambda_i)/\partial v$. Thus while Eqs. (22), (35) and (47) may express the dependence of the μ_i, $\bar{E}$ and ζ upon the composition of the fluid with some accuracy, the compressibility calculated from Eqs. (47) and (48) may be a much poorer approximation. Quite formally, we may write

$$\left(\frac{\partial p}{\partial v}\right)_T = -kT \left\{ \sum_{i=1}^{\nu} \frac{N_i}{v^2} + \sum_{i,k=1}^{\nu} \frac{N_i N_k}{v^3} \int_0^1 \left[B_{ik}(\lambda_i) - v \frac{\partial B_{ik}(\lambda_i)}{\partial v} \right] d\lambda_i \right\}. \tag{49}$$

In case the fluid under consideration is a gas, we know that as the volume is increased to infinity, the pressure decreases continuously to zero. In this case we may integrate Eq. (49) between the limits v and infinity. After a simple partial integration, the following equation of state is obtained.

$$\frac{p\bar{v}}{RT} = 1 + \sum_{i,\,k=1}^{\nu} \frac{x_i x_k}{\bar{v}} \left\{ \int_0^1 N \left[B_{ik}(\lambda_i) + \bar{v}^2 \int_{\infty}^{\bar{v}} \frac{B_{ik}(\lambda_i)}{\bar{v}^3}\, d\bar{v} \right] d\lambda_i \right\} \qquad (50)$$

$$n_i = N_i/N; \qquad x_i = n_i/\sum n_k; \qquad v = v/\sum n_k,$$

where N is Avogadro's number, n_i the number of moles of component i present in the gas and x_i the mole fraction of that component. Eq. (50) may be made the basis for a statistical calculation of the equation of state of a real gas mixture. When the potentials $W_i^k(\lambda_i)$ in the $B_{ik}(\lambda_i)$ are approximated simply by $\lambda_i V_{ik}$ the usual expressions for the second virial coefficients are obtained.

IV.

The present method provides a particularly simple means of determining the equation of state of a real gas mixture. We shall derive expressions for the second and third coefficients in the virial expansion of the equation of state, indicating how the method may be extended to higher coefficients. Results are obtained which are in agreement with those of Ursell, who has treated the same problem from a somewhat different point of view.[8]

If the function $W_i^k(\lambda_i)$ is approximated by Eq. (39), we obtain the following expression for $B_{ik}(\lambda_i)$.

$$B_{ik}(\lambda_i) = \frac{1}{\sigma_k kT} \int V_{ik} \exp \left\{ -\beta\lambda_i V_{ik} + \sum_{s=1}^{\nu} \frac{N_s}{v\sigma_s} \int (1 - e^{-\beta\lambda_i V_{is}})(1 - e^{-\beta V_{ks}}) d\omega_s \right\} d\omega_k. \qquad (51)$$

Substitution of this expression in Eqs. (22) and (50) would yield the chemical potentials of the several components and the equation of state of the gas mixture. We should expect the equation of state, although approximate, to be much more satisfactory than a virial expansion. However, the integrals involved cannot be expressed in terms of elementary functions, and we shall not concern ourselves with their simplification here. We note that Eq. (39) is exact to terms in $1/v^2$, so that the first two terms of an expansion of the right-hand side of Eq. (51) are exact. The expansion is

$$B_{ik}(\lambda_i) = \frac{1}{kT} \left\{ \frac{1}{\sigma_k} \int V_{ik} e^{-\beta\lambda_i V_{ik}} d\omega_k + \sum_{s=1} \frac{N_s}{v} \frac{1}{\sigma_s \sigma_k} \int\int V_{ik} e^{-\beta\lambda_i V_{ik}} (1 - e^{-\beta\lambda_i V_{is}})(1 - e^{-\beta V_{ks}}) d\omega_k d\omega_s + O(1/v^3) \right\}. \qquad (52)$$

[8] Ursell, *Proc. Camb. Phil. Soc.* **23**, 685 (1927); R. H. Fowler, *Statistical Mechanics*, Cambridge University Press (1929), p. 173.

Substitution of this expansion in Eq. (22), integration with respect to λ_i and a rearrangement of terms yields[9]

$$\mu_i = kT\left\{\log N_i/v + \sum_{k=1}^{\nu} \frac{N_k}{v\sigma_k}\int(1 - e^{-\beta V_{ik}})d\omega_k\right.$$

$$+ \frac{1}{2}\sum_{k,s=1}^{\nu} \frac{N_k N_s}{v^2}\frac{1}{\sigma_s\sigma_k}\int\int(1 - e^{-\beta V_{ik}})(1 - e^{-\beta V_{is}})(1 - e^{-\beta V_{ks}})d\omega_k d\omega_s$$

$$\left. + O(1/v^3)\right\}. \quad (53)$$

When the approximate expressions for the μ_i given by Eq. (53) are introduced into Eqs. (47) and (48), we obtain

$$\left(\frac{\partial p}{\partial v}\right)_T = -kT\left\{\sum_{i=1}^{\nu}\frac{N_i}{v^2} + \sum_{i,k=1}^{\nu}\frac{N_i N_k}{v^3}\frac{1}{\sigma_k}\int(1 - e^{-\beta V_{ik}})d\omega_k\right.$$

$$+ \sum_{i,k,s=1}^{\nu}\frac{N_i N_k N_s}{v^4}\frac{1}{\sigma_k\sigma_s}\int\int(1 - e^{-\beta V_{ik}})(1 - e^{-\beta V_{is}})(1 - e^{-\beta V_{ks}})d\omega_s d\omega_k$$

$$\left. + O(1/v^5)\right\}. \quad (54)$$

---

[9] After integration with respect to λ_i, the terms in μ_i involving $1/v^2$ have the form

$$\sum_{\substack{k,s=1\\ k\neq s\neq i}}^{N} \frac{1}{v^2\sigma_k\sigma_s}\int\int(1 - e^{-\beta V_{ks}})\left\{\frac{V_{ik}}{V_{ik}+V_{is}}(e^{-\beta(V_{ik}+V_{is})} - 1) - (e^{-\beta V_{ik}} - 1)\right\}d\omega_k d\omega_s,$$

where the original summation indices, referring to the individual molecules, have been restored for clearness. For every term in the sum with the integrand

$$\left\{\frac{V_{ik}}{V_{ik}+V_{is}}(e^{-\beta(V_{ik}+V_{is})} - 1) - (e^{-\beta V_{ik}} - 1)\right\}(1 - e^{-\beta V_{ks}}),$$

corresponding to any specified pair of molecules k and s, there is also a term involving the same pair, having the form

$$\left\{\frac{V_{is}}{V_{is}+V_{ik}}(e^{-\beta(V_{ik}+V_{is})} - 1) - (e^{-\beta V_{is}} - 1)\right\}(1 - e^{-\beta V_{ks}}).$$

The sum of this pair of terms is readily seen to be

$$(1 - e^{-\beta V_{ik}})(1 - e^{-\beta V_{is}})(1 - e^{-\beta V_{ks}})$$

so that the double sum may be rearranged as follows:

$$\frac{1}{2}\sum_{\substack{k,s=1\\ k\neq s\neq i}}^{N}\frac{1}{v^2\sigma_k\sigma_s}\int\int(1 - e^{-\beta V_{ks}})(1 - e^{-\beta V_{is}})(1 - e^{-\beta V_{ik}})d\omega_k d\omega_s.$$

This sum contains $(N - 1)(N - 2)$ terms of similar magnitude. It differs from the sum over molecular types appearing in Eq. (55) by $(3N - 2)$ terms of the same magnitude. The aggregate of these terms bears a ratio of the order of $1/N$ to either sum and is consequently entirely negligible.

Integration between the volume limits ∞ and v leads to the following equation of state

$$\frac{p\bar{v}}{RT} = 1 + \sum_{i,k=1}^{\nu} \frac{x_i x_k}{\bar{v}} B_{ik}{}^0 + \sum_{i,k,s=1}^{\nu} \frac{x_i x_k x_s}{\bar{v}^2} C_{iks}{}^0 + O(1/\bar{v}^3)$$

$$B_{ik}{}^0 = \frac{N}{2\sigma_k} \int (1 - e^{-\beta V_{ik}}) d\omega_k \tag{55}$$

$$C_{iks}{}^0 = \frac{N^2}{3\sigma_k \sigma_s} \int\int (1 - e^{-\beta V_{ik}})(1 - e^{-\beta V_{is}})(1 - e^{-\beta V_{ks}}) d\omega_k d\omega_s.$$

If the method of approximating $W_i{}^k(\lambda_i)$ embodied in Eq. (39) is carried one stage farther, one more term may be retained in the expansion of $B_{ik}(\lambda_i)$ and the fourth virial coefficient may be calculated. The process can be continued indefinitely, but of course the algebraic operations become tedious, and the final expressions unwieldy. The method consists simply of continued substitution and expansion. If one wishes a virial expansion including terms of the order of $1/v^n$, one begins by approximating the $W^s{}_{ik\ldots l}$, involving n fixed molecules, by sums of the form $\lambda_i V_{is} + \sum_{l=1}^{n-1} V_{ls}$. These expressions, substituted in an equation similar to (38), yield an approximate $W^s{}_{ik\ldots l}$ involving $(n - 1)$ fixed molecules. Continued substitution finally leads to an expression for $W_i{}^k(\lambda_i)$, which when expanded in powers of $1/v$, is exact to terms involving $1/v^n$. It is only necessary to have the expression for $W^s{}_{ik\ldots l}$ involving $(n - 1)$ molecules, exact to terms in $1/v$, since in the final expansion, it is multiplied by a factor $1/v^{n-1}$.

V.

It is interesting to investigate the form of the molecular pair distribution function, $e^{-\beta W_i{}^k}$ by means of the approximation, Eq. (39). Although Eq. (39) can scarcely be accurate at liquid densities, we might expect it to be adequate up to moderately high densities. Moreover, even where inexact, it should serve to illustrate the form of the distribution function.

We shall restrict our attention to a pure fluid, consisting of spherically symmetrical molecules. For such a fluid, Eq. (39) reduces to the following expression when λ_i is equal to unity

$$W(r) = V(r) - (NkT/v) \times \int (1 - e^{-\beta V(r_{13})})(1 - e^{-\beta V(r_{23})}) dv_3,$$

$$r = |\mathbf{r}_1 - \mathbf{r}_2|;\ r_{13} = |\mathbf{r}_1 - \mathbf{r}_3|;\ r_{23} = |\mathbf{r}_2 - \mathbf{r}_3|. \tag{56}$$

Since all molecules are of the same type, $W_i{}^k$ and V_{ik} have the same functional form for every molecular pair, and we may omit the indices i and k. We shall suppose the molecules to be rigid spheres of diameter b, so that when r is less than b, $V(r)$ becomes positively infinite. Attractive forces outside of the sphere a should properly be represented by a potential of the form, $-\gamma/r^6$. However to simplify calculations, we shall represent this potential by a trough of depth u_0 and width, $a - b$. Between the concentric spheres of radii

b and a, $V(r)$ is thus equal to $-u_0$. The potential $V(r)$, upon which the following calculations are based is represented by the following step function.

$$\begin{aligned} V(r) &= \infty, && 0 \leqslant r \leqslant b \\ &= -u_0, && b \leqslant r \leqslant a \\ &= 0, && a < r. \end{aligned} \tag{57}$$

With this potential, the integral on the left-hand side of Eq. (56) may be expressed in terms of the volumes of intersection of spheres of radii a and b.

$$\begin{aligned} W(r)/kT &= V(r)/kT - (N\omega_0/v)J(r), \\ \omega_0 &= 4\pi b^3/3, \\ J(r) &= \frac{1}{\omega_0}\{\omega_{bb} + 2(\omega_{ab} - \omega_{bb})(1 - e^{\beta u_0}) \\ &\qquad + (\omega_{aa} - 2\omega_{ab} + \omega_{bb})(1 - e^{\beta u_0})^2\}, \end{aligned} \tag{58}$$

where ω_{bb} is volume of intersection of two spheres of equal radii b, ω_{aa} that of two spheres of equal radii a, and ω_{ab} that of two spheres of unequal radii a and b, the distance between the centers of each pair of spheres being r. A simple calculation yields

$$\begin{aligned} \frac{\omega_{bb}}{\omega_0} &= 1 - 3r/4b + \tfrac{1}{16}(r/b)^3; \quad 0 < r \leqslant 2b \\ &= 0, \quad r > 2b \\ \frac{\omega_{aa}}{\omega_0} &= (a/b)^3[1 - 3r/4a + \tfrac{1}{16}(r/a)^3]; \quad 0 < r \leqslant 2a \\ &= 0, \quad r > 2a \\ \frac{\omega_{ab}}{\omega_0} &= \tfrac{1}{2}\{[1 - \tfrac{3}{4}(1 - (\alpha/r^2))(r/b) + \tfrac{1}{16}(1 - (\alpha/r^2)^3(r/b)^3] + (a/b)^3 \\ &\times [1 - \tfrac{3}{4}(1 + (\alpha/r^2))(r/a) + \tfrac{1}{16}(1 + (\alpha/r^2))^3(r/a)^3]\}; \\ &\qquad (a^2 - b^2)^{\frac{1}{2}} < r \leqslant a + b \\ &= 0, \quad r > a + b; \quad \alpha = a^2 - b^2. \end{aligned} \tag{59}$$

By means of Eqs. (58) and (59), $W(r)/kT$ may be computed as a function of the ratios, r/b, a/b, $N\omega_0/v$ and u_0/kT. The probability distribution function, which we shall designate by $G(r)$ may then be calculated from the relation $G(r) = e^{-W(r)/kT}$. We note that $N\omega_0$ is equal to eight times the total volume of the molecules, their radii being $b/2$. For most liquids the ratio $N\omega_0/v$ would have a value between 4 and 6. Moreover, we should expect u_0/kT to be at least unity in liquids. The ratio a/b is somewhat arbitrary. However, in order to make the rectangular trough approximate the actual potential of the attractive forces, which diminishes rapidly with increasing distance, a/b cannot differ much from unity. In order to approach conditions in the liquid state, we assign the following values to the constants in question: $N\omega_0/v = 2$;

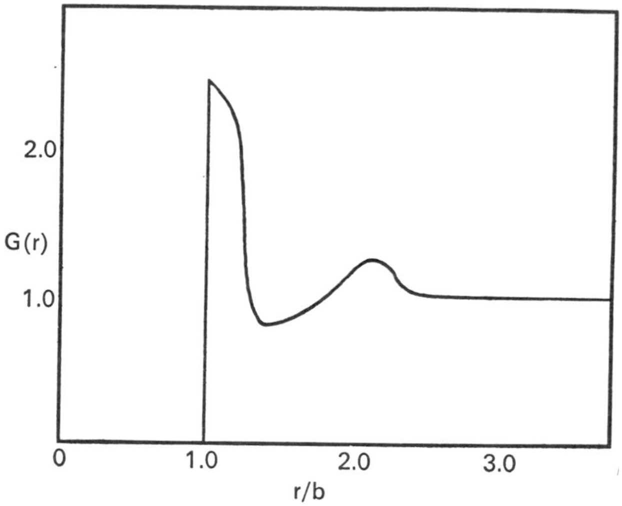

FIG. 1. Molecular pair distribution function based upon Eq. (58).

$u_0/kT = 1$; $a/b = 1.25$. The above value of $N\omega_0/v$ corresponds to a density about a third of ordinary liquid densities. With the above values of the constants, $G(r)$ has been calculated with the aid of Eqs. (58) and (59). It is plotted as a function of r/b in Fig. 1, and tabulated in Table I. Actually there

TABLE I.

r/b	$G(r)$	r/b	$G(r)$
0.0	0.00	1.6	0.86
0.8	0.00	1.8	0.98
1.0	2.48	2.0	1.20
1.2	2.23	2.2	1.25
1.4	0.81	2.4	1.03
		2.5	1.00

is a discontinuity in the curve at $r/b = 1.25$, arising from the artificial nature of the step function potential. In the figure, this discontinuity has been eliminated by drawing a smooth curve through points calculated at r/b intervals of 0.2. It will be observed that the calculated $G(r)$ bears a close resemblance to the molecular distribution functions in liquids derived from measurements of x-ray scattering, exhibiting the characteristic maxima and minima of the empirically determined functions. While we realize that at the temperature and density of the above calculation, the approximation (39) is being pushed to the limit of its applicability, we believe that it adequately illustrates the mechanism by which the intermolecular forces operate to establish molecular pair distribution functions in dense fluids.

It is interesting to observe that the attractive van der Waals forces play a dominant role in the production of the secondary maximum and minimum in the $G(r)$ of Fig. 1. On the basis of Eq. (39), the distribution function in a fluid of rigid spheres with no attractive forces would exhibit a single maximum at $r = b$. The absence of secondary maxima and minima for rigid spheres is of course the fault of Eq. (39). If the approximation were carried one stage farther, they would begin to appear. However, the point to be emphasized is that probability distribution functions derived from the packing of rigid spheres can scarcely be applied to actual fluids, where the attractive forces play a dominant role in determining the form of the distribution function.

A further limitation of the approximation (39) is that it fails to produce more than a single pair of secondary maxima and minima. For a more exact calculation, it is suggested that the distribution function derived from Eq. (39) be used as a starting point for the self-consistent solution of the more exact integral Eqs. (41) and (42). Thus, it will be observed that tertiary maxima and minima would doubtless arise from the secondary maximum and minimum of the approximate $W(r, \lambda)$ based on Eq. (39), if the latter function were substituted in the integral of Eq. (42). The computational difficulties involved in the self-consistent solution of Eq. (42) are unfortunately rather serious, since even for spherically symmetrical molecules, a triple numerical or mechanical integration is required at each stage of the process. However, these difficulties are not insurmountable.

The formulation of a theory of solutions on the basis of the present ideas offers intriguing possibilities. Several methods of approach are open, the direct use of our expressions for the chemical potentials being the most obvious. An alternative and more phenomenological treatment applicable to dilute solutions has also been undertaken. These investigations will be described in a future article.

Note added in proof:

(a) A remark about the normalization of the molecular pair distribution functions is perhaps worth while. In defining the potential of mean force, $W_i^k(\lambda_i)$, an arbitrary constant is at our disposal. This constant has been so chosen that

$$(1/v\sigma_k)\int e^{-\beta W_i^k(\lambda_i)} d\omega_k = 1$$

a relation which may be verified by reference to Eq. (20b). The approximate forms for $W_i^k(\lambda_i)$ of course do not exactly satisfy this condition.

(b) At sufficiently high temperatures, the exponentials of Eq. (41) may be expanded and the following approximate linear integral equation is obtained

$$W_i^k(\lambda_i) = \lambda_i V_{ik} - \frac{\lambda_i}{kT} \sum_s \frac{N_s}{v} \frac{1}{\sigma_s} \int V_{is} W_k^s(1) d\omega_s$$

where regions in which W_i^s and W_k^s become infinite due to repulsive forces, are excluded from the integration. If we apply the equation to the ions of an electrolyte solution, the solvent being treated as a continuous medium of dielectric constant D, we know that V_{ik} is equal $e_i e_k / D r_{ik}$ where e_i and e_k are the ionic charges. For this potential, it may be verified without difficulty that the above set of linear integral equations has the following solutions

$$W_i^k(\lambda_i) = \lambda_i \frac{e_i e_k}{D r_{ik}} e^{-\kappa r_{ik}}; \quad \kappa^2 = \frac{4\pi}{DkT} \sum_s \frac{N_s}{v} e_s^2$$

if molecular size is neglected. These solutions, together with Eq. (22) lead to the Debye-Hückel limiting law for the chemical potentials of the ions.

Statistical Mechanics of Liquid Solutions*

JOHN G. KIRKWOOD, *Department of Chemistry, Cornell University, Ithaca, New York*

(Received October 17, 1936)

I. INTRODUCTION

In the formulation of a molecular theory of solutions, there are two main problems to be considered. The first is the calculation of intermolecular forces from a knowledge of molecular structure, and the second is the correlation of the macroscopic properties of a thermodynamic system with the behavior of a dynamical system, consisting of many molecules executing thermal motion under known intermolecular and external forces. In the calculation of certain types of intermolecular force, for example, between ions and between molecules containing low-frequency electric multipole moments, simple electrostatics suffice. A more comprehensive theory of intermolecular forces is furnished by quantum mechanics. The nature of van der Waals forces between non-polar molecules and of the repulsive forces, which determine molecular size, is now well understood. It is true that computational difficulties stand in the way of exact calculations for all but the simplest molecules. Nevertheless, rather good approximations to the potential of van der Waals force can be obtained in terms of a few simple molecular constants, such as polarizability and ionization potential. What is perhaps more important, the approximate form of the potential of intermolecular force as a function of the molecular coordinates is known.

In the present article, we shall be chiefly concerned with the second problem, which lies within the province of statistical mechanics. In the study of liquids at ordinary temperatures it is usually sufficient to use classical statistical mechanics. This is permissible when the motion of the molecules involves only a high frequency and a low frequency type, in the sense of van Vleck's definition. The high frequency type of motion is characterized by the fact that the interval between adjacent energy levels is large relative to kT, the product of Boltzmann's constant and the absolute temperature. Under these circumstances there is no appreciable thermal excitation above the lowest energy state. The low frequency type of motion, on the other hand, is characterized by energy intervals very small relative to kT. The internal motion, electronic and vibrational, of most molecules is of the high frequency type at ordinary temperatures, while the translational and rotational motion is of the low frequency type.

In an earlier article[1] a method for the statistical treatment of liquids was developed on the basis of the classical canonical ensemble. This method provides a suitable basis for the formulation of a general theory of solutions.

---

* Presented at the Ninety-second Meeting of the American Chemical Society in Pittsburgh, September, 1936, on the occasion of the presentation of the American Chemical Society Award in Pure Chemistry for 1936.

[1] J. G. Kirkwood, *J. Chem. Physics*, **3**, 300 (1935).

In addition to yielding a number of new results, it embraces those of older special theories as parts of a unified whole. Both electrolytes and non-electrolytes fit naturally into the scheme. We shall undertake the formulation of the theory as well as a discussion of some of its applications, particularly to electrolyte solutions. While there still remain a number of obstacles to be overcome, the theory is at present sufficiently well developed to yield some interesting results.

II. GENERAL THEORY

The Helmholtz free energy F_N of a liquid solution consisting of N molecules is related to the potential of intermolecular force, V_N, by the method of the canonical ensemble, in the following manner

$$e^{-\beta F_N} = \left[\prod_{s=1}^{\nu} \frac{f_s(T)^{N_s}}{N_s!}\right] Z_N$$

$$Z_N = \int \cdots \int e^{-\beta V_N}\, dv_1 \cdots dv_N \tag{1}$$

where β is equal to $1/kT$, and $N_1, \cdots N_\nu$ are the numbers of molecules of the several components of the solution. The function $f_s(T)$ is a product of the internal partition function of a molecule of type s and the classical momentum phase integral associated with its low frequency translational and rotational degrees of freedom. The familiar phase integral Z_N extends over the translational and rotational configuration space of each molecule, bounded by the volume v of the solution. We denote by dv_i a differential element of this configuration space, divided by 4π for diatomic molecules and linear polyatomic molecules or by $8\pi^2$ for non-linear polyatomic molecules.

It has been previously shown[1] that the chemical potential of a component i of the solution may be expressed in the form

$$\mu_i = -kT \log\left[\frac{f_i(T)}{N_i}\frac{Z_N}{Z_{N-i}}\right] \tag{2}$$

where Z_{N-i} is the phase integral of the system with a single molecule of type i removed, the temperature, volume, and numbers of molecules of the remaining components being the same as in Z_N. We suppose that the potential of intermolecular force may be represented as the sum of terms V_{ik}, each depending upon the relative coordinates of a single molecular pair

$$V_N = \sum_{\substack{i<k\\=1}}^{N} V_{ik} \tag{3}$$

This is no real restriction on the method, for it may be easily extended to include terms V_{ikl} depending upon the coordinates of three molecules, and so on. For simplicity, we shall not include such terms. In treating chemically saturated molecules, terms of the form V_{ikl} are probably needed only when it is desired to take account of the induced or optical polarization of molecules in a system containing ions or dipoles. Such interactions are usually unimportant in comparison with other intermolecular forces. The form of equation (3) might be questioned for the repulsive forces, which operate at small intermolecular distances and determine molecular "size". However, these repulsive forces generally act in such a manner as to make the molecules behave as hard impenetrable objects. Thus their role consists in making $e^{-\beta V_N}$ vanish whenever the relative coordinates of any molecular pair are within the region of repulsion. This may be accomplished with a potential of the form of equation (3), in which each V_{ik} assumes a large value V_R whenever the relative coordinates of the pair are within the region of repulsion of volume ω_{ik}. Strictly speaking, V_R should be infinite, but for practical purposes it is only necessary to assume it very large relative to kT, a procedure which avoids a certain amount of mathematical hedging.

It is convenient to introduce a fictitious potential

$$V_N(\lambda_i) = V_{N-1} + \lambda_i V_i$$

$$V_i = \sum_{k=1}^{N} V_{ik} \tag{3a}$$

where λ_i is an arbitrary parameter, and V_{N-1} is the potential of intermolecular force in a system containing one less molecule of type i than the original one. Corresponding to $V_N(\lambda_i)$ we may construct a phase integral $Z_N(\lambda_i)$ which is equal to Z_N when λ_i has the value unity and to Z_{N-i} when λ_i is zero. Following the methods of the earlier paper,[1] we finally obtain for the chemical potential of the component i

$$\mu_i = kT \log N_i/v + \sum_{k=1}^{\nu} \frac{N_k}{v} (J_{ik} + G_{ik}) + \varphi_i(T)$$

$$J_{ik} = \int_0^1 \int_0^{\omega_{ik}} V_{ik} e^{-\beta W_i^k(\lambda_i)}\, dv_k\, d\lambda_i \tag{4}$$

$$G_{ik} = \int_0^1 \int_{\omega_{ik}}^{v} V_{ik} e^{-\beta W_i^k(\lambda_i)}\, dv_k\, d\lambda_i$$

$$\varphi_i(T) = -kT \log f_i(T)$$

where the integral J_{ik} extends only over the region of repulsion ω_{ik}, and G_{ik} extends over the rest of the volume of the solution. The function $W_i^k(\lambda_i)$ is the potential of average force between i and k, defined as follows

$$e^{-\beta W_i^k(\lambda_i)} = \frac{v \int \cdots \int e^{-\beta V_N(\lambda_i)}\, dv_1 \cdots dv_{N-2}}{\int \cdots \int e^{-\beta V_N(\lambda_i)}\, dv_1 \cdots dv_{N-1}} \tag{5}$$

where the integral in the numerator extends over all molecules except i and k, while that in the denominator extends over all molecules except i. In the earlier article[1] it is shown that $W_i^k(\lambda_i)$ satisfies the following equation

$$W_i^k(\lambda_i) = \lambda_i V_{ik} + \sum_{l=1}^{\nu} \frac{N_l}{v} \int_0^{\lambda_i} \int_0^{v} V_{il} (e^{-\beta W_{ik}^l(\lambda_i)} e^{-\beta W_i^l(\lambda_i)})\, dv_l\, d\lambda_i \tag{6}$$

where $W_{ik}^l(\lambda_i)$ is the potential of average force acting on a molecule l in the neighborhood of the fixed pair i and k. It is defined by a relation similar to equation (5). A set of integral equations for the $W_i^k(\lambda_i)$ of the several types of pairs in the solution may be obtained if $W_{ik}^l(\lambda_i)$ is approximated by $W_i^l(\lambda_i) + W_k^l(1)$:

$$W_i^k(\lambda_i) = \lambda_i V_{ik} + \sum_{l=1}^{\nu} \frac{N_l}{v} \int_0^{\lambda_2} \int_0^v V_{il} e^{-\beta W_i^l(\lambda_i)} (e^{-\beta W_k^l(1)} - 1)\, dv_l\, d\lambda_i \tag{7}$$

The nature of the superposition approximation, upon which this equation is based, has been discussed elsewhere.[1] It may happen that outside the regions of repulsion, βW_i^l and βW_k^l are small enough to permit expansion of the exponentials with the neglect of terms in the second and higher powers of β. When this is done a set of approximate linear integral equations is obtained,

$$W_i^k(\lambda_i) = V'_{ik}(\lambda_i) - \beta \sum_{l=1}^{\nu} \frac{N_l}{v} \left\{ \int_0^{\omega'_{il}} K_{il} W_k^l(1)\, dv_l + \lambda_i \int_{\omega_{il}, \omega_{kl}}^{v} V_{il} W_k^l(1)\, dv_l \right\}$$

$$V'_{ik}(\lambda_i) = \lambda_i V_{ik} + \sum_{l=1}^{\nu} \frac{N_l}{v} \left\{ \lambda_i \int_0^{\omega'_{kl}} V_{il}\, dv_l - \int_0^{\omega_{ikl}} K_{il}\, dv_l \right\} \tag{8}$$

$$K_{il}(\lambda_l) = \int_0^{\lambda_i} V_{il} e^{-\beta W_i^l(\lambda_i)}\, d\lambda_i; \quad l \text{ in } \omega_{il}$$

where ω'_{il} and ω'_{kl} are the non-overlapping parts of the regions of repulsion for l around i and k, and ω_{ikl} is the overlapping part of these regions. Solution of these equations for several types of intermolecular forces has been undertaken. The case of electrolytes will be discussed in a later section of this article. Fortunately we do not need to know K_{il} in this case. Solution has also been attempted for a system of spherical molecules with short-range attractive forces. In this case K_{il} must be known and has been estimated with some success for pure liquids. This work will be reported in a later article.

For the calculation of the integrals G_{ik} and J_{ik} appearing in equation (4), it is necessary to know the potential $W_i^k(\lambda_i)$ both inside and outside the sphere of exclusion ω_{ik}. While considerable progress has been made in the calculation of the G_{ik}, direct attempts to evaluate the J_{ik} have not yet been successful. Inside ω_{ik}, $W_i^k(\lambda_i)$ is of course positive and very large except when λ_i is near zero, so that the integrand $V_{ik} e^{-\beta W_i^k(\lambda_i)}$ has a sharp peak near $\lambda_i = 0$ and vanishes elsewhere. A crude approximation, not valid at liquid densities, is obtained by setting $W_i^k(\lambda_i)$ equal to $\lambda_i V_{ik}$, yielding $J_{ik} = kT\omega_{ik}$. Indirect methods of approach have yielded fair approximations to J_{ik} in pure liquids, but in mixtures the problem has not been solved, except under certain arbitrary assumptions about the entropy of solvation.

We return to equation (4) for the chemical potential, which we write in the following form

$$\mu_i = kT \log x_i + \sum_{k=1}^{\nu} \frac{N_k}{v} G_{ik} + \mu_i^*$$

$$\mu_i^* = kT \log \bar{v} + \sum_{k=1}^{\nu} \frac{N_k}{v} J_{ik} + \varphi_i(T) \tag{9}$$

where $\bar{v}$ is the mean molal volume of the solution, and $x_1, \cdots x_2$ are the mole fractions of the several components. Let us now suppose that our solution contains N_i' molecules which are of the same shape and volume as molecules of type i but which exert no attractive forces on their neighbors. Although such molecules may have arbitrary shape, we shall find it convenient to refer to them as hard spheres. For a hard sphere all G_{ik} are zero. Referring again to equation (4), we find for the chemical potential of a hard sphere

$$\mu_i' = kT \log x_i' - kT \log \bar{v}' + \sum_{k=1}^{\nu+1} \frac{N_k}{v} J_{ik} + \varphi_i(T) \tag{10}$$

where x_i' is the mole fraction of the hard spheres and $\bar{v}'$ is the mean molal volume of the solution augmented by N_i' hard spheres, the summation over all components of course including them. We now observe that the limit of

$$\mu_i' - kT \log x_i'$$

as $x_i' \to 0$ is simply μ_i^* of equation (9). Thus μ_i^* is the non-ideal part of the chemical potential of hard spheres of type i at infinite dilution in a solvent consisting of the solution under investigation.[2]

For thermodynamic purposes, it is convenient to choose some reference value of the chemical potential, μ_i^0, and to define an activity coefficient which measures the departure of $\mu_i - \mu_i^0$ from its ideal value $kT \log x_i$. When the mole fraction of the component is large, or when solutions are to be studied in which its mole fraction varies over a wide range, it is customary to choose μ_i^0 as the chemical potential of the pure liquid component at the same temperature and pressure as the solution,

$$\mu_i = kT \log f_i x_i + \mu_i^0 \tag{11}$$

where the activity coefficient f_i approaches unity as the mole fraction x_i tends to unity. On the other hand, if one component, the solvent, is present in large excess at all compositions of interest, it is convenient to choose the reference value, μ_i^0, for a solute component as the limit of $\mu_i - kT \log x_i$ as the mole fraction of the solvent, x_s, approaches unity.

$$\begin{aligned} \mu_i &= kT \log \gamma_i x_i + \mu_i^0 \\ \mu_i^0 &= \lim_{x_s \to 1} \mu_i - kT \log x_i \end{aligned} \tag{12}$$

where γ_i is an activity coefficient which approaches unity as the solution becomes infinitely dilute with respect to all solute species. It is often convenient to use the molarity or the concentration of species i in place of its mole fraction. In dilute solution these variables are nearly proportional to one another and the corresponding activity coefficients are nearly equal. From equation (9), we obtain for the first choice of μ_i^0, the chemical potential of pure liquid i,

$$\mu_i^0 = NG_{ii}^0/\bar{v}_i^0 + \mu_i^{*0}$$

[2] The formal and thermodynamic aspects of the separation of the chemical potential into parts arising from different types of intermolecular force are discussed by Bell and Gatty (*Phil. Mag.* **19**, 66 (1935)). Our hard sphere species corresponds to the solute with "limited interaction" of Bell and Gatty.

where G^0_{ii} is to be calculated with a distribution function $e^{-\beta W_i^k(\lambda_i)}$ appropriate to the pure liquid component and μ_i^* is the non-ideal part of the chemical potential of a hard sphere of the same size as molecules of type i, at infinite dilution in pure i. By subtraction and use of the relation

$$1/\bar{v}_i = N_i/v + \sum_{\substack{k \neq i \\ =1}}^{\nu} N_k \bar{v}_k / v \bar{v}_i$$

we obtain

$$kT \log f_i/f_i^* = \sum_{k=1}^{\nu} \frac{N_k}{v}\left(G_{ik} - \frac{\bar{v}_k}{\bar{v}_i} G_{ii}\right) + \frac{NG_{ii}}{\bar{v}_i} - \frac{NG^0_{ii}}{\bar{v}^0_i} \tag{13}$$

$$kT \log f_i^* = \mu_i^* - \mu_i^{*0}$$

If the μ_i^0 is chosen at infinite dilution in a solvent s, we have

$$\mu_i^0 = NG^0_{is}/\bar{v}^0_s + \mu_i^{*(s)} \tag{14}$$

where $\mu_i^{*(s)}$ is the chemical potential of a hard sphere of type i at infinite dilution in the pure solvent. We then obtain for the activity coefficient γ_i the following expression.

$$kT \log \frac{\gamma_i}{\gamma_i^*} = \sum_{\substack{k=1 \\ \neq s}}^{\nu} \frac{N_k}{v}\left(G_{ik} - \frac{\bar{v}_k}{\bar{v}_s} G_{is}\right) + \frac{NG_{is}}{\bar{v}_s} - \frac{NG^0_{is}}{\bar{v}^0_s}$$

$$kT \log \gamma_i^* = \mu_i^* - \mu_i^{*(s)} \tag{15}$$

For exact calculations, we must be able to say something about the chemical potential μ_i^* of the hard spheres. Since direct calculations of the J_{ik} have not yet been successful, only provisional statements about μ_i^* may be made. At this point it is of interest to mention an empirical means of estimating $\mu_i^* - \mu_i^{*(s)}$ similar to a method due to Scatchard,[3] who recognized the need for such a correction in the case of electrolytes. He proposed to use the solubilities of the noble gases for this purpose. The noble gases approximate hard spheres, at least in polar solvents, since their attractive forces are weak relative to those between polar molecules. In the present formulation γ_i^* would be equal to the limit of p^*/p_0^* as the pressure of the noble gas tends to zero, where p^* and p_0^* are the gas fugacities in equilibrium with equal mole fractions of the dissolved gas in the actual solution and in the pure solvent. This limit is equal to K/K_0, the ratio of the Henry's law constants of the gas for the solution and for the pure solvent. By a process of size interpolation among the several noble gases, it should be possible to pick a value appropriate to the size of a given solute molecule. Given the data, this would at least provide a means of estimating errors introduced by the customary neglect of the term $\mu_i^* - \mu_i^{*(s)}$ in theories of dilute solutions.[4]

There is another method of estimating μ_i^*, based upon certain assumptions about the entropy of solvation of a hard sphere. From thermodynamics we know that μ_i is equal to $\bar{H}_i - T\bar{S}_i$ or to an adequate approximation in condensed system, $\bar{E}_i - T\bar{S}_i$, where $\bar{H}_i$, $\bar{E}_i$, and $\bar{S}_i$ are the partial molal heat

[3] G. Scatchard, *Physik. Z.* **33**, 22 (1932).

[4] A similar method was first proposed by Bjerrum and his coworkers (*Trans. Faraday Soc.* **23**, 445 (1927); *Z. physik. Chem.* **127A**, 358 (1927); **159**, 194 (1932)).

content, energy, and entropy of component i. Now the energy of a solution is easily calculated as

$$E = \frac{1}{2} \sum_{\substack{k, l \\ =1}}^{\nu} \frac{N_k N_l}{v} B_{kl} + \sum_{k=1}^{N} N_k E_k^0(T)$$

$$B_{kl} = \int_{\omega_{kl}}^{v} V_{kl} e^{-\beta W_k^l(1)} \mathrm{d}v_l \tag{16}$$

where $E_k^0(T)$ is the sum of the internal energy and the average rotational and translational kinetic energy of a molecule of type k, depending only on the temperature. The B_{ik} are calculated with the distribution function $W_i^k(1)$, which always makes $e^{-\beta W_i^k(1)}$ vanish in the region of repulsion ω_{ik}, so that no contribution to the integral arises from this region. The B_{ik} all vanish for a hard sphere. If we imagine hard spheres of type i to be present, they can influence the energy of the solution only by their effect on the volume and on the relative distribution of the other molecules. Neglecting the latter effect, and calculating $\bar{E}_i^*$ for a hard sphere of type i, we obtain

$$\bar{E}_i^* = \left(\frac{\partial E}{\partial N_i}\right)_{T,p,N_k \cdots} = -\frac{\bar{v}_i^*}{2v^2} \sum_{\substack{k, l \\ =1}}^{\nu} N_k N_l B_{kl} + E_i^0(T) \tag{17}$$

where, since $\bar{E}_i^*$ is to be taken at infinite dilution with respect to the hard spheres, the B_{kl} and v are those of the actual solution. The partial molal volume $\bar{v}_i^*$ of the hard spheres is not necessarily equal to $\bar{v}_i$, that of the actual species i, but in many cases the two will be very nearly equal. We now tentatively assume that $\bar{S}_i^*$ is the same for all solutions and pure liquids at the same temperature and pressure, remembering that $\bar{S}_i^*$ is the non-ideal part of the partial molal entropy of the hard spheres at infinite dilution in the given solution. This assumption cannot as yet be justified by exact reasoning, and it probably is not valid or only approximately valid when one has to do with components of unequal molecular size. When applied to solutions whose components are identical in molecular size and shape, the assumption is entirely reasonable, for since the hard sphere exerts no attractive forces on the other molecules of the solution, its motion in the system is determined solely by the repulsive forces exerted on it by the other molecules, in other words by their size, shape, and packing. Under this assumption the chemical potential of a hard sphere depends upon the solution in which it is immersed only through $\bar{E}_i^*$. This term arises from the pushing of the other molecules of the solution apart, an effect which may be likened to that of the introduction of a microscopic bubble into the solution. The corresponding values of f_i^* and γ_i^* are the following

$$kT \log f_i^* = -\frac{\bar{v}_i^*}{2}\left[\sum_{\substack{k, l \\ =1}}^{\nu} \frac{N_k N_l}{v^2} B_{kl} - \frac{N^2 B_{ii}^0}{\bar{v}_i^{02}}\right]$$

$$k \log \gamma_i^* = -\frac{\bar{v}_i^*}{2}\left[\sum_{\substack{k, l \\ =1}}^{\nu} \frac{N_k N_l}{v^2} B_{kl} - \frac{N^2 B_{is}^0}{\bar{v}_s^2}\right] \tag{18}$$

where $\bar{v}_i^*$ is assumed to have the same value in the solution and in the reference liquid, in the first case pure liquid i, and in the second pure solvent. For future reference, we shall express $kT \log \gamma_i^*$ in a form suitable for dilute solutions in which only solute concentrations appear.

$$kT \log \gamma_i^* = -\frac{\bar{v}_i^*}{\bar{v}_s^2} \sum_{\substack{k=1 \\ \neq s}}^{\nu} \frac{N_k}{v} [\bar{v}_s B_{ks} - \bar{v}_k B_{ss}]$$

$$- \frac{\bar{v}_i^*}{2\bar{v}_s^2} \sum_{\substack{k,l \\ \neq s}}^{\nu} \frac{N_k N_l}{v^2} [\bar{v}_s^2 B_{kl} + \bar{v}_l^2 B_{ss} - 2\bar{v}_k \bar{v}_l B_{ks}] \tag{19}$$

where all molal volumes are assumed independent of composition.

Scatchard[5] and Hildebrand and Wood[6,7] have proposed an equation for non-electrolyte mixtures, based upon two primary assumptions: (a) the entropy of mixing is ideal; (b) the probability distribution is the same for all molecular pairs in the solution and is independent of composition. In our notation the Scatchard-Hildebrand equation may be written

$$kT \log f_i = \frac{\bar{v}_i}{2} \sum_{\substack{k,l \\ =1}}^{\nu} \frac{N_k N_l \bar{v}_k \bar{v}_l}{v^2} \left[\frac{2B_{ik}^0}{\bar{v}_i \bar{v}_k} - \frac{B_{kl}^0}{\bar{v}_k \bar{v}_l} - \frac{B_{ii}^0}{\bar{v}_i^2} \right] \tag{20}$$

where the partial molal volumes are assumed independent of composition and the B_{kl}^0 are computed with a distribution function appropriate to any one of the pure liquid components. It is interesting to note the conditions under which our equations (13) and (18) reduce to the Scatchard–Hildebrand equation. This occurs when all $W_i^k(\lambda_i)$ are independent not only of composition, but also of λ_i. When the $W_i^k(\lambda_i)$ are independent of composition the term

$$G_{ii}/\bar{v}_i - G_{ii}^0/\bar{v}_i^0$$

vanishes. When they are independent of λ_i, the G_{ik} reduce to the corresponding B_{ik}. If, in addition, we suppose that the partial molal volume $\bar{v}_i^*$ is equal to $\bar{v}_i$, and that all $\bar{v}_k$ are independent of composition, our equations (9) and (18) reduce to equation (20) after some algebraic transformations involving the relation

$$1/\bar{v}_i = \left(N_i + \sum_{k \neq i}^{\nu} N_k \bar{v}_k / \bar{v}_i \right) \Big/ v$$

An investigation of the $W_i^k(\lambda_i)$ in liquids consisting of spherical molecules with short-range attractive forces, now in progress, has shown that when the attractive forces between different components do not differ greatly, the function $W_i^k(\lambda_i)$ is determined primarily by molecular size. This conclusion is not especially remarkable, and has been reached by others on qualitative grounds. However, when this is true, we find that $W_i^k(\lambda_i)$ is practically independent of λ_i except when λ_i is nearly zero, which requires the G_{ik} to

[5] G. Scatchard, *Chem. Rev.* **8**, 321 (1931).
[6] J. H. Hildebrand and S. E. Wood, *J. Chem. Physics* **1**, 817 (1933).
[7] J. H. Hildebrand, *Chem. Rev.* **18**, 315 (1936).

reduce effectively to the B_{ik}. When all components of the solution are of the same molecular size, $W_i^k(\lambda_i)$ also becomes independent of composition, and the two major conditions for the validity of the Scatchard–Hildebrand equation are fulfilled.

Guggenheim[8] has developed an interesting theory of solutions, which makes no attempt to go into the fine points of molecular distribution. His theory bears a marked resemblance to lattice theories of the solid state, as does a somewhat earlier theory of Heitler.[9] Guggenheim confirms the Scatchard-Hildebrand equation for equal molecular sizes and random distribution of pairs of the type previously discussed. He also proposes an approximate method for taking departures from random distribution into account when the attractive forces between like and unlike pairs are considerably different. Guggenheim's approach is quite different from ours and in many ways simpler. However, while it is probably adequate to deal with problems concerning the energy of mixing and solution, it fails to take account of the non-ideal entropy of mixing in a formally satisfactory manner. We shall present briefly an extension of the Guggenheim theory, which takes formal account of the entropy of mixing, a step which is necessary in estimating its possibilities.

Guggenheim assumes that as in crystals V_N, the potential of intermolecular forces, has a number of sharp minima of equal depth in the configuration space of the system of N molecules. In perfect crystals, there are just $\prod_{k=1}^{\nu} N_s!$ of these minima, one for each permutation of molecules of the same species, which just cancels out this factor in the denominator of the right-hand side of equation (1). On the other hand, in some liquid mixtures, where attractive forces between like and unlike molecules are not very different from those between like molecules, the minima in V_N occur for permutations of unlike molecules as well so that they are $\left(\sum_{s=1}^{\nu} N_s\right)!$ in number. The phase integral of equation (1) is then equal to $\left(\sum_{s=1}^{\nu} N_s\right)!I_N$, where I_N is the value of Z_N taken over the region in the neighborhood of one of the minima. From equation (1) we then obtain for the free energy of the solution

$$F_N = +\sum_{k=1}^{\nu} N_k kT \log x_k - kT \log I_N + \sum_{k=1}^{\nu} N_k \varphi_k(T) \tag{21}$$

where factorials have been approximated by Sterling's formula. Guggenheim then approximates I_N by $e^{-\beta \bar{V}_N} v^N$ where $\bar{V}_N$ is its value at the minimum (also the average potential energy in this theory), and v is a proper volume in which a molecule is free to move. For the theory to be of value, the dependence of this quantity v on composition must be investigated. Guggenheim applies his theory only to cases in which it is reasonable to assume v independent of composition. However, it is possible to get a deeper insight into this question in the following manner. In order to evaluate I_N by peak integration, it is necessary to expand V_N in a Taylor's series in normal coordinates $q_1 \cdots q_{3N}$ specifying the displacement of the system of N molecules

---

[8] E. A. Guggenheim, *Proc. Roy. Soc. London* **148A**, 304 (1935).

[9] W. Heitler, *Ann. Physik.* [4], **80**, 630 (1928).

from the point in configuration space corresponding to the minimum value of V_N and the maximum of $e^{-\beta V_N}$,

$$V_N = \bar{V}_N + \tfrac{1}{2} \sum_{s=1}^{3N} \left(\frac{\partial^2 V_N}{\partial q_s^2} \right)_0 q_s^2 + \cdots\cdots \tag{22}$$

where the linear terms in the q_k do not appear, since all first derivatives of V_N vanish at the minimum, and, by the use of normal coordinates, all cross derivatives $(\partial^2 V_N/\partial q_s \partial q_k)_0$ are made to vanish. The derivatives $(\partial^2 V_N/\partial q_i^2)_0$ are equal to $2\pi^2 M_s \nu_s^2$, where M_s is a function of the masses of the N molecules, and the ν_s is one of the normal frequencies, in terms of which the vibration of the system around the position of minimum V_N is described, in other words one of the Debye frequencies of the solution. In the peak integration, the q_s are followed to range between $-\infty$ and $+\infty$ with the result

$$I_N = e^{-\beta \bar{V}_N} \left[\prod_{s=1}^{3N} \cdot \frac{1}{\nu_s} \right] \prod_{s=1}^{3N} \left(\frac{kT}{2\pi M_s} \right)^{1/2} \tag{23}$$

Substitution of this expression into equation (21) gives

$$F_N = \sum_{k=1}^{\nu} N_k kT \log x_k + \bar{V}_N + \sum_{s=1}^{3N} kT \log \nu_s + \sum_{k=1}^{\nu} N_k \varphi_k(T) \tag{24}$$

where the factors $(kT/2\pi M_s)^{1/2}$ are absorbed into the temperature functions $\varphi_k(T)$. Thus Guggenheim's effective volume v is proportional to the mean reciprocal of the Debye frequencies of the solution

$$\log v = \frac{1}{N} \sum_{s=1}^{3N} \log \nu_s^{-1} \tag{25}$$

except for an additive constant dependent only on the temperature. It is no easy task to determine the dependence of the mean Debye frequency on composition, and it should be pointed out that not only molecular size, but also the attractive forces must enter into such a calculation. However, in a nearly ideal solution, where the assumption of approximately equal depths for all minima of V_N is justified, it is reasonable to suppose that v is rather insensitive to changes in composition of the solution. This is not necessarily true in Guggenheim's extension of his theory to take into account the inequalities in the depths of the minima for unequal attractive forces. Moreover, in the latter case the Debye frequencies must be averaged, not only over all normal modes for a single permutation of the molecules, but also over all such permutations. It appears that an exact treatment of the entropy of mixing, into which the v must enter, is even more difficult by the Guggenheim method than by our own.

III. THE RÔLE OF ELECTROSTATIC FORCES

We shall for the present be concerned with moderately dilute solutions. Let us denote γ_i/γ_i^* by γ_i'. It is also convenient to write equation (15) in a slightly different form.

$$kT \log \gamma_i' = \sum_{\substack{k \neq s \\ =1}}^{\nu} \frac{N_k}{v} G_{ik} + \frac{N_s}{v} G_{is} - \frac{N G_{is}^0}{\bar{v}_s^0} \tag{26}$$

We shall not attempt to calculate the hard sphere contribution γ_i^*, but we should remember that to obtain the true activity coefficient γ_i' must be multiplied by this quantity. An estimate of γ_i^* in dilute solutions is given by equation (19).

In this section we shall be particularly interested in solutions containing ions and dipoles. While for non-polar solutions the difference between G_{is} and G_{is}^0 may often be ignored, this is not true in solutions containing ions or dipole molecules, for the pair distribution functions $W_i^k(\lambda_i)$ are no longer even approximately independent of composition. Let us consider a solution consisting of a mixed electrolyte furnishing ν ionic species of charges e_k in a solvent consisting of dipole molecules. The potentials of intermolecular force for the different types of molecular pairs are the following,

$$\begin{aligned} V_{ik} &= e_i e_k / r_{ik} \\ V_{is} &= e_i \boldsymbol{\mu}_s \cdot \nabla_s \left(\frac{1}{r_{is}}\right) \end{aligned} \tag{27}$$

where r_{ik} is the distance between the ion pair i and k, and r_{is} is the distance between an ion i and a solvent molecule of dipole moment $\boldsymbol{\mu}_s$. For $N_s G_{is}/v$, we have from equations (4) and (27)

$$\frac{N_s G_{is}}{v} = \int_0^1 \int_{\omega_{is}}^{v} \frac{N_s}{v} e_i \boldsymbol{\mu}_s \cdot \nabla_s \left(\frac{1}{r_{is}}\right) e^{-\beta W_i^s(\lambda\,)} \mathrm{d}v_s \, \mathrm{d}o_s \tag{28}$$

where for clearness we indicate the orientation of a solvent molecule explicitly, $\mathrm{d}o_s$ being a normalized differential element of its orientation space, while $\mathrm{d}v_s$ refers only to its translational configuration space. We remark that

$$\frac{N_s e^{-\beta W_i^s(\lambda_i)}}{v}$$

is the average density of solvent molecules having a specified orientation at a specified distance, r_{is}, from ion i. Thus the integral

$$(N_s/v) \int \boldsymbol{\mu}_s e^{-\beta W_i^s(\lambda_i)} \mathrm{d}o_s$$

is the average density of electric moment or local polarization ${}^i\mathbf{P}$ of the solvent in the vicinity of ion i, charged to a fraction λ_i of its full charge e_i, and we may write

$$\frac{N_s G_{is}}{v} = \int_0^1 \int_{\omega_{is}}^{v} e_i \, {}^i\mathbf{P} \cdot \nabla_s \left(\frac{1}{r_{is}}\right) \mathrm{d}v_s \, \mathrm{d}\lambda_i \tag{29}$$

If ${}^i\mathbf{D}(r_{is})$ is the local dielectric displacement, we may define a local dielectric constant, ${}^i\epsilon$ by the relation

$${}^i\mathbf{P} = \frac{1}{4\pi} \frac{{}^i\epsilon - 1}{{}^i\epsilon} {}^i\mathbf{D} \tag{30}$$

where the local dielectric constant, ${}^{i}\epsilon$, may of course differ from the macroscopic dielectric constant, ϵ, of the solution and may depend upon ${}^{i}\mathbf{D}$ if there is electrical saturation. Except for possible terms of dipole symmetry, the local dielectric displacement is equal to the sum of $-\lambda_i e_i \nabla_s(1/r_{is})$ and the mean values of $-e_k \nabla_s(1/r_{ks})$, arising from the other ions k, averaged with i fixed

$$
{}^{i}\mathbf{D}(r_{is}) = -\lambda_i e_i \nabla_s \left(\frac{1}{r_{is}}\right) - \sum_{k=1}^{\nu} \frac{N_k}{v} e_k \int_{\omega_{ik}}^{v} \nabla_s \left(\frac{1}{r_{ks}}\right) e^{-\beta W_i^k(\lambda_i)} \, dv_k \tag{31}
$$

Substitution of equations (30) and (31) in equation (29) yields

$$
\begin{aligned}
\frac{N_s G_{is}}{v} = &- \int_0^1 \int_{\omega_{ik}}^{v} \lambda_i \frac{{}^{i}\epsilon - 1}{4\pi\,{}^{i}\epsilon} \frac{e_i^2}{r_{is}^4} \, dv_s \, d\lambda_i \\
&- \sum_{k=1}^{\nu} \frac{N_k e_i e_k}{v} \int_0^1 \int_{\omega_{ik}}^{v} \int_{\omega_{is}}^{v} \frac{{}^{i}\epsilon - 1}{4\pi\,{}^{i}\epsilon} \nabla_s \left(\frac{1}{r_{is}}\right) \cdot \nabla_s \left(\frac{1}{r_{ks}}\right) e^{-\beta W_i^k(\lambda_i)} \, dv_s \, dv_k \, d\lambda_i
\end{aligned} \tag{31a}
$$

We remark that if the regions of repulsion ω_{ik} and ω_{is} are small spheres of arbitrary radius, it is easy to carry out the integration over s by means of Green's theorem, which transforms it to a surface integral on the spheres, ω_{is}.

$$
\int_{\omega_{is}}^{v} \nabla_s \left(\frac{1}{r_{is}}\right) \cdot \nabla_s \left(\frac{1}{r_{ks}}\right) = \frac{4\pi}{r_{ik}} \tag{32}
$$

Using this relation, we may write

$$
\begin{aligned}
\frac{N_s G_{is}}{v} &= \sum_{k=1}^{\nu} \frac{N_k}{v} [G_{ik}^{(s)} - G_{ik}] + A_{is} \\
G_{ik} &= \int_0^1 \int_{\omega_{ik}}^{v} \frac{e_i e_k}{r_{ik}} e^{-\beta W_i^k(\lambda_i)} \, dv_k \, d\lambda_i \\
G_{ik}^{(s)} &= \int_0^1 \int_{\omega_{ik}}^{v} V_{ik}^{(s)} e^{-\beta W_i^k(\lambda_i)} \, dv_k \, d\lambda_i \\
V_{ik}^{(s)} &= \frac{e_i e_k}{\epsilon r_{ik}} + \frac{e_i e_k}{4\pi} \int_{\omega_{is}}^{v} \frac{\epsilon - {}^{i}\epsilon}{\epsilon\, {}^{i}\epsilon} \nabla_s \left(\frac{1}{r_{is}}\right) \cdot \nabla_s \left(\frac{1}{r_k}\right) dv_s \\
A_{is} &= -\frac{e_i^2}{4\pi} \int_0^1 \int_{\omega_{is}}^{v} \frac{{}^{i}\epsilon - 1}{{}^{i}\epsilon} \frac{1}{r_{is}^4} \, dv_s \, d\lambda_i
\end{aligned} \tag{33}
$$

where ϵ is the macroscopic dielectric constant of the solution. If the deviation of the local dielectric constant ${}^{i}\epsilon$ from ϵ can be neglected, $V_{ik}^{(s)}$ reduces simply to $e_i e_k / \epsilon r_{ik}$, the electrostatic energy of a pair of charges in a uniform dielectric continuum. As the distance r_{ik} increases, ${}^{i}\epsilon$ must approach ϵ. Near ion i, it may be expected to deviate from ϵ, owing to electrical saturation and to variations of the local density of the solvent from its average density. To investigate this effect from a molecular point of view, it is necessary to study the potential of average force and torque on a solvent dipole in the vicinity of an ion. Without detailed calculation, it is easy to see that the deviation of $V_{ik}^{(s)}$ from $e_i e_k / \epsilon r_{ik}$ will have only the effect of imposing a short-range force upon the Coulomb force, for since $\epsilon - {}^i\epsilon$ approaches zero at large values of r_{ik}, the integral certainly decreases more rapidly than $1/r_{ik}$.

For an ionic constituent of an electrolyte solution in a polar solvent we may therefore write

$$\left.\begin{aligned} kT \log \gamma_i' &= \sum_{k=1}^{\nu} \frac{N_k}{v} G_{ik}^{(s)} + A_{is} - A_{is}^0 \\ A_{is} - A_{is}^0 &= \frac{e_i^2}{4\pi} \int_0^1 \int_{\omega_{is}}^{v} \left[\frac{1}{{}^i\epsilon} - \frac{1}{{}^i\epsilon_0} \right] \frac{1}{r_{is}^4} \, dv_s \, d\lambda_i \end{aligned}\right\} \tag{34}$$

where ${}^i\epsilon_0$ is the local dielectric constant of the pure solvent near an ion i at infinite dilution. We have assumed that the polarization of the solution was due entirely to the permanent dipole moments of the solvent molecules, and have ignored the small contribution due to induced polarization of the solvent and the solute. This may be taken into account by introducing terms of the form V_{iks} into V_N, where V_{iks} is of the form $\alpha_s \nabla_s(1/r_{is}) \cdot \nabla_s(1/r_{ks})$, α_s being the polarizability of a solvent molecule. By an analysis similar to the preceding one, equation (34) is again obtained, the local dielectric constant ${}^i\epsilon$ including the effect of induced polarization. It should also be mentioned that short-range van der Waals forces between the ions can be included by adding their potential to $V_{ik}^{(s)}$. It is possible to take account of the influence of the solvent on the potential of average force $W_i^k(\lambda_i)$, through the potential $V_{ik}^{(s)}$. We may write equation (6) for a pair of solute molecules in the following form.

$$\left.\begin{aligned} W_i^k(\lambda_i) &= \lambda_i V_{ik} + \sum_{l=1}^{\nu} \frac{N_l}{v} \int_0^{\lambda_i} \int_0^v V_{il} \left(e^{-\beta W_k^l(\lambda_i)} - e^{-\beta W_i^l(\lambda_i)} \right) dv_l \, d\lambda_i \\ &+ \frac{N_s}{v} \int_0^{\lambda_i} \int_0^v V_{is} \left(e^{-\beta W_{ik}^s(\lambda_i)} - e^{-\beta W_i^s(\lambda_i)} \right) dv_s \, do_s \, d\lambda_i \end{aligned}\right\} \tag{35}$$

The last integral

$$(N_s/v) \int^{\lambda_i} \int_0^v V_{is} \, e^{-\beta W_i^s(\lambda_i)} \, dv_s \, do_s \, d\lambda_i$$

is equal to $N_s G_{is}/v$ and is given by equation (33). To obtain the first integral we proceed in a similar manner

$$\frac{N_s}{v} \int^{o_s} V_{is} \, e^{-\beta W_{ik}^s(\lambda_i)} \, do_s = e_i {}^{ik}\mathbf{P} \cdot \nabla_s \left(\frac{1}{r_{is}} \right) \tag{36}$$

where ${}^{ik}\mathbf{P}$ is the average local polarization of the solvent near the fixed ion pair i and k. There will be a corresponding local dielectric constant ${}^{ik}\epsilon$, and the dielectric displacement is

$${}^{ik}\mathbf{D} = -\lambda_i e_i \nabla_s \left(\frac{1}{r_{is}} \right) - e_k \nabla_s \left(\frac{1}{r_{ks}} \right) - \sum_{l=1}^{\nu} \frac{N_l}{v} \int^v e_l \nabla_s \left(\frac{1}{r_{sl}} \right) e^{-\beta W_{ik}^l(\lambda_i)} \, dv_l \tag{37}$$

Substitution of $[({}^{ik}\epsilon - 1)/4\pi{}^{ik}\epsilon]{}^{ik}\mathbf{D}$ for ${}^{ik}\mathbf{P}$ in equation (36) and integration over s leads to an expression similar to equation (33), with some additional terms. Finally one obtains equation (35) in the following form

$$W_i^k(\lambda_i) = \lambda_i V_{ik}^{(s)}({}^{ik}\epsilon) + A_{is}({}^{ik}\epsilon) - A_{is}({}^{i}\epsilon) \qquad (38)$$
$$+ \sum_{l=1}^{\nu} \frac{N_l}{v} \int_0^{\lambda_i} \int [V_{il}^{(s)}({}^{ik}\epsilon)e^{-\beta W_{ik}^l(\lambda_i)} - V_{il}^{(s)}({}^{i}\epsilon)e^{-\beta W_i^l(\lambda_i)}]\, dv_l\, d\lambda_i$$

where $V_{ik}^{(s)}$ and A_{is} are again given by equation (33), the notation $V_{ik}^{(s)}({}^{ik}\epsilon)$ meaning that the local dielectric constant ${}^{ik}\epsilon$ appears instead of ${}^{i}\epsilon$. Finally, if the deviations of the local dielectric constants from the macroscopic dielectric constant can be neglected, the equation takes the form

$$W_i^k(\lambda_i) = \lambda_i V_{ik}^{(s)} + \sum_{l=1}^{\nu} \frac{N_l}{v} \int_0^{\lambda_i} \int_0^{v} V_{il}^{(s)}[e^{-\beta W_{ik}^l(\lambda_i)} - e^{-\beta W_i^l(\lambda_i)}]dv_l\, d\lambda_i \qquad (39)$$
$$V_{ik}^{(s)} = V_{ik}/\epsilon$$

the equation for the potential of average force between a pair of ions, in which the solvent plays the rôle of a dielectric continuum, the sole effect of which is to multiply the V_{ik} by a factor $1/\epsilon$. We shall presently undertake the solution of equation (39) with certain approximations.

Not only when the solute molecules are ions, but whenever the attractive forces between them are principally electrostatic in nature, equations (39) and (34) may be used for the calculation of the potential of average force and the activity coefficients, the $G_{ik}^{(s)}$ being given by

$$G_{ik}^{(s)} = \int_0^1 \int_{\omega_{ik}}^{v} V_{ik}^{(s)}\, e^{-\beta W_i^k(\lambda_i)}\, dv_k\, d\lambda_i \qquad (40)$$

If the local dielectric constants are approximated by the macroscopic dielectric constant, $V_{ik}^{(s)}$ is reduced to V_{ik}/ϵ. Electrostatic forces between solute molecules are generally of predominant importance only for electrolytes and polar molecules. The three most important types of interaction are therefore those between two ions, between an ion and a dipole, and between dipoles. The first has already been considered. The other two types of forces have potential $V_{ik}^{(s)}$ of the form

$$V_{ik}^{(s)} = \frac{e_i}{\epsilon}\mu_k \cdot \nabla_k\left(\frac{1}{r_{ik}}\right);\ \text{ion–dipole} \qquad (41)$$
$$V_{ik}^{(s)} = \frac{1}{\epsilon}(\mu_i \cdot \nabla_i)(\mu_k \cdot \nabla_k)\left(\frac{1}{r_{ik}}\right);\ \text{dipole–dipole}$$

It should be remembered, however, that it is a much poorer approximation to neglect the deviation of the local dielectric constant from the macroscopic one, in the case of ion–dipole and dipole–dipole interaction than in the case of ion–ion interaction, since the former are themselves short-range forces. Also, the effect of the discontinuity of the dielectric constant at the surface of the dipole molecule has been neglected in the above expressions

(41), the dipole having been supposed to consist of a pair of charges encased in non-overlapping small spheres, since otherwise the dielectric displacement $^i\mathbf{D}$ of equation (31) cannot be expressed simply as a sum of Coulomb terms arising from the individual charges of the molecules, but there will be contributions arising from the effect of the cavity made by the molecule in the statistical continuum of the solvent. The effect of the cavity can be calculated easily only if the local dielectric constant is assumed to be ϵ, and the boundary conditions of electrostatics are applied at the surface of the molecule. (Continuity of the potential, the tangential component of the electric field, and the normal component of the dielectric displacement.) For dipole molecules of spherical shape, this leads to corrected expressions for $V_{ik}^{(s)}$.

$$\begin{aligned} V_{ik}^{(s)} &= \left[\frac{3\epsilon}{2\epsilon+1}\right]\frac{e_i}{\epsilon}\,\mu_k\cdot\nabla_k\left(\frac{1}{r_{ik}}\right); \text{ ion–dipole} \\ V_{ik}^{(s)} &= \left[\frac{3\epsilon}{2\epsilon+1}\right]^2\frac{1}{\epsilon}\,(\mu_i\cdot\nabla_i)(\mu_k\cdot\nabla_k)\left(\frac{1}{r_{ik}}\right); \text{ dipole–dipole} \end{aligned} \tag{42}$$

The method also leads to an expression for the polarization energy of solvent by a dipole molecule. If the molecule is a sphere, we obtain

$$A_{is} = \frac{\mu_i^2}{a^3}\,\frac{1-\epsilon}{2\epsilon+1} \tag{43}$$

The potentials of ion–dipole and dipole–dipole interaction are those of short-range forces. For this reason $W_i^k(\lambda_i)$ of equation (39) may be approximated by $\lambda_i V_{ik}^{(s)}$ for an ion–dipole or a dipole–dipole pair. With this approximation, the integrals $G_{ik}^{(s)}$ take the form

$$G_{ik}^{(s)} = kT\int_{\omega_{ik}}^{v}(1 - e^{-\beta V_{ik}^{(s)}})\,dv_k \tag{44}$$

a form reminiscent of the second virial coefficient of gases. If the salting-out term $A_{is} - A_{is}^0$, depending upon the influence of the solute on the dielectric constant of the solution is ignored, the following limiting law for the activity coefficient of a dipole molecule i in a dilute solution, is obtained

$$\log \gamma_i' = \sum_{k=1}^{\nu}\frac{N_k}{v}\int_{\omega_{ik}}^{v}(1 - e^{-\beta V_{ik}^{(s)}})\,dv_k \tag{45}$$

where the sum extends over all solute components of the solution, which may include both ions and dipoles. It should be pointed out that this is not a true limiting law for the salting-out term $A_{is} - A_{is}^0$ and the hard sphere factor γ_i^* (equation (19)) both contain terms proportional to the solute concentrations N_k/v. Only when these additional terms are small, can equation (45) be a good approximation. This probably is only true for large dipoles such as zwitterions, the electric moments of which are very large in comparison with those of the solute molecules, or perhaps for smaller dipoles when the solvent is non-polar. Equation (45) was first proposed by Fuoss[10] for solutions containing only dipole solutes. His argument was based upon the

[10] R. Fuoss, *J. Am. Chem. Soc.* **56**, 1027 (1934); **58**, 982 (1936).

van't Hoff analogy between the osmotic pressure of a solution and the pressure which the solute would exert as a gas in the same volume. Fuoss' calculation of the osmotic pressure therefore closely parallels the Keesom theory of the equation of state of dipole gases. Fuoss has given asymptotic expressions for the integral

$$\int_{\omega_{ik}}^{v} (1 - e^{-\beta V_{ik}^{(s)}})\, dv_k$$

for elongated elliptical molecules, and has tabulated it for spherical dipole molecules as a function of the parameter $\mu^2/\epsilon a^3 kT$, where μ is the dipole moment and a is the molecular diameter.

One of the most interesting applications of equation (45) is found in the study of the influence of electrolytes upon the activity coefficients of the aliphatic amino acids. It is well established that these acids exist in zwitterionic form in solvents of high dielectric constant. Zwitterions differ from true ions in that they possess no resultant charge, but they are characterized by dipole moments of great magnitude, of the order of 15.0×10^{-18} E.S.U. for α-amino acids. Calculation of $\log \gamma_i$ for spherical zwitterions with the use of equations (42) and (45) leads to a limiting law in agreement with that obtained by the author[11] on the basis of the Debye–Hückel theory. The calculations have been extended to non-spherical zwitterions, account being taken of the finite separation of the charged groups. The resulting formulas have been applied with success to experimental results of Cohn[12] and his co-workers on the influence of salts upon the solubilities of the amino acids and their peptides. This work will be reported in detail at a later time.

It is of interest to remark that a better approximation to the salting-out term $A_{is} - A_{is}^0$, which represents the difference between the energy of polarization in the given solution and in the pure solvent, can be obtained by incorporating a term to take care of it in $V_{ik}^{(s)}$. This may be done by taking the sizes of both molecules i and k into account in the calculation of their electrostatic energy $V_{ik}^{(s)}$ in a medium of dielectric constant ϵ. If the molecules are spherical in shape and a_{is} and a_{ks} are the radii of the respective cavities which they form in the solvent, one obtains for ions the following expression for $V_{ik}^{(s)}$, by applying the boundary conditions of electrostatics

$$V_{ik}^{(s)} = \frac{e_i e_k}{\epsilon r_{ik}} - \frac{1}{2} \frac{e_i^2 a_{ks}^3 + e_k^2 a_{is}^3}{2\epsilon + 1} \frac{\epsilon - 1}{\epsilon} \frac{1}{r_{ik}^4} \tag{46}$$

Similar, but more complicated, expressions may be obtained for ion–dipole and dipole–dipole pairs. If these $V_{ik}^{(s)}$ are used in equation (34), salting out is automatically taken care of and the term $A_{is} - A_{is}^0$, a cruder estimate of the effect, does not appear.

IV. STRONG ELECTROLYTES

The potential of mean force $W_i^k(\lambda_i)$ between a pair of ions cannot be approximated by $\lambda_i V_{ik}^{(s)}$, because the long-range character of the interionic forces causes the

$$\int_{\omega_{ik}}^{\infty} (1 - e^{-\beta V_{ik}^{(s)}})\, dv_k$$

[11] J. G. Kirkwood, *J. Chem. Physics* **2**, 351 (1934).
[12] E. J. Cohn, *Annual Review of Biochemistry*, Vol. IV, p. 93 (1935).

to diverge. We therefore turn to equation (39) for a better approximation. Equation (39) differs from equation (4) only by the substitution of $V_{ik}^{(s)}$ and $V_{il}^{(s)}$ for V_{ik} and V_{il}. By the same set of approximations,

$$W_{ik}^{l}(\lambda_i) = W_{i}^{l}(\lambda_i) + W_{k}^{l}(1)$$

and expansion of the exponentials, equation (39) may be transformed into a linear equation like equation (7). Introducing $e_i e_l / \epsilon r_{il}$ for the $V_{il}^{(s)}$, we obtain for ions of equal size

$$W_i^k(\lambda_i) = \lambda_i \frac{e_i e_k}{\epsilon r_{ik}} - \frac{\lambda_i}{kT} \sum_{l=1}^{\nu} \frac{N_l}{v} e_i e_l \int_{\omega_{ik}, \omega_{il}}^{v} \frac{W_k^l(1)}{r_{il}} \, dv_l \tag{47}$$

where the integrals over the regions of repulsion are omitted for brevity. For ions of equal size, they vanish because of electrical neutrality

$$\sum_{l=1}^{\nu} N_l e_l = 0$$

when the solutions $W_i^k(\lambda_i)$ have the form

$$W_i^k(\lambda_i) = \lambda_i \frac{e_i e_k}{\epsilon} g(r_{ik}) \tag{48}$$

where $g(r_{ik})$ is the same function for all ionic species. A more general solution of equation (7) may be obtained by adding to equation (48) a term independent of the ionic charges, $W_i^{k^0}(\lambda_i)$ satisfying the equation

$$\begin{aligned} W_i^{k^0}(\lambda_i) &= u(r_{ik}) - \sum_{l=1}^{\nu} \frac{N_l}{v} \int_0^{\omega'_{il}} K_{il} W_k^{l^0}(1) \, dv_l \\ u(r_{ik}) &= - \sum_{l=1}^{\nu} \frac{N_l}{v} \int_0^{\omega_{ikl}} K_{il} \, dv_l \end{aligned} \tag{49}$$

Thus $W_i^{k^0}(\lambda_i)$ is just the potential of average force between a pair of hard spheres. We shall be interested here only in the part of $W_i^k(\lambda_i)$ dependent upon the ionic charges. It is interesting to remark that a rather tedious analysis shows that the terms neglected in approximating W_{ik}^l by $W_i^l + W_k^l$ are of the same magnitude as the non-linear terms neglected in the expansion of exponentials to obtain equations (47) and (49), so that equations (7), (47), and (49) are exact as linear approximations to equations (4) and (39).

We now introduce the form of equation (48) into equation (47). Since all ions are assumed identical as to size and shape, ω_{ik} and ω_{il} are independent of the ionic species l, as are the integrals

$$\int_{\omega_{ik}, \omega_{il}}^{\infty} [g(r_{kl})/r_{il}] \, dv_l$$

so that equation (47) becomes

$$\begin{aligned} g(R) &= \frac{1}{R} - \frac{\kappa^2}{4\pi} \int_{\omega_{13}, \omega_{23}}^{\infty} \frac{g(r_{13})}{r_{23}} \, dv_3 \\ \kappa^2 &= \frac{4\pi}{\epsilon kT} \sum_{l=1}^{\nu} \frac{N_l e_l^2}{v} \end{aligned} \tag{50}$$

where R, r_{13}, and r_{23} have been introduced for r_{ik}, r_{kl}, and r_{il}. We remark that κ is identical with the corresponding function in the Debye–Hückel theory. We now assume that the ions are spherical in shape so that ω_{13} and ω_{23} are spherical regions of equal radius a, separated by a distance R, which are to be excluded from the region of integration in equation (50). Introducing r_{13} and r_{23} as variables of integration, we have

$$\mathrm{d}v_3 = (2\pi/R) r_{13} r_{23} \mathrm{d}r_{13} \mathrm{d}r_{23}$$

By integration over r_{23}, with proper regard to the influence of ω_{23} upon the limits of integration, we obtain the following integral equation. For simplicity we designate the single remaining variable of integration, r_{13}, by r.

$$g(R) = \varphi(R)/R$$

$$\varphi(R) = 1 - \kappa^2 \int_a^\infty K(R, r)\varphi(r)\, \mathrm{d}r \tag{51}$$

where the kernel $K(R, r)$ has the form

$$\begin{aligned} a \leq R < 2a\colon K(R, r) &= (r + R - a)/2 & a \leq r < R + a \\ &= R & R + a \leq r < \infty \\ 2a \leq R < \infty\colon K(R, r) &= r & a \leq r < R - a \\ &= (r + R - a)/2 & R - a \leq r < R + a \\ &= R & R + a \leq r < \infty \end{aligned} \tag{52}$$

If we had neglected the size of one of the ions and extended the integration over ω_{23}, the kernel $K(R, r)$ would have the simpler form

$$\begin{aligned} &a \leq R < \infty \\ &\quad K(R, r) = r; \quad a \leq r < R \\ &\qquad\qquad = R; \; R \leq r < \infty \end{aligned} \tag{53}$$

With the approximate kernel (53), equation (51) is equivalent to the linear Poisson–Boltzmann equation with boundary conditions, of the Debye–Hückel theory. The unique solution is

$$\varphi(R) = \frac{e^{-\kappa(R-a)}}{1 + \kappa a} \tag{54}$$

a result which may be verified by direct substitution. The corresponding value of $W_i^k(\lambda_i, R)$ is

$$W_i^k(\lambda_i, R) = \frac{\lambda_i e_i e_k}{\epsilon R} \frac{e^{-\kappa(R-a)}}{1 + \kappa a} \tag{55}$$

With the omission of the salting-out term and the hard sphere term, the activity coefficient of a spherical ion of type i may be obtained from equations (40), (33), and (34),

$$kT \log \gamma_i' = \frac{4\pi e_i}{\epsilon} \sum_{k=1}^{v} \frac{N_k}{v} e_k \int_0^1 \int_a^\infty R(e^{-\beta W_i^k(\lambda_i)} - 1)\, \mathrm{d}R \mathrm{d}\lambda_i \tag{56}$$

where, because of electrical neutrality of the solution, the vanishing term $(4\pi e_i/\epsilon) \sum_{k=1}^{\nu} (N_k e_k)/v \int_0^1 \int_a^\infty R \mathrm{d}R \mathrm{d}\lambda_i$ has been subtracted from the left-hand side of equation (56). If $W_i^k(\lambda_i, R)$ has the form (48), and non-linear terms in the expansion of the exponential can be neglected, we have

$$kT \log \gamma_i' = -\frac{e_i^2}{2\epsilon} \kappa^2 \int_a^\infty \varphi(R) \, \mathrm{d}R \tag{57}$$

where $\varphi(R)$ satisfies the integral equation (51). With the solution (54) corresponding to the approximate kernel (53), in which the size of one of the ions is neglected, we obtain the Debye–Hückel[13] result

$$kT \log \gamma_i' = -\frac{e_i^2}{2\epsilon} \frac{\kappa}{1 + \kappa a} \tag{58}$$

The mean activity coefficient of any electrolyte which may be formed from the ions in the solution may be calculated from the individual ion activity coefficients in the usual way.

The solution of equation (51) with the kernel (52), which takes the sizes of both ions of the pair into account, is considerably more difficult. It is found that the solution may be expressed in the form

$$\varphi(R) = \sum_{n=1}^{\infty} A_n e^{-z_n R} \tag{59}$$

where the sum extends over all roots z_n, with positive real parts, of the transcendental equation

$$z^2 - \kappa^2 \cosh za = 0 \tag{60}$$

It is convenient to order the roots according to the magnitudes of their real parts. Several of the denumerably infinite set of roots are tabulated below:

$$z_n = \alpha_n + i\beta_n$$

κa	0.10	1.00	1.03	2.00
$\alpha_1 a$	0.10	1.62	2.07	1.06
$\beta_1 a$	0.00	0.00	0.00	+2.08
$\alpha_2 a$	9.88	2.56	2.07	1.06
$\beta_2 a$	0.00	0.00	0.00	−2.08
$\alpha_3 a$	11.11	6.26		4.84
$\beta_3 a$	±14.42	±14.90		±15.07

When κa is less than 1.03, there are two real roots, one of which remains very nearly equal to κa in dilute solutions. At κa equal to 1.03, the real roots merge into a repeated root, while for greater values of κa, all roots are complex. For small values of κa, all roots except z_1 have very large real parts, so that their contributions to $\varphi(R)$, equal to $e^{-z_n R}$, will decay rapidly as R

[13] P. Debye and E. Hückel, *Physik. Z.* **24**, 185, 305 (1923).

increases, and so can be important only for small values of R. In more concentrated solutions, $\kappa a > 1.03$, all roots are complex, imparting to $\varphi(R)$ an oscillatory form, characteristic of radial distribution functions in liquids.

By substitution of the form (59) in the integral equation (51) with the kernel (52) for $R > 2a$, it is found that only one condition is imposed upon the coefficient A_n.

$$\sum_{n=1}^{\infty} \frac{A_n}{z_n^2} e^{z_n a}(1 + z_n a) = 1/\kappa^2 \tag{61}$$

However, in order that (59) be a solution in the interval $a \leq R < 2a$, an infinite set of conditions is imposed upon the A_n. Since the $e^{-z_n R}$ doubtless form a complete set of functions, they could be orthogonalized by linear combination in the interval $a \leq R < 2a$, and the properties of orthogonal sets could be used in conjunction with the integral equation for the determination of the A_n. However, this process is rather laborious and cumbersome. A better method, suggested to the writer by Dr. Warschawski of Cornell University, is to calculate the Laplace transform $\int_0^\infty \varphi(R)e^{-uR}dR$, which is then inverted by means of the Fourier integral theorem. This procedure transforms the integral equation (51) entirely onto the interval $a \leq R < 2a$. Although the resulting integral equation cannot be solved in finite terms, it leads immediately to the desired set of linear relations between the A_n, for a solution of the form (59).

We shall be content here with the construction of an approximate solution, involving only the first two terms of the series (59). Using the two roots z_n, with smallest real parts, we can make the solution

$$\varphi(R) = A_1 e^{-z_1(R-a)} + A_2 e^{-z_2(R-a)} \tag{62}$$

fit at the two ends of the interval, $R = a$ and $R = 2a$, and everywhere outside, $R > 2a$. By substitution in equation (51) with the kernel appropriate to $a \leq R < 2a$, the condition that equation (62) be a solution at $R = a$ imposes one linear relation upon the coefficients. A second relation is furnished by equation (61), and we remember that any linear combination of the form (59) is a solution of $R = 2a$ and for all greater values of R. After making some transformations with the aid of equation (60), we have

$$\begin{gathered} A_1(1 + z_1 a)/z_1^2 + A_2(1 + z_2 a)/z_2^2 = 1/\kappa^2 \\ A_1 e^{z_1 a}/z_1^2 + A_2 e^{z_2 a}/z_2^2 = 1/\kappa^2 \end{gathered} \tag{63}$$

with solutions

$$\begin{aligned} A_1 &= \frac{z_1^2}{\kappa^2} \frac{e^{-z_1 a} - e^{-(z_1+z_2)a}(1 + z_2 a)}{(1 + z_1 a)e^{-z_1 a} - (1 + z_2 a)e^{-z_2 a}} \\ A_2 &= \frac{z_2^2}{\kappa^2} \frac{e^{-z_2 a} - e^{-(z_1+z_2)a}(1 + z_1 a)}{(1 + z_2 a)e^{-z_2 a}(1 + z_1 a)e^{-z_1 a}} \end{aligned} \tag{64}$$

when $\kappa a < 1.03$, z_1 and z_2 are real, equal to α_1 and α_2. $W_i^k(\lambda_i, R)$ and $\log \gamma_i'$ may be computed by substitution of equations (62) and (64) into (48) and (57).

$$W_i^k(\lambda_i, R) = \lambda_i \frac{e_i e_k}{\epsilon R} [A_1 e^{-\alpha_1(R-a)} + A_2 e^{-\alpha_2(R-a)}] \tag{65}$$

For the activity coefficient, we obtain

$$kT \log \gamma_i' = -\frac{e_i^2}{2\epsilon} \frac{\alpha_1 e^{-\alpha_1 a}(1 - e^{-\alpha_2 a}) - \alpha_2 e^{-\alpha_2 a}(1 - e^{-\alpha_1 a})}{(1 + \alpha_1 a)e^{-\alpha_1 a} - (1 + \alpha_2 a)e^{-\alpha_2 a}} \tag{66}$$

In dilute solutions, reference to the table of roots shows that $(\alpha_2 a - \alpha_1 a)$ is very large, amounting to about 9.0. Under these circumstances all terms involving $e^{-\alpha_2 a}$ are completely negligible and we have

$$kT \log \gamma_i' = -\frac{e_i^2}{2\epsilon} \frac{\alpha_1}{1 + \alpha_1 a} \tag{67}$$

a result which differs from the Debye–Hückel expression only by the appearance of α_1 instead of κ. But in dilute solutions α_1 differs inappreciably from κ so that the Debye–Hückel result is obtained. When κa is equal to 1.03, the roots z_1 and z_2 merge into a repeated root, and equations (63) have no solutions. However, the expressions (65) and (66) for $W_i^k(\lambda_i, R)$ and the activity coefficient both converge for $\kappa a = 1.03$, although A_1 and A_2 individually diverge. Beyond $\kappa a = 1.03$, the roots z_1 and z_2 become complex conjugates, $\alpha \pm i\beta$ and equations (63) again have solutions. Then $W_i^k(\lambda_i, R)$ takes the form

$$W_i^k(\lambda_i, R) = \lambda_i \frac{e_i e_k}{\epsilon R} e^{-\alpha(R-a)}[A_1 \cos \beta(R - a) + A_2 \sin \beta(R - a)]$$

$$A_1 = \frac{1}{\kappa^2} \frac{(\alpha^2 - \beta^2)[\sin \beta a - \beta a e^{-\alpha a}] - 2\alpha\beta[\cos \beta a - (1 + \alpha a)e^{-\alpha a}]}{(1 + \alpha a) \sin \beta a - \beta a \cos \beta a} \tag{68}$$

$$A_2 = \frac{1}{\kappa^2} \frac{(\alpha^2 - \beta^2)[\cos \beta a - (1 + \alpha a)e^{-\alpha a}] + 2\alpha\beta[\sin \beta a - \beta a e^{-\alpha a}]}{(1 + \alpha a) \sin \beta a - \beta a \cos \beta a}$$

For the activity coefficient, we obtain the expression

$$kT \log \gamma_i' = -\frac{e_i^2}{2\epsilon} \frac{\alpha \sin \beta a - \beta(\cos \beta a - e^{-\alpha a})}{(1 + \alpha a) \sin \beta a - \beta a \cos \beta a} \tag{69}$$

In figure 1, equations (66) and (69) are compared with the Debye–Hückel formula (58). In dilute and moderately dilute solutions, $\kappa a < 0.5$, $\log \gamma_i'$ does not differ much from the Debye–Hückel value. However, at higher concentrations, $\kappa a > 1.03$, the deviation becomes appreciable, and $\log \gamma_i'$ fails to approach the Debye–Hückel asymptotic value $-e_i^2/\epsilon a k T$.

The periodic factor in $W_i^k(\lambda_i, R)$, for $\kappa a > 1.03$, is particularly interesting. As κa increases, the real part, α, of z_1 and z_2 diminishes, and the exponential decay becomes less rapid. In other words the ionic atmosphere expands. At the same time the period of oscillation $2\pi/\beta$, at first very long, tends to a distance slightly exceeding the ionic diameter, a. When κa becomes equal to 2.79, α vanishes and equation (68) is no longer a solution of (51). At higher concentrations, a liquid type of distribution function, if one exists at all, must be constructed from the higher roots of equation (60). For values of κa just less than 2.79, the exponential factor is effectively unity over many molecular diameters, and the corresponding distribution is suggestive of a microcrystalline distribution, with "local" long-range order extending over many molecular diameters. This brings up the intriguing question: Do very concentrated electrolyte solutions ($\kappa a > 2.79$) possess long-range crystalline order in the distribution of the ions, which they contain? A loosely bound statistical lattice might still leave the solution with the elastic properties of a viscous fluid, manifesting itself chiefly in the optical properties. The answer to this question is probably in the negative, for the solution (68), in which only the first two roots of equation (60) are employed, very likely has only qualitative significance at very high concentrations. The value, $\kappa a = 2.79$, predicted by equation (68) as the limiting concentration for a liquid type of distribution seems altogether too low. Thus in a uni-univalent electrolyte solution with $e_i^2/\epsilon akT$ equal to unity, this value of κa corresponds to a volume about 2.3 times greater than the ions would occupy if packed in a face-centered cubic lattice, with an interionic distance equal to the diameter a.

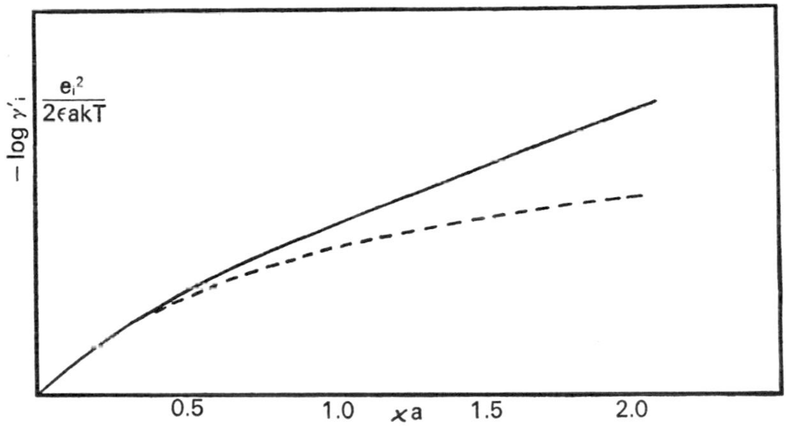

FIG. 1

- - - - - Debye-Hückel equation (58)

———— Equations (66) and (69).

Better approximations to the solution of equation (51), may be obtained by including terms $e^{-z_n R}$ involving the higher roots of equation (60). The best way to do this is to employ a general method based upon the Laplace transformation. However, the method employed here could be extended by including the terms $e^{-z_n R}$ involving the first m roots (ordered according to the magnitude of their real parts) and determining the coefficients A_n by making the sum $\sum_{n=1}^{m} A_n e^{-z_n(R-a)}$ a solution of equation (51) at m points on the interval $a \leq R < 2a$. However, even an exact solution of equation (51), although a step in the right direction, could be applied only with caution to very concentrated electrolyte solutions. There is always the question of the error arising from approximating the local dielectric constant by the macroscopic one. This error is doubtless serious when the mole fraction of the electrolyte becomes comparable with that of the solvent. Moreover, even if the macroscopic dielectric constant can be used, it may become so small in very concentrated solutions that it is not permissible to approximate the exponentials in equation (39) by the first two terms of their series expansions. Under these circumstances equation (51) no longer furnishes an adequate approximation to $W_i^k(\lambda_i)$. Another point should be borne in mind. The γ_i' of equation (57) is not the actual activity coefficient, but must be corrected for salting out and multiplied by the hard sphere factor γ_i^*, before comparison with experiment can be made. These latter influences are not negligible in comparison with the pure electrostatic effect, at very high concentrations.

In spite of the fact that equation (51) can be attributed only to qualitative significance in extremely concentrated solutions, it seems reasonable to suppose that it can be used quantitatively in moderately dilute solutions, let us say up to concentrations of 1 mole per liter, as long as $e_i e_k/\epsilon akT$ is small relative to unity for all ion pairs. When this condition is not fulfilled, either equation (39) must be solved without expansion of the exponentials, or a method of the Bjerrum[14] type must be used. Since the error involved in approximating W_{ik}^l by $W_i^l + W_k^l$ is of the same order of magnitude as the non-linear terms in the expansion of the exponentials of equation (39), the former method is almost hopelessly complicated. The Bjerrum method seems therefore to be the most promising.

V. STATISTICAL MASS ACTION AND THE BJERRUM THEORY OF ION ASSOCIATION

If the potential V_{ik} has a minimum of depth large relative to kT for certain values of the relative coordinates of the molecular pair i and k, and if for this configuration, they exert together only a small attractive force upon neighboring molecules, W_i^k may be approximated by an expression which leads to simple mass action. It is a matter of considerable interest to investigate the nature of this approximation.

Reference to equation (18) of "Statistical Mechanics of Fluid Mixtures"[1] allows us to write the chemical potential of a component i in the form

$$\mu_i = kT \log f_i(1) C_i + \varphi_i(T)$$

$$kT \log f_i(\lambda) = \int_0^\lambda \overline{V_i(t)}\, dt = \sum_{k=1}^{\nu} \frac{N_k}{v} \int_0^\lambda \int_0^v V_{ik} e^{-\beta W_i^k(t,1)}\, dv_k\, dt \qquad (70)$$

where C_i is the concentration of component i, in any units, conversion factors being absorbed into $\varphi_i(T)$, and $f_i(\lambda)$ is the activity coefficient of a partially coupled molecule i. Let us now consider a potential of average force $W_i^k(\lambda_i, \lambda_k)$, defined for a potential of intermolecular force $V_N(\lambda_i, \lambda_k)$ (equation (7), "Statistical Mechanics of Fluid Mixtures"), in which only the coupling parameters λ_i and λ_k for a single pair of molecules differ from unity.

$$e^{-\beta W_i^k(\lambda_i,\lambda_k)} = \frac{v^2 \int \cdots \int e^{-\beta V_N(\lambda_i,\lambda_k)}\, dv_1 \cdots dv_{N-2}}{\int \cdots \int e^{-\beta V_N(\lambda_i,\lambda_k)}\, dv_1 \cdots dv_N}$$

$$V_N(\lambda_i, \lambda_k) = V_{N-2} + \lambda_i \lambda_k V_{ik} + \lambda_i V_i' + \lambda_k V_k' \qquad (71)$$

$$V_i' = \sum_{\substack{l=1 \\ \neq k}}^{N} V_{il} \qquad V_k' = \sum_{\substack{l=1 \\ \neq i}}^{N} V_{kl}$$

---

[14] N. Bjerrum, *Kgl. Danske Videnskab. Selskab.* 7, 9 (1926).

Equations similar to equation (29) ("Statistical Mechanics of Fluid Mixtures") may be obtained by partial differentiation of equation (71)

$$\begin{aligned} \frac{\partial W_i^k(\lambda_i, \lambda_k)}{\partial \lambda_i} &= \lambda_k V_{ik} + \overline{{}^{ik}V_i'(\lambda_i, \lambda_k)} - \overline{V_i'(\lambda_i)} \\ \frac{\partial W_i^k(\lambda_i, \lambda_k)}{\partial \lambda_k} &= \lambda_i V_{ik} + \overline{{}^{ik}V_k'(\lambda_i, \lambda_k)} - \overline{V_k'(\lambda_k)} \end{aligned} \tag{72}$$

It is unnecessary to indicate the dependence of $\overline{V_i'(\lambda_i, \lambda_k)}$ on λ_k since, except for a term of zero order, it will be independent of the coupling with any single molecule of type k. On the other hand $\overline{{}^{ik}V_i'(\lambda_i, \lambda_k)}$, an average with i and k held fixed, will depend on both λ_i and λ_k when the two molecules are in each other's neighborhood. In order to calculate $W_i^k(\lambda, 1)$, we remember that $W_i^k(\lambda_i, \lambda_k)$ must vanish when either λ_i or λ_k is zero. We choose a path of integration in the (λ_i, λ_k) plane consisting of the straight line $\lambda_i = \lambda t$; $\lambda_k = t$ extending from the origin to the point $(\lambda, 1)$. Using this path and the partial derivatives of equation (72), we obtain

$$\begin{aligned} W_i^k(\lambda, 1) = \lambda V_{ik} &+ \int_0^1 [\lambda \overline{{}^{ik}V_i'(\lambda t, t)} + \overline{{}^{ik}V_k'(\lambda t, t)}]\, dt \\ &- \int_0^\lambda \overline{V_i'(t)}\, dt - \int_0^1 \overline{V_k'(t)}\, dt \end{aligned} \tag{73}$$

We note that $\lambda V_i' + V_k'$ is the mutual potential energy of the molecular pair i and k with all the other molecules of the solution. Let us write

$$kT \log f_{ik}(\lambda, 1, q_{ik}) = \int_0^1 [\lambda \overline{{}^{ik}V_i'(\lambda t, t)} + \overline{{}^{ik}V_k'(\lambda t, t)}]\, dt \tag{74}$$

By reference to equation (70), we see that $f_{ik}(\lambda, 1, q_{ik})$ could be interpreted as an activity coefficient of the compound molecule (ik), in which the relative coordinates q_{ik} of the pair have some fixed value. This interpretation, while correct is, however, unessential. Referring again to equation (70) and remembering that $\overline{V_i'(t)}$ and $\overline{V_k'(t)}$ can be identified with $\overline{V_i(t)}$ and $\overline{V_k(t)}$ (since in an average in which no molecules are held fixed, any single term $\overline{V_{ik}}$ is of negligible order), we may write equation (73) in the form

$$W_i^k(\lambda, 1) = \lambda V_{ik} + kT \log \frac{f_{ik}(\lambda, 1, q_{ik})}{f_i(\lambda) f_k(1)} \tag{74}$$

The usefulness of this expression is apparent, for if V_{ik} has a deep minimum for some particular configuration q_{ik}, and at the same time f_{ik} is practically unity, $W_i^k(\lambda' 1)$ can be approximated by $\lambda V_{ik} - kT \log f_i(\lambda) f_k(1)$. As will presently be shown, it is this approximation which leads to simple mass action.

From now on, we shall limit our attention to a system of only two components. Using equations (70) and (74), and separating the region of integration for unlike pairs into a region v_0 for small values of their relative coordinates and $v - v_0$ for large values, we may write

$$kT \frac{d \log f_1(\lambda)}{d\lambda} = C_2 f_1(\lambda) f_2(1) \int_0^{v_0} \frac{V_{12}}{f_{12}} e^{-\beta\lambda V_{12}} dv + kT \frac{d \log \overline{f_1(\lambda)}}{d\lambda}$$

$$kT \log \overline{f_1(\lambda)} = C_2 \int_0^{\lambda} \int_{v_0}^{v} V_{12} e^{-\beta W^2(t,1)} dv\, dt + C_1 \int_0^{\lambda} \int_0^{v} V_{11} e^{-\beta W^1(t,1)} dv\, dt \tag{75}$$

where C_1 and C_2 are the bulk concentrations of the two components in molecules per cubic centimeter. The expression (74) has been introduced only for W_1^2 in the region v_0. It could have been used for all W_i^k, but this would not be a very useful procedure. A similar equation may be constructed for $f_2(\lambda)$. Integration of equation (75) and the similar one for $f_2(\lambda)$ with regard for the fact that $f_1(0)$ and $f_2(0)$ have the value unity, leads to the result

$$\frac{1}{f_1} - \frac{1}{\bar{f}_1} = K_1 f_2 C_2$$

$$\frac{1}{f_2} - \frac{1}{\bar{f}_2} = K_2 f_1 C_1$$

$$K_1 = -\frac{1}{kT} \int_0^1 \int_0^{v_0} V_{12} g_{12}(t, 1)^{-1} e^{-\beta t V_{12}} dv\, dt \tag{76}$$

$$K_2 = -\frac{1}{kT} \int_0^1 \int_0^{v_0} V_{12} g_{21}(t, 1)^{-1} e^{-\beta t V_{12}} dv\, dt$$

$$g_{12}(t, 1) = \frac{f_{12}(t, 1, q_{12}) \overline{f_1(1)}}{\overline{f_1(t)}}; \qquad g_{21}(t, 1) = \frac{f_{12}(1, t, q_{12}) \overline{f_2(1)}}{\overline{f_2(t)}}$$

where all activity coefficients refer to $\lambda = 1$, since it is these that we finally desire. The functions K_1 and K_2 depend in general upon the composition of the solution. We shall assume them to be equal. It seems probable that this could be proved generally true, and it is certainly true when $e^{-\beta t V_{12}}$ has a strong peak at $t = 1$, the most important case. We now define quantities C_{12} and $\bar{f}_{12}$ by the relations

$$f_1 C_1 = \bar{f}_1 (C_1 - C_{12})$$

$$f_2 C_2 = \bar{f}_2 (C_2 - C_{12})$$

$$\bar{f}_{12} = \frac{K}{K_1} = \frac{K}{K_2} \tag{77}$$

where K is an arbitrarily chosen equilibrium constant. Equations (77) over-define C_{12}, but substitution in equations (76) shows that both relations are satisfied. The substitution leads to the following equation for C_{12}

$$\frac{\bar{f}_{12} C_{12}}{\bar{f}_1 \bar{f}_2 (C_1 - C_{12})(C_2 - C_{12})} = K \tag{78}$$

which is the generalized mass action equation, C_{12} having a phenomenological interpretation as the concentration of compound pairs defined with reference to the equilibrium constant K. Up to this point we have made use of purely formal operations, and, except for the assumption of equality of K_1 and K_2, the results are rigorously true within the frame of classical statistical mechanics. While equation (78) could of course be written down at once, on formal thermodynamic grounds, our rather tedious analysis is necessary for the correlation of the activity coefficients $\bar{f}_1$, $\bar{f}_2$, and $\bar{f}_{12}$ with intermolecular forces.

A suitable choice of the equilibrium constant K is evidently the following

$$K = \int_0^{v_0} (e^{-\beta V_{12}} - 1)\, dv$$

$$\bar{f}_{12} = \frac{\displaystyle\int_0^1 \int_0^{v_0} V_{12} e^{-\beta t V_{12}}\, dv\, dt}{\displaystyle\int_0^1 \int_0^{v_0} V_{12} g_{12}^{-1} e^{-\beta t V_{12}}\, dv\, dt} \tag{79}$$

With this equilibrium constant, we obtain simple mass action if $\bar{f}_1$, $\bar{f}_2$, and $\bar{f}_{12}(t, 1)$ do not deviate appreciably from unity. Again, if V_{12} has a sharp minimum of depth, large relative to kT, inside v_0, $e^{-\beta t V_{12}}$ will have a sharp peak for this configuration as well as at $t = 1$ in the interval $0 \leq t \leq 1$, and we have

$$\bar{f}_{12} = f_{12}(1, 1, q_{12}^0) \tag{80}$$

where q_{12}^0 specifics the relative coordinates of the pair at which V_{12} has its minimum. It may happen that $\bar{f}_{12}$, $\bar{f}_1$, $\bar{f}_2$ do not deviate much from unity, or much less from unity than f_1 or f_2, so that simple mass action will furnish a good first approximation in the calculation of f_1 and f_2. This will be true for an ion pair when $-e_i e_k / \epsilon a k T$ is large relative to unity, since $\bar{f}_{12}$ is then the activity coefficient of a dipole under the influence of ions. Again in the case of a pair of dipole molecules, for which V_{12} has a sharp minimum in the antiparallel orientation, $\bar{f}_{12}$ will be the activity coefficient of a quadrupole in the presence of dipoles. The choice of v_0 is arbitrary. Any change in $\bar{f}_{12}$ caused by a change in v_0 will be compensated by changes in $\bar{f}_1$ and $\bar{f}_2$. However, the method is likely to prove useful only when V_{12} has such a deep maximum that K and $\bar{f}_{12}$ are very insensitive to the choice of v_0. For short-range forces, v_0 may conveniently be expanded to include the entire volume v of the solution, provided $\bar{f}_{12}$ does not differ sensibly from unity for any configuration in which V_{12} differs effectively from zero. This is not true of interionic forces.

We shall now discuss the application of the theory just outlined to electrolyte solutions. When certain conditions are fulfilled it leads to the theory of ionic association first proposed by Bjerrum[14], and so successfully extended and applied by Kraus and Fuoss.[15] Although we have considered a system of only two components, an argument similar to that used in section II allows us to apply the theory to two solute components in the presence of an excess of solvent, $V_{ik}^{(s)}$ replacing the V_{ik}, and $\mu_i^0(T, p)$, the non-ideal part of the

[15] C. Kraus and R. Fuoss, *J. Am. Chem. Soc.* 55, 476, 1019, 2837, 3614 (1933).

chemical potential at infinite dilution, replacing $\varphi_i(T)$ as the reference value of the chemical potential. For brevity we shall omit the superscript s on the V_{ik} in what follows. We shall consider a uni-univalent electrolyte at a molecular concentration C in a solvent of dielectric constant ϵ. The bulk concentrations of both positive and negative ions are then both equal to C. Under these circumstances, we obtain from equations (77) and (78) for the activity coefficient of either ionic species, also $f_{\pm}$, the mean activity coefficient,

$$f_1 = (1 - \alpha)\bar{f}_1$$

$$\frac{\bar{f}_{12}\,\alpha}{\bar{f}_1\bar{f}_2(1 - \alpha)^2} = Kc \tag{81}$$

$$K = 4\pi \int_a^{r_0} (e^{e_1^2/\epsilon rkT} - 1)r^2\,\mathrm{d}r$$

where v_0 is taken as a sphere of radius r_0, and α is equal to c_{12}/c. For the present we suppose merely that r_0 is chosen so that W_1^2/kT is small relative to unity for all greater values of the interionic distance, so that the exponentials in equation (75) defining $\bar{f}_1$ may be expanded with retention of only the first two terms. For ions of the same valence type, we may suppose that for distances less than r_0, W_1^1/kT is large and positive relative to unity so that $e^{-\beta W_1^1}$ is effectively zero, while outside r_0 the exponential may be expanded. Taking account of electrical neutrality, we then have

$$kT \log \bar{f}_1 = -\kappa^2 \int_0^1 \int_{r_0}^{\infty} [W_1^1(t, 1) - W_1^2(t, 1)]r\,\mathrm{d}r\,\mathrm{d}t \tag{82}$$

where κ is the Debye kappa for a uni-univalent electrolyte. It would be necessary to have recourse to equation (39) for a satisfactory investigation of W_1^2 and W_1^1 when $r > r_0$. Since this involves difficulties which have not yet been overcome, we shall limit ourselves to some semi-quantitative remarks. By analogy with the simple Debye formula, equation (58), Bjerrum assumed

$$kT \log \bar{f}_1 = -\frac{e_1^2}{2\epsilon}\frac{\kappa'}{1 + \kappa' r_0}$$

$$\kappa' = (1 - \alpha)^{1/2}\,\kappa \tag{83}$$

where κ' is an effective kappa, computed with the concentration of "free" ions, $c - c_{12}$. This result follows from equation (82) if the potentials of average force have the form

$$W_1^1(t, 1) = -W_1^2(t, 1) = t\,\frac{e_1^2(1 - \alpha)}{\epsilon R}\,\frac{e^{-\kappa'(R - r_0)}}{1 + \kappa' r_0} \tag{84}$$

It may be verified without difficulty that $W_1^1 = e_1\overline{\psi(R)}$ and $W_1^2 = -e_1\overline{\psi(R)}$ where $\overline{\psi(R)}$ is the mean electrostatic potential in the neighborhood of a sphere of radius r_0 containing a total charge $te_1(1 - \alpha)$, when the Poisson–Boltzmann equation holds for $r > r_0$ and the boundary conditions of electrostatics are satisfied at $r = r_0$. This is a reasonable approximation, for $\pm e_1(1 - \alpha)$ is indeed the average charge carried by the sphere r_0 around any ion, α being the probability that an ion is "associated," that is, that another ion of opposite charge lies within the sphere, r_0. Further, the appearance of the effective kappa, κ', means that the other ions in the solution screen with this same average charge, $\pm e_1(1 - \alpha)$. With the Bjerrum result, equation (83), we obtain

$$\log f_1 = - \frac{e_1^2}{2\epsilon kT} \frac{\kappa'}{1 + \kappa' r_0} + \log (1 - \alpha) \tag{85}$$

where α is to be calculated by equation (81). In the original Bjerrum theory f_{12} was assumed to be unity. Fuoss, however, has made estimates of f_{12} by considering the interaction of an ion pair in contact with remaining "free" ions in the solution. It is difficult to judge the adequacy of Bjerrum's approximation to f_1. It is probably adequate in dilute solutions, when α is small relative to unity, but should be used with caution for values of α intermediate between zero and unity. When α is nearly unity, it is again adequate, for then it is sufficient to know that f_1 is virtually unity and its form as a function of concentration is unimportant.

We have remarked that r_0 must be sufficiently large to permit the expansion of $e^{-\beta W_1^2}$ and $e^{-\beta W_1^1}$ for greater interionic distances. This condition is satisfied by Bjerrum's value

$$r_0 = e_1^2/2\epsilon kT$$

Otherwise the choice of r_0 is arbitrary, any change being absorbed in f_{12}, f_1, and f_2. However, it should be remembered that an unfortunate choice of r_0, for example too large a value, can make it impossible to approximate f_{12} by unity or by the activity coefficient of a dipole consisting of an ion pair in contact. The simple Bjerrum theory will be useful only when this can be done. If $e^{-\beta V_{12}}$ has a strong peak when the ions are in contact, both K and f_{12} are very insensitive to the choice of r_0, provided it remains a length of molecular order of magnitude, and under these circumstances the theory leads to unambiguous results. An illuminating discussion of this point has been made by Fuoss,[16] with the aid of a distribution function, specifying the probability that an ion pair be separated by a distance R, while no other ions be within the sphere of radius R.

---

[16] R. Fuoss, *Trans. Faraday Soc.* **30**, 967(1934).
W. H. Keesom, *Physik. Z.* **22**, 129, 643 (1921).
J. G. Kirkwood, *J. Chem. Physics* **2**, 767 (1934).
S. Levine, *Proc. Roy. Soc. London* **152A**, 529 (1935).
L. Onsager, *Chem. Rev.* **13**, 73 (1933).

Order and Disorder in Liquid Solutions*

JOHN G. KIRKWOOD, *Department of Chemistry, Cornell University, Ithaca, New York*

(Received October 1, 1938)

I.

A large number of non-polar liquid mixtures conform approximately to the laws of the regular solution, originally formulated by Hildebrand[1] on the basis of thermodynamic considerations. The regular solution has been treated from a molecular point of view by Scatchard,[2] by Hildebrand and Wood,[3] and by Guggenheim.[4] A regular solution is primarily characterized by the fact that it possesses the entropy of mixing of an ideal solution. This implies the existence of a random molecular distribution in the solution. By random distribution we mean that the neighbors of each molecule are, on the average, distributed among the various molecular species of the mixture in the proportion of their mole fractions, the average local composition in the vicinity of the molecule being identical with the bulk composition of the solution. In real solutions with non-vanishing heats of mixing, random distribution can scarcely provide more than an approximate description of the actual situation. In seeking an explanation for the departure of actual solutions from regular behavior, it is therefore of importance to study the influence of deviations from random distribution on the thermodynamic functions of the system. The present investigation is concerned with this problem.

The average distribution of the neighbors of a molecule in solution, among the various molecular species present, is determined by two opposing influences—the disordering effect of thermal motion and the ordering effect of intermolecular forces. For example, in a binary solution in which the intermolecular attraction between unlike molecules is greater than that between like molecules, each molecule will exert an ordering influence in its vicinity resulting in a local composition richer in molecules of the opposite species than the solution in bulk. On the other hand, if the attraction between like molecules is greater than between unlike, a local composition in the vicinity of each molecule, richer in molecules of the same species, will result. The extent to which local segregation of this sort can be established depends upon the violence of thermal motion and will be greater the lower the temperature. At sufficiently low temperatures it may manifest itself on a macroscopic scale by causing the solution to separate into two phases.

---

* Presented at the Symposium on Intermolecular Action, held at Brown University, Providence, Rhode Island, December 27–29, 1938, under the auspices of the Division of Physical and Inorganic Chemistry of the American Chemical Society.

[1] J. H. Hildebrand, Solubility. American Chemical Society Monograph, 2nd edition. The Chemical Catalog Co., Inc., New York (1936).

[2] G. Scatchard, *Chem. Rev.* **8**, 321 (1931).

[3] J. H. Hildebrand and S. E. Wood, *J. Chem. Phys.* **1**, 817 (1933).

[4] E. A. Guggenheim, *Proc. Roy. Soc.* (*London*) **A148**, 304 (1935).

The problem of local order or order of neighbors was discussed by Bethe[5] from a quantitative point of view in his theory of superlattices in solid solutions. Into this problem there entered another type of order, long-range order, relating to the segregation of the components on interpenetrating lattices in the crystal. Since there can be no question of the establishment of long-range order in liquid solutions, we need only concern ourselves with local order. An alternative method of treating order and disorder in solid solutions, developed by the writer,[6] is particularly well adapted to the investigation of local order in liquid solutions. Although, in the meantime, the problem has been treated by Rushbrooke,[7] using Bethe's method, it seems worthwhile to discuss the question from the standpoint of our method if only because of its simplicity and directness.

II.

We consider a non-polar binary liquid solution composed of N_1 molecules of type 1 and N_2 molecules of type 2, the total number of molecules $N_1 + N_2$ being designated by N. Following the general lines of Guggenheim's method,[4] we span the volume v occupied by the solution by a virtual lattice, dividing it into N cells of equal size. Neglecting configurations in which two or more molecules occupy a single cell, we may express the partition function of the system as follows[8]

$$f = \sum_{c} e^{-\beta E(c)} Q(c)$$

$$\beta = 1/kT \tag{1}$$

where the sum extends over all configurations, c, of the system, the term "configuration" being employed in a special sense here to designate a specific distribution of the cells among the N molecules.[9] $E(c)$ is the energy of the system in the given configuration when each molecule is situated at the origin of the cell which it occupies, and $Q(c)$ is a vibrational partition function appropriate to the given configuration, analogous to the lattice vibrational partition function of a crystal. In the theory of Guggenheim $Q(c)$ is assumed independent of configuration and composition and is expressed in the following form

$$Q(c) = (2\pi m_1 kT)^{3N_1/2}(2\pi m_2 kT)^{3N_2/2} v^{N_1+N_2} \tag{2}$$

where m_1 and m_2 are the masses of the two molecular types and v is the free volume of a molecule in any cell.[10] On the basis of equation (2) and the

---

[5] H. Bethe, *Proc. Roy. Soc.* (*London*) **A150**, 552 (1935).

[6] J. G. Kirkwood, *J. Chem. Phys.* **6**, 70 (1938).

[7] Rushbrooke, *Proc. Roy. Soc.* (*London*) **A166**, 296 (1938).

[8] The formulation, equation 1, is really of value only for spherically symmetric molecules of equal size. However, if formally applied to non-spherical molecules, the factors, $Q(c)$, are understood to include rotational contributions to the partition function in the given configuration, and the free volume factors, v, in equation 2 should properly include a factor in rotational configuration space.

[9] By considering the distribution of cells among molecules rather than molecules among cells, we avoid the necessity of dividing by $N_1!N_2!$, since we make no distinction between configurations differing only in the permutation of identical molecules.

[10] The free volume v differs from that of Eyring and Hirschfelder, since the latter authors give equal weight to configurations in which two or more molecules are in a single cell. (See Rice: *J. Chem. Phys.* **6**, 476 (1938).) The distinction is of no practical importance in the present discussion, since the free volume does not appear in the free energy of mixing.

assumption that the energy $E(c)$ is independent of configuration, Guggenheim deduces the laws of the regular solution of Hildebrand. We shall employ the first assumption, embodied in equation (2), but not the second. By taking account of the fluctuations in energy among the various configurations, we are able to investigate the ordering effect of a given molecule on its neighbors and the resulting deviations from the laws of the regular solution.

A configuration of the system may be uniquely specified by a set of numbers $\eta_1 \ldots \eta_N$, stating the numbers of molecules of type 1 in each of the N cells. Each variable η_a may assume one of two values, zero or unity. Equally suitable for the purpose is the set $\rho_1 \ldots \rho_N$, stating the number of molecules of type 2 in each cell. Obviously these sets are not independent, but for each cell a the relation, $\eta_a + \rho_a = 1$, holds. Nevertheless, for the sake of symmetry in notation, we shall find it convenient to employ both sets of variables. The following sum relations, satisfied by the η's and the ρ's, are important.

$$\sum_{a=1}^{N} \eta_a = N_1; \qquad \sum_{a=1}^{N} \rho_a = N_2 \tag{3}$$

where the sums extend over all cells.

In calculating the energy, $E(c)$, of a given configuration, we shall neglect the interaction of each molecule with all but its z nearest neighbors, an approximation which is fairly good, since we are concerned with non-polar molecules coupled by short-range intermolecular forces. If there is no volume change on mixing the pure liquid constituents 1 and 2, the energy then has the form

$$E = E_0 + NV_0 p$$

$$V_0 = z[V_{12} - \tfrac{1}{2}(V_{11} + V_{22})] \tag{4}$$

where E_0 is the energy, $E_1 + E_2$, of the two pure liquids before mixing, V_{11}, V_{22} and V_{12} are the mutual energies of the indicated types of nearest neighbor pair, and p is a variable depending upon configuration in the following manner

$$p = (1/Nz) \sum_{a,\, b=1}^{N} \lambda_{ab} \eta_a \rho_b \tag{5}$$

where λ_{ab} is unity if the cells a and b are neighbors, and zero otherwise. Evidently we may write

$$\sum_{b=1}^{N} \lambda_{ab} = z \tag{6}$$

for any cell a.

The Gibbs free energy of mixing, ΔF, equal to ΔA, the work content change, if there is no volume change on mixing,[11] is related to the partition functions of the solution and the pure liquids before mixing, f, f_1, and f_2, respectively, in the following manner

$$e^{-\beta \Delta F} = f/(f_1 f_2)$$

$$f_1 = (2\pi m_1 kT)^{3N_1/2} v^{N_1} \tag{7}$$

$$f_2 = (2\pi m_2 kT)^{3N_2/2} v^{N_2}$$

[11] G. Scatchard, *Trans. Faraday Soc.* **33**, 160 (1937).

and f is given by equations (1) and (2). Equations (1), (2), (4), and (7) then allow us to write

$$e^{-\beta \Delta F} = \sum_p \omega(p) e^{-N\alpha p}$$

$$\alpha = V_0/kT \tag{8}$$

where the sum extends over all values of p consistent with condition (3), and $\omega(p)$ is the number of configurations corresponding to a given value of p. Evidently we have

$$\sum_p \omega(p) = \binom{N}{N_1} \tag{9}$$

where the binomial coefficient $\binom{N}{N_1}$ is the total number of configurations of the system, equal to the number of ways in which the N cells may be distributed among N_1 molecules of type 1 and N_2 molecules of type 2. We define a distribution function, $\varphi(p)$, normalized to unity by the relation

$$\omega(p) = \binom{N}{N_1} \varphi(p) \tag{10}$$

The free energy of mixing, ΔF, may then be written

$$\Delta F/kT = N_1 \log x_1 + N_2 \log x_2 - \log \sigma \tag{11}$$

$$\sigma = \sum_p \varphi(p) e^{-N\alpha p}$$

where the factorials of large numbers in $\binom{N}{N_1}$ have been evaluated by Stirling's formula and x_1 and x_2 are the mole fractions N_1/N and N_2/N of the two components.

The extreme difficulty of determining the distribution function, $\varphi(p)$, prevents the direct evaluation of the sum σ. However, its logarithm may be expanded in a power series in α, the coefficients of which involve the moments of $\varphi(p)$.

$$\log \sigma = \sum_{n=1}^{\infty} \frac{\lambda_n}{n!} (-N\alpha)^n \tag{12}$$

where the quantities, λ_n, are the semi-invariants of Thiele,[12] which are related to the moments M_n of $\varphi(p)$ by the following set of linear equations

$$\sum_{m=1}^{n} \binom{n-1}{m-1} \lambda_m M_{n-m} = M_n; \quad n = 1, 2, \cdots$$

$$M_n = \sum_p p^n \varphi(p) \tag{13}$$

[12] See A. Fisher: Mathematical Theory of Probabilities, 2nd edition. The Macmillan Co., New York (1926).

Solution of equations (13) yields for the first few semi-invariants

$$\begin{aligned}\lambda_1 &= M_1\\ \lambda_2 &= M_2 - M_1^2\\ \lambda_3 &= M_3 - 3M_1M_2 + 2M_1^2\end{aligned} \tag{14}$$

For the calculations of the moments, M_n (equation (13)), it is convenient to introduce the variables $\eta_1 \ldots . \eta_N$ as indices of summation, since p depends upon these variables (equation (5)). From the definitions of $\varphi(p)$ and $\omega(p)$ we may write

$$M_n = \binom{N}{N_1}^{-1} \sum_{\substack{\eta_1 \cdots \eta_N = 0 \\ \sum_{a=1}^{N} \eta_a = N_1}}^{1} [p(\eta_1, \cdots \eta_N)]^n \tag{15}$$

We note that if m is a positive exponent

$$\eta_a{}^m = \eta_a; \qquad \rho_a{}^m = \rho_a \tag{16}$$

since η_a and ρ_a are restricted to the values zero and unity. This fact, together with equation (5), leads to the following expression for the moments,

$$M_n = (1/Nz)^n \sum_{r=1}^{n} \sum_{s=1}^{n} \nu_{rs}^{(n)} y_{rs}$$

$$y_{rs} = \binom{N}{N_1}^{-1} \sum_{\substack{\eta_1 \cdots \eta_N = 0 \\ \sum_{a=1}^{N} \eta_a = N_1}}^{1} \eta_{a_1} \cdots \eta_{a_r} \rho_{b_1} \cdots \rho_{b_s} \tag{17}$$

where $\nu_{rs}^{(n)}$ is the number of terms in

$$\left(\sum_{a,b=1}^{N} \lambda_{ab} \eta_a \rho_b \right)^n$$

involving $r + s$ distinct indices (cells) $a_1, \ldots a_r$, $b_1, \ldots b_s$. The validity of equation (17) of course assumes that y_{rs} is independent of the particular set of $r + s$ cells involved. This we shall show to be the case. The product, $\eta_{a_1} \ldots . \eta_{a_r}$, $\rho_{b_1} \ldots . \rho_{b_s}$ is unity if r specified cells $a_1 \ldots a_r$ are occupied by molecules of type 1 and s specified cells $b_1 \ldots b_s$ are occupied by molecules of type 2. Otherwise it is zero, since it vanishes if any of the $r + s$ factors is zero. Thus the sum on the right-hand side of equation (17) is exactly equal to the number of ways in which $N - r - s$ specified cells may be distributed among $N_1 - r$ molecules of type 1 and $N_2 - s$ molecules of type 2, equal to $\binom{N - r - s}{N_1 - r}$, multiplied by the number of ways r specified cells may be distributed among r molecules of type 1 and s specified cells among s molecules of type 2, equal to unity. Thus we have the following expression for y_{rs}:

$$y_{rs} = \binom{N}{N_1}^{-1} \binom{N - r - s}{N_1 - r} \tag{18}$$

a result which is independent of the particular set of $r + s$ specified cells involved. We shall not attempt to give a general expression for the coefficients $\nu_{rs}^{(n)}$, merely calculating them for certain specific values of n. The first moment, M_1, is easily calculated, $\nu_{11}^{(1)}$ being equal to Nz, the total number of terms in the sum (equation (5)). Thus we have by equations (17) and (18),

$$M_1 = \binom{N}{N_1}^{-1} \binom{N-2}{N_1 - 1} = x_1 x_2 \left(1 + \frac{1}{N}\right) + O(1/N^2) \tag{19}$$

where $O(1/N^2)$ denotes terms bearing a ratio or order $1/N^2$ to the initial term. For the calculation of the second moment M_2, we find by inspection of the second power of the sum in equation (5)

$$\begin{aligned} \nu_{11}^{(2)} &= Nz \\ \nu_{12}^{(2)} = \nu_{21}^{(2)} &= Nz(z-1) \\ \nu_{22}^{(2)} &= N^2 z^2 - 4Nz^2 + 2Nz \end{aligned} \tag{20}$$

We note that the sum of the $\nu_{rs}^{(n)}$ is less than the total number of terms, $(Nz)^n$, in the sum,

$$\left(\sum_{a,b=1}^{N} \lambda_{ab} \eta_a \rho_b \right)^n$$

since any term in which an index a is equal to an index b vanishes by virtue of the relation $\eta_a + \rho_a = 1$, requiring $\eta_a \rho_a$ always to vanish. By equations (17), (18), and (20) we obtain, after some algebraic reductions,

$$M_2 = x_1^2 x_2^2 \left(1 + \frac{2(z+1)}{Nz}\right) + O(1/N^2) \tag{21}$$

The moment M_3 may be calculated by a similar procedure. Finally we obtain with the aid of equation (14) the following expressions for the semi-invariants.

$$\begin{aligned} \lambda_1 &= x_1 x_2 \\ \lambda_2 &= 2x_1^2 x_2^2 / Nz \\ \lambda_3 &= -4x_1^2 x_2^2 (x_1 - x_2)^2 / N^2 z^2 \end{aligned} \tag{22}$$

In the calculation of λ_3, the details of which have not been given, it is necessary to retain terms of order N^{-2} in M_1 and M_2. The method just described for the calculation of the moments is similar in principle to that employed by Van Vleck in his treatment of the Heisenberg theory of ferro-magnetism. An alternative method has been described by the writer in an earlier article which involves the use of interpenetrating lattices. It may equally well be used in the present calculations.

Equations (11), 12), and (22) lead to the following expression for the free energy of mixing of the solution:

$$\Delta F/NkT = x_1 \log x_1 + x_2 \log x_2 + \alpha x_1 x_2 - (\alpha^2/z)x_1^2 x_2^2 - (2\alpha^3/3z^2)x_1^2 x_2^2 (x_1 - x_2)^2 \quad (23)$$

Equation (23) is valid to terms in the fourth and higher powers of α. By means of the thermodynamic formulas

$$E = \partial(F/T)/\partial(1/T)$$

and

$$S = -\partial F/\partial T$$

expressions for the average energy and entropy of mixing may be obtained.

$$\begin{aligned} \Delta E/NkT &= \alpha x_1 x_2 - (2\alpha^2/z)x_1^2 x_2^2 - (2\alpha^3/z^2)x_1^2 x_2^2 (x_1 - x_2)^2 \\ \Delta S/Nk &= -x_1 \log x_1 - x_2 \log x_2 - (\alpha^2/z)x_1^2 x_2^2 - (4\alpha^3/3z^2)x_1^2 x_2^2 (x_1 - x_2)^2 \end{aligned} \quad (24)$$

The chemical potentials of the two components may be obtained by differentiation of ΔF with respect to N_1 and N_2, respectively, at constant temperature, pressure, and number of moles of the other component.

$$\left.\begin{aligned} (\mu_1 - \mu_1^0)/RT &= \log x_1 + \alpha x_2^2 - (\alpha^2/z)x_1 x_2^2 (3x_2 - 1) + \ldots. \\ (\mu_2 - \mu_2^0)/RT &= \log x_2 + \alpha x_1^2 - (\alpha^2/z)x_1^2 x_2 (3x_1 - 1) + \ldots. \end{aligned}\right\} \quad (25)$$

where μ_1^0 and μ_2^0 are the chemical potentials of the pure liquid components. The retention of terms in the first power of α alone in equations (23), (24), and (25) leads to the laws of the regular solution. The terms in the higher powers of α represent the ordering effect of each molecule on its neighbors and the resulting deviation from random distribution.

The constant V_0, equal to αkT, may be computed from the heat of solution at any temperature by means of equation (24). Since there is no volume change on mixing, ΔE is equal to ΔH, the negative of the integral heat of solution. If we designate by L the negative of the integral heat of solution per mole of an equimolal mixture of the components and retain only terms in α^2 in equation (24), we obtain

$$\alpha = z[1 - (1 - 8L/zRT)^{1/2}] \quad (26)$$

In the greater number of non-polar liquid mixtures L is positive, corresponding to a negative heat of solution, and α and V_0 are also positive.

When α is positive there exists a critical solution temperature below which the solution separates into two phases. Although in most non-polar liquid mixtures this temperature lies so low that the solution is unstable with respect to solid phases before it is reached, a discussion of the question is not without theoretical interest. For the coexistence of two liquid phases γ and ϵ, the conditions of heterogeneous equilibrium require

$$\begin{aligned} \mu_1^{(\gamma)} &= \mu_1^{(\varepsilon)} \\ \mu_2^{(\gamma)} &= \mu_2^{(\varepsilon)} \end{aligned} \quad (27)$$

where $\mu_1^{(\gamma)}$, $\mu_2^{(\varepsilon)}$, etc., are the chemical potentials of the components in the respective phases. From the symmetry of equations (25), remark that in either phase

$$\mu_1^{(\gamma)} - \mu_1^0 = \mu(x_1^{(\gamma)}) \tag{28}$$

$$\mu_2^{(\gamma)} - \mu_2^0 = \mu(x_2^{(\gamma)})$$

$$\mu(x)/RT = \log x + \alpha(1-x)^2 - (\alpha^2/z)x(1-x)^2(2-3x)$$

Thus equations (27) reduce to

$$\begin{aligned} \mu(x_1^{(\gamma)}) &= \mu(x_1^{(\varepsilon)}) \\ \mu(x_2^{(\gamma)}) &= \mu(x_2^{(\varepsilon)}) \\ x_1^{(\gamma)} + x_2^{(\gamma)} &= 1 \\ x_1^{(\varepsilon)} + x_2^{(\varepsilon)} &= 1 \end{aligned} \tag{29}$$

Equations (29) are satisfied if

$$\begin{aligned} \mu\left(\frac{1+\delta}{2}\right) &= \mu\left(\frac{1-\delta}{2}\right) \\ x_1^{(\gamma)} &= x_2^{(\varepsilon)} \\ x_2^{(\gamma)} &= x_1^{(\varepsilon)} \\ x_1^{(\gamma)} + x_2^{(\gamma)} &= 1 \end{aligned} \tag{30}$$

where δ is the difference, $x_1^{(\gamma)} - x_1^{(\varepsilon)}$ or $x_2^{(\varepsilon)} - x_2^{(\gamma)}$, in composition of the two phases. Equations (28) and (30) lead to the following condition on δ:

$$\begin{aligned} \delta &= \tan h\,(B\delta) \\ B &= \tfrac{1}{2}[\alpha - (\alpha^2/z)(1-\delta^2)] \end{aligned} \tag{31}$$

For two phases to coexist, equation (31) must have a real solution differing from zero, the vanishing solution corresponding to the trivial case in which the phases are identical. A non-vanishing real solution exists only if B is greater than unity. Thus there exists a critical value α_c which must be exceeded for two phases to coexist, satisfying the equation

$$\begin{aligned} \alpha_c^2 - 2z\alpha_c + 4z &= 0 \\ \alpha_c &= z[1 - (1 - 4/z)^{1/2}] \end{aligned} \tag{32}$$

and a critical solution temperature, T_c, below which two phases can coexist.

$$T_c = V_0/k\alpha_c \tag{33}$$

For a regular solution in which only the linear term in α is retained, T_c is equal to 0.5 V_0/k. However, from equation (32) we calculate for α_c a value, 2.34, with body-centered packing, $z = 8$, and a critical solution temperature 0.427 V_0/k. This is lower than the regular solution value by 15 per cent.

Thus the local order established by a molecule among its neighbors opposes the tendency of the solution to separate into two phases. The latter process may be regarded as a macroscopic mechanism for establishing order, satisfying the tendency of a molecule to make its environment rich in its own species when α is positive. This tendency may be partially satisfied without separation into two phases through the microscopic ordering mechanism by means of which a molecule establishes a local composition richer in its own species than the solution in bulk.

A remark about the relative magnitudes of the various terms in the free energy of mixing, equation (23), is perhaps appropriate. We shall consider only the regular solution term $\alpha x_1 x_2$ and the quadratic term $(\alpha^2/z)x_1{}^2x_2{}^2$. The latter term bears a ratio of $\alpha x_1 x_2/z$ to the regular solution term. With z equal to eight in an equimolar mixture at the critical solution temperature, this ratio is equal to 0.07. Thus the local order effect produces a rather small deviation from the regular solution, smaller, indeed, than one might surmise on qualitative grounds.

Rushbrooke[7] obtains an expression for the free energy of mixing in which the local order contribution involves an exponential. When the exponential is expanded and notations are brought into correspondence, his equation and equation (23) are in agreement in the linear and quadratic terms in α. However, the cubic terms in α do not agree, and indeed Rushbrooke's term depends upon composition in an entirely different manner from our own. Since the present treatment provides an exact method for the expansion of the free energy in powers of α, within the frame of the simplifying assumptions underlying both theories, it would appear that not much significance can be attached to the higher powers of α or $1/T$ in the expansion of Rushbrooke's exponential. The conclusions based upon the two treatments are, however, essentially the same.

When we come to consider the influence of the local order effect on the deviation of actual solutions from regular behavior, we find that it is generally overshadowed by other effects. An analysis of the data on a large number of non-polar liquid mixtures by Professor Scatchard[13] shows that in solutions for which ΔE and α are positive, the entropy of mixing, in excess of the ideal value, $R[-x_1 \log x_1 - x_2 \log x_2]$, is in general positive, whereas the local order contribution, $-(\alpha^2/z)x_1^2x_2^2$, from equation (24) is always negative. We shall not speculate on the nature of the other effects at the present. However, they are doubtless concealed in the vibrational factors $Q(c)$ of the partition function (equation (1)). Moreover it seems certain that the Guggenheim approximation, in which these factors are treated as independent of both composition and configuration, is far too drastic to provide an exact theory.

In conclusion, we remark that although the local order effect is relatively small and generally overshadowed by other influences, an analysis of the type which has been described seems not without value, since these conclusions could scarcely have been reached by qualitative reasoning.

---

[13] G. Scatchard and W. J. Hamer, *J. Am. Chem. Soc.* **57**, 1805 (1935).

Light Scattering Arising from Composition Fluctuations in Multi-Component Systems

JOHN G. KIRKWOOD AND RICHARD J. GOLDBERG
The Gates and Crellin Laboratories of Chemistry, California Institute of Technology, Pasadena, California

(Received May 6, 1949)

A general theory of Rayleigh scattering due to composition fluctuations in multi-component systems is developed with the aid of the grand canonical ensemble of Gibbs. It reduces to the usual expression for systems of two components, but contains previously neglected terms arising from thermodynamic interactions between solutes in systems of more than two components. The theory is used to interpret the turbidity measurements of polystyrene in benzene-methanol mixtures of Ewart, Roe, Debye, and McCartney.

I.

The utility of light scattering measurements in the determination of molecular weights and in the study of thermodynamic interactions in solutions of macromolecules has been clearly demonstrated in recent years. Correct theoretical interpretation of the measurements has been achieved for two-component systems composed of one macromolecular solute in a solvent of low molecular weight. However, attempts to extend the two-component theory to multi-component systems have led to certain errors and misconceptions, the correction of which is one of the purposes of the present article.

A general theory of composition fluctuations in multi-component systems will be developed with the use of the grand canonical ensemble of Gibbs. The theory provides a complete thermodynamic description of Rayleigh scattering without the use of supplementary molecular assumptions, although the latter may be of importance in interpreting the thermodynamic information obtained from the light scattering measurements.

It is found that thermodynamic interaction between a macromolecular solute and a solute of low molecular weight may cause the former to induce composition fluctuations with respect to the latter of the same order of magnitude as composition fluctuations with respect to the macromolecular species itself. This effect, which has been neglected in previous theories, is shown to be of importance in interpreting turbidity measurements of solutions of macromolecules in mixed solvents. To illustrate the use of the theory, an analysis is made of the turbidity measurements of solutions of polystyrene in benzene-methanol mixtures obtained by Ewart, Roe, Debye, and McCartney.[1]

---

[1] Ewart, Roe, Debye, and McCartney, *J. Chem. Phys.* **14**, 687 (1946); P. Debye, *J. Phys. Coll. Chem.* **51**, 18 (1947).

II.

The turbidity τ_0 of a fluid arising from Rayleigh scattering of light of wave-length λ is determined by the well-known relation,[2] based on the theory of Einstein,

$$\tau_0 = (8\pi^3/3\lambda^4)V\langle\Delta\epsilon^2\rangle_{\mathrm{Av}}, \tag{1}$$

where $\langle\Delta\epsilon^2\rangle_{\mathrm{Av}}$ is the dielectric constant fluctuation in a region of volume V. We shall be concerned here only with those contributions to $\langle\Delta\epsilon^2\rangle_{\mathrm{Av}}$ arising from composition and density fluctuations. If we denote by $m_0, \cdots m_\nu$ the average masses and by $N_0, \cdots N_\nu$ the numbers of molecules of the several components in the region V, and define

$$\begin{aligned} c_i &= m_i/m_0; \quad i = 1, \cdots \nu, \\ m_i &= M_i\langle N_i\rangle_{\mathrm{Av}}/N, \\ \Delta N_i &= N_i - \langle N_i\rangle_{\mathrm{Av}}, \\ \xi_i &= \Delta N_i/\langle N_i\rangle_{\mathrm{Av}} - \Delta N_0/\langle N_0\rangle_{\mathrm{Av}}, \\ \xi &= \sum_{k=0}^{\nu} \bar{v}_k \Delta N_k/NV; \end{aligned} \tag{2}$$

where N is Avogadro's number and $\bar{v}_k$ the partial molar volume of component k, we may write,

$$\langle\Delta\epsilon^2\rangle_{\mathrm{Av}} = \frac{\langle\xi^2\rangle_{\mathrm{Av}}}{\kappa^2}\left(\frac{\partial\epsilon}{\partial p}\right)^2_{T,c} + \sum_{\substack{i,k\\=1}}^{\nu} c_i c_k \langle\xi_i\xi_k\rangle_{\mathrm{Av}} \left(\frac{\partial\epsilon}{\partial c_i}\right)_{T,\,p,\,c_j}\left(\frac{\partial\epsilon}{\partial c_k}\right)_{T,\,p,\,c_j}, \tag{3}$$

where κ is the compressibility of the fluid, and the sum extends over all solute species, $k = 1, \cdots \nu$, the subscript zero denoting solvent. The first term of Eq. (3) arises from density fluctuations at constant composition, and the second from composition fluctuations. Except for critical phases, Eq. (3) is exact to terms of statistically negligible order of magnitude. We now define in the customary manner the turbidity τ due to composition fluctuations,

$$\begin{aligned} \tau_0 &= \tau + \frac{8\pi^3 V}{3\lambda^4}\frac{\langle\xi^2\rangle_{\mathrm{Av}}}{\kappa^2}\left(\frac{\partial\epsilon}{\partial p}\right)^2_{T,\,c} \\ \tau &= \frac{8\pi^3 V}{3\lambda^4}\sum_{\substack{i,k\\=1}}^{\nu} c_i c_k\langle\xi_i\xi_k\rangle_{\mathrm{Av}}\left(\frac{\partial\epsilon}{\partial c_i}\right)_{T,\,p,\,c_j}\left(\frac{\partial\epsilon}{\partial c_k}\right)_{T,\,p,\,c_j}, \end{aligned} \tag{4}$$

where the second term of the first of Eqs. (4) is the turbidity arising from pure density fluctuations. In Eqs. (3) and (4), we have anticipated the result, $\langle\xi\xi_i\rangle_{\mathrm{Av}} = 0$, presently to be proved.

In order to determine the composition fluctuations we employ the theory of the grand canonical ensemble in a manner which has been earlier described

[2] See, for example, Doty, Zimm, and Mark, *J. Chem. Phys.* **13**, 159 (1945).

by one of us.[3] The probability that an open region V in an infinite mass of fluid contain exactly $N_0, N_1, \cdots N_\nu$ molecules of the several components, considered as an example of a grand canonical ensemble, is

$$P = \exp([\Omega + \sum_{i=0}^{\nu} N_i\mu_i' - A(N_0 \cdots N_\nu)]/kT),$$
$$\Omega = -pV + kT \log \sigma, \tag{5}$$

where k is Boltzmann's constant, T the temperature, μ_i' the chemical potential of component i, per molecule, and A is the Helmholtz free energy of the region when it contains the specified numbers of molecules. The term $kT \log \sigma$ is of statistically negligible magnitude relative to pV, but is important for normalization in the order required for the calculation of the composition fluctuations. Expansion of the exponent of the right-hand side of Eq. (5) in the variables $N_i - \langle N_i \rangle_{Av}$ yields, with the neglect of terms of higher degree than quadratic, which, except for critical phases make statistically negligible contributions to mean values,

$$P = \sigma \exp(-\tfrac{1}{2} \sum_{\substack{i,k\\=0}}^{\nu} \beta_{ik}{}^0 \Delta N_i \Delta N_k),$$
$$\Delta N_i = N_i - \langle N_i \rangle_{Av}, \tag{6}$$
$$kT\beta_{ik}{}^0 = \left(\frac{\partial^2 A}{\partial N_i \partial N_k}\right)_{T,\,V,\,N_j} = \left(\frac{\partial \mu_i'}{\partial N_k}\right)_{T,\,V,\,N_j} = \left(\frac{\partial \mu_k'}{\partial N_i}\right)_{T,\,V,\,N_j}$$

We now make use of the mathematical relation,

$$\left(\frac{\partial \mu_i'}{\partial N_k}\right)_{T,\,V,\,N_j} = \frac{\bar{v}_i \bar{v}_k}{N^2 \kappa V} + \frac{M_k}{N^2 m_0}\left(\frac{\partial \mu_i}{\partial c_k}\right)_{T,\,p,\,c_j}, \tag{7}$$

where N is Avogadro's number, $\bar{v}_i$ the partial molar volume of component i, M_i the molecular weight, and μ_i is the chemical potential per mole of that component. The coefficients $\beta_{ik}{}^0$ may then be expressed in the form,

$$\beta_{ik}{}^0 = \frac{\bar{v}_i \bar{v}_k}{N^2 \kappa VkT} + \frac{Nm_0}{2} \frac{\beta_{ik}}{\langle N_i \rangle_{Av} \langle N_k \rangle_{Av}},$$
$$\beta_{ik} = \frac{c_i c_k}{M_i RT}\left(\frac{\partial \mu_i}{\partial c_k}\right)_{T,\,p,\,c_j} = \frac{c_i c_k}{M_k RT}\left(\frac{\partial \mu_k}{\partial c_i}\right)_{T,\,p,\,c_j}, \tag{8}$$
$$\sum_{k=0}^{\nu} \beta_{ik} = 0; \quad \beta_{00} = \sum_{\substack{i,k\\=1}}^{\nu} \beta_{i0}\beta_{k0},$$

where the sum rules for the coefficients β_{ik} follow from the Gibbs-Duhem equation. Introducing the composition fluctuation variables ξ_i and the

[3] J. G. Kirkwood, mimeographed notes, "Lectures on statistical mechanics" delivered at Princeton University (Spring term, 1947).

reduced density fluctuation variable ξ, of Eq. (2)

$$\begin{aligned} \xi_i &= \Delta N_i/\langle N_i\rangle_{\text{Av}} - \Delta N_0/\langle N_0\rangle_{\text{Av}}, \\ \xi &= \sum_{k=0}^{\nu} \bar{v}_k \Delta N_k/NV; \end{aligned} \tag{9}$$

we obtain from Eqs. (6) and (8) the fluctuation distribution function,

$$\begin{aligned} P(\xi_1 \cdots \xi_\nu, \xi) &= \frac{(2\pi)^{-(\nu+1/2)}(\kappa VkT)^{-\frac{1}{2}}}{|\beta|^{\frac{1}{2}}} \\ &\times \exp\Big(-(Nm_0/2)\sum_{\substack{i,k\\=1}}^{\nu} \beta_{ik}\xi_i\xi_k - V\xi^2/2\kappa kT\Big) \\ |\beta| &= |\beta_{ik}|, \end{aligned} \tag{10}$$

where $|\beta|$ is the determinant of the thermodynamic coefficients β_{ik}. It will be remarked that the transformation, Eq. (9), has eliminated non-diagonal terms in the Gaussian distribution involving the composition fluctuations ξ_i and the density fluctuation ξ.

The distribution function, Eq. (10), yields with the aid of the theory of quadratic forms the following mean values,

$$\begin{aligned} V\langle \xi_i\xi_k\rangle_{\text{Av}} &= (V/Nm_0)(|\beta|_{ik}/|\beta|); \quad i, k = 1 \cdots \nu, \\ V\langle \xi^2\rangle_{\text{Av}} &= \kappa kT, \\ \langle \xi\xi_i\rangle_{\text{Av}} &= 0, \end{aligned} \tag{11}$$

where $|\beta|_{ik}$ is the appropriate co-factor of the determinant $|\beta|$. Substitution of the density and composition fluctuations of Eq. (11) into Eqs. (1) and (3) yields the following expressions for the turbidity,

$$\begin{aligned} \tau_0 &= \tau + (8\pi^3/3\lambda^4)(kT/\kappa)(\partial\epsilon/\partial p)^2{}_{T,\,c}, \\ \tau &= \frac{8\pi^3}{3\lambda^4}\frac{1}{N\rho_0}\sum_{\substack{i,k\\=1}}^{\nu} c_i c_k \frac{|\beta|_{ik}}{|\beta|}\left(\frac{\partial\epsilon}{\partial c_i}\right)_{T,\,p,\,c_j}\left(\frac{\partial\epsilon}{\partial c_k}\right)_{T,\,p,\,c_j}, \end{aligned} \tag{12}$$

where ρ_0 is the mass of solvent in unit volume. Equations (12) give a complete description of Rayleigh scattering arising from density and composition fluctuations in terms of thermodynamically defined quantities and the derivatives $(\partial\epsilon/\partial c_i)_{T,\,p,\,c_j}$. The non-diagonal terms which have previously been neglected in the analysis of Rayleigh scattering in multi-component systems, make it possible for a solute of high molecular weight to induce significant composition fluctuations with respect to a second solute of low molecular weight as the result of strong thermodynamic interaction between the two.

III.

We shall now present several applications of Eq. (12), which illustrate the manner in which the turbidity of a multi-component fluid may be used to obtain thermodynamic information relating to the dependence of the chemical potentials of the components on composition. For the case of two components, Eq. (12) of course reduces to the expression,

$$\tau = \frac{8\pi^3 RT}{3\lambda^4 N\rho_0}\left(\frac{\partial\epsilon}{\partial c_1}\right)^2_{T,\,p} M_1 \Big/ \left(\frac{\partial\mu_i}{\partial c_1}\right)_{T,\,p}, \tag{13}$$

given by the elementary theory of composition fluctuations and which has been extensively used in light scattering studies. In order to simplify Eq. (12) in the multi-component case, we suppose all solutes to be non-electrolytes and expand the excess chemical potentials in power series in the concentrations c_i,

$$\begin{aligned} \mu_i &= RT\log\gamma_i c_i + \mu_i^0(T, p), \\ \mu_i^0 &= \lim_{c_1\cdots c_\nu}[\mu_i - RT\log c_i], \\ \log\gamma_i &= \sum_{k=1}^{\nu} A_{ik}c_k + 0(c_kc_j), \end{aligned} \tag{14}$$

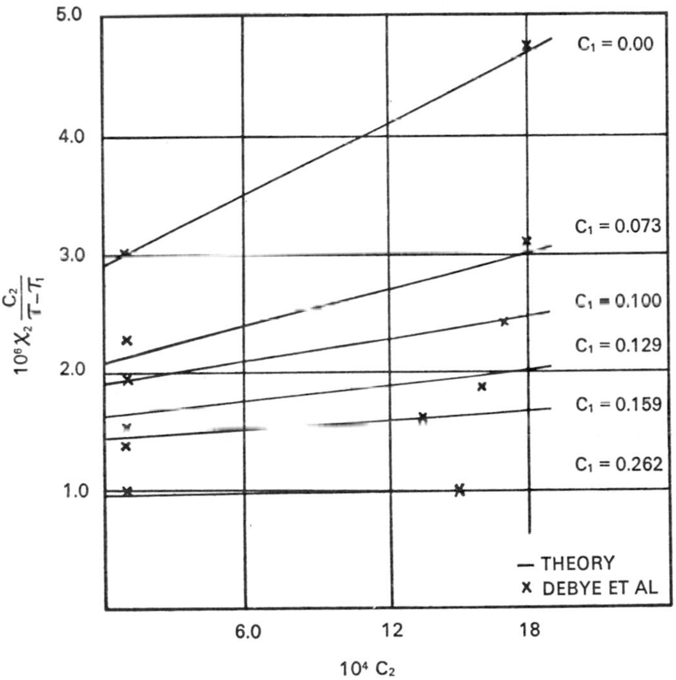

FIG. 1. Turbidity-composition curves of solutions of polystyrene in benzene-methanol mixtures.

retaining only linear terms in the expansions of $\log\gamma_i$. In this approximation, we may write,

$$\begin{aligned} (\partial\mu_i/\partial c_k) &= (RT/c_i)\delta_{ik} + A_{ik}, \\ M_kA_{ik} &= M_iA_{ki}, \end{aligned} \tag{15}$$

where, as henceforth, we abbreviate the derivatives $(\partial\mu_i/\partial c_k)_{T,\ p,\ c_j}$ as

$\partial\mu_i/\partial c_k$. Using Eq. (15), we find

$$|\beta|_{ik}/|\beta| = M_i\delta_{ik}/c_i - M_iA_{ki},$$

$$\tau = \frac{8\pi^3}{3N\rho_0\lambda^4}\left\{\sum_{k=1}^{\nu} M_k c_k\left(\frac{\partial\epsilon}{\partial c_k}\right)^2 - \tfrac{1}{2}\sum_{i,k=1}^{\nu} M_k A_{ik}\frac{\partial\epsilon}{\partial c_i}\frac{\partial\epsilon}{\partial c_k}c_ic_k\right\}, \tag{16}$$

where we abbreviate $(\partial\epsilon/\partial c_i)_{T,\,p,\,c_j}$ by $\partial\epsilon/\partial c_i$. In the case of a polymer with a molecular weight distribution, where it is appropriate to treat $\partial\epsilon/\partial c_i$ as independent of i in first approximation, we obtain

$$\frac{Hc}{\tau} = \frac{1}{\langle M\rangle_{\mathrm{Av}}} + \frac{c}{\langle M\rangle_{\mathrm{Av}}^2}\sum_{i,k=1}^{\nu} M_kA_{ik}f_if_k,$$

$$c = \sum_{k=1}^{\nu} c_k; \quad \langle M\rangle_{\mathrm{Av}} = \sum_{k=1}^{\nu} f_kM_k, \tag{17}$$

$$H = (8\pi^3/3N\rho_0\lambda^4)(\partial\epsilon/\partial c)^2,$$

where f_i is the weight fraction of component of molecular weight M_i. In a previous attempt to adapt two-component fluctuation theory to this case,[4] the non-diagonal terms in the sum of Eq. (17) were overlooked.

TABLE I. Thermodynamic interaction coefficients in benzene-methanol-polystyrene solutions.*

A_{12}	A_{22}	B_{212}	B_{222}
1.1	340	5100	0.0

* Subscript 1, methanol; subscript 2, polystyrene; $M_2 = 3.45 \times 10^5$.

We now turn our attention to the system of three components. In this case Eq. (12) may be put in the form,

$$\Delta\tau = \frac{H_2M_2RT}{\partial\mu_2/\partial c_2}\,\frac{1 - 2\alpha\omega_1 + \alpha^2\omega_1^2}{1 - (M_2/M_1)\omega_1\omega_2},$$

$$\Delta\tau = \tau - \tau_1; \quad H_2 = \frac{32\pi^3n^2}{3N\rho_0\lambda^4}\left(\frac{\partial n}{\partial c_2}\right)^2; \quad \epsilon = n^2, \tag{18}$$

$$\omega_1 = (\partial\mu_1/\partial c_2)/(\partial\mu_1/\partial c_1),$$

$$\omega_2 = (\partial\mu_1/\partial c_2)/(\partial\mu_2/\partial c_2),$$

$$\alpha = (\partial n/\partial c_1)/(\partial n/\partial c_2),$$

[4] B. Zimm and P. Doty, *J. Chem. Phys.* **12**, 203 (1944).

where τ_1 is given by Eq. (13). If all components are non-electrolytes, and we employ the power series,

$$\log \gamma_i = \sum_{k=1}^{2} A_{ik} c_k + \sum_{j,k=1}^{2} B_{ijk} c_j c_k + \cdots, \qquad (19)$$

$$\alpha = \alpha_0 + \alpha_1 c_1 + \alpha_2 c_2,$$

for the activity coefficients, γ_i, and the refractive index ratio, α, we obtain the following expansion of Eq. (19).

$$H_2 c_2/\Delta\tau = 1M_2\{1 + G_{10}c_1 + G_{01}c_2 + G_{20}c_1^2 + G_{11}c_1c_2 + G_{02}c_2^2\};$$
$$G_{10} = 2\alpha_0 A_{12}; \quad G_{01} = A_{22}; \quad G_{02} = 2B_{222};$$
$$G_{20} = 4\alpha_0 B_{112} - 2\alpha_0 A_{11} A_{12} + 2\alpha_1 A_{12} + 3\alpha_0^2 A_{12}^2; \qquad (20)$$
$$G_{11} = 2(1 + 2(M_1/M_2)\alpha_0)B_{212} - (M_2/M_1)A_{12}^2 + 2\alpha_0 A_{12} A_{22} + 2\alpha_2 A_{12}.$$

We have analyzed the light scattering data of Ewart, Roe, Debye, and McCartney[1] on solutions of polystyrene in benzene-methanol mixtures, by means of Eq. (20), supplemented by an additional cubic term of the order $c_1^2c_2$, the coefficient of which we do not interpret theoretically, although this could easily be done. The curves from which the coefficients are determined are compared with experiment in Fig. 1. It will be observed that the measurements are reasonably well reproduced. The coefficients of the refractive index increment ratio α were estimated to be $\alpha_0 = -1.9$; $\alpha_1 = 4.8$; $\alpha_2 = 0$. The values of the thermodynamic interaction coefficients, A_{ik} and B_{ijk}, of Eq. (20), calculated from the experimentally determined coefficients G_{ik} of Eq. (20) are presented in Table I. The coefficients A_{ik} and B_{ijk} are, of course, dimensionless, but it should be remembered that the numerical values are appropriate to concentrations c_i expressed in grams of solute per gram of benzene.

The calculations which have been presented exhibit the manner in which turbidity measurements may be used in conjunction with the present theory to obtain thermodynamic data in multi-component systems containing at least one macromolecular component. The positive value of the interaction coefficient A_{12} for polystyrene and methanol, when interpreted from the molecular standpoint, means, as Debye surmised, that a polystyrene molecule exhibits a preference for benzene molecules in its statistical environment. Such qualitative considerations should, however, be regarded as supplementing the thermodynamic theory presented here, rather than the basis for an exact analysis of turbidity.

Solutions of Nonelectrolytes*

By FRANK P. BUFF, *Department of Chemistry, University of Rochester, Rochester, New York*
AND
JOHN G. KIRKWOOD, *Gates and Crellin Chemical Laboratories, California Institute of Technology, Pasadena, California*†

Introduction.—The year 1950 has been marked by extensive contributions to the field of solutions of nonelectrolytes which frequently confirm earlier generalizations but also point to the need for more refined treatments to account for interesting discrepancies between existing solution theories and experimental measurements. A great wealth of experimental data and a useful summary of various theoretical treatments will be found in the long awaited third edition of Hildebrand's *The Solubility of Nonelectrolytes*[1] written in collaboration with Scott. In view of the wide variety of subjects that fall into the field to be reviewed, the various contributions will be discussed under appropriate headings. The authors express the hope that not too many significant papers have been overlooked.

General.—Within the last decade, it has been found useful from both the experimental and theoretical standpoint to employ volume fraction expansions for the excess chemical potentials of the components of a solution. It has been customary to neglect terms higher than quadratic, which leads to the familiar Flory-Huggins equation for a binary system

$$\mu_1(T, p, \phi_1) - \mu_1{}^0(T, p) = RT\left[\log \phi_1 + \left(1 - \frac{V_1}{V_2}\right)\phi_2\right] + V_1\Delta_{12}\phi_2{}^2 \qquad (1)$$

where $\phi_1 = x_1V_1/(x_1V_1 + x_2V_2)$ and $\mu_1(T, p, \phi_1)$ is the chemical potential of the solvent 1, x and V are mole fraction and molar volume, respectively, and Δ_{12} is a specific parameter for the system under consideration. It will be noted that even when a quadratic expansion may suffice for the chemical potential, the corresponding expressions for derived thermodynamic functions are in general more complex:

$$\begin{aligned} \bar{S}_1(T, p, \phi_1) &- S_1{}^0(T, p) \\ &= -R\left[\log \phi_1 + \left(1 - \frac{V_1}{V_2}\right)\phi_2\right] - V_1\phi_2{}^2\left[\left(\frac{\partial \Delta_{12}}{\partial T}\right)_p \right. \\ &\quad \left. + RT\,\frac{(\alpha_1 - \alpha_2)(V_2 - V_1)}{V_1V_2} + \Delta_{12}(\alpha_1 + 2(\alpha_2 - \alpha_1)\phi_1)\right] \end{aligned} \qquad (2)$$

* The survey of the literature pertaining to this review was concluded in December, 1950.
† Contribution No. 1518.
[1] J. H. Hildebrand and R. L. Scott, *The Solubility of Nonelectrolytes* (Reinhold Publishing Corp., New York, 488 pp. 1950).

$$\bar{V}_1(T, p, \phi_1) - V_1^0(T, p) \tag{3}$$

$$= V_1\phi_2^2\left[\left(\frac{\partial \Delta_{12}}{\partial p}\right)_T + RT\,\frac{(\kappa_1 - \kappa_2)(V_2 - V_1)}{V_1 V_2} + \Delta_{12}(\kappa_1 + 2(\kappa_2 - \kappa_1)\phi_1)\right]$$

where $\bar{S}_1$ and $\bar{V}_1$ are the partial molar entropy and volume of the solvent and α and κ are the coefficients of thermal expansion and isothermal compressibility of the pure components.

An expansion of the type 1 may be justified on the basis of molecular theory. Kirkwood & Buff[2] have shown from the theory of the grand ensemble that Δ_{12} is given by

$$\Delta_{12} = \frac{RT}{2}\left[\frac{1}{V_1} - \frac{2}{V_2}\left(1 - \frac{\bar{V}_2^0}{V_2}\right) + \frac{NG_{22}^0 - RT\kappa_1}{V_2^2}\right] \tag{4}$$

$$G_{22}^0 = \int [g_{22}(\vec{R}_{12}) - 1]dV_{12}$$

where $\bar{V}_2^0$ is the partial molar volume of the solute at an infinite dilution in the solvent, and k is Avogadro's number. G_{22}^0 is the "second virial coefficient" of the osmotic pressure expansion,[3] which may be calculated from the pair correlation function $g_{22}(\vec{R}_{12})$ of two solute molecules at infinite dilution in the solvent. While the partial molar volumes and isothermal compressibility of the solution may be similarly related to integrals of molecular distribution functions, the partial molar entropies must be computed in terms of the temperature derivatives of these integrals. The important coefficient G_{22}^0 is receiving increasing attention. Isihara[4] has extended Zimm's earlier work[5] to high polymer molecules treated as rigid ovaloids and Flory and Krigbaum[6] have carried out approximate calculations of G_{22}^0 for dilute polymer solutions.

The first two terms of equation (1), Flory's formula,[7] arose from approximate calculations of the entropy of mixing of athermal solutions when it is assumed that open chain molecules occupy m sites in a quasi-lattice of coordination number z with solvent molecules occupying single lattice sites. The more refined result is due to Huggins[8] and Guggenheim[9]:

$$\bar{S}_1 - S_1^0 = -R\left[\log\phi_1 - \frac{z}{2}\log\left(1 + \frac{2}{z}\left(\frac{1}{m} - 1\right)\phi_2\right)\right]$$

$$= -R\left[\log\phi_1 + \left(1 - \frac{1}{m}\right)\phi_2 + \frac{1}{z}\left(1 - \frac{1}{m}\right)^2\phi_2^2 + \cdots\right]. \tag{5}$$

[2] J. G. Kirkwood and F. P. Buff, *Statistical Mechanical Theory of Solutions*. (Presented at the 118th Meeting, Am. Chem. Soc., September, 1950.)

[3] W. G. McMillan and J. E. Mayer, *J. Chem. Phys.* **13**, 276–305 (1945).

[4] A. Isihara, *J. Chem. Phys.* **18**, 1446–49 (1950).

[5] B. H. Zimm, *J. Chem. Phys.* **14**, 164–79 (1946).

[6] P. J. Flory and W. R. Krigbaum, *J. Chem. Phys.* **18**, 1086–94 (1950).

[7] P. J. Flory, *J. Chem. Phys.* **10**, 51–61 (1942).

[8] M. L. Huggins, *Ann. N. Y. Acad. Sci.* **43**, 1–32 (1942).

[9] E. A. Guggenheim, *Proc. Roy. Soc.* (*London*) [A]**183**, 203–12 (1944).

Guggenheim and McGlashan[10] have extended this theory to chain molecules having the shapes of equilateral triangles, regular tetrahedra, and squares. The essential assumption of the treatment is that if two sites are not occupied by the same molecule, then the relative probabilities of being occupied or vacant are independent for the two sides. On the basis of this analysis, these authors concluded that Flory's formula, which corresponds formally to letting the co-ordination number tend to infinity, leads to slightly high values for the total entropy of mixing. Their treatment did not confirm Staverman's extension of equation (5) to molecules containing rings.[11]

Recently Münster[12–16] published a series of investigations concerning the properties of binary solutions on the basis of the quasi-lattice picture. He emphasized that the theory of strictly regular solutions predicts entropy changes upon mixing which at times even differ in sign from the experimental observations. Since a re-examination of this theory led to results in agreement with the earlier work of Rushbrooke[17] and Kirkwood,[18] he suggested that orientation effects might remove the discrepancies for certain types of systems. Three types of interaction are considered: (*a*) two solute molecules orient each other; at sufficiently low concentrations the theory of strictly regular solutions still applies; (*b*) the solvent molecules are oriented by the solute molecules, although free rotation occurs in the pure solvent; (*c*) in the pure solvent, co-operative orientation takes place which is disturbed by the solute molecules. His treatment for type (*b*) replaces the assumption of spherical symmetry of the interaction potential employed in the theory of strictly regular solutions by the assumption that the solvent molecules can take up p orientations of equal energy in the pure phase and that, for those solvent molecules which are neighbors of a solute molecule, one of the orientations has an additional energy W_{or}/N, where N is Avogadro's number. With W/N the interaction energy of two solute molecules, Münster developed the following expression for the free energy of mixing, ΔF_{mix},

$$\frac{\Delta F_{\text{mix}}}{RT} = x_1 \log x_1 + x_2 \log x_2 - z\left\{\frac{W}{2RT} + \log\left[\frac{\exp\left(\frac{-W_{or}}{RT}\right) + p - 1}{p}\right]\right\}x_2$$
$$- \frac{z}{2}\left\{\frac{p^2 \exp\left(\frac{-W}{RT}\right)}{\left[\exp\left(-\frac{W_{or}}{RT}\right) + p - 1\right]^2} - 1\right\}x_2^2 + \cdots. \tag{6}$$

Reasonable values for the adjustable parameters of equation (6) led to good agreement with the experimental results for the heat of mixing and excess

[10] E. A. Guggenheim and M. L. McGlashan, *Proc. Roy. Soc.* (*London*) [A]**203**, 435–54 (1950).
[11] A. J. Staverman, *Rec. trav. chim.* **69**, 163–74 (1950).
[12] A. Münster, *Z. physik. Chem.* **195**, 67–87 (1950).
[13] A. Münster, *Z. physik. Chem.* **196**, 106–26 (1950).
[14] A. Münster, *Z. Elektrochem.* **54**, 443–49 (1950).
[15] A. Münster, *Proc. Cambridge Phil. Soc.* **46**, 319–30 (1950).
[16] A. Münster, *Trans. Faraday Soc.* **46**, 165–74 (1950).
[17] G. S. Rushbrooke, *Proc. Roy. Soc.* (*London*) [A]**166**, 296–315 (1938).
[18] J. G. Kirkwood, *J. Phys. Chem.* **43**, 97–107 (1939).

entropy of dilution of the system chloroform and acetone. Münster's corresponding treatment of type (*c*) again abandoned the assumption of spherical symmetry of the interaction potential and postulated two different orientations for the solvent molecules instead. Denoting the energy that induces two neighboring molecules to take up identical orientation by $W_{or}|/N$, he found on the basis of a generalized quasi-chemical equation,

$$\frac{\Delta F_{\text{mix}}}{RT} = x_1 \log x_1 + x_2 \log x_2 - \frac{z}{2RT}\left(W + \frac{W_{or}}{2} - \frac{WW_{or}}{4RT} - \frac{W_{or}^2}{4RT}\right)x_2 + \frac{z}{2RT}\left(W + \frac{W_{or}}{2} - \frac{W^2}{2RT} - \frac{WW_{or}}{RT} - \frac{W_{or}^2}{2RT}\right)x_2^2 + \cdots. \tag{7}$$

Comparison with the system cyclohexane-benzene led to fair agreement, particularly for the entropy of mixing.

Prigogine and Garikian[19] have published an approach to the theory of solutions which employs a more realistic model of liquids than is provided by the quasi-lattice approximation. They presented an approximate extension of the Lennard-Jones and Devonshire[20] free volume theory to binary mixtures of spherical molecules at temperatures far from the critical point. On the basis of rough calculations, they were able to show that the concentration dependence of both the change of volume upon mixing and of the vibrational frequency of the molecules in the mean field of their nonidentical neighbors leads to appreciably larger entropy changes than would be predicted from the theory of strictly regular solutions. They state that the molecular parameters they employed in their calculations correspond to the system carbon tetrachloride-neopentane, which is also being studied experimentally.

In many applications of equation (1), refinements of the preceding type have been neglected, and the third member of this equation has been represented by a van Laar-Hildebrand-Scatchard heat term for solutions without specific interaction. Primarily with the approximation of spherical symmetry of the intermolecular forces and other simplifying assumptions which are discussed by Hildebrand in his book[1] and recent review article,[21] Δ_{12} has been represented by

$$\Delta_{12} = (\delta_1 - \delta_2)^2, \quad \delta_\alpha = (\Delta E_\alpha / V_\alpha)^{1/2}, \quad \alpha = 1, 2 \tag{8}$$

where ΔE_α is the molar energy of vaporization of component α, and V_α is its molar volume. Hildebrand's regular solution equation is obtained by employing the approximation, equation (8), in equation (1):

$$\mu_1 - \mu_1^0 = RT\left[\log \phi_1 + \left(1 - \frac{V_1}{V_2}\right)\phi_2\right] + V_1(\delta_1 - \delta_2)^2\phi_2^2. \tag{9}$$

A wealth of experimental data indicates the usefulness of this relation for relatively simple systems, although particularly for mixtures containing

[19] I. Prigogine and G. Garikian, *Physica*, **16**, 239–48 (1950).
[20] J. E. Lennard-Jones and A. F. Devonshire, *Proc. Roy. Soc.* (*London*) [A]**163**, 53–70 (1937).
[21] J. H. Hildebrand, *Proc. Natl. Acad. Sci.* **36**, 7–15 (1950).

paraffin hydrocarbons, Hildebrand[22] has pointed out that the solubility parameter δ is to be properly regarded as an empirical constant. When the molar volumes of the components do not differ appreciably, equation (9) may be replaced by the more frequently used older relation

$$\mu_1 - \mu_1{}^0 = RT \log x_1 + V_1(\delta_1 - \delta_2)^2\phi_2{}^2. \tag{10}$$

Although the expansion underlying equation (1) fails to converge in the immediate vicinity of the consolute point, equation (10) has been employed to calculate Δ_{12} from critical mixing point data. The corresponding relations[23] that may be derived from equation (9) are

$$x_2{}^{\text{crit}} = \frac{V_1{}^{3/2}}{V_1{}^{3/2} + V_2{}^{3/2}} = \frac{V_1}{V_1 + V_2} + \frac{1}{4}\left(\frac{V_1 - V_2}{V_1 + V_2}\right) + \frac{5}{16}\left(\frac{V_1 - V_2}{V_1 + V_2}\right)^3 + \cdots \tag{11}$$

a relation independent of Δ_{12} which relates the critical composition $x_2{}^{\text{crit}}$ to the molar volumes, and

$$\begin{aligned} RT_c &= \frac{2\Delta_{12}}{(V_1{}^{-1/2} + V_2{}^{-1/2})^2} \\ &= \frac{\Delta_{12}(V_1 + V_2)}{4}\left(1 - \frac{3}{4}\left(\frac{V_1 - V_2}{V_1 + V_2}\right)^2 - \frac{13}{16}\left(\frac{V_1 - V_2}{V_1 + V_2}\right)^4 - \cdots\right) \end{aligned} \tag{12}$$

where T_c is the consolute temperature.

Among more qualitative treatments of solutions during 1950, we note a paper by Drenan and Hill[24] who treated binary systems on the basis of a generalized van der Waals equation in a manner similar to the analogous work of Wall and Stent.[25] A semi-empirical formula relating the activities of a binary system has been proposed by Martell.[26]

Hydrocarbons and fluorocarbons.—Recent experimental work on solutions containing paraffin hydrocarbons has brought out some discrepancies between existing theories and experiments designed to test various refinements. Van der Waals and Hermans[27] measured the integral heats of mixing, ΔH_{mix}, for the binary alkane systems *n*-hexane-*n*-hexadecane, *n*-heptane-*n*-hexadecane, *n*-octane-*n*-hexadecane, *n*-decane-*n*-hexadecane, *n*-decane-*n*-dotriacontane, and 2,2,4-trimethylpentane-*n*-hexadecane. They commented on the marked decrease with temperature of ΔH_{mix} and showed that ΔH_{mix} for hexane, heptane, octane, and decane as the one component, and hexadecane as the other component, could be well fitted by a Brønsted-Koefoeld[28] type expression: ΔH_{mix} (20°C.) $= 5.1$ $(k_1 - k_2)^2 x_1 x_2$ joule per mole of mixture, where k_1 and k_2 are the number of carbon atoms in the molecules of the two components. The dependence of ΔH_{mix} on the chain length of the

[22] J. H. Hildebrand, *J. Chem. Phys.* **18**, 1337–38 (1950).
[23] J. H. Hildebrand, B. B. Fisher and H. A. Benesi, *J. Am. Chem. Soc.* **72**, 4348–51 (1950).
[24] J. W. Drenan and T. L. Hill, *J. Phys. and Colloid Chem.* **54**, 1132–48 (1950).
[25] F. T. Wall and G. S. Stent, *J. Chem. Phys.* **17**, 1112–16 (1949).
[26] A. E. Martell, *J. Phys. and Colloid Chem.* **54**, 459–66 (1950).
[27] J. H. van der Waals and J. J. Hermans, *Rec. trav. chim.* **69**, 949–70 (1950).
[28] J. N. Brønsted and J. Koefoeld, *Kgl. Danske Videnskab. Selskab, Mat.-fys. Medd.* **22**(17), 1–32 (1946).

constituent molecules did not agree with Tompa's theory[29] for heats of mixing in n-alkane systems based on the quasi-lattice model. Additional vapor pressure determinations[30] on some of these systems, open to the criticism that the vapor phase was not completely eliminated, showed that the entropy of mixing for hexane-hexadecane and heptane-hexadecane could be very well accounted for with Flory's formula or equation (5), although this agreement cannot persist at temperatures appreciably higher than 20°C. in view of the strong temperature dependence of the heat of mixing. However, the weakness of the quasi-lattice model was illustrated by the system 2,2,4-trimethylpentane-hexadecane, which, although it closely obeys Raoult's law at 25°C., has a far greater excess entropy of mixing than would be obtained for n-octane-hexadecane.

Similar experiments carried out by Mathot and Prigogine[31, 32] were designed to determine the influence on the excess entropy of mixing of the molecular symmetry rather than the size of the constituents. The two systems selected both showed positive excess free energies of mixing and one, cyclohexane-n-hexane, also had a positive excess entropy and integral heat of mixing. However, the other system, tetraethylmethane-n-octane, had both negative excess entropy and integral heat of mixing. These authors have suggested that, since both systems should have a nearly ideal entropy of mixing on the basis of the athermal quasi-lattice model, the origin of the entropy terms should be imputed to the heat of mixing. The effect of the internal partition functions will be checked spectroscopically in their laboratory.

Simons and Dunlap's thorough investigation of the system perfluoro-n-pentane-n-pentane[33] led to data for the excess chemical potentials, partial molar enthalpies and volumes, and the mutual solubility diagram. Even though large volume changes were observed, the vapor pressure measurements could be well fitted by equation (10) and led to a value for Δ_{12} in good

TABLE I. Solubility Parameters at Critical Solution Temperatures

System	t_c°C.	$\delta_2-\delta_1$ (obs.*)	$\delta_2-\delta_1$ (theor.†)	Reference
n-C_5H_{12}-n-C_5F_{12}	− 7.7	2.79	1.32	32
n-C_7H_{16}-n-C_7F_{16}	+50.0	2.61	1.58	23
i-C_8H_{18}-n-C_7F_{16}	23.7	2.48	1.01	23
CCl_4-n-C_7F_{16}	58.7	2.68	2.97	23
$CHCl_3$-n-C_7F_{16}	78.5	3.22	3.19	23
C_6H_6-n-C_7F_{16}	113.5	3.11	3.15	23

* Differences calculated from Equation (12).
† Differences calculated from theoretical solubility parameters.

agreement with that obtained from equation (12). No attempt was made to calculate Δ_{12} from the azeotropic data. These authors found that the experimental Δ_{12} differed appreciably from the theoretical solubility parameter prediction, and they ascribed the discrepancy to unusual peripheral interpenetration of the hydrocarbon molecules with attendantly small free volume

[29] H. Tompa, *Trans. Faraday Soc.* **45**, 101–9 (1949).
[30] J. H. van der Waals and J. J. Hermans, *Rec. trav. chim.* **69**, 971–1002 (1950).
[31] V. Mathot, *Bull. soc. chim. Belges*, **59**, 111–39 (1950).
[32] I. Prigogine and V. Mathot, *J. Chem. Phys.* **18**, 765–66 (1950).
[33] J. H. Simons and R. D. Dunlap, *J. Chem. Phys.* **18**, 335–46 (1950).

for the liquid. Similar effects were noted by Hildebrand, Fisher and Benesi[23] from the solubility of perfluoro-*n*-heptane with *n*-heptane and 2,2,4-trimethylpentane. Table I illustrates this irregularity in the solvent powers of the paraffins, the subscript 1 referring to the fluorocarbon while the other components are denoted by the subscript 2. Hildebrand[22] has shown that "a simple, practical means of dealing with the solubility relations of paraffins is to derive their solubility parameters from known solubility data with a reasonable expectation that values so derived will prove applicable to new cases".

Cox and DeVries[34] were able to account for the solubility of solid ethane in liquid nitrogen remarkably well on the basis of the regular solution equation (10). Similar solubility measurements of solid ethane, ethylene, and propylene in liquid oxygen led to an experimental Δ_{12} appreciably larger than the value predicted from theoretical solubility parameters. While some improvement may be achieved with use of equation (9), in view of this difference between oxygen and nitrogen, additional experimental confirmation would be desirable, particularly since some of the measurements reported by Cox and DeVries do not agree with earlier work.

TABLE II. Solubility Parameter of Iodine Calculated from its Solubility in Regular Solutions

Solvent	$100x_2$	δ_1	δ_2
n-C_7F_{16}	0.0182	5.8	14.4
$(CH_3)_3CC_2H_5$	0.469	6.7	13.1
iso-C_8H_{18}	0.592	6.8	13.0
n-C_6H_{14}	0.452	7.3	13.6
n-C_7H_{16}	0.679	7.4	13.5
cyclo-C_6H_{12}	0.918	8.2	14.0
$SiCl_4$	0.499	7.6	13.9
CCl_4	1.147	8.6	14.2
$CHCl_3$	2.28	9.0	14.1
trans-$C_2H_2Cl_2$	1.417	9.0	14.5
cis-$C_2H_2Cl_2$	1.441	9.1	14.5
1,1-$C_2H_4Cl_2$	1.531	9.0	14.4
1,2-$C_2H_4Cl_2$	2.20	9.8	14.9
$TiCl_4$	2.15	9.0	14.1
CS_2	5.58	9.9	14.1
1,2-$C_2H_4Br_2$	7.82	10.4	14.1
$CHBr_3$	6.16	10.5	14.1
		Av.	14.0
I_2	25.8	$\left\{\frac{\Delta E_2}{V_2}\right\}^{1/2}$	$=13.6$

Calingaert and Wojciechowski[35] presented evidence for negative azeotropy in the system 2,2,3-trimethylbutane and 2,4-dimethylpentane whose pure components boil less than 0.4° apart under atmospheric pressure.

Iodine solutions.—Investigations of iodine solutions provide a particularly useful test of the theory of regular solutions, since a wide range of solubilities is encountered, and furthermore, departure from the violet color of iodine

[34] A. L. Cox and T. DeVries, *J. Phys. and Colloid Chem.* **54**, 665–70 (1950).
[35] G. Calingaert and M. Wojciechowski, *J. Am. Chem. Soc.* **72**, 5310–11 (1950).

vapor indicates specific interaction effects. Table II, taken from a paper by Hildebrand, Benesi and Mower,[36] summarizes the results of solubility determinations of iodine in a wide variety of violet solutions and also indicates the usefulness of the regular solution approximation. The theoretical solubility parameter of the solvent is represented by δ_1, and δ_2 is calculated from equation (10). The moderate deviations from the average value of δ_2 encountered in the case of the paraffins could be somewhat improved by employing modified parameters for the solvent.

Spicer and Kruger[37] obtained liquid-vapor equilibrium data for the system bromine-carbon tetrachloride and found the formation of an azeotrope as had been anticipated from the boiling points and solubility parameters of the pure components.

TABLE III. Equilibrium Constants for Halogen-Aromatic Complexes in CCl_4 Solutions

Aromatic	I_2*	Br_2†	ICl‡
Benzene	1.72	1.04	4.76
Toluene		1.44	7.97
o-Xylene		2.29	15.4
m-Xylene		2.16	16.0
p-Xylene		2.26	13.4
Mesitylene	7.2		
Chlorobenze		0.90	2.24
Bromobenzene		1.18	3.43

* Taken from Benesi & Hildebrand (38).
† Taken from Keefer & Andrews (40).
‡ Taken from Keefer & Andrews (41).

The last few years have seen great interest in the brownish solutions of iodine, which are also found to deviate from the regular solubility-temperature curves. The discovery by Benesi and Hildebrand[38] of a specific ultraviolet absorption peak at about 300 mμ for solutions of iodine in aromatic hydrocarbons has stimulated further work which has pretty well established that this peak is due to a one-to-one complex formed between the solvent and the halogen molecule. The original explanation put forth by these authors[39] that the molecular addition compound is due to an acid-base interaction in the electron donor-acceptor sense also appears to have been substantiated, as can be seen from Table III, taken from papers by Benesi and Hildebrand[38] and Keefer and Andrews.[40, 41] The equilibrium constant for the equilibrium $X_2 + A \rightleftarrows X_2 \cdot A$, where A denotes the aromatic solvent and X_2 the halogen, has been obtained from spectrophotometric measurements and varies in accordance with the acid-base interaction picture. Fairbrother[42] has presented some evidence for the analogous behavior of iodine cyanide in electron donor solvents. Hildebrand, Benesi and Mower [36] showed

[36] J. H. Hildebrand, H. A. Benesi and L. M. Mower, *J. Am. Chem. Soc.* **72**, 1017–20 (1950).
[37] W. M. Spicer and J. Kruger, *J. Am. Chem. Soc.* **72**, 1855–58 (1950).
[38] H. A. Benesi and J. H. Hildebrand, *J. Am. Chem. Soc.* **71**, 2703–7 (1949).
[39] H. A. Benesi and J. H. Hildebrand, *J. Am. Chem. Soc.* **70**, 2832–33 (1948).
[40] R. M. Keefer and L. J. Andrews, *J. Am. Chem. Soc.* **72**, 4677–81 (1950).
[41] R. M. Keefer and L. J. Andrews, *J. Am. Chem. Soc.* **72**, 5170–73 (1950).
[42] F. Fairbrother, *J. Chem. Soc.* 180–5 (1950).

the consistency of the equilibrium constants with the solubility of iodine in benzene and mesitylene after making appropriate corrections with equation (10).

Cromwell and Scott[43] calculated the heat of formation of the iodine-benzene complex from spectrophotometric data obtained at different temperatures. Hartley and Skinner[44] carried out calorimetric measurements of the heats of solution of iodine in several organic solvents. After subtracting the regular solution contribution, equation (10), they found that the rather approximate heats of complex formation increased with the intensity of the brown color of the solution. The order of increasing heats of formation was benzene, toluene, methyl alcohol, ethyl acetate, ethyl alcohol, methyl acetate, nitrobenzene, dioxane, diethyl ether, and pyridine. In the case of pyridine, they suggested the formation of a salt.

Various structures for the molecular addition compounds have been proposed. Keefer and Andrews[40] prefer to describe the benzene-halogen complex as a resonance hybrid of the many different resonance forms based on the general formula

$$(C_6H_6^{+}):\ddot{\underset{\cdot\cdot}{\mathrm{X}}}::\ddot{\underset{\cdot\cdot}{\mathrm{X}}}:^{-}$$

in which the centers of the benzene ring and the two halogen atoms (10) lie on a straight line. Mulliken[45] has treated the specific interaction complexes of iodine, bromine, iodine monochloride, and iodine monobromide with simple benzene derivatives, ethers, alcohols, water, and ketones on the basis of valence theoretical considerations. He regards the above structure as unlikely, since he believes that the intense absorption bands of these complexes in the neighborhood of 300 mμ may in part be explained in terms of a loss of symmetry by the benzene ring on forming the complex. Instead, he favors a type of structure in which the halogen molecule is located in a position parallel to the plane of the aromatic nucleus, with the center of the molecule on the sixfold symmetry axis of the ring. In connection with predictions of the structure of the acetone-iodine complex, it is of interest to note that Benesi and Hildebrand[46] have shown that there is a rapid chemical reaction between iodine and acetone and that the single intense absorption peak at 363 mμ they previously reported for this system[38] is due to the triiodide ion. Bayliss[47] has treated the red shift of absorption in solution on the basis of quantum mechanics and classical dispersion theory. This effect, which is nonspecific in nature, cannot account for the specific one-to-one interaction of the halogen complexes.

Two-phase equilibria.—The solubility of gases in liquids has received some attention. Gjaldbaek and Hildebrand[48] determined the solubility of chlorine in perfluoro-*n*-heptane and showed that regular solution theory, equation (9), could account fairly well for the observed solubilities and their temperature dependence. The rather concentration-dependent partial molar volume of chlorine in perfluoro-*n*-heptane was found to be near that of liquid chlorine, while the partial molar volumes of nitrogen, methane, and ethane

---

[43] T. M. Cromwell and R. L. Scott, *J. Am. Chem. Soc.* **72**, 3825–26 (1950).

[44] K. Hartley and H. A. Skinner, *Trans. Faraday Soc.* **46**, 621–25 (1950).

[45] R. S. Mulliken, *J. Am. Chem. Soc.* **72**, 600–8 (1950).

[46] H. A. Benesi and J. H. Hildebrand, *J. Am. Chem. Soc.* **72**, 2273–74 (1950).

[47] N. S. Bayliss, *J. Chem. Phys.* **18**, 292–96 (1950).

[48] J. C. Gjaldbaek and J. H. Hildebrand, *J. Am. Chem. Soc.* **72**, 609–11 (1950).

in perfluoro-n-heptane, n-hexane, and carbon disulfide decreased strongly with increasing solubility parameters of the solvents.[49] The solubility of hydrogen bromide in n-hexane, n-octane, and n-decane, measured by Boedeker and Lynch,[50] is also in qualitative agreement with regular solution theory. Their heats of solution, obtained from the temperature dependence of the solubility at a constant partial pressure p_2, are only qualitative since Henry's law did not hold rigorously. This objection is readily apparent from the approximate, though adequate, thermodynamic relationship

$$H_2 \text{ (vap.)} - \bar{H}_2 \text{ (liq.)} = \frac{1}{RT}\left(\frac{\partial \mu_1}{\partial \log x_1}\right)_{T,\,p} \left\{\frac{\partial R \log x_2}{\partial \frac{1}{T}}\right\}_{p2} \tag{13}$$

where x_2 is the mol fraction of the gas in the liquid.

The freezing points of the systems *cis*- and *trans*-decahydronaphthalene, dotriacontane and *cis*-decahydronaphthalene, and tetracosane and *cis*-decahydronaphthalene were examined by Seyer, Yip and Pyle[51] and were found to be very close to the ideal state. Similar ideality was found from the freezing points of *cis*- and *trans*-1,2-dichloroethene, investigated by Broers, Ketelaar and van Velden.[52] The entropies of fusion, computed from the slopes of the melting point-composition diagram of this system, could be ascribed to more rotational freedom for the *trans* molecule. Mathot[53] has pointed out that when the entropy of fusion of one component of a binary ideal system is less than 4 cal. per M per degree, a point of inflection may result in the eutectic phase diagram. This prediction appears to be verified for the system methylcyclohexane-cyclohexane.

Witnauer and Swern[54] found that the isomeric 9,10-epoxyoctadecanols lead to a simple eutectic, and Cilento[55] found that phthalic anhydride-thiophthalic anhydride, phthalimide-phthalic anhydride, phthalimide-thiophthalic anhydride, triphenylthiophosphate-triphenylphosphate, triphenylselenophosphate-triphenylphosphate, and tri-p-tolylthiophosphate-tri-p-tolylphosphate also lead to simple eutectics while selenophthalic anhydride-thiophthalic anhydride and triphenylselenophosphate-triphenyl-thiophosphate yield a Roozeboom type 1 diagram.

Small deviations from ideality were found from liquid-vapor studies of the binary systems pyridine-acetic anhydride,[56] tetradecane-1-hexadecene,[57] ethylene oxide-acetaldehyde,[58] and binary solutions with H_2, D_2, and HD as constituents.[59] Wise, Puck and Failey[60] employed a novel dew point method in a liquid-vapor equilibrium investigation of water-2,2′-ethylene dioxydi-ethanol that indicated negative deviations from Raoult's law. Bent and

---

[49] J. C. Gjaldbaek and J. H. Hildebrand, *J. Am. Chem. Soc.* **72**, 1077–78 (1950).
[50] E. R. Boedeker and C. C. Lynch, *J. Am. Chem. Soc.* **72**, 3234–36 (1950).
[51] W. F. Seyer, S. Yip and G. Pyle, *J. Am. Chem. Soc.* **72**, 3162–64 (1950).
[52] G. H. J. Broers, J. A. A. Ketelaar and P. F. van Velden, *Rec. trav. chim.* **69**, 1122–26 (1950).
[53] V. Mathot, *Bull. soc. chim. Belges* **59**, 137–39 (1950).
[54] L. P. Witnauer and D. Swern, *J. Am. Chem. Soc.* **72**, 3364–68 (1950).
[55] G. Cilento, *J. Phys. and Colloid Chem.* **54**, 564–69 (1950).
[56] P. A. Nelson and A. E. Markham, *J. Am. Chem. Soc.* **72**, 2417–18 (1950).
[57] R. R. Rasmussen and M. Van Winkle, *Ind. Eng. Chem.* **42**, 2121–24 (1950).
[58] K. F. Coles and F. Popper, *Ind. Eng. Chem.* **42**, 1434–38 (1950).
[59] R. D. Arnold and H. J. Hoge, *J. Chem. Phys.* **18** 1295 (1950).
[60] H. Wise, T. T. Puck and C. F. Failey, *J. Phys. and Colloid Chem.* **54**, 734–41 (1950).

Krinbill[61] have remarked that in binary liquid-vapor systems whose chemical potentials may be represented by equation (1), the ratio of the vapor pressures of the pure components is independent of Δ_{12} at a liquid composition $x_1 = V_2^{1/2}(V_1^{1/2} + V_2^{1/2})$. They applied this observation to the determination of the vapor pressure of pure diphenyl ether at 50°C., employing "mustard gas" as reference liquid. Minimum boiling azeotropes were found at 1 atm. in the systems water-2-methyl-3-butyn-2-ol and water-3-hydroxy-3-methyl-2-butanone,[62] while phase rule studies of the water-ethene system[63, 64] led to the determination of the composition, $C_2H_4 \cdot 7H_2O$, for the dissociating compound found by these substances.

Metallic solutions.—Employing the electromotive force method, Kleppa[65] studied the liquid tin-gold system up to 78 atomic per cent gold. From these data, activities, relative partial molar and integral heats of mixing were determined at 600°C. This system shows very large negative deviations from Raoult's law consistent with the presence of stable intermetallic phases which give rise to a maximum in the binary phase diagram. Kleppa[66] also measured ultrasonic velocities of sound in equiatomic liquid mixtures of tin-cadmium, tin-mercury, tin-bismuth, and tin-lead and found that the rule of additivity was only approximately valid.

Hauffe's technique[67] of using glass as an electrolyte for activity determinations of liquid alloys has been utilized by him and Vierk.[68] They determined the activity of potassium in amalgams containing 0.260 to 0.988 atomic per cent potassium by means of the chain

$$\text{K (liq.)}|\ \text{"Thüringer" glass (3.5 wt. per cent } K_2O)|\ \text{K-Hg (liq.) 325°C.}$$

Although the strong negative deviations from Raoult's law they found are expected, since KHg lies in the composition range investigated, their results disagree with earlier work by Pedder and Barrat[69] and Millar.[70] The exchange of sodium ions by potassium ions in the glass is being studied by these authors. Vierk[71] employed the chain

$$\text{Tl (liq.)}|\text{"Thüringer" glass containing Tl ions}|\ \text{Tl-Bi (liq.) 459°C.}$$

and found thallium activities in good agreement with earlier work by Wagner and Engelhardt[72] and Hildebrand and Sharma.[73]

The equilibrium solubility of pure iron in mercury was determined from 25° to 700°C. by Marshall, Epstein and Norton[74] and large positive deviations from Raoult's law were found in these extremely dilute solutions. Johnson,

---

[61] H. E. Bent and C. A. Krinbill, Jr., *J. Am Chem. Soc.* **72**, 2757–60 (1950).
[62] A. Z. Conner, P. J. Elving, J. Benischeck, P. E. Tobias and S. Steingiser, *Ind. Eng. Chem.* **42**, 106–10 (1950).
[63] G. A. M. Diepen and F. E. C. Sheffer, *Rec. trav. chim.* **69**, 593–603 (1950).
[64] G. A. M. Diepen and F. E. C. Sheffer, *Rec. trav. chim.* **69**, 604–9 (1950).
[65] O. J. Kleppa, *J. Am. Chem. Soc.* **72**, 3346–52 (1950).
[66] O. J. Kleppa, *J. Chem. Phys.* **18**, 1331–36 (1950).
[67] K. Hauffe, *Z. Elektrochem.* **46**, 348–56 (1940).
[68] A. L. Vierk and K. Hauffe, *Z. Elektrochem.* **54**, 383–86 (1950).
[69] J. S. Pedder and S. Barrat, *J. Chem. Soc.* 537–46 (1933).
[70] R. W. Millar, *J. Am. Chem. Soc.* **49**, 3003–10 (1922).
[71] A. L. Vierk, *Z. Elektrochem.* **54**, 436–37 (1950).
[72] C. Wagner and G. Engelhardt, *Z. physik Chem.* [A]**159**, 241–67 (1932).
[73] J. H. Hildebrand and J. N. Sharma, *J. Am. Chem. Soc.* **51**, 462–71 (1929).
[74] A. L. Marshall, L. F. Epstein and F. J. Norton, *J. Am. Chem. Soc.* **72**, 3514–16 (1950).

Meyer and Martens[75] measured the density of solutions of lithium in liquid ammonia at −33.2°C. and of saturated solutions of sodium and potassium in liquid ammonia at temperatures ranging from about −32° to −51°C.

Surface and critical phenomena.—Recently, Kirkwood and Buff[76] developed the statistical mechanical theory of surface phenomena, which, in the case of solutions of nonelectrolytes, leads to results which are not readily amenable to numerical evaluation. For the purpose of obtaining relatively simple expressions, several authors[77, 78, 79] have employed the quasi-crystalline lattice approximation with the assumption that the interfacial region consists of a unimolecular layer having the same lattice properties as the bulk of the solution, but differing, in general, in its composition. The expression for the surface tension of a strictly regular solution derived by Guggenheim[79] on the basis of this model has been tested on the system ether-acetone by Prigogine[80] with excellent agreement. Defay and Prigogine[81] have re-examined the implications of these approximations and have shown that the assumption of a unimolecular layer as the surface phase separating a strictly regular solution from its vapor phase is in contradiction with the Gibbs adsorption equation. When, however, the possible presence of several unimolecular layers in the surface phase is taken into account, this discrepancy is removed with little modification of the surface tension expression, although the relative adsorption is altered significantly.

Prigogine and Defay[82] have utilized the layer model for the calculation of the interfacial tension between the immiscible phases of binary strictly regular solutions. Prigogine and Sarolea[83, 83a] also have examined the surface tension of a solution where one component occupies one place and the other two places of a quasi-crystalline lattice with good agreement between theory and experiment for the system benzene-diphenyl. The contribution of permanent dipoles to the relative adsorption of polar-dipole solutions has been calculated by Hartmann[84] in a manner similar to Wagner's theory[85] of the relative adsorption of strong electrolyte solutions. Hartmann's comparison of this result with a rough estimate of the relative adsorption of the cyclohexane-nitrobenzene system is doubtful in view of the neglect of the van der Waals force contribution to the adsorption.

The symposium on critical phenomena held at the 116th meeting of the American Chemical Society was recently published in the *Journal of Physical and Colloid Chemistry*. Rice[86] presented a general survey of the field with particular emphasis on the association theory, and Tisza[87] reviewed the

---

[75] W. C. Johnson, A. W. Meyer and R. D. Martens, *J. Am. Chem. Soc.* **72**, 1842–43 (1950).
[76] J. G. Kirkwood and F. P. Buff, *J. Chem. Phys.* **17**, 338–43 (1949).
[77] J. W. Belton and M. G. Evans, *Trans. Faraday Soc.* **41**, 1–12 (1945).
[78] A. A. Schuchowitzky, *Acta Physicochim. U.R.S.S.* **19**, 176–207 (1944).
[79] E. A. Guggenheim, *Trans. Faraday Soc.* **41**, 150–56 (1945).
[80] I. Prigogine, *Trans. Faraday Soc.* **44**, 626–28 (1948).
[81] R. Defay and I. Prigogine, *Trans. Faraday Soc.* **46**, 199–204 (1950).
[82] I. Prigogine and R. Defay, *Bull. soc. chim. Belges* **59**, 255–62 (1950).
[83] I. Prigogine, *J. Chem. Phys.* **47**, 33–40 (1950).
[83a] I. Prigogine and L. Sarolea, *J. chim. phys.* **47**, 807–15 (1950).
[84] H. Hartmann, *Z. physik. Chem.* **195**, 53–57 (1950).
[85] C. Wagner, *Physik. Z.* **25**, 474–77 (1924).
[86] O. K. Rice, *J. Phys. and Colloid Chem.* **54**, 1293–1305 (1950).
[87] L. Tisza, *J. Phys. and Colloid Chem.* **54**, 1317–23 (1950).

theory of fluctuations near the critical point. Zimm's important investigation[88] of light scattering near the critical mixing point of a binary system and its bearing on Mayer's theory of critical phenomena[3] has already been discussed in detail by Hildebrand and Scott[89] in their review article for 1950. Boyd[90] discussed retrograde condensation of binary mixtures and presented a qualitative formulation of this phenomenon in terms of the van der Waals equation of state. Atack and Schneider[91] reported solubility measurements in the neighborhood of T_M, the temperature at which the meniscus disappears. Employing ethane as solvent and 1-chloro-4-iodobenzene containing some radioactive iodine as solute, they found that vigorous stirring is required in order to obtain a uniform density gradient at temperatures larger than 0.3°C. above T_M. Furthermore, at temperatures less than 0.3°C., they presented evidence for an equilibrium density gradient in the vicinity of the point where the meniscus disappears at T_M and suggested that the gradient might be ascribed to the effect of the gravitational field on large clusters of molecules.

Wentorf, Buehler, Hirschfelder and Curtiss[92] carried out extensive calculations of the Lennard-Jones and Devonshire[20] equation of state of compressed gases and liquids and found the expected result that the theory is unsatisfactory near the critical point but improves at higher densities. Ono[93, 94, 95] has examined critical and surface phenomena on the basis of the quasi-lattice approximation and free volume theories with particular reference to the lower critical mixing point.

Miscellaneous.—Kittsley and Golden[96] have extended Hildebrand's system[97] of seven liquid phases in stable equilibrium to eight phases. The eight liquid layers, indefinitely stable at 45°C., in order of increasing density are paraffin oil, silicone oil, water, aniline, perfluorodimethylcyclohexane, white phosphorus, gallium, and mercury.

Gross and Taylor[98] measured the dielectric constants of aqueous hydrogen peroxide solutions from 30° to 65°C. and found a broad maximum at intermediate concentrations in the dielectric constant-composition diagram. Similar dielectric constant measurements were carried out by LaRochelle and Vernon[99] for the system methyl alcohol-benzene.

Fineman[100] has modified equation (8) for the calculation of heats of formation of alkali halide solid solutions by employing solubility parameters computed from energies of sublimation. The rather poor agreement with experiment was of the same order of magnitude as calculations based on recent lattice theories.[101]

---

88 B. H. Zimm, *J. Phys. and Colloid Chem.* **54**, 1306–17 (1950).
89 J. H. Hildebrand and R. L. Scott, *Ann. Rev. Phys. Chem.* **1**, 75–92 (1950).
90 C. A. Boyd, *J. Phys. and Colloid Chem.* **54**, 1347–57 (1950).
91 D. Atack and W. G. Schneider, *J. Phys. and Colloid Chem.* **54**, 1323–36 (1950).
92 R. H. Wentorf, Jr., R. J. Buehler, J. O. Hirschfelder and C. F. Curtiss, *J. Chem. Phys.* **18**, 1484–1500 (1950).
93 S. Ono, *Mem. Faculty Eng., Kyushu Imp. Univ.* **10**, 195–255 (1947).
94 S. Ono, *Mem. Faculty Eng., Kyushu Imp. Univ.* **12**, 1–8 (1950).
95 S. Ono, *Mem. Faculty Eng., Kyushu Imp. Univ.* **12**, 201–13 (1950).
96 S. L. Kittsley and H. A. Golden, *J. Am. Chem. Soc.* **72**, 4841–42 (1950).
97 J. H. Hildebrand, *J. Phys. and Colloid Chem.* **53**, 944–67 (1949).
98 P. M. Gross, Jr., and R. C. Taylor, *J. Am. Chem. Soc.* **72**, 2075–80 (1950).
99 J. H. LaRochelle and A. A. Vernon, *J. Am. Chem. Soc.* **72**, 3293–94 (1950).
100 M. Fineman, *J. Chem. Phys.* **18**, 771–72 (1950).
101 W. E. Wallace, *J. Chem. Phys.* **17**, 1095–99 (1949).

Haase[102] has given a lucid discussion of the general Gibbs coexistence and stability conditions for multicomponent systems, and this author, Meijering,[103] and Münster[104] also treated the segregation in ternary systems on the basis of this thermodynamic theory and approximate analytic expressions for the chemical potentials.

102 R. Haase, *Z. Naturforsch.* **5a**, 109–24 (1950).
103 J. L. Meijering, *Philips Research Reports* **5**, 333–56 (1950).
104 A. Münster, *J. Polymer Sci.* **5**, 333–53 (1950).

The Statistical Mechanical Theory of Solutions. I

JOHN G. KIRKWOOD AND FRANK P. BUFF,* *Gates and Crellin Laboratories of Chemistry, California Institute of Technology, Pasadena, California*†

(Received March 26, 1951)

A general statistical mechanical theory of solutions is developed with the aid of the theory of composition fluctuations in the grand canonical ensemble. It is shown that the derivatives of the chemical potentials and osmotic pressure with respect to concentrations, the partial molar volumes, and compressibility may be expressed in terms of integrals of the radial distribution functions of the several types of molecular pairs present in the solution. Explicit coefficients of a q-fraction expansion of the thermodynamic variables are presented in a detailed treatment of the two-component system.

I.

This paper will be concerned with the development of a general statistical mechanical theory of solutions which is applicable to all types of intermolecular interaction and is valid both classically and quantum mechanically. The theory of the grand canonical ensemble is employed on the one hand to relate composition fluctuations to derivatives of the chemical potentials of the components and on the other hand to relate them to integrals of the radial distribution functions of the several types of molecular pairs present in the solution. When the composition fluctuations are themselves eliminated from these relations, expressions for the derivatives of the chemical potentials and osmotic pressure with respect to concentrations, the partial molar volumes, and compressibility are obtained in terms of integrals of the radial distribution functions. For short-range intermolecular forces, these integrals may be developed in power series in the concentrations of the solutes, the coefficients of which involve distribution functions of sets n of molecules at infinite dilution in the solvent. The resulting expansion for the osmotic pressure is identical with that given earlier by McMillan[1] and Mayer in their valuable paper on solution theory.

In Part II of this article, following a discussion of notation and the definition of various molecular distribution functions, we present a review of the theory of composition fluctuations in the grand ensemble. The results are subsequently employed to evaluate important thermodynamic variables of a multicomponent system in terms of integrals of the radial distribution functions. The theory provides an alternative to the familiar charging process encountered in electrolyte theory, while in the absence of long-range inter-

---

* AEC Postdoctoral Fellow, 1949–1950. Present address: Department of Chemistry, University of Rochester, Rochester, New York.

† Contribution No. 1548.

[1] W. G. McMillan, Jr., and J. E. Mayer, *J. Chem. Phys.* **13**, 276 (1945).

molecular forces, expansions of the excess chemical potentials, partial molar volumes and compressibility in terms of the q-fractions of the solute components may be obtained.

In Part III of the article the two-component system will be treated in detail. Here, anticipating the results of a future publication, we present the dominant q-fraction expansion coefficients of the thermodynamic variables.

II.

We first wish to formulate the relations between average densities in systems of molecules and the fluctuations in density. We shall treat explicitly those relations involving the number density in the configuration space of molecular pairs. The results may be generalized without difficulty to densities in the configuration space of sets of n molecules and fluctuations of higher order. We consider an open region of volume v, which is a part of a system of infinite extent, and we select an example of the grand ensemble representing its statistical behavior, for which v contains exactly $N_1, \cdots N_\nu$ molecules of the ν-species of the multicomponent system. For specified configurations, $\mathbf{R}_{i_\alpha}$, of all of the molecules, the singlet density $\nu_\alpha^{(1)}(\mathbf{R}_1)$ of species α at a point $\mathbf{R}_1$ in v and the density $\nu_{\alpha\beta}^{(2)}(\mathbf{R}_1, \mathbf{R}_2)$ of ordered pairs of molecules of species $\alpha\beta$ at a point $\mathbf{R}_1$ and species β at $\mathbf{R}_2$ are given by

$$\begin{aligned} \nu_\alpha^{(1)}(\mathbf{R}_1) &= \sum_{i_\alpha=1}^{N_\alpha} \delta(\mathbf{R}_{i_\alpha} - \mathbf{R}_1), \\ \nu_{\alpha\beta}^{(2)}(\mathbf{R}_1, \mathbf{R}_2) &= \sum_{\substack{i_\alpha=1 \\ i_\alpha \neq k_\alpha}}^{N_\alpha} \sum_{k_\beta=1}^{N_\beta} \delta(\mathbf{R}_{i_\alpha} - \mathbf{R}_1)\delta(\mathbf{R}_{k_\beta} - \mathbf{R}_2), \end{aligned} \tag{1}$$

where $\delta(\mathbf{R}_{i_\alpha} - \mathbf{R}_1)$ is the three-dimensional Dirac delta-function. These densities possess by virtue of their definitions the following integrals,

$$\begin{aligned} \int^v \nu_\alpha^{(1)}(\mathbf{R}_1) dv_1 &= N_\alpha, \\ \int^v \int^v \nu_{\alpha\beta}^{(2)}(\mathbf{R}_1, \mathbf{R}_2) dv_1 dv_2 &= N_\alpha N_\beta - N_\alpha \delta_{\alpha\beta}, \end{aligned} \tag{2}$$

where $\delta_{\alpha\beta}$ is the Kronecker delta, unity for $\alpha = \beta$ and zero for $\alpha \neq \beta$. We denote by $\rho_\alpha^{(1)}(\mathbf{R}_1)$ and $\rho_{\alpha\beta}^{(2)}(\mathbf{R}_1, \mathbf{R}_2)$ the average number densities in the singlet and pair spaces,

$$\begin{aligned} \rho_\alpha^{(1)}(\mathbf{R}_1) &= \langle \nu_\alpha^{(1)} \rangle_{\text{Av}}, \\ \rho_{\alpha\beta}^{(2)}(\mathbf{R}_1, \mathbf{R}_2) &= \langle \nu_{\alpha\beta}^{(2)} \rangle_{\text{Av}}, \end{aligned} \tag{3}$$

where the averages are understood to be taken over all numbers of molecules $N_1 \cdots N_\nu$ and over the accessible phase space of each set of molecules with the probability distribution function, P, of the grand canonical ensemble,

$$P = \exp([\Omega + \sum_{\alpha=1}^{\nu} N_\alpha \mu_\alpha - H_{N_1 \cdots N_\nu}]/kT), \tag{4}$$

where μ_α is the chemical potential of species α, per molecule, $H_{N_1 \cdots N_\nu}$ is the Hamiltonian of the set of molecules, $N_1 \cdots N_\nu$, and Ω is equal to $-pv$ to within terms of thermodynamically negligible order of magnitude. Calculation of the mean values of both sides of Eqs. (3) yields the following expressions for the integrals of the mean densities,

$$\int^v \rho_\alpha^{(1)}(\mathbf{R}_1)dv_1 = \langle N_\alpha\rangle_{\text{Av}},$$

$$\int^v\int^v \rho_{\alpha\beta}^{(2)}(\mathbf{R}_1, \mathbf{R}_2)dv_1dv_2 = \langle N_\alpha N_\beta\rangle_{\text{Av}} - \delta_{\alpha\beta}\langle N_\alpha\rangle_{\text{Av}}, \tag{5}$$

$$\int^v\int^v \{\rho_{\alpha\beta}^{(2)}(\mathbf{R}_1, \mathbf{R}_2) - \rho_\alpha^{(1)}(\mathbf{R}_1)\rho_\beta^{(1)}(\mathbf{R}_2)\}dv_1dv_2$$
$$= [\langle N_\alpha N_\beta\rangle_{\text{Av}} - \langle N_\alpha\rangle_{\text{Av}}\langle N_\beta\rangle_{\text{Av}}] - \delta_{\alpha\beta}\langle N_\alpha\rangle_{\text{Av}}.$$

For a fluid system, liquid solution, or gas mixture, the mean densities have the form

$$\rho_\alpha^{(1)}(\mathbf{R}_1) = \langle N_\alpha\rangle_{\text{Av}}/v = c_\alpha,$$
$$\rho_{\alpha\beta}^{(2)}(\mathbf{R}_1, \mathbf{R}_2) = c_\alpha c_\beta g_{\alpha\beta}^{(2)}(R), \tag{6}$$
$$R = (\mathbf{R}_2 - \mathbf{R}_1),$$

where c_α is bulk molecular concentration of species α, and $g_{\alpha\beta}^{(2)}(R)$ is the radial distribution function of species α and β, dependent only on the scalar distance R between the pair of type $\alpha\beta$. With the use of Eq. (6), the last of Eq. (5) assumes the form

$$\int [g_{\alpha\beta}^{(2)}(R) - 1]dv = v\,\frac{\langle N_\alpha N_\beta\rangle_{\text{Av}} - \langle N_\alpha\rangle_{\text{Av}}\langle N_\beta\rangle_{\text{Av}}}{\langle N_\alpha\rangle_{\text{Av}}\langle N_\beta\rangle_{\text{Av}}} - \frac{\delta_{\alpha\beta}}{c_\alpha}, \tag{7}$$

where the integral extends over all relative coordinates of a pair of type $\alpha\beta$. These are the desired relations between the radial distribution functions and the density fluctuations, which form the basis of the present theory. It is to be remarked that although the integral extends only over the relative centers of mass of the molecules of the pair, it has not been assumed that they possess only translational degrees of freedom. The effect of hindered relative rotation for molecules possessing internal degrees of freedom is implicit in the radial distribution functions $g_{\alpha\beta}^{(2)}(R)$, which is to be interpreted as the integral of a more general pair correlation function over all relative orientations of the pair. It is the task of a detailed molecular theory of the molecular distribution functions to determine the implicit influence of hindered rotation, which in many cases is of decisive importance on $g_{\alpha\beta}^{(2)}$.

Next we recall that the composition fluctuations of a thermodynamically open system of volume v are directly related to thermodynamic variables by means of the Gibbs grand canonical ensemble.[2–4] The well-known relations are

$$\langle N_\alpha N_\beta\rangle_{\text{Av}} - \langle N_\alpha\rangle_{\text{Av}}\langle N_\beta\rangle_{\text{Av}} = |A|_{\alpha\beta}/|A|,$$
$$|A| = |A_{\alpha\beta}|; \quad A_{\alpha\beta} = (1/kT)(\partial\mu_\alpha/\partial N_\beta)_{T,V,N_\gamma}, \tag{8}$$

[2] H. C. Brinkman and J. J. Hermans, *J. Chem. Phys.* **17**, 574 (1949).
[3] J. G. Kirkwood and R. J. Goldberg, *J. Chem. Phys.* **18**, 54 (1950).
[4] W. H. Stockmayer, *J. Chem. Phys.* **18**, 58 (1950).

where $|A|_{\alpha\beta}$ symbolizes the cofactor of $A_{\alpha\beta}$ in the determinant $|A|$, μ_α is the chemical potential, per molecule, of species α, T is the thermodynamic temperature, and k is Boltzmann's constant.

Elimination of the composition fluctuations from Eq. (8) immediately leads to expressions for useful thermodynamic variables. Upon taking the inverse of Eq. (8) we obtain for an infinite system, with the use of Eq. (7),

$$(1/kT)(\partial\mu_\alpha/\partial N_\beta)_{T,V,N_\gamma} = |B|_{\alpha\beta}/v|B|,$$

$$B_{\alpha\beta} = c_\alpha\delta_{\alpha\beta} + c_\alpha c_\beta G_{\alpha\beta}, \tag{9}$$

$$G_{\alpha\beta} = \int [g_{\alpha\beta}^{(2)}(R) - 1]dv.$$

In order to obtain expressions for variables measured at the constant pressure p we employ the Gibbs-Duhem equation,

$$\sum_{\alpha=1}^{\nu} N_\alpha\left(\frac{\partial\mu_\alpha}{\partial N_\beta}\right)_{T,p,N_\gamma} = 0 \tag{10}$$

and the mathematical relation

$$(\partial\mu_\alpha/\partial N_\beta)_{T,V,N_\gamma} = (\partial\mu_\alpha/\partial N_\beta)_{T,p,N_\gamma} + \bar{v}_\alpha\bar{v}_\beta/\kappa v, \tag{11}$$

where $\bar{v}_\alpha$ is the partial molar volume, per molecule, of species α and κ is the compressibility of the solution. Use of Eqs. (9), (10), and (11) leads after a straightforward transformation to the desired expressions for the partial molar volumes, compressibility, and derivatives of the chemical potentials,

$$(v/kT)(\partial\mu_\alpha/\partial N_\beta)_{T,p,N_\gamma} = |\Delta|_{\alpha\beta}/c_\alpha c_\beta|\Delta|; \quad \alpha, \beta = 2, \cdots \nu, \tag{12}$$

$$\Delta_{\alpha\beta} = (\delta_{\alpha\beta}/c_\alpha) + (1/c_1) + G_{\alpha\beta} + G_{11} - G_{1\alpha} - G_{1\beta},$$

$$\bar{v}_\alpha = \sum_{\beta-1}^{\nu} c_\beta|B|_{\alpha\beta}/\sum_{\beta,\gamma=1}^{\nu} c_\beta c_\gamma|B|_{\beta\gamma}, \tag{13}$$

$$\kappa kT = |B|/\sum_{\alpha,\beta=1}^{\nu} c_\alpha c_\beta|B|_{\alpha\beta}. \tag{14}$$

The derivative of the osmotic pressure π of a solution, solvent 1 and solutes 2, $\cdots$ may be calculated in a similar manner from Eq. (9) and the thermodynamic equation,

$$\left(\frac{\partial\pi}{\partial c_\alpha}\right)_{T,\mu_1,c_\gamma} = \sum_{\beta=2}^{\nu} c_\beta\left(\frac{\partial\mu_\beta}{\partial c_\alpha}\right)_{T,\mu_1,c_\gamma} \tag{15}$$

with the result

$$\left(\frac{\partial\pi}{\partial c_\alpha}\right)_{T,\mu_1,c_\gamma} = kT\sum_{\beta=2}^{\nu}\frac{c_\beta|B'|_{\alpha\beta}}{|B'|}, \tag{16}$$

$$B_{\alpha\beta}' = c_\alpha\delta_{\alpha\beta} + c_\alpha c_\beta G_{\alpha\beta}.$$

It will be noted that this expression does not contain explicitly solvent-solvent and solvent-solute interaction terms.

III.

We shall now present a more detailed treatment of the two component system, solvent 1 and solute 2. In this case Eqs. (12), (13), (14), and (16) may be exhibited in the form

$$\bar{v}_1 = \frac{1 + (G_{22} - G_{12})c_2}{c_1 + c_2 + c_1c_2(G_{11} + G_{22} - 2G_{12})}, \tag{17}$$

$$c_1\bar{v}_1 + c_2\bar{v}_2 = 1,$$

$$\kappa kT = \frac{1 + G_{11}c_1 + G_{22}c_2 + (G_{11}G_{22} - G_{12}^2)c_1c_2}{c_1 + c_2 + (G_{11} + G_{22} - 2G_{12})c_1c_2}, \tag{18}$$

$$(\partial\pi/\partial c_2)_{T,\mu 1} = kT/(1 + G_{22}c_2), \tag{19}$$

$$\frac{1}{kT}\left(\frac{\partial\mu_2}{\partial c_2}\right)_{T,p} = \frac{1}{c_2} + \frac{G_{12} - G_{22}}{1 + c_2(G_{22} - G_{12})}, \tag{20}$$

$$\frac{1}{kT}\left(\frac{\partial\mu_1}{\partial c_1}\right)_{T,p} = \frac{1}{c_1} + \frac{G_{12} - G_{11}}{1 + c_1(G_{11} - G_{12})}, \tag{21}$$

$$\frac{1}{kT}\left(\frac{\partial\mu_2}{\partial x_2}\right)_{T,p} = \frac{1}{x_2} + \frac{c_1(2G_{12} - G_{11} - G_{22})}{1 + c_1x_2(G_{11} + G_{22} - 2G_{12})}, \tag{22}$$

where $x_\alpha = N_\alpha/(N_1 + N_2)$, is the mole fraction of component α.

The preceding relations are completely general, and it is of interest to remark that in electrolyte theory Eq. (20) provides an alternative to the usual charging process. For example, the well-known limiting law immediately follows when G_{22} is calculated by means of the Debye-Huckel radial distribution function. In the absence of long-range intermolecular forces, the integrals $G_{\alpha\beta}$ may be developed in power series in c_2 the coefficients of which involve distribution functions of sets n of molecules at infinite dilution in the solvent. This development, which leads to the solution theory of McMillan and Mayer[1] as a special case, constitutes a generalization of the methods of Part II and will be described in a forthcoming paper. In the remainder of this article these results will be anticipated, and we shall give the explicit expansion coefficients involving the cluster integrals of sets of 3 molecules. The following additional integrals are encountered:

$$\begin{aligned} vG_{\alpha\beta\gamma} = (1/c_\alpha c_\beta c_\gamma)\int\int\int \{&\rho_{\alpha\beta\gamma}{}^{(3)}(\mathbf{R}_1, \mathbf{R}_2, \mathbf{R}_3) - \rho_{\alpha\beta}{}^{(2)}(\mathbf{R}_1, \mathbf{R}_2)\rho_\gamma{}^{(1)}(\mathbf{R}_3) \\ &+ 2\rho_\alpha{}^{(1)}(\mathbf{R}_1)\rho_\beta{}^{(1)}(\mathbf{R}_2)\rho_\gamma{}^{(1)}(\mathbf{R}_3) - \rho_{\alpha\gamma}{}^{(2)}(\mathbf{R}_1, \mathbf{R}_2)\rho_\beta{}^{(1)}(\mathbf{R}_3) \\ &- \rho_{\beta\gamma}{}^{(2)}(\mathbf{R}_1, \mathbf{R}_2)\rho_\alpha{}^{(1)}(\mathbf{R}_3)\}dv_1dv_2dv_3, \end{aligned} \tag{23}$$

where $\rho_{\alpha\beta\gamma}{}^{(3)}$ is the mean density of ordered triplets which, when expressed in terms of the generalized correlation functions of the centers of mass of the molecules, simplify for a fluid system,

$$G_{\alpha\beta\gamma} = \iiint \{2 + g_{\alpha\beta\gamma}{}^{(3)}(\mathbf{R}_{12}, \mathbf{R}_{13}) - g_{\alpha\beta}{}^{(2)}(R_{12})$$

$$- g_{\alpha\gamma}{}^{(2)}(R_{13}) - g_{\beta\gamma}{}^{(2)}(R_{23})\} dv_{12} dv_{13}, \tag{24}$$

$$\rho_{\alpha\beta\gamma}{}^{(3)} = c_\alpha c_\beta c_\gamma g_{\alpha\beta\gamma}{}^{(3)}.$$

It is found that the osmotic pressure π is given by

$$\pi = c_2 kT\{1 - \tfrac{1}{2}G_{22}{}^0 c_2 - \tfrac{1}{3}(G_{222}{}^0 - 3G_{22}{}^{02})c_2{}^2 + \cdots\}, \tag{25}$$

where the superscript 0 denotes that the cluster integrals are evaluated in the infinitely dilute solvent. Similar expansions in powers of c_2 may be obtained for the other variables, but in most applications it is more convenient to employ expansions in powers of the q_2-fraction which is defined by the relation,

$$q_2 = x_2/(x_1 + mx_2),$$

$$m = \bar{v}_2{}^0/\bar{v}_1{}^0; \quad \bar{v}_2{}^0 = \lim_{c_2=0} \bar{v}_2 = \bar{v}_1{}^0 + G_{11}{}^0 - G_{22}{}^0. \tag{26}$$

The theory leads to the following expansions for the chemical potentials:

$$\mu_2 = kT \log q_2 + \mu_2{}^E + \mu_2{}^0(T, p), \quad \mu_2{}^0 = \lim_{q_2=0} [\mu_2 - kT \log q_2], \tag{27}$$

$$\mu_1 = kT \log(1 - mq_2) + \mu_1{}^E + \mu_1{}^0(T, p), \tag{28}$$

where

$$\mu_2{}^E/kT = a_1 q_2 + a_2 q_2{}^2 + \cdots, \tag{29}$$

$$\mu_1{}^E/kT = b_1 q_2 + b_2 q_2{}^2 + b_3 q_2{}^3 + \cdots, \tag{30}$$

and

$$a_1 = (G_{12}{}^0 - G_{22}{}^0)/\bar{v}_1{}^0,$$

$$a_2 = (\tfrac{1}{2}\bar{v}_1{}^{02})[3G_{122}{}^0 + G_{111}{}^0 - 3G_{112}{}^0 - G_{222}{}^0$$
$$+ 3(G_{22}{}^0 - G_{12}{}^0)^2 - (G_{11}{}^0 - G_{12}{}^0)^2$$
$$+ (G_{11}{}^0 - G_{12}{}^0)(G_{22}{}^0 - G_{12}{}^0)$$
$$+ \bar{v}_1{}^0(G_{11}{}^0 + G_{22}{}^0 - 2G_{12}{}^0)],$$

$$b_1 = (G_{11}{}^0 - G_{12}{}^0)/\bar{v}_1{}^0,$$

$$b_2 = (\tfrac{1}{2}\bar{v}_1{}^{02})[(G_{11}{}^0 - G_{12}{}^0)^2 + \bar{v}_1{}^0(G_{22}{}^0 + G_{22}{}^0 - 2G_{12}{}^0)],$$

$$b_3 = (\tfrac{1}{3}\bar{v}_1{}^{03})\{(G_{11}{}^0 - G_{12}{}^0)^3 + \bar{v}_1{}^0[3(G_{112}{}^0 - G_{221}{}^0)$$
$$+ 3(G_{11}{}^0 - G_{12}{}^0)^2 - 3(G_{22}{}^0 - G_{12}{}^0)^2 + G_{222}{}^0 - G_{111}{}^0]\}.$$

Similarly, the partial molar volumes are given by

$$\bar{v}_2 = \bar{v}_2{}^0 + d_1 q_2 + \cdots, \tag{31}$$

$$\bar{v}_1 = \bar{v}_1{}^0 - \tfrac{1}{2} d_1 q_2{}^2 + \cdots, \tag{32}$$

where

$$\bar{v}_2{}^0 = \bar{v}_1{}^0 + G_{11}{}^0 - G_{12}{}^0,$$

$$d_1 = 2G_{12}{}^0 - G_{11}{}^0 - G_{22}{}^0 + (1/\bar{v}_1{}^0)[2G_{12}{}^0 G_{22}{}^0 + 2G_{112}{}^0 + G_{11}{}^{02} - 2G_{12}{}^{02} - G_{122}{}^0 - G_{111}{}^0 - G_{11}{}^0 G_{22}{}^0].$$

Finally, the compressibility is found to be

$$\kappa kT = \kappa^0 kT + e_1 q_2 + \cdots, \tag{33}$$

where

$$\kappa^0 kT = \bar{v}_1{}^0 + G_{11}{}^0,$$

$$e_1 = G_{12}{}^0 - G_{11}{}^0 + (1/\bar{v}_1{}^0)[G_{112}{}^0 + G_{11}{}^{02} - G_{111}{}^0 - G_{12}{}^{02}].$$

While mole fraction expansions are not as useful as the preceding expressions, for the sake of completeness we present the expansion for the chemical potential

$$\mu_1/kT = \log x_1 + f_2 x_2{}^2 + f_3 x_2{}^3 + \cdots + \mu_1{}^0/kT, \tag{34}$$

where

$$f_2 = [G_{11}{}^0 + G_{22}{}^0 - 2G_{12}{}^0]/2\bar{v}_1{}^0,$$

$$f_3 = (\tfrac{1}{3}\bar{v}_1{}^{02})[3G_{112}{}^0 + 3(G_{11}{}^0 - G_{12}{}^0)^2 - G_{111}{}^0 - 3G_{221}{}^0 - 3(G_{22}{}^0 - G_{12}{}^0)^2 + G_{222}{}^0 + 3(G_{12}{}^0 - G_{11}{}^0)(G_{11}{}^0 + G_{22}{}^0 - 2G_{12}{}^0)].$$

APPENDIX

Equation (8) is readily derived from the grand partition function,

$$e^{\Omega'} = \sum_{\substack{N_1 \cdots N_\nu \\ =0}}^{\infty} \prod_{\alpha=1}^{\nu} \lambda_\alpha{}^{N_\alpha} \exp\left[-\frac{A(N_1 \cdots N_\nu, T_1 v)}{kT} \right], \tag{A1}$$

$$\Omega' = pv/kT; \quad \lambda_\alpha = \exp(\mu_\alpha/kT),$$

where $A(N_1 \cdots N_\nu, T_1 v)$ is the Helmholtz free energy of a member of the grand ensemble. Repeated differentiation of Ω with respect to the absolute activity λ_α leads to mean values of the composition fluctuations:

$$\lambda_\alpha(\partial\Omega'/\partial\lambda_\alpha)_{T,v,\lambda_\gamma} = \langle N_\alpha \rangle_{\text{Av}},$$

$$\lambda_\alpha\lambda_\beta(\partial^2\Omega'/\partial\lambda_\alpha\partial\lambda_\beta)_{T,v,\lambda_\gamma} + \lambda_\alpha(\partial\Omega'/\partial\lambda_\alpha)_{T,v,\lambda_\gamma}\delta_{\alpha\beta} = \langle N_\alpha N_\beta \rangle_{\text{Av}} - \langle N_\alpha \rangle_{\text{Av}} \langle N_\beta \rangle_{\text{Av}}. \tag{A2}$$

Next by equating the mathematical identity, we obtain

$$\left(\frac{\partial^2\Omega'}{\partial N_\alpha \partial N_\beta}\right)_{T,v,N_\gamma} = \frac{1}{(kT)^2} \sum_{\sigma,\rho=1}^{\nu} \left[\lambda_\sigma\lambda_\rho\left(\frac{\partial^2\Omega'}{\partial\lambda_\sigma\partial\lambda_\rho}\right)_{T,v,N_\gamma} + \lambda_\sigma\left(\frac{\partial\Omega'}{\partial\lambda_\sigma}\right)_{T,v,N_\gamma}\delta_{\sigma\rho}\right]\left(\frac{\partial\mu_\sigma}{\partial N_\alpha}\right)_{T,v,N_\gamma}\left(\frac{\partial\mu_\rho}{\partial N_\beta}\right)_{T,v,N_\gamma} + \frac{1}{kT}\sum_{\sigma=1}^{\nu}\lambda_\sigma\left(\frac{\partial\Omega'}{\partial\lambda_\sigma}\right)_{T,v,N_\gamma}\left(\frac{\partial^2\mu_\sigma}{\partial N_\alpha\partial N_\beta}\right)_{T,v,N_\gamma} \tag{A3}$$

to the result obtained by differentiating the Gibbs-Duhem equation

$$kT\left(\frac{\partial^2\Omega'}{\partial N_\alpha\partial N_\beta}\right)_{T,v,N_\gamma} = \left(\frac{\partial\mu_\alpha}{\partial N_\beta}\right)_{T,v,N_\gamma} + \sum_{\sigma=1}^{\nu} N_\sigma\left(\frac{\partial^2\mu_\sigma}{\partial N_\alpha\partial N_\beta}\right)_{T,v,N_\gamma}. \tag{A4}$$

We finally obtain with use of Eq. (A2)

$$\frac{1}{kT}\left(\frac{\partial\mu_\alpha}{\partial N_\beta}\right)_{T,v,N_\gamma} = \sum_{\sigma,\rho=1}^{\nu}\frac{1}{k^2T^2}[\langle N_\sigma N_\rho\rangle_{\text{Av}} - \langle N_\sigma\rangle_{\text{Av}}\langle N_\rho\rangle_{\text{Av}}] \times\left(\frac{\partial\mu_\sigma}{\partial N_\beta}\right)_{T,v,N_\gamma}\left(\frac{\partial\mu_\rho}{\partial N_\alpha}\right)_{T,v,N_\gamma}, \quad \alpha,\beta = 1,\cdots\nu. \tag{A5}$$

This set of equations is equivalent to the matrix equation,

$$A = ABA,$$
$$A_{\alpha\beta} = A_{\beta\alpha} = (1/kT)(\partial\mu_\alpha/\partial N_\beta)_{T,v,N_\gamma}, \tag{A6}$$
$$B_{\sigma\rho} - B_{\rho\sigma} - \langle N_\sigma N_\rho\rangle_{\text{Av}} - \langle N_\sigma\rangle_{\text{Av}}\langle N_\rho\rangle_{\text{Av}}.$$

with the solution,

$$B = A^{-1}; \quad B_{\sigma\rho} = |A|_{\sigma\rho}/|A|.$$

ADDENDUM TO PAPER NUMBER 6

The grand ensemble distribution function given in Eq. (4) is expressed in terms of the Hamiltonian of the system, implying that the theory is applicable only to classical systems. However, as one of the authors[5] has remarked, the formulation given in this paper is completely general and equally applicable to quantum as well as classical systems.

---

[5] F. P. Buff and R. Brout, *J. Chem. Phys.* **23**, 458 (1955).

The Free Volume Theory of Multicomponent Fluid Mixtures*

ZEVI W. SALSBURG AND JOHN G. KIRKWOOD, *Sterling Chemistry Laboratory, Yale University, New Haven, Connecticut*

(Received May 15, 1952)

The free volume theory of the liquid state is extended to multicomponent mixtures by using the method of moments in the treatment of the order-disorder problem. Retention of only the first moment yields an approximation to the partition function which has recently been studied by Prigogine and Garikian and by Prigogine and Mathot. An approximation equivalent to retaining the third moment is given, and the calculation of the thermodynamic functions from the first moment approximation is discussed.

Although in principle an exact theory of the liquid state can be given within the framework of statistical mechanics, the mathematical difficulties encountered in trying to obtain explicit results have prompted the use of intuitively plausible models. One of these models in the form of the free volume theory developed by Eyring[1] and co-workers and by Lennard-Jones and Devonshire[2] has provided a useful approximate description of the thermodynamic properties of pure liquids.

One[3] of us has shown that the free volume theory can be derived from the general principles of statistical mechanics by means of well-defined approximations. This general insight into the nature of the free volume theory has provided the basis for extending the theory to multicomponent fluid mixtures. The results of this extension are given in this article.

Recently, Prigogine[4,5] and co-workers have given expressions for the excess thermodynamic properties of binary liquid solutions by extending the Lennard-Jones and Devonshire cell method. In their derivation they assumed, as a first approximation, a random mixing and thus neglected short-range order. In general the cooperative phenomena exhibited by fluid mixtures can be treated (within the framework of the free volume theory) by the order-disorder methods developed in the theory of the solid state. The expansion given by the method of moments[6,7] will be used in the following development.

We consider a closed system of N monatomic molecules and r different species. We let N_i denote the number of molecules of species i $(i = 1, 2 \cdots, r)$, where $\sum_i N_i = N$. We span the physical volume v by means of a virtual lattice

---

* This work was carried out with support from the ONR under Contract Nonr-410(00) with Yale University.

[1] H. J. Eyring and O. Hirschfelder, *J. Chem. Phys.* **4**, 250 (1937).
[2] Lennard-Jones and Devonshire, *Proc. Roy. Soc.* (*London*) **A163**, 53 (1937); **165**, 1 (1938).
[3] J. G. Kirkwood, *J. Chem. Phys.* **18**, 380 (1950).
[4] I. Prigogine and Garikian, *Physica* **16**, 239 (1950).
[5] I. Prigogine and V. Mathot, *J. Chem. Phys.* **20**, 49 (1952).
[6] J. G. Kirkwood, *J. Chem. Phys.* **6**, 70 (1938).
[7] J. G. Kirkwood, *J. Phys. Chem.* **43**, 97 (1939).

which divides this volume into N cells of equal size. The partition function Q for this system is given by the theory of the classical canonical ensemble in the form

$$Q = \prod_{i=1}^{r} \left(\frac{2\pi m_i kT}{h^2}\right)^{3N_i/2} \frac{Z_{N_1,\, N_2,\, \cdots,\, N_r}}{\prod_{i=1}^{r} N_i!},$$

where (1)

$$Z_{N_1,\, N_2,\, \cdots,\, N_r} = \int^{v} \cdots \int^{v} e^{-\beta V} \prod_{k=1}^{N} dv_k,$$

$$\beta = 1/kT.$$

$Z_{N_1,\, N_2,\, \cdots,\, N_r}$ is the Gibbs phase integral in configuration space, m_i is the mass of a molecule of species i, T the thermodynamic temperature, k the Boltzmann constant, h Planck's constant, and V the potential of intermolecular force.

If we denote the volume of each of the above virtual cells by Δ, the integral over the volume may be replaced by a sum of integrals over the cells. We then obtain for the Gibbs phase integral the expression

$$Z_{N_1,\, \cdots,\, N_r} = \sum_{l_1=1}^{N} \cdots \sum_{l_N=1}^{N} \int^{\Delta l_1} \cdots \int^{\Delta l_N} e^{-\beta V} \prod_{k=1}^{N} dv_k. \tag{2}$$

In general, Eq. (2) may be expressed in terms of integrals of the type

$$Z_{N_1,\, N_2,\, \cdots,\, N_r}^{(\xi_1{}^1,\, \cdots,\, \xi_N{}^1,\, \xi_1{}^2,\, \cdots,\, \xi_N{}^2,\, \cdots,\, \xi_1{}^r,\, \cdots,\, \xi_N{}^r)},$$

where $\xi_s{}^i$ is the number of molecules of species i occupying the cell Δ_s. We may then write

$$\frac{Z_{N_1,\, \cdots,\, N_r}}{\prod_{i=1}^{r} N_i!} = \sum_{\xi_1{}^1,\, \cdots,\, \xi_N{}^1 - 0}^{N_1} \cdots \sum_{\xi_1{}^r,\, \cdots,\, \xi_N{}^r - 0}^{N_r} \frac{Z_{N_1,\, \cdots,\, N_r}^{(\xi_1{}^1,\, \cdots,\, \xi_N{}^r)}}{\prod_{i=1}^{r} \prod_{s=1}^{N} \xi_s{}^i!}$$

(3)

$$\sum_{s} \xi_s{}^i = N_i \quad (i = 1, 2, \cdots, r)$$

$$\sum_{i} \xi_s{}^i = \text{no. of molecules in cell } s.$$

We denote by $Z^{(1)}$ the sum containing the integrals for all distinguishable configurations corresponding to single occupancy of each cell.

$$Z^{(1)} = \sum_{\xi_1{}^1,\, \cdots,\, \xi_N{}^1 = 0}^{1} \cdots \sum_{\xi_1{}^r,\, \cdots,\, \xi_N{}^r = 0}^{1}$$

$$\times \int^{\Delta_1} \cdots \int^{\Delta_N} e^{-\beta V(r_1,\, \cdots,\, r_N,\, \xi)} \prod_{k=1}^{N} dv_k \tag{4}$$

$$\sum_{s=1}^{N} \xi_s{}^i = N_i \quad (i = 1, 2, \cdots, r)$$

$$\sum_{i=1}^{r} \xi_s{}^i = 1 \qquad (s = 1, 2, \cdots, N),$$

where $V(\mathbf{r}, \xi)$ is the potential of intermolecular force for an arbitrary configuration, $\xi_1^1, \cdots, \xi_N^1, \cdots, \xi_1^r, \cdots, \xi_N^r$.

Formally we can define a parameter σ by the relation

$$(\sigma)^N = \sum_{\xi_1^1, \cdots, \xi_N^1=0}^{N_1} \cdots \sum_{\xi_1^r, \cdots, \xi_N^r=0}^{N_r} \frac{1}{\prod_{i=1}^{r} \prod_{s=1}^{N} \xi_s^i!} \times \frac{Z_{N_1, \cdots, N_r}^{(\xi_1^1, \cdots, \xi_N^r)}}{Z^{(1)}} \tag{5}$$

$$\sum_{s=1}^{N} \xi_s^i = N_i \quad (i = 1, 2, \cdots, r),$$

and write

$$\frac{Z_{N_1, \cdots, N_r}}{\prod_{i=1}^{r} N_i!} = (\sigma)^N Z^{(1)}. \tag{6}$$

σ has the value 1 if, as at high densities, intermolecular repulsive forces exclude multiple occupancy by causing all

$$Z_{N_1, \cdots, N_r}^{(\xi_1^1, \cdots, \xi_N^r)}$$

except those corresponding to single occupancy to vanish. However, as the density tends to zero and all

$$Z_{N_1, \cdots, N_r}^{(\xi_1^1, \cdots, \xi_N^r)}$$

become equal, σ approaches the value e. The problem of obtaining the exact value of σ[8] is left open for the present and we will confine our attention to the analysis of the free volume approximation to $Z^{(1)}$.

Corresponding to a given configuration, $\xi_1^1, \cdots, \xi_N^r$, there will exist the phase integral $Z^{(1)}(\xi)$ which is related to a relative probability density in configuration space, $P^{(1)}(\xi, \mathbf{r}_1, \cdots, \mathbf{r}_N)$, in the following manner.

$$p^{(1)}(\xi, \mathbf{r}_1, \cdots, \mathbf{r}_N) = \exp[\beta(A^{(1)}(\xi) - V(\xi, \mathbf{r}_1, \cdots, \mathbf{r}_N))]$$
$$\exp[-\beta A_r^{(1)}(\xi)] = Z^{(1)}(\xi), \tag{7}$$

where

$$A^{(1)}(\xi) = E^{(1)}(\xi) - TS^{(1)}(\xi),$$

$$E^{(1)}(\xi) = \int^{\Delta_1} \cdots \int^{\Delta_N} V(\xi, \mathbf{r}_1, \cdots, \mathbf{r}_N) \times P^{(1)}(\xi, \mathbf{r}_1, \cdots, \mathbf{r}_N) \prod_{k=1}^{N} dv_k,$$

$$S^{(1)}(\xi) = -k \int^{\Delta_1} \cdots \int^{\Delta_N} P^{(1)}(\xi, \mathbf{r}_1, \cdots, \mathbf{r}_N) \times \log P^{(1)}(\xi, \mathbf{r}_1, \cdots, \mathbf{r}_N) \prod_{k=1}^{N} dv_k,$$

[8] For a discussion of this problem for the case of a pure liquid see (a) J. A. Pople, *Phil. Mag.* **42**, 459 (1951). (b) P. Janssens and I. Prigogine, *Physica* **16**, 895 (1950).

and

$$\sum_{\xi_1^1,\cdots,\xi_N^1=0}^{1} \cdots \sum_{\xi_1^r,\cdots,\xi_N^r=0}^{1} \exp[-\beta A^{(1)}(\xi)] = Z^{(1)},$$

$$\sum_{i=1}^{r} \xi_s^i = 1 \qquad (s = 1, 2, \cdots, N),$$

$$\sum_{s=1}^{N} \xi_s^i = N_i \quad (i = 1, 2, \cdots, r).$$

From Eqs. (1) and (6) we obtain the following expression for the total free energy, $A_{N_1, N_2, \cdots, N_r}$.

$$A_{N_1, \cdots, N_r} = -kT \log\left[\prod_{i=1}^{r} \left(\frac{2\pi m_i kT}{h^2}\right)^{3N_i/2}\right] - NkT \log \sigma - kT \log Z^{(1)} \tag{8}$$

We now introduce the approximation[3]

$$\prod_{s=1}^{N} \varphi(\mathbf{r}_s, \xi) = P^{(1)}(\xi, \mathbf{r}_1, \cdots, \mathbf{r}_N). \tag{9}$$

$\varphi(\mathbf{r}_s, \xi)$ depends only on the position $\mathbf{r}_s$ of the molecule in the cell s, referred to some convenient origin in that cell, and on the given configuration $\{\xi\}$. $\varphi(\mathbf{r}_s, \xi)$ is also subject to the following normalization condition

$$\int^{\Delta} \varphi(r, \xi) dv = 1.$$

We will now assume that the intermolecular potential $V(\xi, \mathbf{r}_1, \cdots, \mathbf{r}_N)$ for a given configuration $\{\xi\}$, can be expressed in the form

$$V(\xi, \mathbf{r}_1, \cdots, \mathbf{r}_N) = \sum_{k<s} \sum_{i, l=1}^{r} \xi_k^i \xi_s^l V_{il}(|\mathbf{R}_{sk}|) \tag{10}$$

$$\sum_{i=1}^{r} \xi_s^i = 1 \quad (s = 1, \cdots, N).$$

$V_{il}|\mathbf{R}_{sk}|$ is the intermolecular potential for a pair of molecules of type i and l, respectively, located in cells s and k.

$$|\mathbf{R}_{sk}| = |\mathbf{R}_{sk}^0 + \mathbf{r}_k - \mathbf{r}_s|,$$

where $\mathbf{R}_{sk}^0$ is the vector from the origin in the cell s to the origin in cell k.

Following the analysis outlined,[3] we extremalize $A^{(1)}(\xi)$ with respect to the functions $\varphi(\mathbf{r}_s, \xi)$, obtaining the set of simultaneous integral equations

$$\varphi(\mathbf{r}_s, \xi) = e^{\beta[\alpha(\xi) - \psi(r_s, \xi)]} \quad (s = 1, \cdots, N), \tag{11}$$

where

$$e^{-\beta\alpha(\xi)} = \int^{\Delta_s} e^{-\beta\psi(\mathbf{r},\xi)} dv$$

$$\psi(\mathbf{r}_s, \xi) = \int^{\Delta_s} w_s(\mathbf{r} - \mathbf{r}_s) e^{\beta[\alpha(\xi) - \psi(r,\xi)]} dv$$

$$w_s(\mathbf{r} - \mathbf{r}_s) = E(\mathbf{r} - \mathbf{r}_s) - \bar{E}_s$$

$$\bar{E}_s = \int^{\Delta_s} \int^{\Delta} E(\mathbf{r} - \mathbf{r}_s) \varphi(\mathbf{r}, \xi) dv dv_s$$

$$E(\mathbf{r}) = \sum_{\substack{k=1 \\ \neq s}}^{N} \sum_{i,l=1}^{r} \xi_k^i \xi_s^l V_{il}(|\mathbf{R}_{sk}^0 + \mathbf{r}|)$$

$$\sum_{i=1}^{r} \xi_s^i = 1 \quad (s = 1, \cdots, N).$$

If $\varphi(\mathbf{r}, \xi)$ is sharply peaked in the vicinity of the cell origin, it may be set equal to $\delta(\mathbf{r})$, the Dirac delta function, in a zero approximation. It has been shown[3] that this approximation leads to the Lennard-Jones Devonshire theory.

Since

$$A^{(1)}(\xi) = \sum_{s=1}^{N} \left\{ \alpha(\xi) + \frac{\bar{E}_s(\xi)}{2} \right\}, \tag{12}$$

$$Z^{(1)} = \int^{\Delta_1} \cdots \int^{\Delta_N} \sum_{\xi_1^1, \cdots, \xi_N^1 = 0}^{1} \cdots$$

$$\times \sum_{\xi_1^r, \cdots, \xi_N^r = 0}^{1} e^{-\beta W(\xi, r_1, \cdots, r_N)} \prod_{k=1}^{N} dv_k, \tag{13}$$

$$\sum_{s=1}^{N} \xi_s^i = N_i \quad (i = 1, \cdots, r),$$

$$\sum_{i=1}^{r} \xi_s^i = 1 \quad (s = 1, \cdots, N),$$

where

$$W(\xi, \mathbf{r}_1, \cdots, \mathbf{r}_N) = \sum_{s=1}^{N} \sum_{\substack{k=1 \\ \neq s}}^{N} \sum_{i,\, l=1}^{r} \xi_k^i \xi_s^l \epsilon_{sk}^{il}(\mathbf{r}_s),$$

$$\sum_{i=1}^{r} \xi_s^i = 1 \quad (s = 1, \cdots, N),$$

$$\epsilon_{sk}^{il}(\mathbf{r}_s) = V_{il}(|\mathbf{R}_{sk}^0 - \mathbf{r}_s|) - \tfrac{1}{2} V_{il}(|\mathbf{R}_{sk}^0|).$$

The integrand in Eq. (13) can be expanded by the method of moments[6,7] in the following manner, where it is to be understood that in this calculation the vectors of the set $\{\mathbf{r}_1, \cdots, \mathbf{r}_N\}$ are held fixed. Let the exponential $e^{-\beta W}$ in the integrand of Eq. (13) be expanded in powers of βW. Hence

$$\sum_{\xi_1^1,\cdots,\xi_N^1=0}^{1} \cdots \sum_{\xi_1^r,\cdots,\xi_N^r=0}^{1} e^{-\beta W} = \frac{N!}{\prod_{i=1}^{i} N_i!} \sum_{n=0}^{\infty} \frac{M_n}{n!} (-\beta)^n,$$

$$\sum_{s=1}^{N} \xi_s^i = N_i \quad (i = 1, \cdots, r), \tag{14}$$

$$\sum_{i=1}^{r} \xi_s^i = 1 \quad (s = 1, \cdots, N),$$

where

$$M_n = \frac{\prod_{i=1}^{r} N_i!}{N!} \sum_{\xi_1^1,\cdots,\xi_N^1=0}^{1} \cdots \sum_{\xi_1^r,\cdots,\xi_N^r=0}^{1} (W)^n,$$

$$\sum_{s=1}^{N} \xi_s^i = N_i \quad (i = 1, \cdots, r),$$

$$\sum_{i=1}^{r} \xi_s^i = 1 \quad (s = 1, \cdots, N).$$

We can rewrite this expansion using the semi-invariants or cumulants, λ_n, of Thiele.

$$\frac{N!}{\prod_{i=1}^{r} N_i!} \sum_{n=0}^{\infty} \frac{M_n}{n!} (-\beta)^n = \frac{N!}{\prod_{i=1}^{r} N_i!} \exp\left[\sum_{n=1}^{\infty} \frac{\lambda_n}{n!} (-\beta)^n\right]. \tag{15}$$

The semi-invariants, λ_n, are expressible[6] in terms of the moments M_n. The first few are given by

$$\lambda_1 = M_1,$$

$$\lambda_2 = M_2 - M_1^2, \tag{16}$$

$$\lambda_3 = M_3 - 3M_1M_2 + 2M_1^3.$$

From Eqs. (13), (14), and (15) we obtain

$$Z^{(1)} = \frac{N!}{\prod_{i=1}^{r} N_i!} \int^{\Delta_1} \cdots \int^{\Delta_N} \times \exp\left[\sum_{n=1}^{\infty} \left(\frac{\lambda_n}{n!}\right) (-\beta)^n\right] \prod_{k=1}^{N} dv_k. \tag{17}$$

From Eq. (14), we have

$$M_n = \langle W^n \rangle_{\mathrm{Av}}, \tag{18}$$

where the average denotes an a priori average over all configurations. Since

$$\langle \xi_s{}^i \rangle_{\text{Av}} = x_i \quad (s = 1, \cdots, N),$$

$$M_1 = \sum_{s=1}^{N} \sum_{\substack{k=1 \\ \neq s}}^{N} \sum_{i,l=1}^{r} x_i x_l \epsilon_{sk}{}^{il}(\mathbf{r}), \tag{19}$$

where x_i is the mole fraction of species i.

At sufficiently high temperatures or when the differences in interaction will not alter a random distribution of the r species among nearest neighbors, one is justified in retaining only the first moment in the above theory. Retention of only the first moment has been shown[6,7] to be equivalent to the Bragg-Williams approximation. Employing this approximation, a simplified extension of the Lennard-Jones and Devonshire smoothed potential is obtained by replacing the summation over k in Eq. (19) by an integral over a sphere of radius equal to the mean distance between molecules.[3] For a binary solution this procedure yields precisely the expression first used by Prigogine and Garikian.[4]

One[9] of us has given an alternative approach to the order-disorder problem. This method gives an approximation equivalent to retaining the third moment and has been shown[9] to be equivalent to the method of local configurations of Bethe[10] and the quasi-chemical method of Fowler and Guggenheim.[11,12]

Eq. (13) may be rewritten in the form

$$Z^{(1)} = \int^{\Delta_1} \cdots \int^{\Delta_N} \Phi(\mathbf{r}, 0) \times \exp\left[\int_0^1 \frac{\partial \log \Phi(\mathbf{r}, \lambda)}{\partial \lambda} d\lambda\right] \prod_{k=1}^{N} dv_k, \tag{20}$$

where

$$\Phi(\mathbf{r}, \lambda) = \sum_{\xi_1{}', \cdots, \xi_N{}'=0}^{1} \cdots \sum_{\xi_1{}^r, \cdots, \xi_N{}^r=0}^{1} e^{-\beta\lambda W(\xi, r_1, \ldots, r_N)}$$

$$\sum_{s=1}^{N} \xi_s{}^i = N_i \quad (i = 1, 2, \cdots, r)$$

$$\sum_{i=1}^{r} \xi_s{}^i = 1 \quad (s = 1, \cdots, N).$$

$\Phi(\mathbf{r}, 0)$ reduces to the total number of configurations among the cells

$$\Phi(\mathbf{r}, 0) = \frac{N!}{\prod_{i=1}^{r} N_i!}.$$

The procedure for evaluating $\partial \log \Phi(\mathbf{r}, \lambda)/\partial\lambda$ is given in detail[9] in the computation of $\partial \log f/\partial\alpha$, and in the case of a binary mixture yields the result

$$Z^{(1)} = \binom{N}{N_1} \prod_{s=1}^{N} \left\{\int^{\Delta_s} \exp\left[-\beta \sum_{\substack{k=1 \\ \neq s}}^{N} U_{sk}(\mathbf{r})\right] dv_s\right\}, \tag{21}$$

---

[9] J. G. Kirkwood, *J. Chem. Phys.* **8**, 623 (1940).
[10] Bethe, *Proc. Roy. Soc.* (*London*) **A145**, 699 (1934).
[11] Guggenheim, *Proc. Roy. Soc.* (*London*) **A169**, 304 (1938).
[12] Fowler and Guggenheim, *Proc. Roy. Soc.* (*London*) **A174**, 189 (1940).

where

$$U_{sk}(\mathbf{r}) = \frac{1}{\beta[\epsilon_{sk}^{11}(\mathbf{r}) - 2\epsilon_{sk}^{12}(\mathbf{r}) + \epsilon_{sk}^{22}(\mathbf{r})]}$$

$$\times \left[\left\{ q \log \frac{\varphi - q}{1 - q} + \log \frac{\varphi + 1}{2} \right\} \epsilon_{sk}^{11}(\mathbf{r}) \right.$$

$$+ \left\{ (1 + q) \log \frac{2(\varphi + q)}{(1 + q)(\varphi + 1)} \right.$$

$$\left. + (1 - q) \log \frac{2(\varphi - q)}{(1 - q)(\varphi + 1)} \right\} \epsilon_{sk}^{12}(\mathbf{r})$$

$$\left. + \left\{ \log \frac{\varphi + 1}{2} - q \log \frac{\varphi + q}{1 + q} \right\} \epsilon_{sk}^{22}(\mathbf{r}) \right]$$

$$\varphi = [q^2 + (1 - q^2) \exp - \beta\{\epsilon_{sk}^{11}(\mathbf{r}) - 2\epsilon_{sk}^{12}(\mathbf{r}) + \epsilon_{sk}^{22}(\mathbf{r})\}]^{\frac{1}{2}}$$

$$q = x_1 - x_2$$

$$\beta = 1/kT.$$

Retaining only the first moment and using Eqs. (18), (17), and (19) we obtain for the total free energy

$$A_{N_1, \cdots, N_r} = NkT \sum_{i=1}^{r} x_i \log x_i + A^*_{N_1, \cdots, N_r} + A^E_{N_1, \cdots, N_r}$$

$$A^*_{N_1, \cdots, N_r} = -kT \sum_{i=1}^{r} N_i \log \left\{ e \left(\frac{2\pi m_i kT}{h^2} \right)^{\frac{3}{2}} v \right\}$$

$$A^E_{N_1, \cdots, N_r} = -NkT \log \frac{\sigma}{e} - NkT \log \frac{1}{v} \int^{\Delta} e^{-\beta w_0(r)} dv \qquad (22)$$

$$+ \frac{N}{2} E_0(N_1, \cdots, N_r)$$

$$w_C(r) = \sum_{k=2}^{N} \sum_{i,l=1}^{r} x_i x_l \{ V_{il}(|\mathbf{R}_{1k}^0 - \mathbf{r}|) - V_{il}(|\mathbf{R}_{1k}^0|) \}$$

$$E_0(N_1, \cdots, N_r) = \sum_{k=2}^{N} \sum_{i,l=1}^{r} x_i x_l V_{il}(|\mathbf{R}_{1k}^0|).$$

For spherical nonpolar molecules the intermolecular potential for a pair of molecules, $V_{il}(|\mathbf{R}_{1k}^0 - \mathbf{r}_1|)$, can be represented by the Lennard-Jones potential

$$V_{il}(|\mathbf{R}_{1k}^0 - \mathbf{r}_1|) = 4\epsilon_{il} \left[\left(\frac{a_{il}}{R} \right)^{12} - \left(\frac{a_{il}}{R} \right)^{6} \right], \qquad (23)$$

where $R = |\mathbf{R}_{1k}^0 - \mathbf{r}_1|$ is the scalar distance between the molecule in cell 1 and the molecule in cell k, ϵ_{il} is the maximum energy of interaction, and a_{il} is the value of R for which $V_{il}(R) = 0$.

Following the procedure given by Wentorf, Buehler, Hirschfelder, and Curtiss,[13] we replace the sum over k in the definition of $w_0(\mathbf{r})$, Eq. (20), by an integral over the first, second, and third shells of nearest neighbors situated at distances a, $\sqrt{2}a$, and $\sqrt{3}a$, respectively. Then

$$w_0(r) = \sum_{i,l=1}^{r} x_i x_l 12\epsilon_{il}\left\{\left(\frac{v_{il}^0}{v}\right)^4 L(y) - 2\left(\frac{v_{il}^0}{v}\right)^2 M(y)\right\},$$

where (24)

$$L(y) = l(y) + \frac{1}{128}l\left(\frac{y}{2}\right) + \frac{2}{729}l\left(\frac{y}{3}\right)$$

$$M(y) = m(y) + \frac{1}{16}m\left(\frac{y}{2}\right) + \frac{2}{27}m\left(\frac{y}{3}\right)$$

$$l(y) = (1 + 12y + 25.2y^2 + 12y^3 + y^4)(1 - y)^{-10} - 1$$

$$m(y) = (1 + y)(1 - y)^{-4} - 1$$

$$y = \left(\frac{r}{a}\right)^2$$

$$v_{il}^0 = Na_{il}^3.$$

$w_0(r)$ can be written in the form

$$w_0(r) = 12\bar{\epsilon}\left\{\left(\frac{\bar{v}^0}{v}\right)^4 L(y) - 2\left(\frac{\bar{v}^0}{v}\right)^2 M(y)\right\}, \tag{25}$$

where $\bar{\epsilon}$ and $\bar{v}^0$ are determined by the two equations

$$\bar{\epsilon}\bar{v}^0 = \sum_{i,l=1}^{r} x_i x_l \epsilon_{il} v_{il}^{04}$$

$$\bar{\epsilon}\bar{v}^{02} = \sum_{i,l=1} x_i x_l \epsilon_{il} v_{il}^{02}.$$

Formally the theory for a multicomponent system becomes identical in form with the Lennard-Jones and Devonshire theory for a pure liquid with constants $\bar{\epsilon}$ and $\bar{v}^0$. Extensive tables[13] are available for the calculations of thermodynamic functions of a pure liquid and can be used without modification to obtain the properties of solutions for which the first moment approximations are valid.

As a first approximation in determining $\bar{\epsilon}$ and $\bar{v}^0$, we adopt the familiar expressions

$$(\epsilon_{il})^2 = \epsilon_{ii}\epsilon_{ll}$$

$$a_{il} = (a_{ii} + a_{ll})/2. \tag{26}$$

In the applications discussed by Prigogine[4,5] and his co-workers it was assumed that $a_{11} = a_{12} = a_{22}$. While the cells in this theory are taken to be equal in size, the limitation on the relative sizes of the molecules is not nearly

[13] Wentorf, Buehler, Hirschfelder, and Curtiss, *J. Chem. Phys.* **18**, 1484 (1950).

as severe. The only complication introduced is in the definition of $\bar{\epsilon}$ and $\bar{v}^0$ which now have the form

$$\bar{v}^0 = \left[\frac{\sum_{i,l=1}^{r} x_i x_l \epsilon_{il} v_{il}^{0^4}}{\sum_{i,l=1}^{r} x_i x_l \epsilon_{il} v_{il}^{0^2}} \right]^{\frac{1}{2}}$$

$$\bar{\epsilon} = \frac{\left[\sum_{i,l=1}^{r} x_i x_l \epsilon_{il} v_{il}^{0^2} \right]^2}{\sum_{i,l=1}^{r} x_i x_l \epsilon_{il} v_{il}^{0^4}}. \tag{27}$$

With these definitions the Helmholtz free energy A can be calculated from the expression

$$A^E{}_{N_1, \cdots, N_r} = -NkT \log \frac{\sigma}{e} - NkT \log \frac{2\pi\sqrt{2}G}{N} + \frac{N}{2} E_0(N_1, \cdots, N_r)$$

$$E_0 = 12\bar{\epsilon} \left\{ 1.0109 \left(\frac{\bar{v}^0}{v} \right)^4 - 2.4090 \left(\frac{\bar{v}^0}{v} \right)^2 \right\}, \tag{28}$$

where

$$G = \int_0^{0.30544} y^{\frac{1}{2}} \exp[-\beta w_0(y)] dy.$$

The chemical potential μ_i of component i can be obtained from Eq. (28) and the relation

$$\mu_i = (\partial A / \partial N_i)_{T,\, V,\, N_j}.$$

The result is

$$\mu_i - \mu_i^* + kT \log x_i + \mu_i^E,$$

$$\mu_i^* = -kT \log \left\{ \left(\frac{2\pi m_i kT}{h^2} \right)^{\frac{3}{2}} v \right\},$$

$$\mu_i^E = -kT \log \frac{2\pi\sqrt{2}G}{N} - kT \log \frac{\sigma}{e}$$

$$- 12\bar{\epsilon} \left[1.2045 \left(\frac{\bar{v}^0}{v} \right)^2 - \left(1.51635 + \frac{2g_L}{G} \right) \left(\frac{\bar{v}^0}{v} \right)^4 \right]$$

$$- \sum_{l=1}^{r} x_l 12\epsilon_{li} \left[\left(2.4090 + \frac{4g_M}{G} \right) \left(\frac{v_{li}{}^0}{v} \right)^2 - \left(1.0109 + \frac{2g_L}{G} \right) \left(\frac{v_{li}{}^0}{v} \right)^4 \right], \tag{29}$$

$$g_L = \int_0^{0.30544} y^{\frac{1}{2}} L(y) \exp[-\beta w_0(y)] dy,$$

$$g_M = \int_0^{0.30544} y^{\frac{1}{2}} M(y) \exp[-\beta w_0(y)] dy.$$

Moments of higher order than the first can be computed by methods previously presented[4,5] and are limited only in so far as they necessitate extensive numerical computations. A more serious restriction is placed upon the relative sizes of the molecules, since the theory is limited to cells of equal size. In addition, we have bypassed the problem of calculating the communal entropy. Although the limitations of the free volume theory are evident, further modifications to this theory would be of minor practical importance without solutions to the two problems just mentioned.

ADDENDUM TO PAPER NUMBER 7

By ZEVI W. SALSBURG, *William Marsh Rice University, Houston, Texas*

In considering the formulation of the free volume theory for mixtures we first derived a Free Volume Integral Equation, Eq. (11), for each possible distribution $\{\xi\}$ of molecules among the cells following the procedure outlined by Kirkwood in his critique of the Free Volume Theories (Paper number 00). We could have then formulated the partition function for single occupancy either in the form given by Eq. (13) or the equivalent form (obtained by interchanging the integrations and summations),

$$Z^{(1)} = \sum_{\{\xi\}} \prod_{s=1}^{N} v_f^s(\xi)$$

$$v_f^s(\xi) = \int^{\Delta_s} e^{-\beta\psi(r_s,\xi)} dv_s$$

$$\psi(r_s, \xi) = \sum_{\substack{k=1 \\ \neq s}}^{N} \xi_k^i \xi_s^l \epsilon_{sk}^{il}(r_s).$$

An appropriate approximation for the dependence of the free volumes $v_f^s(\xi)$ on the occupation variables leads directly to the formulation of Prigogine and his co-workers.[1]

The reason for considering the order-disorder problem under the integration as indicated in Eq. (13) was that this led directly to the corresponding-states formalism expressed in Eq. (25).

We later realized that this order-disorder analysis could be carried out for any set of position vectors $\{\mathbf{R}_1 \cdots, \mathbf{R}_M\}$ and presented this analysis in paper number 142. Thus, in many ways the article on the free volume theory of mixtures is obsolete. One can obtain the same results in a simpler manner, by first formulating the pseudo single fluid potential characteristic of the mixture as described in paper number 142 and then using Kirkwood's free volume theory directly for this potential.

---

[1] I. Prigogine, *The Molecular Theory of Solutions* (Interscience Publishers, Inc., New York, 1957).

Applications of the Free Volume Theory of Binary Mixtures*

ZEVI W. SALSBURG† AND JOHN G. KIRKWOOD, *Sterling Chemistry Laboratory, Yale University, New Haven, Connecticut*

(Received June 11, 1953)

Detailed calculations for the free volume theory of binary mixtures are presented and compared with experimental results. It is found that this theory predicts heats of mixing and volumes of mixing larger in magnitude than the observed values and excess entropies of mixing which are smaller than the experimental results. The theory, however, does predict a volume contraction, a negative excess entropy of mixing and a positive heat of mixing for solutions of carbon tetrachloride and neopentane in qualitative agreement with recent observations.

The free volume theory[1–3] has provided a useful description of the thermodynamic properties of dense gases and liquids. To facilitate the application of this theory Wentorf, Buehler, Hirschfelder, and Curtiss[4] prepared tables of all the pertinent thermodynamic properties over a wide range of temperatures and densities. Comparison with experimental results shows that the theoretical calculations are unsatisfactory in the critical region but improve at high densities. These calculations have been applied only to spherical non-polar molecules where the energy of interaction between a pair of molecules, i and j, can be represented satisfactorily by the Lennard-Jones type potential,

$$V_{ij}(R) = 4\epsilon_{ij}\left[\left(\frac{a_{ij}}{R}\right)^{12} - \left(\frac{a_{ij}}{R}\right)^{6}\right]. \tag{1}$$

In view of these results and the simplicity of the numerical calculations, it seemed advisable to extend this theory to liquid mixtures in order to try to calculate the excess thermodynamic properties of simple liquid nonelectrolyte solutions. By combining the Lennard-Jones and Devonshire cell method[2] with the order-disorder theory of the crystalline state, we[5] have recently derived expressions for the excess thermodynamic properties of fluid mixtures. The purpose of this article is to present in detail the numerical calculations based upon this theory and to give a comparison with experimental results.

---

* This work was carried out with support from the U.S. Office of Naval Research under Contract with Yale University.

† National Science Foundation Fellow, 1952–1953. Material herein presented is contained in the thesis of Zevi W. Salsburg presented for the degree of Doctor of Philosophy in Yale University. Present address: University of Amsterdam, Amsterdam, Holland.

[1] H. J. Eyring and J. O. Hirschfelder, *J. Chem. Phys.* **4**, 250 (1937).

[2] J. E. Lennard-Jones and A. F. Devonshire, *Proc. Roy. Soc.* (*London*) **A163**, 53 (1937); **A165**, 1 (1938).

[3] J. G. Kirkwood, *J. Chem. Phys.* **18**, 380 (1950).

[4] Wentorf, Buehler, Hirschfelder, and Curtiss, *J. Chem. Phys.* **18**, 1484 (1950).

[5] Z. W. Salsburg and J. G. Kirkwood, *J. Chem. Phys.* **20**, 1538 (1952).

In general this theory predicts heats of mixing larger than the experimental values and excess entropies of mixing which are smaller than the experimental results.

The simple theory of nonpolar mixtures developed by Hildebrand[6] and his co-workers states that it is the square of the difference between the square roots of the cohesive energy densities of the components which determines the deviations from ideality. However, the treatment of nearly ideal solutions makes too drastic a demand on this simple theory since it requires a small difference between large numbers. One finds that the quantitative calculations based on Hildebrand's theory give only about a fifth of the measured values for the heats of mixing (e.g., see reference 22). The model considered in this semi-empirical approach neglects deviations from a random distribution of molecules in the neighborhood of a given molecule and also neglects effects that give rise to volume changes on mixing. In addition, the interpretation of this theory in terms of statistical mechanics is obscure.

Using the cell method of Lennard-Jones and Devonshire, Prigogine and his co-workers[7–10] have recently formulated a solution theory which is closely related to our development. In addition to the random mixing hypothesis they have assumed that the Lennard-Jones potential parameters a_{ij} [see Eq. (1)] for all the components are equal. While the cells in the free volume theory are all equal in size, the relative sizes of the molecules are not nearly as severely limited. We shall see that small variations in the relative sizes of the components have an appreciable effect on the mixing properties of the solutions. The simplified model considered by Prigogine *et al.*, however, does show that the effects related to a change of volume on mixing at constant pressure can give rise to important entropy and heat changes.

In mixture theories in which the intermolecular potential is assumed to be a sum of pair potentials there arises the problem of determining the parameters which describe the interaction between unlike pairs of molecules. The analysis of the dispersion forces by London indicates that, for the energy parameter ϵ_{ij}, the geometric mean approximation

$$\epsilon_{ij} = (\epsilon_{ii}\epsilon_{jj})^{\frac{1}{2}} \tag{2}$$

may be used for similar type molecules. The experimental work on the measurement of second virial coefficients for gaseous mixtures[11] supports this assumption and moreover indicates that a suitable approximation to a_{ij} is given by

$$a_{ij} = (a_{ii} + a_{jj})/2. \tag{3}$$

The article by Prigogine and Mathot[8] considers the qualitative effects due to deviations of ϵ_{ij} from the value given by Eq. (2). This problem has also been treated in a recent article by Rowlinson[12] who, in the same manner as

[6] J. H. Hildebrand and R. L. Scott, *The Solubility of Nonelectrolytes* (Reinhold Publishing Corporation, New York, 1950), third edition.
[7] I. Prigogine and V. Mathot, *J. Chem. Phys.* **20**, 49 (1950).
[8] I. Prigogine and G. Garikian, *Physica* **16**, 236 (1950).
[9] I. Sarolea, *J. Chem. Phys.* **21**, 182 (1953).
[10] J. Nasielski, *J. Chem. Phys.* **21**, 184 (1953).
[11] R. H. Fowler and E. A. Guggenheim, *Statistical Thermodynamics* (Cambridge University Press, Cambridge, 1939), *pp.* 296–300.
[12] J. S. Rowlinson, *Proc. Roy. Soc.* (*London*) **A214**, 192 (1952).

Prigogine, assumes that all a_{ij} are equal. The errors introduced by this assumption are of the same order of magnitude as those effects which Prigogine and Rowlinson attribute to deviations from the geometric mean approximation. In fact, the numerical calculations will show that small changes in the relative value of $a_{ii} - a_{jj}$ in certain cases can change the sign of the predicted volumes and excess entropies of mixing.

I. EQUATIONS FOR THE THERMODYNAMIC FUNCTIONS

In a recent article[5] we have extended the free volume theory to multicomponent fluid mixtures. The expressions for the thermodynamic functions on which our numerical calculations are based were obtained under the following approximations.

(a) The communal free energy, $RT \ln \sigma$ [see Eq. (5) or reference 5], which contains the corrections due to multiple occupancy of the cells is approximated by its low density value, $\sigma = e$. This approximation is identical to that originally made by Eyring and Hirschfelder.[1] However, there is reason to believe that for common liquids the high density value of $\sigma = 1$ would be more appropriate. In any case, if one approximates σ by a constant the excess entropy of mixing is independent of this constant.

(b) Under the restriction of single occupancy for each cell, the relative probability density in configuration space $P^{(1)}$ is approximated by a product of distribution functions for the individual cells. That is

$$P^{(1)} = \prod_{s=1}^{N} \varphi_s,$$

where φ_s depends only on the position of the molecule in cell s and on the given distribution of molecules in the neighboring cells. By minimizing the Helmholtz free energy at constant temperature and volume one obtains a set of simultaneous integral equations for the cell distribution functions.

(c) An approximate solution to this set of integral equations which is identical in form with the Lennard-Jones and Devonshire[2] cell distribution function is used. Mayer and Careri[13] have recently given an alternative approximation to this function which may prove to give better quantitative results.

(d) The method of moments[14,15] is used to solve the order-disorder problem for the distribution of molecules among cells. For our approximate calculations we have only retained the first moment. This is equivalent to the random mixing assumption made by Prigogine *et al.*[7,8] For the case of a quasi-lattice model, the problem of nonrandom mixing has been studied by Kirkwood,[15] Rushbrooke,[16] and Guggenheim.[17] These results indicate that the corrections due to nonrandomness are small compared to the free volume corrections. This numerical comparison can be seen in Table VIII. A recent analysis by Sarolea,[9] who used the theory developed by Prigogine, supports the view that these corrections are small.

---

[13] J. E. Mayer and G. Careri, *J. Chem. Phys.* **20**, 1001 (1952).
[14] J. G. Kirkwood, *J. Chem. Phys.* **6**, 70 (1938).
[15] J. G. Kirkwood, *J. Phys. Chem.* **43**, 97 (1939).
[16] G. S. Rushbrooke, *Proc. Roy. Soc.* (*London*) **A166**, 296 (1938).
[17] E. A. Guggenheim, *Proc. Roy. Soc.* (*London*) **A148**, 304 (1935).

The results of our treatment are identical in form with the Lennard-Jones and Devonshire theory for a pure liquid in which the potential constants (or parameters) are given by certain averages of the constants for the individual components. For a system containing N_1 molecules of type 1, N_2 of type 2, $\cdots$, N_r of type r, the free energy can be written in the form

$$A_{N_1 \cdots, N_r} = NkT \sum_{i=1}^{r} x_i \ln x_i + A^*_{N_1, \cdots, N_r} + A^E_{N_1, \cdots, N_r}, \tag{4}$$

where

$$A^*_{N_1, \cdots, N_r} = -kT \sum_{i=1}^{r} N_i \ln \left\{ ev \left(\frac{2\pi m_i kT}{h^2} \right)^{\frac{3}{2}} \right\}, \tag{4a}$$

$$A^E_{N_1, \cdots, N_r} = -NkT \ln \frac{2\pi\sqrt{2}G}{N} + \frac{N}{2} E_0(N_1, \ldots, N_r). \tag{4b}$$

T is the thermodynamic temperature, k the Boltzmann constant, m_i the mass of a molecule of species i, and v is the volume of the system. x_i is the mole fraction of species i.

$$E_0 = 12\bar{\epsilon} \left\{ 1.0109 \left(\frac{\bar{v}^0}{v} \right)^4 - 2.4090 \left(\frac{\bar{v}^0}{v} \right)^2 \right\}, \tag{5}$$

$$G = \int_0^{0.030544} y^{\frac{1}{2}} \exp[-\beta w_0(y)] dy \tag{6}$$

where

$$\beta = 1/kT,$$

$$w_0(y) = 12\bar{\epsilon} \left\{ \left(\frac{\bar{v}^0}{v} \right)^4 L(y) - 2 \left(\frac{\bar{v}^0}{v} \right)^2 M(y) \right\}$$

and

$$L(y) = l(y) + \frac{1}{128} l\left(\frac{y}{2}\right) + \frac{2}{729} l\left(\frac{y}{3}\right),$$

$$M(y) = m(y) + \frac{1}{16} m\left(\frac{y}{2}\right) + \frac{2}{27} m\left(\frac{y}{3}\right),$$

$$l(y) = (1 + 12y + 25.2y^2 + 12y^3 + y^4)(1 - y)^{-10} - 1,$$

$$m(y) = (1 + y)(1 - y)^{-4} - 1.$$

The average constants $\bar{\epsilon}$ and $\bar{v}^0$ are functions of the Lennard-Jones constants for the individual types of molecular pairs and the mole fractions of the components,

$$\bar{v}^0 = \left\{ \frac{\sum_{i,l=1}^{r} x_i x_l \epsilon_{il} v_{il}^{0^4}}{\sum_{i,l=1}^{r} x_i x_l \epsilon_{il} v_{il}^{0^2}} \right\}^{\frac{1}{2}}, \tag{7}$$

$$\bar{\epsilon} = \frac{\{\sum_{i,l=1}^{r} x_i x_l \epsilon_{il} v_{il}^{0\,2}\}^2}{\sum_{i,l=1}^{r} x_i x_l \epsilon_{il} v_{il}^{0\,4}}, \tag{8}$$

where

$$v_{il}^0 = N a_{il}^3,$$

$$N = \sum_{i=1}^{r} N_i.$$

The equation of state is given by the relation

$$\frac{pv}{NkT} = 1 - \frac{12\bar{\epsilon}}{kT}\left[2.4090\left(\frac{\bar{v}^0}{v}\right)^2 - 2.0219\left(\frac{\bar{v}^0}{v}\right)^4\right]$$

$$- \frac{48\bar{\epsilon}}{kT}\left[\left(\frac{\bar{v}^0}{v}\right)^2\left(\frac{g_M}{G}\right) - \left(\frac{\bar{v}^0}{v}\right)^4\left(\frac{g_L}{G}\right)\right], \tag{9}$$

where

$$g_M = \int_0^{0.30544} y^{\frac{1}{2}} M(y) \exp[-\beta w_0(y)]dy$$

$$g_L = \int_0^{0.30544} y^{\frac{1}{2}} L(y) \exp[-\beta w_0(y)]dy.$$

The internal energy of gas imperfection per mole takes the form

$$E^E = \frac{N}{2} E_0 + 12 N\bar{\epsilon}\left[\left(\frac{\bar{v}^0}{v}\right)^4 \frac{g_L}{G} - 2\left(\frac{\bar{v}^0}{v}\right)^2 \frac{g_M}{G}\right]. \tag{10}$$

The excess entropy, S^E, is defined in such a way that it is zero in the limit of large volume. From Eq. (4) we obtain

$$S^E = Nk \ln \frac{G}{G_\infty} + \frac{N}{T} 12\bar{\epsilon}\left[\left(\frac{\bar{v}^0}{v}\right)^4 \frac{g_L}{G} - 2\left(\frac{\bar{v}^0}{v}\right)^2 \frac{g_M}{G}\right] \tag{11}$$

$$G_\infty = \lim_{v\to\infty} G = (2\pi\sqrt{2})^{-1}.$$

The chemical potential μ_i of component i can be obtained from Eq. (4) and the thermodynamic relation

$$\mu_i = (\partial A/\partial N_i)_{T,v,N_j}.$$

The result is

$$\mu_i = \mu_i^* + kT \ln x_i + \mu_i^E \tag{12}$$

where

$$\mu_i^* = -kT \ln v\left\{\left(\frac{2\pi m_i kT}{h^2}\right)^{\frac{3}{2}}\right\}.$$

μ_i^E is the excess chemical potential referred to the ideal gas as a standard state.

$$\mu_i{}^E = -kT \ln \frac{2\pi\sqrt{2}G}{N} - 12\bar{\epsilon}\left\{1.2045\left(\frac{\bar{v}^0}{v}\right)^2 - \left(1.51635 + \frac{2g_L}{G}\right)\left(\frac{\bar{v}^0}{v}\right)^4\right\}$$

$$- \sum_{l=1}^{r} x_l 12\epsilon_{li}\left\{\left(2.4090 + \frac{4g_M}{G}\right)\left(\frac{v_{li}{}^0}{v}\right)^2 - \left(1.0109 + \frac{2g_L}{G}\right)\left(\frac{v_{li}{}^0}{v}\right)^4\right\}.$$

In the simple theory proposed by Hildebrand[6] the cohesive energy density plays a central role. This quantity can be obtained by means of the relation

$$\frac{v}{NkT}\left(\frac{\partial E^E}{\partial v}\right)_T = 1 - \frac{pv}{NkT} - 4\left(\frac{12\bar{\epsilon}}{kT}\right)^2\left(\frac{\bar{v}^0}{v}\right)^4 B, \tag{13}$$

where

$$B = \left(\frac{\bar{v}^0}{v}\right)^4\left[\left(\frac{g_L}{G}\right)^2 - \frac{g_{LL}}{G}\right]$$

$$+ 3\left(\frac{\bar{v}^0}{v}\right)^2\left[\frac{g_{ML}}{G} - \frac{g_M}{G}\frac{g_L}{G}\right] + 2\left[\left(\frac{g_M}{G}\right)^2 - \frac{g_{MM}}{G}\right]$$

and

$$g_{LL} = \int_0^{0.30544} y^{\frac{1}{2}}[L(y)]^2 \exp[-\beta w_0(y)]dy,$$

$$g_{ML} = \int_0^{0.30544} y^{\frac{1}{2}}L(y)M(y) \exp[-\beta w_0(y)]dy,$$

$$g_{MM} = \int_0^{0.30544} y^{\frac{1}{2}}[M(y)]^2 \exp[-\beta w_0(y)]dy.$$

The excess heat capacity at constant volume, $C_v{}^E$, can be computed from the relation

$$\frac{C_v{}^E}{Nk} = \left(\frac{12\bar{\epsilon}}{kT}\right)^2\left(\frac{\bar{v}_0}{v}\right)^4\left\{\left(\frac{\bar{v}^0}{v}\right)^4\left[\frac{g_{LL}}{G} - \left(\frac{g_L}{G}\right)^2\right]\right.$$

$$\left. + 4\left(\frac{\bar{v}^0}{v}\right)^2\left[\frac{g_L}{G}\frac{g_M}{G} - \frac{g_{ML}}{G}\right] + 4\left[\frac{g_{MM}}{G} - \left(\frac{g_M}{G}\right)^2\right]\right\}. \tag{14}$$

Equations (4) and (9) through (14) enable one to calculate all the pertinent thermodynamic functions of the system. The enthalpy of the system can be obtained from Eqs. (9) and (10) together with the thermodynamic definition $H = E + pv$. The excess internal energy and entropy of mixing per mole of solution are defined by

$$\Delta E^E = E^E - \sum_{i=1}^{r} x_i E_i{}^E, \tag{15}$$

$$\Delta S^E = S^E - \sum_{i=1}^{r} x_i S_i{}^E, \tag{16}$$

where $E_i{}^E$ and $S_i{}^E$ are the molal internal energy and entropy of gas imperfection for pure component i.

II. CALCULATION OF THE THERMODYNAMIC FUNCTIONS

It is convenient to express the volume, temperature, and pressure in the reduced forms,

$$q = \frac{v}{\bar{v}^0} \tag{17}$$

$$\theta = \frac{kT}{\bar{\epsilon}} \tag{18}$$

$$p^* = \frac{p}{p_1} = \left(\frac{pv}{NkT}\right)\left(\frac{kT}{\bar{\epsilon}}\right)\left(\frac{\bar{v}^0}{v}\right) \tag{19}$$

Here p_1 is the characteristic pressure of the substance defined as

$$p_1 = 136.23\left(\frac{\bar{\epsilon}}{k}\right)\frac{1}{\bar{a}^3} \text{ atmos.}; \quad \bar{a} = (\bar{v}^0/N)^{\frac{1}{3}},$$

where $\bar{\epsilon}/k$ is given in degrees Kelvin and $\bar{a}$ is given in Angströms.

The magnitudes of the excess mixing properties of the simple solutions we wish to treat are very small in comparison with the total thermodynamic quantities. Therefore, unless the calculations are carried out with extreme accuracy the error in the calculation will be greater than the mixing property itself. Although Wentorf, Buehler, Hirschfelder, and Curtiss[4] have compiled extensive tables of the free volume thermodynamic functions, the accuracy of these tables does not permit the calculation of the excess mixing properties of solutions. In addition, these tables omit calculations for $\theta < 0.70$ since this represents the experimental triple point for simple monatomic solids (argon, neon, etc.). In view of these considerations we have undertaken the numerical program of calculating the thermodynamic properties in the region of interest.

The integrals were computed using the sixteen-point Gauss integration formula.[18] The upper limit of integration was adjusted to neglect values of the independent variable corresponding to negligible values of the integrand. If one uses y as a variable of integration some difficulty in the integration often occurs near $y = 0$ for the integrand of G varies here as $y^{\frac{1}{2}}$. This difficulty can be avoided if one chooses $y^{\frac{1}{2}}$ as the variable of integration. In this manner, our calculations procedure differs from previous ones.[4] Eight significant digits were carried in each operation and we believe that the results are good to five significant figures. As an aid to computation we present six digits in our tables. The values of the integrals are presented in Table I and the corresponding thermodynamic functions are given in Table II.

Experimental measurements are almost invariably carried out under conditions of constant pressure (about 1 atmos). For this reason we have limited our calculations to the region around 1-atmos pressure. The corresponding values of p^* for a typical range of $\bar{\epsilon}$ and $\bar{a}$ are given in Table III.

---

[18] W. E. Milne, *Numerical Calculus* (Princeton University Press, Princeton, 1949), pp. 285–289.

TABLE I. Integrals.[a]

q	θ	G	gL/G	gM/G	gLL/G	gMM/G	gLM/G
0.94	0.15	1.80198(−5)	2.45168(−2)	5.78886(−3)	2.34147(−4)	5.50469(−5)	9.96033(−4)
0.94	0.16	1.98287(−5)	2.60955(−2)	6.15693(−3)	2.65860(−4)	6.24343(−5)	1.13218(−3)
0.94	0.17	2.16375(−5)	2.76741(−2)	6.52500(−3)	2.97572(−4)	6.98217(−5)	1.26832(−3)
0.94	0.19	2.54453(−5)	3.08077(−2)	7.25357(−3)	3.67852(−4)	8.61471(−5)	1.57090(−3)
0.94	0.20	2.74158(−5)	3.23657(−2)	7.61509(−3)	4.05500(−4)	9.48743(−5)	1.73333(−3)
0.95	0.25	4.11491(−5)	4.23101(−2)	9.91102(−3)	6.87426(−4)	1.59887(−4)	2.95609(−3)
0.95	0.26	4.35368(−5)	4.39150(−2)	1.02797(−2)	7.39664(−4)	1.71875(−4)	3.18377(−3)
0.95	0.27	4.59614(−5)	4.55142(−2)	1.06466(−2)	7.93557(−4)	1.84225(−4)	3.41898(−3)
0.95	0.30	5.34458(−5)	5.02778(−2)	1.17365(−2)	9.64945(−4)	2.23395(−4)	4.16906(−3)
0.96	0.30	5.80065(−5)	5.30378(−2)	1.23661(−2)	1.07122(−3)	2.47611(−4)	4.63558(−3)
0.96	0.31	6.07780(−5)	5.46948(−2)	1.27434(−2)	1.13784(−3)	2.62761(−4)	4.92860(−3)
0.96	0.32	6.35833(−5)	5.63458(−2)	1.31187(−2)	1.20614(−3)	2.78272(−4)	5.22947(−3)
0.96	0.34	6.92917(−5)	5.96303(−2)	1.38639(−2)	1.34773(−3)	3.10358(−4)	5.85440(−3)
0.97	0.36	8.16214(−5)	6.69336(−2)	1.55072(−2)	1.71499(−3)	3.92771(−4)	7.49188(−3)
0.97	0.37	8.46323(−5)	6.79788(−2)	1.57493(−2)	1.74066(−3)	3.98990(−4)	7.59705(−3)
0.97	0.38	8.78604(−5)	6.96747(−2)	1.61307(−2)	1.82649(−3)	4.18272(−4)	7.97930(−3)
0.97	0.40	9.44046(−5)	7.30485(−2)	1.68879(−2)	2.00313(−3)	4.57870(−4)	8.76752(−3)
0.98	0.40	1.02234(−4)	7.69190(−2)	1.77544(−2)	2.21419(−3)	5.05068(−4)	9.71180(−3)
0.98	0.42	1.09411(−4)	8.04291(−2)	1.85376(−2)	2.41532(−3)	5.49901(−4)	1.06146(−2)
0.98	0.43	1.13042(−4)	8.21747(−2)	1.89263(−2)	2.51845(−3)	5.72841(−4)	1.10784(−2)
0.98	0.44	1.16700(−4)	8.39141(−2)	1.93131(−2)	2.62325(−3)	5.96122(−4)	1.15504(−2)
0.98	0.45	1.20385(−4)	8.56473(−2)	1.96980(−2)	2.73970(−3)	6.19738(−4)	1.20305(−2)
0.99	0.48	1.42283(−4)	9.55052(−2)	2.18778(−2)	3.37126(−3)	7.61460(−4)	1.49366(−2)
0.99	0.49	1.46355(−4)	9.72932(−2)	2.22714(−2)	3.49481(−3)	7.88627(−4)	1.54988(−2)
0.99	0.50	1.50451(−4)	9.90749(−2)	2.26630(−2)	3.62001(−3)	8.16123(−4)	1.60693(−2)
1.00	0.50	1.62553(−4)	1.04134(−1)	2.37726(−2)	3.98429(−3)	8.94962(−4)	1.77327(−2)
1.00	0.52	1.71433(−4)	1.07838(−1)	2.45819(−2)	4.26324(−3)	9.56872(−4)	1.90112(−2)
1.00	0.53	1.75909(−4)	1.09679(−1)	2.49836(−2)	4.40529(−3)	9.87826(−4)	1.96635(−2)
1.00	0.54	1.80408(−4)	1.11515(−1)	2.53832(−2)	4.54902(−3)	1.01910(−3)	2.03246(−2)
1.00	0.55	1.84929(−4)	1.13344(−1)	2.57810(−2)	4.69442(−3)	1.05070(−3)	2.09942(−2)
1.01	0.57	2.09337(−4)	1.22820(−1)	2.78340(−2)	5.47818(−3)	1.22041(−3)	2.46172(−2)
1.01	0.58	2.14254(−4)	1.24709(−1)	2.82413(−2)	5.64187(−3)	1.25570(−3)	2.53772(−2)
1.01	0.60	2.24151(−4)	1.28467(−1)	2.90501(−2)	5.97430(−3)	1.32721(−3)	2.69239(−2)

TABLE I. Integrals.[a] (*continued*)

1.02	0.60	2.41605(−4)	1.34781(−1)	3.04052(−2)	6.54796(−3)	1.45030(−3)	2.96004(−2)
1.02	0.62	2.52286(−4)	1.38670(−1)	3.12326(−2)	6.91648(−3)	1.52903(−3)	3.13272(−2)
1.02	0.63	2.57657(−4)	1.40605(−1)	3.16483(−2)	7.10329(−3)	1.56886(−3)	3.22044(−2)
1.04	0.70	3.42112(−4)	1.68941(−1)	3.76303(−2)	1.00867(−2)	2.19869(−3)	4.63555(−2)
1.04	0.71	3.48390(−4)	1.70978(−1)	3.80556(−2)	1.03208(−2)	2.24760(−3)	4.74774(−2)
1.04	0.72	3.54682(−4)	1.73008(−1)	3.84788(−2)	1.05566(−2)	2.29679(−3)	4.86080(−2)
1.04	0.75	3.73649(−4)	1.79058(−1)	3.97366(−2)	1.12737(−2)	2.44605(−3)	5.20603(−2)
1.06	0.76	4.37885(−4)	1.98116(−1)	4.36719(−2)	1.36496(−2)	2.93715(−3)	6.35728(−2)
1.06	0.77	4.45198(−4)	2.00554(−1)	4.41615(−2)	1.40165(−2)	3.01006(−3)	6.54288(−2)
1.06	0.78	4.52319(−4)	2.02411(−1)	4.45507(−2)	1.42191(−2)	3.05388(−3)	6.63567(−2)
1.08	0.82	5.52485(−4)	2.30142(−1)	5.01750(−2)	1.81154(−2)	3.84562(−3)	8.55693(−2)
1.08	0.83	5.60685(−4)	2.32405(−1)	5.06291(−2)	1.84550(−2)	3.91395(−3)	8.72611(−2)
1.08	0.84	5.68895(−4)	2.34661(−1)	5.10809(−2)	1.87964(−2)	3.98254(−3)	8.89639(−2)
1.08	0.85	5.77112(−4)	2.36909(−1)	5.15307(−2)	1.91395(−2)	4.05138(−3)	9.06776(−2)
1.08	0.87	5.93572(−4)	2.41382(−1)	5.24237(−2)	1.98307(−2)	4.18978(−3)	9.41372(−2)
1.10	0.87	6.78814(−4)	2.62710(−1)	5.66589(−2)	2.32288(−2)	4.86658(−3)	1.11238(−1)
1.10	0.88	6.88048(−4)	2.65092(−1)	5.71272(−2)	2.36287(−2)	4.94533(−3)	1.13268(−1)
1.10	0.89	6.97288(−4)	2.67465(−1)	5.75933(−2)	2.40302(−2)	5.02471(−3)	1.15310(−1)
1.10	0.90	7.06532(−4)	2.69830(−1)	5.80571(−2)	2.44336(−2)	5.10412(−3)	1.17364(−1)
1.10	0.91	7.15780(−4)	2.72188(−1)	5.85187(−2)	2.48386(−2)	5.18376(−3)	1.19428(−1)
1.12	0.90	8.05431(−4)	2.93018(−1)	6.25838(−2)	2.84815(−2)	5.89754(−3)	1.38070(−1)
1.12	0.93	8.36377(−4)	3.00538(−1)	6.40344(−2)	2.98751(−2)	6.16776(−3)	1.45277(−1)
1.12	0.94	8.46693(−4)	3.03028(−1)	6.45133(−2)	3.03431(−2)	6.25826(−3)	1.47705(−1)
1.12	0.95	8.57010(−4)	3.05510(−1)	6.49898(−2)	3.08129(−2)	6.34896(−3)	1.50133(−1)
1.14	0.95	9.73295(−4)	3.30938(−1)	6.98526(−2)	3.57253(−2)	7.29335(−3)	1.75773(−1)
1.14	0.96	9.84738(−4)	3.33570(−1)	7.03504(−2)	3.62609(−2)	7.39528(−3)	1.78596(−1)
1.14	0.97	9.96178(−4)	3.36192(−1)	7.08450(−2)	3.67983(−2)	7.49839(−3)	1.81433(−1)
1.14	1.00	1.03047(−3)	3.44006(−1)	7.23157(−2)	3.84209(−2)	7.80485(−3)	1.90023(−1)
1.16	0.97	1.12800(−3)	3.63444(−1)	7.59690(−2)	4.24813(−2)	8.57284(−3)	2.11562(−1)
1.16	0.99	1.15326(−3)	3.68982(−1)	7.69967(−2)	4.37026(−2)	8.80127(−3)	2.18113(−1)
1.16	1.00	1.16587(−3)	3.71770(−1)	7.75069(−2)	4.43159(−2)	8.91573(−3)	2.21410(−1)
1.18	1.02	1.34356(−3)	4.06829(−1)	8.39656(−2)	5.23174(−2)	1.04002(−2)	2.64694(−1)
1.18	1.03	1.35738(−3)	4.09716(−1)	8.44895(−2)	5.30133(−2)	1.05277(−2)	2.68506(−1)
1.18	1.05	1.38498(−3)	4.15462(−1)	8.55296(−2)	5.44104(−2)	1.07831(−2)	2.76176(−1)

[a] Note.—The number in parentheses is the power of 10 by which the corresponding entry is to be multiplied.

TABLE II. Thermodynamic functions.[a]

q	θ	p^*	pv/NkT	E^E/N	S^E/Nk
0.94	0.15	−3.14400(−1)	−1.97024(0)	−8.36897	−6.27571
0.94	0.16	−2.23784(−1)	−1.92911(−1)	−8.35471	−7.18237
0.94	0.17	−1.29167(−1)	−7.14220(−2)	−8.34044	−7.09714
0.94	0.19	5.49524(−2)	5.49524(−2)	−8.31207	−6.93932
0.94	0.20	1.73333(−1)	6.89030(−1)	−8.29794	−6.86684
0.95	0.25	−2.62737(−2)	−9.98400(−2)	−8.20821	−6.47479
0.95	0.26	6.31745(−2)	2.30830(−1)	−8.19437	−6.42051
0.95	0.27	1.52362(−1)	5.36090(−1)	−8.18057	−6.36842
0.95	0.30	4.18421(−1)	1.32500(0)	−8.13937	−6.22372
0.96	0.30	−1.52141(−1)	−4.86850(−1)	−8.11426	−6.14615
0.96	0.31	−6.46447(−2)	−2.00190(−1)	−8.10068	−6.10159
0.96	0.32	2.26000(−2)	6.78000(−2)	−8.08713	−6.05857
0.96	0.34	1.96356(−1)	5.54416(−1)	−8.06013	−5.97673
0.97	0.36	−1.21557(−1)	−3.27528(−1)	−7.99813	−5.80752
0.97	0.37	−6.55609(−2)	−1.71876(−1)	−7.99014	−5.78821
0.97	0.38	1.94819(−2)	4.97300(−2)	−7.97688	−5.75274
0.97	0.40	1.88859(−1)	4.57982(−1)	−7.95047	−5.69499
0.98	0.40	−2.83935(−1)	−6.95640(−1)	−7.91633	−5.61121
0.98	0.42	−1.17080(−1)	−2.73186(−1)	−7.89024	−5.54757
0.98	0.43	−3.40033(−2)	−7.74960(−2)	−7.87724	−5.51697
0.98	0.44	4.88391(−2)	1.08778(−1)	−7.86428	−5.48696
0.98	0.45	1.31456(−1)	2.86282(−1)	−7.85134	−5.45808
0.99	0.48	−5.53484(−2)	−1.14156(−1)	−7.77524	−5.30378
0.99	0.49	2.55295(−2)	5.15800(−2)	−7.76254	−5.27747
0.99	0.50	1.06189(−1)	2.10254(−1)	−7.74987	−5.25258
1.00	0.50	−2.86667(−1)	−5.73334(−1)	−7.70888	−5.24551
1.00	0.52	−1.27733(−1)	−2.45640(−1)	−7.68386	−5.13255
1.00	0.53	−4.85946(−2)	−9.16880(−2)	−7.67139	−5.10910
1.00	0.54	3.03275(−2)	5.61620(−2)	−7.65896	−5.08588
1.00	0.55	1.09034(−1)	1.98244(−1)	−7.64655	−5.06283
1.01	0.57	−9.45805(−2)	−1.67590(−1)	−7.57835	−4.95116
1.01	0.58	−1.73966(−2)	−3.02940(−2)	−7.56615	−4.92995
1.01	0.60	1.36352(−1)	2.29526(−1)	−7.54184	−4.88878
1.02	0.60	−1.91406(−1)	−3.25390(−1)	−7.49581	−4.82234
1.02	0.62	−4.02988(−2)	−6.62980(−2)	−7.47186	−4.78308
1.02	0.63	3.49539(−2)	5.65920(−2)	−7.45993	−4.76396
1.04	0.70	−2.33760(−2)	−3.47300(−2)	−7.28029	−4.51314
1.04	0.71	4.84568(−2)	7.09790(−2)	−7.26883	−4.49693
1.04	0.72	1.20099(−1)	1.73477(−1)	−7.25740	−4.48088
1.04	0.75	3.33939(−1)	4.63062(−1)	−7.22325	−4.43447
1.06	0.76	−7.71816(−2)	−1.07648(−1)	−7.10882	−4.29880
1.06	0.77	−5.01226(−5)	−6.90000(−5)	−7.09611	−4.28198
1.06	0.78	6.03095(−2)	8.19590(−2)	−7.08677	−4.27011
1.08	0.82	−6.87335(−2)	−9.05270(−2)	−6.93570	−4.10015
1.08	0.83	−2.84198(−3)	−3.69800(−3)	−6.92508	−4.08726
1.08	0.84	6.28802(−2)	8.08460(−2)	−6.91448	−4.07455
1.08	0.85	1.28438(−1)	1.63192(−1)	−6.90391	−4.06204
1.08	0.87	2.59065(−1)	3.21598(−1)	−6.88283	−4.03756
1.10	0.87	−7.54543(−2)	−9.54020(−2)	−6.77283	−3.92752
1.10	0.88	−1.22768(−2)	−1.53460(−2)	−6.76260	−3.91584
1.10	0.89	5.07405(−2)	6.27130(−2)	−6.75240	−3.90429
1.10	0.90	1.13600(−1)	1.38845(−1)	−6.74221	−3.89292
1.10	0.91	1.76305(−1)	2.13116(−1)	−6.73205	−3.88163
1.12	0.90	−1.61915(−1)	−2.01494(−1)	−6.63031	−3.78726
1.12	0.93	2.01362(−2)	2.42500(−2)	−6.60071	−3.75491
1.12	0.94	8.05186(−2)	9.59370(−2)	−6.59088	−3.74417
1.12	0.95	1.40751(−1)	1.65938(−1)	−6.58108	−3.73396
1.14	0.95	−8.96850(−2)	−1.07622(−1)	−6.46895	−3.63316

TABLE II. Thermodynamic functions.[a]—*contd.*

q	θ	p^*	pv/NkT	E^E/N	S^E/Nk
1.14	0.96	−3.14307(−2)	−3.73240(−2)	−6.45944	−3.62324
1.14	0.97	2.66801(−2)	3.13560(−2)	−6.44995	−3.61341
1.14	1.00	2.00160(−1)	2.28182(−1)	−6.42159	−3.58462
1.16	0.97	−1.61715(−1)	−1.93391(−1)	−6.33768	−3.51656
1.16	0.99	−4.95051(−2)	−5.80060(−2)	−6.31930	−3.49783
1.16	1.00	6.39310(−3)	7.41600(−3)	−6.31014	−3.48832
1.18	1.02	−4.10567(−2)	−4.74970(−2)	−6.18102	−3.37822
1.18	1.03	1.26934(−2)	1.45420(−2)	−6.17218	−3.36963
1.18	1.05	1.19806(−1)	1.34639(−1)	−6.15455	−3.35258

[a] Note.—The number in parentheses is the power of 10 by which the corresponding entry is to be multiplied.

For convenience in calculation we will consider the properties of the mixture at $p^* = 0$. With this approximation we are neglecting the small variation of the mixing properties with pressure. Although this approximation does not affect the general conclusions given in this article an accurate study of a given mixture can be readily obtained from Tables I and II and should be carried out when necessary.

TABLE III. p^* as a function of $\bar{\epsilon}/k$ and $\bar{a}$ a one-atmosphere pressure.

$\bar{\epsilon}/k$ °K	$\bar{a}$ A	p^*
300	4.50	2.23×10^{-3}
400	5.00	2.29×10^{-3}
500	6.00	3.17×10^{-3}

The values of the thermodynamic variables at $p^* = 0$ were computed by inverse interpolation using a table of three-point and four-point Lagrangian interpolation coefficients[19] and are given in Table IV.

III. CALCULATION OF THE EXCESS MIXING PROPERTIES OF BINARY MIXTURES AND COMPARISON WITH EXPERIMENT

By using Eqs. (15) and (16) together with Table IV the excess internal energy and enthalpy, together with the excess entropy of mixing, at $p^* = 0$ can be computed. At $p^* = 0$ the internal energy and enthalpy of mixing are exactly equal and since the change in volume on mixing is very small (or the order of 1 or 2 cc per mole), they can be set equal to within the error of the calculation for pressures around one atmosphere.

The major problem in calculating the thermodynamic functions is the determination of the individual Lennard-Jones parameters. Ideally, these parameters can be determined from second virial coefficient measurements, but little has been done with substances of experimental interest in solutions. As a result we are forced to adopt an approximation for the mixed parameters (e.g., see Eqs. (2) and (3)) and to determine the parameters for the pure components by some empirical means. In this article we will first use Eqs. (2) and (3) to determine $\bar{\epsilon}$ and $\bar{v}^0$ indirectly. In connection with the use of these equations we will consider two empirical methods of determining the Lennard-Jones constants for the pure substances. The first method uses

[19] L. J. Briggs and A. N. Lowan, *Tables of Lagrangian Interpolation Coefficients* (Math. Tables Project, W.P.A., 1944).

the experimentally determined critical temperature and pressure; the second method will use the experimental values of the heat of vaporization and molal volume at a given temperature.

TABLE IV. Thermodynamic functions at $p^* = 0$.

q	θ	E^E/N	S^E/N
0.94	0.1840	−8.3200	−6.9870
0.95	0.2530	−8.2039	−6.4590
0.96	0.3175	−8.0910	−6.0704
0.97	0.3741	−7.9795	−5.7638
0.98	0.4340	−7.8719	−5.5042
0.99	0.4858	−7.7664	−5.2850
1.00	0.5315	−7.6635	−5.0950
1.01	0.5804	−7.5643	−4.9252
1.02	0.6250	−7.4661	−4.7723
1.04	0.7031	−7.2764	−4.5075
1.06	0.7700	−7.0961	−4.2820
1.08	0.8304	−6.9240	−4.0871
1.10	0.8819	−6.7612	−3.9133
1.12	0.9261	−6.6035	−3.7634
1.14	0.9652	−6.4539	−3.6179
1.16	0.9989	−6.3111	−3.4893

A. Use of Critical Constant Data

The problem of obtaining a semi-empirical method for the determination of the potential-energy curve has been examined by Hill.[20] He remarks that the law of corresponding states requires that the Lennard-Jones parameters be related to the critical point by the equations

$$a = c_5(T_c/p_c)^{\frac{1}{3}}, \qquad \epsilon/k = c_4 T_c. \tag{20}$$

The constants c_4 and c_5 are determined empirically by Hill from the measured properties of neon, argon, nitrogen, and methane. Using a geometric mean to determine an average c_4 and an arithmetic mean to determine c_5, Hill obtains

$$a(A) = 2.633\left[\frac{T_c(°K)}{p_c(\text{atmos.})}\right]^{\frac{1}{3}}, \qquad \epsilon/k(°\text{K}) = 0.780T_c(°\text{K}). \tag{21}$$

If we anticipate section B of this discussion which determines the values of the Lennard-Jones parameters from the experimental heat of vaporization and molal volume of the liquid, we can compute empirical values for c_4 and c_5 for various common nonpolar substances. These results are given in Table V. Although the error introduced by the free volume equation of state for the liquid may be large, the relative discrepancies among the values indicate, roughly, the failure of the law of corresponding states, which reflects the use of the two parameter Lennard-Jones potential to represent the

[20] T. L. Hill, *J. Chem. Phys.* **16**, 399 (1948).

TABLE V. Empirical relation between critical constants and Lennard-Jones potential parameters (see Sec. II-A).[a]

Substance	T_c[b] °K	p_c[b] atms	a A	ϵ/k °K	c_5	c_4
CCl_4	556.3	45.0	5.411	485.7	2.340	0.873
C_6H_{12}	554.2	40.4	5.624	485.7	2.349	0.876
C_6H_6	561.7	47.7	5.260	493.6	2.312	0.879
$SnCl_4$	591.9	37.0	5.818	582.6	2.309	0.984
n-hexane	508.0	29.5	5.964	462.1	2.309	0.910
CS_2	546.2	76.0	4.580	413.7	2.373	0.757
n-octane	569.2	24.6	6.500	604.6	2.281	1.062
n-heptane	540.0	26.8	6.241	538.1	2.294	0.996

[a] The Lennard-Jones parameters were computed from the experimental heats of vaporization and molal volumes using the free volume expressions for the thermodynamic functions.
[b] *Handbook of Chemistry and Physics* (1947), thirtieth edition, p. 1807.

interaction between a pair of molecules. This potential is at best a rough approximation and from a qualitative examination of Table V we expect the calculations for mixtures of carbon tetrachloride, benzene, and cyclohexane to be more reliable than for several other mixtures we will consider.

Returning to Eq. (21) which is based upon second virial coefficient measurements, we use Eqs. (2) and (3), determine $\bar{\epsilon}$ and $\bar{v}^0$ and then calculate the mixing properties of various solutions. A brief summary of the results together with the experimental values is given in Table VI. The experimental values were obtained from the various references given in the table. The agreement between the calculated and the experimental values is very poor. However, a detailed examination of the calculations reveals that the mixing properties are very sensitive to small variations in the Lennard-Jones parameters (this will be discussed in more detail in a later section). For this reason the results given in Table VI may be regarded as tentative until accurate second virial coefficient measurements on the vapors have been performed.

TABLE VI. Excess thermodynamic properties of equimolal mixtures $T = 298.2$°K (see Sec. II-A).[a]

Mixture	$\bar{\epsilon}/k$ °K	v^0 cc	$100\Delta v/v_0^0$ calc	$100\Delta v/v_0^0$ exp	ΔH^E cal/mole calc	ΔH^E cal/mole exp	$\Delta S^E/R$ calc	$\Delta S^E/R$ exp
CCl_4—C_6H_6	430.8	143.8	0.37	0.003	40	30	0.010	0.018
CCl_4—C_6H_{12}	435.5	132.9	0.11	0.16	10	34	0.004	0.030
C_6H_6—C_6H_{12}	430.2	141.0	0.75	0.65	97	176	0.024	0.171
CCl_4—$SnCl_4$	433.4	159.0	2.60	0.40	257	..	0.073	..

$v_0^0 = x_1v_1 + x_2v_2$

[a] The Lennard-Jones parameters for the pure components were computed from the experimental critical constants of the pure liquids. The experimental values of the mixing properties were taken from reference (6) and from Scatchard, Wood, and Mochel, *J. Am. Chem. Soc.* **62**, 712 (1940).

B. Use of Heats of Vaporization and Molal Volumes of the Pure Liquids

Using the energy of vaporization and the molal volume of a liquid at 25°C or 20°C, the free volume expressions for the excess internal energy and the equation of state at $p^* = 0$ can be solved to give ϵ and v^0. In practice these equations were solved graphically and the results can be found in Table V. The thermodynamic properties of equimolar mixtures calculated on this

TABLE VII. Excess thermodynamic properties of equimolal mixtures [see Sec. II(B)].[a]

Mixture	T °K	$\bar{\epsilon}/k$ °K	v^0 cc	$100\Delta v/v_0^0$ calc	$100\Delta v/v_0^0$ exp	ΔH^E cal/mole calc	ΔH^E cal/mole exp	$\Delta S^E/R$ calc	$\Delta S^E/R$ exp	$\Delta S^E/R$ non-random[b]
CCl_4—C_6H_6	298.2	487.9	91.74	0.25	0.003	30	30	0.007	0.018	−0.0003
CCl_4—C_6H_{12}	298.2	482.4	101.70	0.46	0.16	52	34	0.013	0.030	−0.0002
C_6H_6—C_6H_{12}	298.2	479.9	98.43	1.32	0.65	171	176	0.042	0.171	−0.0061
CCl_4—$SnCl_4$	298.2	521.0	108.90	3.00	0.40	233	...	0.042	...	
CCl_4—$SiCl_4$	298.2	462.0	104.3	0.66	0.02	101	32	0.024	0.020	
C_6H_{12}—n-hexane	293.2	466.7	118.3	0.90	...	129	48	0.034	0.055	
C_6H_{12}—dioxane	293.2	509.1	96.70	−0.88	...	174	280	0.032	0.081	
CCl_4—CS_2	293.2	401.7	82.20	9.60	...	857	76	0.250	...	
CCl_4—$C(CH_3)_4$	293.2	405.9	103.34	−2.96	...	16	...	−0.174	...	

[a] The Lennard-Jones parameters for the pure components were obtained from the experimental heats of vaporization and molal volumes of the pure liquids. The experimental values listed in this table were taken from reference (6) and from the following: Scatchard, Wood, and Mochel, *J. Am. Chem. Soc.* **62**, 712 (1940). V. W. Schulze, *Z. anorg. Chem.* **261**, 297 (1950). J. H. Simons and J. B. Hickman, *J. Phys. Chem.* **56**, 420 (1952). R. D. Vold, *J. Am. Chem. Soc.* **59**, 1515 (1937). Anna-Luise Vierk, *Z. anorg. Chem.* **261**, 283 (1950). J. H. Hildebrand and J. M. Carter, *J. Am. Chem. Soc.* **59**, 1510 (1937). I. Prigogine and V. Mathot, *J. Chem. Phys.* **18**, 765 (1950).

[b] Contribution to the excess entropy of mixing as calculated from the Kirkwood (reference 4) quasi-lattice theory.

empirical basis are summarized in Table VII together with the experimental results. As mentioned earlier we have included a few examples of the contribution due to nonrandom mixing as calculated[21] from the Kirkwood[14] quasi-lattice theory of solutions.

C. Empirical Use of the Heats and Volumes of Mixing

The average Lennard-Jones constants $\bar{\epsilon}/k$ and $\bar{v}^0$ can be computed empirically from the knowledge of the heat of mixing and volume of mixing of the solution in the same manner in which one obtains ϵ/k and $\bar{v}^0$ for a pure liquid using the energy of vaporization and the molal volume. The results of this calculation for several equimolar mixtures are summarized in Table VIII.

TABLE VIII. Excess thermodynamic properties of equimolal mixtures $T = 298.2°K$ (see Sec. II-C).[a]

Mixture	$\bar{\epsilon}/k$ °K	v^0 cc	$\Delta S^E/R$	δ/k
CCl_4—C_6H_6	487.90	91.52	0.007	−0.008
CCl_4—C_6H_{12}	483.62	101.38	0.009	−0.006
C_6H_6—C_6H_{12}	478.10	97.77	0.043	−0.034
CCl_4—$SiCl_4$	469.38	101.03	0.0018	−0.094

[a] The average potential parameters, $\bar{\epsilon}/k$ and $\bar{v}^0$ for the mixture were computed empirically from the measured heats and volumes of mixing.

It is possible to empirically attribute the discrepancies between the experimental and theoretical values for the heats of mixing and volumes of mixing to the failure of the approximation given by Eq. (2). If we let

$$\epsilon_{12} = (\epsilon_{11}\epsilon_{22})^{\frac{1}{2}} + \delta, \tag{22}$$

then δ can be determined by means of the equation

$$\delta = \frac{\bar{\epsilon}_e\bar{v}_e^{0 2} - \bar{\epsilon}\bar{v}^{0 2}}{2x_1x_2v_{12}^{0 2}}, \tag{23}$$

where $\bar{\epsilon}_e$ and $\bar{v}_e^0$ are the values determined from the experimental properties of the mixture (see Table VIII) and $\bar{\epsilon}$ and $\bar{v}^0$ are computed using Eqs. (2) and (3) and the experimental properties of the pure components. Several values of δ are given in Table VIII.

IV. COMMENTS

The calculated volumes, heats, and entropies of mixing given in this paper are only correct to two significant digits. We have not fully exploited the accuracy which can be obtained from the functions given in Tables I and II, for the agreement with the experimental results permits one to draw only qualitative conclusions about the theory. As a general feature, with only one or two exceptions, we find that the predicted volumes and heats of mixing are too large, and the calculated entropies of mixing are always too small. It is possible to explain the discrepancies in terms of the small deviations from the mixture approximation given in Eqs. (2) and (3). However, this is

[21] Scatchard, Wood, and Mochel, *J. Am. Chem. Soc.* **62**, 712 (1940).

purely an empirical assignment and is misleading in view of the sensitivity of the mixing properties to variations in the Lennard-Jones parameters. In order to illustrate the dependence upon these potential parameters we have prepared Figs. 1 and 2 which give the behavior of the heat of mixing and volume of mixing for a typical case.

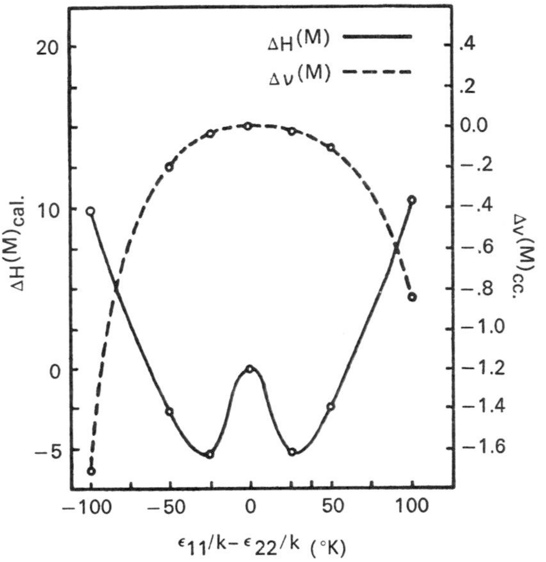

FIG. 1. Typical variation of $\Delta H^{(M)}$ and $\Delta v^{(M)}$ with $\epsilon_{11}/k - \epsilon_{22}/k$.

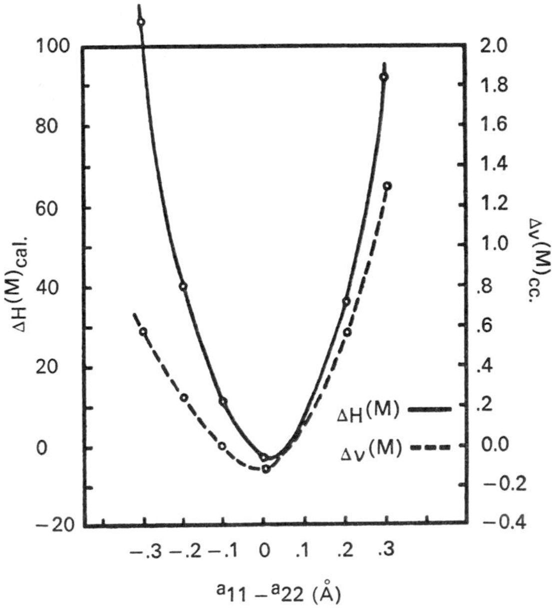

FIG. 2. Typical variation of $\Delta H^{(M)}$ and $\Delta v^{(M)}$ with $a_{11} - a_{22}$.

The entropy of mixing is consistently too low. Scatchard[21] *et al.* have remarked that the experimental evidence, in the case of C_6H_6, CCl_4 and C_6H_{12} solutions, indicates that the relatively large excess entropies of mixing are not caused by preferential orientation in the pure liquids. A possible improvement in the predicted entropy might be expected by using a simple extension of the present theory, namely the introduction of vacant cells or "holes." However, the fraction of vacant cells, x_0, which is obtained by minimizing the free energy at constant temperature and volume is extremely small. The hole fraction, x_0, in the region of interest and at $p^* = 0$ is given in Table IX. The largest correction due to holes comes from a term which corresponds to the ideal entropy of mixing of holes and molecules. When x_0

TABLE IX. "Hole" fraction at $p^* = 0$.

q	θ	x_0
1.00	0.5315	3.352(−9)[a]
1.01	0.5804	1.568(−8)
1.02	0.6250	5.416(−8)
1.04	0.7031	3.532(−7)
1.06	0.7700	1.374(−6)
1.08	0.8304	4.017(−6)
1.10	0.8819	9.358(−6)
1.12	0.9261	1.852(−5)
1.14	0.9652	3.337(−5)
1.16	0.9989	5.489(−5)

[a] Note.—The number in parentheses is the power of 10 by which the corresponding entry is to be multiplied.

is very small this term is given by

$$\frac{\Delta S_0{}^E}{R} = x_1 x_0{}^{(1)} \ln x_0{}^{(1)} + x_2 x_0{}^{(2)} \ln x_0{}^{(2)} - x_0 \ln x_0, \tag{24}$$

where $x_0{}^{(1)}$, $x_0{}^{(2)}$ and x_0 are the fractions of vacant cells in pure liquid 1, pure liquid 2, and the solution, respectively. For an equimolar mixture of benzene and carbon tetrachloride this term increases the excess entropy of mixing by 2.9×10^{-8} units in $\Delta S/R$, which is a negligible contribution.

As a final comment we would like to point to the lack of experimental data on simple solutions to which one might expect this theory to apply. The wide class of tetrahalides might be considered as approaching the symmetrical requirements although there is some doubt as to whether the forces between molecules are of the central type. In the absence of experimental techniques which can treat mixtures of liquid argon, neon, methane, etc. a careful experimental study of some group of symmetrical molecules would be appropriate to the present state of the theory of solutions.

Since repulsive forces play an important role at the densities under consideration, a better approximation for the effectively spherical nonpolar molecules can be obtained by considering the three-parameter intermolecular potential

$$V(R) = -\frac{\mu}{R^6} + P \exp\left[-\frac{R}{\rho}\right]. \tag{25}$$

This extension of the theory is possible with modern calculating facilities, but the unknown errors inherent in the cell method itself places some doubt on the value of such a program.

Theory of Multi-Component Fluid Mixtures. I. Statistical Order-Disorder Analysis in Multi-Component Fluid Mixtures*

ZEVI W. SALSBURG,† *Department of Chemistry, The Rice Institute, Houston, Texas*
AND
PETER J. WOJTOWICZ‡ AND JOHN G. KIRKWOOD, *Sterling Chemical Laboratory, Yale University, New Haven, Connecticut*

(Received November 2, 1956)

Recent theories of solutions (Prigogine and co-workers: Scott) have been developed without specific reference to a molecular model by the use of a corresponding states procedure which relates the properties of the solution to the properties of one of the pure components. These considerations have been based exclusively upon intuitive postulates which have been formulated by analogy from previous "cell" theories of solutions.

The basis for a corresponding states treatment is examined in a rigorous manner by the use of statistical mechanics. A general method is given for reducing the multi-component configurational partition function to a form peculiar to a system of one component. Two types of approximations to the rigorous theory that are amenable to numerical calculations are developed on a strictly mathematical basis, and are used to estimate the magnitudes of the correction terms to a corresponding states analysis.

I. INTRODUCTION

Within recent years there have appeared several theoretical treatments of nonelectrolyte solutions. Hildebrand's semiempirical Regular solution theory[1] was among the first. The more rigorous quasi-chemical method was applied to the strictly Regular solution by Guggenheim[2] and Rushbrooke.[3] Prigogine and Garikian,[4] Rowlinson,[5] Pople,[6] and Salsburg and Kirkwood[7,8] have approached the problem from the lattice-model or cell-theory point of view. An alternative development for the statistical treatment of mixtures is

* Contribution No. 1408 from the Sterling Chemistry Laboratory, Yale University, New Haven, Connecticut.

† This work has been carried out in part under the auspices of the U.S. Atomic Energy Commission at the Los Alamos Scientific Laboratory of the University of California.

‡ National Science Foundation Predoctoral Fellow 1953–1956. Present address: RCA Laboratories, Princeton, New Jersey.

[1] J. H. Hildebrand and R. L. Scott, *The Solubility of Nonelectrolytes* (Reinhold Publishing Corporation, New York, 1950), third edition.

[2] E. A. Guggenheim, *Mixtures* (Oxford University Press, New York, 1952).

[3] G. S. Rushbrooke, *Proc. Roy. Soc.* (*London*) **A166**, 296 (1938).

[4] I. Prigogine and G. Garikian, *Physica* **16**, 239 (1950).

[5] J. S. Rowlinson, *Proc. Roy. Soc.* (*London*) **A214**, 192 (1952).

[6] J. A. Pople, *Trans. Faraday Soc.* **49**, 591 (1953).

[7] Z. W. Salsburg and J. G. Kirkwood, *J. Chem. Phys.* **20**, 1538 (1952).

[8] Z. W. Salsburg and J. G. Kirkwood, *J. Chem. Phys.* **21**, 2169 (1953).

contained in a series of articles by Longuet-Higgins[9–11] on the theory of conformal solutions. Discussions of the relative merits and applicability of a number of these theories have been given by Scott[12] and Rowlinson.[13]

The restriction of some of these considerations to the framework of the cell model has, however, obscured some of the general aspects of the mixture theory. It is certainly of interest to reconsider these points in an independent manner. The conformal solution theory, on the other hand, is independent of any molecular model. However, being only a first-order perturbation theory, it de-emphasizes the fundamental problem of averaging over geometrical configurations which differ only by an interchange of the positions of individual molecules.

These generalizations have been recognized and intuitively considered in three recent articles by Prigogine *et al.*,[14] by Rice,[15] and by Scott.[16] However, the development of these results from fundamental statistical mechanical principles in terms of well-defined approximations has thus far been omitted.

In this communication the problem of a multi-component fluid is examined in a general way by the use of statistical mechanics and several devices from the order-disorder theory of the solid state. A general method is given for reducing the multi-component configurational partition function to a form peculiar to a system of one component, the intermolecular potential of which is a function of the actual potentials, the composition, and the temperature. Unlike the crystalline order-disorder theory, or the several cell theories, however, we shall not need to appeal to the existence of a real or virtual lattice. Two types of approximations to the rigorous theory that are amenable to numerical calculations are developed on a strictly mathematical basis. These approximations are based upon the method of moments[17] and a generalization[18] of this method.

II. EXACT STATISTICAL MECHANICAL DEVELOPMENT

We consider a closed fluid system composed of N molecules of r different species and occupying a volume v. We let N_s denote the number of molecules of species s ($s = 1, 2, \cdots, r$) in the system. Under the assumption that the internal degrees of freedom of the molecules are independent of the configurational state of the mixture, the partition function Q_{N} for a petite canonical ensemble of these systems is given by the expression

$$\begin{aligned} Q_{\mathrm{N}} &= Z_{\mathrm{N}} \prod_{s=1}^{r} [N_s! \lambda_s^{3N_s} \psi_s^{-N_s}]^{-1} \\ Z_N &= \int^v \cdots \int^v \exp[-\beta V_N] \prod_{k=1}^{N} dv_k \qquad (1) \\ \lambda_s &= h/(2\pi m_s kT)^{\frac{1}{2}} \\ \beta &= 1/kT \end{aligned}$$

---

[9] H. C. Longuet-Higgins, *Proc. Roy. Soc.* (*London*) **A205**, 247 (1951).
[10] D. Cook and H. C. Longuet-Higgins, *Proc. Roy. Soc.* (*London*) **A209**, 28 (1951).
[11] W. B. Brown and H. C. Longuet-Higgins, *Proc. Roy. Soc.* (*London*) **A209**, 416 (1951)
[12] R. L. Scott, *Discussions Faraday Soc.* **15**, 44 (1953).
[13] J. S. Rowlinson, *Discussions Faraday Soc.* **15**, 52 (1953).
[14] Prigogine, Bellemans, and Englert-Chwoles, *J. Chem. Phys.* **24**, 518 (1956).
[15] S. A. Rice, *J. Chem. Phys.* **24**, 357, 1283 (1956).
[16] R. L. Scott, *J. Chem. Phys.* **25**, 193 (1956).
[17] J. G. Kirkwood, *J. Chem. Phys.* **6**, 70 (1938); *J. Phys. Chem.* **43**, 97 (1939).
[18] J. G. Kirkwood, *J. Chem. Phys.* **8**, 623 (1940).

where V_N is the potential of intermolecular force acting between the molecules, and is a function of the intermolecular distances (and orientations). The function $\psi_s(T)$ is the internal molecular partition function of species s and m_s the molecular mass of species s; h is Planck's constant, k is Boltzmann's constant, and T the thermodynamic temperature; $\mathbf{N}$ denotes the set $\{N_1, N_2, \cdots, N_r\}$.

We describe an arbitrary configuration of the N molecules in the system by specifying a set of N-position vectors, $\{\mathbf{R}\} = \{\mathbf{R}_1, \cdots, \mathbf{R}_N\}$ (orientation coordinates may be included if needed), and associating with each vector $\mathbf{R}_i$ a set of occupation parameters $\xi_i^1, \cdots, \xi_i^r$ defined as follows:

$$\xi_i^s = \begin{cases} 1, \text{ if a molecule of species } s \text{ is located at } \mathbf{R}_i \\ 0, \text{ otherwise.} \end{cases} \tag{2}$$

Let $\{\xi\}$ denote the set of occupation parameters, $\xi_1^1, \cdots, \xi_N^1, \cdots, \xi_1^r, \cdots, \xi_N^r$. Specification of $\{\mathbf{R}\}$ and $\{\xi\}$, then, completely determines the configuration of the system. We shall assume that the potential of intermolecular force V_N can be written as a sum of pair potentials in the form

$$V_N(\mathbf{R},\boldsymbol{\xi}) = \sum_{i<j} \sum_{s=1}^{r} \sum_{t=1}^{r} \xi_i^s \xi_j^t V_{st}(R_{ij}) \tag{3}$$

where $V_{st}(R_{ij})$ is the pair interaction potential between molecules of types s and t located respectively at the positions i and j and $R_{ij} = |\mathbf{R}_i - \mathbf{R}_j|$. Because of the two-valued nature of ξ_i^s, the only nonzero term in the summations over s and t is the term which gives the interaction between the molecules actually located at i and j.

Although we have written the intermolecular potential as a function of the occupation parameters $\{\boldsymbol{\xi}\}$, the Gibbs phase integral Z_{N} is independent of these parameters. Specifying the set $\{\boldsymbol{\xi}\}$ can be viewed simply as a method of identifying the order of integration (i.e., identifying each variable of integration with a given type of molecule). Since each integration is carried out over the entire physical volume v, the phase integral is independent of the order in which the integrations are performed and thus independent of the ξ's.

Hence, Z_{N} may be formally written as

$$Z_{\mathrm{N}} = (\prod_{s=1}^{r} N_s!/N!) \sum_{\{\xi\}}{}' \int^{v} \cdots \int^{v} \times \exp[-\beta V_N(\mathbf{R},\boldsymbol{\xi})] \prod_{k=1}^{N} dv_k \tag{4}$$

where the primed summation is given by

$$\sum_{\{\xi\}}{}' = \sum_{\xi_1^1, \cdots, \xi_N^1 = 0}^{1} \; \sum_{\xi_1^2, \cdots, \xi_N^2 = 0}^{1} \cdots \sum_{\xi_1^r, \cdots, \xi_N^r = 0}^{1}$$

subject to the restrictions

$$\begin{aligned} &\sum_{i=1}^{N} \xi_i^s = N_s \quad (s = 1, 2, \cdots, r) \\ &\sum_{s=1}^{r} \xi_i^s = 1 \qquad (i = 1, 2, \cdots, N). \end{aligned} \tag{5}$$

Each of the terms in the summation make equal contributions to Z_N and there are $N!/\prod_{s=1}^{r} N_s!$ terms. By interchanging the order of integration and summation in Eq. (4) we obtain

$$Z_N = \int^v \cdots \int^v \exp[-\beta\Phi_N(\mathbf{R})] \prod_{k=1}^{N} dv_k$$

$$\exp[-\beta\Phi_N] = \left(\prod_{s=1}^{r} N_s!/N!\right) \sum_{\{\xi\}}{}' \exp[-\beta V_N(\mathbf{R},\boldsymbol{\xi})]. \tag{6}$$

$\Phi_N(R)$, defined in Eq. (6), may be thought of as a pseudo single-component potential function. The major consequence of Eq. (6) lies in the observation that the Gibbs phase integral Z_N for the mixture can now be expressed in a form peculiar to a system of a single component whose intermolecular potential is given by Φ_N. The evaluation of $\exp[-\beta\Phi_N(R)]$ for a fixed set $\{\mathbf{R}\}$ is mathematically equivalent to the determination of the configurational partition function for a mixed crystal. Here, however, $\{\mathbf{R}\}$ need not form a lattice.

It is instructive to examine the relation between the "pseudopotential" and the average intermolecular potential for a fixed set $\{\mathbf{R}\}$. This can be obtained by first forming

$$\frac{\partial(\beta\Phi_N)}{\partial\beta} = \langle V_N \rangle_{\text{Av}} \tag{7}$$

where

$$\langle V_N \rangle_{\text{Av}} = \frac{\sum_{\{\xi\}}' V_N \exp[-\beta V_N]}{\sum_{\{\xi\}}' \exp[-\beta V_N]}$$

is the average intermolecular potential for fixed $\{\mathbf{R}\}$. When β equals zero, $\beta\Phi_N$ is zero. Thus, integration of Eq. (7) yields

$$\Phi_N = \frac{1}{\beta}\int_0^\beta \langle V_N \rangle_{\text{Av}}\, d\beta. \tag{8}$$

This relation will be used in Sec. IV, where the method of pair distribution functions is used to approximate Φ_N.

III. APPROXIMATION BY THE MOMENT EXPANSION

A consistent sequence of approximations can be obtained by expanding Φ_N in a power series in β and considering the nth partial sums ($n = 0, 1, 2, \cdots$). This is a particular application of a general perturbation theory[17] and is implicitly used in the theory of conformal solutions.[9]

By expanding $\exp[-\beta V_N]$ in a power series we obtain from Eq. (6),

$$\exp[-\beta\Phi_N] = \sum_{k=0} \frac{M_k}{k!} (-\beta)^k \tag{9}$$

where the kth moment M_k is given by

$$M_k = (\prod_{s=1}^{r} N_s!/N!) \sum_{\{\xi\}}{}'(V_N)^k. \tag{10}$$

We have emphasized the temperature dependence by writing this expansion as a power series in $\beta = 1/kT$ which implies rapid convergence at high temperatures. However, it must be remarked that, in reality, the rate of convergence of this series depends upon the magnitude of βV_N and in the regions of high compression V_N may be very large, which in turn implies slow convergence of Eq. (9) for very high densities.

Φ_N may be written as a power series in $(-\beta)$ of the form

$$\Phi_N = \sum_{n=1}^{\infty} \frac{\lambda_n}{n!}(-\beta)^{n-1} \tag{11}$$

where the coefficients λ_n can be expressed in terms of the moments M_k in a straightforward manner. The details of this procedure are outlined elsewhere.[17,19] For the first two terms one obtains

$$\lambda_1 = M_1 \tag{12}$$

$$\lambda_2 = M_2 - M_1^2.$$

The methods used to compute the moments in the order-disorder theory of regular solutions[17] can be applied directly to the present theory (see Appendix A). The results of this calculation for M_1 and M_2 can be used with Eqs. (11) and (12) to obtain the following approximations for Φ_N.

A. Zeroth Approximation

When all terms of order β are neglected in Eq. (11) we have

$$\Phi_N = \sum_{i<j} \varphi(ij)$$

$$\varphi(ij) = \sum_{s=1}^{r} \sum_{t=1}^{r} x_s x_t V_{st}(ij) \tag{13}$$

$$x_s = N_s/N.$$

The pseudo pair potential $\varphi(R_{ij})$ is a quadratic function of the mole fractions and is independent of the temperature. This expression for Φ_N has been shown[17] to be equivalent to the random mixing approximation used in the theory of solutions.

In another article[20] the theoretical and practical aspects of the zeroth approximation are developed and discussed. In particular, a principle of corresponding states is shown to be a consequence of this approximation.

---

[19] R. W. Zwanzig, *J. Chem. Phys.* **22**, 1420 (1954).
[20] Wojtowicz, Salsburg, and Kirkwood, *J. Chem. Phys.* (to be published).

B. First Approximation

When all terms of order β^2 are neglected in Eq. (11) we obtain

$$\Phi_N = \tfrac{1}{2} \sum_{ij}{}^* \varphi(ij) - \beta\{\tfrac{1}{2} \sum_{ij}{}^* \varphi^{\ddagger}(ij) + \sum_{ijk}{}^* \varphi^{\dagger}(ij;jk)\}$$

$$\varphi^{\ddagger} = \sum_{s=1}^{r} \sum_{t=1}^{r} x_s x_t [V_{st}]^2 - \varphi^2 \tag{14}$$

$$\varphi^{\dagger}(R;R') = \sum_{s=1}^{r} \sum_{t=1}^{r} \sum_{u=1}^{r} x_s x_t x_u V_{st}(R) V_{tu}(R') - \varphi(R)\varphi(R')$$

where $\sum^*$ denotes a summation where the indices take on all values such that no two indices are equal. Thus we see that when Φ_N is written as a power series in β, the first correction to the random mixing approximation contains terms which can no longer be written as a sum of pair potentials. This complication is a serious obstacle to any practical application of the higher order approximation obtained by this procedure.

At high temperature, or when the differences in interaction will not alter a random distribution of molecules, Eq. (13) will be an adequate approximation. For mixtures which deviate appreciably from random mixing, higher moments or an alternative approximation procedure must be used.

IV. APPROXIMATION BY PAIR CORRELATIONS

An alternative procedure for computing Φ_N can be obtained by adopting a general method for cooperative phenomena which has been developed by Kirkwood.[18] This procedure involves the approximate evaluation of a pair distribution function which we formally introduce in the following development.

The potential of intermolecular force, Eq. (3), may, for convenience in our later discussions, be rewritten as follows:

$$V_N = \tfrac{1}{4} \sum_{i,j}{}^* \sum_{s=1}^{r} \sum_{t=1}^{r} \xi_i{}^s \xi_j{}^t J_{st}(ij) + \tfrac{1}{2} \sum_{i,j}{}^* \sum_{s=1}^{r} \xi_i{}^s V_{ss}(ij) \tag{15}$$

$$J_{st}(R) = 2V_{st}(R) - V_{ss}(R) - V_{tt}(R)$$

where we have made use of the restriction on $\xi_i{}^s$ given by Eq. (5). From Eqs. (15) and (8) we can write $\beta\Phi_N$ in the form

$$\beta\Phi_N = \tfrac{1}{2} \sum_{i,j}{}^* \left\{ \tfrac{1}{2} \sum_{s,t} J_{st}(ij) \int_0^{\beta} \langle \xi_i{}^s \xi_j{}^t \rangle_{\mathrm{Av}} d\beta + \sum_{s} \int_0^{\beta} \langle \xi_i{}^s \rangle_{\mathrm{Av}} d\beta \right\} \tag{16}$$

where the average of any function y is given by

$$\langle y \rangle_{\mathrm{Av}} = \sum_{\xi_i{}^s=0}^{1} \sum_{\xi_j{}^t=0}^{1} y(\xi_i{}^s, \xi_j{}^t) P^{(2)}(\beta; \xi_i{}^s, \xi_j{}^t)$$

where $P^{(2)}(\beta; \xi_i{}^s, \xi_j{}^t)$ is the probability that the positions i and j will have the specified occupation $[\xi_i{}^s, \xi_j{}^t]$ irrespective of the occupation of the remaining positions and is defined by

$$P^{(2)}(\beta; \xi_i{}^s, \xi_j{}^t) = \frac{\sum_{\{\xi\}}'' \exp[-\beta V_N]}{\sum_{\{\xi\}}' \exp[-\beta V_N]}. \tag{17}$$

The symbol $\sum''$ indicates a summation over all the occupation variables except ξ_i^s and ξ_j^t subject to the restrictions which require that, consistent with the fixed values of $[\xi_i^s, \xi_j^t]$, the entire system have exactly N_u molecules of type u ($u = 1, \cdots, r$) and there be one and only one molecule at each position.

An alternative representation for $P^{(2)}(\beta; \xi_i^s, \xi_j^t)$ can be obtained by considering the following derivative with respect to β.

$$-\frac{\partial \Psi}{\partial \beta} = \langle V_N(\xi_i^s,\xi_j^t)\rangle_{\text{Av}} - \langle V_N\rangle_{\text{Av}}$$

$$\Psi(\beta;\xi_i^s,\xi_j^t) = \ln P^{(2)}(\beta;\xi_i^s,\xi_j^t) \tag{18}$$

where

$$\langle V_N(\xi_i^s,\xi_j^t)\rangle_{\text{Av}} = \frac{\sum''_{\{\xi\}} V_N \exp[-\beta V_N]}{\sum''_{\{\xi\}} \exp[-\beta V_N]} \tag{19}$$

is the average intermolecular potential consistent with fixed molecular positions, $\{\mathbf{R}\}$, and fixed values of ξ_i^s and ξ_j^t in a petite canonical ensemble of closed systems. When β is equal to zero, $P^{(2)}$ reduces to the ratio of the number of configurations consistent with the specified values of ξ_i^s and ξ_j^t to the total number of configurations—both calculations are carried out for fixed molecular positions. This combinatorial problem is straightforward but tedious (see Appendix B). The solution can be expressed in the form

$$\Psi(0;\xi_i^s,\xi_j^t) = \ln[(1 - x_s)(1 - x_t)] + \xi_i^s \ln \frac{x_s}{1 - x_s} + \xi_j^t \ln \frac{x_t}{1 - x_t}. \tag{20}$$

The desired formulation for $P^{(2)}$ can then be obtained by integrating Eq. (18) with the use of Eq. (20).

$$\Psi(\beta;\xi_i^s,\xi_j^t) = (1 - \xi_i^s) \ln(1 - x_s) + (1 - \xi_j^t) \ln(1 - x_t) + \xi_i^s \ln x_s + \xi_j^t \ln x_t - \beta\psi(\beta;\psi\xi_i^s,\xi_j^t) \tag{21}$$

$$\psi(\beta;\xi_i^s,\xi_j^t) = \frac{1}{\beta}\int_0^\beta [\langle V_N(\xi_i^s,\xi_j^t)\rangle_{\text{Av}} - \langle V_N\rangle_{\text{Av}}]d\beta.$$

The pair distribution function, and thus also ψ, are subject to the normalization condition

$$\sum_{\xi_i^s=0}^{1} \sum_{\xi_j^t=0}^{1} P^{(2)}(\beta;\xi_i^s,\xi_j^t) = 1. \tag{22}$$

Since each ξ has a domain of two values only, zero and unity, we may express ψ as a function of these variables in the following form

$$\psi = -w_{00}(st) + w_{10}(st)\xi_i^s + w_{01}(st)\xi_j^t - w_{11}(st)\xi_i^s\xi_j^t. \tag{23}$$

The four values of the function ψ depend upon the positions i and j as well as the coordinates of all the other molecules in the system. For the sake of brevity of notation we have suppressed this dependence in writing Eq. (23). Since ψ is subject to Eq. (22), only three of four values of ψ are independent. We arbitrarily choose w_{10}, w_{01}, and w_{11} as the independent functions and from Eq. (22) obtain

$$\exp[-\beta w_{00}] = (1 - x_s)(1 - x_t) + (1 - x_s)x_t \exp[-\beta w_{01}]$$
$$+ (1 - x_t)x_s \exp[-\beta w_{10}] + x_s x_t \exp[\beta(w_{11} - w_{10} - w_{01})]. \tag{24}$$

In order to calculate w_{01}, w_{10}, and w_{11}, it is necessary to determine $\langle V_N(\xi_i^s, \xi_j^t)\rangle_{\text{Av}}$. This could be done by a continuation of the method employed in the calculation of $\langle V_N\rangle_{\text{Av}}$ and would lead to the consideration of the distribution function for four positions. Further continuation of this process would lead to a chain of equations and, therefore, for practical considerations it is necessary to terminate this process at some convenient point by means of a suitable approximation. We propose to approximate $\langle V_N(\xi_i^s, \xi_j^t)\rangle_{\text{Av}}$ by expanding this function in a power series in β and neglecting terms of $O(\beta)$. This leads to the equation,

$$\langle V_N(\xi_i^s,\xi_j^t)\rangle_{\text{Av}} = \frac{1}{\Omega} \sum_{\{\xi\}}'' V_N + O(\beta) \tag{25}$$

where Ω is the number of configurations consistent with the given values of ξ_i^s and ξ_j^t. V_N as a function of the occupation variables, is given by Eq. (3). The details of this calculation (see Appendix B) are similar to those used in the calculation of the moments M_k. The final result can be expressed in the form

$$w_{01}(ts) = w_{10}(st) = \sum_{k\neq i,j} \sum_{u} x_u V_{su}(jk) + \sum_{v\neq t} \frac{x_v}{1 - x_t} V_{sv}(ij)$$
$$- \sum_{u\neq s} \sum_{v\neq t} \frac{x_u}{1 - x_s} \frac{x_v}{1 - x_t} V_{uv}(ij) + O(\beta)$$

$$- w_{11}(st) = V_{st}(ij) - \sum_{v\neq t} \frac{x_v}{1 - x_t} V_{sv}(ij) - \sum_{u\neq s} \frac{x_u}{1 - x_s} V_{ut}(ij)$$
$$+ \sum_{u\neq s} \sum_{v\neq t} \frac{x_u}{1 - x_s} \frac{x_v}{1 - x_t} V_{uv}(ij) + O(\beta). \tag{26}$$

In the usual order-disorder theory of a solid lattice these parameters are no longer independent, but are restrained by the condition that all lattice sites are equivalent in the average crystal (i.e., the average value of each occupation variable must be independent of the lattice site). For our general theory of mixtures, where lattice sites are replaced by arbitrary positions of the molecules, this restraint no longer holds. But the advantages of introducing an approximation expressed by this restraint are twofold; (1) a result that in the limit of a crystalline configuration is equivalent to the familiar quasi-chemical approximation is obtained and (2) this procedure yields an expression for Φ_N that can be written as a sum of pair potentials and thus compared directly with the random mixing approximation. Moreover, unless some type of restraint is introduced at this point the resulting expressions for the pair distribution functions will not, in the limit of a crystalline-lattice configuration, satisfy the condition that all lattice sites must be equivalent. In the absence of any further knowledge, therefore, we find it convenient to adopt this quasi-crystalline approximation which can be expressed mathematically by the equations

$$\langle \xi_i^s \rangle_{\text{Av}} = x_s; \quad \langle \xi_j^t \rangle_{\text{Av}} = x_t. \tag{27}$$

This will be a particularly bad distortion for configurations in which an interchange of a large and a small molecule will lead to an appreciable repulsion or overlapping between neighboring molecules. However, it is reasonable to postulate that for liquids under normal conditions such configurations do not contribute appreciably to the partition function. If the most important contributions to the partition function come from configurations which are quasi-crystalline then our procedure will lead to a negligible error. In terms of the coefficients in the expansion of ψ, these two conditions can be written in the form

$$\exp[-\beta w_{00}] = (1 - x_t) \exp[-\beta w_{10}] + x_t \exp[\beta(w_{11} - w_{10} - w_{01})] \tag{28a}$$

$$\exp[-\beta w_{00}] = (1 - x_s) \exp[-\beta w_{01}] + x_s \exp[\beta(w_{11} - w_{10} - w_{01})]. \tag{28b}$$

By means of Eqs. (24), (28a), and (28b), the coefficients w_{10}, w_{01}, and w_{00} may be expressed in terms of w_{11}.

$$\begin{aligned} \exp[\beta w_{10}] &= x_s/(\exp[-\beta w_{00}] + x_s - 1) \\ \exp[\beta w_{01}] &= x_t/(\exp[-\beta w_{00}] + x_t - 1) \\ \exp[-\beta w_{00}] &= \tfrac{1}{2}(\eta + p \exp[-\beta w] - p + 1) \end{aligned} \tag{29}$$

where

$$\eta = \{q^2 + (1 - p^2 - q^2) \exp[-\beta w] + p^2 \exp[-2\beta w]\}^{\frac{1}{2}}$$

$$p = x_s + x_t - 1$$

$$q = x_s - x_t.$$

For simplicity in notation, the symbol $w_{11}(s,t)$ has been replaced by w. From Eqs. (29), (21), and (16) we obtain

$$\langle \xi_i^s \xi_j^t \rangle_{\text{Av}} = \frac{(u^2 - q^2) \exp[\beta w]}{2(u + 1 - p)} \tag{30}$$

$$u = \eta + p \exp[-\beta w].$$

The integral of $\langle \xi_i^s \xi_j^t \rangle_{\text{Av}}$ can now be evaluated by elementary means. After some algebraic transformations this leads to the following expression for Φ_N.

$$\Phi_N = \sum_{i<j} \varphi(ij)$$

$$\varphi(ij) = \tfrac{1}{2} \sum_{s=1}^{r} \sum_{t=1}^{r} G_{st}(ij) J_{st}(ij) + \sum_{s=1}^{r} x_s V_{ss}(ij)$$

$$G_{st}(ij) = \frac{1}{\beta w}\left\{ \ln\left[\frac{u+1-p}{2}\right] - \frac{1+p-q}{2} \ln\left[\frac{u-q}{1+p-q}\right] - \frac{1+p+q}{2} \ln\left[\frac{u+q}{1+p+q}\right]\right\} \tag{31}$$

$$J_{ss} = 0 \quad (s = 1, 2, \cdots, r)$$

and where [see Eq. (26)],

$$w = w(st) = \frac{-1}{(1-x_s)(1-x_t)} \{V_{st} - \sum_u x_u(V_{su} + V_{ut}) + \sum_u \sum_v x_u x_v V_{uv}\}.$$

We remark that for a binary mixture the parameter w reduces to

$$w(12) = -J$$
$$J = 2V_{12} - V_{11} - V_{22} \tag{32}$$

which is the usual energy parameter encountered in the order-disorder theory of solids.

It is anticipated that considerations of the type presented here will prove to be especially valuable for calculations at high densities when used with the Monte Carlo methods[21] for calculating the thermodynamic properties of a pure liquid.

In order to illustrate qualitatively the effect of introducing this type of approximation for the pair correlations we consider a 50–50 binary mixture of $CO_2(1)$ and $CO(2)$. We will assume that a Lennard-Jones 6–12 potential,

$$V(R) = 4\epsilon\left[\left(\frac{\sigma}{R}\right)^{12} - \left(\frac{\sigma}{R}\right)^{6}\right] \tag{33}$$

with the parameters

$$\epsilon_{11}/k = 189°\text{K}; \qquad \sigma_{11} = 4.486 \text{ A}$$

$$\epsilon_{22}/k = 100.2°\text{K}; \quad \sigma_{22} = 3.763 \text{ A}$$

adequately describes the interactions between like molecules of species 1 and 2, respectively. We further assume that for the interaction between unlike

[21] M. N. Rosenbluth and A. W. Rosenbluth, *J. Chem. Phys.* **22**, 881 (1954).

molecules we can use Eq. (33) with the parameters,

$$\epsilon_{12} = (\epsilon_{11}\epsilon_{22})^{\frac{1}{2}}; \quad \sigma_{12} = \tfrac{1}{2}(\sigma_{11} + \sigma_{22}). \tag{34}$$

The results of this calculation are given in Table I. Since the pair correlation approximation is temperature dependent we have arbitrarily chosen 300°K for the purpose of illustration. The calculations were carried out on the following basis.

For a binary 50–50 mixture ($x_1 = x_2 = \frac{1}{2}$) the parameters p and q are identically zero. Therefore the pseudo pair potential function reduces to

$$\begin{aligned} \varphi_{\text{p.c.}} &= \tfrac{1}{2}(V_{11} + V_{22}) + G_{12}J_{12} \\ G_{12} &= -\frac{1}{\beta J_{12}} \ln[(e^{\gamma} + 1)/2] + \tfrac{1}{2} \\ \gamma &= \beta J_{12}/2 \end{aligned} \tag{35}$$

TABLE I. A comparison of the "random mixing" and "pair correlation" potential functions for a equimolar binary mixture of CO_2 and CO. $T = 300$°K.

R A	$\varphi_{\text{r.m.}}/\bar{\epsilon}$	$(\varphi_{\text{p.c.}} - \varphi_{\text{r.m.}})/\bar{\epsilon}$
4.0	3.432463	−0.936860
4.1	1.794707	−0.482336
4.2	0.703155	−0.237773
4.3	−0.014119	−0.112791
4.4	−0.474713	−0.050868
4.5	−0.759464	−0.021622
4.6	−0.924155	−0.008185
4.7	−1.007417	−0.002614
4.8	−1.036048	−0.000575
4.9	−1.028648	−0.000016
5.0	−0.998112	−0.000098
5.1	−0.953371	−0.000344
5.2	−0.900564	−0.000546
5.3	−0.843874	−0.000764
5.4	−0.786127	−0.000825
5.5	−0.729178	−0.000992
5.6	−0.674218	−0.000890
5.7	−0.621968	−0.000847
5.8	−0.572831	−0.000789
5.9	−0.526984	−0.000720
6.0	−0.484458	−0.000647

where the subscript p.c. denotes the pair correlation approximation. Similarly the random mixing approximation (denoted by r.m.) is given by

$$\varphi_{\text{r.m.}} = \tfrac{1}{4}(V_{11} + V_{22} + 2V_{12}). \tag{36}$$

Thus we find that

$$(\varphi_{\text{p.c.}} - \varphi_{\text{r.m.}})/\bar{\epsilon} = -\frac{k}{\bar{\epsilon}}\,[J_{12}/4k + T\ln(e^{-\gamma} + 1)/2] \tag{37}$$

where $\bar{\epsilon}$ is an average energy depth chosen to obtain a convenient scale for φ. For the calculations summarized in Table I, $\bar{\epsilon}/k = 126.2$°K.

The correction term to the random mixing approximation is always negative. The minimum ϵ in the pair potential function is lowered by approximately 0.5% and the effective collision diameter σ is reduced from 4.298 A to 4.279 A, again a change of less than 0.5%. Thus we see that the higher order approximations have little effect in the neighborhood of the minimum of the potential curve. However, the pair correlation function is not completely specified by the two parameters ϵ and σ. Further examination of Table I shows that the correction terms become appreciable when the repulsive forces are dominant. For example when $\varphi_{\text{r.m.}}$ is approximately equal to kT we obtain a correction of about 27% when pair correlations are introduced.

From this analysis we conclude that the random mixing approximation is adequate for simple mixtures like CO_2 and CO under atmospheric pressure. However, at high densities where the repulsive forces are important one must consider the higher order approximations.

APPENDIX A

The development given in Sec. III involves the evaluation of the moments M_k defined by Eq. (10). Although a general formulation for all k has not been developed, we can readily express the first two moments M_1 and M_2 as functions of the composition variables, $x_1, \cdots, x_r$, where x_s is the mole fraction of species s.

Considering the intermolecular potential V_N as a function of the occupation variables [see Eq. (3)] and the definition of M_k, Eq. (10), we can form

$$M_1 = \tfrac{1}{2} \sum_{i,j}{}^{*} \sum_{s,t=1}^{r} [\xi_i{}^s \xi_j{}^t]_{\text{Av}} V_{st}(i,j) \tag{A-1}$$

and

$$\begin{aligned} M_2 = \tfrac{1}{4} \sum_{i,j,k,l}{}^{*} \sum_{s,t,u,v} [\xi_i{}^s \xi_j{}^t \xi_k{}^u \xi_l{}^v]_{\text{Av}} V_{st}(i,j) V_{uv}(kl) \\ + \sum_{i,j,k}{}^{*} \sum_{s,t,u} [\xi_i{}^s \xi_j{}^t \xi_k{}^u]_{\text{Av}} V_{st}(i,j) V_{tu}(j,k) \\ + \tfrac{1}{2} \sum_{i,j}{}^{*} \sum_{s,t} [\xi_i{}^s \xi_j{}^t]_{\text{Av}} [V_{st}(i,j)]^2 \end{aligned} \tag{A-2}$$

where $\sum^*$ represents a summation over all the indicated indices with no two of the indices allowed to be equal. In obtaining this expression for M_2, Eq. (A-2), we have made use of the relation

$$\xi_i{}^u \xi_j{}^t = \xi_j{}^t \delta_{tu}$$

where δ_{tu} is the Kronecker delta. This equation expresses the restriction that only one type of molecule can occupy a given position. We find, therefore, that one has to consider the following unweighted averages,

$$[\xi_i{}^s \xi_j{}^t \cdots \xi_k{}^u]_{\text{Av}} = \frac{\prod_{s=1}^{r} N_s!}{N!} \sum_{(\xi)}{}' \xi_i{}^s \xi_j{}^t \cdots \xi_k{}^u \tag{A-3}$$

where $i, j, \cdots, k$ are n distinct positions. The product of ξ's which occurs in each term in Eq. (A-3) will be unity if position i is occupied by a molecule of type s, position j by a molecule of type t, etc. Otherwise, it is zero. Therefore, the sum over configurations is exactly equal to the number of ways in which $N - n$ specified positions may be distributed among the molecules not occupying positions $k, j, \cdots, k$. When $s, t, \cdots, u$ are all distinct, the solution to this combinatorial problem is given by

$$\frac{(N-n)!}{(N_s-1)!(N_t-1)!\cdots(N_u-1)! \prod_{v \neq s,t,\cdots,u} N_v!}. \tag{A-4}$$

If $N \gg n$, we may write as an approximation,

$$[\xi_i{}^s \xi_j{}^t \cdots \xi_k{}^u]_{\text{Av}} \cong x_s x_t \cdots x_u. \tag{A-5}$$

In case some of the positions $(i, j, \cdots, k)$ are occupied by molecules of the same type (i.e., two or more of the indexes $s, t, \cdots, u$ are equal), we find that Eq. (A-5) still holds when the assumption, $N_s \gg n$ for all s, is valid.

From Eqs. (A-1), (A-2), and (A-5) we then obtain

$$M_1 = \tfrac{1}{2} \sum_{i,j}{}^* \sum_{s,t=1}^{r} x_s x_t V_{st}(ij) \tag{A-6}$$

and

$$M_2 = \tfrac{1}{4} \sum_{i,j,k,l}{}^* \sum_{s,t,u,v} x_s x_t x_u x_v V_{st}(ij) V_{uv}(jk) + \sum_{i,j,k}{}^* \sum_{s,t,u} x_s x_t x_u V_{st}(ij) V_{tu}(jk)$$
$$+ \tfrac{1}{2} \sum_{i,j}{}^* \sum_{s,t} x_s x_t [V_{st}(ij)]^2. \tag{A-7}$$

With these expressions for M_1 and M_2, together with Eq. (12) we can calculate λ_1 and λ_2. The result is given by

$$\lambda_1 = M_1 = \tfrac{1}{2} \sum_{i,j}{}^* \sum_{s,t} x_s x_t V_{st}(ij) \tag{A-8}$$

and

$$\lambda_2 = M_2 - M_1{}^2 = \sum_{i,j,k}{}^* \sum_{s,t,u} x_s x_t x_u V_{st}(ij) \times \{V_{tu}(jk) - \sum_v x_v V_{uv}(jk)\}$$
$$+ \tfrac{1}{2} \sum_{i,j}{}^* \sum_{s,t} x_s x_t V_{st}(ij) \times \{V_{st}(ij) - \sum_u \sum_v x_u x_v V_{uv}(ij)\}. \tag{A-9}$$

Equations (13) and (14) can then be obtained directly from Eqs. (A-8) and (A-9).

APPENDIX B

(1) In the development of Eq. (20) we encounter the problem of computing the logarithm of the total number of configurations, $\ln \Omega(s,t)$, consistent with the specified values of $\xi_i{}^s$, $\xi_j{}^t$. Therefore we write,

$$\ln \Omega(s,t) = \xi_i^s \xi_j^t \ln \Omega_{11} + \xi_i^s(1 - \xi_j^t) \ln \Omega_{10} + \xi_j^t(1 - \xi_i^s) \ln \Omega_{01} + (1 - \xi_i^s)(1 - \xi_j^t) \ln \Omega_{00} \tag{B-1}$$

where

Ω_{11} equals the number of configurations consistent with having a molecule of type s at position i and a molecule of type t at position j.

Ω_{10} equals the number of configurations consistent with having a molecule of type s at position i and *not* having a molecule of type t at position j.

Ω_{01} equals the number of configurations consistent with *not* having a molecule of type s at position i but having a molecule of type t at position j.

Ω_{00} equals the number of configurations consistent with the condition that position i cannot be occupied by a molecule of type s and position j cannot be occupied by a molecule of type t.

These four terms cover all possible cases and are mutually exclusive. For a given ξ_i^s and ξ_j^t only one term is nonzero. When $s \neq t$ the individual Ω's are given by

$$\begin{aligned}
\Omega_{11} &= \frac{(N-2)!}{\prod\limits_{u \neq s,t} N_u!(N_s - 1)!(N_t - 1)!} \\
\Omega_{10} &= \frac{(N-1)!}{\prod\limits_{u \neq s} N_u!(N_s - 1)!} - \Omega_{11} \\
\Omega_{01} &= \frac{(N-1)!}{\prod\limits_{u \neq t} N_u!(N_t - 1)!} - \Omega_{11} \\
\Omega_{00} &= \frac{N!}{\prod\limits_{u} N_u!} - \Omega_{10} - \Omega_{01} - \Omega_{11}.
\end{aligned} \tag{B-2}$$

The form of Ω_{10}, for example, was obtained by first computing the number of configurations consistent with the condition that position i is occupied by a molecule of type s, and then subtracting the number of configurations in which position i is occupied by a molecule of types s and position j is occupied by a molecule of type t. The other expressions were obtained in a similar manner. When Eqs. (B-1) and (B-2) are combined and we assume that

$$N_s - 1 \cong N_s \quad \text{for all } s$$

we obtain after some algebraic rearrangement,

$$\ln \Omega(s,t) = \ln(1 - x_s)(1 - x_t) + \xi_i^s \ln \frac{x_s}{1 - x_s} + \xi_j^t \ln \frac{x_t}{1 - x_t} + \ln \frac{N!}{\prod\limits_u N_u!}. \tag{B-3}$$

Equation (20) is then obtained by forming

$$\ln\{\Omega(st) \prod_u N_u!/N!\}. \tag{B-4}$$

(2) We propose here to outline the calculation which leads to Eq. (26). The intermolecular potential V_N can be written in a manner which explicitly

displays its dependence upon the variables $\xi_i{}^s$ and $\xi_j{}^t$. When this is done, Eq. (25) can be written in the form,

$$\langle V_N(\xi_i{}^s,\xi_j{}^t)\rangle_{\mathrm{Av}} = \xi_i{}^s\xi_j{}^t V_{st}(ij)$$

$$+ \xi_i{}^s\{ \sum_{k\neq i,j} \sum_{u=1}^{r} [\xi_k{}^u]_{\mathrm{Av}}{}^{(s,t)} V_{su}(ik) + \sum_{\substack{u=1\\ \neq t}}^{r} [\xi_j{}^u]_{\mathrm{Av}}{}^{(s,t)} V_{su}(ij)\}$$

$$+ \xi_j{}^t\{ \sum_{k\neq i,j} \sum_{u=1}^{r} [\xi_k{}^u]_{\mathrm{Av}}{}^{(s,t)} V_{tu}(jk) + \sum_{\substack{u=1\\ \neq s}}^{r} [\xi_i{}^u]_{\mathrm{Av}}{}^{(s,t)} V_{tu}(ij)\}$$

$$+ \sum_{\substack{k<l\\ \neq ij}} \sum_{u,v=1}^{r} [\xi_k{}^u\xi_l{}^v]_{\mathrm{Av}}{}^{(s,t)} V_{uv}(kl) + \sum_{\substack{u=1\\ \neq s}}^{r} \sum_{\substack{v=1\\ \neq t}}^{r} [\xi_i{}^u\xi_j{}^t]_{\mathrm{Av}}{}^{(s,t)} V_{u,v}(ij) + O(\beta) \quad \text{(B-5)}$$

where

$$[y]_{\mathrm{Av}}{}^{(s,t)} = \frac{1}{\Omega} \sum_{\{\xi\}}{}'' y$$

indicates an unweighted average of y over all configurations consistent with the given values of $\xi_i{}^s$ and $\xi_j{}^t$.

The unweighted average value of a function of the occupation variables for positions different from either i or j is independent of the specified values of $\xi_i{}^s$ and $\xi_j{}^t$. This may be verified by enumerating in detail the various possible cases and counting the necessary number of configurations. However, this result becomes evident when one realizes that, since the averages are unweighted, a specified occupation of the positions i and j does not influence, through molecular interactions, the average occupation of neighboring positions. For this case, therefore, we are essentially considering a system composed of $N - 2$ molecules with a composition which differs negligibly from the original composition. Explicitly, we find

$$[\xi_k{}^u]_{\mathrm{Av}}{}^{(s,t)} \cong x_u \quad (u = 1, \cdots, r); \quad k \neq i, j \quad \text{(B-6)}$$

and

$$[\xi_k{}^u\xi_l{}^v]_{\mathrm{Av}}{}^{(s,t)} \cong x_u x_v \quad (u, v = 1, \cdots, r); \quad k, l \neq i, j.$$

However, the average value of a function of the occupation variables for position i or j does depend upon the specified values of $\xi_i{}^s$ and $\xi_j{}^t$.

Examining each case separately, we find first,

$$[\xi_j{}^u]_{\mathrm{Av}}{}^{(s,t)} \cong (1 - \xi_j{}^t) \frac{N_u}{N - N_t} = (1 - \xi_j{}^t) \frac{x_u}{1 - x_t} \quad (u \neq t) \quad \text{(B-7)}$$

which is obtained by considering the configurations in which the $N - N_t$ molecules not of type t can occupy position j. This average is only nonzero when position j is not occupied by a molecule of type t. In a similar manner we have

$$[\xi_i{}^u]_{\mathrm{Av}}{}^{(s,t)} \cong (1 - \xi_i{}^s) \frac{x_u}{1 - x_s} \quad (u \neq s) \quad \text{(B-8)}$$

and

$$[\xi_i{}^u\xi_j{}^v]_{\mathrm{Av}}{}^{(s,t)} \cong (1 - \xi_i{}^s)(1 - \xi_j{}^t) \frac{x_u}{1 - x_s} \frac{x_v}{1 - x_t}. \quad \text{(B-9)}$$

When Eqs. (B-6) through (B-9) are substituted into Eq. (B-5) we obtain

$$\langle V_N(\xi_i^s,\xi_j^t)\rangle_{\text{Av}} = W_{00} + \xi_i^s W_{10} + \xi_j^t W_{01} + \xi_i^s \xi_j^t W_{11}$$

$$W_{00} = \sum_{\substack{k<l \\ \neq i,j}} \sum_{u,v} x_u x_v V_{uv}(k,l) + \sum_{u\neq s} \sum_{v\neq t} \frac{x_u}{1-x_s}\frac{x_v}{1-x_t} V_{uv}(ij)$$

$$W_{01}(t,s) = W_{10}(s,t) = \sum_{k\neq i,j} \sum_{u} x_u V_{su}(jk) + \sum_{v\neq t} \frac{x_v}{1-x_t} V_{sv}(ij) - \sum_{u\neq s} \sum_{v\neq t} \frac{x_u}{1-x_s}\frac{x_v}{1-x_t} V_{uv}(ij) \tag{B-10}$$

$$W_{11} = V_{st}(ij) - \sum_{v\neq t} \frac{x_v}{1-x_t} V_{sv}(ij) - \sum_{u\neq s} \frac{x_u}{1-x_s} V_{tu}(ij) + \sum_{u\neq s} \sum_{v\neq t} \frac{x_u}{1-x_s}\frac{x_v}{1-x_t} V_{uv}(ij).$$

Neglecting terms of 0 (β) we can carry out the integration indicated in Eq. (21) to obtain the function ψ. Comparing the result with Eq. (23) we obtain the three parameters w_{10}, w_{01}, and w_{11} given by Eq. (26).

ADDENDUM TO PAPER NUMBER 9

The general theory outlined in this paper has been examined in detail by Fickett[1] in connection with his studies of the detonation properties of condensed explosives. In this study he calculated several examples of the pair correlation approximation [Eq. (31) of paper number 142] on an IBM 7090 computer. An interesting comparison of the various theories for an effective single potential function for mixtures in which the molecules interact with a Lennard-Jones pair potential can be found in Fig. 3.4 (page 51) of the Fickett report. Qualitatively the effective potential given by Eq. (31) [paper number 142] yields an appropriate representation of both the repulsive and attractive parts of the interactions. However, because of its complicated nature it has not received extensive use.

[1] W. Fickett, Los Alamos Scientific Laboratory Report, LA-2712 (1962).

Theory of Multi-Component Fluid Mixtures
II. A Corresponding States Treatment*

PETER J. WOJTOWICZ,† *Sterling Chemistry Laboratory, Yale University, New Haven, Connecticut*
ZEVI W. SALSBURG, *Department of Chemistry, The Rice Institute, Houston, Texas*
AND
JOHN G. KIRKWOOD, *Sterling Chemistry Laboratory Yale University, New Haven, Connecticut*

(Received November 8, 1956)

The theoretical basis for a theorem of corresponding states for mixtures is examined in a rigorous manner by the use of statistical mechanics. With the aid of the general theory of mixtures presented in a previous paper, the theorem of corresponding states is found to be a consequence of the following assumptions: (a) the internal molecular partition functions depend only on the temperature, (b) the system is in a condition of random mixing, and (c) the several intermolecular interactions can be described by a set of pair-potentials of the same analytical form.

In addition to providing a firm theoretical foundation for the corresponding states treatments of Prigogine *et al.* and Scott, several new approaches to the use of corresponding states in the statistical thermodynamics of mixtures are also presented. In particular, the chemical potentials in binary mixtures of molecules of equal size, and of unequal sizes, are developed. The coefficients in the Margules expansion of the activity coefficients are found to be expressible as functions of the intermolecular interaction parameters and certain experimentally determined thermodynamic properties of the pure components.

The relationships of the Regular solution and Conformal solution theories to the present development are also demonstrated.

I. INTRODUCTION

In recent years the theorem of corresponding states has assumed an increasingly important role as a basis for the theoretical treatment of nonelectrolyte solutions. The first application of this theorem was made by Longuet-Higgins[1–3] in the first-order perturbation treatment of Conformal solutions. More recently Prigogine, Bellemans, and Englert-Chwoles,[4] and Rice[5] have assumed the existence of a theorem of corresponding states for

---

* This paper is part of a dissertation submitted by Peter J. Wojtowicz in partial fulfillment of the requirements for the degree of Doctor of Philosophy in Chemistry at Yale University.

† National Science Foundation Predoctoral Fellow, 1953–1956. Present address: Radio Corporation of America, RCA Laboratories, Princeton, New Jersey.

[1] H. C. Longuet-Higgins, *Proc. Roy. Soc.* (*London*) **A205**, 247 (1951).

[2] D. Cook and H. C. Longuet-Higgins, *Proc. Roy. Soc.* (*London*) **A209**, 28 (1951).

[3] W. B. Brown and H. C. Longuet-Higgins, *Proc. Roy. Soc.* (*London*) **A209**, 416 (1951).

[4] Prigogine, Bellemans, and Englert-Chwoles, *J. Chem. Phys.* **24**, 518 (1956).

[5] S. A. Rice, *J. Chem. Phys.* **24**, 357, 1283 (1956); *Ann. N.Y. Acad. Sci.* **65**, 33 (1956).

the cell partition functions of molecules in solution. Scott,[6] on the other hand, has assumed this theorem for mixtures in a manner somewhat independent of the cell model. The results of the above theories have been found to agree favorably with experiment, and it is quite clear at the present time that the corresponding states treatments will prove to be of great utility in the practical computation of the thermodynamic properties of fluid mixtures. These treatments are especially attractive since they form the first realistic method for obtaining the properties of mixtures from the experimentally determined properties of pure components.

Although these theories have been shown to be successful in their predictions of experimental facts, their relation to rigorous molecular theory has not been established. Moreover, the use of the corresponding states theorem has not, as yet, been satisfactorily divorced from the cell-theory point of view. The main purpose of this investigation, therefore, is to demonstrate the validity of the principle of corresponding states for mixtures by deriving this theorem from fundamental statistical mechanics by the use of certain general assumptions and mathematical approximations. Several new approaches to the use of corresponding states in the formulation of the statistical thermodynamics of mixtures shall also be indicated.

In a previous communication,[7] we have considered the problem of multicomponent fluid mixtures in a general way by the use of statistical mechanics and several devices from solid state order-disorder theory. The multicomponent configurational partition function is reduced to a form corresponding to a system of only one component. The concept of the "pseudo-potential" is introduced, and the dependence of this quantity on the true intermolecular potentials, the composition, and the temperature is determined. Several mathematical approximations to the formal theory that are amenable to numerical computation are also developed. In particular, a certain approximation (equivalent to the assumption of random-mixing) is found to yield an especially simple form of pseudo potential. Using these results of I, we shall show in this paper that the principle of corresponding states for mixtures is a natural consequence of the following general assumptions; (a) the internal molecular partition functions depend only on the temperature, (b) the solution is in the condition of random-mixing, and (c) the various intermolecular interactions can be described by a set of pair potentials of similar but restricted form. In addition, we shall also describe several equivalent ways in which this principle may be stated with regard to the thermodynamic functions of the mixture and pure components. The chemical potential for the case of binary mixtures will be treated in some detail. A general method will be given for obtaining the coefficients appearing in the Margules expansion of this quantity. The coefficient of the first term will be calculated explicitly.

In the derivation of the formal mixture theory described in I, it was sufficient to assume that the potentials of intermolecular force acting on the system could be written as a sum of pair potentials. Here, however, it is necessary to restrict the form of potentials more severely. In order to establish the principle of corresponding states, all the pair potentials must be of the same general form, namely $\epsilon\gamma(R/a)$, where ϵ and a are characteristic energy

---

[6] R. L. Scott, *J. Chem. Phys.* **25**, 193 (1956).

[7] Salsburg, Wojtowicz, and Kirkwood, *J. Chem. Phys.* **26**, 1553 (1957); hereafter referred to as I.

and size parameters, different for the several interactions, and $\gamma(R/a)$ is the same function of the reduced intermolecular distance, R/a for all interactions. The potentials acting between spherical nonpolar molecules are of this type. In the discussion of the thermodynamic applications, however, the presentation will be limited to potentials of the type $\epsilon g(R)$; all components have the same molecular size. This restriction is made for the following reasons, primarily, the mathematical details will be less complex, there being no need to consider unequal size parameters. The basic reasoning behind the calculation will be easier to follow. Secondly, it is only for molecules of reasonably equal size and spherical symmetry that the condition of random mixing can be expected to obtain. The final equations of a similar development for mixtures of molecules of unequal sizes (Lennard-Jones potentials) will be given, however, although the results must be considered applicable only in so far as departures from random mixing can be neglected.

Before beginning the detailed mathematical considerations, it is worthwhile to examine here the sort of results which have been found using the corresponding states principle. The forms obtained for the chemical potential in particular serve as good examples of the variety of practical problems that can be treated by these methods.

For binary mixtures the chemical potential of one of the components (say that of component one) may be expressed as

$$\begin{aligned} \mu_1(T,p,x_1) &= \mu_1{}^0(T,p) + RT \ln f_1 x_1, \\ RT \ln f_1 &= A_{12} x_2{}^2 + A_{13} x_2{}^3 + \cdots, \end{aligned} \tag{1}$$

where $\mu_1{}^0$ is the chemical potential of pure 1 at the same temperature and pressure as that of the mixture, and f_1 is the activity coefficient of component 1, the logarithm of which we have represented as a power series (Margules expansion) in the mole fraction of component 2. The coefficients in the Margules expansion are found to be expressible as functions of the intermolecular interaction parameters and the thermodynamic properties of the pure components (at the *same* temperature and pressure as the mixture). The first coefficient, A_{12}, has been developed for mixtures of molecules of equal and of unequal sizes.

For mixtures of molecules of equal size the coefficient A_{12} is found to be given by the following:

$$A_{12}(T,p) = 2w_1[TC_{v1}{}^e + v_1\kappa_1(p - T\alpha_1/\kappa_1)^2] + u_1\Delta E_1{}^v, \tag{2}$$

where α_1, κ_1, and v_1 are the coefficient of expansion, the isothermal compressibility, and the molar volume, respectively, of the pure component one, at the same T and p as that of the mixture. $\Delta E_1{}^v$ is the internal energy of vaporization from pure liquid 1 to its vapor in the ideal gas state, while $C_{v1}{}^e$ is the excess heat capacity at constant volume, equal to $-(\partial \Delta E_1{}^v/\partial T)_v$. The parameters w_1 and u_1 are certain functions of the interaction parameters, and are fully described in Sec. III. For mixtures of molecules of unequal sizes A_{12} is given by

$$\begin{aligned} A_{12}(T,p) = \tfrac{1}{2}\{&(D_1' + D_1{}^2)\Delta E_1{}^v - B_1'(pv_1 - RT) \\ &+ D_1{}^2(TC_{v1}{}^e + v_1\kappa_1[p - T\alpha_1/\kappa_1]^2) \\ &+ B_1{}^2(p\kappa_1 - 1)pv_1 + 2B_1D_1(T\alpha_1 - p\kappa_1)pv_1\}, \end{aligned} \tag{3}$$

where α_1, κ_1, v_1, $\Delta E_1{}^v$, and $C_{v1}{}^0$ have the same significance as in Eq. (2), and B_1, B_1', D_1, and D_1' are certain functions of the interaction parameters for this case, and are given in detail in section IV. Thus the chemical potential and hence all other thermodynamic partial molal quantities may now be determined from experimental data on the pure components alone. Equations (2) and (3) have been written in forms which are most convenient for practical computations. Other representations are possible, and in the case of Eq. (2), an equivalent expression has been obtained, which, as shall be shown later, appears to lend considerable insight into the theoretical interpretation of the Regular solution[8] hypothesis.

II. PRINCIPLE OF CORRESPONDING STATES

In this section the principle of corresponding states will be obtained from the general mixture theory of I by the incorporation of the several assumptions enumerated in the previous section. A brief review of the pertinent results of I will be given first. The principle will then be derived for mixtures of molecules of equal size, and the application of these results to thermodynamics will be given.

The system in which we are interested is a fluid composed of N molecules (N is Avogadro's number so that we treat a mean mole of mixture) of r different species occupying a volume v. We let N_s be the number of molecules of species s ($s = 1, \cdots, r$) in the system, and let x_s be the mole fraction, N_s/N, of species s. Then, if the internal degrees of freedom of the molecules are unaffected by the configurational state of the mixture (assumption *a*), the theory of the petit canonical ensemble gives the mean molar Helmholtz free energy as

$$A(T,v,\mathbf{x}) = \sum_{s=1}^{r} x_s[RT \ln x_s + A_s^*(T)] - kT \ln Z_N,$$

$$A_s^*(T) = -RT \ln\left[\frac{e}{N}\left(\frac{2\pi m_s kT}{h^2}\right)^{\frac{3}{2}} \psi_s(T)\right], \tag{4}$$

$$Z_N = \int^v \cdots \int^v \exp[-\beta V_N] \prod_{k=1}^{N} dv_k,$$

where V_N is the potential of intermolecular force acting between the molecules, and is a function of the intermolecular distances. The function $\psi_s(T)$ is the internal molecular partition function of species s, and m_s is the molecular mass of species s. h is Planck's constant, k is Boltzmann's constant, T is the thermodynamic temperature, and $\beta = 1/kT$. $\mathbf{N}$ and $\mathbf{x}$ denote the sets $\{N_1, \cdots, N_r\}$ and $\{x_1, \cdots, x_r\}$, respectively. The free energy is seen to be decomposed into two parts, the first part dependent on the temperature alone, and a second part which depends on the configurational state of the system through the Gibbs phase integral, Z_N. The major problem in mixture theories is, of course, the evaluation of that part of the free energy which is dependent on Z_N.

According to I, the multicomponent Z_N may be treated in the following way. We introduce a set of position vectors, $\{\mathbf{R}\} = \mathbf{R}_1, \cdots, \mathbf{R}_N$, which give

[8] J. H. Hildebrand and R. L. Scott, *The Solubility of Nonelectrolytes* (Reinhold Publishing Corporation, New York, 1950), third edition.

the locations of the N molecules in the system without regard to their chemical identity. Associated with each vector $\mathbf{R}_i$ is a set of occupation parameters, $\xi_i^1, \cdots, \xi_i^r$ which give the identity of the molecule actually located at $\mathbf{R}_i$. ξ_i^s is defined to be unity if a molecule of species s is at $\mathbf{R}_i$, and zero otherwise. We let $\{\boldsymbol{\xi}\}$ denote the set of Nr parameters $\xi_1^1, \cdots, \xi_1^r, \cdots, \xi_N^1, \cdots, \xi_N^r$. Specification of $\{\mathbf{R}\}$ and $\{\boldsymbol{\xi}\}$ completely determines the configuration of the system. In the pair potential approximation the intermolecular potential energy for the configuration $\{\mathbf{R}\}$, $\{\boldsymbol{\xi}\}$ can then be written

$$V_N(\mathbf{R},\boldsymbol{\xi}) = \sum_{i<j}^{N} \sum_{s,t}^{r} \xi_i^s \xi_j^t V_{st}(R_{ij}), \tag{5}$$

where $V_{st}(R_{ij})$ is the potential acting between two molecules of species s and t separated by the distance $R_{ij} = |\mathbf{R}_j - \mathbf{R}_i|$. The Gibbs phase integral may now be obtained by forming the function $\exp[-\beta V_N(\mathbf{R}, \boldsymbol{\xi})]$ and summing over all distinguishable configurations, that is summing over all values of the set of parameters $\{\boldsymbol{\xi}\}$, and then integrating over the configuration space of the set $\{\mathbf{R}\}$. Following I, Z_N may then be expressed as

$$Z_N = \int^v \cdots \int^v \exp[-\beta\Phi_N(\mathbf{R})] \prod_{k=1}^{N} dv_k, \tag{6}$$

$$\exp[-\beta\Phi_N(\mathbf{R})] = \frac{\prod_{s=1}^{r} N_s!}{N!} \sum_{\{\boldsymbol{\xi}\}} \exp[-\beta V_N(\mathbf{R},\boldsymbol{\xi})]$$

in terms of the pseudo single component potential $\Phi_N(\mathbf{R})$. Thus the Gibbs phase integral is reduced to a form corresponding to that for a single component system having the intermolecular potential energy $\Phi_N(\mathbf{R})$. The pseudopotential, $\Phi_N(\mathbf{R})$, for a fixed configuration $\{\mathbf{R}\}$, can be determined from the second of Eqs. (6) by the well-known methods employed in the study of cooperative phenomena. Indeed, several mathematical approximations to Φ_N have been constructed and described in I.

For the purpose of this investigation, it is necessary to consider only the lowest approximation to Φ_N. By the use of the moment expansion, it was shown in I that if the mixture could be described as being in a condition of random mixing (assumption b), the pseudo potential assumed the following simple form:

$$\begin{aligned} \Phi_N(\mathbf{R}) &= \sum_{i<j}^{N} \varphi(R_{ij}), \\ \varphi(R_{ij}) &= \sum_{s=1}^{r} \sum_{t=1}^{r} x_s x_t V_{st}(R_{ij}). \end{aligned} \tag{7}$$

That is, $\Phi_N(\mathbf{R})$ becomes a sum of pseudo *pair* potentials which are quadratic functions of the mole fractions, and are temperature independent. The Gibbs phase integral, Eq. (6), is then seen to have the form exactly corresponding to that for a system of one component whose intermolecular *pair* interactions are described by the function $\varphi(R_{ij})$. At high temperatures or when the differences in interaction are not sufficient to alter a random distribution of molecules, the approximation given in Eq. (7) will be adequate. For mixtures which deviate appreciably from random mixing, alternative procedures of higher approximation and greater complexity must be used.[7]

On the basis of Eq. (7) it is possible to establish a principle of corresponding states if the various intermolecular pair potentials acting in the system can all be described by functions of the same form (assumption *c*). In this section the procedure will be considered for mixtures of spherical nonpolar molecules of equal size. The pair potentials for this case are given by

$$V_{st}(R) = \epsilon_{st} g(R), \quad (s, t = 1, \cdots, r), \tag{8}$$

where ϵ_{st} is the characteristic energy parameter for the $s - t$ interaction, and $g(R)$ is the same function of the intermolecular distance R for all interactions. The pseudo pair potential, $\varphi(R)$, may then be written in the same functional form as the real potentials,

$$\varphi(R) = \tilde{\epsilon} g(R), \qquad \tilde{\epsilon} = \sum_{s=1}^{r} \sum_{t=1}^{r} x_s x_t \epsilon_{st}, \tag{9}$$

where $\tilde{\epsilon}$ is the pseudo energy parameter for the mixture. By combining Eqs. (6), (7), and (9), the Gibbs phase integral for the multi-component system at temperature T and volume v may be expressed as

$$Z_N(T,v,\mathbf{x}) = \int^v \cdots \int^v \times \exp\left[-\frac{\tilde{\epsilon}}{kT} \sum_{i<j}^{r} g(R_{ij})\right] dv_1 \cdots dv_N. \tag{10}$$

Moreover, the Gibbs phase integral for a mole of one of the pure components, say component one, at a temperature T_1 and volume v has the form

$$Z_1(T_1,v) = \int^v \cdots \int^v \times \exp\left[-\frac{\epsilon_{11}}{kT_1} \sum_{i<j}^{N} g(R_{ij})\right] dv_1 \cdots dv_N, \tag{11}$$

where the subscripts, 1, refer to quantities for the system of pure component 1. Clearly,

$$Z_N(T,v,\mathbf{x}) = Z_1(T_1,v), \tag{12}$$

if the temperatures of the two systems are related by

$$T_1 = (\epsilon_{11}/\tilde{\epsilon})T. \tag{13}$$

When Eqs. (12) and (13) are satisfied, we say that the mixture and the pure component are in corresponding states, and call T and T_1 corresponding temperatures.

The molar Helmholtz free energy of pure component 1 may be written in the same form as Eq. (4),

$$A_1(T_1,v) = A_1^*(T_1) - kT_1 \ln Z_1(T_1,v). \tag{14}$$

Substituting Eqs. (12) and (14) into Eqs. (4) yields the mean molar Helmholtz free energy of the mixture in terms of the molar free energy of pure 1 (at corresponding temperature, T_1):

$$A(T,v,\mathbf{x}) = \sum_{s=1}^{r} x_s[RT \ln x_s + A_s^*(T)] + \tilde{\epsilon}/\epsilon_{11}[A_1(T_1,v) - A_1^*(T_1)]. \quad (15)$$

Differentiation of Eq. (15) with respect to volume at constant temperature and composition gives the relation between the corresponding pressures of the two systems:

$$p(T,v,\mathbf{x}) = (\tilde{\epsilon}/\epsilon_{11})p_1(T_1,v). \quad (16)$$

Thus by using Eq. (16), the equation of state of mixtures, either liquid or gas, may be determined from a knowledge of the characteristic energy parameters, ϵ_{k1}, and the experimentally determined equation of state of one of the pure components. By adding pv to both sides of Eq. (15), and using Eqs. (13) and (16), the mean molar Gibbs free energy may be obtained,

$$F(T,p,\mathbf{x}) = \sum_{s=1}^{r} x_s[RT \ln x_s + A_s^*(T)] + (\tilde{\epsilon}/\epsilon_{11})[F_1(T_1,p_1) - A_1^*(T_1)], \quad (17)$$

where $F_1(T_1, p_1)$ is the molar Gibbs free energy of pure 1 at the corresponding state, T_1 and p_1. Other thermodynamic functions may be derived from Eqs. (15) and (16) by the appropriate differentiations, as shall be shown later for the more general case of unequal sizes.

Another useful way of expressing the principle of corresponding states is to consider the thermodynamic functions in excess of their ideal gas values. For an ideal system (no intermolecular interactions) the Gibbs phase integral is simply v^N, while its contribution to the free energy is $-RT \ln v$. Thus, for the ideal free energies of the mixture and of pure component 1,

$$A^i(T,v,\mathbf{x}) = \sum_{s=1}^{r} x_s[RT \ln x_s + A_s^*(T)] - RT \ln v, \quad (18)$$

$$A_1^i(T_1,v) = A_1^*(T_1) - RT_1 \ln v.$$

Adding $RT \ln v$ to both sides of Eq. (15), and using (18), the following corresponding states relationship is obtained for the excess free energies of the mixture and pure component 1,

$$A^e(T,v,\mathbf{x}) = (\tilde{\epsilon}/\epsilon_{11})A_1^e(T_1,v), \quad (19)$$

where $A_1^e = A_1 - A_1^i$ and $A^e = A - A^i$. Again, differentiation will yield similar forms for other excess thermodynamic quantities.

III. CHEMICAL POTENTIAL

In this section we shall derive the chemical potentials for a system composed of only two components having equal molecular sizes. The form to be considered is that illustrated by Eq. (1). The chemical potential of component one may be defined in terms of the mean molar Gibbs free energy,

$$\mu_1 = F + (1 - x_1)(\partial F/\partial x_1)_{T,p}. \quad (20)$$

Substitution from Eq. (17) with $r = 2$ yields

$$\mu_1 = RT \ln x_1 + A_1^*(T) + G_1 + (1 - x_1)(\partial G_1/\partial x_1)_{T,p}, \qquad (21)$$

$$G_1 = (\tilde{\epsilon}/\epsilon_{11})[F_1(T_1,p_1) - A_1^*(T_1)].$$

The quantity G_1 and its derivative are expanded, at constant T and p (of the mixture), in a Taylor series about the point $x_1 = 1$:

$$G_1(x_1) = G_1(1) + (1 - x_1)\left(\frac{\partial G_1}{\partial(1 - x_1)}\right)_{T,p}\bigg|_{x_1=1} + \tfrac{1}{2}(1 - x_1)^2\left(\frac{\partial^2 G_1}{\partial(1 - x_1)^2}\right)_{T,p}\bigg|_{x_1=1} + \cdots, \qquad (22)$$

$$\left(\frac{\partial G_1}{\partial x_1}\right)_{T,p} = \left(\frac{\partial G_1}{\partial x_1}\right)_{T,p}\bigg|_{x_1=1} + (1 - x_1)\left(\frac{\partial^2 G_1}{\partial x_1 \partial(1 - x_1)}\right)_{T,p}\bigg|_{x_1=1} + \cdots.$$

Substitution of Eq. (22) in Eq. (21), and use of the relation between mole fractions, $x_1 + x_2 = 1$, gives

$$\mu_1(T,p,x_1) = RT \ln x_1 + A_1^*(T) + G_1(1) - \tfrac{1}{2}x_2^2(\partial^2 G_1/\partial x_1^2)_{T,p}|_{x_1=1} + \cdots. \qquad (23)$$

With the aid of Eqs. (9), (13), and (16), we observe that for $x_1 = 1$,

$$G_1(x_1 = 1) = F_1(T,p) - A_1^*(T). \qquad (24)$$

Since $F_1 = \mu_1^0$, substitution of Eq. (24) in Eq. (23), and comparison with Eq. (1), enables us to write for the coefficient of x_2^2 in the expansion of $RT \ln f_1$,

$$A_{12}(T,p) = -\tfrac{1}{2}(\partial^2 G_1/\partial x_1^2)_{T,p}|_{x_1=1} \qquad (25)$$

Coefficients of terms of higher order in x_2 will be proportional to the higher derivatives of the quantity G_1 (all evaluated at $x_1 = 1$).

The explicit calculation of the coefficient A_{12} will now be presented in some detail. Noting that G_1 is the product of two factors, we have for the first derivative,

$$\left(\frac{\partial G_1}{\partial x_1}\right)_{T,p} = \frac{\tilde{\epsilon}}{\epsilon_{11}}\left\{\frac{d \ln \tilde{\epsilon}}{dx_1}[F_1 - A_1^*] + \left(\frac{\partial}{\partial x_1}[F_1 - A_1^*]\right)_{T,p}\right\}. \qquad (26)$$

Since $[F_1 - A_1^*]$ is an explicit function of T_1 and p_1, we must use the following for the second term in Eq. (25),

$$(\partial/\partial x_1)_{T,p} = (\partial T_1/\partial x_1)_{T,p}(\partial/\partial T_1)_{p_1} + (\partial p_1/\partial x_1)_{T,p}(\partial/\partial p_1)_{T_1}. \qquad (27)$$

But T_1 and p_1 are functions of x_1 through their dependence on $\tilde{\epsilon}$, Eqs. (13) and (16), so that

$$(\partial T_1/\partial x_1)_{T,p} = -T_1(d \ln \tilde{\epsilon}/dx_1),$$

$$(\partial p_1/\partial x_1)_{T,p} = -p_1(d \ln \tilde{\epsilon}/dx_1),$$

and

$$(\partial/\partial x_1)_{T,p} = -(d \ln \tilde{\epsilon}/dx_1) \times [T_1(\partial/\partial T_1)_{p_1} + p_1(\partial/\partial p_1)_{T_1}]. \tag{28}$$

Use of Eq. (28) in Eq. (26) gives

$$(\partial G_1/\partial x_1)_{T,p} = (\tilde{\epsilon}/\epsilon_{11})(d \ln \tilde{\epsilon}/dx_1) \times [F_1 - A_1^* + T_1(S_1 - S_1^*) - p_1 v], \tag{29}$$

where S_1 is the molar entropy of pure 1 at T_1 and p_1, and S_1^* is that portion of the entropy given by $-(dA_1^*/dT_1)$. Collection of terms in the brackets yields the following,

$$(\partial G_1/\partial x_1)_{T,p} = (\tilde{\epsilon}/\epsilon_{11})(d \ln \tilde{\epsilon}/dx_1) \times [E_1(T_1,p_1) - E_1^*(T_1)], \tag{30}$$

where E_1 is the molar internal energy of pure 1, and E_1^* is that part of the internal energy given by $A_1^* + T_1S_1^*$. The quantity in the brackets, however, is just the excess internal energy, since by differentiation of Eq. (18),

$$\left(\frac{\partial(A_1^i/T_1)}{\partial(1/T_1)}\right)_v = E_1^i = E_1^*. \tag{31}$$

By use of the foregoing procedure, the following is obtained for the second derivative:

$$\left(\frac{\partial^2 G_1}{\partial x_1^2}\right)_{T,p} = \frac{\tilde{\epsilon}}{\epsilon_{11}}\left\{E_1^e(T_1,p_1)\left[\frac{d^2 \ln \tilde{\epsilon}}{dx_1^2} + \left(\frac{d \ln \tilde{\epsilon}}{dx_1}\right)^2\right] - \left(\frac{d \ln \tilde{\epsilon}}{dx_1}\right)^2\left[T_1\left(\frac{\partial E_1^e}{\partial T_1}\right)_{p_1} + p_1\left(\frac{\partial E_1^e}{\partial p_1}\right)_{T_1}\right]\right\}. \tag{32}$$

Passing to the limit of $x_1 \to 1$, we note that $\tilde{\epsilon} \to \epsilon_{11}$, $T_1 \to T$, and $p_1 \to p$, so that Eqs. (25) and (32) give, for the desired coefficient,

$$\begin{aligned} A_{12}(T,p) &= 2w_1\left(T\left[\frac{\partial E_1^e}{\partial T}\right)_p + p\left(\frac{\partial E_1^e}{\partial p}\right)_T\right] - u_1 E_1^e, \\ u_1 &= \frac{1}{2}\left[\frac{d^2 \ln \tilde{\epsilon}}{dx_1^2} + \left(\frac{d \ln \tilde{\epsilon}}{dx_1}\right)^2\right]_{x_1=1} = \frac{\epsilon_{11} + \epsilon_{22} - 2\epsilon_{12}}{\epsilon_{11}}, \\ w_1 &= \frac{1}{4}\left(\frac{d \ln \tilde{\epsilon}}{dx_1}\right)^2_{x_1=1} = \left(\frac{\epsilon_{11} - \epsilon_{12}}{\epsilon_{11}}\right)^2, \end{aligned} \tag{33}$$

where E_1^e and its derivatives are now functions of T, p, the temperature and pressure of the mixture. Thus the chemical potential, Eq. (1), has been evaluated as a function of the parameters of the intermolecular interactions and certain thermodynamic properties of the pure components. We remark that the chemical potential of component 2 may be obtained from Eqs. (1) and (33) by interchange of all subscripts 1 and 2.

For the practical computation of the thermodynamic properties of mixtures, a transformed expression for the coefficient A_{12} is more convenient:

$$A_{12}(T,p) = 2w_1[TC_{v_1}{}^e + v_1\kappa_1(p - T\alpha_1/\kappa_1)^2] + u_1\Delta E_1{}^v, \tag{34}$$

where $C_{v_1}{}^e$, α_1, κ_1, and v_1 are the excess heat capacity at constant volume, the coefficient of expansion, the isothermal compressibility, and the molar volume, respectively, of the pure liquid 1 at the T and p of the mixture. $\Delta E_1{}^v$ is the molar internal energy of vaporization of pure liquid 1 to its vapor in the ideal gas state. Equation (34) is obtained from Eq. (33) by the use of the thermodynamic identities

$$\begin{aligned}(\partial E_1{}^e/\partial T)_p &= C_{v_1}{}^e + Tv_1\alpha_1{}^2/\kappa_1 - pv_1\alpha_1,\\ (\partial E_1{}^e/\partial p)_T &= pv_1\kappa_1 - Tv_1\alpha_1,\\ E_1{}^e &= -\Delta E_1{}^v.\end{aligned} \tag{35}$$

If desirable, the terms in the brackets of Eq. (34) may also be replaced by their equivalents:

$$[TC_{p_1}{}^e + pv_1\kappa_1(p - T\alpha_1/\kappa_1)], \tag{36}$$

where $C_{p_1}{}^e$ is the excess heat capacity of pure 1 at constant pressure.

Another form of expression for Eq. (33), which is of interest from the theoretical standpoint, may be obtained from the following considerations. Under the usual assumption that the energy parameter for the mixed interaction is given by $\epsilon_{12} = (\epsilon_{11}\epsilon_{22})^{\frac{1}{2}}$, the parameters u_1 and w_1 of Eq. (33) reduce to

$$u_1 = w_1 = (\epsilon_{11}{}^{\frac{1}{2}} - \epsilon_{22}{}^{\frac{1}{2}})^2/\epsilon_{11}. \tag{37}$$

Now, just as Eqs. (13), (16), and (19), were established between mixture and pure 1, so also Eq. (11) can be used to show that the principle of corresponding states obtains between the pure components, component 1 at T, p, and component 2 at T_2, p_2,

$$\begin{aligned}T_2 &= (\epsilon_{22}/\epsilon_{11})T,\\ p_2 &= (\epsilon_{22}/\epsilon_{11})p,\\ \Delta E_{2v}(T_2,p_2) &= (\epsilon_{22}/\epsilon_{11})\Delta E_1{}^v(T,p).\end{aligned} \tag{38}$$

Substitution of Eq. (37) into Eq. (33) and use of the Eq. (38) yields the following:

$$\begin{aligned}A_{12} = \{[\Delta E_1{}^v]^{\frac{1}{2}} - [\Delta E_2{}^v]^{\frac{1}{2}}\}^2 + 2\{[-T(\partial\Delta E_1{}^v/\partial T)_p]^{\frac{1}{2}}\\ - [-T_2(\partial\Delta E_2{}^v/\partial T_2)_{p2}]^{\frac{1}{2}}\}^2 + 2\{[-p(\partial\Delta E_1{}^v/\partial p)_T]^{\frac{1}{2}}\\ - [-p_2(\partial\Delta E_2{}^v/\partial p_2)_{T2}]^{\frac{1}{2}}\}^2,\end{aligned} \tag{39}$$

where the quantities for component 1 are evaluated at the T and p of the mixture, while those for component 2 are to be evaluated at the corresponding state, T_2 and p_2. The form of Eq. (39) is quite reminiscent of the results obtained from the theory of Regular solutions. Indeed, the Regular solution expression[8] for the activity coefficient (for components of equal molar volumes) may be obtained from Eqs. (1) and (39) by neglecting all terms of $0(x_2^3)$ and all terms containing derivatives of $\Delta E_{1,2}^v$, and by expanding ΔE_2^v in a Taylor series about $T_2 = T$, $p_2 = p$ and ignoring terms of $0(\epsilon_{22} - \epsilon_{11})$:

$$(RT \ln f_1)_{\text{Reg}} = x_2^2\{[\Delta E_1^v]^{\frac{1}{2}} - [\Delta E_2^v]^{\frac{1}{2}}\}^2, \quad (40)$$

where both energy quantities now pertain to the T and p of the mixture. The development leading to Eq. (40), therefore, illustrates to what degree of approximation the Regular solution results are consistent with detailed molecular theory. It is clear that in the limit of vanishing difference of energies of intermolecular interaction, the terms neglected will be of minor importance, and the Regular solution result can be expected to approximate well the actual properties of solutions. For mixtures of nonpolar substances commonly encountered, however, it can be shown that the terms neglected are of the same order of magnitude as those retained.

IV. MIXTURES OF MOLECULES OF UNEQUAL SIZES

We now shall consider mixtures of spherical nonpolar molecules of unequal sizes. All of the details will not be given since the development is entirely analogous to, but more tedious than, the previous considerations concerning the case of equal sizes.

The most commonly used approximation to the potential functions of spherical nonpolar molecules is the Lennard-Jones potential:

$$V_{st}(R) = \epsilon_{st}\gamma(R/a_{st}); \quad (s, t = 1 \cdots r), \quad (41)$$

$$\gamma(y) = 4[y^{-12} - y^{-6}],$$

where ϵ_{st} is the maximum energy of the $s - t$ interaction, and a_{st} is the value of R for which $V_{st}(R) = 0$ (the a_{st} are measures of the molecular sizes). Equation (7) gives the formula for the pseudo pair potential for this case. Written in the same form as Eq. (41), it is given by

$$\varphi(R) = \tilde{\epsilon}\gamma(R/\tilde{a}),$$

$$\tilde{\epsilon} = [\sum_s^r \sum_t^r x_s x_t \epsilon_{st} a_{st}^6]^2 / \sum_s^r \sum_t^r x_s x_t \epsilon_{st} a_{st}^{12}, \quad (42)$$

$$\tilde{a}^6 = \sum_s^r \sum_t^r x_s x_t \epsilon_{st} a_{st}^{12} / \sum_s^r \sum_t^r x_s x_t \epsilon_{st} a_{st}^6,$$

where $\tilde{\epsilon}$ and $\tilde{a}$ are the pseudo energy and size parameters, respectively, for the mixture. The Gibbs phase integrals of the mixture and pure component 1 at temperatures and volumes T, v and T_1, v_1, respectively, may be written as

$$Z_N(T,v,\mathbf{x}) = \int^v \cdots \int^v \times \exp\left[-\frac{\tilde{\epsilon}}{kT}\sum_{i<j}^N \gamma(R_{ij}/\tilde{a})\right] dv_1 \cdots dv_N,$$

$$Z_1(T_1,v_1) = \int^v \cdots \int^{v1} \times \exp\left[-\frac{\epsilon_{11}}{kT_1}\sum_{i<j}^N \gamma(R_{ij}/a_{11})\right] dv_1 \cdots dv_N. \quad (43)$$

It is apparent that

$$Z_N(T,v,\mathbf{x}) = (\tilde{a}/a_{11})^{3N} Z_1(T_1,v_1) \tag{44}$$

when the temperatures and volumes of the two systems are related by

$$\begin{aligned} T_1 &= \epsilon_{11} T/\tilde{\epsilon}, \\ v_1 &= (a_{11}/\tilde{a})^3 v. \end{aligned} \tag{45}$$

The mixture and pure component 1 are said to be in corresponding states when Eqs. (44) and (45) are satisfied. We note that since the Lennard-Jones potential is a two parameter potential, two conditions are now required to establish corresponding states.

The mean molar Helmholtz free energy for the mixture may be obtained as previously by using Eqs. (4), (14), (44), and (45),

$$\begin{aligned} A(T,v,\mathbf{x}) = \sum_{s=1}^{r} x_s[RT \ln x_s + A_s^*(T)] \\ - RT \ln\left(\frac{\tilde{a}}{a_{11}}\right)^3 + \frac{\tilde{\epsilon}}{\epsilon_{11}}[A_1(T_1,v_1) - A_1^*(T_1)]. \end{aligned} \tag{46}$$

Differentiation with respect to volume at constant temperature and composition yields

$$p(T,v,\mathbf{x}) = (\tilde{\epsilon} a_{11}^3/\epsilon_{11}\tilde{a}^3) p_1(T_1,v_1), \tag{47}$$

the relation between the corresponding pressures of the mixture and pure component 1 when in corresponding states. With Eq. (45), Eq. (47) also forms the basis for the determination of the equation of state of the mixture, liquid or gas, in terms of the potential constants, and the known experimentally determined equation of state of one of the pure components.

By the addition of pv to both sides of Eq. (46), and use of Eqs. (45) and (47), the mean molar Gibbs free energy of the mixture is found to be

$$\begin{aligned} F(T,p,\mathbf{x}) = \sum_{s=1}^{r} x_s[RT \ln x_s + A_s^*(T)] \\ - RT \ln\left(\frac{\tilde{a}}{a_{11}}\right)^3 + \frac{\tilde{\epsilon}}{\epsilon_{11}}[F_1(T_1,p_1) - A_1^*(T_1)]. \end{aligned} \tag{48}$$

Differentiating with respect to temperature at constant pressure and composition yields the mean molar entropy of the mixture,

$$\begin{aligned} S(T,p,\mathbf{x}) = \sum_{s=1}^{r} x_s[-R \ln x_s + S_s^*(T)] \\ + R \ln\left(\frac{\tilde{a}}{a_{11}}\right)^3 + S_1(T_1,p_1) - S_1^*(T_1), \end{aligned} \tag{49}$$

where S_1 is the molar entropy of pure 1, and $S_s^* = -dA_s^*/dT$. Adding TS to both sides of Eqs. (46) and (48), and using (49), the mean molar internal energy and the enthalpy are obtained:

$$E(T,v,\mathbf{x}) = \sum_{s=1}^{r} x_s E_s^*(T) + \frac{\tilde{\epsilon}}{\epsilon_{11}} [E_1(T_1,v_1) - E_1^*(T_1)],$$

$$H(T,p,\mathbf{x}) = \sum_{s=1}^{r} x_s E_s^*(T) + \frac{\tilde{\epsilon}}{\epsilon_{11}} [H_1(T_1,p_1) - E_1^*(T_1)], \quad (50)$$

where E_1 and H_1 are the molar internal energy and enthalpy, respectively of pure 1, and $E_s^* = A_s^* + TS_s^*$. Other thermodynamic functions could also be obtained by the continuation of the foregoing general procedure. Thus, all the properties of the mixture may be determined from a knowledge of the analogous properties of the pure components, at corresponding states.

In the same manner as previously, corresponding states relations between excess thermodynamic quantities are also found to be possible,

$$A^e(T,v,\mathbf{x}) = (\tilde{\epsilon}/\epsilon_{11}) A_1{}^e(T_1,v_1),$$

$$F^e(T,p,\mathbf{x}) = (\tilde{\epsilon}/\epsilon_{11}) F_1{}^e(T_1,p_1). \quad (51)$$

It is of interest to digress at this point to examine the relationship of the treatment of Scott[6] to the present development. Scott begins his argument by assuming that the mixture and the pure components obey a law of corresponding states which is equivalent to our statement of this law in terms of the excess functions, Eq. (51). To complete his statement of corresponding states, Scott further assumes three alternative models by which the potential parameters of the mixture, and hence the corresponding temperatures and pressures may be computed. These models are the "single liquid," "two liquid," and "three liquid" solution models previously considered in the cell theories of mixtures. The single liquid prescription for determining the potential parameters is exactly the same as Eq. (42) which we have derived here from our general theory under the three added assumptions previously enumerated. Thus, all of Scott's results which are based on the single liquid model are completely equivalent to those obtained in this investigation, and are consistent with the correct statistical mechanics provided the three assumptions concerning the mixture are not violated.

Scott has also reported some detailed numerical calculations of the thermodynamic properties of a number of real solutions. The results of his three models are compared with experiment and several other mixture theories. The agreement with experiment is generally good for the single and two liquid models, the latter being found to be somewhat the better. Now, it is shown by Scott that the single liquid or random-mixing approximation gives an upper bound for the excess free energy of the mixture. That the two liquid model is found to yield better numerical results, however, should not be construed to mean that this model is necessarily an approximation of greater validity. That it probably is not may be seen quite clearly by comparing the simple formula for the pseudo potential parameters in the two liquid model with the rather complicated results obtained by us[7] for approximations of higher order than that of random mixing. Indeed, it is shown in I that the pursuit of more realistic approximations to the pseudo potential, Φ_N, leads to forms which cannot even be decomposed into sums of pseudo *pair* potentials.

Returning to the presentation of the results obtained for the case of unequal sizes, we consider next the chemical potentials in binary mixtures. The form exhibited in Eq. (1) is also applicable in this case. Here, however, the coefficients A_{12} in the Margules expansion is calculated to be

$$A_{12}(T,p) = -\frac{1}{2}\left(\frac{\partial^2}{\partial x_1^2}\left\{\frac{\tilde{\epsilon}}{\epsilon_{11}}[F_1(T_1,p_1) - A_1^*(T_1)] - RT\ln\left(\frac{\tilde{a}}{a_{11}}\right)^3\right\}\right)_{T,p}\Bigg|_{x_1=1}. \tag{52}$$

The coefficients of higher powers of x_2 in Eq. (1) will be proportional to the higher derivatives of the quantity in the braces. The actual evaluation of A_{12} is accomplished in the same manner as previously, except that here there is an additional dependence of the thermodynamic quantities on x_1 through $\tilde{a}$. Also, the derivatives of $\tilde{\epsilon}$ and $\tilde{a}$, Eq. (42) are much more complex. The final result for A_{12} given in the same form as Eq. (34) is

$$\begin{aligned}
A_{12}(T,p) = \tfrac{1}{2}\{&(D_1' + D_1^2)\Delta F_1^v - B_1'(pv_1 - RT) \\
&+ D_1^2(TC_{v1}^e + v_1\kappa_1[p - T\alpha_1/\kappa_1]^2) \\
&+ B_1^2(p\kappa_1 - 1)pv_1 + 2B_1D_1(T\alpha_1 - p\kappa_1)pv_1\},
\end{aligned}$$

$$\begin{aligned}
D_1 &= \frac{d\ln\tilde{\epsilon}}{dx_1}\bigg|_{x_1=1} = 2\left[1 - \frac{\epsilon_{12}}{\epsilon_{11}}\left(2\frac{a_{12}^6}{a_{11}^6} - \frac{a_{12}^{12}}{a_{11}^{12}}\right)\right] \\
B_1 &= \frac{d\ln\tilde{a}^3}{dx_1}\bigg|_{x_1=1} = \frac{\epsilon_{12}}{\epsilon_{11}}\left[\frac{a_{12}^6}{a_{11}^6} - \frac{a_{12}^{12}}{a_{11}^{12}}\right] \\
D_1' &= \frac{d^2\ln\tilde{\epsilon}}{dx_1^2}\bigg|_{x_1-1} = 4\gamma_1 - 2\delta_1 - 2 \\
B_1' &= \frac{d^2\ln\tilde{a}^3}{dx_1^2}\bigg|_{x_1=1} = \delta_1 - \gamma_1, \\
\gamma_1 &= \frac{\epsilon_{22}a_{22}^6}{\epsilon_{11}a_{11}^6} + 2\frac{\epsilon_{11}\epsilon_{12}a_{11}^6a_{12}^6 - \epsilon_{12}^2a_{12}^{12}}{\epsilon_{11}^2a_{11}^{12}} \\
\delta_1 &= \frac{\epsilon_{22}a_{22}^{12}}{\epsilon_{11}a_{11}^{12}} + 2\frac{\epsilon_{11}\epsilon_{12}a_{11}^{12}a_{12}^{12} - \epsilon_{12}^2a_{12}^{24}}{\epsilon_{11}^2a_{11}^{24}},
\end{aligned} \tag{53}$$

where ΔE_1^v, C_{v1}^e, α_1, κ_1, and v_1 have the same significance as in Eq. (34), and are to be evaluated at the same temperature and pressure as that of the mixture. ϵ_{11}, a_{11}, ϵ_{22}, and a_{22} are the Lennard-Jones constants for the pure 1 and pure 2 interactions, respectively, while suitable approximations to the mixed interaction constants are given by

$$\begin{aligned}
a_{12} &= (a_{11} + a_{22})/2, \\
\epsilon_{12} &= (\epsilon_{11}\epsilon_{22})^{\frac{1}{2}}a_{11}^3a_{22}^3/a_{12}^6.
\end{aligned} \tag{54}$$

The second equation deviates from the familiar $\epsilon_{12} = (\epsilon_{11}\epsilon_{22})^{\frac{1}{2}}$ since we believe that it should be the entire attractive term, $-\epsilon_{12}(a_{12}/R)^6$, that should be approximated by the square root of the product, and not merely ϵ_{12} itself.

Equation (53) is written in a form which seems most convenient for numerical computation; the needed thermodynamic quantities of the pure components are directly available or readily calculable. Moreover, it is apparent that only the ratios of the interaction parameters are required rather than the absolute values. A form for Eq. (53), analogous to Eq. (39), for the case of equal sizes, however, does not appear to be possible, so that for this case the reduction to the Regular solution theory is not so obviously achieved. The relationship of the Conformal solution theory to the present case, however, will be discussed briefly in the last section. We remark, also, that the chemical potential of component 2 may be obtained by interchange of all subscripts 1 and 2, while other partial molal thermodynamic functions may be obtained by the appropriate differentiation of Eqs. (1) and (53).

The coefficients of higher terms in the Margules expansion have not been explicitly derived here. They may be obtained by the general method used for A_{12}, of course, but will be rather more complex and cumbersome. Estimates of the magnitudes of the coefficients of the cubic terms, A_{13} and A_{23}, may be obtained, however, from the following considerations. If terms of order x_1^4 and x_2^4 are neglected,

$$RT \ln f_1 = A_{12}x_2^2 + A_{13}x_2^3,$$

$$RT \ln f_2 = A_{22}x_1^2 + A_{23}x_1^3.$$

The activity coefficients must, however, satisfy the Gibbs-Duhem equation at constant temperature and pressure,

$$x_1 d \ln f_1 + x_2 d \ln f_2 = 0.$$

Substitution and comparison of terms of equal order in x_1 or x_2 yields the following for the desired coefficients:

$$A_{13} = -A_{23} = 2(A_{22} - A_{12})/3. \tag{55}$$

Equation (55) can then be used as a test to determine whether the computation of higher terms will be required for particular mixtures.

A preliminary numerical computation has been made in order to test the accuracy of Eq. (53). Neglecting terms of order $x_{1,2}^3$ in the Margules expansion, the mean molar free energy of mixing (in excess of the ideal part) is given by

$$\Delta F_M^e = x_1x_2(x_2A_{12} + x_1A_{22}). \tag{56}$$

Equations (53) and (56) were then combined, and the excess free energy of mixing at 25°C. and 1 atmos was computed for the three equimolar mixtures of benzene, cyclohexane, and carbon tetrachloride. The thermodynamic quantities for the pure components were obtained from the usual standard reference tables, while the ratios of the Lennard-Jones constants were obtained from the ratios of the critical constants of the pure substances. The critical point was assumed to be a corresponding state for the pure components. The results of this computation are summarized in Table I where comparison is made with Scott's single liquid and two liquid approximations, and with the experimentally observed values. The agreement of our results with experiment is about as good as that obtained by Scott. We believe, however, that a great deal of improvement could be achieved by the use of more accurate interaction constants. Certainly, the assumption that the critical point is a corresponding state is not the best way to obtain the interaction constants. Until more accurate information concerning the intermolecular potential functions of nonpolar molecules is available, a truly satisfactory test of Eq. (53) cannot be made.

V. CONFORMAL SOLUTION TREATMENT

A procedure which helps to clarify the approximations behind the Conformal solution treatment of Longuet-Higgins[1–3] has been presented in I. It is still of interest, however, to examine the relation of that development to the present corresponding states treatment for the case of unequal sizes. In this last section, an expansion method which illustrates this relation will be given.

We begin with Eq. (51) for the excess Gibbs free energy, in terms of the pure component s, which after use of the definition of F_s^e, may be written as

$$F^e(T,p,\mathbf{x}) = (\tilde{\epsilon}/\epsilon_{ss})[F_s(T_s,p_s) - A_s^*(T_s)] + RT\ln v - RT\ln(\tilde{a}/a_{ss})^3. \qquad (57)$$

We define

$$\omega_s = \frac{\tilde{\epsilon}}{\epsilon_{ss}} - 1, \quad \sigma_s = \left(\frac{\tilde{a}}{a_{ss}}\right)^3 - 1, \qquad (58)$$

which are the differences from unity of the ratios of the energy and size parameters, respectively, of the mixture and pure component s. By the use of Eqs. (45) and (47), T_s and p_s are expressible as functions of the differences, ω_s and σ_s,

$$\begin{aligned} T_s - T &= -T(\omega_s/1 + \omega_s), \\ p_3 - p &= p(\sigma_s - \omega_s/1 + \omega_s). \end{aligned} \qquad (59)$$

Now, $F_s(T_s, p_s) - A_s^*(T_s)$ is expanded in a Taylor series about the point $T_s = T, p_s = p$:

$$\begin{aligned} F_s(T_s,p_s) - A_s^*(T_s) &= F_s(T,p) - A_s^*(T) + (p_s - p)v_s \\ &\quad + (T_s - T)[- S_s(T,p) + S_s^*(T)] + \cdots. \end{aligned} \qquad (60)$$

TABLE I. Excess free energy of mixing of equimolar mixtures at 25°C. and 1 atmos (in cal/mole).

	CCl_4–C_6H_6	CCl_4–C_6H_{12}	C_6H_6–C_6H_{12}
Scott (single liquid)	20	46	126
Scott (two liquid)	10	23	63
This paper, Eq. (53)	8	39	95
Observed	19	17	74

If Eqs. (57) through (60) are collected, and the result expressed only to first order in the differences, σ_s and ω_s, one obtains

$$F^e(T,p,\mathbf{x}) = F_s^e(T,p) + \omega_s E_s^e(T,p) + \sigma_s(pv_s - RT) + O(\omega^2,\sigma^2,\sigma\omega). \qquad (61)$$

Instead of using only component s as the reference component, it is also permissible to use each component, $1\cdots r$, in proportion to its composition in the mixture, so that

$$F^e(T,p,\mathbf{x}) - \sum_{s=1}^{r} x_s F_s^e(T,p) = \Delta F_M^e,$$
$$\Delta F_M^e = \sum_{s=1}^{r} x_s[\omega_s E_s^e(T,p) + \sigma_s(pv_s - RT)], \qquad (62)$$

where ΔF_M^e is the Gibbs free energy of mixing in excess of the ideal part, and, as written, is valid only to first order in the differences of the ratios of the constants from unity.

The Conformal solution result for this quantity is given by the following,[1]

$$\Delta F_M^e = f_0 E_0^e(T,p) + g_0(pv_0 - RT),$$
$$f_0 = \sum_{s<t}^{r} x_s x_t(2f_{st} - f_{ss} - f_{tt}), \qquad (63)$$
$$g_0 = 3\sum_{s<t}^{r} x_s x_t(2g_{st} - g_{ss} - g_{tt}),$$

where f_{st} and g_{st} are the ratios of the energy and size parameters, ϵ_{st} and a_{st}, to those of the reference fluid, ϵ_0 and a_0. E_0^e is the excess internal energy of the reference fluid, while v_0 is its molar volume at T, p. The result is stated to be valid only to terms of first order in the differences of the f_{st}, g_{st} from unity.

Apart from the difference that we have taken all pure components as reference fluids, rather than just one of them, the two expressions do agree in their dependence on the thermodynamic quantities of the reference fluid. The Conformal solution expression does not agree with our result, however, in its dependence on composition and the differences in interaction parameters. The reason for this discrepancy lies for the most part in the fact that the perturbation technique used in Conformal solution theory does not take into account the exact dependence of the potentials on the intermolecular distance. Our development does, of course, consider the exact form of the pair potentials in the computation of $\tilde{\epsilon}$ and $\tilde{a}$. This discrepancy disappears in the limit of vanishing differences in the size parameters of the components; here the exact dependence of potential on intermolecular separation is not important. For the case of equal sizes then, the two methods will give exactly the same results (to first order in ω_s or f_0).

Although the expansion method presented above indicates that the Conformal solution result can be obtained as a special case of our random mixing approximation, we do not mean to imply, however, that the random mixing approximation is necessary to derive the Conformal solution theory. As has been shown in I, the Conformal solution theory may be obtained from our exact development by a straightforward perturbation calculation which does not utilize the moment expansion.

ADDENDUM TO PAPER NUMBER 10

Some of the statements in Section V about the conformal solution theory are misleading. This was brought to the attention of the authors by Byers-Brown.[1] In particular, the third paragraph on page 150 should be corrected, since the conformal solution theory is rigorously correct and does take account of the exact dependence of the potentials on the intermolecular distance. The random mixing approximation is correct only to first-order terms in the expansion discussed in Section V. It disagrees with the conformal solution theory in the second-order terms because of the random mixing approximation itself.

[1] W. Byers-Brown, Private communications (1957).

Introduction to the "Electrolyte Solution Theory" Section of the "Collected Papers of John Gamble Kirkwood"

By JACQUES C. POIRIER, *Duke University, Durham, North Carolina*

I. GENERAL COMMENTS

All but two of the papers in this section may be divided into two logically separate but chronologically intertwined groups, both concerned with the theory of equilibrium properties of solutions of charge-bearing molecular species.

(A) Contributions which follow the Debye-Hückel methodology. This group consists of papers 11, 12, 14, 15, 16, 17, and 18.

Paper 11, historically the first of Kirkwood's papers on solutions, attacks the problem of calculating the electrostatic contribution to the activity coefficient of an ion (or molecule) having a *non*-spherically symmetrical charge distribution. By using a relatively simple model (two point charges separated by a fixed distance, each surrounded by an impenetrable sphere),[1] Scatchard and Kirkwood demonstrate that (1) the Debye-Hückel limiting law expression for a divalent ion is recovered at low concentration if the point charges are of like sign, and hence the limiting law does not require ions to have spherically symmetrical charge distributions, and (2) if the point charges are of opposite sign and the model thus represents a zwitterion, then the $\sqrt{c}$ term vanishes in the expansion of the logarithm of the activity coefficient, leaving a leading term proportional to c as in the case of nonelectrolytes—but of larger magnitude. In paper 12 Kirkwood presents a more general analysis of a more general model; the central ion is represented by an arbitrary distribution of point charges (the extension to continuous charge distributions is clearly indicated) imbedded in a spherical cavity of dielectric constant differing from that of the external solvent. Particularizations of the general formulas, with the assumption that the cavity dielectric constant is unity and negligible compared to the dielectric constant of the solvent, lead to predictions of the effect of added electrolyte on the solubility of zwitterions (and vice versa) and the effect of solvent dielectric constant on zwitterion solubility. From the data of Cohn (whose experimental work during the period stimulated interest in the zwitterion problem; see the references in papers 11, 12, and 16) reasonable values of the structural parameters of the moderately spherical glycine zwitterion are deduced. In paper 16, Kirkwood again considers dipolar ions, but in a different manner. The coupling parameter approach, introduced in earlier papers is utilized. If only valid limiting laws are desired, the electrostatic problem simplifies to the interaction of a dipole with a single external

[1] For entertaining comments, see G. Scatchard, *J. Chem. Phys.* **33**, 1280 (1960).

ion, the Poisson-Boltzmann equation being avoided entirely. It then becomes feasible to include the interaction of the external ion with its image in the spherical, low dielectric constant cavity surrounding the dipole, which ultimately results in a "salting-out" term. Ellipsoidal dipoles are treated without this latter refinement, and amino acid and peptide data are structurally interpreted.

The Kirkwood-Westheimer theory of dissociation constants, exposed in papers 14 and 15, is based on the observation that the logarithm of the ratio of the dissociation constants of two acids is the Gibbs free energy of transferring a proton from one anion to the other. For two structurally similar acids, this free energy can be approximated by the sum of a simple entropy term (depending on the gross symmetries) and an electrostatic work term. This idea, dating back to Bjerrum,[2] and used with a primitive ionic model, had required unreasonable structural parameters to fit data on ionization constants of some dibasic acids. The more refined spherical cavity model (developed in paper 12) is shown in paper 14 to lead to reasonable structural parameters for these acids as well as acids differing by a dipolar group. In paper 15, the same approach is carried through for pairs of acids of ellipsoidal shape. In reply to a rather critical article, Westheimer and Kirkwood in paper 18 substantiate the view that although the theory may not be "good," it is the best in existence in this area, a view still current.[3] In paper 17 the Kirkwood-Westheimer theory is used in deriving an explicit form for a function determining all acid-base equilibria of an ampholyte solute containing an equal number of two types of sites for protons, randomly distributed on a spherical surface.

(B) Contributions transcending the Debye-Hückel methodology. This group consists of papers 13, 20, and 22.

Paper 13 contains Kirkwood's outstanding early analysis of the statistical mechanical basis of the Debye-Hückel theory and of some earlier criticism of it, as well as possible approaches to a more exact solution of the general problem. In paper 20 Kirkwood and Poirier return to the statistical mechanical basis of the Debye-Hückel theory, using more elegant mathematical apparatus devised in the intervening years largely by Kirkwood. It is pointed out that the Poisson-Boltzmann equation (solutions of which fail to satisfy conditions of integrability) results from taking the Laplacian of an integral equation which is not self-consistent, whereas the *linearized* Poisson-Boltzmann equation (solutions of which *do* satisfy conditions of integrability) results from taking the Laplacian of the *linearized* integral equation, which is now self-consistent. A systematic method of obtaining better approximations to the potential of mean force is presented, but the promised solution has never appeared.

Starting with much the same approach as paper 20, Stillinger and Kirkwood present in paper 22 a detailed molecular theory of the diffuse (Gouy) double layer near a plane electrode, apparently the first formal treatment with this degree of rigor.

The two remaining papers of this section are, in the sense of the present organization, hybrids. In paper 19 Kirkwood and Mazur investigate the

---

[2] N. Bjerrum, *Z. Physik. Chem.* **106**, 219 (1923).

[3] See, for example, Jack S. Hine, *Physical Organic Chemistry* (McGraw-Hill Book Company, Inc., New York, 1962), 2nd ed., p. 61.

interaction of charged macromolecules with each other by solving the Born-Green integral equation by computer iteration. The influence of the simple electrolyte ions, also present in the solution of macromolecules, is implicitly and approximately given by the Debye-Hückel methodology because the Verwey-Overbeek pair potential is used for the macromolecules. The resulting macromolecular radial distribution function reveals local ordering. The theory of the heat of transport of electrolytic solutions presented in paper 21 by Helfand and Kirkwood devolves from the investigations on transport properties collected elsewhere in this volume. The non-equilibrium perturbations to the pair correlation function of two ions and to the mean electrostatic potential, necessary to obtain the ion-ion contribution to the heat of transport, are determined to the accuracy necessary in a limiting law.

Das Verhalten von Zwitterionen und von mehrwertigen Ionen mit weit entfernten Ladungen in Elektrolytlösungen

VON GEORGE SCATCHARD* UND JOHN G. KIRKWOOD†

Die Moleküle mit weit entfernten Ladungen sind sehr wichtig für die organische und besonders für die biologische Chemie.[1] Meistens enthalten die mehrwertigen organischen Ionen mehrere mehr oder weniger getrennte einzelne Ladungen desselben Zeichens. Seit Adams' Annahme,[2] daß die aliphatischen Aminosäuren Zwitterionen sind, das heißt, daß sie zwei weit getrennte Ladungen von entgegengesetzten Zeichen enthalten, haben sich die Beweise dafür gehäuft. Es ist auch sehr wahrscheinlich, daß die Eiweißkörper sogar im isoelektrischen Zustand mehrere weit entfernte Ladungen enthalten.

In einer schönen Arbeit hat Bjerrum[3] gezeigt, daß das Verhalten eines solchen Moleküls sich dem von einzelnen unabhängigen Ionen nähert, sowie die Entfernung sich vergrößert. Bjerrum sagt weiter[4], daß, wenn die Entfernung der Ladungen e von Null an zunimmt, das Debye-Hückelsche Grenzgesetz sich verändert von $\frac{\kappa}{2D}\left[\sum e\right]^2$ nach $\frac{\kappa}{2D}\sum e^2$.

Den ersten Schluß Bjerrums bestätigen wir, den zweiten dagegen nicht Wir finden, daß der Effekt der Entfernung sich mit der Konzentration des Elektrolyts ändert und sogar so, daß das Grenzgesetz weder von der Entfernung der Ladungen noch von der Form des Moleküls, sondern nur von der Gesamtladung abhängt. Die Wirkung eines Zwitterions ist also in verdünnten Lösungen nicht der Wurzel der Konzentration, sondern der Konzentration selbst proportional, und irgendein mehrwertiges Ion verhält sich ungefähr so wie ein kugelsymmetrisches Ion, dessen Durchmesser von der Ladungstrennung, sowie von der Molekülgröße abhängt.

Diese Schlüsse kann man aus der Debye-schen Annahme der Ionenatmosphäre fast sofort ziehen. In verdünnten Lösungen wirken die übrigen Ionen auf ein kugelsymmetrisches Ion von der Ladung e ebenso wie eine über eine Kugel vom Halbdurchmesser $1/\kappa$ symmetrisch ausgebreitete

---

* Massachusetts Institute of Technology; Guggenheim Fellow, z. Z. Physikal. Inst. Leipzig.

† International Research Fellow, z. Z. Physikal. Inst. Leipzig.

[1] An diesem Problem wurden wir durch unseren Freund Professor E. J. Cohn, Harvard Medical School, und seinen Mitarbeitern im Laboratory of Physical Chemistry interessiert in Zusammenhang mit dessen Untersuchungen über das Verhalten von Aminosäuren und Eiweißkörpern. Den Vergleich der Experimente mit der von uns gegebenen Theorie überlassen wir den Veröffentlichungen jenes Laboratoriums. Zusammenfassende Berichte über dessen Arbeiten siehe: E. J. Cohn, *Erg. Physiol.* **33**, 828 (1931), sowie Naturwissenschaften März 1932 (im Druck). [Ed. note: E. J. Cohn, *Naturwissenschaften* **20**, 663 (1932).]

[2] E. Q. Adams, *Jour. Amer. Chem. Soc.* **38**, 1503 (1916).

[3] N. Bjerrum, *Zeitschr. f. physik. Chem.* **104**, 147 (1923).

[4] N. Bjerrum, *ibid.* **108**, 82 (1924).

Ladung $-e$. Deshalb nennt Debye $1/\kappa$ die Dicke der Ionenatmosphäre. $1/\kappa$ ist gegeben durch die Gleichung:

$$\kappa^2 = \frac{4\pi\epsilon^2}{DkT} \sum_j c_j z^2{}_j.$$

Dabei ist D die Dielektrizitätskonstante des Lösungsmittels, c_j die Zahl der Ionen im cm^3 von der Wertigkeit z_j, k die Boltzmannsche Konstante, T die Temperatur und ϵ die Protonenladung. Die Wirkung der Ladungsentfernung muß von ihrem Verhältnis zu dieser Dicke abhängen. Ist der Abstand, verglichen mit $1/\kappa$, sehr groß, so wirken die Ladungen unabhängig voneinander; wenn aber der Abstand relativ klein ist, so wirken die Ladungen so, als ob sie in einem Punkt konzentriert wären. Da κ der Wurzel der Konzentration proportional ist, so ist $1/\kappa$ bei der Konzentration Null unendlich groß und deshalb sehr groß gegen irgendeine endliche Entfernung der Ladungen. In wäßrigen Lösungen ist $1/\kappa$ ungefähr $3 \cdot 10^{-8}\ \text{cm}/\sqrt{\mu}$, wobei μ die Ionenstärke ist. Die Entfernung der Ladungen kann also nur für Riesenmoleküle groß gegen $1/\kappa$ in verdünnten Lösungen sein.

Man sieht auch physikalisch, daß die Anordnung der Ladungen in den übrigen Molekülen das Grenzgesetz nicht beeinflussen kann. Das Potential irgendeines Ions, sogar eines symmetrischen, sollte in der Tat von der Ladungstrennung der übrigen Ionen abhängen, aber nicht im Konzentrationsgebiete, worin $1/\kappa$ sehr groß gegen diese Trennung ist.

Man kann die Methode von Debye und Hückel auf die Untersuchung der Verteilung von Ionen in der Nähe irgendeines Moleküls anwenden, das sich in einer Lösung symmetrischer Ionen befindet, sofern die rein elektrostatischen Kräfte für diese Verteilung maßgebend sind. Für unsere Zwecke wird das Molekül durch eine Fläche S von willkürlicher Gestalt charakterisiert, innerhalb deren kein in der Lösung vorhandenes Ion eindringen kann, und außerhalb deren nur die Coulombschen Kräfte maßgebend sind, sowie durch eine Reihe von Ladungen $e_1, \cdots e_m$, die auf beliebige Weise innerhalb dieser Fläche angeordnet sind.

Ist ψ das mittlere elektrostatische Potential in der Nähe dieses Moleküls, außerhalb der Grenzfläche S, so können wir nach Debye und Hückel näherungsweise schreiben

$$\Delta\psi - \kappa^2\psi = 0. \tag{1}$$

Wegen der Linearität der Gleichung (1) können wir schreiben

$$\psi = \sum_{j=1}^{m} \psi_j, \tag{2}$$

wobei ψ_j das von der Ladung e_j entstehende Potential bedeutet. Wählen wir ein Koordinatensystem $[r_j, \vartheta_j, \varphi_j]$ mit Ursprung in der Ladung e_j, und machen wir ferner den Ansatz

$$\psi_j = R(r_j)\Theta(\vartheta_j)\Phi(\varphi_j), \tag{3}$$

so erhalten wir aus Gleichung (1)

$$\Theta = P_n^p(\cos \vartheta_j); \quad \Phi = e^{-p\varphi_j}, \quad n \geq p \geq -n$$

wo $P_n^p(\cos\vartheta_j)$ die zugeordnete Kugelfunktion bedeutet, und R der folgenden Differentialgleichung genügt:

$$\frac{d^2R}{dr_j^2} + \frac{2}{r_j}\frac{dR}{dr_j} - \left[\kappa^2 + \frac{n(n+1)}{r_j^2}\right]R = 0. \tag{4}$$

Diese Gleichung hat die folgenden Lösungen

$$\frac{e^{-\kappa r_j}}{r_j^{n+1}} L_n(\kappa r_j) \text{ und } \frac{e^{+\kappa r_j}}{r_j^{n+1}} K_n(\kappa r_j), \tag{5}$$

wo

$$L_n(\kappa r_j) = \sum_{l=0}^{n} a_l(\kappa r_j)^l;$$

$$K_n(\kappa r_j) = \sum_{l=0}^{n} a_l(-\kappa r_j)^l;$$

mit der Rekursionsformel

$$a_l = \frac{2}{l}\frac{n-l+1}{2n-l+1} a_{l-1}. \tag{6}$$

Von diesen Lösungen genügt nur die erste der Randbedingung

$$\psi_{(\infty)} = 0.$$

Lösungen von Gleichung (1), die dieser Randbedingung genügen, lassen sich folgendermaßen darstellen

$$\psi_j = \sum_{n=0}^{\infty}\sum_{p=-n}^{+n} A_j(n,p)\frac{e^{-\kappa r_j}}{r_j^{n+1}} L_n(\kappa r_j) P_n^p(\cos\vartheta_j)e^{ip\varphi_j}. \tag{7}$$

Die physikalische Bedeutung dieses Potentials besteht darin, daß es aus der Punktladung e_j und einer Serie von Multipolmomenten entsteht, deren elektrische Schwerpunkte mit e zusammenfallen.

Innerhalb der Fläche S muß das Potential ψ' der Laplaceschen Gleichung

$$\Delta\,\psi' = 0 \tag{8}$$

genügen. Hier können wir auch schreiben

$$\psi' = \sum_{j=1}^{m} \psi_j',$$

und wir erkennen physikalisch, daß jedes ψ_j' die folgende Form haben muß

$$\psi_j' = \frac{e_j}{Dr_j} + \sum_{n=0}^{\infty}\sum_{p=-n}^{+n} B_j(n,p) r_j^n P_n^p(\cos\vartheta_j)e^{ip\varphi_j}. \tag{9}$$

Die Koeffizienten $A_j(n, p)$ und $B_j(n, p)$ sind durch die folgenden Randbedingungen zu bestimmen: nämlich 1. die Potentiale ψ und ψ', sowie die normalen Komponenten ihrer Gradienten sollen sich auf der Grenzfläche S stetig anschließen, da keine Ladungsverteilung auf dieser Fläche möglich ist;

2. beide Potentiale sollen bei $\kappa = 0$ in die folgende Form übergehen

$$\psi_0 = \psi_0' = \sum_{j=1}^{m} \frac{e_j}{Dr_j}. \tag{10}$$

Die Bestimmung der Koeffizienten wird im allgemeinen Falle sehr umständlich. Wenn man aber die Potentiale nach Potenzen von κ entwickelt, kann man beweisen, daß der Koeffizient der ersten Potenz von κ weder von der Form der Grenzfläche noch von der Anordnung der Ladungen abhängt, sondern nur von der gesamten Ladung des Moleküls. Die Glieder, die höhere Potenzen von κ enthalten, zeigen sich jedoch gegen die Form der Grenzfläche empfindlich. Wir gehen hier nicht weiter in der allgemeinen Behandlung, sondern begnügen uns mit den vorhergehenden physikalischen Überlegungen.

Wir betrachten jetzt ein einfaches zwei Ladungen enthaltendes Modell

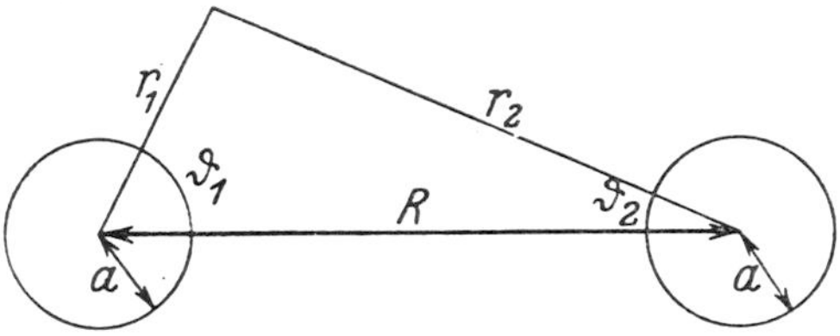

FIG. 1

näher, und zwar dasjenige, das zwei unabhängigen Ionen am ähnlichsten ist. Betrachten wir zwei Kugeln mit gleichem Radius a, deren Zentren durch einen festen Abstand R getrennt werden. In der ersten Kugel soll eine Ladung $z\epsilon$ kugelsymmetrisch verteilt werden, und in der zweiten eine Ladung $w\,z\epsilon$. Dabei ist $w = \pm 1$. Wenn w den Wert $+1$ annimmt, entspricht das System einem zweiwertigen Ion, und wenn w den Wert -1 hat, stellt es ein Zwitterion dar. Nehmen wir an, daß das System sich in einer Elektrolytlösung befindet, und wählen wir den Radius a auf solche Weise, daß kein in der Lösung liegendes Ion in die zwei Kugeln eindringen kann, so können wir die vorangehenden Überlegungen auf unser Modell anwenden. Wenn R genügend groß gegen a ist, lassen sich die Grenzbedingungen in guter Näherung erfüllen, wenn wir nur die ersten Glieder der Potentiale (7) und (9) berücksichtigen. Es kommen hier nur die ersten drei Glieder zur Betrachtung. Wir schreiben also nach Gleichung (2), (6), (7) und (9) mit Berücksichtigung der Symmetrie des Systems

$$\psi = e^{-\kappa r_1}\left\{\frac{A_0}{r_1} + A_1\frac{1+\kappa r_1}{r_1^2}\cos\vartheta_1 + A_2\frac{1+\kappa r_1+\kappa^2 r_1^2/3}{r_1^3}(3\cos^2\vartheta_1 - 1)\right\}$$

$$+ we^{-\kappa r_2}\left\{\frac{A_0}{r_2} + A_2\frac{1+\kappa r_2}{r_2^2}\cos\vartheta_2 + A_2\frac{1+\kappa r_2+\kappa^2 r_2^2/3}{r_2^3}(3\cos^2\vartheta_2 - 1)\right\} \tag{11}$$

$$\psi_1 = \frac{z\epsilon}{Dr_1} + B_{01} + B_{11}r_1\cos\vartheta_1 + B_{21}r_1^2(3\cos^2\vartheta_1 - 1) \tag{12}$$

$$\psi_2 = \frac{wz\epsilon}{Dr_2} + B_{02} + B_{12}r_2\cos\vartheta_2 + B_{22}r_2^2(3\cos^2\vartheta_2 - 1), \tag{13}$$

wobei ψ in der äußeren Lösung, ψ_1 in der ersten Kugel und ψ_2 in der zweiten Kugel gilt. Dabei bedeuten r_1 den Abstand des betreffenden Punkts vom Zentrum der ersten Kugel und r_2 den Abstand vom Zentrum der zweiten, während ϑ_1 bzw. ϑ_2 die Winkel bedeuten, die r_1 bzw. r_2 mit R bilden.

Auf der Oberfläche der ersten Kugel gilt

$$r_2 = (r_1^2 + R^2 - 2Rr_1 \cos \vartheta_1)^{\frac{1}{2}}; \quad \cos \vartheta_2 = \frac{R - r_1 \cos \vartheta_1}{r_2}. \tag{14}$$

Wir können also auf dieser Fläche die Funktionen von r_2 und ϑ_2, die im Potential ψ auftreten, nach Potenzen von r_1/R entwickeln. Nachdem diese Entwicklung durchgeführt ist, sorgen wir dafür, daß die Koeffizienten jeder in den Potentialen auftretenden Potenz von $\cos \vartheta_1$ den Grenzbedingungen 1 and 2 unabhängig genügen. Dabei werden diese Bedingungen auf der Kugelfläche überall erfüllt.[5] Endlich erhalten wir

$$\left.\begin{aligned}
A_0 &= \frac{z\epsilon}{D}\frac{e^{\kappa a}}{1 + \kappa a - w\kappa^2 a^3 e^{-\kappa(R-a)}/3R}; \quad A_1 = A_2 = 0 \\
B_{01} &= \frac{z\epsilon}{D}\frac{-\kappa + \dfrac{w}{R}\left\{e^{-\kappa(R-a)}\left[1 + \kappa^2 a^2\left(\dfrac{1}{2} + \dfrac{wa}{3R}\right)\right] - 1 - \kappa a\right\}}{1 + \kappa a - w\kappa^2 a^3 e^{-\kappa(R-a)}/3R} \\
B_{11} &= \frac{z\epsilon}{D}\frac{w}{R^2}\frac{(1 + \kappa R)e^{-\kappa(R-a)}}{1 + \kappa a - w\kappa^2 a^3 e^{-\kappa(R-a)}/3R} \\
B_{21} &= \frac{z\epsilon}{D}\frac{w}{2R^3}\frac{(1 + \kappa R + \kappa^2 R^2/3)e^{-\kappa(R-a)}}{1 + \kappa a - w\kappa^2 a^3 e^{-\kappa(R-a)}/3R}.
\end{aligned}\right\} \tag{15}$$

Aus der Form der Koeffizienten B sollte man erwarten, daß das Potential ψ_1 überall in der ersten Kugel gut konvergiert, wenn a/R klein ist.

Da die Ladung $z\epsilon$ mit Kugelsymmetrie innerhalb der Kugel (1) verteilt ist, liefern die Glieder $B_{11} \cos \vartheta_1$ und B_{21} $(3 \cos^2 \vartheta_1 - 1)$ des Potentials ψ_1 keinen Beitrag zu der Energie dieser Ladung, weil die Mittelwerte von $\cos \vartheta_1$ sowie $(3 \cos^2 \vartheta_1 - 1)$ auf irgendeiner Kugel Null sind. Wir brauchen also nur B_{01} und B_{02} zu betrachten, um die elektrische Energie des Systems abzuschätzen, die von der Anwesenheit der anderen Ionen abhängt. Man findet ohne Mühe, daß der Koeffizient B_{02} einfach $B_{01}\,w$ ist. Nach dem Güntelberg-Müllerschen Ladungsprozeß ergibt sich der elektrostatische

[5] Wenn man den Einfluß aller Multipolglieder vernachlässigt, erhält man eine erste etwas grobere Näherung, wobei das gesamte Potential einfach gleich der Summe der Potentiale zweier unabhängiger Ionen ist. Dann lautet es so:

$$A_0 = \frac{z\epsilon}{D}\frac{e^{\kappa a}}{1 + \kappa a}$$

$$B_{01} = \frac{z\epsilon}{D}\frac{-\kappa + \dfrac{w}{R}\left(e^{-\kappa(R-a)} - 1 - \kappa a\right)}{1 + \kappa a}.$$

Beitrag μ_e zu dem chemischen Potential unseres Moleküls, sowie der entsprechende Aktivitätskoeffizient γ_e

$$\mu_e = kT \log \gamma_e = \frac{z\epsilon}{2} (B_{01} + w\, B_{02}) = z\epsilon\, B_{01}$$

$$\mu_e = -\frac{z^2\epsilon^2}{D} \frac{\kappa - \frac{w}{R}\left\{e^{-\kappa(R-a)}\left[1 + \kappa^2 a^2\left(\frac{1}{2} + \frac{wa}{3R}\right)\right] - 1 - \kappa a\right\}}{1 + \kappa a - \kappa^2 w a^3 e^{-\kappa(R-a)}/3R}. \tag{16}$$

Bei kleinem κ können wir diesen Ausdruck nach Potenzen von κ entwickeln. Das erste Glied dieser Reihe lautet

$$\mu_e = kT \log \gamma_e = -\frac{z^2\epsilon^2}{D} \kappa(1 + w). \tag{17}$$

Wenn $w = +1$, entspricht unser Modell einem Ion mit der Valenz $z_0 = 2z$, und Gleichung (17) geht über in

$$\mu_e = kT \log \gamma_e = -\frac{z_0^2\epsilon^2}{2D} \kappa. \tag{18}$$

Diese Beziehung zeigt sich identisch mit dem gewöhnlichen Debye-Hückelschen Grenzgesetz und hängt nicht von der Entfernung der Kugeln ab.

Wenn $w = -1$, was einem Zwitterion entspricht, verschwindet das Glied, das von κ abhängt. In diesem Falle fängt das Grenzgesetz mit κ^2 an, d. h. mit der ersten Potenz der Konzentration, wie bei gewöhnlichen Nichtelektrolyten. Um das Verhalten eines Zwitterions in konzentrierteren Elektrolytlösungen besser vor Augen zu halten, haben wir das Verhältnis des aus

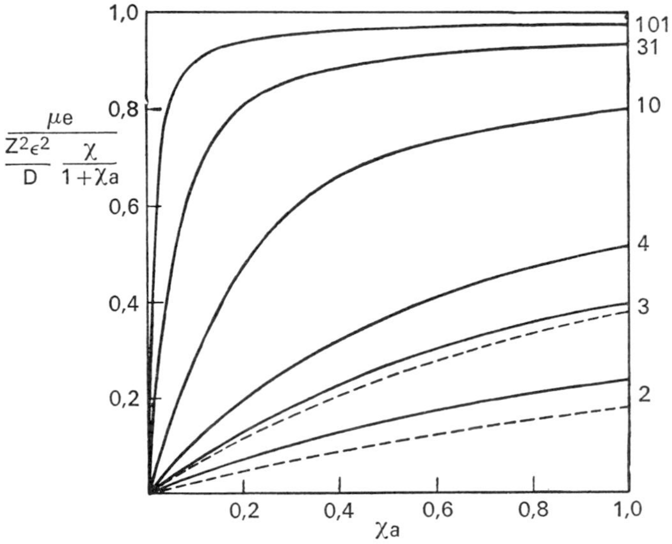

FIG. 2

Gleichung (16) gerechneten Wertes von μ_e oder $kT \log \gamma_e$ zu dem den zwei unabhängigen Ionen entsprechenden Wert $-\frac{z^2\epsilon^2}{D}\frac{\kappa}{1+\kappa a}$ ausgerechnet. Wir haben dieses Verhältnis für verschiedene Werte von R/a als Funktion von κa in Fig. 2 aufgetragen. Dabei ist daran zu erinnern, daß in wäßrigen Lösungen, wenn a den wahrscheinlichen Wert $3 \cdot 10^{-8}$ cm hat, κa der Quadratwurzel der Ionenstärke gleicht, und daß es immer dieser proportional ist. Man sieht, daß ein Zwitterion sich in verdünnten Lösungen gar nicht wie zwei unabhängige Ionen verhält, und daß sich das Verhältnis mit zunehmender Konzentration stark verändert bis es sogar fast eins ist, obwohl für mäßige Entfernungen die entsprechenden Konzentrationen groß sind. Die gestrichelten Linien in Fig. 2 entsprechen der ersten Näherung (s. Anmerkung Seite 299) [Ed. note: see footnote 5]. Für größere Entfernungen genügt diese Näherung so gut, daß der Unterschied von der dritten Annäherung in diesem Bild nicht sichtbar ist.

Nach unserem Modell verhält sich ein mehrwertiges Ion mit getrennten Ladungen nicht wie zwei einzelne Ionen, sondern vielmehr—obwohl nicht genau so—wie ein kugelsymmetrisches Ion, dessen Durchmesser mit R sowie mit a zunimmt. In erster Näherung ist sein chemisches Potential gleich dem eines gleichwertigen Ions mit der ganzen Ladung innerhalb einer Kugel vom Halbmesser a minus demjenigen eines Zwitterions derselben Ladungstrennung R. Die Veränderung der dritten Annäherung für ein mehrwertiges Ion ist ungefähr eineinhalbmal so groß als für ein Zwitterion.

Das hier beschriebene Modell ist nur als schematisch anzusehen. Wir glauben nicht, daß die Dimensionen wirklicher mehrwertiger Ionen oder Zwitterionen aus unseren Formeln für das chemische Potential berechnet werden können. Es sind nicht nur die Ladungskonfiguration und die Form eines solchen Moleküls viel komplizierter als unser einfaches Vorbild, sondern, außer dem zu der ersten Potenz von κ proportionalen Glied, sind die anderen Wechselwirkungen (gewöhnliche van der Waalssche Kräfte) derselben Größenordnung wie die reine elektrostatische Wechselwirkung. Wir glauben immerhin, daß unsere Darstellung den allgemeinen Charakter des Verhaltens solcher Molekeln wiedergibt. Wir glauben auch an die allgemeine Gültigkeit des Schlusses, daß das zu κ proportionale Glied des chemischen Potentials weder von der gegenseitigen Entfernung der Ladungen noch von der Form des Moleküls, sondern nur von der Gesamtladung abhängt.

Theory of Solutions of Molecules Containing Widely Separated Charges with Special Application to Zwitterions*

JOHN G. KIRKWOOD, *Research Laboratory of Physical Chemistry, Massachusetts Institute of Technology*

(Received March 24, 1934)

The electrical contribution to the chemical potential of an ion having an arbitrary charge distribution is calculated with the aid of the Debye-Hückel theory. The calculation is based upon a general solution in polar coordinates of the approximate Debye-Hückel equation, $\Delta\psi - \kappa^2\psi = 0$. In addition, the Born relation between the free energy of solvation of a spherical ion and the dielectric constant of the solvent, is generalized to include ions of arbitrary charge distribution. Application of the theory to a study of the influence of simple electrolytes, and of the dielectric constant of the solvent on the solubilities of the aliphatic amino-acids in alcohol water mixtures, is discussed.

I.

The aliphatic amino-acids, as well as a number of related compounds, exhibit many of the properties of strong electrolytes when dissolved in solvents of high dielectric constant such as water or alcohol. But unlike electrolytes, they do not appreciably increase the electrical conductivity of the solution. Evidently then, these substances do not produce real ions in solution. To account for this peculiar behavior, Adams[1] and Bjerrum[2] suggested that both the acidic and basic groups of an amino-acid molecule are completely ionized in certain solvents, giving rise to a hybrid ion with no resultant charge. Although it cannot contribute to the conductivity of the solution, the hybrid ion is surrounded by a strong electrostatic field, because of the wide separation of its charged groups. Therefore, large deviations from the ideal solution laws arising from electrostatic interaction between the hybrid ions, the solvent, and real ions present in the solution, might be expected. Hybrid ions of this type have been called Zwitterions.

In recent years much evidence in favor of the Zwitterionic hypothesis has accumulated.[3] Perhaps the most convincing argument in its favor is furnished by measurements of the dielectric constants of amino-acid solutions.[4] The high dielectric constants of these solutions can be explained if one attributes an enormous electric moment of the order of 20×10^{-18} e.s.u. to an α-amino

* Contribution No. 331.

[1] E. Q. Adams, *J. Am. Chem. Soc.* **38**, 1503 (1916).

[2] N. Bjerrum, *Zeits. f. physik. Chemie* **104**, 147 (1923).

[3] E. J. Cohn, *Ergebnisse der Physiologie* **33**, 781 (1931); *Naturwiss.* **20** (36), 44 (1932).

[4] Hedestrand, *Zeits. f. physik. Chemie* **135**, 36 (1928); Wyman and McMeekin, *J. Am. Chem. Soc.* **55**, 915 (1933); **53**, 3292 (1931); Devoto, *Gazz. Chim. Ital.* **60**, 520 (1930); **61**, 897 (1932).

acid molecule and still larger moments to those of the β and γ-acids. Dipole moments of this magnitude could scarcely be produced except by amphoteric ionization leading to the formation of Zwitterions.

In an earlier article, the influence of salts upon the activity of Zwitterions in solution was investigated from the standpoint of the Debye-Hückel theory.[5] Although the theory predicts a large electrical contribution to the chemical potential of a Zwitterion, the logarithm of its activity coefficient is found to contain no term proportional to the square root of the ionic strength of the salt. It was therefore concluded that a Zwitterion behaves more like a highly polar non-electrolyte molecule than like a real ion in salt solutions of low ionic strength. The Zwitterion was represented by a highly simplified model consisting of two oppositely charged spheres with a rigid connection between their centers. This model was chosen because of its close resemblance to two independent ions. It has, however, certain disadvantages from a mathematical point of view. The electrostatic potential in the neighborhood of the Zwitterion is most conveniently expressed in terms of polar coordinates, and the boundary conditions lead to an infinite set of linear equations which are very difficult to solve unless the boundary of the ion has spherical symmetry.

In the present article the influence of salts and of the dielectric constant of the solvent upon the activity of a spherical ion, having a complex charge distribution, is investigated. When the net charge of the complex ion is zero, and its dipole moment is large, it corresponds to a Zwitterion. The discussion is limited to solutions in which the concentration of the complex ions, in particular Zwitterions, is so low that their mutual electrostatic interaction can be neglected. It should be possible to treat the mutual interaction of Zwitterions at least approximately by means of Keesom's theory of dipole gases.[6] This, however, will not be undertaken here.

II.

We consider a solution of complex ions at low concentration in a solvent of dielectric constant D. For the present purposes the ion is schematically represented by sphere of radius b, having a dielectric constant D_i, within which are situated M discrete point charges $e_1 \cdots e_M$. A polar coordinate system with origin at the center of the sphere b may be conveniently employed to describe the configuration of the charges $e_1 \cdots e_M$. The position of each charge e_k is then given by three coordinates r_k, ϑ_k, and φ_k. The orientation of the coordinate system is quite arbitrary, and does not enter into the final result. The electrostatic potential at any point (r, ϑ, φ) inside the sphere b satisfies Laplace's equation and is given by

$$V_1 = \sum_{k=1}^{M} \frac{e_k}{D_i |r - r_k|} + \psi$$

$$\psi = \sum_{n=0}^{\infty} \sum_{m=-n}^{+n} B_{nm} r^n P_n^m(\cos \vartheta) e^{im\varphi}, \tag{1}$$

where $|r - r_k|$ is the distance of the charge e_k from the point (r, ϑ, φ), and ψ is the contribution to the potential arising from charge distributions in the solution outside of the sphere b. The $P_n^m(\cos \vartheta)$ are the associated Legendre

[5] G. Scatchard and J. G. Kirkwood, *Phys. Zeits.* **33**, 297 (1932).
[6] W. H. Keesom, *Phys. Zeits.* **22**, 129, 643 (1921).

functions and i is the imaginary unit, $(-1)^{\frac{1}{2}}$. The constants B_{nm} are to be determined by the proper boundary conditions. If there is no space charge in the surrounding solution, and the dielectric constant of the ion D_i is identical with that of the solvent D, then ψ vanishes. This, however, is not in general true.

We now suppose that in addition to the complex ions, the solution contains a simple electrolyte which produces ions of the valence types $Z_1 \cdots Z_i$, present at the molal concentrations $C_1 \cdots C_i$. These ions are supposed not only to be spherical in shape, but also to possess spherically symmetrical charge distributions. In other words their multipole electric moments, dipole, quadrupole, etc., are all assumed to be zero. If the mean distance of closest approach of these ions to the complex ion is a, there will exist a second spherical boundary of radius a, concentric with the sphere b, within which no ions penetrate. In the spherical shell, bounded by the spheres a and b, the potential V_2 must therefore satisfy Laplace's equation. When expanded in spherical harmonics it must have the form

$$V_2 = \sum_{n=0}^{\infty} \sum_{m=-n}^{+n} \{C_{nm}/r^{n+1} + G_{nm}r^n\} P_n{}^m(\cos\vartheta)e^{im\varphi}, \tag{2}$$

where r, ϑ, φ are the coordinates of a point in this region. We also remember that the dielectric constant in this region is D, that of the solvent.

In the solution outside of the sphere a, interaction of the complex ion with the simple electrolyte ions produces a mean space charge. The potential V_3 in this region satisfies Poisson's equation. If we assume that the mean space charge in the neighborhood of the complex ion is given by the Boltzmann distribution formula in the form employed by Debye, and further if nonlinear terms in V_3 appearing in the expansion of the Boltzmann factor are dropped, we may employ the approximate equation of the Debye-Hückel theory to determine this potential.

$$\Delta V_3 - \kappa^2 V_3 = 0, \quad \kappa^2 = (4\pi N\epsilon^2/1000DkT) \sum_i Z_i^2 C_i, \tag{3}$$

where Δ is the Laplacian operator,[7] and κ^2 is a function of the ionic strength, $\sum_i Z_i^2 C_i/2$ of the electrolyte, as well as of Avogadro's number N, the electronic charge ϵ, Boltzmann's constant k, the absolute temperature T, and the dielectric constant of the solution D. If we ignore the influence of the electrolyte on the dielectric constant, D is equal to the dielectric constant of the solvent. After separation of variables, a general solution of Eq. (3) in polar coordinates can be effected.[5] All solutions which vanish at infinity, a necessary boundary condition, may be expressed in the form

$$\begin{aligned} V_3 &= \sum_{n=0}^{\infty} \sum_{m=-n}^{+n} (A_{nm}/r^{n+1})e^{-\kappa r} K_n(\kappa r) P_n{}^m(\cos\vartheta)e^{im\varphi}, \\ K_n(x) &= \sum_{s=0}^{n} \frac{2^s n!(2n-s)!}{s!(2n)!(n-s)!} x^s, \end{aligned} \tag{4}$$

---

[7] For example in polar coordinates

$$\Delta = \frac{1}{r^2}\frac{\partial}{\partial r}\left(r^2 \frac{\partial}{\partial r}\right) + \frac{1}{r^2 \sin\vartheta}\frac{\partial}{\partial\vartheta}\left(\sin\vartheta \frac{\partial}{\partial\vartheta}\right) + \frac{1}{r^2\sin^2\vartheta}\frac{\partial^2}{\partial\varphi^2}.$$

where r, ϑ, φ are the coordinates of any point in the solution outside the sphere a, referred to the polar system with origin at the center of this sphere.[8] The polynomials $K_n(x)$ and their first derivatives $K_n'(x)$ satisfy the following recurrence relations which will later be of use.

$$(2n + 1 + x)K_n(x) - xK_n'(x) = (2n + 1)K_{n+1}(x),$$
$$K_{n+1}(x) - K_n(x) = x^2K_{n-1}(x)/(2n + 1)(2n - 1); \quad n > 0. \tag{5}$$

In the three potentials V_1, V_2 and V_3 there are four constants A_{nm}, C_{nm}, G_{nm}, and B_{nm} to be determined for every set of indices n and m. These constants are fixed by the following boundary conditions. On the surface of the sphere a, V_3 and V_2 as well as their gradients shall be equal:

$$\left.\begin{aligned} V_3 &= V_2 \\ \nabla V_3 &= \nabla V_2 \end{aligned}\right\} \quad r = a. \tag{6}$$

On the surface of the sphere b, V_2 and V_1, the tangential components of their gradients, and the normal components of the dielectric displacement (dielectric constant multiplied by the field strength) shall be equal.[9]

$$\left.\begin{aligned} V_2 = V_1; \quad \frac{1}{r}\frac{\partial V_2}{\partial \vartheta} &= \frac{1}{r}\frac{\partial V_1}{\partial \vartheta} \\ \frac{1}{r \sin \vartheta}\frac{\partial V_2}{\partial \varphi} &= \frac{1}{r \sin \vartheta}\frac{\partial V_1}{\partial \varphi}; \quad r = b \\ D\frac{\partial V_2}{\partial r} &= D_i\frac{\partial V_1}{\partial r}. \end{aligned}\right. \tag{7}$$

Since some of them are equivalent, relations (6) and (7) furnish just four independent conditions. Before applying them we note that the first part of the potential V_1 may be expanded in spherical harmonics in the following form in the neighborhood of the surface of the sphere b, provided all of the r_k are less than b.

$$\sum_{k=1}^{M} \frac{e_k}{D_i|r - r_k|} = \sum_{n=0}^{\infty} \sum_{m=-n}^{+n} \frac{E_{nm}}{D_i r^{n+1}} P_n{}^m(\cos \vartheta)e^{im\varphi}, \tag{8}$$

where

$$E_{nm} = [(n - |m|)!/(n + |m|)!] \sum_{k=1}^{M} e_k r_k{}^n P_n{}^m(\cos \vartheta_k)e^{-im\varphi_k}. \tag{9}$$

We now apply the boundary conditions, which are at once seen to be satisfied independently by every harmonic component of the potentials. For every set

---

[8] The radial factors of the solutions of Eq. (3) are related to the Bessel functions $r^{-\frac{1}{2}}I_{n+\frac{1}{2}}(\kappa r)$ or $r^{-\frac{1}{2}}J_{n+\frac{1}{2}}(i\kappa r)$. However, these functions as customarily defined do not satisfy the boundary conditions of the present problem.

[9] See for example Abraham-Becker, *Theorie der Elektrizität*, I, §32, p. 72.

of indices m and n, four equations are obtained:

$$A_{nm}e^{-\kappa a}K_n(\kappa a) = C_{nm} + a^{2n+1}G_{nm},$$

$$A_{nm}e^{-\kappa a}[(n+1+\kappa a)K_n(\kappa a) - \kappa a K_n'(\kappa a)] = (n+1)C_{nm} - na^{2n+1}G_{nm},$$

$$E_{nm}/D_i + b^{2n+1}B_{nm} = C_{nm} + b^{2n+1}G_{nm}, \tag{10}$$

$$(n+1)E_{nm} - nD_i b^{2n+1}B_{nm} = (n+1)DC_{nm} - nDb^{2n+1}G_{nm}.$$

Solution of these equations and use of the recurrence formulas (5) lead to the following expression for the constants B_{nm}, which are the only ones we require

$$B_{nm} = \frac{E_{nm}}{D_i b^{2n+1}} \frac{(n+1)(D_i - D)}{(n+1)D + nD_i} - \frac{E_{nm}}{Da^{2n+1}} \frac{2n+1}{2n-1}\left[\frac{D}{(n+1)D + nD_i}\right]^2 \frac{\kappa^2 a^2 K_{n-1}(\kappa a)}{K_{n+1}(\kappa a) + \dfrac{n(D - D_i)}{(n+1)D + nD_i}\left(\dfrac{b}{a}\right)^{2n+1} \dfrac{\kappa^2 a^2 K_{n-1}(\kappa a)}{(2n-1)(2n+1)}}$$

except for $n = 0$, where (11)

$$B_{00} = \frac{E_{00}}{b}\left(\frac{1}{D} - \frac{1}{D_i}\right) - \frac{E_{00}}{Da}\frac{\kappa a}{1 + \kappa a}.$$

It is to be noted that only B_{00} contains a term proportional to κ, the square root of the ionic strength. In every other B_{nm} the lowest power of κ is the second.

The mutual electrostatic energy of the complex ion and the medium in which it is immersed arises from the ionic space charge in the solution outside the sphere a, and from a surface charge of polarization on the sphere b depending upon the difference between D_i and D. This energy is determined by the potential ψ, the second term of Eq. (1). It can therefore be expressed as a function of the B_{nm} of Eq. (11), upon which ψ depends. It is easily verified that the B_{nm} are linear functions of the charges $e_1 \cdots e_M$, constituting the ion, so that ψ also is a linear function of these charges. By a hypothetical charging process of the Guntelberg-Müller type, one finds that the mutual electrostatic energy of the ion and the medium, equal to a work of charging, is given by one-half the sum of the products of each e_l by the value of ψ at the point $(r_l, \vartheta_l, \varphi_l)$.[10]

$$W = \tfrac{1}{2} \sum_{l=1}^{M} e_l \psi(r_l, \vartheta_l, \varphi_l). \tag{12}$$

[10] Self-energy terms for the charge distribution $e_1 \cdots e_M$ are omitted. They arise from the first term of V_1 and are independent of the medium. Further, because of the crudity of the molecular model, they have no physical significance.

Introducing ψ from Eq. (1) and using the values of B_{nm} given by Eq. (10), we obtain

$$W = W_0 + W(\kappa),$$

$$W_0 = \tfrac{1}{2} \sum_{n=0}^{\infty} \frac{(n+1)Q_n(D_i - D)}{D_i b^{2n+1}[(n+1)D + nD_i]}, \tag{13}$$

$$W(\kappa) = -(Q_0/2D)\kappa/(1+\kappa a)$$

$$- \tfrac{1}{2} \sum_{n=1}^{\infty} \frac{Q_n}{Da^{2n-1}} \frac{2n+1}{2n-1} \left[\frac{D}{(n+1)D + nD_i}\right]^2$$

$$\frac{\kappa^2 K_{n-1}(\kappa a)}{K_{n+1}(\kappa a) + \dfrac{n(D - D_i)}{(n+1)D + nD_i}\left(\dfrac{b}{a}\right)^{2n+1} \dfrac{\kappa^2 a^2 K_{n-1}(\kappa a)}{(2n-1)(2n+1)}},$$

$$Q_n = \sum_{k=1}^{M} \sum_{l=1}^{M} e_k e_l r_k{}^n r_l{}^n \sum_{m=-n}^{+n} \frac{(n-|m|)!}{(n+|m|)!} P_n{}^m(\cos \vartheta_k) P_n{}^m(\cos \vartheta_l) e^{im(\varphi_k - \varphi_l)}.$$

By the addition theorem of spherical harmonics, the Q_n may be written more simply as

$$Q_n = \sum_{k=1}^{M} \sum_{l=1}^{M} e_k e_l r_k{}^n r_l{}^n P_n(\cos \vartheta_{kl}), \tag{14}$$

where the $P_n(\cos \vartheta)$ are the ordinary Legendre functions and ϑ_{kl} is the angle between r_k and r_l, the lines drawn from the center of the sphere b to the charges e_k and e_l. Thus the final expression is independent of the orientation of the coordinate system (r, ϑ, φ). The early members of the function system $P_n(x)$ have the form

$$\begin{aligned} P_0(x) &= 1, \\ P_1(x) &= x, \\ P_2(x) &= (3x^2 - 1)/2, \\ P_3(x) &= (5x^3 - 3x)/2. \end{aligned} \tag{15}$$

Thus we find that Q_0 is simply $(\sum_k e_k)^2$ or $Z^2 \epsilon^2$ where Z is the valence of the complex ion. The terms in Eq. (13), corresponding to $n = 0$, are seen to be identical with those of the ordinary Debye-Hückel theory, applied to an ion having a spherically symmetric charge distribution. If the net charge of the complex ion is zero, in which case it would correspond to a hybrid ion, the term for $n = 0$ vanishes and the first term of importance is the one involving Q_1. Q_1 is readily seen to be equal to the square of the dipole moment of the ion. The succeeding Q_n's involve the higher order multipole moments.

It should be remarked here that the foregoing analysis is in no way restricted to ions consisting of discrete point charges e_k. A slight modification of the argument permits one to treat a complex ion whose charge distribution is a continuous function of position, $\rho_0(r, \vartheta, \varphi)$. Since we are interested here only in electrostatic contributions to the energy and do not take van der Waals forces into account, we may use a ρ_0 averaged over the high frequency motion of the electrons. Appropriate distribution functions of this type have been calculated with the aid of quantum mechanics by Hartree.[11] If ρ_0 is known the potential inside the ion must satisfy Poisson's equation

$$\Delta V_1 = -4\pi\rho_0. \tag{16}$$

The solution of this equation which replaces the V_1 of Eq. (1) is

$$V_1 = \int \frac{\rho_0(r', \vartheta', \varphi')}{|r' - r|} dv' + \psi, \tag{17}$$

where ψ is the same function as before, and the integration is extended over all of space. Actually, we may suppose $\rho_0(r, \vartheta, \varphi)$ to be effectively zero outside of a sphere of radius b. The potentials outside of the sphere b remain the same as before, and the same expression for W, Eq. (13), is obtained, except that the Q_n's are now given by integrals of the form

$$Q_n = \iint \rho_0(r, \vartheta, \varphi)\rho_0(r', \vartheta', \varphi')r^n r'^n P_n[\cos(\vartheta - \vartheta')]dv'dv \tag{18}$$

instead of by sums over discrete point charges. One would still want to represent the atomic nuclei by point charges, so that in general the Q_n's would consist of an integral over the electronic distribution and a discrete sum over the nuclear point charges. For the present purposes, this generalization is unimportant, since we do not try to calculate the multipole moments Q_n explicitly from atomic structure. However, it is of interest to know that the results have the same form, whether we employ the crude point charge model or a more refined one, consistent with modern theories of molecular structure.

We may inquire as to the significance of the dielectric constant of the ion D_i. By assigning a value greater than unity to D_i, we have a crude means of taking the polarization of the ion into account. Henceforth we shall neglect this effect and assign a value unity to D_i. Further, since we shall be interested in solutions having dielectric constants greater than 25, we may simplify our formulas by neglecting D_i/D in comparison with unity, without introducing much error.

We are now able to calculate the change in the chemical potential of a complex ion attending its transfer from one solution to another, under the assumption that this change is equal to the difference between the works of charging, Eq. (13), in the two mediums. If we choose a standard state as a solution in which the chemical potential of the complex ion is μ^0, the activity coefficient, γ, in a second solution, in which the chemical potential is μ, is defined by the relation

$$\mu - \mu^0 = kT \log \gamma x/x^0 = kT \log \gamma + kT \log x/x^0, \tag{19}$$

where x^0 and x are the mol fractions of the complex ion type in the respective solutions. If in addition to the ideal term $kT \log x/x^0$, the only change in chemical potential is assumed to be that associated with electrostatic forces, we have

$$\log \gamma = (W - W^0)/kT, \tag{20}$$

where W and W^0 are the respective works of charging in the two solutions.

[11] D. R. Hartree, *Proc. Camb. Phil. Soc.* **24**, 89 (1928).

We shall first investigate the influence of simple electrolytes on the activity coefficient of the complex ion. We choose the standard state as a solution in which the ionic strength of the simple electrolyte is zero, and the concentration of the complex ions is sufficiently small to allow the neglect of their mutual interactions. From Eqs. (13) and (20) we obtain the following expression for $\log \gamma$ in a solution containing the simple electrolyte at an ionic strength proportional to κ^2, under the assumption that the dielectric constant of the solution is that of the pure solvent, D, and that the concentration of the complex ions remains small.[12]

$$\log \gamma = W(\kappa)/kT = -(Q_0/2DkT)\kappa/(1 + \kappa a) \tag{21}$$

$$-\frac{\kappa^2}{2DkT}\sum_{n=1}^{\infty}\frac{(2n+1)Q_n}{(2n-1)(n+1)^2a^{2n-1}}\frac{K_{n-1}(\kappa a)}{K_{n+1}(\kappa a)+\dfrac{nb^{2n+1}\kappa^2K_{n-1}(\kappa a)}{(n+1)(2n-1)(2n+1)a^{2n-1}}}.$$

In this expression, the above-mentioned approximation of neglecting D_i in

[12] The fact that we have employed the Guntelberg-Müller charging process rather than that of Debye perhaps requires some comment. The Guntelberg-Müller process yields the chemical potential of the complex ion directly, while the Debye process requires an intermediate calculation of the total free energy of the solution (complex ions and simple electrolyte). We cannot calculate the total free energy statistically, without first investigating the influence of complex ions upon the potential in a simple electrolyte ion. This problem is somewhat more complicated than that of the influence of the simple electrolyte on the potential in a complex ion. So far it has not been solved by means of the Debye theory.

We may assume that the two charging processes lead to the same result if the condition of integrability is fulfilled. If ψ_i is the potential in a simple electrolyte ion i, and ψ_s is the potential in a complex ion s, this principle requires that

$$\partial\psi_s/\partial e_i = \partial\psi_i/\partial e_s,$$

where e_i is the charge on the ion i, and e_s is a common factor of the ensemble of charges making up the complex ion. It should be pointed out that e_i refers to the charge on a single ion i, and not to the charge of the ion type. (Onsager, *Chem. Rev.* **13**, 73 (1933); Halpern, *J. Chem. Phys.* **2**, 85 (1934).) Since solutions of the Debye linear equation, Eq. (3), generally satisfy the condition of integrability, we might reasonably suppose that the integrability condition is satisfied, without explicitly calculating ψ_i.

It is nevertheless interesting to investigate the matter further by means of a semi-thermodynamic argument suggested to the writer by Professor Scatchard. Without reproducing the argument in detail, we shall give an outline of it for the case when the complex ion is a Zwitterion. At Zwitterion concentrations sufficiently small that may neglect the dependence of the chemical potential, μ_z, on the Zwitterion concentration, we may write by thermodynamics

$$F = F_0 + \int_0^{n_z}\mu_z dn_z = F_0 + n_z\mu_z,$$

where F is the electrical free energy of the solution, F_0 the electrical free energy of the simple electrolyte solution in the absence of Zwitterions, μ_z the electrical part of the chemical potential of a Zwitterion, and n_z their number. The potential ψ_i in an ion may then be calculated from F by the following relation:

$$\psi_i = \partial F/\partial e_i = \psi_i^0 + n_z\partial\mu_z/\partial e_i,$$
$$\psi_i^0 = -(e_i/D)\kappa/(1 + \kappa a_i).$$

To avoid undue complication, we neglect small terms in the denominators of Eq. (22) depending on $(b/a)^{2n+1}$, and write

$$\mu_z - \mu_z^0 = kT\log\gamma_z = -\frac{\kappa^2}{2D}\sum_{n=1}^{\infty}\frac{(2n+1)Q_n}{(2n-1)(n+1)^2a^{2n-1}}\frac{K_{n-1}(\kappa a)}{K_{n+1}(\kappa a)}.$$

comparison with D has been introduced. It is perhaps worth while at this point to give explicit expressions for some of the polynomials $K_n(x)$. We have from Eq. (4)

$$\begin{aligned} K_0(x) &= 1, \\ K_1(x) &= 1 + x, \\ K_2(x) &= 1 + x + x^2/3, \\ K_3(x) &= 1 + x + 2x^2/5 + x^3/15, \\ K_4(x) &= 1 + x + 3x^2/7 + 2x^3/21 + x^4/105. \end{aligned} \tag{22}$$

If we are interested in the influence of the simple electrolyte upon the solubility of Zwitterions, we have

$$\log (N/N_0) = -\log \gamma, \tag{23}$$

where N_0 is the solubility at zero ionic strength of the simple electrolyte, and N is the solubility at a finite ionic strength. The solubilities are to be expressed as mol fractions.

The influence of the complex ions upon the activity of a simple electrolyte ion may be obtained in a similar manner. We treat only the case in which the complex ion is a Zwitterion ($Q_0 = 0$), and the ionic strength of the electrolyte is very small. Under these conditions, each of the polynomials $K_n(\kappa a)$ is closely approximated by unity. Moreover, the mutual interaction of the electrolyte ions can be ignored. Choosing the standard state of the electrolyte as a solution in which the Zwitterion concentration is zero, we have for the

---

Differentiation with respect to e_i and multiplication by n_z yields

$$\psi_i = -(e_i/D)\kappa/(1 + \kappa a_i) - \frac{4\pi e_i n_z}{D^2kTv}\left\{\frac{3}{4}\frac{Q_1}{a}\frac{1 - \kappa a/2 + \kappa^2a^2(1 + \kappa a)/6}{1 + \kappa a + \kappa^2a^2/3}\right.$$

$$\left. + \sum_{n=2}^{\infty} \frac{(2n + 1)Q_n}{(2n - 1)(n + 1)^2a^{2n-1}} \frac{K_{n-1}(\kappa a) + \kappa^2a^2[K_n(\kappa a)/(2n + 1) - K_{n-2}(\kappa a)/(2n - 1)]}{K_{n+1}(\kappa a)}\right\}.$$

The limiting form of this expression is used in the following section to obtain the influence of Zwitterions on the activity of slightly soluble salts.

The above value of ψ_i automatically fulfills the condition of integrability, when μ_z is calculated by the Guntelberg process, but it would be arguing in a circle to say that we have proved that the integrability condition is satisfied by this calculation. However, we can get at the matter in another way. Thus the chemical potential of the ion i is given by $\mu_i = \mu_i^0 + n_z(\partial\mu_z/\partial n_i)$. By the Guntelberg process,

$$\psi_i = \partial\mu_i/\partial e_i = \psi_i^0 + n_z(\partial^2\mu_z/\partial e_i\partial n_i).$$

The ψ_i calculated by this relation agrees with the above expression to terms of order $1/n_i$, where n_i is the number of ions of the ith type present. Thus the two calculations of ψ_i agree except for a quantity of completely negligible order. Applying the condition of integrability to the latter expression for ψ_i, we find that it requires $\partial\psi_s/\partial e_i = \partial^2\psi_s/\partial e_i\partial n_i$. We find that this condition is fulfilled by our ψ_s with the neglect of terms of order $1/n_i$, due to the fact that ψ_s is of the form $e_s f(\kappa)$. It should be remarked that this would not be true for an arbitrary ψ_s, for example, one containing terms of the Gronwall-La Mer type. Thus we have shown that the Guntelberg process gives a result which is consistent with the integrability condition, in the present case. Although the question cannot be definitely settled without an independent statistical calculation of ψ_i we may assume with some confidence that our result is independent of the charging process.

activity coefficient of an ion of type i in a solution containing Zwitterions at a molal concentration C,

$$\log \gamma_i = -\frac{2\pi N Z_i^2 \epsilon^2}{1000 D^2 k^2 T^2} C \sum_{n=1} \frac{(2n+1)Q_n}{(2n-1)(n+1)^2 a^{2n-1}}. \tag{24}$$

This expression is useful in determining the influence of Zwitterions on the solubility of a slightly soluble salt. If N is the solubility of the salt in a solution containing Zwitterions, and N_0 is its solubility in the absence of Zwitterions, we have

$$\log(N/N_0) = -\log \gamma_\pm = -(1/\sum_i \nu_i)\sum_i \nu_i \log \gamma_i, \tag{25}$$

where $\gamma\pm$ is the mean activity coefficient of the salt ions, and ν_i is the number of ions of the ith type produced by a salt molecule.

We now turn our attention to the influence of the dielectric constant of the solvent upon the chemical potential of the complex ion, in the absence of the electrolyte. In this case κ vanishes and W reduces to the first term, W_0, of Eq. (12). If we choose as the standard state a solution of the complex ion at low concentration in a solvent of dielectric constant D_0, we have from Eqs. (13) and (20),

$$\log \gamma = \frac{1}{2kT} \sum_{n=0}^{\infty} \frac{(n+1)Q_n}{b^{2n+1}} \left\{ \frac{1-D}{(n+1)D+n} - \frac{1-D_0}{(n+1)D_0+n} \right\} \tag{26}$$

as the expression for the activity coefficient in a solvent of dielectric constant D. Here again the dielectric constant of the complex ion has been assigned the value unity. The first term of Eq. (26) corresponds to Born's result for an ion having a spherically symmetrical charge distribution.[13] The remaining terms depend upon the multipole electric moments of the ion. For the ratio of the solubilities N and N_0 of Zwitterions in solvents having the respective dielectric constants D and D_0, we may write

$$\log(N/N_0) = -\log \gamma, \tag{27}$$

where $\log \gamma$ is given by Eq. (26). The rate of change of $\log(N/N_0)$ with the reciprocal dielectric constant is

$$\frac{d \log(N/N_0)}{d(1/D)} = -\frac{1}{2kT} \sum_{n=1}^{\infty} \frac{2n+1}{n+1} \frac{Q_n}{b^{2n+1}} \frac{1}{(1+n/(n+1)D)^2}. \tag{28}$$

Thus, as long as D is large, we may expect $\log(N/N_0)$ to be virtually a linear function of $1/D$.[14]

[13] M. Born, *Zeits. f. Physik.* **1**, 45 (1920).

[14] R. P. Bell, *Trans. Faraday Soc.* **27**, 797 (1931), has obtained an equation corresponding to Eq. (26) for the influence of the solvent dielectric constant on the chemical potential of a dipole molecule. Bell's expressions for the electrostatic potentials near the boundary of the molecule agree with the dipole terms ($n = 1$) of our potentials in the limit $\kappa = 0$. However, his value for the electrostatic energy of the dipole differs from ours by a factor $\frac{1}{3}$. To obtain the electrostatic energy, he integrates $DE^2/8\pi$ over all of space. This should and does give the same result as summing $\frac{1}{2}e\psi$ over all charges of the molecule, where ψ is the potential in the interior of the molecule due to external charge distributions. Bell's factor $\frac{1}{3}$ appears to arise from a faulty estimate of $\int DE^2/8\pi dv$ in the interior of the molecule. Thus he extends the integral over the volume occupied by the charges constituting the dipole, which is not permissible, and also uses an expression for the potential which does not converge near these charges.

We should expect Eqs. (21) and (26) to provide a refinement of the simple Debye-Hückel theory in the case of real ions possessing asymmetric charge distributions. Here, however, the terms depending upon the multipole moments of the ion would in general be of the nature of small corrections to the initial terms, depending upon the net charge. In the case of Zwitterions on the other hand, the total charge is zero, and the terms of Eqs. (21) and (26) containing Q_0 vanish. Thus the entire electrical contribution to the chemical potential arises from the multipole moments. For this reason, Eqs. (21) and (26) find their most interesting application to the case of Zwitterions. Of course the present theory is highly simplified and could only be expected to give precise results if the following conditions were exactly fulfilled. (1) The Zwitterions have spherical boundaries. (2) They are present in the solution at such low concentration that their mutual interaction is negligible. (3) Their multipole electric moments are very large relative to those of a solvent molecule. (4) Non-electrostatic deviations from the ideal solution laws are insignificant. (5) Corrections of the Gronwall-La Mer type arising from non-linear terms in the Poisson-Boltzmann equation can be neglected. However, it often happens that these conditions are approximately fulfilled, so that our equations furnish the basis for a semi-quantitative theory of Zwitterionic solutions.

According to the Zwitterionic hypothesis, the aliphatic amino acids exist as hybrid ions in solvents of high dielectric constant. Thus an α-amino acid $RNH_2CHCOOH$ forms a Zwitterion of the structure $R\overset{+}{N}H_3CHCO\overset{-}{O}$. The simplest member of this class of substances is glycine which forms the

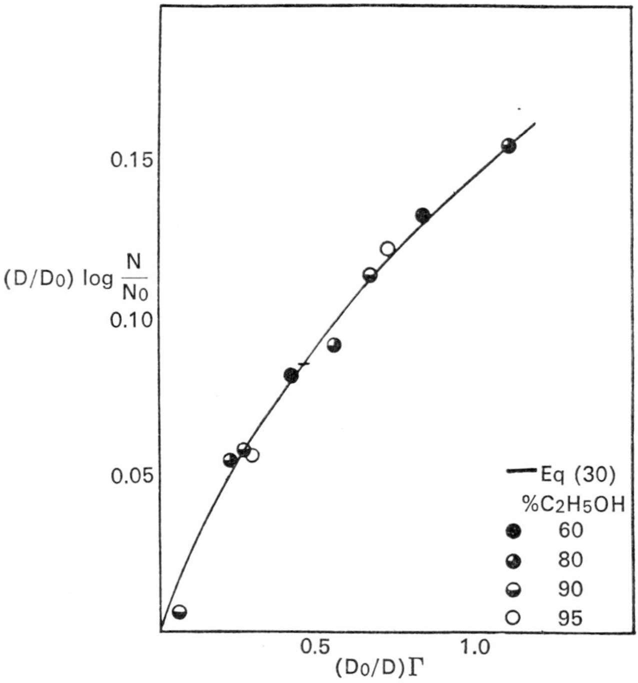

FIG. 1. Solubility of glycine in alcohol-water mixtures containing LiCl at 25°C.

Zwitterion $\overset{+}{N}H_3CH_2C\overset{-}{O}O$. Among the aliphatic amino acids, glycine furnishes the most favorable example for the application of the present theory. Not only may the nonelectrostatic deviation from the ideal solution laws be expected to be a minimum, but also the boundary of the glycine Zwitterion can be roughly approximated by a spherical surface. This is not obvious from the formula, but examination of a steric model makes it plausible. An extensive experimental study of the solubility relations of the aliphatic amino acids in alcohol-water mixtures has been carried out by E. J. Cohn and his co-workers.[15] Professor Cohn has kindly placed at our disposal his data, in part unpublished, relating to the influence of salts and of the dielectric constant of the solvent upon the solubility of glycine.

An interesting property of Eq. (21) provides a means of correlating measurements of the influence of salts on the solubility of glycine in different solvents. By definition, Eq. (3), κ^2 is proportional to Γ/D, where Γ, the ionic strength of the salt, is defined as $\sum_i Z_i^2 C_i/2$. Thus according to Eq. (21), $D \log \gamma$ or $D \log(N/N_0)$ should be the same function of Γ/D for all solvents. This conclusion is confirmed by Cohn's measurements at 25°C. of the solubility of glycine in alcohol-water mixtures containing lithium chloride. In Fig. 1, the experimental values of $(D/D_0) \log(N/N_0)$ in solutions of alcohol content varying from sixty to ninety-five percent, are plotted as a function of $(D_0/D)\Gamma$. The dielectric constant, D_0, of water at 25° has been introduced merely as a convenient scale factor. It is seen that the points fall very nearly upon a single curve up to ionic strengths, which doubtless lie beyond the region of validity of the present theory. Measurements in pure water do not fall upon the curve. This, however, is not to be expected. While the absolute solubility of glycine in solutions of high alcohol content is very low, its solubility in solutions of high water content is so high that the mutual interaction of the glycine hybrid ions can no longer be neglected, and Eq. (21) is no longer applicable.

Unless the charge distribution is concentrated very near the boundary of the ion, the sums in Eq. (21) and Eq. (26) converge quite rapidly, so that it is only necessary to retain the first few terms. For a Zwitterion, Q_0 is of course zero, while Q_1 is equal to the square of the dipole moment μ, and is independent of the position of the electric center of the charge distribution. The constants Q_2, Q_3, etc., are functions of the higher order multipole moments. They depend not only upon the relative charge distribution, but also upon the distance of the electric center from the boundary of the ion. If we approximate the charge distribution of a simple Zwitterion by two point charges $+e$ and $-e$ separated by a distance R, and situated at equal distances r from the center of the boundary sphere b, the constants Q_n have the following values

$$\begin{aligned} Q_0 &= 0, \\ Q_1 &= \mu^2 = \epsilon^2 R^2, \\ Q_2 &= 3\mu^2[r^2 - R^2/4], \\ Q_3 &= 6\mu^2[r^4 - 5r^2R^2/8 + 5R^4/48]. \end{aligned} \tag{29}$$

The Q_n of higher order may be calculated without difficulty from Eq. (14), for this or for any other simple charge distribution. If we neglect terms involving Q_n of higher order than the second, we obtain from Eqs. (21) and

[15] E. J. Cohn, *Naturwiss.* **20**, 44 (1932).

(23), after converting to common logarithms

$$(D/D_0)\log_{10} N/N_0 = A\Gamma'\left\{\frac{Q_1}{a}\frac{1}{1+(B\Gamma')^{\frac{1}{2}}+[1+\frac{1}{2}(b/a)^3]B\Gamma'/3}\right.$$

$$\left.+\frac{20}{81}\frac{Q_2}{a^3}\frac{1+(B\Gamma')^{\frac{1}{2}}}{1+(B\Gamma')^{\frac{1}{2}}+2[1+(1/9)(b/a)^5]B\Gamma'/5+[1+\frac{2}{3}(b/a)^5](B\Gamma')^{\frac{3}{2}}/15}\right\}$$

$$A = 3\pi N\epsilon^2/2303 D_0{}^2k^2T^2 = (3.00\times 10^{34})/D_0{}^2T^2,$$

$$B = 8\pi N\epsilon^2a^2/1000 D_0kT = 2.53\times 10^{19}(a^2/D_0T), \qquad (30)$$

$$\Gamma' = (D_0/D)\Gamma$$

where Q_1 and Q_2 are given by Eq. (29), and the remaining symbols have their usual significance.

In the case of glycine, it is sufficient to retain only the first term of Eq. (30). With a proper choice of the constants Q_1, a and b, Eq. (30) yields the curve of Fig. 1, which fits the experimental points very satisfactorily. The radius, b, of the glycine hybrid ion is estimated from the partial molal volume to lie between 2.6 and 2.8A, depending upon whether a correction for the electrostriction of the solvent is made or not.[16] We therefore assign it a value of 2.7A. The course of the solubility curve is very insensitive to the explicit value of b, being chiefly determined by Q_1 and a. The limiting slope is determined by the ratio Q_1/a and the curvature by a. From the curve, Fig. 1, we obtain a value, 15.0×10^{-18} e.s.u. for the dipole moment, μ, of the glycine Zwitterion, and a value, 3.3A for the mean radius, a, of the salt ions and the Zwitterion. This value of the dipole moment differs but little from Wyman's estimate, 20×10^{-18} e.s.u., based upon measurements of the dielectric constants of an α-amino acid solution.[17] If we divide μ by the electronic charge, we obtain a value, 3.17A, for the effective separation of the positive charge on the basic group and the negative charge on the acidic group of the glycine Zwitterion. From a steric model of glycine, one finds that if the center of gravity of the positive charge is on the nitrogen atom of the amino group and that of the negative charge lies between the oxygen atoms of the carboxyl group, this distance should be about 3.3A. Due to internal polarization of the molecule, the effective separation of the two charges should certainly be less than this. Thus the value, 3.17A, obtained from solubility data with the aid of Eq. (30) furnishes a very reasonable estimate of the effective separation of the charged groups, although it is probably somewhat too large.

We now turn our attention to the influence of the dielectric constant of the solvent upon the solubility of glycine in the absence of salts. If multipoles of higher order than the quadrupole are neglected and common logarithms are introduced, Eq. (28) becomes

$$\frac{d\log_{10}(N/N_0)}{d(1/D)} = -\frac{2.374\times 10^{15}}{T}\left\{\frac{Q_1}{b^3}\frac{1}{(1+1/2D)^2}+\frac{10}{9}\frac{Q_2}{b^5}\frac{1}{(1+2/3D)^2}\right\}. \qquad (31)$$

If $\log(N/N_0)$ were plotted as a function of D^{-1}, the slope of the resulting curve should, according to Eq. (31), be independent of the choice of standard state. Moreover, in solvents of dielectric constant greater than that of alcohol,

[16] E. J. Cohn, *Science* **79**, 83 (1934).

[17] J. Wyman, *J. Am. Chem. Soc.* **56**, 536 (1934).

the factors $(1 + n/(n + 1)D)^{-2}$ vary only slightly from unity. Thus in alcohol-water mixtures, the curve, although slightly concave upward, should differ very little from a straight line. Cohn's measured values of $\log(N/N_0)$ for glycine in alcohol water mixtures at 25°C do not exhibit exactly this type of curve when plotted against $1/D$. In solvents rich in water, the curvature, although in the same direction, is much larger than could be accounted for by Eq. (31). This is probably due to mutual interaction of the glycine Zwitterions, not taken into account in this equation. In solvents rich in alcohol, on the other hand, there is a slight downward curvature not predicted by Eq. (31). This is probably due to a selective effect of the glycine Zwitterion upon the molecules of the mixed solvent, which would tend to make the solution in its immediate neighborhood richer in water than the bulk of the solution. This effect is also neglected in Eq. (31). However, in solvents ranging in alcohol content from forty to eighty percent, the slope is nearly constant, and has a mean value -96.4. If the quadrupole term is neglected, and Eq. (31) is provisionally applied, this slope should be proportional to Q_1/b^3. Using the value of Q_1 previously obtained from the solubility of glycine in salt solutions, we calculate a value, 2.6A, for the radius b of the glycine Zwitterion. This is in good agreement with the estimates of this quantity from the molal volume, which range from 2.6 to 2.8A. The difference, $a - b$, equal to 0.7A, furnishes an estimate of the effective radii of the lithium and chloride ions. If a^{-1} is calculated as the mean reciprocal of b and ionic radii obtained from crystal structure data, this difference, $b - a$, should be about 1A instead of 0.7A. This discrepancy could be removed by assigning a value, 3.6A, to a, instead of 3.3A. If this were done, the dipole moment calculated from the limiting slope of the salt curve, Fig. 1, would become 15.7×10^{-18} e.s.u., differing from the previous value by only five percent. However, the theoretical curve would then fall below the experimental points at the higher ionic strengths. This latter difficulty could perhaps be removed by taking the influence of higher multipole moments and the effect of the salt on the dielectric constant into account. However, such refinements do not seem worth while, in view of other approximations in the theory, such as the neglect of van der Waals forces and of the selective effect of the Zwitterion on the mixed solvent.

From the foregoing discussion, it is seen that the present theory gives an approximate account of the solubility relations of glycine in alcohol-water mixtures, both in the presence and in the absence of salts, as long as the glycine concentration is small. Moreover, it yields values of the dipole moment and of the size of the glycine Zwitterion, which are of reasonable magnitude. The calculated value of the dipole moment, 15×10^{-18} e.s.u., although it may be in error by fifteen or twenty percent, is perhaps the most reliable estimate as yet available. The theory also gives the qualitative aspects of the solubility relations of the other aliphatic amino acids, although, due to their hydrocarbon chains, the boundaries of these molecules cannot be approximated by spherical surfaces. Moreover, there is evidence that nonelectrostatic deviations from ideality in alcohol-water solutions of these acids increase with the length of the hydrocarbon chain. Quantitative agreement with the present theory is therefore not to be expected.

In conclusion, the writer wishes to acknowledge his indebtedness to Professor George Scatchard and to Professor E. J. Cohn for their interest and cooperation in this work.

On the Theory of Strong Electrolyte Solutions*

John G. Kirkwood, *Research Laboratory of Physical Chemistry, Massachusetts Institute of Technology*

(Received June 15, 1934)

The nature of the approximations involved in the derivation of the Poisson-Boltzmann equation of the Debye-Hückel theory is investigated in detail from the standpoint of classical statistical mechanics. The validity of the initial Debye approximation, under the restrictions originally imposed upon it, is confirmed. Deviations arising from fluctuation terms and van der Waals forces are roughly estimated. An alternative to the Bjerrum method for the treatment of ions of small size and high valence is outlined.

I.

Although the Debye-Hückel[1] theory furnishes a strikingly satisfactory account of many of the properties of strong electrolyte solutions, it is based upon physical assumptions, which, though plausible, are not in exact accord with the formal theory of statistical mechanics. This discrepancy has exposed the theory to a certain amount of adverse criticism in recent years. Although some of this criticism has certainly been of value in bringing the imperfections of the theory to light, none of it has been very successful in estimating their quantitative importance. It is the object of the present article to investigate in some detail the approximations involved in the derivation of the Debye-Hückel equations from statistical mechanics, and to estimate, insofar as possible, their quantitative importance.

The formulation of a statistical theory of electrolyte solutions offers little difficulty in itself. However, obstacles are immediately encountered in the evaluation of certain phase integrals. Until these are evaluated the theory remains formal and somewhat impotent. In order to obtain integrals, which can be treated with much hope of success, it is necessary to idealize the solvent as a continuous medium characterized only by its dielectric constant. Let us suppose that a solution of volume v consists of N ions dissolved in a solvent of dielectric constant D. Let F be the Helmholtz free energy, $E - TS$, of the solution when all ions bear their full charges $e_1, \cdots e_N$, and F_0 be the free energy when all ions are completely discharged. For convenience, we exclude from F a constant term of the form $\sum_{k=1}^{N} e_k^2/2Db_k$ arising from the self-energy of the ions. If we assume that the system of N ions, in thermal equilibrium with a temperature T, can be represented by a classical canonical

---

* No. 334.

[1] Debye and Hückel, *Phys. Zeits.* **24**, 185, 305 (1923).

ensemble, we may write

$$e^{-\beta(F-F_0)} = Z_N/Z_N^\circ,$$

$$Z_N = \int \cdots \int e^{-\beta V_N} dv_1 \cdots dv_N, \tag{1}$$

$$Z_N^\circ = \int \cdots \int e^{-\beta U_N} dv_1 \cdots dv_N,$$

where β is equal to $1/kT$, V_N is the mutual potential energy of the fully charged ions, and U_N is the mutual potential energy of the completely discharged ions, consisting only of the terms in V_N, arising from short range van der Waals forces. Integration in the configuration space v_k of each ion is to be extended over the volume, v, occupied by the solution.

The position of any ion k can be specified by a set of configuration coordinates, q_k, for example the three components of a vector $\mathbf{r}_k$, drawn from some arbitrary origin and terminating at the center of the ion k. For simplicity we assume that the ions have no internal degrees of freedom, and that they are spherically symmetrical. Their mutual potential energy may then be expressed as a function of the configuration coordinates $q_1 \cdots q_N$ in the following manner.

$$V_N = \tfrac{1}{2} \sum_{k=1}^{N} [e_k \psi_k(q_k) + U_k(q_k)],$$

$$\psi_k(q_k) - \sum_{\substack{l=1 \\ \neq k}}^{N} \frac{e_l}{D|\mathbf{r}_l - \mathbf{r}_k|}, \tag{2}$$

$$U_k(q_k) = \sum_{\substack{l=1 \\ \neq k}}^{N} u_{kl}(|\mathbf{r}_k - \mathbf{r}_l|),$$

where e_k is the charge on an ion k, and $|\mathbf{r}_l - \mathbf{r}_k|$ is the distance between the ion pair k and l. Thus $\psi_k(q_k)$ is the electrostatic potential produced in the interior of the ion k by the charges on the other ions. The potential of the short range van der Waals and polarization forces can be represented to a very close approximation, as in the theory of imperfect gases, by a sum of terms of the type u_{kl}, each depending only upon the relative coordinates of the ion pair k and l.

Eq. (1) is of course purely formal and is of little value unless it is possible to evaluate the phase integrals Z_N and Z_N°. The integral Z_N°, involving only short range van der Waals forces, may be obtained by the methods employed in the statistical theory of imperfect gases. This method is not applicable in the case of Z_N, which unfortunately is very difficult to treat. Kramers[2] has attempted to evaluate Z_N and van Rysselberghe,[3] using a similar method, has attempted to calculate the osmotic pressure directly without the intermediate calculation of Z_N. Both methods are based upon dimensional considerations, which fail to account satisfactorily for the rôle of the van der

[2] H. A. Kramers, *Proc. Amst. Acad. Sci.* **30**, 145 (1927).
[3] P. van Rysselberghe, *J. Chem. Phys.* **1**, 205 (1933).

Waals forces between the ions. Moreover, unless these forces, which determine the size of the ions, are taken into account, Z_N clearly diverges. Thus, while very ingenious, the investigations of both Kramers and van Rysselberghe fail to do much more than confirm the Debye-Hückel limiting law at low concentrations, without indicating how a better approximation may be obtained.

Instead of basing the calculation of the free energy F on a direct determination of Z_N, it is possible to start from the mean electrostatic potential in an ion, defined as follows:

$$\bar{\psi}_k = \frac{\int \cdots \int \psi_k(q_k) e^{-\beta V_N} dv_1 \cdots dv_N}{\int \cdots \int e^{-\beta V_N} dv_1 \cdots dv_N}. \tag{3}$$

From (1), it is easily demonstrated that

$$\begin{aligned} \partial F / \partial e_k &= \bar{\psi}_k, && \text{(a)} \\ \partial \bar{\psi}_k / \partial e_l &= \partial \bar{\psi}_l / \partial e_k. && \text{(b)} \end{aligned} \tag{4}$$

These relations have been derived and discussed in detail by Onsager[4] and later by Halpern.[5] If the charges on the ions are varied in an arbitrary manner, we have from (4a)

$$\delta F = \sum_{k=1}^{N} \frac{\partial F}{\partial e_k} \delta e_k = \sum_{k=1}^{N} \bar{\psi}_k \delta e_k. \tag{5}$$

From (4b), the condition of integrability, we may conclude that the integral of δF in any charging process depends only upon the initial and final values of the charges, and not upon the method of charging. Thus the difference $F - F_0$, where F is the free energy of the solution when all ions have the full charges $e_1 \cdots e_N$, and F_0, the free energy when all ions are completely discharged, may be obtained by integrating $\sum_{k=1}^{N} \bar{\psi}_k \delta e_k$ along any path. The Debye charging process is the one most commonly employed. In this process, all ions are charged simultaneously by equal fractions of their final charge, so that

$$F - F_0 = \sum_{k=1}^{N} \int_0^1 e_k \overline{\psi_k(\lambda e_1, \cdots \lambda e_N)} d\lambda. \tag{6}$$

It is often possible to assume that F_0 is the free energy of an ideal solution, or when this is not permissible to treat it by empirical methods, applicable to ordinary non-electrolyte solutions. It is to be emphasized that the charging process need not be attributed physical significance, but can be regarded simply as a mathematical device for calculating the free energy function, F, defined by Eq. (1). The method outlined here, although somewhat indirect, has distinct advantages, since it is easier to calculate $\bar{\psi}_k$, at least approximately, than it is to calculate Z_N.

II.

The foundation for a precise statistical calculation of $\bar{\psi}_k$, the mean potential produced in an ion k, by the other ions in the solution, was laid by Fowler.[6]

[4] Onsager, *Chem. Rev.* **13**, 73 (1933).
[5] Halpern, *J. Chem. Phys.* **2**, 85 (1934).
[6] R. H. Fowler, *Statistical Mechanics*, 8.7, 8.8, Cambridge University Press (1929).

We shall have occasion to use the mean Poisson equation of Fowler's theory, Eqs. (582) and (584), which we derive here in a slightly different and somewhat more direct manner. From this point on, we depart from Fowler, employing a method of treating the statistical space charge around an ion, which leads to somewhat more concrete results.

We begin by considering the electrostatic potential at some fixed point, q, in the solution

$$\psi(q) = \sum_{l=1}^{N} (e_l/D|\mathbf{r}_l - \mathbf{r}|), \tag{7}$$

where $|\mathbf{r}_l - \mathbf{r}|$ is the distance of the lth ion from the point q. The mean value of $\psi(q)$, when a selected ion k is fixed at a point q_k is given by

$$\overline{\psi(q)}^{k} = \frac{\int\cdots\int\psi(q)e^{-\beta V_N}dv_1\cdots dv_{N-1}}{\int\cdots\int e^{-\beta V_N}dv_1\cdots dv_{N-1}} \tag{8}$$

where the integrations are extended over the coordinates of all ions except those of the selected ion, k. We define $\psi_k(q)$ as the potential at q, arising from all ions except the fixed ion k.

$$\psi_k(q) = \psi(q) - e_k/D|\mathbf{r} - \mathbf{r}_k|. \tag{9}$$

The term $e_k/D|\mathbf{r} - \mathbf{r}_k|$ is a constant as long as ion k remains fixed, and is unaffected by a mean value operation of the type (8). Suppose that $\overline{\psi_k(q)}^{k}$ has been determined everywhere in the neighborhood of the ion k, and let $\overline{\psi_k(q_k)}^{k}$ be its value in the interior of the ion k. From Eqs. (3) and (8) we obtain the relation

$$\frac{\int \overline{\psi_k(q_k)}^{k}[\int\cdots\int e^{-\beta V_N}dv_1\cdots dv_{N-1}]dv_k}{\int\cdots\int e^{-\beta V_N}dv_1\cdots dv_N} = \overline{\psi}_k. \tag{10}$$

If $\overline{\psi_k(q_k)}^{k}$ is independent of q_k, we may write immediately

$$\overline{\psi_k}^{k} = \overline{\psi}_k. \tag{11}$$

We may assume without formal proof that $\overline{\psi_k}^{k}$ is independent of q_k, that is, of the position of k relative to the boundaries of the solution, except in a surface region of negligible volume. Otherwise direct contradictions with experiment would result, such as concentration gradients in the bulk of the solution. Therefore Eq. (11) may be accepted as valid, except for a quantity of negligible order.

We may rewrite Eq. (8), which defines $\overline{\psi(q)}^{k}$, in a somewhat different manner.

$$\begin{aligned}\overline{\psi(q)}^{k} &= \sum_{\substack{l=1\\ \neq k}}^{N} \int \frac{\overline{\rho_l(q_l)}^{k}}{D|\mathbf{r}_l - \mathbf{r}|}\, dv_l + \frac{e_k}{D|\mathbf{r}_k - \mathbf{r}|},\\ \overline{\rho_l(q_l)}^{k} &= e_l \frac{\int\cdots\int e^{-\beta[V_{N-1}+V_l(q_l)]}dv_1\cdots dv_{N-2}}{\int\cdots\int e^{-\beta V_N}dv_1\cdots dv_{N-1}}.\end{aligned} \tag{12}$$

In the expression for $\overset{k}{\overline{\rho_l(q_l)}}$, the coordinates of both k and l remain fixed in the integral in the numerator, while only those of k remain fixed in the integral in the denominator. For clearness we have expressed V_N as a sum of two terms, V_{N-1}, which is independent of q_l, and $V_l(q_l)$ which is given by

$$V_l(q_l) = e_l\psi_l(q_l) + U_l(q_l).$$

This is merely a rearrangement of terms, which may be carried out for any one of the N ions. Eq. (12) is precisely the solution of the following Poisson equation:[7]

$$\nabla^2 \overset{k}{\overline{\psi(q)}} = -(4\pi/D)\, \overset{k}{\overline{\rho(q)}},$$

$$\overset{k}{\overline{\rho(q)}} = \sum_{l=1}^{N} e_l \frac{\int\cdots\int e^{-\beta[V_{N-1}+V_l(q)]}dv_1\cdots dv_{N-2}}{\int\cdots\int e^{-\beta V_N}dv_1\cdots dv_{N-1}}. \tag{13}$$

In general, there will be several ion types present in the solution. If N_i be the number of ions of the ith type, N_i/v is the bulk concentration C_i of that type. Moreover, $\overset{k}{\overline{\rho_l(q)}}$ is the same function $\overset{k}{\overline{\rho_i(q)}}$ for all ions of the ith type. Therefore we may write

$$\overset{k}{\overline{\rho(q)}} = \sum_i c_i e_i \zeta_{ki}(q),$$

$$\zeta_{ki}(q) = \frac{v\,\overset{k}{\overline{\rho_i(q)}}}{e_i} = \frac{v\int\cdots\int e^{-\beta[V_{N-1}+V_i(q)]}dv_1\cdots dv_{N-2}}{\int\cdots\int e^{-\beta V_N}dv_1\cdots dv_{N-1}} \tag{14}$$

and the Poisson Eq. (13) becomes $\nabla^2 \overset{k}{\overline{\psi(q)}} = -(4\pi/D)\sum_i c_i e_i \zeta_{ki}(q)$, (15)

where the sum is extended over all ion types. Properly, the selected ion k should be omitted from the sum, but its omission would alter the concentration of the type to which it belongs by a quantity of the order C_i/N_i, which can be ignored altogether.

---

[7] The passage from (12) to (13) follows from a well-known transformation in potential theory, depending upon the fact that $\nabla^2|\mathbf{r}_l - \mathbf{r}|^{-1}$ is zero except when $\mathbf{r}_l = \mathbf{r}$, where it has a singularity. Thus in any integral of the form

$$\int F(q_l)\nabla^2|\mathbf{r}_l - \mathbf{r}|^{-1}dv_l$$

the integrand is zero except in the immediate neighborhood of the point $\mathbf{r}_l = \mathbf{r}$. The integral in the vicinity of this point may be transformed by Green's theorem and evaluated as $J = -4\pi F(q)$. This may be represented symbolically by saying that $\nabla^2|\mathbf{r}_l - \mathbf{r}|^{-1}$ is a delta-function

$$\nabla^2|\mathbf{r}_l - \mathbf{r}|^{-1} = -4\pi\delta(\mathbf{r}_l - \mathbf{r}),$$

where $\delta(\mathbf{r}_l - \mathbf{r})$ has the property

$$\int F(q_l)\delta(\mathbf{r}_l - \mathbf{r})dv_l = F(q).$$

Thus the $\rho(x)$ in the integrand of Fowler's Eq. (584) is simply

$$-4\pi \sum_{\substack{l=1\\ \neq k}}^{N} \delta(\mathbf{r}_l - \mathbf{r}).$$

It is sometimes convenient to define a function V_{ki} by means of the following relation

$$e^{-\beta V_{ki}} = \zeta_{ki}. \tag{16}$$

It may be shown that V_{ki} is the potential of the mean force acting on the ion i at the point q.[4] When the ζ_{ki} are expressed in the form (16), Eq. (15) becomes identical in form with Fowler's Eqs. (583) and (584). From Eqs. (14) and (16) one obtains by differentiation of ζ_{ki}

$$\nabla^2 V_{ki} + 4\pi e_i \rho_{ki}/D = -\beta[\,{}^{ik}\overline{(\nabla V_i)^2} - (\nabla V_{ki})^2],$$

$$\rho_{ki} = -\frac{D}{4\pi e_i}\,{}^{ik}\overline{\nabla^2 V_i}, \tag{17}$$

where the mean values are taken with the ion i fixed at the point q and the ion k fixed at the point q_k. Eq. (17) is identical with Fowler's Eqs. (585) and (586). If the quantities ρ_{ki} and ${}^{ik}\overline{(\nabla V_i)^2}$ were known, ${}^{k}\overline{\psi(q)}$ could be determined by the simultaneous solution of Eqs. (15), (16), and (17) with appropriate boundary conditions. Unfortunately, we do not have the necessary information about ρ_{ki} and ${}^{ik}\overline{(\nabla V_i)^2}$, nor does there seem to be any practicable means of obtaining it. For this reason, we prefer to study the charge density ${}^{k}\overline{\rho(q)}$ of Eq. (14) by another method, which utilizes the properties of the functions ζ_{ki} themselves and not those of their derivatives.

The familiar Poisson-Boltzmann equation of the Debye-Hückel theory follows immediately from Eqs. (15) and (16) when $e_i\,{}^{k}\overline{\psi(q)}$ is substituted for V_{ki} in ζ_{ki}. This is admittedly an approximation, for it involves the assumption that the potential of the mean force is equal to the mean potential. However, the approximation

$$V_{ki} = e_i\,{}^{k}\overline{\psi(q)} \tag{18}$$

is by no means as objectionable as the approximation attributed to Debye and Hückel by Fowler (*Statistical Mechanics*, Eq. (587))

$$\nabla^2 V_{ki} = -(4\pi e_i/D)\,{}^{k}\overline{\rho(q)} = e_i \nabla^2\,{}^{k}\overline{\psi(q)}. \tag{19}$$

Thus two functions may be approximately equal over a large interval even though their second derivatives are not. The approximate validity of (18), for example at large distances from the selected ion k, is not subject to the validity of (19) nor would it even follow from (19), unless all boundary values of the two functions $e_i\,{}^{k}\overline{\psi(q)}$ and V_{ki} were equal.

Fowler's criticism of the Debye-Hückel theory was based upon Eqs. (17) and (19). In order for these equations to be consistent it is necessary that $\beta[\,{}^{ik}\overline{(\nabla V_i)^2} - (\nabla V_{ki})^2] + 4\pi e_i \rho_{ki}/D$ be equal to $4\pi e_i\,{}^{k}\overline{\rho(q)}/D$. If ρ_{ki} and ${}^{k}\overline{\rho(q)}$ were approximately equal, the fluctuation in the force acting upon the ion i would have to be small. However, it turns out that this requirement is not necessary, for ρ_{ki} is quite different from ${}^{k}\overline{\rho(q)}$ and always much smaller. As Onsager[4] has pointed out Eq. (17) is meaningless, unless van der Waals forces of the repulsive type are taken into account. By the method employed in the derivation of Eq. (13), it is readily shown[8] that these repulsive forces, which give the ions their finite size, cause the Coulomb contribution to ρ_{ki} to vanish. Thus Eq. (17) should actually be written in the following manner:

$$-\beta[\overline{{}^{ik}(\nabla V_i)^2} - (\nabla V_{ki})^2] = \nabla^2 V_{ki} - \overline{{}^{ik}\nabla^2 U_i}, \tag{17a}$$

where $U_i(q)$ is the potential of the short range forces acting upon the ion i. This circumstance makes it even more difficult to determine whether Eqs. (17) and (19) are consistent, but it removes the restriction that the fluctuation in the force must be small. Finally, when it is emphasized that Debye and Hückel wished to obtain a differential equation for $\overline{{}^{k}\psi(q)}$, not V_{ki}, and that their result follows directly from Eqs. (15) and (18), it becomes clear that the adequacy of their approximation should not be judged on the basis of Eq. (19). Thus to conclude that the two functions V_{ki} and $e_i\,\overline{{}^{k}\psi(q)}$ could not be approximately equal in an extensive region of the solution simply because their second derivatives may not be equal, would to say the least, put the Debye-Hückel approximation in an unjustifiably unfavorable light.

III.

Solution of the Poisson Eq. (15) requires a knowledge of the mean charge density, $\overline{{}^{k}\rho(q)}$, which is expressible in terms of the functions ζ_{ki}. We shall now investigate the relation of these functions to the mean potential $\overline{{}^{k}\psi(q)}$. The method to be employed is in certain respects similar to a general method

---

[8] The density function ρ_{ki} in Eq. (17) is equal to $-\dfrac{D}{4\pi e_i}\overline{{}^{ik}\nabla^2 V_i(q)}$.

$$\overline{{}^{ik}\Delta^2 V_i} = \frac{\int\cdots\int \nabla^2 V_i(q) e^{-\beta V_N(q_i=q)} dv_1 \cdots dv_{N-2}}{\int\cdots\int e^{-\beta V_N(q_i=q)} dv_1 \cdots dv_{N-2}}, \tag{a}$$

where the ions i and k remain fixed during the averaging process. Since

$$V_i(q) = e_i \sum_{\substack{l=1\\ \neq i}}^{N} \frac{e_l}{D|\mathbf{r}_l - \mathbf{r}|} + U_i(q), \tag{b}$$

we may write (see reference 7)

$$\nabla^2 V_i = -\frac{4\pi e_i}{D} \sum_{\substack{l=1\\ \neq i}}^{N} e_l \delta(\mathbf{r}_l - \mathbf{r}) + \nabla^2 U_i. \tag{c}$$

Thus

$$\overline{{}^{ik}\nabla^2 V_i} = -\frac{4\pi e_i}{D} \sum_{\substack{l=1\\ \neq i}}^{N} e_l \frac{\int\cdots\int e^{-\beta V_N(q_l=q_i=q)} dv_1 \cdots dv_{N-3}}{\int\cdots\int e^{-\beta V_N(q_i=q)} dv_1 \cdots dv_{N-2}} + \overline{{}^{ik}\nabla^2 U_i}. \tag{d}$$

Now due to van der Waals forces V_N contains terms of the form $u_{il}(q_i - q_l)$. Whenever any $|q_i - q_l|$ becomes zero as for example when $q_i = q_l = q$, there is always a term which becomes positively infinite and makes $e^{-\beta V_N(q_i=q_l)}$ vanish. Thus the first term of (d), arising from electrostatic forces, always vanishes and we are left with

$$\rho_{ki} = -(D/4\pi e_i)\overline{{}^{ik}\nabla^2 U_i}. \tag{e}$$

proposed by Onsager.[4] We differentiate ζ_{ki} with respect to e_i, the charge on the ion i. Remembering Eqs. (2) and (14), we obtain

$$\frac{\partial\zeta_{ki}}{\partial e_i} = -\beta\zeta_{ki}[{}^{ik}\overline{\psi_i(q)} - {}^{k}\overline{\psi_i(q_i)}], \tag{20}$$

$${}^{k}\overline{\psi_i(q_i)} = \frac{\int\cdots\int\psi_i(q_i)e^{-\beta V_N}dv_1\cdots dv_{N-1}}{\int\cdots\int e^{-\beta V_N}dv_1\cdots dv_{N-1}},$$

$${}^{ik}\overline{\psi_i(q)} = \frac{\int\cdots\int\psi_i(q)e^{-\beta[V_{N-1}+V_i(q)]}dv_1\cdots dv_{N-2}}{\int\cdots\int e^{-\beta[V_{N-1}+V_i(q)]}dv_1\cdots dv_{N-2}}. \tag{21}$$

Thus ${}^{ik}\overline{\psi_i(q)}$ is the mean value of the potential at the point q, when the ion i is fixed at that point, and the ion k is fixed at the point q_k. The subscript i in $\psi_i(q)$ means as before that the term, $e_i/D|\mathbf{r}_i - \mathbf{r}|$ is omitted. For certain purposes it is convenient to express this potential in a somewhat different form. The mean potential at any point q', when the ions i and k are fixed at any points q_i and q_k is

$${}^{ik}\overline{\psi_i(q'; q_i, q_k)} = \frac{\int\cdots\int\psi_i(q')e^{-\beta V_N(q_i,\cdots q_k\cdots)}dv_1\cdots dv_{N-2}}{\int\cdots\int e^{-\beta V_N(q_i,\cdots q_k\cdots)}dv_1\cdots dv_{N-2}}. \tag{22}$$

The potential ${}^{ik}\overline{\psi_i(q)}$ is evidently equal to ${}^{ik}\overline{\psi_i(q; q, q_k)}$, that is the value of (22) when $q' = q_i = q$. Moreover, it is clear that this latter potential must depend only on the relative coordinates $|q - q_k|$ of the ions i and k (except in the surface region of the solution). It therefore remains unaltered by an interchange of the coordinates of i and k, or by a shift of their center of gravity.

$${}^{ik}\overline{\psi_i(q; q, q_k)} = {}^{ik}\overline{\psi_i(q_i; q_i, q')}, \qquad |q - q_k| = |q' - q_i|, \tag{23}$$

so that one may write

$${}^{ik}\overline{\psi_i(q)} = \frac{\int\cdots\int\psi_i(q_i)e^{-\beta[V_{N-1}+V_k(q')]}dv_1\cdots dv_{N-2}}{\int\cdots\int e^{-\beta[V_{N-1}+V_k(q')]}dv_1\cdots dv_{N-2}}, \tag{24}$$

subject to the condition that $|q' - q_i| = |q - q_k|$. We shall have occasion to use both of the alternative expressions (21) and (24) in discussing the properties of ${}^{ik}\overline{\psi_i(q)}$.

We may integrate Eq. (20) at once to obtain

$$\zeta_{ki} = \zeta_{ki}^{\circ}e^{-\beta\int_0^{e_i}[{}^{ik}\overline{\psi_i(q)} - {}^{k}\overline{\psi_i(q_i)}]de_i}, \tag{25}$$

$$\zeta_{ki}^{\circ} = \frac{v\int\cdots\int e^{-\beta[V_{N-1}+u_i(q)]}dv_1\cdots dv_{N-2}}{\int\cdots\int e^{-\beta[V_{N-1}+u_i(q_i)]}dv_1\cdots dv_{N-1}},$$

$$= \frac{\int\cdots\int e^{-\beta[V_{N-1}+u_i(q)]}dv_1\cdots dv_{N-1}}{\int\cdots\int e^{-\beta[V_{N-1}+u_i(q_i)]}dv_1\cdots dv_{N-1}}. \tag{26}$$

In the second equality (26), the v factor has simply been written as an integration over q_i. This can be done since the integrand $e^{-\beta[V_{N-1}+u_i(q)]}$ is independent of q_i, the running coordinates of the i ion having been replaced by q. It may be noted that ζ_{ki}° is formally the mean value, when $e_i = 0$, of the following function

$$\zeta_i^\circ = e^{-\beta[u_i(q)-u_i(q_i)]}; \qquad \zeta_{ki}^\circ = \overline{\zeta_i^\circ}^{k}\Big|_{e_i=0}. \tag{27}$$

Substitution of (25) in Eq. (15) yields

$$\nabla^2 \overline{\psi(q)}^{k} = -\frac{4\pi}{D} \sum_i c_i e_i \zeta_{ki}^\circ e^{-\beta\int_0^{e_i} [\overline{\psi_i(q)}^{ik} - \overline{\psi_i(q_i)}^{k}]de_i}. \tag{28}$$

This is an exact form of the Poisson equation for the mean potential $\overline{\psi(q)}^{k}$. We note that each of the ζ_{ki}° contains a factor $e^{-\beta u_{ki}(q-q_k)}$. When $|q - q_k|$ becomes small, van der Waals repulsion makes $u_{ki}(q - q_k)$ positively infinite and each ζ_{ki}° vanishes. Thus "inside" the ion k, the right-hand side of Eq. (28) vanishes, and it becomes Laplace's equation. Outside of the ion k, the ζ_{ki}° are effectively unity except for a small term depending upon van der Waals forces. Without going into the details of the calculation, which would divert us from our main purpose, we may state that ζ_{ki}° is approximately given by[9]

$$\zeta_{ki}^\circ = 1 - 2\sum_j B_{ij} C_j(\zeta_{kj} - 1) + \cdots, \tag{29}$$

where the B_{ij} have the same form as the second virial coefficients of an imperfect gas, and C_j is the bulk concentration of the ion type j. If van der Waals forces of the attractive type are ignored and the ions are treated as rigid spheres, one may write

$$B_{ij} = (2\pi/3)a_{ij}^3, \tag{30}$$

where a_{ij} is the mean diameter of ions of types i and j.

---

[9] The function $\zeta_{ki}^\circ - 1$ has the form

$$\zeta_{ki}^\circ - 1 = \frac{\int\cdots\int e^{-\beta V_{N-1}}[e^{-\beta u_i(q)} - e^{-\beta u_i(q_i)}]dv_1\cdots dv_{N-1}}{\int\cdots\int e^{-\beta[V_{N-1}+u_i(q_i)]}dv_1\cdots dv_{N-1}}.$$

Making use of the identity

$$e^{-\beta u_i(q)} - e^{-\beta u_i(q_i)} = (e^{-\beta u_i(q)} - 1) - (e^{-\beta u_i(q_i)} - 1)$$

we may write

$$\zeta_{ki}^\circ - 1 = \frac{\int\cdots\int e^{-\beta V_{N-1}}[e^{-\beta u_i(q)} - 1]dv_1\cdots dv_{N-1}}{\int\cdots\int e^{-\beta[V_{N-1}+u_i(q_i)]}dv_1\cdots dv_{N-1}} - \frac{\int\cdots\int e^{-\beta V_{N-1}}[e^{-\beta u_i(q_i)} - 1]dv_1\cdots dv_{N-1}}{\int\cdots\int e^{-\beta[V_{N-1}+u_i(q_i)]}dv_1\cdots dv_{N-1}}.$$

Now $U_i(q) = \sum_{j=1,\,\neq i}^{N} u_{ij}(q_j - q)$, where the potentials, $u_{ij}(q_j - q)$, of the short range forces are effectively zero unless the distance $|\mathbf{r}_j - \mathbf{r}|$ is very small, of the order of a molecular diameter. Thus $e^{-\beta u_i(q)} - 1$ is zero unless at least one distance $|\mathbf{r}_j - \mathbf{r}|$ is of the order of a molecular diameter. Likewise $e^{-\beta u_i(q_i)} - 1$ is zero unless at least one interionic distance $|\mathbf{r}_j - \mathbf{r}_i|$

We are chiefly interested in the properties of the mean potentials $\overline{{}^{ik}\psi_i(q)}$ and $\overline{{}^{k}\psi_i(q_i)}$. By means of the following identity, we can relate $\overline{{}^{ik}\psi_i(q)}$ to its values $\overline{{}^{ik}\psi_i(q)}\big|_{e_i=0}$ and $\overline{{}^{ik}\psi_i(q)}\big|_{e_k=0}$, when the charges on the ions i and k are, respectively, zero.

$$\overline{{}^{ik}\psi_i(q)} = \overline{{}^{ik}\psi_i(q)}\Big|_{e_i=0} + \overline{{}^{ik}\psi_i(q)}\Big|_{e_k=0} - \overline{{}^{ik}\psi_i(q)}\Big|_{e_i=0;\ e_k=0} + \int_0^{e_i}\int_0^{e_k} \frac{\partial^2 \overline{{}^{ik}\psi_i(q)}}{\partial e_i \partial e_k}\, de_i de_k. \tag{31}$$

When the charge e_i is zero, we have from Eq. (22)

$$\overline{{}^{ik}\psi_i(q)}\Big|_{e_i=0} = \frac{\int\cdots\int \psi_i(q) e^{-\beta[V_{N-1}+u_i(q)]} dv_1 \cdots dv_{N-2}}{\int\cdots\int e^{-\beta[V_{N-1}+u_i(q)]} dv_1 \cdots dv_{N-2}}. \tag{32}$$

Both numerator and denominator of (32) may be multiplied by v, and since both integrands are independent of q_i, all q_i's having been replaced by q, the v factors may be expressed as integrations over the running coordinates q_i.

$$\overline{{}^{ik}\psi_i(q)}\Big|_{e_i=0} = \frac{\int\cdots\int \psi_i(q) e^{-\beta[V_{N-1}+u_i(q)]} dv_1 \cdots dv_{N-1}}{\int\cdots\int e^{-\beta[V_{N-1}+u_i(q)]} dv_1 \cdots dv_{N-1}}. \tag{33}$$

---

is of the order of a molecular diameter. Thus each of the two parts of $\zeta_{ki}^\circ - 1$ must at least contain the ionic concentration C to a power not lower than the first, and we may state at once $\zeta_{ki}^\circ - 1 = 0(C)$ that is, $\zeta_{ki}^\circ - 1$ is of negligible order if we neglect terms involving the first power of the concentration. However, we can go farther than that. Thus we may write

$$e^{-\beta u_i(q)} = \prod_{\substack{j=1\\ \neq i}}^{N} e^{-\beta u_{ij}(q_j - q)} = \prod_{\substack{j=1\\ \neq i}}^{N} [1 + (e^{-\beta u_{ij}} - 1)].$$

Expansion of the continued product gives as a first approximation

$$e^{-\beta u_i(q)} = 1 + \sum_{\substack{j=1\\ \neq i}}^{N} (e^{-\beta u_{ij}} - 1) + \cdots.$$

Now consider an integral of the form

$$\int f(q_j)[e^{-\beta u_{ij}(q)} - 1] dv_j.$$

Since $(e^{-\beta u_{ij}(q)} - 1)$ is zero except when q_j is in the immediate neighborhood of q, we may write approximately

$$\int f(q_j)[e^{-\beta u_{ij}(q)} - 1] dv_j = -2B_{ij} f(q),$$

$$B_{ij} = \tfrac{1}{2} \int (1 - e^{-\beta u_{ij}}) dv_j.$$

This is a rough but adequate approximation when $f(q_j)$ does not vary rapidly over the small region, in which $u_{ji}(q_j - q)$ is effectively different from zero. It amounts to replacing $f(q_j)$ in this region by its value at the center $q = q_j$. Making this approximation, the function $\zeta_{ki}^\circ - 1$ becomes with the neglect of terms in C^2,

$$\zeta_{ki}^\circ - 1 = -2 \sum_j C_j B_{ij} (\zeta_{kj}' - 1),$$

$$\zeta_{kj}' = \frac{v \int\cdots\int e^{-\beta[V_{N-2}+V_j(q)]} dv_1 \cdots dv_{N-2}}{\int\cdots\int e^{-\beta V_{N-1}} dv_1 \cdots dv_{N-1}}.$$

Thus ζ_{kj}' differs from ζ_{kj}, simply by the removal of the single ion i. This removal can produce a change in ζ_{kj} only of the order of ζ_{kj}/N_i, so that effectively $\zeta_{kj}' = \zeta_{kj}$.

In this expression both q_k and q are of course held fixed during the integrations. With the aid of (2), (27) and (33) we find

$$\overline{{}^{ik}\psi_i(q)}\big|_{e_i=0} = \frac{\overline{{}^{k}\psi_i(q)\zeta_i^\circ}\big|_{e_i=0}}{\zeta_{ki}^\circ} = \overline{{}^{k}\psi_i(q)}\big|_{e_i=0}$$

$$+ \frac{\overline{{}^{k}\psi_i(q)\zeta_i^\circ}\big|_{e_i=0} - \overline{{}^{k}\psi_i(q)}\big|_{e_i=0}\overline{{}^{k}\zeta_i^\circ}\big|_{e_i=0}}{\overline{{}^{k}\zeta_i^\circ}\big|_{e_i=0}}. \qquad (34)$$

The second term in expression (34) depends primarily upon van der Waals forces and is approximately given by

$$\frac{\overline{{}^{k}\psi_i(q)\zeta_i^\circ}\big|_{e_i=0} - \overline{{}^{k}\psi_i(q)}\big|_{e_i=0}\overline{{}^{k}\zeta_i^\circ}\big|_{e_i=0}}{\overline{{}^{k}\zeta_i^\circ}\big|_{e_i=0}} =$$

$$-2\sum_j B_{ij}C_j\zeta_{kj}\left[\frac{3}{2}\frac{e_j}{Da_{ij}} + \overline{{}^{jk}\psi_{ij}(q)}\big|_{ei=0} - \overline{{}^{k}\psi_i(q)}\big|_{ei=0}\right] \qquad (35)$$

where the various symbols have the same meaning as in Eq. (29).[9]

Starting from Eq. (24) instead of from (22), we obtain in a similar manner the following expression for $\overline{{}^{ik}\psi_i(q)}\big|_{e_k=0}$

$$\overline{{}^{ik}\psi_i(q)}\big|_{e_k=0} = \overline{{}^{i}\psi_i(q_i)}\big|_{e_k=0} + \frac{\overline{{}^{i}\psi_i(q_i)\zeta_k^\circ(q')}\big|_{e_k=0} - \overline{{}^{i}\psi_i(q_i)}\big|_{e_k=0}\overline{{}^{i}\zeta_k^\circ(q')}\big|_{e_k=0}}{\overline{{}^{i}\zeta_k^\circ(q')}\big|_{e_k=0}}$$

$$|q' - q_i| = |q - q_k|. \qquad (36)$$

As in (34), the second term of (36) is small, and depends primarily upon van der Waals forces.

The potential $\overline{{}^{ik}\psi_i(q)}|_{e_i=0;\ e_k=0}$ is of course zero if all ions are of equal size, that is if all u_{ki} have the same form. If the sizes are unequal $\overline{{}^{ik}\psi_i(q)}|_{e_i=0,\ e_k=0}$ will consist of a small term proportional to the concentration, arising from a statistical double layer on the surface of the ion i.

Differentiation of Eq. (21) leads to the following expression for $\partial^2\ \overline{{}^{ik}\psi_i(q)}/\partial e_i\partial e_k$

$$\frac{\partial^2\ \overline{{}^{ik}\psi_i(q)}}{\partial e_i\partial e_k} = \beta^2\ \overline{{}^{ik}[\psi_k(q_k) - \overline{{}^{ik}\psi_k(q_k)}][\psi_i(q) - \overline{{}^{ik}\psi_i(q)}]^2}. \qquad (37)$$

This derivative is thus a fluctuation of the third order.

Combining (34), (36) and (37), we obtain, remembering that quantities with the subscript, $e_i = 0$, are independent of e_i

$$\int_0^{e_i} [\overline{{}^{ik}\psi_i(q)} - \overline{{}^{k}\psi_i(q_i)}]de_i$$

$$= e_i\,\overline{{}^{k}\psi_i(q)}\big|_{e_i=0} + \int_0^{e_i} [\overline{{}^{i}\psi_i(q_i)}\big|_{e_k=0} - \overline{{}^{k}\psi_i(q_i)}]de_i + \varphi_{ki}(q), \qquad (38)$$

where

$$\varphi_{ki}(q) = \int_0^{e_i}\int_0^{e_i}\int_0^{e_k} \beta^2\, {}^{ik}\overline{[\psi_k(q_k) - {}^{ik}\overline{\psi_k(q_k)}][\psi_i(q) - {}^{ik}\overline{\psi_i(q)}]^2}\, de_i de_i de_k$$

$$+ e_i\left[\frac{{}^{k}\overline{\psi_i(q)\zeta_i^\circ(q)}\Big|_{e_i=0} - {}^{k}\overline{\psi_i(q)}\Big|_{e_i=0}\, {}^{k}\overline{\zeta_i^\circ(q')}\Big|_{e_i=0}}{{}^{k}\overline{\zeta_i^\circ(q)}\Big|_{e_i=0}} - {}^{ik}\overline{\psi_i(q)}\Big|_{e_i=0,\ e_k=0}\right]$$

$$+ \int_0^{e_i}\left[\frac{{}^{i}\overline{\psi_i(q_i)\zeta_k^\circ(q')}\Big|_{e_k=0} - {}^{i}\overline{\psi_i(q_i)}\Big|_{e_k=0}\, {}^{i}\overline{\zeta_k^\circ(q')}\Big|_{e_k=0}}{{}^{i}\overline{\zeta_k^\circ(q')}\Big|_{e_k=0}}\right] de_i. \qquad (39)$$

It is readily seen that the mean potential ${}^{k}\overline{\psi_i(q)|_{e_i=0}}$ differs from ${}^{k}\overline{\psi(q)}$ by a quantity of order ${}^{k}\overline{\psi(q)}/N_i$ where N_i is the number of ions of the ith type. In an averaging process in which only the k ion is held fixed, all ions of the ith type are equivalent. Thus the discharge of a single i ion would alter the potential only by a quantity of negligible order $(1/N_i)$. (The discharge of a single ion of course destroys the electrical neutrality of the solution but in a completely trivial manner.) For the same reason ${}^{i}\overline{\psi_i(q_i)|_{e_k=0}}$ can be identified with ${}^{i}\overline{\psi_i(q_i)}$. Since by Eq. (11) this latter potential is equal to $\bar{\psi}_i$, we may identify ${}^{i}\overline{\psi_i(q_i)|_{e_k=0}}$ with ψ_i. Further it is clear that ${}^{k}\overline{\psi_i(q_i)}$ also differs from $\bar{\psi}_i$ by a quantity of negligible order. The fixed ion k can influence the potential and distribution in the neighborhood of a particular ion i, only when that ion is in a region around k, having a volume, ω, of molecular order of magnitude. But the ratio of the probability that an ion i will be in this small volume to the probability that it will be elsewhere in the solution is roughly ω/v, or a quantity of negligible order. Since ${}^{i}\overline{\psi_i(q_i)|_{e_k=0}}$ and ${}^{k}\overline{\psi_i(q_i)}$ are both effectively equal to $\bar{\psi}_i$ the second term of (38) vanishes. Further, since ${}^{k}\overline{\psi_i(q)|_{e_i=0}}$ is effectively equal to ${}^{k}\overline{\psi(q)}$, we may write

$$\int_0^{e_i} [\,{}^{ik}\overline{\psi_i(q)} - {}^{k}\overline{\psi_i(q_i)}]de_i = e_i\, {}^{k}\overline{\psi(q)} + \varphi_{ki}(q). \qquad (40)$$

This relation is exact to quantities of order $1/N$, where N is the total number of ions. When relation (40) is introduced into Eq. (28), the mean Poisson equation becomes

$$\nabla^2\, {}^{k}\overline{\psi(q)} = -\frac{4\pi}{D}\sum_i c_i e_i \zeta_{ki}^\circ e^{-\beta[e_i\, {}^{k}\overline{\psi(q)} + \varphi_{ki}(q)]}. \qquad (41)$$

This equation is statistically exact, since only quantities of negligible order of magnitude, $0(1/N)$, have been neglected in its derivation. From now on, we shall begin to make approximations. Suppose we assume the ions to be rigid spheres and neglect van der Waals forces of the attractive type. Let a_k be the mean distance of closest approach of the other ions to ion k. The primary effect of van der Waals forces is to make the ζ_{ki}° vanish inside the sphere a_k. If secondary effects of van der Waals forces in ζ_{ki}° and in φ_{ki} are ignored, Eq. (41) becomes:[10]

$$\nabla^2 \, {}^{k}\overline{\psi(q)} = -\frac{4\pi}{D} \sum_i c_i e_i e^{-\beta[e_i \, {}^{k}\overline{\psi(q)} + \varphi_{ki}(q)]}; \qquad |\mathbf{r} - \mathbf{r}_k| > a_k$$

$$= 0; \qquad |\mathbf{r} - \mathbf{r}_k| \leq a_k; \tag{42}$$

$$\varphi_{ki}(q) = \beta^2 \int_0^{e_i} \int_0^{e_i} \int_0^{e_k} {}^{ik}\overline{[\psi_k(q_k) - {}^{ik}\overline{\psi_k(q_k)}][\psi_i(q) - {}^{ik}\overline{\psi_i(q)}]^2} \, de_i de_i de_k.$$

If the fluctuation terms φ_{ki} are neglected, Eq. (42) reduces to the fundamental equation of the Debye-Hückel theory.

$$\nabla^2 \, {}^{k}\overline{\psi(q)} = -\frac{4\pi}{D} \sum_i e_i c_i e^{-\beta e_i \, {}^{k}\overline{\psi(q)}}; \qquad |\mathbf{r} - \mathbf{r}_k| > a_k \tag{43}$$

$$= 0; \qquad |\mathbf{r} - \mathbf{r}_k| \leq a_k.$$

The nature of this approximation becomes clearer when the fluctuation (37) is expressed in terms of ${}^{ik}\overline{\psi_k(q_k)}$, the mean potential in the ion k, when the ion i is held fixed at the point q. We recall that

$${}^{ik}\overline{\psi_k(q_k)} = \frac{\int \cdots \int \psi_k(q_k) e^{-\beta[V_{N-1} + V_i(q)]} dv_1 \cdots dv_{N-2}}{\int \cdots \int e^{-\beta[V_{N-1} + V_i(q)]} dv_1 \cdots dv_{N-2}}. \tag{44}$$

By differentiation of (44), we find

$${}^{ik}\overline{[\psi_k(q_k) - {}^{ik}\overline{\psi_k(q_k)}][\psi_i(q) - {}^{ik}\overline{\psi_i(q)}]^2} = \frac{1}{\beta^2} \frac{\partial^2 \, {}^{ik}\overline{\psi_k(q_k)}}{\partial e_i^2}. \tag{45}$$

Suppose that ${}^{ik}\overline{\psi_k(q_k)}$ is expanded in a Taylor's series of the form

$$\overline{\psi_k(q_k)} = {}^{ik}\overline{\psi_k(q_k)} \Big|_{e_i=0} + e_i \left[\frac{\partial \, {}^{ik}\overline{\psi_k(q_k)}}{\partial e_i}\right]_{e_i=0} + \sum_{n=2}^{\infty} \frac{e_i^n}{n!} \left[\frac{\partial^n \, {}^{ik}\overline{\psi_k(q_k)}}{\partial e_i^n}\right]_{e_i=0}. \tag{46}$$

If it is a sufficient approximation to neglect all but the first two terms of the expansion (46), the fluctuation (45) and also the integrated fluctuation φ_{ki} vanish. Thus, we see that the neglect of the fluctuation terms is equivalent to assuming that ${}^{ik}\overline{\psi_k(q_k)}$ can be approximated by a linear function of the charge, e_i, on the ion i. When the point q, at which the ion i is situated, is a large distance from the ion k, we should expect this to be a rather good

---

[10] The simplification of (41) when the ions are assumed to have different sizes is more elaborate, but offers no difficulty. Except for the fluctuation terms, the equations are identical with those employed by Scatchard in the treatment of this case. (G. Scatchard, *Phys. Zeits.* **33**, 22 (1932).)

approximation. Moreover, aside from the neglect of certain secondary effects of van der Waals forces, it is the only approximation involved in the derivation of the Debye-Hückel Eq. (43) from statistical mechanics. This is a rather striking fact, for the opinion was generally held that the neglect of the local influence of the ion i, when situated at q, on the potential and distribution in the neighborhood of the ion k, was only one of the defects of the Debye theory. However, it appears that not even this factor is entirely neglected.

It is interesting to remark that φ_{ki} depends entirely upon the screening influence of the statistical space charge on the interaction of the ions i and k, and therefore vanishes at zero ionic concentration. Thus we may write

$$\lim_{c=0} \overline{{}^{ik}\psi_k(q_k)} = \frac{e_i}{Dr}; \quad r = |\mathbf{r} - \mathbf{r}_k|$$

$$\lim_{c=0} \frac{\partial^2 \overline{{}^{ik}\psi_k(q_k)}}{\partial e_i{}^2} = 0 \tag{47}$$

and therefore by Eqs. (42) and (45)

$$\lim_{c=0} \varphi_{ki} = 0. \tag{48}$$

The potential $\overline{{}^{k}\psi(q)}$, on the other hand, approaches e_k/Dr, so that

$$\lim_{c=0} \varphi_{ki}(q)/\overline{{}^{k}\psi(q)} = 0. \tag{49}$$

Eq. (49) suggests that we might use solutions of the Debye-Hückel Eq. (43) to obtain a first approximation to $\overline{{}^{ik}\psi_k(q_k)}$, which we require to obtain an estimate of φ_{ki}. When the distance $|\mathbf{r} - \mathbf{r}_k|$ between the fixed ions i and k is large, we should expect to obtain a fair approximation to $\overline{{}^{ik}\psi_k(q_k)}$ by writing

$$\overline{{}^{ik}\psi_k(q_k)} = \overline{{}^{k}\psi_k(q_k)} + \overline{{}^{i}\psi(q_k)}|_{q_i=q}. \tag{50}$$

This approximation involves the assumption that the statistical space charges around the ions i and k are additive, in other words that they overlap without mutual interference. More exactly, it can be shown to be equivalent to neglecting a fourth order fluctuation of the form

$$\overline{{}^{ik}[\psi_k(q_k) - \overline{{}^{ik}\psi_k(q_k)}]^2[\psi_i(q) - \overline{{}^{ik}\psi_i(q)}]^2}$$

in the derivative, $\partial^2 \overline{{}^{ik}\psi_k(q_k)}/\partial e_i{}^2$.

In this approximation, we have, since the derivatives of $\overline{{}^{k}\psi_k(q_k)}$ with respect to e_i are of negligible magnitude $0(1/N_i)$

$$\frac{\partial^2 \overline{{}^{ik}\psi_k(q_k)}}{\partial e_i{}^2} = \frac{\partial^2 \overline{{}^{i}\psi(q_k)}\big|_{q_i=q}}{\partial e_i{}^2}. \tag{51}$$

Now $\overline{{}^{i}\psi(q_k)}\,|_{q_i=q}$, equal to $\overline{{}^{i}\psi(|\mathbf{r}-\mathbf{r}_k|)}$, satisfies an equation of the type (42). Let us try as an approximation, the Gronwall-La Mer-Sandved[11] solution of the Debye-Hückel Eq. (43).

$$\overline{{}^{i}\psi(q_k)}\,\Big|_{q_i=q} = \sum_{m=1}^{\infty}(-\beta)^{m-1}\left(\frac{e_i}{Da_i}\right)^m \psi_m(a_i, r), \tag{52}$$

$$r = |\mathbf{r}-\mathbf{r}_k|,$$

where the ψ_m (in the Gronwall-La Mer notation $\epsilon^{m-1}\psi_m$) are symmetrical functions of the ionic charges, $e_1\cdots e_N$: and their derivatives with respect to the charge e_j of any single ion are quantities of negligible order of magnitude. From Eqs. (42), (45), (51) and (52), we obtain the following estimate of the integrated fluctuation φ_{ki}.

$$\varphi_{ki}(r) = e_k \sum_{m=2}^{\infty}(-\beta)^{m-1}\left(\frac{e_i}{Da_i}\right)^m \psi_m(a_i, r). \tag{53}$$

No claim is made that this estimate is exact, but it probably is of the right order of magnitude. We see that it does not involve the initial Debye approximation ($m = 1$) at all, but only the Gronwall-La Mer correction terms $m \geqq 2$. Since the $\varphi_{ki}(r)$ of Eq. (53) are not exact, it would not be worth while to employ them in the tedious integration of Eq. (42). However, without detailed calculation, it is easily seen that they cannot influence the initial Debye approximation to $\overline{{}^{k}\psi(q)}$, although they may make contributions comparable with, but probably somewhat smaller than the Gronwall-La Mer correction terms. We should expect their contributions to be small under the same conditions that the Gronwall-La Mer terms are small, namely when

$$e_k e_i/DrkT \ll 1 \text{ for all } e_i. \tag{54}$$

At distances from the ion k, such that the above condition (54) is satisfied, the initial Debye approximations to $\overline{{}^{k}\psi(q)}$ and $\overline{{}^{k}\rho(q)}$ should be adequate and the Poisson Eq. (42) should reduce effectively to the linear equation of the Debye-Hückel theory.

$$\left.\begin{aligned} \nabla^2\,\overline{{}^{k}\psi(q)} - \kappa^2\,\overline{{}^{k}\psi(q)} = 0, \quad \kappa^2 &= \frac{4\pi}{DkT}\sum_i c_i e_i^2, \\ r > r_0; \quad \frac{e_k e_i}{Dr_0 kT} &\ll 1. \end{aligned}\right\} \tag{55}$$

If it happens that the ions are so large that the following condition is fulfilled

$$e_k e_i/Da_k kT \ll 1 \text{ for all } e_i, \tag{56}$$

Eq. (55) would be a good approximation in the entire region outside the boundary sphere a_k, as assumed in the original formulation of the Debye-Hückel theory. These statements cannot be regarded as rigorously established

[11] Gronwall, La Mer and Sandved, *Phys. Zeits.* **29**, 358 (1928).

without an exact calculation of the fluctuation terms, but the present estimate of the φ_{ki} seems reliable enough to make them convincing.

The exact determination of the fluctuation terms, φ_{ki} is very difficult, and no convenient means of calculation has yet been devised. However, it seems worth while to outline a possible method of successive approximation. If the mean potential ${}^{ik}\overline{\psi_k(q_k)}$ is known, φ_{ki} may be calculated from its second derivative with respect to e_i. Now

$$ {}^{ik}\overline{\psi_k(q_k)} = {}^{ik}\overline{\psi_k(q_k;\, q,\, q_k)}, \tag{57} $$

where ${}^{ik}\overline{\psi(q_k;\, q,\, q_k)}$ is the value of the mean potential ${}^{ik}\overline{\psi(q';\, q_i,\, q_k)}$ given by Eq. (22) when $q' = q_k$ and $q_i = q$. By the same methods employed in the derivation of Eq. (28), it may be shown that ${}^{ik}\overline{\psi(q',\, q_i,\, q_k)}$ satisfies the following Poisson equation:

$$ (\nabla')^2\, {}^{ik}\overline{\psi(q';\, q_i,\, q_k)} = -\frac{4\pi}{D} \sum_i c_j e_j \zeta^\circ{}_{ikj} \times e^{-\beta\int_0^{e_j} {}^{ijk}\overline{[\psi_j(q')} - {}^{ik}\overline{\psi_j(q_j)]}\, de_j}. \tag{58} $$

The exact solution of this equation would require the knowledge of fluctuation terms depending on a mean potential ${}^{ijk}\overline{\psi}$, which may be shown to satisfy a Poisson equation similar to (58). By setting up a series of Poisson equations for ${}^{1}\overline{\psi}$, ${}^{2}\overline{\psi}$, $\cdots$ ${}^{n}\overline{\psi}$ in which 1, 2, $\cdots$ n ions are, respectively, held fixed during the averaging process, and neglecting fluctuation terms in the equation for ${}^{n}\overline{\psi}$, one could presumably obtain any desired degree of approximation by making n large enough. To obtain an exact solution, one would have to set up a system of Poisson equations for $N - 1$ mean potentials, ${}^{1}\overline{\psi}$, $\cdots$ ${}^{N-1}\overline{\psi}$ and solve them simultaneously. However, when n becomes of the same order of magnitude as N, one can no longer make the simplifications in the statistical charge density that are possible for small n, and one has a set of simultaneous integro-differential equations, which are virtually impossible to solve.

The solution of Eq. (58) for ${}^{ik}\overline{\psi(q';\, q_i,\, q_k)}$ is difficult, even in the Debye-Hückel approximation corresponding to (43), since two ionic centers are involved. A solution of this equation in the initial Debye approximation corresponding to Eq. (55) has been obtained by Scatchard and Kirkwood.[12] Using their approximation to ${}^{ik}\overline{\psi_k(q_k)}$, we find that φ_{ki} vanishes. A solution of the complete Debye-Hückel equation for two ionic centers by the Gronwall-La Mer method has never been carried out, but it is quite certain that it would lead to a value of φ_{ki} of the same form and magnitude as Eq. (53).

It may be objected that, since we have based our calculation of the φ_{ki} upon solutions of a Poisson equation in which similar fluctuation terms were neglected, we have not definitely shown that they cannot be large. The final answer to this question must await an exact calculation of the φ_{ki} by some independent method. We have shown, however, that the Debye-Hückel Eq. (42) is statistically consistent with values of the fluctuation terms of the magnitude of the Gronwall-La Mer terms, and we believe to have presented convincing, if not conclusive evidence that they cannot influence the initial Debye approximation.

[12] Scatchard and Kirkwood, *Phys. Zeits.* **33**, 297 (1932).

IV.

The significance of the Gronwall-La Mer terms remains somewhat ambiguous, due to the fact that the fluctuation terms may make contributions to $\overline{{}^k\psi(q)}$ of comparable although somewhat smaller magnitude. Moreover, even if the φ_{ki} were known with exactness, the integration of Eq. (42) would be complicated and tedious. It therefore seems very desirable to employ the method of Bjerrum[13] or one similar to it in the treatment of ions of small size and high valence, for which the initial Debye approximation is inadequate. The essential feature of Bjerrum's method consists in neglecting the screening effect of other ions on the interaction of an ion pair, k and i, when the two ions are close together. Bjerrum also makes use of a special hypothesis concerning ionic association, which, though intuitively attractive, is in some respects arbitrary. We shall outline an alternative treatment here, which utilizes Bjerrum's screening approximation, but not his association hypothesis. The method leads to a result which is almost identical with that of Bjerrum at low ionic strengths, but which is somewhat different at higher ionic strengths. Although Bjerrum's special hypothesis concerning association is not employed, ionic association in the classical sense involving a continuum of molecular species without sharply graded dissociation energies is still implicitly taken into account. The method is proposed as an alternative and not necessarily as a substitute for Bjerrum's treatment, for the latter may give better results under conditions favoring a sharply graded binary association of the ions.

The potential $\overline{{}^k\psi_k(r)}$ at a distance r from the ion k, can be expressed in terms of the spherically symmetric charge density, $\overline{{}^k\rho(r)}$, in the following manner

$$\overline{{}^k\psi_k(r)} = \frac{4\pi}{Dr}\int_0^r \xi^2\, \overline{{}^k\rho(\xi)}d\xi + \frac{4\pi}{D}\int_r^\infty \xi\, \overline{{}^k\rho(\xi)}d\xi. \tag{59}$$

Because of the van der Waals forces of the repulsive type, $\overline{{}^k\rho(\xi)}$ vanishes in the neighborhood of $\xi = 0$, so that the above expression converges. The value of the potential at the center of the ion k is therefore

$$\overline{{}^k\psi_k} = \frac{4\pi}{D}\int_0^\infty \xi\, \overline{{}^k\rho(\xi)}d\xi. \tag{60}$$

Further, $\overline{{}^k\rho(\xi)}$ must satisfy the following normalization condition

$$4\pi\int^\infty \xi^2\, \overline{{}^k\rho(\xi)}d\xi = -e_k. \tag{61}$$

This condition is imposed by the electrical neutrality of the solution as a whole. That it is satisfied by the exact charge density, $\overline{{}^k\rho(q)}$ of Eq. (14) is easily verified by direct integration of the ζ_{ki}. When the ions are treated as rigid spheres of diameter a, the charge density $\overline{{}^k\rho(\xi)}$ vanishes when $\xi \leq a$. In this case, the boundary conditions, requiring $\overline{{}^k\psi(q)}$ and the normal component of its gradient to be equal on the two sides of the boundary sphere a,

[13] N. Bjerrum, *Kgl. Dan. Vid. Sels.* VII, 9 (1926).

are automatically fulfilled, when Eqs. (60) and (61) are satisfied. However, these equations are more general than the simple boundary conditions, for they hold even when the ions do not have sharp boundaries.

Let us suppose that r_0 is some distance, beyond which condition (54) is satisfied. Outside of the sphere r_0, the Debye linear equation may be employed to obtain ${}^{k}\overline{\psi(r)}$ and ${}^{k}\overline{\rho(r)}$

$$\left.\begin{aligned} \nabla^2\, {}^{k}\overline{\psi(r)} - \kappa^2\, {}^{k}\overline{\psi(r)} &= 0, \\ {}^{k}\overline{\psi(r)} &= A\,\frac{e^{-\kappa r}}{r}, \\ {}^{k}\overline{\rho(r)} &= -\frac{D\kappa^2 A}{4\pi}\,\frac{e^{-\kappa r}}{r}, \end{aligned}\right\} \qquad r > r_0, \tag{62}$$

where the solution, $e^{+\kappa r}/r$ is excluded since it would make ${}^{k}\overline{\psi(r)}$ infinite as r tends to infinity, a physically impossible situation. With the aid of Eqs. (62) and (14), the relations (60) and (61) become

$$\begin{aligned} {}^{k}\overline{\psi_k} - \frac{1}{D}\sum_i c_i e_i K_{ki} &- \kappa A e^{-\kappa r_0}, \\ -\,e_k = \sum_i c_i e_i G_{ki} &- DA(1 + \kappa r_0)e^{-\kappa r_0}, \\ K_{ki} = 4\pi \int_0^{r_0} &\xi \zeta_{ki}(\xi)d\xi, \\ G_{ki} = 4\pi \int_0^{r_0} &\xi^2 \zeta_{ki}(\xi)d\xi. \end{aligned} \tag{63}$$

Eliminating A from these two equations, and making use of Eq. (11), we obtain[14]

$$\bar{\psi}_k = -\frac{1}{D}\left[e_k + \sum_i c_i e_i G_{ki}\right]\frac{\kappa}{1 + \kappa r_0} + \frac{1}{D}\sum_i c_i e_i K_{ki}. \tag{64}$$

At small concentrations the ζ_{ki} become independent of the ionic strength, and the above expression approaches the limiting law of the Debye-Hückel theory. If the mean diameter of the ions is such that condition (55) is fulfilled, we may take $r_0 = a_k$, and the integrals G_{ki} and K_{ki} vanish. We are then left with the initial Debye approximation to $\bar{\psi}_k$. When (55) is not satisfied, we may obtain approximate expressions for the integrals K_{ki} and G_{ki} by neglecting the influence of screening on the functions ζ_{ki} when r is less than r_0. When screening is neglected, we may write

$${}^{k}\overline{\psi(r)} = e_k/Dr; \quad {}^{ik}\overline{\psi_k(q_k)} = e_i/Dr; \quad \partial^2\, {}^{ik}\overline{\psi_k(q_k)}/\partial e_i^2 = 0; \quad r \leq r_0. \tag{65}$$

[14] It should be remarked that $\Sigma_i e_i c_i G_{ki}$ and $\Sigma_i e_i c_i K_{ki}$ are opposite in sign to e_k, since the integrals G_{ki} and K_{ki} are much greater when e_i is opposite in sign to e_k than when of the same sign.

Thus the neglect of screening causes the fluctuation (45) to vanish, and we have

$$\varphi_{ki}(r) = 0; \quad r \leq r_0. \tag{66}$$

For simplicity, we assume that the molecules are rigid spheres and neglect attractive van der Waals forces. If we denote the mean diameter of the ion k and an ion of the type i by a_{ki}, and remember that ζ_{ki} must vanish when $r \leq a_{ki}$, we may write

$$\begin{aligned} \zeta_{ki} &= e^{-\beta e_i e_k Dr}; \quad a_{ki} < r \leq r_0 \\ &= 0; \quad r \leq a_{ki} \end{aligned} \tag{67}$$

and the integrals K_{ki} and G_{ki} become

$$\begin{aligned} K_{ki} &= 4\pi \int_{a_{ki}}^{r_0} \xi e^{-\beta e_i e_k / D\xi} d\xi, \\ G_{ki} &= 4\pi \int_{a_{ki}}^{r_0} \xi^2 e^{-\beta e_i e_k / D\xi} d\xi. \end{aligned} \tag{68}$$

Except for the fact that condition (54) must be satisfied, the distance r_0, within which screening is neglected, is somewhat arbitrary. It may be chosen in the manner which Bjerrum proposes, or perhaps by some more convenient criterion. As in Bjerrum's theory, the integrals K_{ki} and G_{ki} are fortunately very insensitive to its value. However, we must certainly require that r_0 be less than $1/\kappa$, for the neglect of screening to a distance comparable with $1/\kappa$ would be a rather drastic approximation.

When screening is neglected in the calculation of K_{ki} and G_{ki}, the approximate $\bar{\psi}_k$ no longer satisfies the condition of integrability (4). However, if r_0 is treated as independent of the ionic charges, the integrability condition is satisfied up to terms in κ^3. Bjerrum circumvents this difficulty by means of his association hypothesis, but does not overcome it. In fact it would be somewhat fortuitous if any approximate $\bar{\psi}_k$ exactly satisfied the integrability condition, unless the method of approximation was specifically chosen with that purpose in mind.

Approximate expressions for the logarithm of the activity coefficient of the ion k may be obtained from Eqs. (64) and (68) with the aid of either the Debye or the Güntelberg-Müller charging process. They differ very little from the corresponding expressions of Bjerrum at low ionic strength. We hope to develop the method more fully at a later time, choosing, if possible, better approximations to the integrals K_{ki} and G_{ki}, which are consistent with the condition of integrability.

We recall that Bjerrum's treatment leads to numerical values of activity coefficients, which differ very little from those obtained from the Gronwall-La Mer-Sandved potential, when the latter converges sufficiently rapidly. Since Eq. (64) leads to essentially the same result as the Bjerrum method, when screening is neglected, we have indirect evidence that the Gronwall-La Mer-Sandved potential is probably a fairly good approximation in spite of the neglect of fluctuation terms. In other words, the neglect of all screening effects at small distances, of which the fluctuation terms are a part, leads to a result which differs but little from that of Gronwall and La Mer, who neglected only fluctuation terms. This suggests the conclusion that all screening effects, including fluctuations, are unimportant at small distances, in comparison with the large constant term e_k/Dr in both the mean potential and the potential of the mean force.

V.

It seems worth while to discuss briefly the relation of the general theory of fluctuations to the properties of electrolyte solutions, since it has occasionally been the source of some misunderstanding. Suppose that Y is some additive property of a macroscopic system consisting of N microscopic systems, for example molecules or ions. If y_k is the contribution of the microscopic system k to Y, we may write

$$Y = \sum_{k=1}^{N} y_k, \quad \overline{Y} = \sum_{k=1}^{N} \overline{y_k}, \tag{69}$$

since the averaging process is a linear operation. The same equality does not hold for the mean square fluctuations $\overline{(Y - \overline{Y})^2}$ and $\sum_{k=1}^{N} \overline{(y_k - \bar{y}_k)^2}$, which in general are not only unequal but of entirely different orders of magnitude. We say that Y is a normal property of the macroscopic system (sensibly constant to external observation, with the value $\overline{Y}$) when $\overline{(Y - \overline{Y})^2}$ is very small relative to $\overline{Y}^2$. This in no way implies that $\overline{(y_k - \bar{y}_k)^2}$ must be small relative to $\bar{y}_k^2$. In general, this is not the case, nor would we expect it to be, for a single molecule or a small number of molecules does not have normal properties in the thermodynamic sense. However, the fact that $\overline{(y_k - \bar{y}_k)^2}$ may be of the same or greater magnitude as y_k^2, in no way invalidates Eq. (69). $\overline{Y}$ is still the sum of the $\bar{y}_k$, and Y is a normal property if $\overline{(Y - \overline{Y})^2}/Y^2$ is small. In fact, unless $\overline{(y_k - \bar{y}_k)^2}$ happens to be specifically employed in the calculation of $\bar{y}_k$, its value is quite irrelevant.

Let us consider the mean electrostatic energy of the solution[15]

$$\overline{W} = \sum_{k=1}^{N} \bar{w}_k; \quad \bar{w}_k = \tfrac{1}{2} e_k \bar{\psi}_k. \tag{70}$$

We may write at once

$$\overline{(w_k - \bar{w}_k)^2}/\bar{w}_k^2 = \overline{(\psi_k - \bar{\psi}_k)^2}/\bar{\psi}_k^2, \tag{71}$$

where $\overline{(\psi_k - \bar{\psi}_k)^2}$, which has been calculated by Halpern,[5] is given by

$$\overline{(\psi_k - \bar{\psi}_k)^2} = -kT \partial \bar{\psi}_k / \partial e_k. \tag{72}$$

If the $\bar{\psi}_k$ is assumed, as a first approximation, to be linear in e_k, as for example in the Debye limiting law, we have from relations (71) and (72)

$$\overline{(w_k - \bar{w}_k)^2}/\bar{w}_k^2 = -kT/e_k \bar{\psi}_k. \tag{73}$$

---

[15] $\overline{W}$ is related to the thermodynamic energy of the solution in the following manner:

$$E - E_0 = \overline{W}[1 + (\partial \log D/\partial \log T)_v]$$

where E is the energy when all ions are fully charged and E_0 is the energy when they are completely discharged.

In dilute solutions, $-kT/e_k\bar{\psi}_k$ as estimated from experimental values of the activity coefficient, or from the Debye limiting law, is in general much greater than unity, so that $\overline{(w_k - \bar{w}_k)^2}$ is usually greater than $\bar{w}_k^2$. This fact alone in no way invalidates the Debye limiting law. It should be remarked that if the magnitude of $\overline{(w_k - \bar{w}_k)^2}/\bar{w}_k^2$ were taken as a criterion for the validity of statistical calculations of the type of Eq. (69), it would invalidate not only the Debye limiting law but also any other limiting law. In fact by a similar line of reasoning one could cast doubt upon the ideal gas law, $pv = NkT$, since the fluctuation $\overline{(\epsilon - \bar{\epsilon})^2}$ in the energy of a single gas molecule is equal to $\frac{2}{3}\bar{\epsilon}^2$ where $\bar{\epsilon}$ is the mean energy of a single molecule. Of course, the fluctuation in the total energy of an ideal gas, consisting of N molecules is such that $\overline{(E - \bar{E})^2}/\bar{E}^2 = 2/(3N)$, or negligible if N is large, let us say of the order of 10^{20}.

It is easily shown that, while $\overline{(w_k - \bar{w}_k)^2}/\bar{w}_k^2$ may be large, $\overline{(W - \bar{W})^2}/\bar{W}^2$ is always negligibly small in solutions of finite volume and finite concentration, amenable to thermodynamic measurement. Thus, it is easily demonstrated that

$$\overline{(W - \bar{W})^2} = -\frac{kT}{2}\left\{\frac{\partial}{\partial\lambda}\left[\frac{\bar{W}(\lambda e_1 \cdots \lambda e_N)}{\lambda^2}\right]\right\}_{\lambda=1}. \tag{74}$$

If the mean electrostatic energy $\bar{W}$ is assumed to be a homogeneous function of degree three in the ionic charges, $e_1 \cdots e_N$, as for example, according to the Debye-Hückel limiting law

$$\frac{\bar{W}(\lambda e_1 \cdots \lambda e_N)}{\lambda^2} = \lambda \bar{W}, \quad \frac{\overline{(W - \bar{W})^2}}{\bar{W}^2} = -\frac{1}{2}\frac{kT}{\bar{W}} \sim \frac{1}{N}\left(\frac{1}{2}\frac{kT}{e_k\bar{\psi}_k}\right). \tag{75}$$

Now $-kT/2e_k\bar{\psi}_k$ is of the order of magnitude of $(-\log \gamma_{\pm})^{-1}$, where $\gamma_{\pm}$ is the mean activity coefficient of the ions. Moreover, in all solutions of thermodynamic interest $(-N \log \gamma_{\pm})^{-1}$ is a very small quantity, of an order of magnitude not greater than about 10^{-10} in all solutions of sufficient volume and concentration to be of thermodynamic interest. Thus W is certainly a normal property of electrolyte solutions. Of course, strictly speaking, it ceases to be such at zero electrolyte concentration, but long before mathematically zero concentration is reached both $\bar{W}$ and $\overline{(W - \bar{W})^2}$ become too small for thermodynamic observation.

If it were true that a quadratic fluctuation of the type $\overline{(\psi_k - \bar{\psi}_k)^2}$ had been neglected in the Poisson-Boltzmann equation, there would be an adequate basis for objecting to the Debye limiting law since $\overline{(\psi_k - \bar{\psi}_k)^2}$ is of the order of κ. It is to be emphasized, however, that no such quadratic fluctuation is neglected, but only the difference between the mean potential and the potential of the mean force. We have shown that this difference may be expressed in terms of a third order fluctuation of the potential, which does not affect the initial Debye approximation to the mean potential and is small at large distances from the central ion. Further, this fluctuation term depends entirely upon the screening action of the statistical space charge and therefore its influence on the distribution function at small distances from the central ion is small compared with that of the Coulomb term, e_k/Dr, at low ionic concentrations.

The Electrostatic Influence of Substituents on the Dissociation Constants of Organic Acids. I

J. G. KIRKWOOD AND F. H. WESTHEIMER
Department of Chemistry, University of Chicago, Chicago, Illinois

(Received May 11, 1938)

Bjerrum's theory of the influence of substituents on dissociation constants has been extended and amplified. The molecules and ions entering into the ionization equilibria are treated as cavities of low dielectric constant, rather than as structureless regions of the same dielectric constant as the solvent. The theory gives better results than the simple Bjerrum formulation, especially for the short chain dicarboxylic acids, and in the fact that it permits a satisfactory treatment of the influence of dipolar substituents on dissociation constants.

I

The ratio of the first to the second dissociation constant of a dibasic organic acid is always greater than four, and approaches four as the length of the acid is increased. In 1923 Bjerrum[1] suggested that the ratio of the dissociation constants can be accounted for by the combination of a statistical factor of four and the electrostatic effect of the negative charge of the acid-ion on the dissociation of the second hydrogen, and presented an approximate mathematical discussion. In this paper, following a consideration of the Bjerrum treatment, an extension of the electrostatic theory of dissociation constants will be developed.

A thermodynamic comparison of the dissociation constants K_1 and K_2 of two organic acids HA_1 and HA_2 in the same solvent leads to the following relation

$$RT \log K_1/K_2 = \bar{F}^\circ(HA_1) + \bar{F}^\circ(A_2^-) - \bar{F}^\circ(HA_2) - \bar{F}^\circ(A_1^-), \tag{1}$$

where $\bar{F}^\circ(HA_1)$, $\bar{F}^\circ(A_2^-)$, $\bar{F}^\circ(HA_2)$, and $\bar{F}^\circ(A_1^-)$ are the reference values of the chemical potentials of the respective solute species taken at infinite dilution in the solvent. From a molecular point of view, it is readily seen that $\bar{F}^\circ(HA_1) + \bar{F}^\circ(A_2^-) - \bar{F}^\circ(HA_2) - \bar{F}^\circ(A_1^-)$ is equal to $N\Delta w'$, where N is Avogadro's number and $\Delta w'$ is the average reversible work expended in the transfer of a proton from the carboxylate group of an ion A_2^- to the carboxylate group of an ion A_1^-, situated at an infinite distance from A_2^- in the given solvent. A part of $\Delta w'$ may be regarded as purely electrostatic in origin, that is, work done in moving the proton in the electric field produced by the average charge distributions of the two ions. We may denote this part by Δw. Another contribution arises from an entropy change associated with differences in

---

[1] Bjerrum, *Zeits. f. physik. Chemie* **106**, 219 (1923); see Greenspan, *Chem. Rev.* **12**, 339 (1933).

molecular symmetry, and equal to $k \log[\sigma(HA_1)\sigma(A_2^-)/\sigma(A_1^-)\sigma(HA_2)]$ where $\sigma(HA_1)$, $\sigma(HA_2)$, $\sigma(A_1^-)$ and $\sigma(A_2^-)$ are the symmetry numbers of the respective particles. The symmetry number gives rise, in the ratio of the dissociation constants of a symmetrical dibasic acid, to the well-known statistical factor of four. Finally, and by no means to be overlooked, is the contribution to $\Delta w'$ associated with the intrinsic structure of the carboxyl group and carboxylate ion. However, if the two acids, HA_1 and HA_2, are, let us say, of the form R_1CH_2COOH and R_2CH_2COOH, and the possibility of structural resonance is absent, it is reasonable to suppose that the relatively distant substituent groups R_1 and R_2 will have little influence on the structure of the carboxyl group and carboxylate ion, except perhaps for an electrostatic polarization which may be taken into account in Δw, the electrostatic part of $\Delta w'$. Under these circumstances, the structural contributions to the work expended in detaching the proton from HA_2 will be canceled by a contribution of equal magnitude gained by attaching the proton to A_1^-. The net structural contribution to $\Delta w'$ is then zero, and we may write Eq. (1) in the form

$$
\begin{aligned}
RT \log K_1/\sigma K_2 &= N\Delta w = 2.303RT\Delta pK \\
\Delta w &= W(HA_1) + W(A_2^-) - W(HA_2) - W(A_1^-) \qquad (2) \\
\sigma &= \sigma(HA_1)\sigma(A_2^-)/\sigma(A_1^-)\sigma(HA_2),
\end{aligned}
$$

where $W(HA_1)$, $W(A_2^-)$, $W(HA_2)$ and $W(A_1^-)$ are the electrostatic free energies of the respective molecules in the given solvent. The Bjerrum theory, in its most general form, is summarized by Eq. (2). Although Bjerrum developed his theory on the basis of a somewhat different argument, his fundamental assumption may be expressed in our terms, namely that the intrinsic structure of the carboxyl group and carboxylate ion is the same in the two acids. Although this assumption can certainly be no more than a close approximation to the facts, that it is essentially correct is supported by the observation that the dissociation constants of two aliphatic acids, R_1CH_2COOH and R_2CH_2COOH generally differ but slightly when R_1 and R_2 are nonpolar radicals.

If we are interested in a comparison of the first and second dissociation constants of a symmetrical dibasic acid, we are concerned with the molecular species H_2A, HA^-, $A^=$ and HA^-. Since the symmetry number ratios, $\sigma(H_2A)/\sigma(HA^-)$ and $\sigma(A^=)/\sigma(HA^-)$ each have the value two, the statistical factor becomes four, and Eq. (2) becomes

$$
\begin{aligned}
RT \log K_1/4K_2 &= N\Delta w = 2.303RT\Delta pK \\
\Delta w &= W(H_2A) + W(A^=) - 2W(HA^-).
\end{aligned}
\qquad (3)
$$

Bjerrum's approximation is obtained if Δw is set equal to the electrical work e^2/DR' required to bring the two charges, $-e$, of the acid ions, HA^- from infinity to their distance of separation, R', in the di-ion $A^=$, in a homogeneous medium having the solvent dielectric constant, D. This leads to results of fair accuracy[2] in the case of elongated straight chain dibasic acids, but with short

[2] Gane and Ingold, *J. Chem. Soc.* 2153 (1931).

molecules the values of R' obtained are, in some cases, only a fifth of that expected on the basis of structural considerations.

In the next section we shall describe a more refined calculation of Δw, which, although still somewhat schematic, avoids the treatment of the molecules and ions, in which the charges are imbedded, as structureless regions of dielectric constant D. Instead, we regard the molecules as forming cavities of low dielectric constant, D_i, in the solvent. Of course the introduction of an internal molecular dielectric constant D_i differing from unity is somewhat artificial. Nevertheless, its physical significance is clear, for it provides a crude means of allowing for the polarization of a molecule produced by the average charge distributions of polar or ionic substituent groups. A reasonable estimate of D_i for aliphatic compounds is about 2.00, a value in the neighborhood of the dielectric constant of the liquid paraffin hydrocarbons.

For certain purposes it is convenient to write Eq. (3) in the simple Bjerrum form, with the use of an effective dielectric constant, D_E, defined in terms of Δw, where the distance, R, is the separation of the protons in H_2A

$$\begin{aligned} kT \log K_1/4K_2 &= e^2/D_E R \\ D_E &= e^2/R\Delta w, \end{aligned} \tag{4}$$

rather than that of the negative charges in the di-ion $A^=$. This mode of expression was introduced by Eucken[3] from empirical considerations.

We shall also be concerned with a comparison of the dissociation constants of pairs of monocarboxylic acids similar in structure except for the presence of additional polar groups in one of them. As an example of such a pair, we may mention acetic and chloracetic acids. The statistical factor, σ, is evidently unity in these cases. If we adopt the notation of Eucken, using an effective dielectric constant, D_E, the appropriate form of Eq. (2) is

$$\begin{aligned} kT \log K_1/K_2 &= eM \cos \zeta/D_E R^2 = 2.303kT\Delta pK \\ D_E &= M \cos \zeta/R^2\Delta w, \end{aligned} \tag{5}$$

where M is the dipole moment of the polar group in the acid HA_1, R is the distance from the proton of the point dipole, and ζ its angle of inclination to the line joining it to the proton. We shall also make use of a more complicated form of Eq. (1) in which the charge distribution is not treated merely as a point dipole. Substitution of D, the dielectric constant of the solvent, for D_E leads, as Eucken showed, to calculated values of R as much as six times smaller than might be expected.

Perhaps the most serious approximation in our calculations of Δw which follow is the neglect of possible deviations of the local dielectric constant of the solvent in the neighborhood of a solute molecule from its macroscopic value, D. Such deviations might arise from electrical saturation, electrostriction, and other departures of the local density of the solvent from its bulk value. Ingold[4] has attempted to estimate corrections to the simple Bjerrum formula arising from electrical saturation and electrostriction. However, his calculations are based upon the Clausius-Mosotti equation,

---

[3] Eucken, *Zeits. f. angew. Chemie* **45**, 203 (1932).

[4] Ingold, *J. Chem. Soc.* 2179 (1931).

which is known to be invalid for polar liquids such as water. Further, even were the general method accurate the effect he calculated would be reduced to a fraction of the indicated magnitude if the solvent were excluded from the volume actually occupied by the molecule. It seems, then, entirely possible that he overestimates the importance of these effects. While the neglect of electrical saturation and electrostriction may lead to some inaccuracy, certainly the present treatment must be undertaken before finer adjustments are considered.

II

In order to calculate the electrostatic free energy of a spherical molecule of radius b, with an arbitrary charge distribution and immersed in a solvent of dielectric constant D, we make use of a formula developed by one of us in another connection.[5] A slightly different zero of energy is used here, since we have to consider changes of state involving the addition and removal of charges in the molecule.

$$W = \tfrac{1}{2} \sum_{k,l=1}^{\nu} \frac{e_k e_l}{D_i r_{kl}} + \tfrac{1}{2} \sum_{n=0}^{\infty} \frac{(D_i - D)(n+1) G_n}{D_i b^{2n+1}[(n+1)D + nD_i]}$$

$$G_n = \sum_{k=1}^{\nu} \sum_{l=1}^{\nu} e_k e_l r_k^n r_l^n P_n(\cos \vartheta_{kl}), \tag{6}$$

where the set of point charges $e_1 \cdots e_i$ characterizes the average distribution of charge in the molecule, r_{kl} is the distance between the charges e_k and e_l, r_k and r_l the distances of e_k and e_l from the center of the sphere, and ϑ_{kl} the angle between r_k and r_l. The functions $P_n(\cos \vartheta_{kl})$ are the ordinary Legendre functions, and D_i is the internal dielectric constant of the molecule. If we consider the set of molecules HA_1, HA_2, A_1^- and A_2^- of equal radii b, in which A_1 contains the charges $e_l \cdots e_s$ in excess of those contained in A_2^-, a simple calculation shows that

$$\Delta w = \frac{e}{D_i} \sum_{k=1}^{s} \frac{e_s}{R_k} + \tfrac{1}{2}\left(\frac{1}{D} - \frac{1}{D_i}\right) \sum_{n=0}^{\infty} \frac{(n+1)\Delta G_n}{[(n+1) + nD_i/D] b^{2n+1}}$$

$$\Delta G_n = 2er^n \sum_{k=1}^{s} e_k r_k^n P_n(\cos \vartheta_k), \tag{7}$$

where e is the protonic charge, R_k is the distance between e_k and the proton in HA_1, r and r_k are the lengths of the vectors joining the center of the sphere with the proton and the charge e_k, respectively, and ϑ_k the angle between r and r_k. We note that a similar formulation is possible when the excess of charge of A_1^- over A_2^- is continuously distributed with density ρ. If the ions are those involved in the first and second dissociation of a symmetrical dibasic acid, the charge distribution of the acid-ion HA^-, which corresponds to A_1^-, contains a proton in excess of that of $A^=$, which corresponds to A_2^-. If we denote by x the ratio $(r/b)^2$, where r is the distance of each proton in H_2A from the center of the spherical cavity of radius b, Eq. (7) becomes

$$\Delta w = \frac{e^2}{b}\left\{\frac{1}{D_i} \frac{1}{(2x(1 - \cos \vartheta))^{\frac{1}{2}}} + \left(\frac{1}{D} - \frac{1}{D_i}\right) \sum_{n=0}^{\infty} \frac{(n+1)x^n P_n(\cos \vartheta)}{n + 1 + nD_i/D}\right., \tag{8}$$

[5] Kirkwood, *J. Chem. Phys.* **2**, 351 (1934).

where ϑ is the angle between the lines joining the two protons of H_2A to the center of the molecule. Unless we refer our calculation to the distance between the protons rather than the distance between negative charges in the ions, we neglect the effect of the carboxyl dipole. Although the sum in Eq. (8) may be expressed as a definite integral, an adequate approximation is obtained by expanding in powers of D_i/D, and neglecting all terms in powers of D_i/D higher than the first. Then, making use of the properties of the Legendre functions, the series involved may be summed. When the resulting expression is substituted in Eq. (3), we obtain

$$\log_{10} K_1/4K_2 = \frac{e^2}{2.303\,RkT}\left[\frac{f_1}{D} + \frac{f_2}{D_i}\right]$$

$$f_1 = \frac{2(2x(1-\cos\vartheta))^{\frac{1}{2}}}{(1-2x\cos\vartheta + x^2)^{\frac{1}{2}}} - \frac{(2x(1-\cos\vartheta))^{\frac{1}{2}}}{x} \times \log_e \frac{(1-2x\cos\vartheta+x^2)^{\frac{1}{2}} + x - \cos\vartheta}{1-\cos\vartheta}$$

$$f_2 = 1 - \frac{(2x(1-\cos\vartheta))^{\frac{1}{2}}}{(1-2x\cos\vartheta+x^2)^{\frac{1}{2}}}$$

$$R = b(2x(1-\cos\vartheta))^{\frac{1}{2}}, \tag{9}$$

where R is the distance between the protons in H_2A. If we make use of the notation of Eq. (4), in which an effective dielectric constant appears, we have

$$1/D_E = f_1/D + f_2/D_i. \tag{10}$$

In Fig. 1 the values of D_E are shown for all values of $\sqrt{x}$ from zero to one, and for three values of $\cos\vartheta$, namely, -1, $-1/2$ and 0, corresponding to

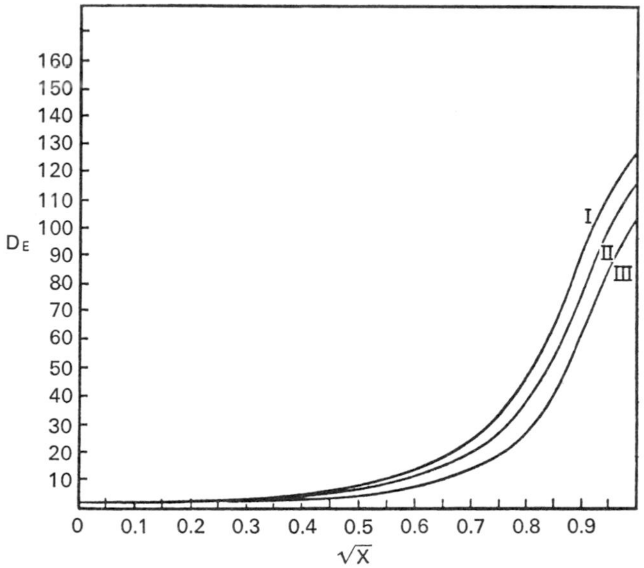

FIG. 1. Plot of D_E for a charged substituent against $\sqrt{x}$. In curve I $\cos\vartheta = -1$, in curve II $\cos\vartheta = -1/2$ and in curve III $\cos\vartheta = 0$. D_i is 2.00 throughout.

the cases in which the protons are on a diameter, placed at an angle, computed from the center, of 120°, and at right angles. D was taken as 78 for water at 25°; D_i was assigned the value 2.00. The effective dielectric constant rises, with increase of $\sqrt{x}$, from D_i when the charges are in the center of the sphere and $\sqrt{x} = 0$ to values above the dielectric constant of water when the charges are on the edge of the sphere and $\sqrt{x} = 1$. The fact that the effective dielectric constant is greater, at the edge of the sphere, than the dielectric constant of the medium may at first glance be surprising. This need cause no concern, for D_E is only a dielectric constant by convention, being so defined that our equations take on the simple Bjerrum form. The result is in no way dependent upon the approximation made when Eq. (8) was expanded in powers of D_i/D. In part IV of this paper, the sum in Eq. (8) is expressed as a definite integral, and the exact value of D_E for charges at the edge of a sphere and on a diameter obtained.

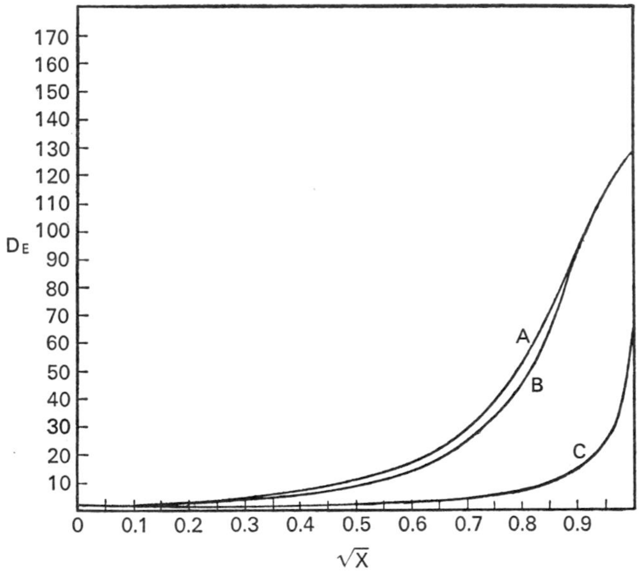

FIG. 2. Curve A, plot of D_E against $\sqrt{x}$ for a charged substituent with $D_i = 2.50$. Curve B, same except $D_i = 2.00$. Curve C, plot of D_E against $\sqrt{x}$ for a dipolar substituent. In all cases $\cos \vartheta = -1$.

In the computation of D_E, no arbitrary parameters enter except the internal molecular dielectric constant, D_i. However, it is assigned a reasonable value, common to all aliphatic molecules, and is not readjusted to meet the demands of individual cases. Further, the value of D_E depends primarily upon the existence of a low internal dielectric constant, and only secondarily upon the exact value assigned to it. In Fig. 2, curve A was computed for charges on a diameter, with $D_i = 2.5$, while curve B was computed for charges on a diameter, with $D_i = 2.0$. The difference, while real, is small.

Besides the effect of substituents bearing a total net charge, we wish to determine the electrostatic free energy difference, Δw, when HA_1 contains a polar group in excess of HA_2. We may regard the dipole as two equal and opposite charges, so placed and of such a magnitude that the product of charge by the distance of separation is equal to the dipole moment. Eq. (18) gives the value of Δw in this case. We can also regard the charge distribution as a point dipole. If we restrict our attention to those cases in which the dipole and proton both lie equidistant from the center on a diameter, then

$$\frac{1}{D_E} = \frac{1}{D_i}\left[1 - \frac{4x^{\frac{3}{2}}}{(1+x)^2}\right] + \frac{1}{D}\left[\frac{8x^{\frac{3}{2}}}{(1+x)^2} + \frac{4x^{\frac{1}{2}}}{1+x} - \frac{4}{x^{\frac{1}{2}}}\log(1+x)\right], \quad (11)$$

where all the symbols have their usual significance. In Fig. 2, curve C is a plot of D_E, obtained from Eq. (11), against $\sqrt{x}$.

III.

From the known dissociation constants of organic acids and Eqs. (4) and (5) an experimental value of D_E can be obtained for the cases in which HA_1 differs from HA_2 either by a charged or by a dipolar substituent. With charged substituents, D_E varies from 15 to about the dielectric constant of water, with dipolar substituents from about 3 to about 10; in both cases D_E is greater for greater values of r/b. For values of r/b between 0.5 and 0.9 which correspond to actual molecules, Figs. 1 and 2 show that D_E, obtained by our theoretical treatment, varies in a similar manner. We note that the effective dielectric constant is much smaller for a dipolar than for a charged substituent at the same value of r/b.[6] In this section we wish to present the computations for the application of our equations to a few simple cases.

The exact location of the proton in the carboxyl group is still open to question. Available evidence[7] seems to favor a double potential energy minimum for the proton adjacent to each of the oxygen atoms, at approximately the position of the proton in the normal O—H bonds. To avoid undue complications in the calculations, we shall adopt the extended chain model, and conventionally place the proton on the extension of the bond between the carboxyl carbon atom and its nearest carbon neighbor. Some convention, of which this is the most convenient, is necessary solely for the purpose of estimating ϑ, the angle between the lines joining the protons to the center.

The selection of a structural distance between the protons of a dicarboxylic acid for comparison with the value computed from the dissociation constant ratio is further complicated by present ignorance relative to internal rotations in the molecule. We obtain a probable upper limit for the structural distance by using the extended chain model with the proton conventionally located at a distance of 1.45A from the respective carboxyl carbon atoms on the extensions of the terminal carbon to carbon bonds. The distance of 1.45A is actually the greatest distance of the projection of the proton on the extension of the terminal carbon-carbon bond, when attached to either oxygen at the covalent distance 0.94A and with an angle of 90° between the C—O and O—H bonds. For the purpose of comparison we have also calculated the root mean square separation of the protons on the basis of free rotation. In this computation, we have employed the following formula for the mean

[6] Smallwood [*J. Am. Chem. Soc.* **54**, 3048 (1932)] has shown by means of a Born cycle that D_E will be unity if certain cancellations in the free energies of solvation, from the hypothetical gaseous state, of the acids and ions occur.

[7] See Price and Evans, *Proc. Roy. Soc.* **A162**, 110 (1937).

square distance $\bar{R}_n^2$ between the terminal atoms in a chain containing n bonds[8]

$$\bar{R}_n^2 = \sum_{k=1}^{n} l_k^2 + 2 \sum_{k=1}^{n} \sum_{s=1}^{k-1} l_k l_s \prod_{m=s}^{k-1} \eta_{m,\, m-1},$$

where $\eta_{m,\, m-1}$ is the cosine of the supplement of the angle between the m and $m - 1$ bonds, and l_k is the length of the k'th bond. We are aware of the fact that the free rotation value does not provide an absolute lower bound for the average structural distance. However, it is not unreasonable to suppose that the average structural separation of the protons lies between the extended chain and the free rotation value. In Table I we have presented the data for a few acids which are at least approximately spherical. It is seen that the distance computed from the dissociation constant ratio by means of our equation do actually fall between the suggested limits, while the values computed with the simple Bjerrum formula lie considerably below the free rotation value and are almost certainly too small on any basis. We remark that the Bjerrum formula is by no means as unsatisfactory for the longer chain acids. We have selected for discussion a group of short chain acids the shapes of which roughly approximate spheres, since it is in these cases that the Bjerrum theory needs refinement. In a later paper, we shall develop a formula on the basis of an ellipsoidal model, which passes asymptotically into the simple Bjerrum formula as the chain length increases. A knowledge of the torques hindering internal rotation would permit a more exact application of our formulas involving a calculation of the average value of ΔpK over all internal configurations of the acids and ions.

TABLE I. Separation of protons in dicarboxylic acids.*
Distance in A.

Acid	Maximum	Free Rotation	This Paper	Bjerrum
Oxalic acid	4.44	3.50	3.85	0.91
Dimethyl malonic acid	4.87	4.12	4.15	1.34
Tetramethyl succinic acid	6.66	4.66	4.80	0.96

* The values in column 4 are given to the nearest 0.05A. Since the computed values of R in Table I refer to a single configuration of the molecule, they are not strictly suitable for comparison with mean distances calculated on the basis of free or inhibited internal rotation. Nevertheless, we have stated the maximum and free rotation distances in order to exhibit a possible range of variation of the interprotonic distance in the acids. With internal rotation, we should properly compute an average value of ΔpK over all internal configurations for comparison with the experimental value. Such a calculation is very tedious and does not seem worth while on the basis of free rotation, since in actual molecules the rotation is doubtless inhibited. We are unable to make the calculation for inhibited rotation, until future information about the hindering torques becomes available.

For these computations it was necessary to estimate the radii of the spheres. In the absence of specific information, we have fallen back on Traube's rule.[9] The partial molar volume of dimethyl malonic acid in water, then, is about 99.1 cc, and the diameter of the molecule, considered as a sphere, is 6.77A. Further, since we have decided, conventionally, to place the protons on the extensions of the terminal carbon to carbon bonds, we may assign the

[8] A special case of the formula developed by Eyring, *Phys. Rev.* **39**, 746 (1932). It is worth while pointing out that for the above formula to be valid, free rotation is not actually necessary. The only requirement is that the mean values of cos φ and sin φ vanish for adjacent bonds, φ being the angle specifying the projection of the $i + 1$'th bond on a plane perpendicular to the i'th bond. This may occur even if the rotation is highly inhibited.

[9] Traube, *Saml. chem. chem-tech., Vortr.* **4**, 255 (1899).

angle $\cos \vartheta = -0.333$ to the lines joining the protons to the center. From Eq. (4) we obtain

$$\sqrt{x} D_E = \frac{e^2}{2.303bkT\Delta pK(2(1 - \cos \vartheta))^{\frac{1}{2}}},$$

$$r/b = \sqrt{x}.$$

Substituting the value of 2.29 for ΔpK for dimethyl malonic acid found by Gane and Ingold[2] in this expression, we find $\sqrt{x} D_E$ equal to 19.1. Values of $\sqrt{x} D_E$ computed with the aid of Eq. (10) are given in Table II for varying $\sqrt{x}$ and $\cos \vartheta$. Using this table, the value of $\sqrt{x}$ can be obtained in any particular case by linear interpolation. The computations for the other acids were carried out in a similar fashion, again using the data of Gane and Ingold. The angle between the protons for oxalic and tetramethyl succinic acids was chosen as 180°.

TABLE II. Values of $\sqrt{x} D_E(x)$.

$\sqrt{x}$	$\cos \vartheta = -1$	$\cos \vartheta = -\frac{1}{2}$	$\cos \vartheta = 0$
0.00	0.00	0.00	0.00
0.10	0.25	0.24	0.23
0.20	0.64	0.60	0.55
0.30	1.31	1.16	1.02
0.40	2.45	2.11	1.76
0.50	4.59	3.82	3.02
0.60	8.79	7.15	5.42
0.70	17.6	14.2	10.6
0.80	37.5	30.9	23.3
0.90	79.2	68.9	56.4
0.95	106.6	96.3	83.2
1.00	127.0	116.3	103.5

TABLE III. Distance between proton and dipole in chloracetic acid in A.

Maximum	Free Rotation	Minimum	This Paper	Bjerrum
3.39	2.99	1.84	2.90	0.55

As an example of the effect of a simple dipolar substituent we present the computations for the ratio of the dissociation constant of acetic to chloracetic acids. Since the molecule does not approach a true sphere, we arbitrarily placed the center at the midpoint of the line joining the proton with the midpoint of the carbon-chlorine bond. We employed the value 1.56×10^{-18} e.s.u. for the dipole moment of the C—Cl bond;[10] the values of the dissociation constants of acetic and chloracetic acids were taken from Landolt-Börnstein.[11] The data for chloracetic acid are given in Table III. Other calculations have shown that, in chloracetic acid, the acidity is relatively little effected by multipole moments of higher order than the second.

[10] Smyth, *Am. Chem. Soc.* Symposium on Molecular Structure, p. 209 (1937).
[11] Landolt-Börnstein, *Physikalische-Chemische Tabellen*, Eg. IIIc.

Finally we may mention that, in common with the previous electrostatic theories of dissociation, the temperature coefficients experimentally determined[12] do not agree with those calculated, on the basis of a constant value of R. Although a real variation of the average value of R with temperature is not unlikely, it may be that a more refined theory is necessary before accurate estimates of temperature coefficients can be made. In any case, the temperature coefficients are not large.

IV.

In this section we shall present some of the mathematical details omitted earlier in the paper. Eq. (7) may be written in the following form.

$$\Delta w = e \sum_{k=1}^{s} e_k H_k$$

$$H_k = \frac{1}{D_i R_k} + \frac{1}{b}\left(\frac{1}{D} - \frac{1}{D_i}\right) S(x_k, \cos \vartheta_k) \tag{12}$$

$$S(x, \alpha) = \sum_{n=0}^{\infty} \frac{(n+1)x^n P_n(\alpha)}{1 + n(1+\omega)},$$

where x_k is equal to rr_k/b^2 and ω is the ratio, D_i/D. From the properties of the Legendre functions, we may write

$$S_0(t, \alpha) = \sum_{n=0}^{\infty} t^n P_n(\alpha) = \frac{1}{(1 - 2\alpha t + t^2)^{\frac{1}{2}}}. \tag{13}$$

It is readily verified that $S(x, \alpha)$ may be expressed in the form

$$S(x, \alpha) = \frac{\partial}{\partial x}\left[x^{\omega/(1+\omega)} \int_0^{x^{1/(1+\omega)}} S_0(t^{1+\omega}, \alpha)dt \right]. \tag{14}$$

Simplification of Eq. (14) leads to

$$S(x, \alpha) = \frac{1}{1+\omega}\left\{ S_0(x, \alpha) + \frac{\omega}{1+\omega} S_1(x, \alpha) \right\}$$

$$S_1(x, \alpha) = x^{-1/(1+\omega)} \int_0^{x} t^{-\omega/(1+\omega)} [1 - 2\alpha t + t^2]^{-\frac{1}{2}} dt. \tag{15}$$

Expansion in powers of ω with the neglect of terms in ω^2 gives

$$S(x, \alpha) = So(x, \alpha) + \omega[S_1^0(x, \alpha) - So(x, \alpha)]$$

$$S_1^0(x, \alpha) = \frac{1}{x}\log\left[\frac{(1 - 2x + x^2)^{\frac{1}{2}} + x - \alpha}{1 - \alpha}\right]. \tag{16}$$

[12] Jones and Soper, *J. Chem. Soc.* 133 (1936).

Evaluation of $S_1(x, \alpha)$ by graphical quadrature shows that the expansion (16) is adequate in all cases of interest although D_E calculated from (10) is 2 per cent high at $x = 1$. Substitution in Eq. (12) gives

$$H_k = \frac{1}{Db}\left\{2[1 - 2x_k \cos \vartheta_k + x_k^2]^{-\frac{1}{2}} - \frac{1}{x_k}\log\left[\frac{(1 - 2x_k \cos \vartheta_k + x_k^2)^{\frac{1}{2}} + x_k - \cos \vartheta_k}{1 - \cos \vartheta_k}\right]\right\} + \frac{1}{D_i}\left\{\frac{1}{R_k} - \frac{1}{b}[1 - 2x_k \cos \vartheta_k + x_k^2]^{-\frac{1}{2}}\right\}. \tag{17}$$

Eq. (9) for the symmetrical dibasic acid follows at once from Eqs. (12) and (17), only one term occurring in the sum of Eq. (12). For a dipolar distribution consisting of two point charges $+e$, and $-e$, Eq. (12) takes the form

$$\Delta w = e^2[H_+ - H_-], \tag{18}$$

where H_+ and H_- are to be computed from Eq. (17) for the respective charges. We note that H_k may be regarded as a function $H(\mathbf{r}_k, \mathbf{r})$ where $\mathbf{r}_k$ and $\mathbf{r}$ are the vectors extending from the center of HA_2 to the charge k and the carboxyl proton, respectively. Thus for a point dipole, we may write

$$\Delta w = e\mathbf{M} \cdot \nabla_1 H(\mathbf{r}_1, \mathbf{r}), \tag{19}$$

where $\mathbf{M}$ is the vector moment and ∇_1 the gradient operator associated with the position $\mathbf{r}_1$ of the dipole. The general expression is rather complicated and will not be given. However, for a molecule in which the proton and dipole are located on a diameter, Eqs. (17) and (19) yield Eq. (11) of Section II.

The Electrostatic Influence of Substituents on the Dissociation Constants of Organic Acids. II

F. H. Westheimer and J. G. Kirkwood, *University of Chicago, Chicago, Illinois*

(Received June 4, 1938)

The theory of the influence of substituents on dissociation constants presented in an earlier article of the same title is extended to acids ellipsoidal in shape. Bjerrum's formula is obtained in the limiting case of unit eccentricity of the elliptical section of a prolate ellipsoid of revolution. The influence of dipolar as well as ionic substituents can satisfactorily be treated.

I.

It has been proposed by Bjerrum[1] that the influence of a polar substituent on the dissociation constant of an organic acid is primarily electrostatic in origin. On the basis of this hypothesis, the ratio of the dissociation constants of two similarly constituted acids may be calculated from electrostatic work necessary to transfer a proton from the first acid to the ion of the second. Because of the fruitfulness of Bjerrum's idea, we considered it desirable to introduce certain refinements into the calculation of the work of transfer. In a previous article, we showed[2] that the electrostatic work is dependent not only upon the charges present and the distance between them, but also upon the shape of the molecule and upon the positions of the charges. We have already presented the equations for a spherical model, and have applied them to several aliphatic acids which approximate a sphere in shape. In the present paper, similar considerations lead to the equations for an ellipsoid of revolution, a model well fitted to treat the longer aliphatic dibasic acids.

We are concerned with four ellipsoids, representing the molecular species HA_1, A_1^-, HA_2 and A_2^-. For the sake of simplicity, we have assumed that the protons of the carboxyl group and the dipoles in the molecules lie on the line connecting the foci of the ellipsoid, and, in the actual computations, have further assumed that the charges are actually at the foci, although this latter limitation is not inherent in the equations developed. In the present discussion, it is convenient to use confocal elliptical coordinates. If r_1 and r_2 are the distances of a point from the two foci, and R the distance between the foci, then $\lambda = (r_1 + r_2)/R$, $\mu = (r_1 - r_2)/R$, and φ is the angle by which the point has been rotated past a fixed plane through the major axis. Since we have chosen an ellipsoid of revolution with all charges on the major axis, the model is axially symmetrical and the angle φ does not enter the formulation.

Following the same reasoning advanced for the spherical model, we approximate the total free energy increment in the reaction $HA_1 + A_2^- \rightleftarrows HA_2 + A_1^-$ by the sum of the electrostatic contribution, Δw, and the

[1] Bjerrum, *Zeits. f. physik. Chemie* **106**, 219 (1923).
[2] Kirkwood and Westheimer, *J. Chem. Phys.* **6**, 506 (1938).

symmetry contribution RT log σ, where σ is the statistical factor, equal to four for symmetrical dibasic acids.

$$kT \log K_1/\sigma K_2 = 2.303\, kT\Delta pK = \Delta w$$

$$\Delta W = W(HA_1) + W(A_2^-) - W(HA_2) - W(A_1^-), \tag{1}$$

where $W(HA_1)$, $W(A_2^-)$, $W(HA_2)$ and $W(A_1^-)$ are the electrostatic free energies of the respective molecular species. In order to determine the electrostatic work, Δw, it is first necessary to solve Laplace's equation in confocal elliptical coordinates. Then, from the electrostatic potential of the charges,

TABLE I. Effective dielectric constant for varying λ_0.

λ_0	D_E (charge)	D_E (dipole)
2.3	7.8	2.7
2.0	11.2	3.3
1.8	15.5	4.0
1.6	25.3	5.7
1.4	51.0	11.2
1.3	74.0	20.4
1.2	94.0	49.0
1.1	94.0	90.0
1.0	78.0	78.0

the electrostatic work can be computed. The actual mathematical treatment is presented in Part III of this paper. In that section it will be shown that, if HA_1 differs from HA_2 by a protonic charge, then

$$\Delta pK = \frac{e^2}{2.303kTR}\left\{\frac{1}{D_i} + \left(\frac{1}{D} - \frac{1}{D_i}\right)\sum_{n=0}^{\infty}\frac{U_n}{1-(D_i/D)C_n}\right\}$$

$$U_n = 2(2n+1)\frac{Q_n(\lambda_0)}{P_n(\lambda_0)}(-1)^n \tag{2}$$

$$C_n = \frac{\lambda_0 - P_{n-1}(\lambda_0)/P_n(\lambda_0)}{\lambda_0 - Q_{n-1}(\lambda_0)/Q_n(\lambda_0)}.$$

Further, if HA_1 differs from HA_2 by a point dipole of moment M inclined at an angle ζ to the major axis of the ellipsoid, then

$$\Delta pK = \frac{eM\cos\zeta}{2.303kTR^2}\left\{\frac{1}{D_i} + \left(\frac{1}{D} - \frac{1}{D_i}\right)\sum_{n=0}^{\infty}\frac{Y_n}{1-(D_i/D)C_n}\right\} \tag{3}$$

$$Y_n = -2n(n+1)(2n+1)\frac{Q_n(\lambda_0)}{P_n(\lambda_0)}(-1)^n.$$

In these formulas, P_n represents a Legendre function of the first kind, D is the dielectric constant of the solvent, D_i the internal molecular dielectric constant[2] and $\lambda = \lambda_0$ is the equation of the ellipsoidal cavity in the solvent created by the molecule.

Q_n represents a Legendre function of the second kind; Q_0 and Q_1 are given by the equations

$$Q_0(\lambda) = \tfrac{1}{2} \log_e \frac{\lambda + 1}{\lambda - 1}$$

$$Q_1(\lambda) = \frac{\lambda}{2} \log_e \frac{\lambda + 1}{\lambda - 1} - 1$$

and the rest can be obtained from the first two by means of the recursion formula,

$$(n + 1)Q_{n+1}(\lambda) = (2n + 1)\lambda Q_n(\lambda) - nQ_{n-1}(\lambda).$$

As in the previous article, an effective dielectric constant, D_E, is defined in terms of the Bjerrum equation.[1,3] For the case in which HA_1 has a charge in excess of HA_2,

$$\Delta pK = e^2/2.303 D_E RkT \tag{4}$$

and in the case in which HA_1 contains a dipole in excess of HA_2

$$\Delta pK = eM \cos \zeta/2.303 D_E R^2 kT. \tag{5}$$

In Table I the values of D_E accurate to 1 percent for molecules in water at 25° computed from Eqs. (2), (3), (4) and (5) for both dipolar and charged substituents are recorded for typical values of λ_0. D_i, as previously, has been set equal to 2.00.

In Fig. 1, D_E has been plotted against λ_0. At large values of λ_0 the charges are brought close together in the medium of low dielectric constant, and D_E

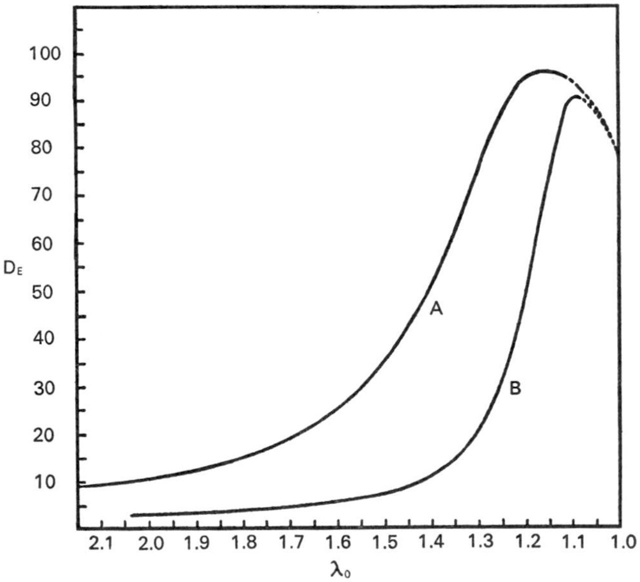

FIG. 1. Curve A is the plot of D_E for a charged substituent against λ_0, curve B is the plot for a dipolar substituent. The slope of the curves at $\lambda_0 = 1$ has not been determined.

[3] Eucken, *Zeits f. angew. Chemie* **45**, 203 (1932).

approaches the internal molecular dielectric constant D_i. On the other hand, as λ_0 decreases toward 1, the ellipsoid thins out into a rod, and at λ_0 equal to 1 disappears altogether, leaving the charges immersed only in the solvent. As in the spherical case, the values of the effective dielectric constant depends primarily upon the existence of a low internal dielectric constant, only secondarily upon its exact value.

With the ellipsoid as with the sphere, values of D_E greater than the dielectric constant of the solvent are obtained. With the ellipsoid, however, since the effective dielectric constant must approach D as the ellipsoid vanishes, the values of D_E go through a maximum.

Here again our theoretical treatment is in agreement with the experimental fact that, for the same value of λ_0 the effective dielectric constant is much greater in the case in which the substituent is charged than in the case in which the substituent contains a dipole.

II.

The equations presented in Part I will now be applied to some actual molecules which approximate an ellipsoid of revolution. We have compared the first and second dissociation constants of three dicarboxylic acids, succinic, glutaric and suberic, and have compared the dissociation constants of chloracetic acid and of β-chlorpropionic acid with the dissociation constants of the corresponding unsubstituted acids. Chloracetic acid, intermediate in shape between a sphere and an ellipsoid, has been treated by both methods. In order to fix the boundaries of the molecules, we have again estimated the partial molar volume in aqueous solution from Traube's rule,[4] and have made use of the following equation relating λ_0, R, and the molecular volume, V, of an ellipsoid of revolution:

$$\lambda_0^3 - \lambda_0 = (6/\pi)(V/R^3). \tag{6}$$

This equation must be solved simultaneously with Eqs. (4) and (5) and with Fig. 1 to obtain the value of R in particular cases. We note that

$$\frac{D_E\text{ (charge)}}{(\lambda_0^3 - \lambda_0)^{\frac{1}{3}}} = \frac{e^2}{2.303kT\Delta pK}\left(\frac{\pi}{6V}\right)^{\frac{1}{3}}$$

and

$$\frac{D_E\text{ (dipole)}}{(\lambda_0^3 - \lambda_0)^{\frac{2}{3}}} = \frac{eM\cos\zeta}{2.303kT\Delta pK}\left(\frac{\pi}{6V}\right)^{\frac{2}{3}}.$$

We have prepared a table of D_E (charge)/$(\lambda_0^3 - \lambda_0)^{\frac{1}{3}}$ and D_E (dipole)/$(\lambda_0^3 - \lambda_0)^{\frac{2}{3}}$ for various values of λ_0 and can, then, estimate the value of λ_0 for any particular case by linear interpolation. From this value of λ_0 and Eq. (6), R is easily obtained. These values are presented in Table II. The values of R, computed for the acids selected, with the aid of Table II, are presented in Table III.

Since the computed values of R in Table III refer to a single configuration of the molecule, they are not strictly suitable for comparison with the mean distances calculated on the basis of free or inhibited rotations. Here, as in the

---

[4] Traube, *Saml. chem. chem-tech., Votr.* **4**, 255 (1899).

TABLE II.

λ_0	D_E (charge)$/(\lambda_0^3 - \lambda_0)^{\frac{1}{3}}$	D_E (dipole)$/(\lambda_0^3 - \lambda_0)^{\frac{2}{3}}$
2.3	3.6	0.60
2.0	6.1	0.99
1.8	9.7	1.58
1.6	18.7	3.1
1.4	46.0	9.2
1.3	77.0	22.0
1.2	117.0	74.0
1.1	154.0	239.0
1.0	∞	∞

TABLE III. *R* in *A*

Acid	ΔpK	Maximum	Free Rotation	This Paper*	Bjerrum
Succinic acid	0.77	6.66	4.66	5.85	3.99
Glutaric acid	0.47	7.39	5.15	7.00	6.53
Suberic acid	0.28	11.46	6.38	9.30	10.9
Chloracetic acid	1.90	3.39	2.99	2.90	0.55
β-Chlorpropionic acid	0.85	4.61	3.69	4.20	1.06

* The values of *R* in this column are given to the nearest 0.05A. For the chloracids, ζ was computed as the angle between the carbon-chlorine bond and the line joining the midpoint of this bond with the point of location of the proton on the extension of the terminal carbon-carbon bond into the carboxyl group. The values of $\cos \zeta$ are 0.59 and 0.94 for chloracetic and β-chlorpropionic, respectively. The carbon-chlorine bond moment was taken as 1.56 Debye units.

previous paper,[2] we have stated the maximum and the free rotation distances in order to exhibit a possible range of variation of the interprotonic distance. The values of ΔpK were taken from Landolt-Börnstein.[5]

It is at once seen that both the Bjerrum formula and the present treatment give reasonable values for the long aliphatic dibasic acids. The advantage of the present treatment over the simple Bjerrum approximation is most clearly exemplified in the cases of the chloro-acids.

The approximations and possible sources of error involved in this formulation have been discussed in the previous paper.[2] They include neglect of electrical saturation and electrostriction, the use of an internal molecular dielectric constant, the use of Traube's rule, and the difficulty in obtaining a structural value of *R* with which to compare our value, due to present ignorance concerning rotation in polyatomic molecules in aqueous solution. We are further limited by the fact that we have placed the charges or dipoles at the foci of the ellipsoid.

III.

In the third part of this paper, we wish to derive the equations presented in Part I. Laplace's equation, in confocal elliptical coordinates for an axially symmetric potential ψ, is

$$(\lambda^2 - 1)\frac{\partial^2 \psi}{\partial \lambda^2} + 2\lambda \frac{\partial \psi}{\partial \lambda} + (1 - \mu^2)\frac{\partial \psi}{\partial \mu^2} - 2\mu \frac{\partial \psi}{\partial \mu} = 0. \tag{7}$$

[5] Landolt-Börnstein, *Physikalische-Chemische Tabellen*, Erg. IIIc.

This equation must be satisfied both inside and outside the ellipsoid, λ_0, forming the boundary between the molecule of dielectric constant D_i and the solvent of dielectric constant D. The potential ψ_i in the interior of the molecule, satisfying Eq. (7) may be written as follows

$$\psi_i = \frac{1}{D_i} \sum_{k=1}^{\nu} \frac{e_k}{|r - r_k|} + \sum_{n=0}^{\infty} B_n P_n(\mu) P_n(\lambda), \tag{8}$$

where the B_n are constants, ψ_i having no singularities except at the positions of the point charges $e_1 \cdots e_2$, characterizing the average charge distribution of the molecule. Since the potential must vanish at an infinite distance from the molecule, the solution, ψ_e, of Eq. (7) outside the boundary ellipsoid may be expressed in the form

$$\psi_e = \sum_{n=0}^{\infty} A_n P_n(\mu) Q_n(\lambda), \tag{9}$$

where the P_n and Q_n are the Legendre functions of the first and second kinds, respectively. The boundary conditions namely, continuity of the potential and of the normal component of the dielectric displacement everywhere on the boundary ellipsoid, λ_0, require the following relations to be satisfied.

$$\begin{aligned} &\psi_i(\lambda_0, \mu) = \psi_e(\lambda_0, \mu) \qquad -1 \leq \mu \leq +1 \\ &D_i \left(\frac{\partial \psi_i}{\partial \lambda}\right)_{\lambda=\lambda_0} = D \left(\frac{\partial \psi_e}{\partial \lambda}\right)_{\lambda=\lambda_0}. \end{aligned} \tag{10}$$

Before applying the boundary condition we introduce into Eq. (8) the Ne mann expansion for each of the terms $1/|r - r_k|$

$$\begin{aligned} \sum_{k=1}^{\nu} \frac{e_k}{|r - r_k|} &= \frac{2}{R} \sum_{n=0}^{\infty} (2n + 1) \beta_n P_n(\mu) Q_n(\lambda) \\ \beta_n &= \sum_{k=1}^{\nu} e_k P_n(\mu_k) \end{aligned} \tag{11}$$

valid when each charge e_k is situated at a point μ_k on the ellipse, $\lambda = 1$, which is the line joining the foci. R is the distance between the foci. Substitution of (8) and (9) into Eq. (10) and use of the property of orthogonality of the $P_n(\mu)$ in the interval, $-1 \leq \mu \leq +1$, yields the following set of linear equations for the determination of the A_n and B_n

$$\begin{aligned} (2/R)(2n + 1)(\beta_n/D_i) Q_n(\lambda_0) + B_n P_n(\lambda_0) &= A_n Q_n(\lambda_0) \\ D_i B_n P_n'(\lambda_0) + (2/R)(2n + 1) \beta_n Q_n'(\lambda_0) &= D A_n Q_n'(\lambda_0). \end{aligned} \tag{12}$$

Solution gives the following expression for the B_n

$$B_n = \frac{2(2n + 1)\beta_n}{R} \left(\frac{1}{D} - \frac{1}{D_i}\right) \frac{Q_n(\lambda_0) Q_n'(\lambda_0)}{P_n(\lambda_0) Q_n'(\lambda_0) - (D_i/D) P_n'(\lambda_0) Q_n(\lambda_0)}, \tag{13}$$

where $P_n'(\lambda_0)$ and $Q_n'(\lambda_0)$ are the first derivatives of the Legendre functions. The derivatives may be eliminated with the aid of the recursion formula,

$$(\lambda^2 - 1)P_n'(\lambda) = n[\lambda P_n(\lambda) - P_{n-1}(\lambda)]$$

$$B_n = \frac{2(2n+1)\beta_n}{R}\left(\frac{1}{D} - \frac{1}{D_i}\right)\frac{Q_n(\lambda_0)}{P_n(\lambda_0)} \times \left[1 - \left(\frac{D_i}{D}\right)\frac{\lambda_0 - P_{n-1}(\lambda_0)/P_n(\lambda_0)}{\lambda_0 - Q_{n-1}(\lambda_0)/Q_n(\lambda_0)}\right]^{-1}. \tag{14}$$

The electrostatic work of charging the molecule is obtained by substitution of Eqs. (8) and (14) into the general formula

$$W = \tfrac{1}{2}\sum_{k=1}^{\nu} e_k \psi_i(1, \mu_k), \tag{15}$$

all charges being located on the line $\lambda = 1$. We are interested in calculating ΔW for a set of molecules HA_1, HA_2, A_1^- and A_2^-.

$$\Delta W = W(HA_1) + W(A_2^-) - W(HA_2) - W(A_1^-). \tag{16}$$

Use of Eqs. (8), (14) and (15) under the assumption that all species have the same size and shape yields

$$\Delta W = \frac{e}{D_i}\sum_{k=1}^{s}\frac{e_k}{r_k} + \frac{1}{R}\left(\frac{1}{D} - \frac{1}{D_i}\right)\sum_{n=0}^{\infty}(2n+1)\alpha_n\frac{Q_n(\lambda_0)}{P_n(\lambda_0)} \times \left[1 - \left(\frac{D_i}{D}\right)\frac{\lambda_0 - P_{n-1}(\lambda_0)/P_n(\lambda_0)}{\lambda_0 - Q_{n-1}(\lambda_0)/Q_n(\lambda_0)}\right]^{-1} \tag{17}$$

$$\alpha_n = 2e\sum_{k=1}^{s} e_k P_n(\mu_k),$$

where the sums extend over the set of charges $e_1 \cdots e_2$ which the acid HA_2 contains in excess of those of HA_1 and r_k is the distance of charge e_k in HA_2 from the proton, e, located at the focus (1, 1) of the ellipsoid. In the symmetrical dibasic acid, the set of charges $e_1 \cdots e_2$ consists of a single proton, e, located at the other focus, (1, —1) and Eq. (17) becomes, since $P_n(-1) = (-1)^n$,

$$\Delta W = \frac{e^2}{R}\left\{\frac{1}{D_i} + \left(\frac{1}{D} - \frac{1}{D_i}\right)\sum_{n=0}^{\infty} 2(2n+1)(-1)^n \times \frac{Q_n(\lambda_0)}{P_n(\lambda_0)}\left[1 - \left(\frac{D_i}{D}\right)\frac{\lambda_0 - P_{n-1}(\lambda_0)/P_n(\lambda_0)}{\lambda_0 - Q_{n-1}(\lambda_0)/Q_n(\lambda_0)}\right]^{-1}.\right. \tag{18}$$

Eqs. (1) and (18) lead to Eq. (2). When HA_2 contains a dipole moment located at the focus (1, —1), in addition to the charges constituting HA_1, we find

$$\alpha_n = 2eM\cos\zeta \lim_{x\to 0}\left\{\frac{1}{x}\left[P_n\left(\frac{2x}{R} - 1\right) - P_n(-1)\right]\right\} = -2(-1)^n n(n+1)\frac{eM\cos\zeta}{R}, \tag{19}$$

where $M\cos\zeta$ is the component of the dipole moment along the axis of the ellipsoid. By symmetry it is readily seen that its component perpendicular to the axis contributes nothing. Eqs. (1), (17) and (19) lead to Eq. (3).

Theoretical Studies upon Dipolar Ions*

J. G. Kirkwood, *Department of Chemistry, Cornell University, Ithaca, New York*

(Received January 30, 1939)

I.

The influence of electrolytes on the behavior of the amino acids and proteins is perhaps one of the most important topics in the physical chemistry of these substances. It has long been known that there is a strong thermodynamic interaction between electrolytes and the amino acids and proteins. In recent years the accurate measurements of Cohn and his co-workers[1,2,3,4,5] have provided a large body of thermodynamic data relating to this question.

With the accumulation of evidence in favor of the dipolar ion or zwitter-ion structure of the amino acids and proteins in the isoelectric condition in solvents of high dielectric constant, it has become apparent that thermodynamic interaction between electrolytes and these substances can, in large measure, be attributed to the strong electrostatic intermolecular forces between dipolar ions and real ions in solution. A dipolar ion, while bearing no net charge, is characterized by electric multipole moments of large magnitude. For example, the glycine dipolar ion, $NH_3^+CH_2COO^-$, possesses a dipole moment of about 15 Debye units, about ten times that of an ordinary polar molecule. Thus a dipolar ion is in a sense a superpolar molecule, surrounded by an intense electrostatic field.

An extension of the Debye-Hückel theory describing the electrostatic interaction of dipolar ions and real ions in solution was developed by Scatchard and the writer[6] and later elaborated in some detail by the writer[7] for dipolar ions of spherical shape. It is the purpose of the present article to review the possible applications of the theory and to extend it to dipolar ions of elongated shape. In this extension of the theory we shall confine ourselves to limiting laws approached at high dilution, making use of a method similar to that developed by Fuoss[8] for the study of dipole–dipole interaction,

* Presented at the Symposium on the Physical Chemistry of the Proteins, held at Milwaukee, Wisconsin, September, 1938, under the auspices of the Division of Physical and Inorganic Chemistry and the Division of Colloid Chemistry of the American Chemical Society.

[1] E. J. Cohn, *Naturwissenschaften* **20**, 663 (1932); *Ann. Rev. Biochem.* **4**, 93 (1935); *Chem. Rev.* **19**, 241 (1936).

[2] E. J. Cohn, T. L. McMeekin, J. T. Edsall, and M. H. Blanchard, *J. Am. Chem. Soc.* **56**, 784 (1934); *J. Biol. Chem.* **100**, Proc. XXVIII (1933).

[3] E. J. Cohn, T. L. McMeekin, J. P. Greenstein, and J. H. Weare, *J. Am. Chem. Soc.* **58**, 2365 (1936).

[4] T. L. McMeekin, E. J. Cohn, and M. H. Blanchard, *J. Am. Chem. Soc.* **59**, 2717 (1937).

[5] R. M. Ferry, E. J. Cohn, and E. S. Newman, *J. Am. Chem. Soc.* **60**, 1480 (1938).

[6] G. Scatchard and J. G. Kirkwood, *Physik. Z.* **33**, 297 (1932).

[7] J. G. Kirkwood, *J. Chem. Phys.* **2**, 351 (1934); *Chem. Rev.* **19**, 275 (1936).

[8] R. Fuoss, *J. Am. Chem. Soc.* **56**, 1027 (1934); **58**, 982 (1936).

rather than the somewhat more complicated method based upon the Debye-Hückel theory.

The theory may be employed in two ways. By means of it the influence of electrolytes upon the chemical potential of a dipolar ion of known electrical structure may be predicted. On the other hand, it may be used to determine the structure, for example, the distance between the charged groups and the dipole moments, of simple dipolar ions from data relating to the influence of electrolytes on their chemical potentials. For the latter purpose we shall make extensive use of the measurements of Cohn and his co-workers.

In this article we shall limit the discussion to the aliphatic amino acids and their peptides, since the proteins present certain ambiguities of interpretation with which we cannot concern ourselves here. Thus, so many parameters are required to specify the charge distribution of protein dipolar ions that they cannot be uniquely determined from the influence of electrolyte upon chemical potential. On the other hand, too little is known at present about the details of protein structure to permit a probable assignment of configuration to the dipolar ionic charges from which to predict the interaction with electrolytes. Nevertheless, as Cohn has shown, certain progress can be made along the latter lines, and observed electrolyte effects can, in the case of egg albumin and hemoglobin,[5] be reproduced by hypothetical though not unique assignments of charge configuration.

II.

We shall be interested in the properties of a solution containing a dipolar ion component i at a molar concentration, c_i, and ν ionic components at molar concentrations, $c_1 \cdots c_\nu$, in a solvent of dielectric constant D. The pertinent thermodynamic properties of the solution may be derived from the chemical potentials of the several components. We shall be particularly concerned with the chemical potential of the dipolar ion species, which may be written in conventional form,

$$\mu_i = RT \log \gamma_i c_i + \mu_i^0(T, p)$$
$$\mu_i^0 = \lim_{\substack{c_1 \cdots c_\nu \\ = 0}} [\mu_i - RT \log c_i] \tag{1}$$

where γ_i, the activity coefficient, is defined by this equation.

We shall make the simplifying assumption that the deviation of the solution from ideal behavior is due to electrostatic intermolecular forces alone. If the solvent is idealized as a structureless dielectric continuum, the logarithm of the activity coefficient, γ_i, may be written as follows,[7]

$$\log \gamma_i = \sum_{k=1}^{\nu+1} B_{ik} c_k$$

$$B_{ik} = \frac{N\beta}{1000} \int_\omega^v \int_0^1 V_{ik} e^{-\beta W_{ik}(\lambda)}\, d\lambda\, dv \tag{2}$$

$$\beta = 1/kT$$

where the sum extends over all $\nu + 1$ solute components. V_{ik} is the electrostatic work required to bring the pair of molecules or ions, i and k, from infinite separation to the given configuration in the pure solvent, and $W_{ik}(\lambda)$ is the average work (potential of average force) expended in the same process in the actual solution, all charges, $e_1 \cdots e_s$, of molecule i having a fraction, λ, of their full values. The integration extends over all values of the relative coordinates of the pair of molecules in the volume, v, of the solution and outside a region, ω, of molecular dimensions determined by the size and shape of the two molecules, into which intermolecular repulsion at short range prevents penetration.[9]

According to the Debye-Hückel theory the potentials of average force, W_{ik}, necessary for the evaluation of the coefficients, B_{ik}, satisfy the following relation,

$$W_{ik}(\lambda) = z_k e \psi_i(\lambda, \mathbf{r}_k) \tag{3}$$

where ψ_i is the average electrostatic potential at the point $\mathbf{r}_k$ from an origin in molecule i and $z_k e$ is the charge of ion k. The potential, ψ_i, satisfies the Poisson-Boltzmann equation of the Debye-Hückel theory, which in its lincar approximation is

$$\nabla^2\psi_i - \kappa^2\psi_i = 0$$

$$\kappa^2 = \frac{4\pi N e^2}{1000\, DkT} \sum_{k=1}^{\nu} c_k z_k^2 \tag{4}$$

outside the region of non-penetration, while in ω Laplace's equation is satisfied.

$$\nabla^2\psi_i = 0 \tag{5}$$

Solution of Eqs. (4) and (5), subject to the boundary conditions of electrostatics on the surface of ω, continuity of the potential and the normal component of the dielectric displacement, yields ψ_i, which may be used in Eq. (2) or (2a) for the calculation of the activity coefficient. This method has been employed by the writer to study the influence of electrolytes on the activity of spherical dipolar ions.[7]

In the present article we propose to use a somewhat simpler method, which yields only a limiting law. Only linear terms in the expansion of the logarithm of the activity coefficient in the concentrations of the various solute species appear, thus allowing the treatment of non-spherical dipolar ions and permitting the inclusion of "salting-out" forces between an ion and a dipolar ion. The latter arise from a repulsion between the ionic charge and an image distribution in the cavity of low dielectric constant created by the dipolar ion in the solvent. It is evident that

$$\lim_{c_1, \cdots c_{\nu+1} = 0} W_{ik}(\lambda) = \lambda V_{ik} \tag{6}$$

[9] Equation (2), while somewhat more convenient for our purposes, is essentially equivalent to the more usual expression, based on the Guntelberg–Müller charging process

$$kT \log \gamma_i = \sum_{l=1}^{s} e_l \int_0^1 \{\psi_l(\lambda e_1, \cdots \lambda e_s) - \psi_l^0(\lambda e_1, \cdots \lambda e_s)\} d\lambda$$

where ψ_l is the average electrostatic potential at the point of location of charge, e_l, of molecule i in the actual solution and ψ_l^0 is its value at infinite dilution, all charges, $e_l \cdots e_s$, having a fraction, λ, of their full values.

If we are content with the linear terms in a power series in the ionic concentrations, we may, therefore, write Eq. (2) in the following form,

$$\log \gamma_i = \sum_{k=1}^{\nu} B_{ik}^0 c_k$$

$$B_{ik}^0 = \frac{N}{1000} \int_{\omega}^{\infty} (1 - e^{-\beta V_{ik}})\, dv \tag{7}$$

$$B_{ik}^0 = \lim_{c_1, \cdots c_{\nu+1}=0} B_{ik}$$

For simplicity we suppose that the term in the sum, Eq. (2), arising from the mutual interaction of dipolar ions is negligible and thus limit ourselves to solutions in which the concentration of dipolar ions is itself small. If desired, the B_{ii}^0 for mutual dipolar interaction may be obtained from Fuoss' calculations for dipole molecules.[8] The development (Eq. (7)) is only possible when the integrals defining the B_{ik} exist. Although they diverge when the component i is a true ion, they exist when it is a dipolar ion, bearing no net charge, and the expansion is suitable for our purposes. In solvents of relatively high dielectric constant at ordinary temperatures, a satisfactory approximation to the B_{ik} may be obtained by expansion of $1 - e^{-\beta V_{ik}}$ with retention of the first two terms alone.

$$B_{ik}^0 = \frac{N}{1000} \int_{\omega}^{\infty} [\beta V_{ik} - \frac{\beta^2}{2} V_{ik}^2]\, dv \tag{8}$$

For a dipolar ion characterized by a set of charges, $e_1 \cdots e_s$, distributed in a cavity, ω_0, of dielectric constant D_0, the electrical work, V_{ik}, required to bring a true ion of charge, $z_k e$, from infinity to a point $\mathbf{r}_k$ from an origin fixed in the dipolar ion i is given by

$$V_{ik} = \frac{1}{2} \left\{ z_k e \psi_e^0 (\mathbf{r}_k) + \sum_{l=1}^{s} e_l \psi_i^0 (\mathbf{r}_l) \right\} \tag{9}$$

where $\psi_i^0(\mathbf{r}_l)$ is the electrostatic potential in the interior of ω_0 at the location of the charge, e_l, and $\psi_e^0(\mathbf{r}_k)$ is the potential at the point $\mathbf{r}_k$ exterior to ω_0, when the ion and dipolar ion are fixed in the given configuration in the pure solvent. Self-energy terms in Eq. (9) are to be omitted, V_{ik} vanishing when the ions are at infinite separation. The potentials ψ_i^0 and ψ_e^0 satisfy Laplace's equation, $\nabla^2 \psi = 0$, both interior and exterior to the surface of ω_0, and fulfill the usual boundary conditions everywhere on this surface,

$$\begin{aligned} \psi_i^0 &= \psi_e^0 \\ D_0 \mathbf{n} \cdot \nabla \psi_i^0 &= D \mathbf{n} \cdot \nabla \psi_e^0 \end{aligned} \tag{10}$$

where $\mathbf{n}$ is a unit vector normal to the surface. In addition, the potentials must have the singularities characteristic of the real charge distributions of the two ions. The details of the determination of the electrostatic potential for dipolar ions of several shapes are given in the appendix.

We first consider a spherical dipolar ion of radius b, the charge distribution of which may be characterized by a point dipole of moment, μ, located at its center. The cavity, ω_0, is thus a sphere of radius b, and the excluded region, ω, in the integral (Eq. (8)) is a sphere of radius a, the sum of the radii of the dipolar ion and the real ion, all real ions in the solution being spheres of the same radius. The potential energy, V_{ik}, has the following form,

$$V_{ik} = \frac{3z_k e\mu \cos\vartheta}{(2D + D_0)r^2} + \frac{z_k^2 e^2 b^3}{2\pi^4} \frac{D - D_0}{D} \sum_{n=0}^{\infty} \frac{n+1}{(n+2)D + (n+1)D_0} \left(\frac{b}{r}\right)^{2n} \tag{11}$$

where r is the distance between the centers of the ion and dipolar ion, and ϑ is the angle between the vectors, $\mathbf{r}$ and $\boldsymbol{\mu}$, the dipole moment. The second member of Eq. (11) represents a repulsion between the real ion and an image distribution in the cavity, ω_0, created by the dipolar ion in the solvent. A similar term, usually of much smaller magnitude, arising from the interaction of the dipolar ion and an image distribution in the ionic cavity has been suppressed.

Substitution of Eq. (11) in Eqs. (7) and (8) and the neglect of small terms in D_0/D in the summation of the resulting series yields the following limiting law for the activity coefficient of the dipolar ion component of the solution,

$$\log_{10} \gamma_i = -B_i \Gamma$$

$$\Gamma = (1/2) \sum_{k=1}^{v} c_k z_k^2 \tag{12}$$

$$B_i = \frac{2\pi N e^2}{2303 DkT} \left\{ \frac{3}{2} \frac{\mu^2}{DakT} - \frac{b^3}{a} \alpha(\rho) \right\}$$

where Γ is the ionic strength of the solution, ρ is the ratio b/a, and $\alpha(\rho)$ is a function tabulated in Table I. Insertion of numerical values for the

TABLE I

$\alpha(\rho) = (\frac{1}{3}\rho^4)\{(\rho^3 - 2)\log(1 + \rho) - (\rho^3 + 2)\log(1 - \rho) - 2\rho^2\}$

ρ	$\alpha(\rho)$
0.0	1.00
0.2	1.01
0.4	1.08
0.6	1.21
0.8	1.54
0.9	1.96

universal constants and the introduction of the dielectric constant of water, D_w, yields at 25°C.

$$B_i = B_i^{(0)} - B_i^{(1)}$$

$$B_i^{(0)} = 5.48 \times 10^{-3}(D_w/D)^2\mu^2/a = 0.125\,(D_w/D)^2 R^2/a \tag{13}$$

$$B_i^{(1)} = 4.66 \times 10^{-3}(D_w/D)(v_i/a)\alpha(\rho)$$

where R is the effective dipole separation, μ/e, and v_i is equal to $4\pi N b^3/3$, the value at infinite dilution of the partial molal volume of the dipolar ion component under the idealization of the solvent as structureless continuum. The units employed in Eq. (13) are the Debye unit for dipole moment and the Ångström unit for the lengths R and a. The term $B_i^{(0)}$ gives rise to a decrease in the chemical potential of the dipolar ion by electrolyte ("salting-in"), while the term $B_i^{(1)}$ gives rise to an increase ("salting-out"). The latter effect was not included in the writer's previous treatment,[7] based on the Debye-Hückel theory. If the term $B_i^{(1)}$ is omitted in Eq. (12), a limiting law in exact agreement with the writer's earlier one is reached.

We next consider a dipolar ion of prolate ellipsoidal shape, characterized by a charge distribution consisting of two charges, $+e$ and $-e$, located at the foci. It is convenient to employ confocal elliptical coordinates in the treatment of this model. Thus a point situated at distances r_1 and r_2 from the respective foci of the ellipsoid and in a plane inclined at an angle, φ, to the reference plane containing the major axis is specified by the coordinates λ, η, and φ.

$$\begin{aligned} \lambda &= (r_1 + r_2)/R \\ \eta &= (r_1 - r_2)/R \end{aligned} \tag{14}$$

where R is the interfocal distance. The cavity, ω_0, is an ellipsoid of eccentricity, ϵ, equal to $1/\lambda_0$, and the region ω, into which ions cannot penetrate is, for simplicity, assumed identical with ω_0, although this is strictly true only for vanishing ion size. The potential energy, V_{ik}, of the dipolar ion and a real ion of charge $z_k e$ is closely approximated by the following expression,

$$V_{ik} = \frac{4 z_k e^2}{DR} \frac{\eta}{\lambda^2 - \eta^2} \lambda_0^{-1} \left[\lambda_0 - \frac{(\lambda_0^2 - 1)}{2} \log \frac{\lambda_0 + 1}{\lambda_0 - 1} \right]. \tag{15}$$

Eq. (15) is exact for the two limiting cases, zero and unit eccentricity, and only slightly inaccurate, owing to the approximate summation of an infinite series, for intermediate eccentricities. The term arising from the interaction of the ion with its image distribution in the dipolar ion cavity, included for the sphere, has been omitted in Eq. (15), since it introduces undue complication, which we postpone for later, in the evaluation of the integral (Eq. (8)). Introduction of the coordinates λ and η as variables of integration in the latter equation leads to the following expression

$$B_{ik}^{0} = -\frac{\pi N \beta^2 R^3}{1000} \int_{\lambda_0}^{\infty} \int_{-1}^{+1} (\lambda^2 - \eta^2) V_{ik}^2 \, d\eta \, d\lambda \tag{16}$$

the term linear in V_{ik} vanishing since it is an odd function of η. Eq. (16), together with Eqs. (7) and (15), yields for the logarithm of the activity coefficient of the dipolar ion,

$$\begin{aligned} \log_{10} \gamma_i &= -B_i \Gamma \\ B_i &= \frac{2\pi N e^4 g(\lambda_0)}{2303 (DkT)^2} R \\ g(\lambda_0) &= \lambda_0^{-2} \left[\lambda_0 - \frac{(\lambda_0^2 - 1)}{2} \log \frac{\lambda_0 + 1}{\lambda_0 - 1} \right]^{-1} \end{aligned} \tag{17}$$

Insertion of numerical values for the constants gives, at 25°C.,

$$B_i = 0.167(D_w/D)^2 g(\lambda_0) R. \tag{18}$$

A tabulation of g as a function of the eccentricity of the ellipsoidal cavity is given in Table II. We remark that for constant eccentricity B_i is proportional to the first power of the distance, R, between the charges of the dipolar ion. For elongated ellipsoids in the neighborhood of unit eccentricity, the function g is approximately unity. For ellipsoids nearly spherical, g may be expanded in a power series in R/a, where a is the shortest distance of either focus to the surface, equal to the radius of the sphere at zero eccentricity. The initial term of the series, $3R/4a$, when substituted in Eq. (18) yields an expression identical with $B_i^{(0)}$ (Eq. (13)) for a dipole at the center of a sphere. No counterpart of $B_i^{(1)}$ is obtained, since we have neglected the "salting-out" influence of image

TABLE II. g as a function of the eccentricity of the ellipsoidal cavity

ϵ	$g(\epsilon)$	$\epsilon(1-\epsilon^2)^{-1/2}g(\epsilon)$
0.00	0.00	0.00
0.20	0.30	0.061
0.33	0.49	0.17
0.50	0.71	0.39
0.60	0.83	0.58
0.70	0.94	0.82
0.80	1.01	1.14
1.00	1.00	

forces in the present case. While we shall not consider the problem in detail in the present article, it seems reasonable to suppose that the magnitude of $B_i^{(1)}$ for an ellipsoid can be roughly estimated by an analog of the spherical formula, Eq. (13), in which v_i/l appears instead of v_i/a, l being a length intermediate between the semi-major and semi-minor axes of the ellipsoid.

We shall also discuss a second model in which the dipolar ion is ellipsoidal in shape but characterized by a charge distribution consisting of a point dipole of moment, μ, situated at one of the foci and parallel to the major axis. The calculations proceed in the same manner as for the first ellipsoidal model except that the potential, V_{ik}, is of the form,

$$V_{ik} = \frac{4\pi z_k e}{DR^2} \frac{\lambda\eta}{(\lambda+\eta)^3} \lambda_0{}^{-1}\left[\lambda_0 - \frac{(\lambda_0^2-1)}{2}\log\frac{\lambda_0+1}{\lambda_0-1}\right]^{-1} \tag{19}$$

The logarithm of the activity coefficient of the dipolar ion is finally calculated to be

$$\log_{10}\gamma_i = -B_i T$$

$$B_i = \frac{3\pi N e^2 u(\lambda_0)}{2303(DkT)^2}\frac{\mu^2}{R} \tag{20}$$

$$u(\lambda_0) = \frac{8}{9}\frac{1+3(\lambda_0^2-1)^{-1}+4(\lambda_0^2-1)^{-2}}{\lambda_0(\lambda_0^2-1)\left[\lambda_0 - \frac{(\lambda_0^2-1)}{2}\log\frac{\lambda_0+1}{\lambda_0-1}\right]}$$

With numerical values for the constants at 25°C., B_i is given by the following equation,

$$B_i = 5.48 \times 10^{-3}(D_w/D)^2 u(\lambda_0)\mu^2/R \tag{21}$$

in which the Debye and the Ångström are the units employed. The function $u(\lambda_0)$ is listed for several eccentricities in Table III. In the limit of zero

TABLE III. Values of the function $u(\lambda_0)$

ϵ	$u(\epsilon)$	$\epsilon(1-\epsilon^2)^{-1/3}[u(\epsilon)]^{-1}$
0.00	0.00	0.50
0.20	0.47	0.43
0.33	1.03	0.33
0.50	2.92	0.19
0.60	6.31	0.11
0.70	16.5	0.053
0.80	81.5	0.014

eccentricity of the ellipsoid, $u(\epsilon)/R$ reduces to $1/a$, where a is the radius of the sphere, and Eqs. (20) and (21) reduce to Eqs. (12) and (13), except for the "salting-out" term.

III.

We are now ready for a brief review of the interpretation of the thermodynamic interaction of dipolar ions and electrolytes by means of the equations put forward in the preceding section. For this purpose we turn to the data of Cohn and his co-workers,[1,2,3] relating to the influence of electrolytes on the solubility of the aliphatic amino acids and the peptides of glycine. If s and s_0 are the solubilities of a dipolar ion in a given solvent in the presence and in the absence of electrolyte, the conditions of heterogeneous equilibrium require that the ratio s_0/s be equal to γ, the activity coefficient in the presence of electrolyte, the solution being assumed ideal when the dipolar ion component is present alone. We may therefore write a limiting solubility law in the following form,

$$\log_{10}(s/s_0) = B\Gamma \tag{22}$$

where Γ is the ionic strength and B is given by one of Eqs. (12), (17), or (20), according to the assumed structure of the dipolar ion. The data of Cohn confirm the form of the limiting law, in which the initial term is linear in the ionic strength, and the coefficient B may be obtained from the limiting slopes of his solubility curves. In order to correlate measurements in solvents of different dielectric constant, it is convenient to introduce a coefficient B_0 equal to $(D/D_w)^2 B$, related to the solubility ratio as follows,

$$B_0 = \lim_{\Gamma=0}\left[\frac{d(D_w/D)\log_{10}(s/s_0)}{d(D/D_w)\Gamma}\right] \tag{23}$$

From Eqs. (12), (17), and (20) we remark that the theory predicts that B_0 should be independent of the dielectric constant of the solvent if "salting-out" forces due to image repulsion are of small magnitude. This independence is approximately confirmed by Cohn's measurements[1] of the solubilities of the amino acids in alcohol–water mixtures, from which we may conclude that the "salting-out" forces are of secondary importance, though not negligible.

We shall first discuss the solubility data for the simplest amino acid, glycine, on the basis of the spherical dipolar ion model. The dipole moment, μ, may be computed from the solubility coefficient, B_0, by Eq. (13).

$$\mu = \sqrt{183 B_0^{(0)} a}$$

$$B_0^{(0)} = (D/D_w)^2 B^{(0)} \tag{24}$$

From the partial molal volume of glycine at infinite dilution in water and the ionic radii of Pauling and Huggins,[10] Cohn[1] estimates a to be 3.90 for glycine and lithium chloride. From the solubility of glycine in the presence of lithium chloride in alcohol–water solvents of decreasing dielectric constant, he determines $B_0^{(0)}$ to be 0.32. Substitution of these values in Eq. (24) yields a value, 15 Debye units, for the glycine dipole moment. This value is in agreement with the dipole moment, calculated on the basis of structural considerations, for the glycine dipolar ion in which the terminal NH_3^+ and COO^- carry residual charges $+e$ and $-e$, respectively. It is also of interest to consider the "salting-out" coefficient $B_0^{(1)}$. Its relative importance becomes greater with increasing dielectric constant of the solvent. Although in water the high solubility of glycine prevents the use of Eq. (22) without a term for the mutual dipolar ion interaction, the coefficient B_0 may be obtained from electromotive force measurements of Joseph[11] and freezing point measurements of Scatchard and Prentiss.[12] For glycine and sodium chloride in water at 25°C., B_0 has the value 0.24. The difference between this value and $B_0^{(0)}$, roughly 0.08, gives the "salting-out" coefficient, $B_0^{(1)}$, on the basis of the present theory. For glycine and sodium chloride Cohn calculates a to be 4.05 and ρ is 0.7. By linear interpolation in Table I, we obtain for $\alpha(\rho)$ a value 1.37. With these values and Cohn's estimate, 57 cc., for the limiting partial molal volume of glycine, corrected for solvent electrostriction, we calculate from Eq. (13) the value 0.08 for $B_0^{(1)}$. Thus in water the "salting-out" contribution arising from image forces amounts to about 25 per cent of the "salting-in" contribution to the solubility coefficient, $B_0^{(0)}$, arising from the interaction of the ions of the electrolyte and the true charges of the dipolar ion.

We shall now discuss glycine and its peptides on the basis of the first ellipsoidal model, in which two charges of opposite sign are situated at the foci. The calculations will be somewhat more approximate than those for glycine on the spherical model, since the ion size of the electrolyte is neglected and the "salting-out" influence of image forces is not included. The distance R between the foci of an ellipsoid of eccentricity ϵ and volume v/N may be expressed in the following manner

$$R = \epsilon p (1 - \epsilon^2)^{-\frac{1}{3}} \tag{25}$$

where the length p is equal to $(6v/N\pi)^{\frac{1}{3}}$ and is to be expressed in Ångström units. With numerical values for the constants, we have

$$p = 1.47\, v^{\frac{1}{3}} \tag{26}$$

[10] L. Pauling, and M. L. Huggins, *Z. Krist. Miner. Petrog.* **A87**, 205 (1934).
[11] N. R. Joseph, *J. Biol. Chem.* **111**, 479, 489 (1935).
[12] G. Scatchard and S. S. Prentiss, *J. Am. Chem. Soc.* **56**, 1486, 2314 (1934).

where the molal volume v is in cubic centimeters. For a sphere p is the diameter. From Eqs. (18), (25), and (26), we may write

$$B_0 = 0.167\epsilon p(1 - \epsilon^2)^{-\frac{1}{3}}g(\epsilon)$$

$$R = \epsilon p(1 - \epsilon^2)^{-\frac{1}{3}} \qquad (27)$$

$$p = 1.47v^{\frac{1}{3}}$$

From the first of these equations and the experimental value of B_0 the eccentricity of the molecular ellipsoid may be obtained by linear interpolation in Table II. From the eccentricity and the molal volume, the charge separation of the dipolar ion may then be computed with the second of the equations. Calculations for glycine, diglycine, triglycine, and β-alanine are summarized in Table IV. They are based on Cohn's experimental values of B_0 and on his estimates of molal volumes corrected for solvent electrostriction.[1] The distance, 2.8 Å., for glycine, corresponds to a dipole moment of 13, which differs only slightly from the value 15 obtained on the basis of the spherical model. A significant part of the difference between the two values is due to the neglect of electrolyte ion size in the ellipsoidal calculation. It therefore appears that we cannot conclude much as to the shape of the glycine dipolar ion from the influence of salts on its activity. However, owing to this very insensitivity to shape, we can place considerable confidence in the value of the dipole moment computed from the salt effect. The distances 4.7 and 6.4 computed for diglycine and triglycine are considerably below the values, 6.7 and 10.2, estimated by Cohn[1] for an extended chain configuration. Thus

TABLE IV. Values of B_0, v, and R for four dipolar ions

	B_0	v	R
Glycine	0.32	57	2.8
Diglycine	0.58	93	4.7
Triglycine	0.80	130	6.4
β-Alanine	0.43	73	3.6

our calculations suggest that the extended chain configuration is not the preferred one, but that, owing to internal rotation, the average separation of the charges in these dipolar ions lies intermediate between the extended chain value and the free rotation value. Under these circumstances the computed distances have only formal significance as average distances unless a single preferred configuration should happen to dominate all others in probability. To take internal rotation properly into account, we should compute a B_0 for each internal configuration and then average over all configurations with an appropriate distribution function for comparison with the experimental value of B_0. At present it is not possible to do this; moreover, the ellipsoidal model would be an extremely rough approximation for "crumpled" configurations.

Finally we shall discuss a series of the aliphatic alpha-amino acids on the basis of the second ellipsoidal model in which a point dipole is located at one focus. We represent glycine by a sphere with a point dipole at its center, 2.8 Å. from the surface of the molecule, and the homologs of glycine by ellipsoids with point dipoles at a focus located at the same distance, 2.8 Å., as in glycine, from the surface of the molecule measured along the major axis. The eccentricity of the ellipsoid is then determined by the relation

$$(1 - \epsilon)(1 - \epsilon^2)^{-\frac{1}{3}} = 2l/p \tag{28}$$

where p is defined by Eq. (26) in terms of the molecular volume, and l, the distance of a focus from the surface, is 2.8 Å. in the subsequent calculations. Eq. (28) may be roughly solved by linear interpolation in Table V. From

TABLE V. l/p as a function of the eccentricity of the ellipsoidal cavity

$2(l/p)$	ϵ	$2(l/p)$	ϵ
1.00	0.00	0.46	0.60
0.81	0.20	0.38	0.70
0.70	0.33	0.28	0.80
0.55	0.50		

TABLE VI. Calculated values of the dipole moment

Acid	B^0	p	Dipole Moment
Glycine	0.32	5.6	13
α-Alanine	0.31	6.1	13
α-Aminobutyric acid	0.31	6.6	13
Leucine	0.30	7.3	13

Eqs. (21) and (25) the following relation between the dipole moment of the dipolar ion is obtained

$$\mu = \sqrt{183 B_0 \epsilon p (1 - \epsilon^2)^{-\frac{1}{3}} [u(\epsilon)]^{-1}} \tag{29}$$

Calculations based upon Eq. (29) and Cohn's values of B_0 and molecular volumes for glycine, α-alanine, α-aminobutyric acid, and leucine are listed in Table VI. The discrepancy between the dipole moment values 13 and 15, both based upon the spherical model, is merely due to the neglect of electrolyte ion size in the present calculation, a procedure which we see does not lead to great error. It is interesting that the calculated dipole moments of glycine and of the other aliphatic alpha-amino acids turn out to have identical values. This is essentially what would be expected on the basis of structural considerations, although small differences could possibly arise from induction effects in the different aliphatic chains. The problem of internal rotation does not enter explicitly into the determination of the dipole moments of the alpha-amino acids as it did in the case of the peptides of glycine. However, the average configuration of the aliphatic chain to which the glycine residue is attached will determine how closely the actual molecule conforms to the ellipsoidal shape, which is at best an approximation.

APPENDIX

We shall present here some of the mathematical details in the calculation of V_{ik}, the electrostatic work required to bring a dipolar ion i and a real ion k from infinite separation in the pure solvent to a given relative configuration. The real ion is represented by a point charge $z_k e$ and the dipolar ion by a charge distribution $e_1 \cdots e_s$ located in a cavity ω_0, of dielectric constant D_0, in the solvent of dielectric constant D. The potential V_{ik} is then given by

$$V_{ik} = W - W_0 \tag{30}$$

where W is the work of charging the system in the given configuration and W_0 the work of charging when the two ions are infinitely separated. W is to be calculated by means of the formula

$$W = \tfrac{1}{2}\left\{z_k e \psi_e(\mathbf{r}_k) + \sum_{l=1}^{s} e_l \psi_i(\mathbf{r}_l)\right\} \tag{31}$$

where $\psi_i(\mathbf{r}_l)$ is the electrostatic potential in the interior of ω_0 at the point $\mathbf{r}_l$ of location of charge e_l and $\psi_e(\mathbf{r}_k)$ is the potential exterior to ω_0 at the point of location $\mathbf{r}_k$ of the real ion. The potentials ψ_i and ψ_e both satisfy Laplace's equation,

$$\nabla^2 \psi_i = 0 \tag{32}$$

$$\nabla^2 \psi_e = 0$$

as well as the boundary conditions

$$\psi_i(\mathbf{r}) = \psi_e(\mathbf{r}) \tag{33}$$

$$D_0 \mathbf{n} \cdot \nabla \psi_i(\mathbf{r}) = D \mathbf{n} \cdot \nabla \psi_e(\mathbf{r})$$

on the surface of the cavity ω_0.

Sphere

When the cavity ω_0 is a sphere of radius b, it is convenient to employ polar coordinates (r, ϑ, φ) with origin at the center of the sphere. Potentials ψ_i and ψ_e satisfying Laplace's equation and possessing the appropriate singularities are

$$\begin{aligned}
\psi_i &= \sum_{l=1}^{s} \frac{e_l}{D_0|\mathbf{r} - \mathbf{r}_l|} + \sum_{n=0}^{\infty} \sum_{m=-n}^{+n} B_{nm} r^n P_n^m (\cos\vartheta) e^{im\varphi} \\
\psi_e &= \frac{z_k e}{D|\mathbf{r} - \mathbf{r}_k|} + \sum_{n=0}^{\infty} \sum_{m=-n}^{+n} \frac{A_{nm}}{r^{n+1}} P_n^m (\cos\vartheta) e^{im\varphi}
\end{aligned} \tag{34}$$

where the $P_n^m(\cos\vartheta)$ are the associated Legendre functions of the first kind. On the boundary of the sphere b, we have

$$\psi_e(b, \vartheta, \varphi) = \psi_i(b, \vartheta, \varphi)$$

$$D\left(\frac{\partial \psi_e}{\partial r}\right)_{r=b} = D_0\left(\frac{\partial \psi_i}{\partial r}\right)_{r=b} \tag{35}$$

for all values of ϑ and φ in the intervals 0 to π and 0 and 2π. On the surface of the sphere we may employ the following harmonic expansions

$$\frac{z_k e}{D|\mathbf{r} - \mathbf{r}_k|} = \sum_{n=0}^{\infty} \sum_{m=-n}^{+n} F_{nm} r^n P_n^m (\cos \vartheta) e^{im\varphi}$$

$$F_{nm} = \frac{z_k e}{D r_k^{n+1}} \frac{(n - |m|)!}{(n + |m|)!} P_n^m (\cos \vartheta_k) e^{-im\varphi_k}$$

$$\sum_{l=1}^{s} \frac{e_l}{D_0 |\mathbf{r} - \mathbf{r}_l|} = \sum_{n=0}^{\infty} \sum_{m=-n}^{+n} \frac{G_{nm}}{r^{n+1}} P_n^m (\cos \vartheta) e^{im\varphi} \tag{36}$$

$$G_{nm} = \frac{1}{D_0} \frac{(n - |m|)!}{(n + |m|)!} \sum_{l=1}^{s} e_l r_l^n P_n^m (\cos \vartheta_l) e^{-im\varphi_l}$$

By substitution of Eqs. (34) and (36) in Eq. (35) and use of the orthogonality of the functions

$$P_n^m (\cos \vartheta) e^{im\varphi}$$

on the surface of the sphere, we obtain the following set of linear equations for the coefficients A_{nm} and B_{nm}

$$A_{nm} + b^{2n+1} F_{nm} = G_{nm} + b^{2n+1} B_{nm}$$

$$(n + 1) A_{nm} - n b^{2n+1} F_{nm} = \sigma [(n + 1) G_{nm} - n b^{2n+1} B_{nm}] \tag{37}$$

$$\sigma = D_0 / D$$

Solution yields

$$B_{nm} = \frac{2n + 1}{n + 1 + n\sigma} F_{nm} + \frac{(n + 1)(\sigma - 1)}{n + 1 + n\sigma} \frac{G_{nm}}{b^{2n+1}} \tag{38}$$

$$A_{nm} = \frac{n(1 - \sigma) b^{2n+1}}{n + 1 + n\sigma} F_{nm} + \frac{(2n + 1)\sigma}{n + 1 + n\sigma} G_{nm}$$

Use of Eqs. (34) and (38) in Eqs. (30) and (31) and application of the addition theorem of spherical harmonics yield, when the dipolar ion has no net charge,

$$V_{ik} = \frac{z_k e}{D r_k} \sum_{n=1}^{\infty} \sum_{l=1}^{s} \frac{(2n + 1) e_l}{n + 1 + n\sigma} \left(\frac{r_l}{r_k}\right)^n P_n (\cos \vartheta_{kl}) + (1 - \sigma) \frac{z_k^2 e^2 b}{2 D r_k^2} \sum_{n=1}^{\infty} \frac{n}{n + 1 + n\sigma} \left(\frac{b}{r_k}\right)^{2n} \tag{39}$$

where r_k is the distance of the real ion $z_k e$ from the center of the sphere, and ϑ_{kl} is the angle between the vectors $\mathbf{r}_k$ and $\mathbf{r}_l$ from the center of the sphere terminating in the real ionic charge $z_k e$ and the charge e_l of the dipolar ion.

When the dipolar ion contains a point dipole at the center, the first sum in Eq. (39) degenerates into

$$\frac{z_k e\mu \cos \vartheta_k}{(2D + D_0)r_k^2} \tag{40}$$

and Eq. (11) results at once from Eq. (39), with a slight change in the summation index in the second sum. In this case the dipolar ion may be regarded as possessing two charges $+e$ and $-e$ situated at equal distances r_0 from the center, with $\vartheta_{k2} = \pi - \vartheta_{k1}$. If we pass to the limit $r_0 = 0$ with

$$\mu = 2 \lim_{r_0 \to 0} (er_0)$$

all terms except for $n = 1$ vanish in first sum of Eq. (39), the first term reducing to Eq. (40) if ϑ_{k1} is designated simply by ϑ_k.

Before leaving the spherical case, it is perhaps desirable to give the general expression for $B_i^{(0)}$ when the charge distribution of the dipolar ion is arbitrary. $B_i^{(1)}$ is still given by Eq. (13).

$$B_i^{(0)} = \frac{4\pi Ne^2}{2303(DkT)^2} \sum_{n=1}^{\infty} \frac{(2n+1)}{(2n-1)(n+1+n\sigma)} \frac{M_n}{a^{2n-1}}$$
$$M_n = \sum_{l,l'=1}^{s} e_l e_{l'} r_l^n r_{l'}^n P_n(\cos \vartheta_{l'l}) \tag{41}$$

where $\vartheta_{l'l}$ is the angle between the vectors of length $r_{l'}$ and r_l, joining the charges $e_{l'}$ and e_l to the center of the sphere. For a molecule of the type of cystine, a model, consisting of two point dipoles of moment μ perpendicular to a common diameter and each situated at a distance l from the center, is useful. In this case Eq. (41) reduces to

$$B_i^{(0)} = \frac{8\pi Ne^2}{2303(DkT)^2} \frac{\mu^2(1 + \cos \varphi)}{a} \sum_{n=0}^{\infty} \frac{2n+3}{(2n+1)[n+2+(n+1)\sigma]} \left(\frac{l}{a}\right)^{2n} \tag{42}$$

where φ is the angle between the two dipole moments.

Ellipsoid

When the cavity ω_0 is ellipsoidal in form, we may conveniently employ confocal elliptical coordinates, λ, η, φ, where $\lambda = (r_1 + r_2)/R$, and $\eta = (r_1 - r_2)/R$, r_1 and r_2 being the distances of the point from the respective foci and R the interfocal distance. The angle φ measures the inclination of the plane of r_1 and r_2 to a chosen reference plane containing the major axis. The cavity ω_0 is then specified by a value λ_0 equal to the reciprocal of the eccentricity of its elliptical section. We suppose the charges $e_1 \cdots e_s$ of the dipolar ion to lie on the major axis of the ellipsoid. We shall further neglect the image distribution induced in the cavity ω_0 by the real ionic charge. Potentials satisfying Laplace's equation and having the proper singularities are the following

$$\psi_s = \sum_{n=0}^{\infty} A_n P_n(\eta) Q_n(\lambda)$$

$$\psi_i = \sum_{l=1}^{\infty} \frac{e_l}{D_0|\mathbf{r} - \mathbf{r}_l|} + \sum_{n=0}^{\infty} B_n P_n(\eta) Q_n(\lambda) \tag{43}$$

where the $P_n(\lambda)$ and $Q_n(\lambda)$ are the Legendre functions of the first and second kinds, respectively.

The boundary conditions are

$$\left.\begin{aligned} \psi_e(\lambda_0, \eta) &= \psi_i(\lambda_0, \eta) \\ D\left(\frac{\partial \psi_e}{\partial \lambda}\right)_{\lambda=\lambda_0} &= D_0\left(\frac{\partial \psi_i}{\partial \lambda}\right)_{\lambda=\lambda_0} \end{aligned}\right\} -1 \leq \eta \leq +1 \tag{44}$$

On the boundary of ω_0 the initial terms of the second of Eq. (43) may be developed in the Neumann expansion,

$$\begin{aligned} \sum_{l=1}^{s} \frac{e_l}{D_0|\mathbf{r} - \mathbf{r}_l|} &= \frac{2}{R} \sum_{n=0}^{\infty} (2n+1) G_n P_n(\eta) Q_n(\lambda_0) \\ G_n &= \sum_{l=1}^{s} e_l P_n(\eta_l) \end{aligned} \tag{45}$$

where $(1, \eta_l)$ are elliptical coordinates of the dipolar ionic charge e_l. Application of the boundary conditions (44) to Eqs. (43) and (45), use of the orthogonality of the functions $P_n(\eta)$, yields the set of linear equations,

$$\begin{aligned} A_n Q_n(\lambda_0) &= B_n P_n(\lambda_0) + (2/R)(2n+1) G_n Q_n(\lambda_0) \\ A_n Q_n'(\lambda_0) &= \sigma[B_n P_n'(\lambda_0) + (2/R)(2n+1) G_n Q_n'(\lambda_0)] \end{aligned} \tag{46}$$

where $Q_n'(\lambda_0)$ and $P_n'(\lambda_0)$ are the first derivative of the indicated functions, and σ is the ratio D_0/D. Solution of the Eqs. (46) and elimination of the derivative $Q_n'(\lambda_0)$ by means of the formula

$$P_n Q_n' - P_n' Q_n = (1 - \lambda^2)^{-1}$$

yield

$$\begin{aligned} A_n &= \frac{2\sigma}{R} \frac{(2n+1) G_n}{1 + (\lambda_0^2 - 1)(1 - \sigma) P_n'(\lambda_0) Q_n(\lambda_0)} \\ B_n &= \frac{2(\sigma - 1)}{R} \frac{(2n+1) G_n}{1 - \sigma[P_n'(\lambda_0) Q_n(\lambda_0)]/[P_n(\lambda_0) Q_n'(\lambda_0)]} . \end{aligned} \tag{47}$$

We now calculate V_{ik} by means of the formula

$$V_{ik} = z_k e \psi_e(\lambda_k, \eta_k) \tag{48}$$

and obtain, neglecting σ in comparison with unity in the denominators on the right-hand side of Eq. (47)

$$V_{ik} = \frac{2 z_k e}{DR} \sum_{n=1}^{\infty} \frac{(2n+1) G_n P_n(\eta_k) Q_n(\lambda_k)}{1 + (\lambda_0^2 - 1) P_n'(\lambda_0) Q_n(\lambda_0)} \tag{49}$$

The sum begins with n equal to unity since G_0, the total charge of the dipolar ion, vanishes. By a simple algebraic transformation Eq. (49) may be written as follows

$$V_{ik} = \frac{2z_k e}{DR[1 + (\lambda_0^2 - 1)Q_1(\lambda_0)]} \sum_{n=1}^{\infty} (2n + 1)G_n P_n(\eta_k)Q_n(\lambda_k) + Y(\lambda_k, \eta_k)$$

$$Y(\lambda_k, \eta_k) = \frac{2(\lambda_0^2 - 1)z_k e}{DR} \tag{50}$$

$$\times \sum_{n=2}^{\infty} \frac{(2n + 1)G_n[Q_1(\lambda_0) - P_n'(\lambda_0)Q_n(\lambda_0)]}{[1 + (\lambda_0^2 - 1)P_n'(\lambda_0)Q_n(\lambda_0)][1 + (\lambda_0^2 - 1)Q_1(\lambda_0)]} P_n(\eta_k)Q_n(\lambda_k)$$

The term $Y(\lambda_k, \eta_k)$ vanishes for the limiting eccentricities zero and unity of the ellipsoidal cavity ω_0 and can be neglected without great error for intermediate eccentricities. We therefore have, approximately,

$$V_{ik} = \frac{2z_k e}{DR[1 + (\lambda_0^2 - 1)Q_1(\lambda_0)]} \sum_{n=1}^{\infty} (2n + 1)G_n P_n(\eta_k)Q_n(\lambda_k) \tag{51}$$

When the charge distribution of the dipolar ion consists of two charges $+e$ and $-e$ situated at the foci (1, 1) and (1, —1), respectively, we have

$$G_n = e[1 - (-1)^n] \tag{52}$$

and the series in Eq. (51) may be summed to give Eq. (15), when we note that $1 + (\lambda_0^2 - 1)Q_1(\lambda_0)$ is equal to

$$\lambda_0 \left[1 - \frac{\lambda_0^2 - 1}{2} \log \frac{\lambda_0 + 1}{\lambda_0 - 1}\right].$$

On the other hand, when the charge distribution consists of a point dipole of moment μ at the focus (1, —1), the G_n's have the form

$$G_n = \lim_{x \to 0} e\left[P_n\left(-1 + \frac{2x}{R}\right) - (-1)^n\right]$$

$$\mu = \lim_{x \to 0} (ex) \tag{53}$$

and calculation yields

$$G_n = (-1)^n n(n + 1)\mu/R. \tag{54}$$

Summation in Eq. (51) with the G_n of Eq. (54) yields Eq. (19).

Acid-base Equilibrium in Solutions of Ampholytes

By John G. Kirkwood, *from Cornell University*

Important information concerning the structure of the amino acids and proteins is provided by a study of acid-base equilibria in solutions of these ampholytes. In fact, one of the early arguments in favor of the dipolar ion hypothesis[1] was based upon the striking discrepancy between the values of the dissociation constants of the amino acids and those of aliphatic carboxylic acids. The acidic group of the neutral ampholyte was concluded to be NH_3^+ rather than COOH, in agreement with a dipolar ionic structure $NH_3^+RCOO^-$. On the basis of Bjerrum's theory of electrostatic interaction in the dissociation of polybasic acids, it is further to be expected that the negative group COO^- would have a marked influence on the acidic dissociation of the NH_3^+ group, depending upon the distance of separation of the charged groups. From a comparison of the dissociation constants of the dipolar ion $NH_3^+RCOO^-$ and the ion of its ester salt $NH_3^+RCOOCH_3$, the charge separation in the dipolar ion may be calculated. Neuberger[2] has calculated the charge separation for several aliphatic amino acids on the basis of the Bjerrum theory. The distances so obtained were considerably too small. More recently Westheimer and Shookoff[3] using a more refined electrostatic theory, have computed charge separations which agree very satisfactorily with structural estimates from accepted interatomic distances and bond angles. Their calculations thus complete the argument for dipolar ionic structure based upon the magnitude of dissociation constants. It also is possible to extend the electrostatic theory to an ampholyte with an arbitrary number of acidic groups, NH_3^+ and COOH, and thus to provide a semi-quantitative theory of acid-base equilibria in solutions of proteins.

The ionization equilibria of a simple ampholyte HZ with positive ion H_2Z^+ and negative ion Z^- are described by the equations;

$$H_2Z^+ \rightleftarrows HZ + H^+;\ K_1 \qquad (1)$$

$$HZ \rightleftarrows Z^- + H^+;\ K_2.$$

Let $HZ^{\circ +}$ be a monobasic acid with a basic part Z° differing in structure from the ion Z^- only by the absence of the negative charge. Its ionization equilibrium is described by

$$HZ^{\circ +} \rightleftarrows Z^\circ + H^+;\ K_2^\circ. \qquad (2)$$

From thermodynamics we may write

$$RT \log K_2^\circ / K_2 = -\Delta F^\circ \qquad (3)$$

[1] N. Bjerrum, *Zeit. Physik. Chem.* **106**, 219 (1923).
[2] A. Neuberger, *Proc. Roy. Soc.* (*London*) **A158**, 68 (1937).
[3] F. H. Westheimer and M. W. Shookoff, *J. Am. Chem. Soc.* **61**, 555 (1939).

where ΔF° is the standard free energy increment in the reaction,

$$HZ^{\circ+} + Z^- \rightleftarrows HZ + Z^\circ. \tag{4}$$

From a molecular point of view, $\Delta F^\circ/N$ is equal to average work expended in the transport of a proton from the molecule Z° to the ion Z^-. Since Z° and Z^- contain the same basic group, the effect of short range exchange forces bonding the protons in the acids $HZ^{\circ+}$ and HZ may be expected to cancel in the transfer of the proton between them, leaving the electrostatic interaction between the proton and the negative charge of Z^- as the dominant contribution to ΔF°. If R is the distance between proton and the negative charge in the molecule HZ, ΔF° then has the form

$$-\Delta F^\circ = \frac{Ne^2}{\epsilon' R} \tag{5}$$

where ϵ' is an effective dielectric constant. In the Bjerrum theory ϵ' was assumed identical with the macroscopic dielectric constant ϵ of the solvent. In the Kirkwood-Westheimer theory,[4] the molecule HZ is treated as a cavity of low dielectric constant rather than as a structureless system of two point charges in the solvent continuum. Using classical electrostatic theory, these authors have calculated ϵ' for molecules of spherical and ellipsoidal shape. From Eqs. (3) and (5) the quantity Δp_K, equal to $\log_{10} K_2^\circ/K_2$, may be computed from the formula,

$$\Delta p_K = \frac{e^2}{2.303\epsilon' RkT} \tag{6}$$

where ϵ' may be obtained from the tables of Kirkwood and Westheimer. In their spherical model, the molecules HZ and $HZ^{\circ+}$ are regarded as spheres of radius b, each containing a proton at a distance r from their centers. The molecule HZ is assumed to contain a negative charge e, in excess of $HZ^{\circ+}$,

TABLE I. ($x = r/b$) Values of $\sqrt{x\epsilon'}$

$\sqrt{x}/\cos\vartheta$	-1	$-\frac{1}{2}$	0
0.10	0.25	0.24	0.23
0.20	0.64	0.60	0.55
0.30	1.31	1.16	1.02
0.40	2.45	2.11	1.76
0.50	4.59	3.82	3.02
0.60	8.79	7.15	5.42
0.70	17.6	14.2	10.6
0.80	37.5	30.9	23.3
0.90	79.2	68.9	56.4
1.00	127.0	116.3	103.5

situated at a distance r from the center on a vector making an angle ϑ with the vector to the proton. The values of ϵ' in the solvent water at 25° are presented in Table I. They were calculated with an internal molecular dielectric constant equal to 2.00.

[4] F. H. Westheimer and J. G. Kirkwood, *J. Chem. Phys.* **6**, 506 (1938); **6**, 513 (1938).

For the calculation of R from experimental values of K, it is convenient to write Eq. (6) in the form,

$$x\epsilon'(x) = \frac{e^2}{4.606\, bkT\, \Delta p_K \sin \vartheta/2} \tag{7}$$

$$b = \left(\frac{3v}{4\pi N}\right)^{\frac{1}{3}}$$

$$R = 2bx \sin \vartheta/2.$$

where v is the molar volume of the acid HZ. With an appropriate structural assignment of ϑ, the function $\sqrt{x\, \epsilon'(x)}$ may be computed and the corresponding value of x obtained from Table I. From the latter value the intercharge distance R is calculated from the third of Eq. (7).

If the acid HZ is identified with the dipolar ion $NH_3^+RCOO^-$ and the acid $HZ^{\circ +}$ with the ester salt ion $NH_3^+RCOOCH_3$, the theory may be used to calculate the distance between the charged group of the dipolar ion. Such calculations have been made by Westheimer and Shookhoff, using the spherical model for glycine and alanine and the ellipsoidal model for amino acids and peptides of longer chain length. Their results are presented in Table II, together with the distance R_F computed on the basis of free rotation and R_B on the simple Bjerrum theory in which ϵ' is identified with the solvent dielectric constant. The distance 4.05 Å obtained for glycine agrees moderately

TABLE II. Charge Separation in Dipolar Ions from Δp_K Values

	Δp_K	R	R_F	R_B
Glycine	2.02	4.05	3.56	1.53
Alanine	2.07	3.85	3.56	1.50
β-Alanine	1.06	5.15	4.19	2.92
γ-Aminobutyric acid	0.72	6.10	4.72	4.31
δ-Amino valeric acid	0.62	6.55	5.19	5.00
ϵ-Amino caproic acid	0.38	7.85	5.63	8.16
Glycylglycine	0.56	6.50	5.17	5.54

well with the structural value 3.17 and the salting-in value 3.30. The mean charge separations in the amino acids of longer chain length, as those computed from salting-in and from the dielectric constant increment, do not differ greatly from the free rotation values. Finally, we may say that the dissociation constant data on amino acids and their ester salts are entirely in harmony with the dipolar ion hypothesis.

It is possible to extend the ideas which have just been discussed to ampholytes containing an arbitrary number of acidic and basic groups. We shall begin with some preliminary remarks on the thermodynamic aspects of the dissociation of an ampholyte $H_{2\nu}P$ capable of forming a series of ions $H_{2\nu}P \cdots H_nP \cdots P$ with respective charges $n-\nu$. The dissociation equilibria are described by the equations:

$$\begin{array}{l} H_{2\nu}P \rightleftarrows H_{2\nu-1}P + H^+;\ K_1 \\ \quad \vdots \\ H_nP \rightleftarrows H_{n-1}P + H^+;\ K_{2\nu-n+1} \\ \quad \vdots \\ HP \rightleftarrows P + H^+;\ K_{2\nu}. \end{array} \tag{8}$$

If x is the hydrogen ion activity, C_P° the bulk ampholyte concentration, and C_{H_nP} the concentration of the ion H_nP, we may write,

$$C_{H_nP} = x\gamma_{n-1}\, C_{H_{n-1}P}/\gamma_n K_{2\nu-n+1}$$

$$C_P^\circ = \sum_{n=0}^{2\nu} C_{H_nP} \tag{9}$$

where γ_n is the activity coefficient of the ion H_nP. The difference Eqs. (9) for the concentrations C_{H_nP} have the solutions,

$$C_{H_nP} = C_P^\circ\Big(\prod_{s=1}^{n} K_{2\nu-s+1}{}^{-1}\Big)x^n/\gamma_n G(x)$$

$$G(x) = \sum_{k=0}^{2\nu}\Big(\prod_{s=1}^{k} K_{2\nu-s+1}{}^{-1}\Big)\gamma_k{}^{-1}x_k. \tag{10}$$

Thus the fraction f_n of the ampholyte existing in the form of the ion H_nP is

$$f_n = \Big(\prod_{s=1}^{n} K_{2\nu-s+1}{}^{-1}\Big)x^n/\gamma_n G(x). \tag{11}$$

The mean charge $\bar{Z}$ of the ampholyte is evidently given by

$$\bar{Z} = \sum_{n=0}^{2\nu}(n-\nu)f_n = \frac{d\log G}{d\log X} - \nu. \tag{12}$$

The isoelectric point corresponding to vanishing average charge is obtained by solving the algebraic equation

$$\frac{d\log G}{d\log X} - \nu = 0 \tag{13}$$

for x, equal to $10^{-\mathrm{pH}}$. The activity coefficient of the ampholyte, regarded as the neutral species H_nP is $f_v\gamma_v$, which may be written

$$\gamma = \gamma_\nu/(1 + \gamma_\nu\varphi(x))$$

$$\varphi(x) = \sum_{n=0}^{\nu-1}\Big(\prod_{s=n+1}^{\nu} K_{2\nu-s+1}\Big)\gamma_n{}^{-1}x^{n-\nu} + \sum_{n=\nu+1}^{2\nu}\Big(\prod_{s=\nu+1}^{2\nu} K_{2\nu-s+1}{}^{-1}\Big)\gamma_n{}^{-1}x^{n-\nu}. \tag{14}$$

In an aqueous solution containing the ampholyte and a strong acid at a concentration C_A, electrical neutrality requires

$$\sum_{n=0}^{2\nu}(n-\nu)f_n C_P^\circ + C_{H^+} - C_A - C_{OH^-} = 0. \tag{15}$$

The bound hydrogen ion per mole of ampholyte, y, is defined as follows

$$C_{H^+} = X/\gamma_{H^+} = C_A + C_{OH^-} - yC_P{}^\circ \tag{16}$$

and the bound hydrogen ion becomes equal to the average charge, $\bar{Z}$, or

$$y = \frac{d \log G}{d \log X} - \nu. \tag{17}$$

All pertinent information concerning the acid-base equilibria of the ampholyte may thus be calculated from the function $G(x)$

$$G(x) = \sum_{n=0}^{2\nu} B_n x^n \tag{18}$$

$$B_n = \gamma_n{}^{-1} \prod_{s=0}^{n} K_{2\nu-s+1}{}^{-1}.$$

We shall now undertake the development of an approximate statistical theory of the function $G(x)$ for a large spherical ampholyte of radius R, containing ν acidic groups COOH and ν acidic groups $NH_3{}^+$, following the Linderstrøm-Lang[5] treatment. Let us suppose that $K_1{}^\circ$ and $K_2{}^\circ$ are the respective dissociation constants of an isolated COOH group and an isolated $NH_3{}^+$ group in the absence of electrostatic interaction between the protons of the ampholyte ion. In the ion H_nP, the n protons can assume a number of configurations corresponding to the different ways in which the ν basic sites COO^- and the ν basic sites NH_2 may be assigned to them. If W_c is the local free energy of the configuration C, the configurational part of the chemical potential $\mu_n{}^\circ$ of the ion H_nP may be computed from the partition function,

$$e^{[\mu_n{}^\circ - n\mu_{H^+}{}^\circ]/kT} = \sum_c e^{-W_c/kT}$$

$$W_c = n_1 kT \log K_1{}^\circ + n_2 kT \log K_2{}^\circ + V_c \tag{19}$$

where n_1 is the number of protons occupying COO^- sites, n_2 the number occupying NH_2 sites, and V_c is the mutual electrostatic energy of the n protons and of each proton with the negative charges of the COO^- groups other than that occupied by it. The calculation of V_c demands a specification of the location of the basic groups on the surface of the molecule and use of the Kirkwood-Westheimer theory. We shall assume that the basic sites are randomly distributed on the surface of the sphere R. On the Kirkwood-Westheimer theory, the mean electrostatic interaction of any pair of charges averaged over all points on the surface of the sphere is simply $e_1 e_2/2\epsilon R$ where ϵ is the dielectric constant of the solvent. The average electrostatic energy may therefore be roughly approximated by

$$\bar{V} = [n(n-1) - 2n_1(\nu - 1) - 2n_2\nu]e^2/2\epsilon R \tag{20}$$

[5] K. Linderstrøm-Lang, *Compt. rend. trav. lab. Carlsberg* **15**, No. 7 (1923–25).

If fluctuations in V_c are neglected in the calculation of the partition function (19), we may now write

$$e^{-[\mu_n^\circ - n\mu_{H^+}^\circ - \mu_0^\circ]/kT} = e^{\nu 2\alpha - (n-\nu)2\alpha} A_n$$

$$\alpha = e^2/2\epsilon RkT$$

$$A_n = \sum_{\substack{n_1, n_2 \\ =0 \\ n_1+n_2=n}}^{n} \binom{\nu}{n_1}\binom{\nu}{n_2} \lambda_1^{n_1} \lambda_2^{n_2} \tag{21}$$

$$\lambda_1 = (K_1^\circ e^\alpha)^{-1} \qquad \lambda_2 = (K_2^\circ e^{-\alpha})^{-1}$$

since $\binom{\nu}{n_1}\binom{\nu}{n_2}$ is the number of configurations corresponding to n_1 protons on COO^- sites and n_2 on NH_2 sites. By thermodynamics, we have

$$kT \log K_{2\nu-n+1} = \mu_n^\circ - \mu_{n-1}^\circ - \mu_{H^+}^\circ \tag{22}$$

and from Eqs. (21) and (22) we may write

$$K_{2\nu-n+1} = \frac{A_{n-1}}{A_n} e^{(2n-2\nu-1)\alpha} \tag{23}$$

Thus the coefficient B_n in the function $G(x)$ becomes

$$B_n = \gamma_n^{-1} \prod_{s=1}^{n} K_{2\nu-s+1}^{-1} = e^{\nu 2\alpha - (n-\nu)2\alpha - \log \nu_n A_n}. \tag{24}$$

In all calculations the factor $e^{-\nu^2\alpha}$ is of no importance, so that it is sufficient to write

$$G(x) = \sum_{n=0}^{2\nu} e^{-(n-\nu)2\alpha - \log\gamma_n A_n(\lambda_1, \lambda_2) x^n} \tag{25}$$

$$A_n(\lambda_1, \lambda_2) = \text{Coefficient of } t^n \text{ in } (1 + \lambda_1 t)^\nu (1 + \lambda_2 t)^\nu.$$

We shall not discuss in detail the electrostatic effect embodied in the factor $e^{-(n-\nu)^2\alpha}$, except to remark that it favors the dipolar ion form of the ampholyte $H_\nu P$. However, due to the fact that α may be small in a protein molecule, the electrostatic interaction between the protons of the ampholyte may be dominated by the interaction with the electrolytic environment, manifesting itself in the $\log \gamma_n$ term. Thus acid-base equilibrium and the isoelectric points may be expected to be sensitive to the ionic strength of the ampholyte solution. It is perhaps a matter of interest to state the approximation to $G(x)$ with the neglect of electrostatic interaction within the ampholyte molecule and with the environment.

$$G(x) = (1 + x/K_1^\circ)^\nu (1 + x/K_2^\circ)^\nu. \tag{26}$$

By Eq. (12), the mean charge of the ampholyte becomes

$$\bar{Z} = \nu\left\{\frac{x}{K_1^\circ + x} + \frac{x}{K_2^\circ + x} - 1\right\}. \tag{27}$$

For the isoelectric point, $\bar{Z} = o$, we have

$$x = (K_1{}^\circ K_2{}^\circ)^{\frac{1}{2}} \tag{28}$$

a value independent of the ampholyte's specific structure. This corresponds to a pH of approximately 6. The specific behavior of an ampholyte is thus to be attributed to electrostatic interaction between its charges and with its electrolyte environment. The theory may be extended without difficulty to an ampholyte containing acidic groups other than NH_3^+ and COOH, for example, NH_2^+ and SH groups.

The Electrostatic Influence of Substituents on the Dissociation Constants of Organic Acids. A Reply to Wynne-Jones and Rushbrooke.

By F. H. Westheimer and J. G. Kirkwood

(Received May 28, 1946)

I.

Several years ago the authors of the present paper advanced an electrostatic theory to account approximately for the influence which substituents exercise on the dissociation constants of organic acids.[1] This theory is a modification of the one put forward by Bjerrum.[2] It differs from his in that an attempt was made to take into account the fact that solute molecules themselves occupy space in the solution. Since the theory does not consider numerous factors (e.g. electrical saturation, electrostriction, the detailed structure of the solute molecules), it is necessarily only approximate and of restricted application. These limitations were carefully pointed out in the original papers.

Two years ago, Wynne-Jones and Rushbrooke[3] published a "Criticism of the Kirkwood-Westheimer Theory" in which they again pointed out its limitations and approximations. They concluded that "the advantages of the more complex theory of Kirkwood and Westheimer, though real, are small compared with the big discrepancy between theory and experiment which remains". A value judgment such as the one just cited is a personal matter, and therefore scarcely a subject for scientific discussion. Furthermore, the reiteration of the known limitations of our theory would not in itself justify a reply. But the criticisms of Wynne-Jones and Rushbrooke fall chiefly into two categories: those related to changes in ionisation constant with change in dielectric constant, and those related to change in ionisation constant with change in temperature. It appears to us that, with respect to the former, they have inadequately reported the data, and with respect to the latter, their most severe criticism is based on a misunderstanding of the field in which our equations are valid. Hence, it seems useful to review the subject.

II.

A. The application of electrostatic theory to acid strengths is based upon a consideration of the ratio of the ionisation constants of two closely related acids, which differ chiefly in that one contains a charged or highly polar substituent which is absent from the other. In some cases (e.g. in the comparison of symmetrical dibasic acids with their mono-salts) a statistical factor must also be taken into account. The expression $\Delta p\kappa$ has been defined by the equation

$$\Delta p\kappa = \log_{10} K_1/\sigma K_2$$

[1] Kirkwood and Westheimer, *J. Chem. Physics* **6**, 506, 513 (1938).

[2] Bjerrum, *Z. physik. Chem.* **106**, 219 (1923); Eucken, *Z. Angew. Chem.* **45**, 203 (1932).

[3] Wynne-Jones and Rushbrooke, *Trans. Faraday Soc.* **40**, 99 (1944).

where K_1 and K_2 are the two ionisation constants of the acid in question and σ is the statistical factor. Most of the subsequent discussion deals with $\Delta p\text{K}$.

From observed values of $\Delta p\text{K}$, and by means of our theory, reasonable values for r may be obtained, where r is the distance between the two ionisable protons in a symmetric dibasic acid, or the distance between the ionisable proton and the centre of the dipole determined by the polar substituent in a monobasic acid. The results of the computations are far from precise. Changes in the assumptions as to the shape of the molecules or as to the distribution of charge within the dipole (where one is present) cause a change of several tenths of an Ångström unit in the computed value[4] of r. Because of intramolecular rotations, the average value of r (to compare with that which we calculate) cannot be calculated merely from tables of bond distances and bond angles. However, such tables do permit the calculation of a maximum and a minimum for r. In all cases, the new theory gives values of r which fall between the calculated maximum and minimum. In general, these values lie near a "free rotation" value for r computed on the assumption that all configurations are equally probable (see, however, footnote 8, ref. 1). The new theory, therefore, represents a distinct advance over the older theory of Bjerrum and over its extension by Eucken, both of which occasionally fail in the respect mentioned. Furthermore, it arranges the calculated values for r in an order far more plausible than that obtained by the use of any other theory. And lastly, the new theory presents models for solute molecules which (although still schematic) are more realistic than any hitherto proposed.

B. Our electrostatic theory (as well as that of Bjerrum) predicts that $\Delta p\text{K}$ is a linear function of the reciprocal of the dielectric constant of the solvent. The two theories differ in that the older one predicts that $\Delta p\text{K}$ should vary inversely with the dielectric constant of the solvent, D, whereas the newer one predicts that $\Delta p\text{K}$ should vary inversely with an "effective dielectric constant", D_E. This latter quantity can be computed from the dielectric constant of the solvent, D, the volume and shape of the molecule, and the "internal dielectric constant", D_i, a property of the cavity in the solvent occupied by the solute molecules, which "provides a crude means of allowing for the polarisation of a molecule produced by the average charge distribution of polar or ionic substituent groups".[1] For long chain symmetrical dibasic acids (e.g. suberic) the computed value of D_E lies close to the dielectric constant of the solvent used; for short, dipole-substituted acids (e.g. chloroacetic), it lies close to D_i. Shookhoff and one of us pointed out[4] these predictions from our theory and cited the experimental evidence then available showing that (in agreement with the theory) the values of $\Delta p\text{K}$ for the long chain symmetrical dibasic acids increase roughly inversely as the dielectric constant D, whereas the value of $\Delta p\text{K}$ for the chloroacetic-acetic acid pair is essentially independent of the dielectric constant of the solvent. This evidence, as well as some additional data, is presented in greater detail in Table I and in Fig. 1 of the present paper. The fact that a single theoretical development takes correctly into account the widely differing behaviour of these extreme cases strongly supports the validity of the theory.

C. In addition to the extreme cases (suberic and chloroacetic acids) cited, there are some others where, according to our theory, the value of the effective dielectric constant, D_E, does not approximate to either D or D_i, but lies

[4] Westheimer and Shookhoff, *J. Amer. Chem. Soc.* **61**, 555 (1939).

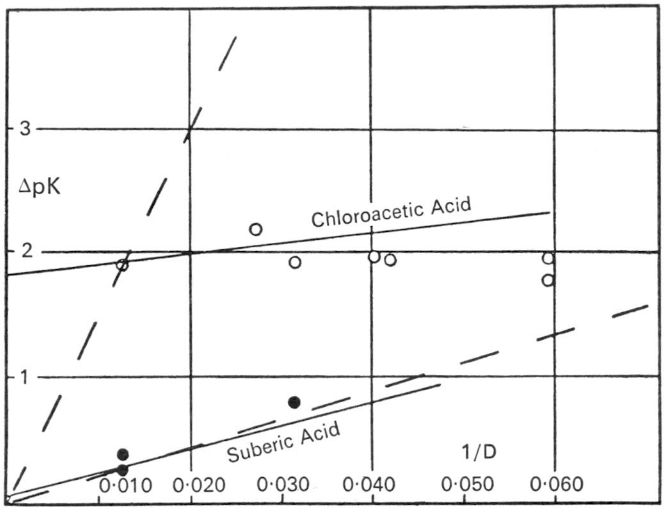

FIG. 1.

Solid line—Kirkwood-Westheimer theory.
Broken line—Bjerrum theory.

intermediate between them. Here it would be predicted that the values of $\Delta p\kappa$ should increase with decreasing dielectric constant, but that the increase should be less rapid than if it were inversely proportional to the dielectric constant of the solvent. Such cases are malonic acid, *m*-iodobenzoic acid (Fig. 2), glycine, and *m*-nitrobenzoic acid (Table I). Here the theory is only in qualitative agreement with the experimental facts. Unfortunately, Wynne-Jones and Rushbrooke discussed principally these and similar acids, to the complete exclusion of acids of the chloroacetic type.

As a matter of fact, it is difficult to state with precision the experimental value of $\Delta p\kappa$ for many symmetrical dibasic acids (including, of course, suberic) in solvents other than water. Malonic acid is a case in point. The data of Schwarzenbach[5] and those of Mizutani[6] refer to dilute non-aqueous solutions, but these authors made no attempt to extrapolate their results to infinite dilution.[7] Further, the two sets of data are not in good agreement. It is difficult to obtain precise values for ionisation constants in water; probably the difficulties for non-aqueous solutions are even greater.

The data for meta- and para-substituted aromatic acids are less ambiguous, since here the salt effects upon $\Delta p\kappa$ are small. Such acids have recently been considered by Sarmousakis,[8] who based his treatment on the same general assumptions which we employed. However, instead of using the prolate spheroidal model which (for lack of a better available approximation) was used by one of us,[9] he carried out the calculation for the more plausible

[5] Schwarzenbach, *Helv. Chim. Acta.* **16**, 522, 529 (1933).

[6] Mizutani, *Z. physik. Chem.* **118**, 318 (1925).

[7] Extrapolation to infinite dilution will probably increase the value of $\Delta p\kappa$ more for non-aqueous than for aqueous solutions. If such is the fact, it would bring our theory closer to the data of Mizutani, but further from those of Schwarzenbach.

[8] Sarmousakis, *J. Chem. Physics* **12**, 277 (1944).

[9] Westheimer, *J. Amer. Chem. Soc.* **61**, 1977 (1939); **62**, 189 (1940).

oblate spheroid. He used the data of Elliot and Kilpatrick,[10] and found that calculations based on either type of spheroid predict for aromatic acids a change in $\Delta p\kappa$ with change in dielectric constant less than that observed. He made the reasonable suggestion that the cavity in the solvent occupied by the molecule should be a little greater for non-aqueous solvents than for water, since the larger solvent molecules probably do not pack so closely around the solute molecules. For the calculations presented here (Table I), the values of the molecular volume, V, have been slightly increased (by 12 A.^3 per molecule) for all solvents other than water, in accordance with the (very approximate) increase in "covolume" given by Traube. This change in covolume is dictated by considerations of self-consistency, for Traube's rule was used in all our computations. The effect of the procedure is to narrow the discrepancy between theory and experiment for the dipole substituted aromatic acids; but the magnitude of the effect is small, and does not significantly affect the agreement between experiment and theory. For example, the change increases the value of $\Delta p\kappa$ for iodobenzoic acid in non-aqueous solutions by only 0·02 log. unit.

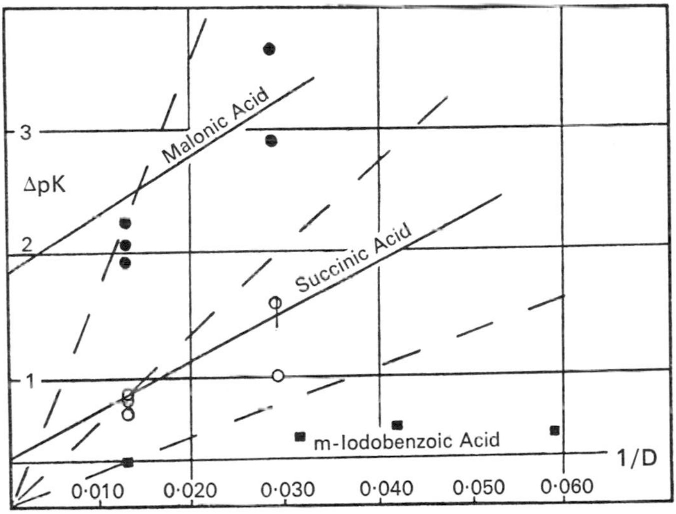

FIG. 2

Solid line—Kirkwood-Westheimer theory.
Broken line—Bjerrum theory.

D. An additional set of facts bearing on the problem of the electrostatic effects of substituents in organic molecules can be obtained from the rates of saponification of the esters of symmetrical dibasic acids.[11] In one particular investigation[12] the rate constants for the saponification of esters of malonic and adipic acids in water and in 80% alcohol were carefully extrapolated to zero ionic strength. Here also, as with the ionisation constants, the value of $\Delta p\kappa$ for the adipates varies inversely with the dielectric constant, whereas

[10] Elliot and Kilpatrick, *J. Physic. Chem.* **45**, 454, 466, 472, 485 (1941); Elliot, *ibid*, **46**, 221 (1942).

[11] Ingold, *J. Chem. Soc.* 1375 (1930); 2170 (1931).

[12] Westheimer, Jones and Lad, *J. Chem. Physics* **10**, 478 (1942).

TABLE I

Acid	r	$\cos\theta$	V H_2O	V Other-wise	Ref.	H_2O			Acetonitrile			80% Ethanol			Methanol			Dioxane-Water			Ethanol			Butanol		
						Obs.	Calc.	*B.*	Obs.	Calc.	*B.*	Obs.	Calc.	*B.*	Obs.	Calc.	*B.*	Obs.	Calc.	*B.*	Obs.	Calc.	*B.*	Obs.	Calc.	*B.*
Malonic	4·10	−1·00	110	122	*a, b, c*	2·25	2·45	(2·25)					3·20	5·10												
					d	1·93						2·90														
					e	2·08						3·62														
Succinic	5·75		137	149	*a, c, f*	0·84	0·90	(0·84)					1·55	1·90												
					d	0·73						1·01														
						0·87						1·59														
Suberic	9·30		244	256	*a*	0·28	0·30	(0·28)								0·65	0·70									
					g										0·81											
					e	0.40																				
Glycine	4·05	−1·00	94	106																						
					i	2·00	2·12					3·2[p]	3·20[p]	5·45[p]												
						2·02																				
Chloroacetic ..	3·00	0·58	100	112	*j*	1·89	1·95	(1·89)		2·10	4·00					2·10	4·65		2·20	5·95		2·20	6·20		2·20	8·70
					k				2·17						1·92			1·95			1·93			1·94		
					l																			1·76		
Cyanoacetic ..	3·80	0·78	100	112	*k*	2·19	2·35	(2·19)							2·26	2·70	5·35	2·37	2·75	6·80				2·42	2·90	10·10
Glycollic					*m*	0·92	0·90	(0·92)								1·05	2·30		1·05	2·95		1·05	3·10			
	3·10	0·36	87	99	*k*	0·88									0·99			1·19			1·17					
m-Nitrobenzoic ..	5·80		255	267	*k*	0·72									1·05						1·17			1·10		
					n		0·72	(0·72)								0·85	1·75					0·90	2·35		0·97	3·30
m-Iodobenzoic ..	5·55		265	277	*k*	0·35	0·34								0·55						0·62			0·57		
					n			(0·35)								0·38	0·95					0·41	1·25		0·42	1·80
Diethyl malonate..	4·90	−1·00	171	183	*o*	1·96	1·90	(1·96)				2·14	2·84	4·40												
Diethyladipate ..	8·20		250	262	*o*	0·39	0·40	(0·39)				0·89	0·80	0·88												

The values of r, $\cos\theta$ and V given in Table I were used to calculate $\Delta p\kappa$ according to our equations; the results are given in the columns marked "calc." Since the values of r have been rounded off to the nearest 0·05 A. unit,[4] the agreement between calculated and observed results in water is not precise. The values of $\Delta p\kappa$, computed according to Bjerrum's or Eucken's equation are listed in the columns marked "*B*". When these equations are used, the values of r necessary to make the agreement precise in water are in most cases considerably less than the values listed in Table I; they are not given here but are tabulated in ref. 4. In several cases, the values of r needed to secure agreement for the Bjerrum-Eucken formulation in water are less than the minimum possible distance of approach of the atoms involved.

(*a*) Gane and Ingold, *J. Chem. Soc.* 2153 (1931).
(*b*) Burton, Hamer and Acree, *J. Res. Nat. Bur. Standards* **16**, 575 (1936).
(*c*) German and Vogel, *J. Amer. Chem. Soc.* **58**, 1546 (1936).
(*d*) Michaelis and Mizutani, *Z. physik. Chem.* **116**, 135 (1925).
(*e*) Schwarzenbach, *Helv. Chim. Acta* **16**, 522, 529 (1933).
(*f*) Jones and Soper, *J. Chem. Soc.* 133 (1936).
(*g*) Ebert, *Ber.* **58**, 175 (1925).
(*h*) Owen, *J. Amer. Chem. Soc.* **56**, 24 (1934).
(*i*) Edsall and Blanchard, *J. Amer. Chem. Soc.* **55**, 2337 (1933).
(*j*) Wright, *J. Amer. Chem. Soc.* **56**, 314 (1934).
(*k*) Elliot and Kilpatrick, *J. Physic. Chem.* **45**, 454, 466, 472, 485 (1941).
(*l*) Wooten and Hammett, *J. Amer. Chem. Soc.* **57**, 2289 (1935).
(*m*) Nims, *J. Amer. Chem. Soc.* **58**, 987 (1936).
(*n*) Sarmousakis, *J. Chem. Physics* **12**, 277 (1944).
(*o*) Westheimer, Jones and Lad, *J. Chem. Physics* **10**, 478 (1942).
(*p*) 90% alcohol instead of 80%. The figure 2.12 for $\Delta p\kappa$ was calculated with the ionisation constant of the methyl ester hydrochloride, that of 2.02 with the ethyl ester hydrochloride.

$\Delta p\text{K}$ for the malonates increases less rapidly. (The symbol $\Delta p\text{K}$ refers to $k_1/\sigma k_2$, where k_1 and k_2 are the first and second saponification constants for the ester, and σ the statistical factor.) The results are at best semi-quantitatively in accord with our theory. No claim was made that the agreement was precise; the phrase used was "the agreement [between theory and experiment] is perhaps not unsatisfactory". It is interesting, however, that for the ionisation constants of malonic acid the observed change of $\Delta p\text{K}$ with change in dielectric constant is probably greater than that predicted by our theory, whereas the corresponding change for the saponification constants of the esters is less.[13]

E. Wynne-Jones and Rushbrooke point out that, according to the data of Schwarzenbach, and in disagreement with our theory, the graph of $\Delta p\text{K}$ against $1/D$ is not linear for some acids (e.g. some of the substituted malonic acids) in alcohol-water mixtures. Since these values of $\Delta p\text{K}$ have not been extrapolated to infinite dilution, it is not certain that the observed departure from linearity is significant. In any event, non-linear plots are probably the exception, not the rule. The fact that (in conformity with electrostatic theory) the plot of $\Delta p\text{K}$ against $1/D$ often is almost linear was long ago suggested by Wynne-Jones.[14]

F. We believe that the following is a fair summary of the success of our admittedly approximate theory in predicting the change in $\Delta p\text{K}$ with change of solvent. The theory is in good quantitative agreement with available experimental data where the effective dielectric constant, D_{E}, is either high or low. Where the effective dielectric constant has intermediate values, the theory is in only qualitative or semi-quantitative agreement with the best data at present known. In such intermediate cases, there may be a general tendency for our theory somewhat to underestimate the effect of the solvent. On the other hand, even for these intermediate cases (e.g. iodobenzoic acid) any theory based on our general assumption will predict the change in ionisation constant with change in solvent more accurately than does any previous theory.

The questions so far treated concern the derivative of the free energy of ionisation with respect to dielectric constant. (Paragraph II **E** concerns a second derivative.) A general discussion of such derivatives is presented in Section III.

III.

A. Wynne-Jones and Rushbrooke in commenting on our work state that "There is an explicit admission in the papers that the formulae do not adequately reproduce the temperature dependence of dissociation constants". Presumably, they refer to the following statement, "Finally, we may mention that, in common with the previous electrostatic theories of dissociation, the temperature coefficients experimentally determined do not agree with those

---

[13] One of the greatest shortcomings (see ref. 12) of our theory is that it fails to account for the fact that Δpk for the saponification of esters is approximately the same as $\Delta p\text{K}$ for the ionisation of the corresponding acids. Because of the greater molecular volume of the esters, the equations based on our theory predict that Δpk should be greater than $\Delta p\text{K}$. The difficulty may be more apparent than real, and may arise at least in part from the mathematically convenient but physically unrealistic assumption that in ellipsoidal molecules, all charges are at the foci.

[14] Wynne-Jones, *Proc. Roy. Soc. A.* **140**, 440 (1933).

calculated, on the basis of a constant value of r. Although a real variation of the average value of r with temperature is not unlikely, it may be that a more refined theory is necessary before accurate estimates of temperature coefficients can be made. In any case, the temperature coefficients are not large."[1] The significance of this last sentence will be taken up in a later paragraph (III C).

Wynne-Jones and Rushbrooke present in detail the data for some amino-acids. They give a series of graphs in which they plot $T\Delta p\text{K}$ against $1/D$, where the dielectric constant chosen was that appropriate to the temperature at which ionisation constants were measured. The graph for alanine (Fig. 7 in their paper) is here reproduced as Fig. 3. They point out that "All these curves are parabolic, or roughly parabolic in form, and it is at once clear that Eq. 3 [an equation based on our theory] from which $T\Delta p\text{K}$ should be a linear function of $1/D$, cannot account for them". Later these authors say that "The most striking discrepancy between experimental data and the predictions of the Kirkwood-Westheimer theory is obviously to be seen in Figs. 5, 6 and 7 . . .". As a matter of fact, however, no equation based on our theory (including Eq. 3 of Wynne-Jones and Rushbrooke) should ever have been applied to the data in question.

Although our theory (as previously stated) does not accurately predict the temperature coefficient of $\Delta p\text{K}$, the "striking discrepancy" cited by Wynne-Jones and Rushbrooke is not a case in point. The values of $T\Delta p\text{K}$ given by them can be reproduced by assuming that the $\Delta p\text{K}$ for an amino-acid refers to the ratio of the first to the second ionisation constant of the amino-acid

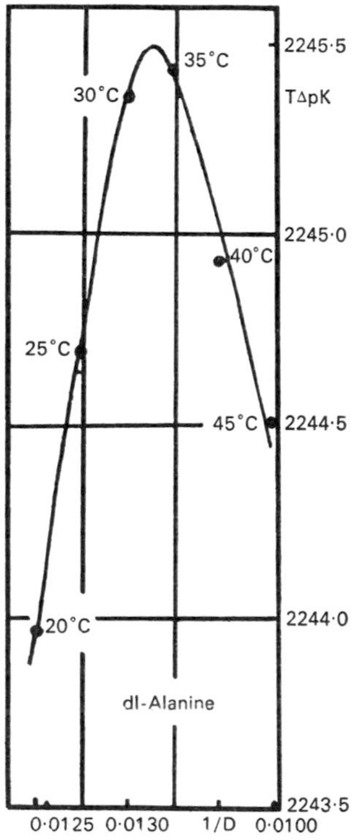

FIG. 3.—Fig. 7 from the article of Wynne-Jones and Rushbrooke.

hydrochloride. But this is not the sort of ratio of ionisation constants which the theory was designed to describe, for the first ionisation constant of alanine hydrochloride refers to the loss of a proton from the carboxyl-group, whereas the second refers to the loss of a proton from an ammonium salt group.

Our whole theory is based on the assumption that both the ionisations used in determining $\Delta p\text{K}$ are the ionisations of groups of the same type. That is, both groups must be carboxyl-groups, or both ammonium salt groups, or both thiol-groups, etc. This restriction is clearly implicit in the treatment given.[1] The data for the amino-acids, previously given by Shookhoff and one of us[4,15] referred to a comparison between the second ionisation constant of an amino-acid hydrochloride and the single ionisation constant of the corresponding amino-ester hydrochloride; in both cases the ionisation was from a positively charged ammonium salt group. (A similar but less attractive comparison is that between the first ionisation constant of an amino-acid hydrochloride and the ionisation constant of the corresponding simple aliphatic acid, e.g. alanine hydrochloride and propionic acid[15]). As can be seen from Fig. 4, a plot of $T\Delta p\text{K}$ against $1/D$, where D is a function of temperature, increases monotonically, with small slope over the small temperature range for which data are available. A similar linear plot with somewhat greater slope is obtained if $p\text{K}$ (propionic acid)$-p\text{K}_1$ (alanine hydrochloride) is set equal to $\Delta p\text{K}$.

It is worth while to examine in detail the questions related to the temperature coefficients of the ratio of the first and second ionisation constants of alanine hydrochloride. This ratio refers to the equilibrium constant for the reaction

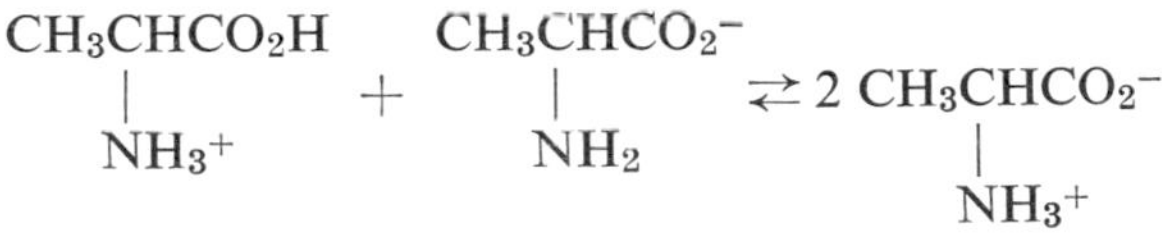

$$
\begin{array}{ccc}
\text{CH}_3\text{CHCO}_2\text{H} & \text{CH}_3\text{CHCO}_2^- \\
\mid & + \quad \mid \\
\text{NH}_3^+ & \text{NH}_2 \\[4pt]
(\text{A}) & (\text{B})
\end{array}
\rightleftarrows 2\,\text{CH}_3\text{CHCO}_2^-
\begin{array}{c}
\\ \mid \\ \text{NH}_3^+
\end{array}
$$

The reaction may be described by saying that a proton is removed from the carboxyl group of molecule A, and placed upon the amino group of molecule

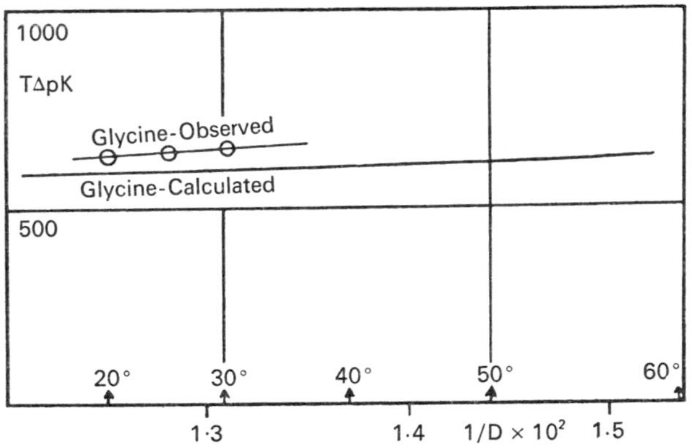

FIG. 4.—$T\Delta p\text{K}$ for glycine as a function of temperature.

[15] Neuberger, *Proc. Roy. Soc. A.* **158**, 68 (1937).

B, infinitely distant from A in a solvent of dielectric constant D. The reversible work for this process may be broken up in the following way:

$$\Delta w = \Delta w_1 + \Delta w_{2(el)} + \Delta w_3 + \Delta w_{4(el)}.$$

Here Δw_1 is the work, due to the intrinsic structure of the carboxyl-group, of removing the ionising proton from A; $\Delta w_{2(el)}$ is the electrostatic work gained because of the interaction of the ionising proton with the positive charge of the ammonium salt group in A; Δw_3 is the work, due to the intrinsic structure of the amino-group, of attaching the proton to B; $\Delta w_{4(el)}$ is the electrostatic work gained in this last process because of the interaction of the proton with the negative charge of the carboxylate ion group in B. Our theory deals only with such terms as $\Delta w_{2(el)}$ and $\Delta w_{4(el)}$. In the cases considered in our earlier publications, the sum of the terms like Δw_1 and Δw_3 vanished, at least approximately, because the groups to which the ionisable proton was attached were very similar. In the case of the amino-acids cited by Wynne-Jones and Rushbrooke, the sum of Δw_1 and Δw_3 does not vanish, since the amino-group and carboxyl-group are in no sense equivalent. Furthermore, the temperature coefficient of the sum of Δw_1 and Δw_3 should not be zero because (if for no other reason) Δw_1 includes a strong electrostatic interaction, which must be dependent on temperature. Our theory, therefore, makes no prediction concerning the temperature coefficient of the ratio of the first and second ionisation constants of an amino-acid hydrochloride; hence, the "striking discrepancy" of Wynne-Jones and Rushbrooke does not exist.[16]

B. Although Wynne-Jones and Rushbrooke's discussion of amino-acids is not pertinent to our theory, we do not wish to minimise the fact that the temperature coefficients computed by us do not agree well with experiment. The data for the temperature coefficients of a number of acids is here presented in Table II. The Bjerrum formulation for electrostatic effects in water solution leads to the equation

$$\frac{d\Delta F(el)}{dt} = -\Delta S = 0{\cdot}0047\,\Delta F(el)$$

where the constant 0·0047 is the value of $d \ln D/dT$.[17] All the equations derived by our treatment (and by Sarmousakis' parallel treatment of the oblate ellipsoid) can be and are here treated in similar fashion. In general, $\frac{d\Delta F(el)}{dT}$ has been set equal to $c\Delta F(el)$. The values of c have been determined from experimental data, and have also been computed by our theory. (The actual temperature coefficients of the ionisation constants of dibasic acids are smaller than would be implied by the values of c in Table II; the experimental data have been corrected by the statistical factor of four, which is independent of temperature.)

It can be seen from Table II that the older Bjerrum theory gives values of c which are in better absolute agreement with experiment than those given by

---

[16] Incidentally, a graph such as Fig. 3 (Fig. 7 of Wynne-Jones and Rushbrooke) may be somewhat misleading. The values for $\Delta p\text{K}$ are all identical within 0.1%. An error of 0·003 log unit in the ionisation constants might completely destroy the indicated parabola. Although the data of Nims and Smith are excellent, it seems more conservative to describe all their values of "$T\Delta p\text{K}$" as identical. The idea (implied in Wynne-Jones' and Rushbrooke's criticism) that our theory should predict changes of the order of magnitude indicated, although flattering, is inconsistent with the avowedly approximate nature of our work.

[17] Akerlöf, *J. Amer. Chem. Soc.* **54**, 4125 (1932).

TABLE II. Temperature Coefficients

Acid	Reference	"c" Obs. (v)	"c" Calc. (v)	"c" Bjerrum
Succinic	*q*	0·0062	0·0023	0·0047
Glutaric	*q*	0·0070	0·0034	0·0047
β,β-Dimethyl glutaric	*q*	0·0025	0·0011	0·0047
Adipic	*q*	0·0070	0·0038	0·0047
cis-Caronic	*q*	0·0027	0·0007	0·0047
trans-Caronic	*q*	0·0051	0·0024	0·0047
Glycine (Me ester)	*s*	0·0026	0·0013	0·0047
Glycine HCl (acetic)	*t*	(0·0046)		
Chloroacetic (acetic)	*t*	0·0020	0·0001	0·0047
Glycollic (acetic)	*t*	0·0041	0·0001	0·0047
m-Nitrobenzoic (benzoic)	*u*	0·0046	0·0004	0·0047
m-Iodobenzoic (benzoic)	*u*	0·0041	0·0003	0·0047
m-Toluic (benzoic)	*u*	0·0000	0·0003	0·0047

The compounds in parentheses are those the ionisation constants of which were used to determine the value of $\Delta p\kappa$ (observed) and therefore of c (observed).
(*q*) Jones and Soper, *J. Chem. Soc.* 133 (1936).
(*s*) Edsall and Blanchard, *J. Amer. Chem. Soc.* 55, 2337 (1933).
(*t*) Harned and Owen, *Physic. Chem. of Electrolyte Solutions*, Reinhold, New York, 1943.
(*u*) Schaller, *Z. physik. Chem.* **25**, 497 (1898). Hammett, *J. Chem. Physics* **4**, 613 (1936). Hammett, *Physical Organic Chemistry*, McGraw-Hill, New York, 1940. Sarmousakis, *J. Chem. Physics* **12**, 277 (1944).
(*v*) c defined by equation $\frac{d\Delta F}{dT} = c\Delta F$.

our theory. On the other hand, our treatment (as indicated by Wynne-Jones and Rushbrooke) places the acids roughly in the correct order. In point of fact, the values of c computed by the new theory seem all to be too low by about 0·003 degree^{-1}.

C. Wynne-Jones and Rushbrooke used our equations and computed the distance, r, from the values of the temperature derivative, c, of the ionisation constants of dibasic acids; the values of r were, as they pointed out, unreasonably small. Their computation, however, reflects the ratio of $c_{\text{obs.}}$ to c_{calc}. In this connection, it is important to point out again (see paragraph A, section III) that the temperature coefficients of $T\Delta p\kappa$ are small. The situation for glycine is shown graphically in Fig. 4, where $\Delta p\kappa$ is the logarithm of the ratio of the ionisation constant of glycine methylester hydrochloride to the second ionisation constant of glycine hydrochloride. The computed and observed curves do not have the same slope; on the other hand, the slopes themselves are small. The difference between the curves increases by only about 0·25 log unit over a range of 100°—an amount not much larger than the experimental uncertainty in $\Delta p\kappa$ (see Tables I and II) and smaller than the uncertainty introduced into the theory by necessary approximations (e.g. choice of a shape for the molecule[4]). When c is computed from our theory, the expression $c_{\text{expt.}}/c_{\text{computed}}$ may be large, but $c_{\text{expt.}}-c_{\text{computed}}$ is small. This sort of situation is typical for approximate theories. Such a theory may reproduce a given function very well, but where the value of the function varies only slightly with change in a given variable Y, the prediction of the derivative with respect to Y may be in error by a large factor. For example, the perfect gas equation, $pv = NRT$, which can be derived from simplified theoretical considerations, is a useful approximation to the behaviour of real gases. Yet the computed derivative of the pressure-volume product with respect to pressure at constant temperature $\text{M} = \left[\frac{\partial(pv)}{\partial p}\right]_T$ is zero, whereas in fact this derivative may be either positive or negative. This ratio $M_{obs.}/M_{computed}$ is then infinite, although $M_{obs.}-M_{computed}$ is small. The desirable refinements which might well be introduced into the electrostatic theory of the ionisation of acids might account for the observed temperature coefficients without greatly affecting the general agreement between the experimental and calculated values of $\Delta p\text{K}$.

IV.

Wynne-Jones and Rushbrooke, after a consideration of the data presented in their paper (which, as already explained, are partly insufficient and partly inapplicable) came to the conclusion that "the Kirkwood-Westheimer theory takes insufficient account of the specific interaction between solvent and solute molecules or ions". Although in our first paper[1] we ourselves pointed out this deficiency, we cannot agree with Wynne-Jones and Rushbrooke as to its quantitative importance. Our reasons coincide closely with those given by Baughan.[18] Wynne-Jones and Rushbrooke make their criticism somewhat more specific by speaking of the " 'clamping' of the solvent, in the neighbourhood of solute ions". But since they do not prescribe a quantitative method for estimating the influence of the "clamping effect" on the chemical potentials of the ions participating in a dissociation equilibrium, it is difficult to apply their ideas.

There seems to be little doubt that any refinement of the theory dealing with the effect of substituents on dissociation constants and reaction rates must be based upon a model similar to ours, but elaborated to include more details of the local solvent structure. Although there is good reason to believe that short range specific interactions between solvent and ions will cancel when the difference between the free energies of ionisation of two similar substances in the same solvent are considered, nevertheless the longer range interactions remain. In a complete theory, these latter should be taken into account by a suitable description in molecular terms of the solvent structure in the close neighbourhood of the ions. In such a description, electrostatic effects such as electrostriction, electrical saturation, and departures of the local dielectric constant from the macroscopic value in the statistical continuum of the solvent should be taken into account. Formidable difficulties remain to be overcome before such a detailed theory can be adequately formulated. Entropy contributions arising from hindered rotation of solvent molecules in the neighbourhood of the ions would probably account largely for the failure of $d\Delta p\text{K}/dT$, as calculated by our theory, to agree with the experimental values.

Until a more refined theory is developed in a form from which quantitative predictions can be made, we see nothing to be gained by objecting that the models on which the newer theory are based are still too simple, and thus minimising the real advantages of the present theory over the less detailed theory of Bjerrum.

Résumé

En réponse à l'article de Wynne-Jones et Rushbrooke, critiquant la théorie de Kirkwood-Westheimer, ces derniers auteurs font remarquer que Wynne-Jones et Rushbrooke ont rapporté de façon inexacte les résultats

[18] Baughan, *J. Chem. Physics* **7**, 951 (1939).

relatifs aux changement de la constante d'ionisation en fonction de la variation de la constante diélectrique et que, en ce qui concerne les changements de la constante d'ionisation avec la température, leur critique est fondée sur une application des équations de Kirkwood-Westheimer dans un domaine où elles ne sont pas valables.

Zusammenfassung

Eine Antwort auf den Artikel von Wynne-Jones und Rushbrooke: "Eine Kritik der Theorie von Kirkwood und Westheimer." Die Autoren wenden ein, dass Wynne-Jones und Rushbrooke die Daten bezüglich Änderungen der Dissoziationskonstante durch Änderung der Dielektrizitätskonstante nur mangelhaft berichtet haben und dass ihre Kritik hinsichtlich der Änderungen der Dissoziationskonstante durch Temperaturänderung auf einem Missverständnis des Gültigkeitsbereichs der Kirkwood-Westheimer'schen Gleichungen beruht.

George Herbert Jones Laboratory,
University of Chicago.

George Fisher Baker Laboratory,
Cornell University.

The Radial Distribution Functions of Electrically Charged Macromolecules in Solution*

JOHN G. KIRKWOOD, *Sterling Chemistry Laboratory, Yale University, New Haven, Connecticut*

AND

JACOB MAZUR, *The Weizmann Institute of Science, Rehovoth, Israel*

(Received June 26, 1952)

The scattering of light by solutions of proteins and other macromolecules as well as the thermodynamic properties of the solutions are determined by the radial distribution function, $g(R)$, which is defined as the ratio of the average local concentration of other macromolecules at a distance R from an arbitrary molecule to the bulk concentration of the macromolecular species. The statistical mechanical theory of distribution functions in fluid mixtures developed in equivalent forms by Kirkwood,[1] Born and Green,[2] Yvon,[3] and Mayer[4] may be employed to determine the radial distribution functions of macromolecules in solution in terms of the potential of average force acting between a pair of macromolecules in an electrolytic solvent of low molecular weight. We shall present here the results of an investigation of the radial distribution functions of electrically charged spherical macromolecules interacting according to a screened Coulomb potential of the Verwey-Overbeek type in a solvent containing electrolytes of low molecular weight. The results are of particular interest in concentrated aqueous solutions of the globular proteins, such as serum albumin. In such concentrated solutions it is found that locally ordered clusters are established through the action of the Coulomb force and the short-range intermolecular repulsion determining the molecular diameter.

We shall employ the Born-Green formulation of the integral equation for the radial distribution function, $g(R)$, for a pair of charged spherical macromolecules in solution in a solvent of low molecular weight. If we define a function $\psi(R)$ by the relation:

$$g(R) = \exp\{-\beta V + \psi(R)/R\}$$

$$\beta = 1/kT \tag{1}$$

the integral equation may be written in the form:[5]

---

* Presented at the Symposium of the Commission on Macromolecules of the International Union of Chemistry, Strasbourg, June 9–11, 1952.

[1] Kirkwood, *J. Chem. Phys.* **3**, 300 (1935).

[2] Born and Green, *Proc. Roy. Soc.* (*London*) **A188**, 10 (1946).

[3] Yvon, *Actualités sci. et ind.* (Hermann et Cie, Paris, 1935).

[4] Mayer, *J. Chem. Phys.* **15**, 187 (1947).

[5] Kirkwood, Maun, and Alder, *J. Chem. Phys.* **18**, 1040 (1950).

$$\psi(R) = \int_0^\infty \{K(|R - r|) - K(R + r)\}\varphi(r)\, dr$$

$$\varphi(r) = r[g(r) - 1] = r[e^{-\beta V + \psi/r} - 1] \tag{2}$$

$$K(t) = \pi\beta c \int_t^\infty (s^2 - t^2) \frac{dV}{ds} g(s)\, ds$$

where c is the macromolecular ion concentration in particles per cubic centimeter and $V(R)$ is the potential of average force between an isolated pair of macromolecules at a distance R apart, averaged over all degrees of freedom of the solvent.

For the potential of mean force between a pair of spherical macromolecular ions, of diameter a, in an aqueous electrolyte medium, we shall use the approximate Verwey-Overbeek potential:[6]

$$V(x) = \infty; \qquad x \leq 1$$

$$V(x) = A(e^{-\kappa a(x-1)}/x); \qquad x > 1$$

$$A = aD\psi_0^2/4 \tag{3}$$

$$\kappa^2 = \frac{4\pi Ne^2}{1000\, DkT} \sum_{i-1}^{v} c_i z_i^2$$

$$x = R/a$$

where ψ_0 is the total potential of the diffuse electric double layer surrounding each macromolecular ion, D the dielectric constant of the solvent, and κ is the Debye-Hückel parameter, determined by the molar concentrations c_i and valences z_i of all ionic species present in the solution.

The solution of Eq. (2) with the interionic potential of Eq. (3) was carried out by the following numerical procedure. After introduction of the reduced variable, $x = R/a$, Fourier transformation of both sides of Eq. (2) leads to the relations:

$$\psi(x) = \frac{2}{\pi} \int_0^\infty F(k) \sin kx\, dk$$

$$F(k) = G(k)H(k)$$

$$F(k) = \int_0^\infty \psi(x) \sin kx\, dx \tag{4}$$

$$H(k) = \int_0^\infty \varphi(x) \sin kx\, dx$$

$$G(k) = \frac{\beta\lambda A}{k^3} \int_0^\infty (kx \cos kx - \sin kx) \frac{(1 + \kappa a x)}{x^2} e^{-\kappa a(x-1)} g(x)\, dx$$

$$\lambda = 4\pi c a^3$$

[6] Verwey and Overbeek, *Theory of Stability of Lyophobic Colloids*. Elsevier, New York-Amsterdam, 1948.

The second equation of (4) was solved by an iterative process based on the following relation:

$$F_{n+1}(k) = \frac{H_n(k) - F_n(k)}{1 - G_n(k)} G_n(k) \tag{5}$$

$$F_0(k) = 0$$

which was found to converge more rapidly than direct iteration by the relation, $F_{n+1} = H_n G_n$. The zero order trial function $\psi_0(x) = 0$ corresponds to the approximation of $g(x)$ by $\exp\{-\beta V\}$. Each state of the iterative process involves the Fourier inversion of $F_n(k)$ to obtain an iterate $\psi_n(x)$ for use in the third and fourth equations of (4) to obtain iterates, $H_n(k)$ and $G_n(k)$ by Fourier transformation. The Fourier transforms were carried out with the use of International Business Machine equipment.[7] Calculations were

TABLE I. Radial Distribution Functions of Spherical Macromolecular Ions in Solution ($\kappa a = 3$)

	$g(x)$			
x	$\lambda = 0.27$ $\beta A = 2.00$	$\lambda = 6.28$ $\beta A = 2.00$	$\lambda = 6.28$ $\beta A = 4.00$	$\lambda = 10.00$ $\beta A = 2.00$
1.00	0.167	0.66	0.21	0.91
1.10	0.375	1.00	0.56	1.36
1.20	0.478	1.24	0.98	1.64
1.30	0.624	1.34	1.33	1.70
1.40	0.747	1.35	1.52	1.60
1.50	0.839	1.29	1.54	1.40
1.60	0.903	1.20	1.45	1.19
1.70	0.947	1.11	1.31	0.99
1.80	0.975	1.02	1.16	0.84
1.90	0.992	0.97	1.02	0.77
2.00	1.004	0.93	0.92	0.73
2.10	—	0.91	0.84	0.74
2.20	1.008	0.91	0.80	0.80
2.30	—	0.93	0.79	0.88
2.40	1.006	0.95	0.82	0.99
2.50	—	0.98	0.87	1.08
2.60	1.004	1.00	0.93	1.16
2.70	—	1.02	0.99	1.17
2.80	1.002	1.03	1.05	1.16
2.90	—	1.03	1.08	1.11
3.00	1.001	1.02	1.10	1.05
3.10	—	1.01	1.10	0.99
3.20	—	1.00	1.07	0.95
3.30	—	1.00	1.05	0.91
3.40	—	0.99	1.03	0.90
3.50	—	0.99	1.00	0.91
3.60	—	0.99	0.99	0.94
3.70	—	0.99	0.96	0.96
3.80	—	1.00	0.95	1.00
3.90	—	1.00	0.95	1.04
4.00	—	1.00	0.96	1.06

[7] Schaeffer, Shomaker, and Pauling, *J. Chem. Phys.* **14**, 648 (1946); **14**, 659 (1946).

carried out at ionic strengths corresponding to $\kappa a = 3$ for several values of the parameters, λ and βA:

$$\lambda = 4\pi c a^3 = 24\Phi$$

$$\beta A = \frac{a D \psi_0^2}{4kT} \tag{6}$$

where Φ is the volume fraction of the macromolecular ions. The radial distributions $g(x)$ for the following parameter sets: $\lambda = 0.27$, $\beta A = 2.00$;

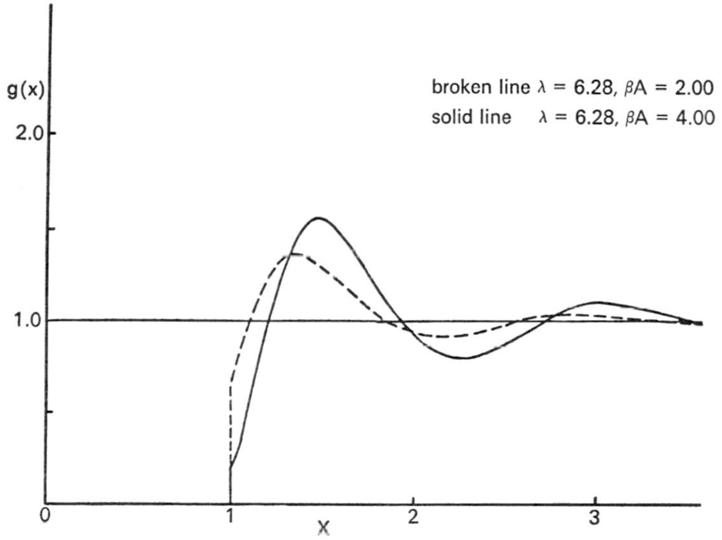

FIG. 1. Influence of electric charge on the radial distribution functions at constant concentration.

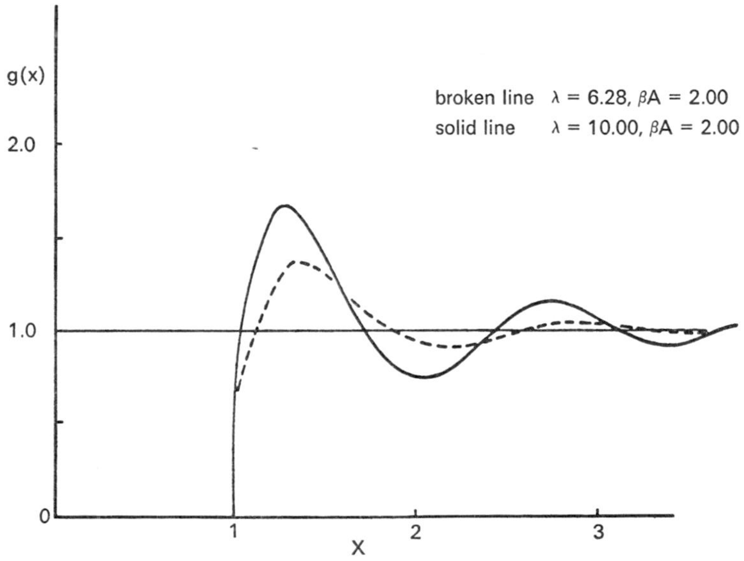

FIG. 2. Influence of concentration on the radial distribution functions at constant charge.

$\lambda = 6.28$, $\beta A = 2.00$; $\lambda = 6.28$, $\beta A = 4.00$; $\lambda = 10.00$, $\beta A = 2.00$ are presented in Table I and in Figs. 1, 2, and 3. It is to be remarked that the macro-ion concentration increases with increasing λ and that its charge increases with increasing βA.

It will be remarked that at low macromolecular concentration the radial distribution function deviates only slightly from exp $\{- V/kT\}$, although at a volume fraction of approximately 0.01 clustering characteristic of liquid-like local order is incipient, as illustrated by Fig. 3. Liquid-like clustering of the macromolecules becomes pronounced at high concentration as illustrated in Figs. 1 and 2. In Fig. 1, the effect of increasing the double layer potential at constant concentration at a volume fraction of approximately 0.26 is presented. The influence of increasing the volume fraction from 0.26 to 0.42 at constant double layer potential is presented in Fig. 2. It will be observed that both an increase in concentration and an increase in

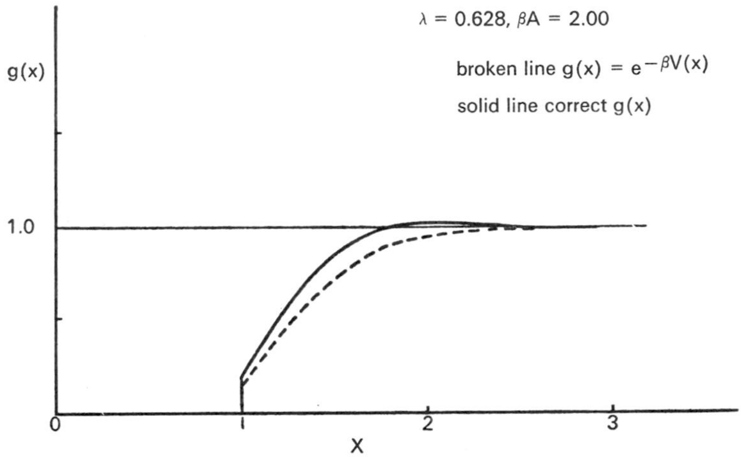

FIG. 3. Radial distribution function at low macro-ion concentration.

the double layer potential enhance the degree of local order in the structure of the clusters, as manifested by the sharpness of the peaks of $g(x)$ and the decrease in their heights with increasing intermolecular distance. For a given magnitude of the double layer potential it is found that a critical concentration exists above which solutions of Eq. (2), for which $x^2(g - 1)$ is integrable, no longer exist. At this point the liquid-like clusters grow cooperatively to produce a transition to a state of long-range order, characteristic of crystalline phases.

Synopsis

Representative radial distribution functions of electrically charged spherical macromolecules, interacting with a screened Coulomb potential, in electrolytic solutions, are determined by means of the statistical mechanical theory of distribution functions in fluid mixtures. At high concentrations locally ordered clusters, characteristic of liquid structure, are established. The degree of local order in the clusters increases with the magnitude of the double layer potential and decreases with increasing ionic strength of the solution.

Résumé

Des fonctions de distribution radiale de macromolécules sphériques chargées électriquement dans une solution électrolytique ont été déterminées au moyen de la théorie de mécanique statistique des fonctions de distribution dans des mélanges fluides. Aux concentrations élevées, des agglomérats, localement ordonnés, et caractéristiques de la structure des liquides ont été établis. Le degré de disposition ordonnée au sein des agglomérats s'accroît avec la grandeur du potentiel de la couche double, et décroit avec une force ionique croissante de la solution.

Zusammenfassung

Representative radiale Verteilungsfunktionen von elektrisch geladenen sphärischen Makromolekülen, die mit einem geschirmten Coulomb'schen Potential zusammenwirken, in elektrolytischen Lösungen, werden mittels der statistischen mechanischen Theorie der Verteilungsfunktionen in Flüssigkeitsgemischen bestimmt. Bei hohen Konzentrationen werden lokal geordnete Anhäufungen gebildet, die für flüssige Struktur charakteristisch sind. Der Grad an lokaler Ordnung in den Anhäufungen nimmt mit der Grösse des Doppelschicht-Potentials zu und nimmt mit zunehmender Ionenstärke der Lösung ab.

The Statistical Mechanical Basis of the Debye-Hückel Theory of Strong Electrolytes

By John G. Kirkwood and Jacques C. Poirier,
Contribution No. 1209 *from the Sterling Chemistry Laboratory,
Yale University, New Haven, Connecticut*

(Received April 19, 1954)

The potentials of mean force of sets of n ions, averaged over the configuration space of all other ions in the system, are expanded as power series in a charging parameter ξ. Equations are derived relating coefficients of the various powers of ξ in these expansions, using the method of semi-invariants. The validity of the linearized Poisson-Boltzmann equation for the coefficient of the first power of ξ in the expansion of the potential of mean force of an ion pair, when ion size is neglected, is demonstrated. The validity of the Debye-Hückel limiting law is thus shown in an unambiguous way. A systematic procedure of obtaining the coefficients of higher powers of ξ is outlined. When ion size is considered, the linearized integral equation for the potential of average force of a pair of ions possesses oscillating solutions at high ionic strength, corresponding to stratifications of average space charge of alternating sign in the neighborhood of each ion.

INTRODUCTION

The Debye–Hückel[1] theory of solutions of strong electrolytes remains one of the outstanding achievements of modern theoretical chemistry. Not only does it provide a general understanding of the unique aspects of electrolyte solutions, arising from the long range Coulomb forces between the ions, but all experimental evidence appears to confirm its limiting laws, as the ionic strength approaches zero, as rigorously exact quantitative relationships. However, although the validity of limiting laws is seldom seriously questioned any longer, their precise theoretical foundation leaves something to be desired. As R. H. Fowler[2] pointed out, the Poisson–Boltzmann equation on which the Debye–Hückel theory is based is not consistent with the exact principles of statistical mechanics, and this is reflected in the failure of the mean electrostatic potentials calculated by the theory to satisfy the conditions of integrability as functions of the ionic charges. Nevertheless, the solutions of the linearized Poisson–Boltzmann equation, upon which the limiting laws are based, do satisfy the conditions of integrability, which is presumptive evidence that only the non-linear terms are in error. Onsager[3] and Kirkwood[4] carried out detailed analyses of the problem along similar lines and reached a

[1] P. Debye and E. Hückel, *Physik. Z.* **24**, 185 (1923).
[2] R. H. Fowler, "Statistical Mechanics," Cambridge University Press, New York, N.Y., 1929, Chap. XIII.
[3] L. Onsager, *Chem. Revs.* **13**, 73 (1933).
[4] J. G. Kirkwood, *J. Chem. Phys.* **2**, 767 (1934).

provisional conclusion that departures from the principle of superposition, upon which the Poisson–Boltzmann equation is based, lead to errors in the potential of mean force between an ion pair, which is of the same order in the ionic charges as the non-linear terms in the Poisson–Boltzmann equation. The principle of superposition states the average force acting upon a third ion in the neighborhood of an ion pair is the sum of the average forces which would act upon it if each ion of the pair were present alone. Their arguments, justifying the validity of the linearized Poisson–Boltzmann equation and the limiting laws, were, however, incomplete in the sense that it was necessary to employ the principle of superposition in order to estimate the error introduced into the Poisson–Boltzmann equation by departures from superposition. Therefore, it was only demonstrated that the use of the approximate principle of superposition was consistent with the rigorous validity of the linearized Poisson–Boltzmann equation, not that this equation was in fact valid. More recently, Mayer[5,6] has presented a theory of strong electrolytes, based upon a cluster development of the partition function of the type used in the theory of imperfect gases and solutions. After forcing convergence of the cluster sums with factors $e^{-\alpha R}$ in the Coulomb potentials of the ions, he was able to obtain the Debye–Hückel limiting law by the summation of selected terms in the cluster development, corresponding to ring graphs alone. However, explicit proof that clusters corresponding to graphs of more complex topological types do not contribute terms of the same order as the limiting law is, to say the least, not transparent and obvious.

For these reasons, it seemed to us worthwhile to re-examine the statistical mechanical basis of the Debye–Hückel theory by means of a systematic development of the potentials of average force in sets of n ions, in power series in the ionic charging parameters, along the lines of the earlier work of Onsager and Kirkwood. In this manner, we shall be able to demonstrate the validity of the linearized Poisson–Boltzmann equation for the coefficient of the first power of the development of the potential of average force of an ion pair in a power series in the charging parameter of either ion, when ion size is neglected, and thus to demonstrate the validity of the Debye–Hückel limiting law in an unambiguous fashion. A systematic method for determining the coefficients of higher powers of the charging parameters is outlined. When ion size is taken into account in a symmetrical manner for both ions of a pair, the linearized integral equation for the potential of average force cannot be converted into a Poisson–Boltzmann equation, but is equivalent to a differential-difference equation which possesses oscillating solutions at high ionic strength, corresponding to stratifications of average space charge of alternating sign in the neighborhood of each ion, simulating the types of radial distribution to be expected in concentrated solutions and in molten salts.

I.

We shall find it profitable to begin with a brief review of some of the general relationships between the excess electrical chemical potentials $\mu_\alpha^{(e)}$ of the ions of the several types $\alpha = 1 \ldots \nu$, present in an electrolyte solution, the mean electrostatic potential $\bar{\psi}_\alpha$ in the neighborhood of an ion of type α, carrying a fraction ξ_1 of its full charge, and the radial distribution functions $g_{\alpha\beta}^{(2)}$

[5] J. E. Mayer, *ibid.* **18**, 1426 (1950).
[6] J. Poirier, *ibid.* **21**, 965 (1953).

of ion pairs, one of which carries a fraction ξ_1 of its full charge. The mean electrostatic potential $\bar{\psi}_\alpha(R)$ at a distance R from an ion of type α, satisfies the exact Poisson equation

$$\nabla^2 \bar{\psi}_\alpha = -\frac{4\pi}{D} \sum_{\beta=1}^{\nu} \frac{N_\beta}{v} e_\beta g_{\alpha\beta}^{(2)}$$

$$g_{\alpha\beta}^{(2)} = e^{-W_{\alpha\beta}^{(2)}/kT} \tag{1}$$

where $W_{\alpha\beta}^{(2)}$ is the potential of mean force acting on an ion pair of type $\alpha\beta$. Equation (1) is valid by definition of the radial distribution functions $g_{\alpha\beta}^{(2)}$, which are so defined that $N_\beta g_{\alpha\beta}^{(2)}/v$ is the average particle density of ions of type β at a distance R from an ion of type α. The excess electrical chemical potential may be determined in several equivalent ways.

$$\mu_\alpha^{(e)} = e_\alpha \int_0^1 \bar{\psi}_\alpha(\xi_1) d\xi_1$$

$$\mu_\alpha^{(e)} = \sum_{\beta=1}^{\nu} \frac{N_\beta}{v} \int_0^1 \int V_{\alpha\beta}^{(1)} [g_{\alpha\beta}^{(2)}(\xi_1, R) - 1] dv \, d\xi_1 \tag{2}$$

where $V_{\alpha\beta}^{(1)}$ is the electrostatic energy of an ion pair of type $\alpha\beta$, and the volume integral extends over all relative configurations of the pair, while the integrals over the charging parameter ξ_1, of one ion of the pair extend from zero to unity, all other ions in the system remaining fully charged (Guntelberg path). As alternative methods, the Debye charging process, in which all ions are charged simultaneously, may be employed, or the general expressions for the chemical potentials of the components of a solution of Kirkwood and Buff[7] may be used. If the exact potentials $\bar{\psi}_\alpha$ or radial distribution functions $g_{\alpha\beta}^{(2)}$ are employed, all methods of determining the chemical potential are consistent and lead to the same result. The Poisson–Boltzmann equation of the Debye–Hückel theory is obtained from Eq. (1) with the use of the approximation

$$W_{\alpha\beta^{(2)}} = e_\beta \bar{\psi}_\alpha(R) \tag{3}$$

An analysis of the limit of validity of this approximation will be the special subject of this investigation.

II.

We suppose that the potential, $V_{\rm N}$, of the intermolecular force acting on a system of N ions occupying a volume v may be expressed in the form

$$V_{\rm N} = \sum_{\substack{i<j\\=1}}^{N} V_{\rm ij}(R_{\rm ij})$$

$$V_{\rm ij} = V_{\rm ij}^{(0)} + V_{\rm ij}^{(1)} \tag{4}$$

where $V_{\rm ij}^{(0)}$ is the potential of the short range intermolecular force, van der Waals and repulsive, acting between the ion pair ij and $V_{\rm ij}^{(1)}$ is the potential of the long range Coulomb force. If the system of ions is immersed in a solvent,

[7] J. G. Kirkwood and F. P. Buff, *ibid.* **19**, 774 (1951).

for example water, the potential V_N is to be interpreted as the potential of mean force, arising both from other ions and the solvent molecules, averaged over all configurations of the solvent molecules in a canonical ensemble. The Coulomb potential $V_{ij}^{(1)}$ may be defined as

$$V_{ij}^{(1)} = \frac{e_i e_j}{D R_{ij}} \tag{5}$$

where e_i and e_j are the charges of the respective ions, R_{ij} the distance between them, and D the macroscopic dielectric constant of the solvent, if we agree conventionally to absorb effects of departures of the local dielectric constant from D in the short-range part $V_{ij}^{(0)}$ of the potential. That such departures contribute only short-range terms, diminishing more rapidly than R_{ij}^{-3} requires separate proof which will not be given here. We shall also neglect departures from superposition, implicit in Eq. (4), arising from the polarization of each ion by the total electric field of all others.

We now assign to each ion i a charging parameter, ξ_i, ranging from zero to unity and introduce the potential $V_N(\xi_1 \ldots \xi_N)$ for the system, in which each ion carries the charge $\xi_i e_i$, a fraction ξ_i if its full value

$$\begin{aligned} V_N(\xi_1 \ldots \xi_N) &= V_N^{(0)} + \sum_{i<j=1}^{N} \xi_i \xi_j V_{ij}^{(1)} \\ V_N^{(0)} &= \sum_{i<j=1}^{N} V_{ij}^{(0)} \\ V_{ij}^{(1)} &= e_i e_j / D R_{ij} \end{aligned} \tag{6}$$

where $V_N^{(0)}$ is the potential of the short-range intermolecular forces.

The potential of mean force $W_N^{(n)}(1 \ldots n)$ for a set of n ions, averaged over the configuration space of the other $N - n$ ions is given by the theory of the canonical ensemble in the following form

$$\begin{aligned} e^{-\beta W_N^{(n)}(1..n)} &= v^n \int^v \cdots \int^v e^{+\beta[A_N - V_N(\xi)]} \prod_{j=n+1}^{N} dv_j \\ \beta &= 1/kT \end{aligned} \tag{7}$$

where the integration extends over the configuration space of the residual set of $N - n$ ions, and it is understood that $W_N^{(n)}$, A_N and V_N depend upon the charging parameters ξ_j of Eq. (6). For brevity, the coordinates of the n ions are denoted by 1, 2, . . n. Properly the potentials of average force should be labeled with the ion types of the set n. However, to avoid excessive complication in notation, this labeling will be introduced explicitly only in our final equations. We now select any one of the ions, say ion 1, of the set n and write

$$\begin{aligned} A_N - V_N &= A_N(0) - V_N(0) + \mu_1^e - \xi_1 \sum_{=2}^{N} \xi_j V_{1j}^{(1)} - \xi_1 V_{1,\,N-n}^{(1)} \\ V_{1,\,N-n}^{(1)} &= \sum_{j=n+1}^{N} \xi_j V_{1j}^{(1)} \end{aligned} \tag{8}$$

where $A_N(0)$ and $V_N(0)$ are the Helmholtz free energy and potential of intermolecular force when ξ_1 is equal to zero, ion 1 uncharged, $\mu_1{}^e$ the electrostatic contribution to the chemical potential of ion 1, equal to $A_N - A_N(0)$, and $V_{1,\,N-n}{}^{(1)}$ is the electrostatic energy arising from the interaction of fully charged ion 1 and the $N - n$ ions of the residual set. Introduction of Eq. (8) into Eq. (7) leads to the expression

$$e^{-\beta W_N{}^{(n)}(1..n)} =$$

$$e^{\beta[\mu_1{}^e - W_N{}^{(n,0)}(1..n) - \xi_1 \sum_{j=2}^{n} \xi_j V_{1j}{}^{(1)}]} < e^{-\beta\xi_1 V_{1,N-n}{}^{(1)}} >_{\xi_1=0}$$

$$e^{-\beta\mu_1{}^e} = < e^{-\beta\xi_1 V_{1,N-1}{}^{(1)}} >_{\xi_1=0}$$

$$< e^{-\beta\xi_1 V_{1,N-n}{}^{(1)}} >_{\xi_1=0} =$$

$$\frac{\int^v \cdots \int^v e^{-\beta\xi_1 V_{1,N-n}{}^{(1)}} e^{+\beta[A_N(0) - V_N(0)]} \prod_{j=n+1}^{N} dv_j}{\int^v \cdots \int^v e^{\beta[A_N(0) - V_N(0)]} \prod_{j=n+1}^{N} dv_j} \tag{9}$$

where $W_N{}^{(n,0)}(1\ldots n)$ is the potential of average force acting on the set n, when ion 1 is discharged, $\xi_1 = 0$, and the averages are to be calculated in an ensemble in which ion 1 is discharged.

By the theory of semi-invariants,[8,9] we may write

$$< e^{-\beta\xi_1 V_{1,N-n}{}^{(1)}} >_{\xi_1=0} = e^{\sum_{s=1}^{\infty} \frac{(-\beta\xi_1)^s}{s!} \Lambda_s{}^{(n)}}$$

$$\sum_{r=1}^{s} \binom{s-1}{r-1} \Lambda_r{}^{(n)} M_{r-s}{}^{(n)} = M_s{}^{(n)};\ s = 1, \cdots \infty$$

$$M_s{}^{(n)} = \frac{\int^v \cdots \int^v [V_{1,N-n}{}^{(1)}]^s e^{\beta[A_N(0) - V_N(0)]} \prod_{j=n+1}^{N} dv_j}{\int^v \cdots \int^v e^{\beta[A_N(0) - V_N(0)]} \prod_{=n+1}^{N} dv_j} \tag{10}$$

$$\Lambda_1{}^{(n)} = M_1{}^{(n)}$$

$$\Lambda_2{}^{(n)} = M_2{}^{(n)} - M_1{}^{(n)2}$$

$$\Lambda_3{}^{(n)} = M_3{}^{(n)} - 3M_2{}^{(n)} M_1{}^{(n)} + 2M_1{}^{(n)3}$$

where the quantities $M_s{}^{(n)}$ are the moments of $V_{1,N-n}{}^{(1)}$, the electrostatic energy of interaction of ion 1 with the $N - n$ ions of the residual set. Eqs. (9)

---

[8] H. Cramer, "Mathematical Methods of Statistics," Princeton University Press, Princeton, N.J., 1946, p. 185.

[9] A similar expansion recently has been used by R. W. Zwanzig in the formulation of a general statistical mechanical perturbation theory, *J. Chem. Phys.* (in press). [Ed. note: *J. Chem. Phys.* **22**, 1420 (1954).]

and (10) lead to the following expressions for the potentials, $W_N{}^{(n)}$

$$W_N{}^{(n)}(1\ldots n) = W_N{}^{(n,0)}(1\ldots n) +$$

$$\xi_1 \sum_{j=2}^{n} \xi_j V_{1j}{}^{(1)} + \sum_{s=1}^{\infty} \frac{(-\beta)^{s-1}}{s!} \xi_1{}^s[\Lambda_s{}^{(n)} - \Lambda_s{}^{(1)}] \tag{11}$$

as power series in the charging parameter ξ_1 of ion 1. Therefore, we may write

$$W_N{}^{(n)}(1\ldots n) = W_N{}^{(n,0)}(1\ldots n) + \sum_{s=1}^{\infty} \xi_1{}^s W_N{}^{(n,s)}(1\ldots n)$$

$$W_N{}^{(n,s)}(1\ldots n) = \frac{(-\beta)^{s-1}}{s!} [\Lambda_s{}^{(n)} - \Lambda_s{}^{(1)}] + \delta_{s1} \sum_{j=2}^{n} \xi_j V_{1j}{}^{(1)} \tag{12}$$

$$\delta_{s1} = \begin{Bmatrix} 1, s = 1 \\ 0, s > 1 \end{Bmatrix}$$

as the desired power series. Although the quantities $\Lambda_s{}^{(n)}$ do not converge individually for Coulomb forces, they may be made to converge by replacing $1/R_{ij}$ by $e^{-\alpha R_{ij}}/R_{ij}$ where α is a positive real number. The differences $\Lambda_s{}^{(n)} - \Lambda_s{}^{(1)}$ do converge in the limit $\alpha = 0$, and are properly defined as such limits.

We now proceed to consider the first of the set of Eq. (12), determining $W_N{}^{(n,1)}(1\ldots n)$, the coefficient of the linear term in ξ_1, which assumes the form

$$W_N{}^{(n,1)}(1\ldots n) = \sum_{j=2}^{n} \xi_j[V_{1j}{}^{(1)} - \bar{V}_{1j}{}^{(1)}] +$$

$$\sum_{j=n+1}^{n} \frac{\xi_j}{v} \int^{v} V_{1j}{}^{(1)}[e^{-\beta[W_N{}^{(n+1,0)}(1..nj) - W_N{}^{(n,0)}(1..n)]} - e^{-\beta W_N{}^{(2,0)}(1j)}]dv_j$$

$$\bar{V}_{1j}{}^{(1)} = \frac{1}{v}\int^{v} V_{1j}{}^{(1)} e^{\ \beta W_N{}^{(2,0)}(1j)} dv_j. \tag{13}$$

The effect of the short-range interactions of uncharged ion 1 with the other ions of the system may be taken into account by a Mayer cluster expansion, which with the neglect of terms of order $1/v$, yields

$$W_N{}^{(n+1,0)}(1\ldots nj) = W_{N-1}{}^{(n)}(2\ldots nj) + \sum_{l=j,2}^{n} V_{1l}{}^{(0)} \tag{14}$$

where $W_{N-1}{}^{(n)}(2\ldots nj)$ is the potential of average force acting on the set of n ions, $2\ldots nj$, in a system of $N - 1$ ions, from which ion 1 is absent. With the neglect of short-range cluster contributions, we may therefore write Eq. (13) in the form

$$W_N{}^{(n,1)}(1\ldots n) = \sum_{j=2}^{n} \xi_j[V_{1j}{}^{(1)} - \bar{V}_{1j}{}^{(1)}]$$

$$+ \sum_{j=n+1}^{n} \frac{\xi_j}{v} \int^{v} V_{1j}{}^{(1)} e^{-\beta V_{1j}{}^{(0)}} [e^{-\beta[W_{N-1}{}^{(n)}(2..nj) - W_{N-1}{}^{(n-1)}(2..n)]} - 1]dv_j \tag{15}$$

If we now expand $W_{N-1}^{(n)}(2\ldots nj)$ in the power series

$$W_{N-1}^{(n)}(2\ldots nj) = W_{N-1}^{(n,0)}(2\ldots nj) + \xi_j W_{N-1}^{(n,1)}(2\ldots nj) + 0\,(\xi_j^2)$$

$$W_{N-1}^{(n,0)}(2\ldots nj) = W_{N-2}^{(n-1)}(2\ldots n) + \sum_{l=2}^{n} V_{jl}^{(0)} \tag{16}$$

in the charging parameter ξ_j of ion j and ignore terms $W_N^{(n)} - W_{N-1}^{(n)}$ and $W_{N-1}^{(n-1)} - W_{N-2}^{(n-1)}$, which bear a ratio of order $1/N$ to terms retained, we obtain the following integral equations

$$W_N^{(n,1)}(1\ldots n) = \sum_{j=2}^{n} \xi_j(V_{1j}^{(1)} - \bar{V}_{1j}^{(1)}) +$$

$$\sum_{j=n+1}^{N} \frac{\xi_j}{v} \int^{v} V_{1j}^{(1)} e^{-\beta V_{1j}^{(0)}} \left[e^{-\beta\xi_j W_N^{(n,1)}(2..nj) - \beta \sum_{l=2}^{n} V_{jl}^{(0)}} - 1 \right] dv_j \tag{17}$$

which are valid with the neglect of terms of the order $\xi_j^2 W_N^{(n,2)}$ in the exponential of the integrand on the right-hand side of Eq. (12). If the short-range intermolecular forces are idealized as those acting between rigid spheres of equal diameter a, and the charging parameters ξ_j are subject to the restraint of electro-neutrality, $\sum_{j=1}^{N} \xi_j e_j = 0$, Eq. (17) simplifies to the form

$$W_N^{(n,1)}(1\ldots n) = \sum_{j=2}^{n} \xi_j V_{1j}^{(1)} + \sum_{j=n+1}^{N} \frac{\xi_j}{v} \int_{\omega_n}^{v} V_{1j}^{(1)}[e^{-\beta\xi_j W_N^{(n,1)}(2..nj)} - 1] dv_j \tag{18}$$

where the region ω_n, bounded by n spheres of radius a, concentric with each of the ions of the set n, is excluded from the domain of integration over the coordinates of each ion j of the residual set, $N - n$. Although there is no difficulty in principle in treating more complicated short-range forces, we shall henceforth restrict ourselves to the case of rigid spheres for the sake of simplicity. If the size of ion 1 is neglected in Eq. (18), and only ω_{n-1}, the region of repulsion of ions $2, \ldots n$, is excluded from the domain of integration of ion j, Eq. (18) may be transformed into the Poisson–Boltzmann equation by taking the Laplacian of both sides

$$\nabla_1^2 W_N^{(n,1)} = -4\pi \sum_{j=n+1}^{N} \frac{\xi_j e_j}{Dv} e^{-\beta\xi_j W_N^{(n,1)}(12..n)}. \tag{19}$$

However, neither Eq. (18) nor Eq. (19) with the neglect of the size of ion 1, is a valid equation for $W_N^{(n,1)}$, since terms of order $\xi_j^2 W^{(n,2)}$ have been discarded in the exponential appearing in the integrand on the right-hand side of Eq. (15). We are therefore only justified in keeping linear terms in ξ_j the expansion of the exponential

$$e^{-\beta[W_{N-1}^{(n)}(2..nj) - W_{N-1}^{(n-1)}(2..n)]}$$

$$= e^{-\beta \sum_{l=2}^{n} V_{jl}^{(0)}} [1 - \beta\xi_j W_{N-1}^{(n,1)}(2\ldots nj) + 0(\xi_j^2)] \tag{20}$$

With the linearization of the exponential of Eq. (18) according to Eq. (20), we obtain the following linear integral equations for the $W_N^{(n,1)}$, valid to terms of the order of ξ_j^3 in the charging parameters of the ions of the residual set, $N - n$

$$W_N^{(n,1)}(1\ldots n) = \sum_{j=2}^{n} \xi_j V_{1j}^{(1)} - \beta \sum_{j=n+1}^{n} \frac{\xi_j^2}{v} \int_{\omega_n}^{v} V_{1j}^{(1)} W_N^{(n,1)}(2\ldots nj)\,dv_j \quad (21)$$

The linear equations (21) constitute a self-consistent set of integral equations, closed for each ion set n, while the non-linear equations, Eq. (18), are inconsistent with the exact statistical mechanical theory in retaining some terms of order ξ_j^3 and higher, but not all, since terms of the order $\xi_j^3 W_N^{(n,2)}$ are neglected. This does not mean that the non-linear equations (18) and (19) may not provide a useful approximation, but accounts for the fact that their solutions fail to satisfy the rigorous criterion of integrability.

In order to proceed to the next higher approximation, terms in $W_N^{(n,2)}$ and $W_N^{(n,1)^2}$ must be retained in the expansion of the exponential, Eq. (20), and the second of Eq. (12) must be employed to determine $W_N^{(n,2)}$

$$W_N^{(n,2)}(1\ldots n) =$$

$$-\frac{\beta}{2} \sum_{j=n+1}^{N} \frac{\xi_j^2}{v} \int_{\omega_n}^{v} V_{1j}^{(1)^2} [e^{-\beta[W_N^{(n)}(2..nj) - W_N^{(n-1)}(2..n)]} - 1]\,dv_j$$

$$-\frac{\beta}{2} \sum_{\substack{j\neq j'\\=n+1}}^{N} \frac{\xi_j \xi_j'}{v^2} \int_{\omega_n}^{v} \int_{\omega_n}^{v} V_{1j}^{(1)} V_{1j'}^{(1)} [e^{-\beta[W_N^{(n+1)}(2..njj') - W_N^{(n-1)}(2..n)]}$$

$$- e^{-\beta W_N^{(2)}(jj')}]\,dv_j dv_{j'} + \frac{\beta}{2} [W_N^{(n,1)}(1\ldots n) - \sum_{j=2}^{n} \xi_j V_{1j}^{(1)}]^2 \quad (22)$$

where terms of negligible order have been neglected and the short-range forces are assumed to be those between rigid spheres as in Eqs. (18) and (21). A rather tedious analysis leads to the following approximation to $W_N^{(n,2)}$, valid to terms in ξ_j^4

$$W_N^{(n,2)}(1\ldots n) = \frac{\beta^2}{2} \sum_{j=n+1}^{N} \frac{\xi_j^3}{v} \int_{\omega_n}^{v} V_{1j}^{(1)^2} W_N^{(n,1)}(2\ldots nj)\,dv_j \quad (23)$$

If terms to the order ξ_j^4 are retained in the expansion of the exponential in the integrand of Eq. (17), and short-range forces are idealized as those between rigid spheres, Eq. (14) becomes

$$W_N^{(n,1)}(1\ldots n) = \sum_{j=2}^{n} \xi_j V_{1j}^{(1)} \quad (24)$$

$$- \beta \sum_{j=n+1}^{N} \frac{1}{v} \int_{\omega_n}^{v} \Big\{ \xi_j^2 V_{1j}^{(1)} W_N^{(n,1)}(2\ldots nj)$$

$$- \xi_j^3 V_{1j}^{(1)} \Big[\frac{\beta}{2} W_N^{(n,1)^2} - W_N^{(n,2)} \Big] \Big\}\,dv_j.$$

Simultaneous solution of Eqs. (23) and (24) would yield a consistent approximation to $W_N^{(n)}(1\ldots n)$ to terms of order ξ_j^3, and would provide correct expression for the terms proportional to $c \log c$ in the excess chemical potential of an unsymmetrical electrolyte present in solution at concentration c. The solution of Eqs. (23) and (24) will be reported in a later article. Extension of the method outlined to the determination of higher approximations to the potentials of mean force could be made in a systematic way, but would be lengthy and tedious.

We now return to the linear integral equations, Eq. (21). The integrals on the right-hand converge in the limit of zero ion size a, and the equations become

$$W_N^{(n,1)}(1\ldots n) = \sum_{j=2}^{n} \xi_j V_{1j}^{(1)} - \beta \sum_{j=n+1}^{N} \frac{\xi_j^2}{v} \int^v V_{1j}^{(1)} W_N^{(n,1)}(2\ldots nj) dv_j \quad (25)$$

Equations (25) may be exactly solved by superposition in the following form

$$W_N^{(n,1)}(1\ldots n) = \sum_{j=2}^{n} w_N^{(n,1)}(1j)$$

$$w_N^{(n,1)}(1j) = \xi_j V_{1j}^{(1)} - \beta \sum_{l=n+1}^{N} \frac{\xi_l^2}{v} \int^v V_{1l}^{(1)} w_N^{(n,1)}(jl)\, dv_l \quad (26)$$

$$w_N^{(n,1)}(1j) = W_{N-n+2}^{(2,1)}(1j)$$

$$W_N^{(2,1)}(12) = \xi_2 \frac{e_1 e_2}{DR_{12}} - \sum_{l=3}^{N} \frac{\xi_1^2 e_1 e_l}{vDkT} \int^v \frac{1}{R_{1l}} W_N^{(2,1)}(2l) dv_l$$

Thus we observe that the entire set of linear integral Equations (25) are rigorously solved by the superposition principle, which was implicit in the original Poisson–Boltzmann equation of the Debye–Hückel theory, if ion size is neglected.

It is of interest to investigate the solutions of Eq. (21) for ion pairs, $n = 2$, without the neglect of ion size. For this purpose we introduce the more explicit notation $W_{\alpha\beta}^{(2,1)}(R_{12})$ for two ions of types α and β, where it is to be understood that there are $N_1, N_2 \ldots N_\nu$ ions of the several types $1\ldots\nu$ present in the volume v, with $N = \sum_{\alpha=1}^{\nu} N_\alpha$, and R_{12} is the distance between the pair of ions. Equations (5) and (21) then lead to the following system of integral equations for the functions $W_{\alpha\beta}^{(2,1)}$ when all ξ_j are set equal to unity, corresponding to full charge for all the ions except ion 1;

$$W_{\alpha\beta}^{(2,1)}(R_{12}) = \frac{e_\alpha e_\beta}{DR_{12}} - \sum_{\gamma=1}^{\nu} \frac{N_\gamma e_\gamma e_\alpha}{DvkT} \int_{\omega_{13},\,\omega_{23}}^{v} \frac{W_{\beta\gamma}^{(2,1)}(R_{23})}{R_{13}} dv_3 \quad (27)$$

$$\alpha, \beta = 1, \ldots \nu$$

where ω_{13} and ω_{23}, spherical regions of radius a, concentric with ions 1 and 2 are to be excluded from the domain of integration in the space of ion 3. The system of Eq. (27) may be solved in the form

$$W_{\alpha\beta}{}^{(2,1)}(R_{12}) = \frac{e_\alpha e_\beta}{DR_{12}}\,\varphi(R_{12})$$

$$\varphi(R) = 1 - \kappa^2 \int_a^\infty K(R,r)\varphi(r)\mathrm{d}r$$

$$K(R,r) = R;\ a \leq R \leq r - a$$

$$= \frac{1}{2}(R + r - a);\ r - a < R \leq r + a \qquad (28)$$

$$= r;\ r + a < R < \infty$$

$$\kappa^2 = \frac{4\pi}{DkT}\sum_{\gamma-1}^{\nu}\frac{N_\gamma e_\gamma{}^2}{\nu}$$

after the introduction of dipolar coordinates, R_{13} and R_{23} in the integration over the configuration space of ion 3, where κ is the familiar Debye–Hückel parameter, proportional to the square root of the ionic strength. The integral equation for $\varphi(R)$ may be solved by the method of Laplace transforms

$$G(z) = \int_a^\infty e^{-zR}\varphi(R)\mathrm{d}R$$

$$G(z) = \frac{B(z)}{z^2 - \kappa^2 \cosh za}$$

$$B(z) - z - \kappa^2 G(0) \quad z^2\sigma(z)$$

$$\sigma(z) = \int_0^a e^{-zR}\,\varphi(R)\mathrm{d}R$$

$$\int_0^a k(R - r)\varphi(r)\mathrm{d}r = f(R);\quad 0 \leq R \leq a$$

$$f(R) = \frac{1}{2\pi i}\int_{c-i\infty}^{c+i\infty}\frac{z - \kappa^2 G(0)}{z^2 - \kappa^2\cosh za}\,e^{zR}\mathrm{d}z \qquad (29)$$

$$k(t) = \frac{1}{2\pi i}\int_{c-i\infty}^{c+i\infty}\frac{e^{zt}}{z^2 - \kappa^2\cosh za}\,\mathrm{d}t$$

where the path of integration is to be taken along a line parallel to the imaginary axes with the constant c lying between zero and the least positive real part of the zeros of the function $z^2 - \kappa^2 \cosh za$. The function $\varphi(R)$ is then given by the expression

$$\varphi(R) = \frac{1}{2\pi i}\int_{c-i\infty}^{c+i\infty} \frac{B(z)e^{zR}}{z^2 - \kappa^2 \cosh za}\,\mathrm{d}z$$

$$\varphi(R) = \sum_{n=1}^{\infty} A_{\mathrm{n}}e^{-z_{\mathrm{n}}R}; \quad R > a \tag{30}$$

$$A_{\mathrm{n}} = \frac{-B(-z_{\mathrm{n}})}{2z_{\mathrm{n}} - \kappa^2 a \sinh z_{\mathrm{n}}a}$$

$$z_{\mathrm{n}}^2 - \kappa^2 \cosh z_{\mathrm{n}}a = 0$$

where the sum extends over all zeros of $z^2 - \kappa^2 \cosh za$ with positive real part. The explicit determination of the coefficients A_{n} may be carried out after numerical solution of the fifth of Eq. (29), an integral equation for $\varphi(R)$ on the finite interval $0 \leq R \leq a$. Since we desire only to discuss the general properties of the function $\varphi(R)$, this calculation will not be presented here.

If we examine the roots z_{n} of the equation

$$z^2 - \kappa^2 \cosh za = 0$$

$$z_{\mathrm{n}} = \alpha_{\mathrm{n}} \pm i\beta_{\mathrm{n}} \tag{31}$$

we find that if a is set equal to zero, there is only one root $z_1 = \kappa$ with positive real part, and the solution, Eq. (27) for $\varphi(R)$ reduces to the Debye–Hückel first approximation $e^{-\kappa R}$. For finite a and small κa there are two positive real roots, the smaller one approximating κ at low ionic strengths, which makes the dominant contribution to $\varphi(R)$, so that $\varphi(R)$ resembles the Debye–Hückel form. As the ionic strength increases, the two real roots approach equality, become equal at $\kappa a = 1.03$ and then move into the complex plane as complex conjugates. For values of κa greater than 1.03, $\varphi(R)$ exhibits the oscillations characteristic of the potentials of mean force in the liquid state, and around each ion there develops a statistical stratification of the average space charge due to the other ions with alternating zones of excess positive and excess negative charge. It is attractive to consider the application of these ideas to an elucidation of the structure of concentrated electrolyte solutions and fused salts, although it would no doubt be necessary to go beyond the linear approximations, Eq. (24) to the potentials of mean interionic forces in order to obtain more than a qualitative description.

Theory of the Heat of Transport of Electrolytic Solutions*

EUGENE HELFAND,† *Bell Telephone Laboratories, Incorporated, Murray Hill, New Jersey*
AND
JOHN G. KIRKWOOD,‡ *Sterling Chemistry Laboratory, Yale University, New Haven, Connecticut*

(Received September 2, 1959)

The limiting concentration dependence of the heat of transport of an ionic component of a dilute solution of electrolyte is determined. The theory is based on recasting the Bearman-Kirkwood statistical mechanical expression for the heat current into a form linear in the particle diffusion currents and identifying the coefficients with the heat of transport. Ion-ion interactions are treated exactly to order $c^{\frac{1}{2}}$ by using a non-equilibrium correlation function determined from the Debye-Hückel radial distribution function by Brownian particle theory. A hydrodynamical model is employed for the analysis of the effect of ion-solvent interactions. Indications are that the latter contributions are often, but not always, negligible. There is accord between the theory and experimental data.

I. INTRODUCTION

Seebeck's measurements of the thermoelectric potential in a metallic circuit were the first recorded systematic observations on an irreversible heat-matter cross effect. Since that time (1824), other manifestations of these effects, such as thermal diffusion, the Soret stationary state, and the Dufour effect, have been the object of extensive research. Agar has reviewed the field, emphasizing the behavior of electrolytic solutions.[1]

In describing the afore-mentioned processes one may use, equivalently, the heat of transport, the transported entropy, the thermal diffusion ratio, the Soret coefficient, or any of a number of quantities which are all related. The heat of transport was first introduced by Eastman in his quasi-thermodynamic studies of thermal diffusion. The utility of this quantity in a systematic formulation of irreversible thermodynamics from the point of view of the linear laws and reciprocal relations is brought out in the monograph of DeGroot.[2]

Recent years have witnessed several important developments in the field of heat-matter cross effects. On the experimental side Agar and co-workers have developed three independent means of measuring the heat of transport of electrolytes in the range of applicability of limiting laws. Further details of these techniques are discussed in Sec. 9.

* Based in part on a dissertation submitted by Eugene Helfand in partial fulfillment of the requirements for the degree of Doctor of Philosophy at Yale University.
† National Science Foundation Predoctoral Fellow, 1955–1958.
‡ Posthumously.

[1] J. N. Agar, *Revs. Pure Appl. Chem.* **8**, 1 (1958).
[2] S. R. DeGroot, *Thermodynamics of Irreversible Processes* (North-Holland Publishing Company, Amsterdam, 1952).

Of more direct relevance to the present work is Bearman, Kirkwood, and Fixman's calculation of the heat of transport of a nonelectrolyte in solution.[3a] Their formulation is based on more comprehensive principles of statistical mechanics than earlier lattice theories [the lattice theories[4,5] amount to a neglect of the difference between singlet and pair space velocities (cf. Sec. 2) and an approximation to the remaining terms], and serves as a basis for the extension to electrolytic solutions.

Although Bearman, Kirkwood, and Fixman adopt a semiphenomenological approach in their paper, the same results may be obtained by application of Brownian motion theory, and it is the latter scheme which we shall employ. There are two new difficulties which arise. The first is that the Fokker-Planck-Chandresekhar equations, from which a statistical theory of the phenomenological coefficients can be derived,[6] is an equation applicable when there are mostly small momentum changes in a force relaxation time,[7] and is therefore not obviously suited for systems containing ionic components. This problem has recently been examined and it is found that the obstacle can be surmounted by treating the short range and the long range forces separately.[8] The former give rise to the usual dissipative terms with friction constants which are autocorrelation functions of the short range part of the forces only. Poisson's equation provides a means of handling the long range Coulomb forces. In this way one obtains equations equivalent to those employed by Debye, Hückel, Onsager, and Falkenhagen in their formulations of the limiting laws for conduction, diffusion, and viscosity.

A second predicament is that the ion-solvent interaction effects cannot be treated solely by means of the method outlined in the previous paragraph. Thus, in the theory of conduction and diffusion one must introduce an electrophoretic drag. So, too, in the theory of the heat of transport it will be found that the ion-solvent effects require special attention. This problem has not been completely solved, but the analysis in Sec. 6 indicates that contributions are small for many salts of interest.

After a brief review of the pertinent principles of the statistical mechanics of irreversible processes and of the phenomenological theory of heat-matter cross terms, we shall present the details of the calculation of the heat of transport of strong electrolytes. As with many other properties of ionic species, a $c^{\frac{1}{2}}$ (c is concentration) limiting behavior in dilute solutions is found. It is this limiting slope which will be specifically calculated.

II. STATISTICAL EXPRESSIONS FOR IRREVERSIBLE FLOWS

Ensemble theory may be profitably applied to systems either in or out of thermodynamic equilibrium. Explicit calculations divide into two parts. The first is the formulation of expressions for the desired properties as tractable functionals of low order distribution functions and the molecular properties. The second is the determination of the required distribution functions. The

[3] (a) Bearman, Kirkwood, and Fixman, *Advances in Chemical Physics* (Interscience Publishers, Inc., New York, 1958), Vol. I, p. 1.

[3] (b) R. J. Bearman and J. G. Kirkwood, *J. Chem. Phys.* **28**, 136 (1958).

[4] K. Wirtz, *Ann. Physik.* **36**, 295 (1939).

[5] K. G. Denbigh, *Trans. Faraday Soc.* **48**, 1 (1952).

[6] J. G. Kirkwood, *J. Chem. Phys.* **14**, 180 (1946).

[7] Reference 6; and John Ross, *J. Chem. Phys.* **24**, 375 (1956).

[8] E. Helfand, dissertation, Yale University (1958).

former task has been performed with about equal success for equilibrium and steady-state systems and this section presents aspects of this previous work which are relevant to the heat of transport calculation. Details may be found in another reference.[3b]

The system under consideration is composed of ν ionic species, in numbers $N_1, \cdots, N_\nu$, and N_0 solvent molecules. Each ion is envisioned as a hard sphere charge so that its microscopic state is specified by three dimensional position and momentum vectors. The solvent molecules will be viewed as point dipoles so that two additional degrees of freedom are relevant. These are specified by a directional vector, for example $\mathbf{e}_\mu$, a unit vector in the direction of the dipole $\boldsymbol{\mu}$, and the conjugate angular momenta (which will not enter into the calculation).

In the treatment of electrolytes in solution, certain phenomena can be taken into account by considering the solvent as a dielectric continuum. The hypothesis is that the effect of preferential orientation of solvent in the neighborhood of an ion can be emulated by introducing a dielectric constant into the mutual interaction potentials, $V_{\alpha\beta}$. This is done after the statistical formulas have been integrated down to pair space.

Statistical mechanically, the properties of the system are described by generic distribution functions, $f_{\alpha\beta}{}^{(2)}$, in the space of pairs. For α and β ionic $f_{\alpha\beta}{}^{(2)}(\mathbf{r}_1, \mathbf{r}_2, \mathbf{p}_1, \mathbf{p}_2)d^3\mathbf{r}_1 d^3\mathbf{r}_2 d^3\mathbf{p}_1 d^3\mathbf{p}_2$ is the probability of simultaneously finding a particle of type α within $d^3\mathbf{r}_1$, $d^3\mathbf{p}_1$ of the state $\mathbf{r}_1$, $\mathbf{p}_1$ and one of type β within $d^3\mathbf{r}_2$, $d^3\mathbf{p}_2$ of $\mathbf{r}_2$, $\mathbf{p}_2$. No time dependence is indicated since consideration will be limited to stationary states. The distribution functions $f_{\alpha 0}{}^{(2)}(\mathbf{r}_1, \mathbf{r}_2, \mathbf{e}_{\mu 2}, \mathbf{p}_1, \mathbf{p}_2)$ and $f_{00}{}^{(2)}(\mathbf{r}_1, \mathbf{e}_{\mu 1}, \mathbf{r}_2, \mathbf{e}_{\mu 2}, \mathbf{p}_1, \mathbf{p}_2)$ contain dependency on the orientation of the solvent.

An integration of $f_{\alpha\beta}{}^{(2)}$ over $\mathbf{r}_2$, $\mathbf{p}_2$, that is over the possible states of β, yields the singlet space generic distribution function $f_\alpha{}^{(1)}$.

If $f_{\alpha\beta}{}^{(2)}$ is integrated over momenta $\mathbf{p}_1$ and $\mathbf{p}_2$, the pair space concentration, $c_{\alpha\beta}{}^{(2)}$, results. A further integration over position of β yields the ordinary particle concentration, c_α. For $\alpha = 0$ (solvent) an integration over orientations, $\mathbf{e}_{\mu 1}$, is required to obtain $c_0(\mathbf{r}_1)$, but in the absence of external fields $c_0(\mathbf{r}_1) = 4\pi c_0(\mathbf{r}_1, \mathbf{e}_{\mu 1})$.

For the description of pair space concentration, it is convenient to introduce a correlation function, $g_{\alpha\beta}{}^{(2)}$, by means of the equation $c_{\alpha\beta}{}^{(2)} = c_\alpha c_\beta g_{\alpha\beta}{}^{(2)}$.

The particle diffusion currents, $\mathbf{j}_\alpha$, which have magnitude equal to the average number of particles of type α crossing unit normal area per unit time, are related to the average velocities, and are given by

$$\mathbf{j}_\alpha = c_\alpha(\mathbf{u}_\alpha - \mathbf{u}) = \int (1/m_\alpha)(\mathbf{p}_1 - m_\alpha \mathbf{u}) f_\alpha{}^{(1)} d^3\mathbf{p}_1. \tag{2.1}$$

The mass average velocity, $\mathbf{u}$, is

$$\mathbf{u} = \sum_{\alpha=0}^{\nu} m_\alpha c_\alpha \mathbf{u}_\alpha \Big/ \sum_{\alpha=0}^{\nu} m_\alpha c_\alpha. \tag{2.2}$$

Similarly, a pair space particle diffusion current may be defined by

$$\mathbf{j}_{\alpha\beta,1}{}^{(2)} = c_{\alpha\beta}{}^{(2)}(\mathbf{u}_{\alpha\beta,1}{}^{(2)} - \mathbf{u}) = \iint (1/m_\alpha)(\mathbf{p}_1 - m_\alpha \mathbf{u}) f_{\alpha\beta}{}^{(2)} d^3\mathbf{p}_1 d^3\mathbf{p}_2. \tag{2.3}$$

Physically, the pair space velocity $\mathbf{u}_{\alpha\beta,1}{}^{(2)}$ is the average velocity of particles of type α at $\mathbf{r}_1$ (with orientation $\mathbf{e}_{\mu 1}$ if solvent) when a particle of type β is at

$\mathbf{r}_2$ (with $\mathbf{e}_{\mu 2}$). The subscript 1 of $\mathbf{j}_{\alpha\beta,1}{}^{(2)}$ and $\mathbf{u}_{\alpha\beta,1}{}^{(2)}$ indicates that the vector is in the space of the particle at $\mathbf{r}_1$.

The heat current density, $\mathbf{q}$, by definition is the total energy flow (relative to the mass average velocity) less the diffusive flow of energy and work. This latter part which is subtracted off for convenience of the thermodynamic theory is

$$\sum \mathbf{j}_\alpha(\bar{E}_\alpha + p\bar{v}_\alpha) = \sum \mathbf{j}_\alpha \bar{H}_\alpha,$$

where $\bar{E}_\alpha$, $\bar{v}_\alpha$, and $\bar{H}_\alpha$ are, respectively, the partial molecular energy, volume, and enthalpy, and p is the pressure.

Irving and Kirkwood[9] derived a statistical expression for the heat current density of a pure fluid by comparing the equation of energy transport obtained from macroscopic considerations with that gotten from the Liouville equation. Bearman and Kirkwood[3b] have generalized this result to mixtures. The form of the heat current density appropriate to the present problem is

$$\mathbf{q} = \mathbf{q}_K + \mathbf{q}_V - \sum_{\alpha=0}^{\nu} \mathbf{j}_\alpha \bar{H}_\alpha, \tag{2.4}$$

$$\mathbf{q}_K = \sum_{\alpha=0}^{\nu} \int (1/2m_\alpha{}^2)(\mathbf{p}_1 - m_\alpha \mathbf{u})^2(\mathbf{p}_1 - m_\alpha \mathbf{u}) \times f_\alpha{}^{(1)}(\mathbf{r}_1, \mathbf{p}_1)d^3\mathbf{p}_1, \tag{2.5}$$

$$\mathbf{q}_V = (\mathbf{q}_V)_{\text{ion-ion}} + (\mathbf{q}_V)_{\text{ion-solv}} + (\mathbf{q}_V)_{\text{solv-solv}}, \tag{2.6}$$

$$(\mathbf{q}_V)_{\text{ion-ion}} = \tfrac{1}{2} \sum_{\alpha=1}^{\nu} \sum_{\beta=1}^{\nu} \int [V_{\alpha\beta}(r)\mathbf{1} - \mathbf{r}\nabla_r V_{\alpha\beta}(r)] \cdot \mathbf{j}_{\alpha\beta,1}{}^{(2)}(\mathbf{r}_1, \mathbf{r}_2)d^3\mathbf{r}, \tag{2.7}$$

$$(\mathbf{q}_V)_{\text{ion-solv}} = \tfrac{1}{2} \sum_{\alpha=1}^{\nu} \int\int [V_{\alpha 0}(\mathbf{r}, \mathbf{e}_\mu)\mathbf{1} - \mathbf{r}\nabla_r V_{\alpha 0}(\mathbf{r}, \mathbf{e}_\mu)] \cdot [\mathbf{j}_{\alpha 0,1}{}^{(2)}(\mathbf{r}_1, \mathbf{r}_2, \mathbf{e}_\mu) + \mathbf{j}_{0\alpha,1}{}^{(2)}(\mathbf{r}_1, \mathbf{r}_2, \mathbf{e}_\mu)]d^3\mathbf{r}d^2\mathbf{e}_\mu, \tag{2.8}$$

$$(\mathbf{q}_V)_{\text{solv-solv}} = \tfrac{1}{2} \int\int\int [V_{00}(\mathbf{r}, \mathbf{e}_{\mu 1}, \mathbf{e}_{\mu 2})\mathbf{1} - \mathbf{r}\nabla_r V_{\alpha 0}(\mathbf{r}, \mathbf{e}_{\mu 1}, \mathbf{e}_{\mu 2})] \cdot \mathbf{j}_{00,1}{}^{(2)}(\mathbf{r}_1, \mathbf{r}_2, \mathbf{e}_{\mu 1}, \mathbf{e}_{\mu 2})d^3\mathbf{r}d^2\mathbf{e}_{\mu 1}d^2\mathbf{e}_{\mu 2}, \tag{2.9}$$

where these equations are to be applied with the dielectric continuum approximation.

The vector $\mathbf{q}_K$ is the mean kinetic energy current density. The flow $\mathbf{q}_V$ arises directly from the mutual interactions. Each of its integrals has two parts. The term containing the potentials $V_{\alpha\beta}$ represents the mean flow of potential energy crossing unit surface with the particles. The portion with the forces, $\nabla_r V_{\alpha\beta}$, arises from work done by particles on one side of a unit surface on those located on the other side. This results in a flow of work, or, equivalently, energy, across this surface.

III. PHENOMENOLOGY OF HEAT OF TRANSPORT

The heat of transport§ of component α, $Q_\alpha{}^*$, may be operationally defined in two seemingly different ways. This duality is a consequence of the Onsager reciprocal relations.

---

[9] J. H. Irving and J. G. Kirkwood, *J. Chem. Phys.* **18**, 817 (1950).

§ Our $Q_\alpha{}^*$ is not DeGroot's $Q_\alpha{}^*$ (reference 2). It is similar to his $Q_\alpha{}^{**}$ except that ours is on a per mole, rather than a per gram, basis, and is not defined relative to a reference component.

The first definition refers to a system in mechanical equilibrium ($\nabla p + \sum c_\alpha \mathbf{X}_\alpha = 0$, where $\mathbf{X}_\alpha$ is the external force on a particle of type α) and in a Soret stationary state (all particle diffusion currents equal to zero). Under such conditions the gradients of total chemical potential are related to the temperature gradient by the proportionality

$$\nabla_T \tilde{\mu}_\alpha = -Q_\alpha^* \nabla \ln T. \tag{3.1}$$

The total chemical potential, $\tilde{\mu}_\alpha$, is equal to a chemical part plus the potential of any external force. The symbol ∇_T indicates that the gradient does not include that part due to the functional dependence of $\tilde{\mu}_\alpha$ on T, so that

$$\begin{aligned} \nabla_T \tilde{\mu}_\alpha &= \nabla \tilde{\mu}_\alpha - (\partial \mu_\alpha / \partial T)_{p,T} \nabla T, \\ &= \nabla \tilde{\mu}_\alpha + T \bar{S}_\alpha \nabla \ln T. \end{aligned} \tag{3.2}$$

The Gibbs-Duhem equation for a system in mechanical equilibrium is

$$\sum c_\alpha \nabla_T \tilde{\mu}_\alpha = 0, \tag{3.3}$$

which may be combined with Eq. (3.1) to yield the relation

$$\sum c_\alpha Q_\alpha^* = 0. \tag{3.4}$$

The above definition, or its extension to systems with diffusion, serves as the basis for most experimental determinations of the heat of transport. It may also be employed in a theoretical development. Work is being done at present on this aspect of the problem, but the tack adopted in this paper revolves about an alternative picture of the heat of transport.

In a system in which no temperature gradients exist the heat flow is given by

$$\mathbf{q} = \sum Q_\alpha^* \mathbf{j}_\alpha. \tag{3.5}$$

Since the particle diffusion currents are not linearly independent [cf. Eqs. (2.1) and (2.2)], the further condition

$$\sum c_\alpha Q_\alpha^* = 0 \tag{3.6}$$

is required to complete the unique specification of the heats of transport.

Comparison of Eqs. (3.5) and (2.4)–(2.9) indicates that if the latter equations can be cast into a form linear in the singlet space particle diffusion currents, then the coefficients will be statistical expressions for the heats of transport providing they are chosen to satisfy the restraint of Eq. (3.6).

IV. KINETIC ENERGY CURRENT

A very simple estimate of the kinetic energy current may be obtained by assuming that the singlet space distribution function is locally Maxwellian; i.e.,

$$f_\alpha^{(1)}(\mathbf{r}_1, \mathbf{p}_1) = [c_\alpha(\mathbf{r}_1)/(2\pi m_\alpha kT)^{\frac{3}{2}}] \exp[-(\mathbf{p}_1 - m_\alpha \mathbf{u}_\alpha)^2 / 2m_\alpha kT]. \tag{4.1}$$

In this case, one finds that to terms linear in diffusion currents

$$\mathbf{q}_K = \tfrac{5}{2} kT \sum_\alpha \mathbf{j}_\alpha, \tag{4.2}$$

A somewhat more sophisticated derivation of this result[8] may be based on the Fokker-Planck-Chandresekhar equation adapted for ionic species. The right-hand side of Eq. (4.2) is the initial term in a series expansion in the reciprocal of the friction constants.

In condensed systems, kinetic terms of totally dissipative processes are very small. The contribution of Eq. (4.2) to the heat flow is exactly balanced by the ideal gas part of the enthalpy, which, according to Eq. (2.4), must be subtracted off.

V. FLOW $(\mathbf{q}_V)_{\text{ion-ion}}$

The problem of obtaining an expression for $\mathbf{q}_V$ which is linear in the singlet space particle diffusion currents is seen to be equivalent to the problem of writing $\mathbf{j}_{\alpha\beta,1}{}^{(2)}$ as a linear form in the $\mathbf{j}_\alpha$'s. The latter desideratum was already encountered in the development of the theories of diffusion, conduction, and viscosity.

According to the Brownian motion theory, for α and β both ionic components of an isothermal system, one has (cf. Appendix 1)

$$\mathbf{j}_{\alpha\beta,1}{}^{(2)} = c_{\alpha\beta}{}^{(2,0)}[(\mathbf{u}_\alpha - \mathbf{u}) + D_\alpha{}^0\nabla_r(g_{\alpha\beta}{}^{(2,1)}(\mathbf{r})/g_{\alpha\beta}{}^{(2,0)}(r)) + (z_\alpha e D_\alpha{}^0/kT)\nabla_r\phi_\beta{}^{(2,1)}(-\mathbf{r})], \qquad (5.1)$$

which is correct to terms linear in nonequilibrium quantities. $D_\alpha{}^0$ is the self-diffusion coefficient of ion α in an infinitely dilute solution, while $z_\alpha e$ is its charge. The vector separation $\mathbf{r}$ is equal to $\mathbf{r}_2 - \mathbf{r}_1$.

In this equation, the correlation function, $g_{\alpha\beta}{}^{(2)}$, has been considered as being equal to its equilibrium value (the radial distribution function) plus a nonequilibrium part; i.e.,

$$g_{\alpha\beta}{}^{(2)}(\mathbf{r}) = g_{\alpha\beta}{}^{(2,0)}(r) + g_{\alpha\beta}{}^{(2,1)}(\mathbf{r}). \qquad (5.2)$$

The electrical potential at a point located at $-\mathbf{r}$ from an ion of type β at $\mathbf{r}_2$ has similarly been split into an equilibrium and nonequilibrium part,

$$\phi_\beta{}^{(2)}(-\mathbf{r}) = \phi_\beta{}^{(2,0)}(r) + \phi_\beta{}^{(2,1)}(-\mathbf{r}). \qquad (5.3)$$

Both $\phi_\beta{}^{(2)}$ and $\phi_\beta{}^{(2,0)}$ satisfy a Poisson's equation so that the difference satisfies the relation

$$\nabla_r{}^2\phi_\beta{}^{(2,1)}(-\mathbf{r}) = -(4\pi e/\epsilon)\sum_{\gamma=1}^{\nu} z_\gamma c_\gamma g_{\beta\gamma}{}^{(2,1)}(-\mathbf{r}), \qquad (5.4)$$

where ϵ is the dielectric constant.

Equation (5.1) for the pair space particle diffusion currents may be obtained[8] from the Fokker-Planck-Chandresekhar equations in singlet and pair space. It has been derived previously by an *ad hoc* extension to molecular species of the theory of the motion of a Brownian particle.[10] The equivalence of the form of Eq. (5.1) with the previous results is demonstrated in Appendix 1.

By reversing the roles of α and β in $\mathbf{j}_{\alpha\beta,1}{}^{(2)}$ and replacing $\mathbf{r}$ by $-\mathbf{r}$ an expression for $\mathbf{j}_{\alpha\beta,2}{}^{(2)}$ is obtained.

Equations for the unknown function $g_{\alpha\beta}{}^{(2,1)}/g_{\alpha\beta}{}^{(2,0)}$ are derived by combining Eq. (5.1) with the pair space equation of continuity, which for a stationary state may be written

$$\nabla_{r_1} \cdot \mathbf{j}_{\alpha\beta,1}{}^{(2)} + \nabla_{r_2} \cdot \mathbf{j}_{\alpha\beta,2}{}^{(2)} = 0. \tag{5.5}$$

In the resulting expressions, some terms may be neglected since they lead to higher $c^{\frac{1}{2}}$ order contributions to the transport properties. These terms are recognized by their order in the ionic charge.[10] The final set of ν^2 coupled equations is

$$\begin{aligned}
&(D_\alpha{}^0 + D_\beta{}^0)\nabla_r{}^2[g_{\alpha\beta}{}^{(2,1)}(\mathbf{r})/g_{\alpha\beta}{}^{(2,0)}(r)] \\
&\quad - (4\pi e^2/\epsilon kT) \sum_{\gamma=1}^{\nu} z_\gamma c_\gamma \{D_\alpha{}^0 z_\alpha [g_{\beta\gamma}{}^{(2,1)}(-\mathbf{r})/g_{\beta\gamma}{}^{(2,0)}(r)] \\
&\qquad + D_\beta{}^0 z_\beta [g_{\alpha\gamma}{}^{(2,1)}(\mathbf{r})/g_{\alpha\gamma}{}^{(2,0)}(r)]\} \\
&\quad = (\mathbf{u}_\beta - \mathbf{u}_\alpha) \cdot \nabla_r \ln g_{\alpha\beta}{}^{(2,0)}, \quad \alpha, \beta = 1, \cdots, \nu.
\end{aligned} \tag{5.6}$$

A solution may be sought in a spherical harmonic series. There obviously is no azimuthal dependence. It appears from Eq. (5.6) and the boundary conditions, which we shall subsequently state, that only the $\cos\theta$ term is nonvanishing. Thus, let us assume that

$$(D_\alpha{}^0 + D_\beta{}^0)[g_{\alpha\beta}{}^{(2,1)}(\mathbf{r})/g_{\alpha\beta}{}^{(2,0)}(r)] = \psi_{\alpha\beta}(r)\mathbf{e}_r \cdot \mathbf{e}_z, \tag{5.7}$$

where the positive z axis is taken in the direction of $\mathbf{q}$ (we restrict considerations to unidirectional macroscopic flow). The insertion of the constant $D_\alpha{}^0 + D_\beta{}^0$ and the spherically symmetric $g_{\alpha\beta}{}^{(2,0)}(r)$ is convenient and innocuous.

Rewriting Eq. (5.6) in terms of $\psi_{\alpha\beta}$, one has

$$\begin{aligned}
&(d^2\psi_{\alpha\beta}/dr^2) + (2/r)(d\psi_{\alpha\beta}/dr) - (2/r^2)\psi_{\alpha\beta} \\
&\quad - (4\pi e^2/\epsilon kT) \sum_{\gamma=1}^{\nu} z_\gamma c_\gamma [z_\beta(D_\beta{}^0/D_\alpha{}^0 + D_\gamma{}^0)\psi_{\alpha\gamma} \quad z_\alpha(D_\alpha{}^0/D_\beta{}^0 + D_\gamma{}^0)\psi_{\beta\gamma}] \\
&\quad = \mathbf{e}_z \cdot (\mathbf{u}_\beta - \mathbf{u}_\alpha)(z_\alpha z_\beta e^2/\epsilon kT)e^{-\kappa r}(1 + \kappa r)/r^2,
\end{aligned} \tag{5.8}$$

where also the Debye-Hückel radial distribution function

$$g_{\alpha\beta}{}^{(2,0)} = \exp[-(z_\alpha z_\beta e^2/\epsilon kT)(e^{-\kappa r}/r)] \tag{5.9}$$

$$\kappa^2 = (4\pi e^2/\epsilon kT) \sum_{\gamma=1}^{\nu} c_\gamma z_\gamma{}^2,$$

[N.B., $\kappa = 0(c^{\frac{1}{2}})$] has been inserted.

The correlation function in both equilibrium and nonequilibrium systems approaches unity at large interparticle distances. One boundary condition which the perturbation part must satisfy, therefore, is

$$\lim_{r\to\infty} \psi_{\alpha\beta}(r) = 0. \tag{5.10}$$

---

[10] H. S. Harned and B. B. Owen, *The Physical Chemistry of Electrolytic Solutions* (Reinhold Publishing Corporation, New York, 1958), Chap. 2.

The second boundary condition in problems such as this is often based on a hydrodynamic requirement.[11] A somewhat simpler condition, which will serve to determine the lowest order terms in κ depends on the requirement that the perturbation part of the correlation function not blow up as the concentration of electrolyte becomes small. This boundary condition is applied by setting equal to zero terms in $\psi_{\alpha\beta}$ which go as $1/\kappa$ for $\kappa \to 0$; mathematically,

$$\lim_{\kappa \to 0} \psi_{\alpha\beta} < \infty. \tag{5.11}$$

Before considering a solution let us note that Poisson's equation, (5.4), indicates that the form of the perturbation to the local potential is

$$\phi_\alpha^{(2,1)}(\mathbf{r}) = -(4\pi e/\epsilon) \sum_{\gamma=1}^{\nu} c_\gamma z_\gamma [\chi_{\alpha\gamma}(r)/(D_\alpha^0 + D_\gamma^0)] \mathbf{e}_r \cdot \mathbf{e}_z, \tag{5.12}$$

which leads to the equation

$$(d^2\chi_{\alpha\gamma}/dr^2) + (2/r)(d\chi_{\alpha\gamma}/dr) - (2/r^2)\chi_{\alpha\gamma} = g_{\alpha\gamma}^{(2,0)}\psi_{\alpha\gamma}. \tag{5.13}$$

The boundary conditions on $\chi_{\alpha\nu}$ are identical with those imposed on $\psi_{\alpha\nu}$ for similar reasons.

In Appendix 2, Eqs. (5.8) and (5.13) are solved to the desired degree of accuracy to obtain expressions for the ψ's and χ's of ionic species as linear functions of the singlet space velocities. Insertion of these results renders the pair space velocity in the form,

$$\begin{aligned} \mathbf{j}_{\alpha\beta,1}^{(2)} &= c_{\alpha\beta}^{(2,0)}(\mathbf{u}_\alpha - \mathbf{u}) \\ &\quad + \frac{D_\alpha^0}{D_\alpha^0 + D_\beta^0} \mathbf{e}_z \cdot \left[\frac{\psi_{\alpha\beta}}{r} \mathbf{1} + \left(\frac{d\psi_{\alpha\beta}}{dr} - \frac{\psi_{\alpha\beta}}{r} \right) \mathbf{e}_r \mathbf{e}_r \right] \\ &\quad + \frac{4\pi z_\alpha e^2 D_\alpha^0}{\epsilon kT} \sum_{\gamma=1}^{\nu} \frac{c_\gamma z_\gamma}{D_\beta^0 + D_\gamma^0} \mathbf{e}_z \cdot \left[\frac{\chi_{\beta\gamma}}{r} \mathbf{1} + \left(\frac{d\chi_{\beta\gamma}}{dr} - \frac{\chi_{\beta\gamma}}{r} \right) \mathbf{e}_r \mathbf{e}_r \right], \end{aligned} \tag{5.14}$$

which is linear in singlet space velocities.

Appendix 3 demonstrates that this leads to a heat current density

$$(\mathbf{q}_V)_{\text{ion-ion}} = \sum_{\alpha=1}^{\nu} \left[\sum_{\beta=1}^{\nu} c_\beta h_{\alpha\beta} + 0(\kappa^2) \right] \mathbf{j}_\alpha, \tag{5.15}$$

$$h_{\alpha\beta} = \tfrac{1}{2} \int_a^\infty (V_{\alpha\beta} - \tfrac{1}{3} r V_{\alpha\beta}') g_{\alpha\beta}^{(2,0)} 4\pi r^2 dr, \tag{5.16}$$

where a is the ion radius (which enters only as $\kappa^2 a^2$ and higher order terms). The term with the h integrals comes from the first term on the right-hand side of Eq. (5.14). It is quasi thermodynamic in the sense that it involves averages over the equilibrium ensemble. The $\mathbf{r}$ dependent parts of the pair space velocity contribute only terms of order κ^2 to the heat of transport.

---

[11] Reference 3(a); reference 10, p. 156.

VI. FLOW $(\varphi_V)_{\text{ion-solv}}$

A detailed knowledge of the equilibrium ion-solvent correlations would be required for a Brownian motion treatment paralleling that of the previous section. Lacking the ability to perform this more rigorous treatment, we shall attempt to obtain as much information as possible from a simplified model.

We seek $\mathbf{j}_{\alpha 0,1}{}^{(2)}(\mathbf{r}_{12}, \mathbf{e}_\mu)$ and $\mathbf{j}_{\alpha 0,2}{}^{(2)}(\mathbf{r}_{12}, \mathbf{e}_\mu)$. Let us first assume that the fixing of a solvent molecule in the neighborhood of an ion instead of averaging over this solvent's position does not significantly affect the ions velocity so that

$$\mathbf{j}_{\alpha 0,1}{}^{(2)} = c_{\alpha 0}{}^{(2)}(\mathbf{r}_{12}, \mathbf{e}_\mu)[\mathbf{u}_\alpha - \mathbf{u}]. \tag{6.1}$$

This approximation is in keeping with a continuum picture of the solvent.

To determine the pair space velocity of a solvent molecule near an ion we adopt the hydrodynamical model used by Debye and Hückel to calculate the electrophoretic force.[12] The solvent is viewed as a uniform continuum of viscosity η (orientation dependencies are thus smoothed). The ions are charged spheres of radius b_α, which may include a solvation shell. To lowest order in electrolyte concentration $\mathbf{u}_{\alpha 0,2}{}^{(2)}$ may be equated to $\mathbf{u}_{\alpha 0,1}{}^{(2)} + \mathbf{v}_\alpha$, where $\mathbf{v}_\alpha(r)$ is the relative average velocity of a volume element located at $\mathbf{r}$ with respect to ion α.

The velocity $\mathbf{v}_\alpha$ may be found as a solution of the Navier-Stokes equation,

$$\eta \nabla \times \nabla \times \mathbf{v}_\alpha = -\nabla p + \mathbf{K}_\alpha. \tag{6.2}$$

The exact nature of the local pressure, $p(\mathbf{r})$, need not concern us. The average volume force on the element is given in terms of two particle average forces[13] by

$$\mathbf{K}_\alpha(\mathbf{r}) = \sum_{\gamma=0}^{\nu} c_\gamma g_{\alpha\gamma}{}^{(2,0)} \overline{\mathbf{F}}_{\alpha\gamma,2}{}^{(2)}. \tag{6.3}$$

In the bulk of the solution $\mathbf{K}_\alpha$ vanishes so that

$$\sum_{\gamma=0}^{\nu} c_\gamma \overline{\mathbf{F}}_\gamma{}^{(1)} = 0. \tag{6.4}$$

On assuming the solvent is uniform and approximating the pair space forces by their singlet space values, we have

$$\mathbf{K}_\alpha = \sum_{\gamma=1}^{\nu} c_\gamma (g_{\alpha\gamma}{}^{(2,0)} - 1) \overline{\mathbf{F}}_\gamma{}^{(1)}. \tag{6.5}$$

The singlet forces may be written, to lowest order in κ, as the negative of the ion-solvent friction constant times the relative singlet velocity of ion and solvent. Thus,

$$K_\alpha = -\sum_{\gamma=1}^{\nu} c_\gamma \zeta_\gamma{}^0 (g_{\alpha\gamma}{}^{(2,0)} - 1)(\mathbf{u}_\gamma - \mathbf{u}_0), \tag{6.6}$$

$$\zeta_\gamma{}^0 = kT/D_\gamma{}^0,$$

into which the linearized Debye-Hückel radial distribution function may be inserted.

---

[12] P. Debye and E. Hückel, *Phys. Z.* **24**, 305 (1923).

[13] Reference 3(a), Eq. (IV.4).

The Navier-Stokes equation is to be solved together with the pair space equation of continuity, which, for a uniform fluid in a stationary state, is

$$\nabla \cdot \mathbf{v}_\alpha = 0. \tag{6.7}$$

The first boundary condition is the asymptotic one

$$\lim_{r\to\infty} \mathbf{v}_\alpha = \mathbf{u}_0 - \mathbf{u}_\alpha. \tag{6.8}$$

The other boundary condition has its origin in the requirement that the viscous fluid will not slip at the ion sphere, so that

$$\mathbf{v}(b_\alpha \mathbf{e}_r) = 0.$$

Solution of these equations[12] and a transformation from $\mathbf{r}$ to $-\mathbf{r}$ yields, when $e^{-\kappa r}$ is expanded as $1 - \kappa r$,||

$$\begin{aligned}\mathbf{j}_{0\alpha,1}{}^{(2)} = c_{\alpha 0}{}^{(2)} \Biggl\{ (\mathbf{u}_\alpha - \mathbf{u}) + \mathbf{e}_z \cdot \Biggl[(\mathbf{u}_0 - \mathbf{u}_\alpha) \\ + \frac{4\pi z_\alpha e^2}{6\pi\eta\kappa\epsilon kT} \sum_{\gamma=1}^{\nu} c_\gamma z_\gamma \zeta_\gamma{}^0 (\mathbf{u}_0 - \mathbf{u}_\gamma) \Biggl\{ \mathbf{e}_r \cos\left(1 - \frac{3b_\alpha}{2r} + \frac{b_\alpha{}^3}{2r^3}\right) \\ - \mathbf{e}_\theta \sin\theta \left(1 - \frac{3b_\alpha}{4r} - \frac{b_\alpha{}^3}{4r^3}\right) \Biggr\} \Biggr] \Biggr\}. \end{aligned} \tag{6.9}$$

The product of inserting the pair space particle diffusion currents (6.1) and (6.9) into $(\mathbf{q}_V)_{\text{ion-solv}}$ is

$$(\mathbf{q}_V)_{\text{ion-solv}} = 2 \sum_{\alpha=1}^{\nu} c_0 h_{\alpha 0} \mathbf{j}_\alpha + \sum_{\alpha=1}^{\nu} (c_\alpha \mathbf{j}_0 - c_0 \mathbf{j}_\alpha)[A_\alpha + \kappa (z_\alpha \zeta_\alpha{}^0 / 6\pi\eta) \tilde{A}], \tag{6.10}$$

$$h_{\alpha 0} = \tfrac{1}{2} \int\int [V_{\alpha 0} - (r/3)(\partial/\partial r) V_{\alpha 0}] g_{\alpha 0}{}^{(2,0)} d^3\mathbf{r} d^2 \mathbf{e}_\mu, \tag{6.11}$$

$$\begin{aligned} A_\alpha = \tfrac{1}{2} \int\int \{ [V_{\alpha 0} - (r/3)(\partial/\partial r) V_{\alpha 0}] \, [1 - (3b_\alpha/2r) + (b_\alpha{}^3/2r^3)] \\ + \tfrac{1}{2} V_{\alpha 0} [(b_\alpha/r) - (b_\alpha{}^3/r^3)] \} g_{\alpha 0}{}^{(2,0)} d^3\mathbf{r} d^2\mathbf{e}_\mu, \end{aligned} \tag{6.12}$$

$$\kappa^2 \tilde{A} = (4\pi e^2/\epsilon kT) \sum_{\gamma=1}^{\nu} c_\gamma z_\gamma A_\gamma. \tag{6.13}$$

This result possesses certain unsatisfactory features which we discuss below, but let us look at its qualitative implications. If details of the ion and solvent structure are ignored then the interaction potential depends only on the square of the ion's charge. In a solution where all the ions are of the same valence type, if the sizes of the ions are the same then the A integrals are the same and by electroneutrality $\tilde{A}$ vanishes. Therefore, to lowest order, $\tilde{A}$ may be considered as linear in differences of ion size, or, in the spirit of Stokes'

|| Equation (6.10) is obtained from either Eq. (6.9) or its precursor with $e^{-\kappa r}$ not expanded. The difference enters as terms of higher order in κ.

Law, linear in the differences of mobility. After completing the theory and comparing with the data, we will be in a position to discuss this term further.

Equation (6.10) has the weakness that major contributions to the integrand come from the region close to the ion. In this portion of space several of the approximations involved in the derivation, such as the neglect of differences between singlet and pair forces and the use of the linearized Debye-Hückel distribution, are questionable. (In contrast, the electrophoretic drag problem leads to integrals with major contributions at distance $1/\kappa$.) The result is probably an over-estimate of the ion-solvent contribution since one expects less κ dependence in the radial distribution function at close distances (compare with the theory of ion pairing where no κ dependence is assumed up close).

VII. FURTHER SOLVENT CONTRIBUTIONS TO HEAT FLOW

The solvent-solvent interactions lead, to the desired order, to a term

$$(\mathbf{q}_V)_{\text{solv-solv}} = c_0 h_{00} \mathbf{j}_0, \tag{7.1}$$

$$h_{00} = \tfrac{1}{2} \int\int\int [V_{00} - (r/3)(\partial/\partial r) V_{00}'] g_{00}^{(2,0)} d^3\mathbf{r} d^2\mathbf{e}_{\mu 1} d^2\mathbf{e}_{\mu 2}. \tag{7.2}$$

If we had attempted a completely molecular treatment of the solvent, we would have had to consider terms like those arising from solvent oriented by an ion interacting with other solvent and ions, but these are the effects which the introduction of the dielectric constant covers.

VIII. HEAT OF TRANSPORT

The results of Secs. 4 to 7 may be united to yield as an expression for the heat current,

$$\mathbf{q} = \sum_{\alpha=0}^{\nu} Q_\alpha^* \mathbf{j}_\alpha, \tag{8.1}$$

$$Q_\alpha^* = (5/2)kT - \bar{H}_\alpha + \sum_{\beta=1}^{\nu} c_\beta h_{\alpha\beta} + 2c_0 h_{\alpha 0} - c_0 A_\alpha$$
$$- (c_0 z_\alpha kT/6\pi\eta D_\alpha^0)\tilde{A}\kappa + 0(\kappa^2) \quad \alpha = 1, \cdots, \nu, \tag{8.2}$$

$$Q_0^* = (5/2)kT - H_0 + c_0 h_{00} + \sum_{\alpha=1}^{\nu} c_\alpha A_\alpha.$$

The heats of transport have been properly identified if Eq. (3.6) is satisfied. Inserting (8.2) and (8.3) reveals

$$\sum_{\alpha=0}^{\nu} c_\alpha Q_\alpha^* = \tfrac{5}{2} kT \sum_{\alpha=0}^{\nu} c_\alpha + \sum_{\alpha,\beta=0}^{\nu} c_\alpha c_\beta h_{\alpha\beta} - \sum_{\alpha=0}^{\nu} c_\alpha \bar{H}_\alpha = 0, \tag{8.4}$$

by using a well-known equilibrium result.[14]

---

[14] Terrill L. Hill, *Statistical Mechanics* (McGraw-Hill Book Company, Inc., New York, 1956), Eqs. (30.10) and (30.20).

For ionic components $h_{\alpha\beta}$ may be evaluated with the coulomb potential and the linearized Debye-Hückel radial distribution function. Part of $c_\beta h_{\alpha\beta}$ diverges when integration is performed over an infinite volume, but upon summing over β these divergencies vanish by electroneutrality. The remaining part is, to order κ,

$$\sum_{\beta=1}^{\nu} c_\beta h_{\alpha\beta} = -2z_\alpha{}^2 e^2\kappa/3\epsilon. \tag{8.5}$$

The integrals $h_{\alpha 0}$ and A_α may be written as their infinite dilution value plus a concentration dependent part. The order of the latter part depends upon how much κ dependence is put into $g_{\alpha 0}{}^{(2,0)}$. This problem is similar to that which arises in the calculation of chemical potential[15] and polarization energy.[16] If we allow the potential of mean force to contain the interaction of solvent and ion atmosphere, we would be taking certain terms into account twice. When properly treated the first concentration dependence of the integrals is $0(\kappa^2)$.

The limiting law for the heat of transport of an ionic species is

$$Q_\alpha{}^* = Q_\alpha{}^{*0} + \mathfrak{s}(Q_\alpha{}^*)\kappa, \tag{8.6}$$

$$\mathfrak{s}(Q_\alpha{}^*) = -\mathfrak{s}(\bar{H}_\alpha) - (2z_\alpha{}^2e^2/3\epsilon) - (c_0 z_\alpha kT\tilde{A}/6\pi\eta D_\alpha{}^0), \tag{8.7}$$

where $\mathfrak{s}(\bar{H}_\alpha)$ is the limiting slope for partial molecular heat content *vs* κ:

$$\mathfrak{s}(\bar{H}_\alpha) = -\frac{3z_\alpha{}^2e^2}{4\epsilon}\left(1 + T\frac{\partial \ln \epsilon}{\partial T} + \frac{T}{3}\frac{\partial \ln v}{\partial T}\right). \tag{8.8}$$

Individual ion heats of transport are experimentally unobtainable. The heat of transport of neutral salts, defined by

$$Q_\pm{}^* = \nu_+ Q_+{}^* + \nu_- Q_-{}^*$$

may be measured (the ν's are standard notation for number of ions in the neutral "molecule"). The slope of the limiting law is

$$\mathfrak{s}(Q_\pm{}^*) = -\,\mathfrak{s}(\bar{H}_\pm) - (2e^2/3\epsilon)\sum \nu_\alpha z_\alpha{}^2 - (c_0 kT\tilde{A}/6\pi\eta)\sum(\nu_\alpha z_\alpha/D_\alpha{}^0). \tag{8.9}$$

The summation in the last term goes as a difference in mobility (recall that $\tilde{A}$ has the same behavior). This further decreases the importance of ion-solvent interaction contributions.

Although neither the single ion entropy $\bar{S}_\alpha$ nor heat of transport $Q_\alpha{}^*$ is measurable separately, the combination

$$\bar{\bar{S}} = \bar{S}_\alpha + (Q_\alpha{}^*/T), \tag{8.10}$$

called the transport entropy, is. We find for the slope of the limiting law for

$$\bar{\bar{S}}_\alpha + k \ln m_\alpha,$$

$$\mathfrak{s}(\bar{\bar{S}}_\alpha) = -\,(z_\alpha{}^2e^2/6\epsilon T) - (c_0 z_\alpha k\tilde{A}/6\pi\eta D_\alpha{}^0). \tag{8.11}$$

[15] J. G. Kirkwood, *Chem. Revs.* **19**, 275 (1936).
[16] A. B. Lidiard, *Phys. Rev.* **112**, 54 (1958).

The ion-solvent term is much more important here than in Eq. (8.9), both because of the lack of the summation factor, and because the ion-ion term is smaller.

A last point to be noted is that from Eq. (8.3), or more simply from Eq. (3.6), it is seen that the heat of transport of the solvent is of order κ^2.

IX. COMPARISON WITH EXPERIMENTS

Results of measurements on the heat of transport of electrolytes in the range of applicability of the limiting laws are scant. The most informative data are those obtained by Agar and Turner[17] using a conductimetric method. Aqueous solutions of NaCl, NaBr, KCl, KBr, and KI were studied at 25°C. and at four concentrations in the range from 0.0025 to 0.02 molar. A value at 0.05 m is available by extrapolation of the thermogravitational results of Alexander.[18] In Columns 5, 6, and 7 of Table I the coefficients of the best least squares quadratic fits to a plot of Q^* (in kcal/mole) *vs* $m^{\frac{1}{2}}$ is presented. A quadratic was chosen because in this concentration range good fits to other electrolytic properties can be obtained by considering only terms to order m. Included also are interval allowances for each value. These are determined by multiplying the square root of the residual mean square by 2.92, the appropriate factor for 90% confidence limits with a mean square error based on two degrees of freedom.

To test the hypothesis that all 1:1 electrolytes have a common slope (except for a small ion-solvent term), the calculation was redone with the constraint that all the curves have the same $m^{\frac{1}{2}}$ coefficient. The coefficients found in this way are reported in Columns 6 and 8, and in Column 3 of $Q_{1:1}^*$. The best common slope is -2.58 ± 0.89. Allowances are calculated with a factor of 1.76 to produce estimates of 90% confidence based on fourteen degrees of freedom. Comparison of the residual mean square for this constrained fit, which is 7.74×10^{-4}, with the average of the mean squares of the unconstrained fits, which is 8.74×10^{-4}, leads one to conclude that the hypothesis of a common limiting slope is statistically tenable.

Considering only the ion-ion term the theory predicts a limiting concentration dependence of 2.57 $m^{\frac{1}{2}}$. Agreement with the individual and common experimental slopes is acceptable. In view of the error margin room for an ion-solvent term exists.

Less complete analysis can be made of the initial and final thermoelectric power experiments of Agar and Breck[19] on $TlClO_4$. These measurements, performed at six concentrations in the range 0.05 and 0.256m, are difficult to interpret because of the higher molarity and the large scatter. The heat of transport and the transported entropy of Tl^+ are shown in Figs. 1 and 2 with the visual curves drawn so as to come in at the values predicted by the ion-ion terms of Eqs. (8.9) and (8.11). Further clarification of these data would be useful.

---

[17] J. N. Agar and J. C. R. Turner (to be published); J. C. R. Turner, dissertation, University of Cambridge (1955); J. N. Agar, in *The Structure of Electrolytic Solutions*, edited by W. J. Hamer (John Wiley and Sons, Inc., New York, 1959).

[18] K. F. Alexander, *Z. physik. Chem.* (*Leipzig*) **203**, 212 (1954). The extrapolation to 25°C. and correction for a 5% error in analysis were performed by Dr. J. N. Agar, whom we thank for supplying these results.

[19] J. N. Agar and W. G. Breck, *Trans. Faraday Soc.* **53**, 167 (1957).

TABLE I. Theoretical predictions and least squares quadratic fit to the data.

1	2	3	4	5	6	7	8
Property	Limiting slope (coefficient of $m^{\frac{1}{2}}$)			Value at infinite dilution		Coefficient of m	
	theoretical ion-ion term	quasitheoretical ion-solvent term	experimental	individual	common slope	individual	common slope
Q_{NaCl}*(kcal/mole)	−2.57	0.18	−4.11±5.39	1.10±0.31	1.01±0.06	5.99±19.13	0.65±3.37
Q_{KCl}*	−2.57	0.001	−2.68±2.49	1.05±0.14	1.04±0.06	2.60±8.84	2.28±3.37
Q_{NaBr}*	−2.57	0.20	−2.32±4.88	0.76±0.28	0.77±0.06	0.77±17.30	1.71±3.37
Q_{KBr}*	−2.57	0.004	−1.63±1.49	0.72±0.09	0.77±0.06	0.35±5.29	3.69±3.37
Q_{KI}*	−2.57	0.002	−2.18±0.98	0.14±0.06	0.20±0.06	2.33±3.48	3.72±3.37
$Q_{1:1}$*	−2.57	..	−2.58±0.89	..	..	..	..
Q_{TlClO_4}*	−2.57	0.01	..	..	..	..	..
Q_{CdSO_4}*	−20.53	1.6	..	..	..	..	..
$\bar{\bar{S}}_{Tl^+}$(eu/mole)	−0.777	−0.33	..	..	..	..	..
$\bar{\bar{S}}_{Cd^{++}}$	−6.22	12.9[a]	6.7[a]	..	..	..	..

[a] Basis for ion-solvent term calculation.

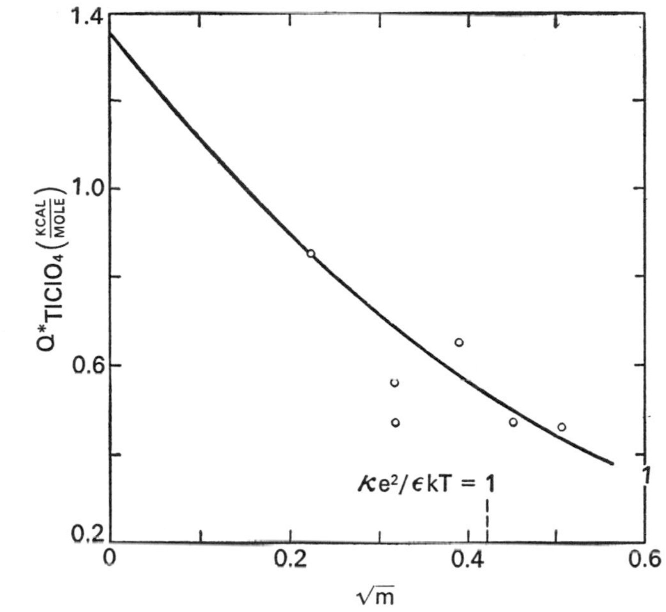

FIG. 1

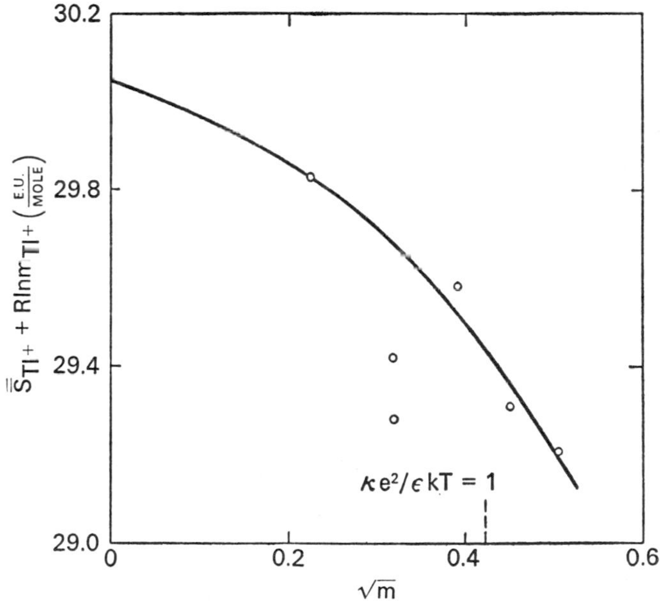

FIG. 2

Breck and Agar[20] have applied the same method to a study of the 2:2 salt $CdSO_4$. The heat of transport and the transported entropy of Cd^{++} are plotted in Figs. 3 and 4. On the abscissa, the point where $\kappa z^2 e^2/\epsilon kT = 1$ is

[20] W. G. Breck and J. N. Agar, *Trans. Faraday Soc.* **53**, 175 (1957).

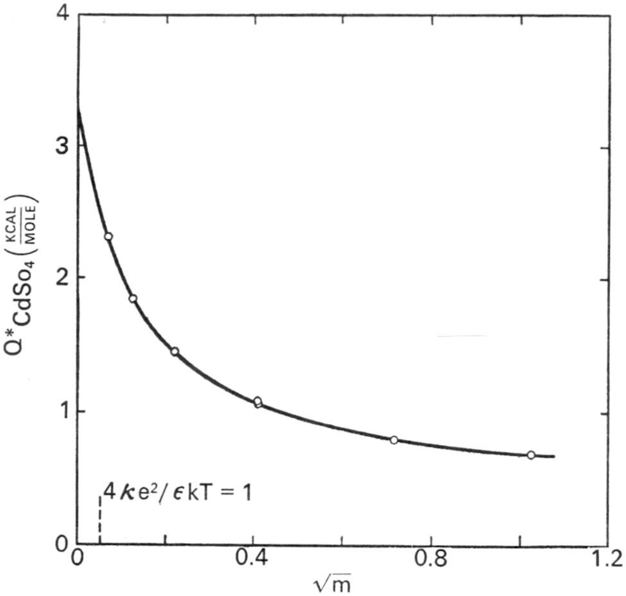

FIG. 3

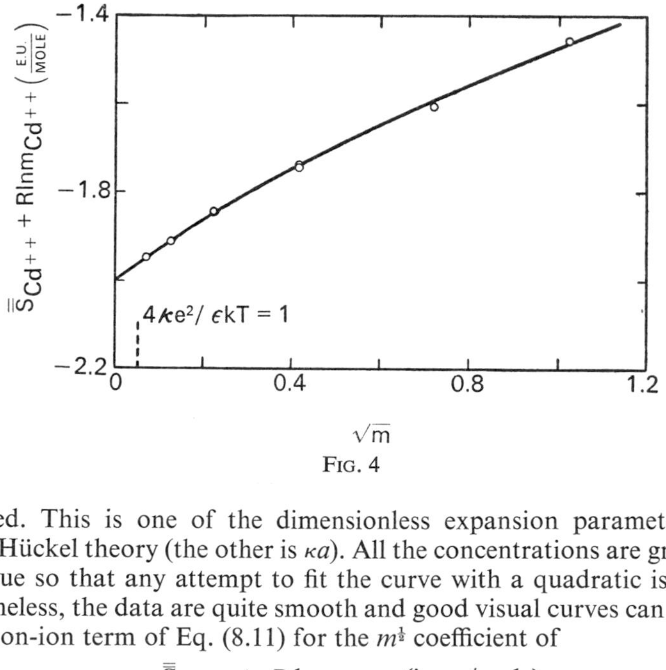

FIG. 4

indicated. This is one of the dimensionless expansion parameters of the Debye-Hückel theory (the other is κa). All the concentrations are greater than this value so that any attempt to fit the curve with a quadratic is unsound. Nevertheless, the data are quite smooth and good visual curves can be drawn.

The ion-ion term of Eq. (8.11) for the $m^{\frac{1}{2}}$ coefficient of

$$\bar{\bar{S}}_{\mathrm{Cd}^{++}} + R \ln m_{\mathrm{Cd}^{++}} \text{ (in eu/mole)}$$

is -6.22 while the slope read off the curve is $+6.7$. A value of $\tilde{A}_{\mathrm{CdSO}_4}$ of 81 is required to explain this difference. When this $\tilde{A}$ is used in the heat of transport equation, the ion-solvent term is 1.6 compared with an ion-ion contribution of -20.53.

If as an approximation, we postulate that for a simple salt with ions of equal valence $\tilde{A}$ is proportional to the magnitude of the charge and to the difference between the self-diffusion constants of the cation and the anion, then from the $CdSO_4$ value of $\tilde{A}$ one obtains the estimates of the ion-solvent contributions to the limiting slope given in Column 3 of Table I. As noted earlier, the solvent effect is much less important for the heat of transport of the salt than for the ion transported entropy.

X. ACKNOWLEDGMENT

The authors would like to express their appreciation to Dr. Martin B. Wilk and Miss Marilyn J. Huyett for performing the statistical analysis of the experimental data.

APPENDIX 1

Equation (5.1) for the pair space diffusion current is given in a somewhat different form in standard references on the theory of electrolytes.[21] One finds (in our notation)

$$\mathbf{u}_{\alpha\beta,1}{}^{(2)} = \mathbf{u} - (D_\alpha{}^0/kT)[kT\nabla_{r_1} \ln c_\beta g_{\alpha\beta}{}^{(2)}(\mathbf{r}) + z_\alpha e\nabla_{r_1}\phi_\beta{}^{(2)}(-\mathbf{r}) + z_\alpha e\nabla_{r_1}\phi_\alpha{}^{(2)}(0) - \mathbf{X}_\alpha]. \tag{A1.1}$$

The equivalence follows after one notes that as $r \to \infty$, this equation becomes

$$\mathbf{u}_\alpha = \mathbf{u} - (D_\alpha{}^0/kT)[kT\nabla_{r_1} \ln c_\beta + z_\alpha e\nabla_{r_1}\phi_\alpha{}^{(2)}(0) - \mathbf{X}_\alpha], \tag{A1.2}$$

while at equilibrium it is

$$\mathbf{u} = \mathbf{u} - (D_\alpha{}^0/kT)[kT\nabla_{r_1} \ln g_{\alpha\beta}{}^{(2,0)}(r) + z_\alpha e\nabla_{r_1}\phi_\beta{}^{(2,0)}(r)]. \tag{A1.3}$$

The latter is one of the basic assumptions behind the Debye-Hückel theory.

The last point involved in establishing the correspondence is that since Eq. (A1.1) is already linear in nonequilibrium quantities, multiplication by $c_{\alpha\beta}{}^{(2)}$ or $c_{\alpha\beta}{}^{(2,0)}$ is equivalent.

APPENDIX 2

The set of Eqs. (5.8) may be written as the one matrix equation

$$L\boldsymbol{\psi} - \kappa^2\mathfrak{A}\boldsymbol{\psi} = \boldsymbol{\Lambda}\, e^{-\kappa r}(1 + \kappa r)/r^2, \tag{A2.1}$$

where we define the differential operator

$$L = (d^2/dr^2) + (2/r)(d/dr) - (2/r^2). \tag{A2.2}$$

The unknown functions have been arranged into a $1 \times \nu^2$ column matrix, $\boldsymbol{\psi}$, which is partitioned into ν equisized parts. The β element of the α partition is $\psi_{\alpha\beta}$. Similarly, $\boldsymbol{\Lambda}$ is the column matrix such that

$$(\boldsymbol{\Lambda})_{\alpha\beta} = (z_\alpha z_\beta e^2/\epsilon kT)(\mathbf{u}_\beta - \mathbf{u}_\alpha) \cdot \mathbf{e}_z. \tag{A2.3}$$

[21] Reference 10, Eqs. (2–3–1) and (2–5–3).

$\mathfrak{A}$ is a $\nu^2 \times \nu^2$ matrix partitioned into ν^2 square parts such that the β, λ element of the α, γ partition is

$$\kappa^2(\mathfrak{U})_{\alpha\gamma\beta\lambda} = (4\pi e^2/\epsilon kT)c_\gamma z_\gamma[\delta_{\alpha\lambda}z_\beta D_\beta{}^0/(D_\alpha{}^0 + D_\gamma{}^0) - \delta_{\beta\lambda}z_\alpha D_\alpha{}^0/(D_\beta{}^0 + D_\gamma{}^0)]. \qquad (A2.4)$$

Define $\mathfrak{B}$ by the equation $\mathfrak{A} = \mathfrak{B}^2$. The unit matrix is $\mathfrak{J}$. $\boldsymbol{\psi}$ and $\boldsymbol{\Lambda}$ may be regarded as vectors of vector elements, while $\mathfrak{A}$ is a matrix of matrix elements.

The solution of Eq. ($A2.1$) which satisfies the boundary conditions (5.10) and (5.11) is

$$\boldsymbol{\psi} = \kappa^{-2}(\mathfrak{B}^2 - \mathfrak{J})^{-1}[\exp(-\kappa\mathfrak{B}r)(\mathfrak{J} + \kappa\mathfrak{B}r)/r^2 - \mathfrak{J}\exp(-\kappa r)(1 + \kappa r)/r^2]\boldsymbol{\Lambda}. \qquad (A2.5)$$

We may now consider the equation for the χ functions which determine the perturbation to the local electrical potential. It can be shown that the approximation of replacing $g_{\alpha\beta}{}^{(2,0)}$ on the right-hand side of Eq. (5.13) by its asymptotic value, unity, is equivalent to approximations which have already been introduced in deriving Eq. (5.8); i.e., terms which yield higher than $c^{\frac{1}{2}}$ contributions to the transport properties are not retained. Therefore, we may write, in matrix form,

$$L\mathbf{X} = \boldsymbol{\psi}, \qquad (A2.6)$$

which has as the solution satisfying boundary conditions (5.10) and (5.11).

$$\mathbf{X} = \kappa^{-4}(\mathfrak{B}^2 - \mathfrak{J})^{-1}\{-\mathfrak{B}^{-2}[1/r^2 - \exp(-\kappa\mathfrak{B}r)(\mathfrak{J} + \mathfrak{B}r)/r^2] + \mathfrak{J}[1/r^2 - \exp(-\kappa r)(1 + \kappa r)/r^2]\}\boldsymbol{\Lambda}. \qquad (A2.7)$$

$\mathfrak{B}$ is singular, but this causes no difficulty since the first term inside the brace is a symbolic representation of the series expansion.

APPENDIX 3

The purpose of this appendix is to derive Eq. (5.15) for the ion-ion potential flow using the results of the previous section. The insertion of Eq. (5.14) into Eq. (2.7) yields

$$\begin{aligned}(\mathbf{q}_V)_{\text{ion-ion}} = \mathbf{e}_z \sum_{\alpha,\beta=1}^{\nu} \{ & c_\alpha c_\beta h_{\alpha\beta}(\mathbf{u}_\alpha - \mathbf{u}) \cdot \mathbf{e}_z \\ & + c_\alpha c_\beta (D_\alpha{}^0/(D_\alpha{}^0 + D_\beta{}^0))\kappa^{-2}\boldsymbol{\Omega}^{\alpha\beta}(\mathfrak{B}^2 - \mathfrak{J})^{-1}[\mathfrak{K}_{\alpha\beta}(\mathfrak{B}) - \mathfrak{K}_{\alpha\beta}(\mathfrak{J})]\boldsymbol{\Lambda} \\ & + (4\pi e^2/\epsilon kT)\sum c_\gamma z_\gamma z_\alpha (D_\alpha{}^0/(D_\beta{}^0 + D_\gamma{}^0))\kappa^{-4}\boldsymbol{\Omega}^{\beta\gamma}(\mathfrak{B}^2 - \mathfrak{J})^{-1} \\ & \cdot (-\mathfrak{B}^{-2}[\mathfrak{K}_{\alpha\beta}(0) - \mathfrak{K}_{\alpha\beta}(\mathfrak{B})] - [\mathfrak{K}_{\alpha\beta}(0) - \mathfrak{K}_{\alpha\beta}(\mathfrak{J})]\boldsymbol{\Lambda}\}, \end{aligned} \qquad (A3.1)$$

$$\begin{aligned}\mathfrak{K}_{\alpha\beta}(\mathfrak{B}) = \int_a^\infty & [\{(V_{\alpha\beta} - \tfrac{1}{3}rV_{\alpha\beta}')\exp(-\kappa\mathfrak{B}r)(\mathfrak{J} + \kappa\mathfrak{B}r)/r^3] \\ & - [(V_{\alpha\beta} - rV_{\alpha\beta}')\exp(-\kappa\mathfrak{B}r)(\mathfrak{J} + \kappa\mathfrak{B}r + \tfrac{1}{3}\kappa^2\mathfrak{B}^2r^2)/r^3]\}\, g_{\alpha\beta}{}^{(2,0)}4\pi r^2 dr,\end{aligned} \qquad (A3.2)$$

and $h_{\alpha\beta}$ is defined in Eq. (5.16). It is convenient to introduce a row matrix $\mathbf{\Omega}^{\alpha\beta}$ with γ elements of the λ partition equal to $\delta_{\alpha\gamma}\delta_{\beta\gamma}$ which picks out the $\alpha\beta$ component from the column matrices of the type defined in Appendix 2.

If we divide $V_{\alpha\beta}$ into a coulombic and a short range part and use the linearized Debye-Hückel radial distribution we find

$$\mathfrak{K}_{\alpha\beta}(\mathfrak{B}) = -\ [(8\pi z_\alpha z_\beta e^2/3\epsilon a) + t_{\alpha\beta}][\mathfrak{J} + 0(\kappa^2\mathfrak{B}^2)], \qquad (A3.3)$$

where $t_{\alpha\beta}$ is a constant arising from the short range forces which is of the same order of magnitude as the constant preceding it. We have purposely refrained from explicitly writing the $\kappa^2\mathfrak{B}^2$ term because the functions in the integral have not been accurately obtained to this order of magnitude.

To finally arrive at Eq. (5.15) one need only substitute and note that $\Lambda = 0(\mathbf{j}_\alpha \cdot \mathbf{e}_z/c_\alpha)$.

Theory of the Diffuse Double Layer*

FRANK H. STILLINGER, JR.† AND JOHN G. KIRKWOOD‡
Sterling Chemistry Laboratory, Yale University, New Haven, Connecticut

(Received December 9, 1959)

The charge moment expansion for potentials of mean force acting between the ions of an electrolyte is reviewed in a form applicable to surface phases. An integral equation is in this manner derived for approximate determination of the average charge distribution near a planar electrode. The solution of the linearized equation is constructed for an electrolyte consisting of charged hard spheres suspended in a dielectric continuum. For very dilute solutions, the predictions of the linearized Poisson-Boltzmann equation are verified; at higher concentrations, the average space charge in the neighborhood of the electrode tends to alternate in sign as a result of local latticelike ion arrangement imposed effectively by short range ion repulsions. Predicted values of the ζ potential relative to those of the linear Poisson-Boltzmann theory are reported.

I. INTRODUCTION

The understanding of the molecular basis of the diffuse, or Gouy, double layer provides insight into a number of phenomena of interest to electrochemists. In particular it is possible to analyze the several electrokinetic phenomena (e.g., electrophoretic migration velocimes and streaming potentials) to predict the stability of lyophobic colloids toward added salt, and to interpret the capacitance of metal electrodes in contact with electrolytic solutions. Theoretical determination of average ion distributions in diffuse double layers typically has employed in the past, the Poisson-Boltzmann equation as adapted to the surface region. Recent developments for the planar interface are concerned either with solution of the Poisson-Boltzmann equation reducing nonlinear terms,[1-3] or, assuming this equation at a basis, with introduction of complicating *ad hoc* physical models to account for such electrolyte parameters as ion size and degree of hydration.[4-6]

Although such extensions are interesting and perhaps intuitively appealing, it is nevertheless true that the Poisson-Boltzmann equation can give at best

* Based upon part of a doctoral thesis submitted by Frank Stillinger, Jr. to the Graduate School Faculty at Yale University.
† Present address: Bell Telephone Laboratories, Murray Hill, New Jersey.
‡ Deceased.
[1] D. C. Grahame, *Chem. Rev.* **41**, 441 (1947).
[2] B.Breyer and F. Gutmann, *J. Chem. Phys.* **21**, 1323 (1953).
[3] J. R. Macdonald and M. K. Brachman, *J. Chem. Phys.* **22**, 1814 (1954).
[4] Freise, *Z. Elektrochem.* **56**, 822 (1952).
[5] R. Schlogl, *Z. Physik.* **202**, 375 (1954).
[6] J. J. Bikerman, *Phil. Mag.* **33**, 384 (1942).

only an approximate description of the molecular situation. The linear terms in the average electrostatic potential (with the Poisson-Boltzmann equation in expanded form) are alone consistent with a rigorous integrability condition satisfied by the excess electrostatic free energy.[7]

The viewpoint adopted in the following analysis involves determination of local ion densities in the double layer region from the well-developed fundamental theory of molecular distribution functions. Specifically, a moment expansion in increasing orders of charge for a particular ion is derived for the potential of mean force acting in a set of particles (including the chosen ion). This is the diffuse double layer version of a similar treatment of bulk electrolytes which has been carried to some length by Kirkwood and Poirier.[8] An alternative approach to our present problem would introduce a conditionally convergent Mayer cluster expansion appropriate to the interfacial region; in order to obtain finite results for the ionic distribution functions, it would be necessary, as is well known, to select certain sets of clusters for partial summation.[9]

By way of illustrating the profound effect that finite ion size can have upon the average charge distribution in the double layer, our distribution function technique is formulated in approximate fashion to deal extensively with an idealized electrolyte. The electrolyte is regarded as consisting of charged rigid spheres suspended in a dielectric continuum, and a planar, uniformly charged electrode produces the double layer in this model fluid. It is in fact then possible to establish that both the ion-exclusion volumes and the electrostatic charges are instrumental in determining even the qualitative features of the distributions of ions. For sufficiently large dilutions, the usual linear Poisson-Boltzmann result is obtained, but as the electrolyte concentration is allowed to increase, the short-range ion-ion repulsions tend to set up a local latticelike structure with alternating layers of positive and negative charge. Numerical computations for the reduced ζ potential clearly reflect the ionic ordering at distances further from the electrode than would be predicted by the linear Poisson-Boltzmann theory.

II. MOMENT EXPANSION

The molecular system to be discussed consists of a large set of N particles of species $1 \cdots \eta$, some of which are electrostatically charged ions). These particles will be enclosed within a volume v. The surface of this volume may be regarded as a mathematical surface of discontinuity in the sense that it may be crossed by none of the particles. It might, for example, be represented by an infinitely steep and high potential barrier. It is necessary to have a certain portion of the containing surface (such as one face of a rectangular solid volume v) correspond to a charged electrode, which induces the Gouy double layer by creating an appropriate external force field.

Each of the N particles comprising our electrolyte is therefore subject to forces arising either from the charged electrode or from the other fluid particles. The total potential of interaction accordingly is split into single-particle, and particle-pair contributions, attributable to these two sources,

---

[7] R. H. Fowler and E. A. Guggenheim, *Statistical Thermodynamics* (The MacMillan Company, New York, 1956), p. 387.

[8] J. G. Kirkwood and J. C. Peirier, *J. Phys. Chem.* **58**, 591 (1954).

[9] In this connection, see F. P. Buff and F. H. Stillinger, Jr., *J. Chem. Phys.* **25**, 312 (1956).

respectively,

$$V_N(1\cdots N) = \sum_{i=1}^{N} V_{\alpha_i}{}^{(1)}(i) + \sum_{i<j=1}^{N} V_{\alpha_i\alpha_j}{}^{(2)}(ij),$$

$$\alpha_i,\ \alpha_j = 1\cdots\eta. \tag{1}$$

Here, α_i and α_j denote the species of particles i and j. Each of the singlet and pair potentials, furthermore, may be separated into parts of electrostatic (e), and short-range (s) character.

$$V_{\alpha_i}{}^{(1)}(i) = V_{\alpha_i}{}^{(1,s)}(i) + \xi_i V_{\alpha_i}{}^{(1,e)}(i),$$

$$V_{\alpha_i\alpha_j}{}^{(2)}(ij) = V_{\alpha_i\alpha_j}{}^{(2,s)}(ij) + \xi_i\xi_j V_{\alpha_i\alpha_j}{}^{(2,e)}(ij). \tag{2}$$

We have, for the sake of convenience, introduced charging parameters ξ_i for each of the particles in the ionic fluid, such that the charge on i will be $\xi_i e$ ($-e$ is the electronic charge). For neutral solvent species, ξ_i will of course vanish.

Specifically, the electrostatic interactions $V^{(1,e)}$ and $V^{(2,e)}$ will be written (including a dielectric constant appropriate to the fluid medium)

$$V_{\alpha_i}{}^{(1,e)}(i) = V^{(1,e)}(x_i) = -(2\pi\sigma e/D)x_i + A, \tag{3}$$

$$V_{\alpha_i\alpha_j}{}^{(2,e)}(ij) = V^{(2,e)}(r_{ij}) = e^2/Dr_{ij}. \tag{4}$$

The singlet and pair electrostatic interactions therefore are species independent. The potential $V^{(1,e)}$ has been chosen as that for a uniformly charged (σ esu/cm^2) planar electrode, with distance x_i measured normal to its surface and directed inward toward the solution. The value of the additive constant A depends upon the choice of a zero of potential energy; its magnitude can in no way affect the ionic distributions.

The probability of observing a set of n particles such as $1\cdots n$ (the first particle is species α, $\cdots$, the nth particle is species ν) in a given set of positions $\mathbf{r}_1\cdots\mathbf{r}_n$ in the system, is conveniently expressed in terms of a molecular correlation function $g_{\alpha\cdots\nu}{}^{(n)}(1\cdots n)$. $g^{(n)}$ is normalized to unity when each member of the set $1\cdots n$ is far both from other members of the set, and from the double layer region. $g^{(n)}$ may be written as a phase space integral of the normalized canonical distribution, over the configurations of the remaining $N-n$ particles, correct to terms of order N^{-1},

$$g_{\alpha\cdots\nu}{}^{(n)}(1\cdots n) = \exp[-\beta W_{\alpha\cdots\nu}{}^{(n)}(1\cdots n)]$$

$$= \frac{v^n \int_v \cdots \int_v \exp[-\beta V_N(1\cdots N)]dv_{n+1}\cdots dv_N}{\int_v \cdots \int_v \exp[-\beta V_N(1\cdots N)]dv_1\cdots dv_N},$$

$$\beta = (kT)^{-1}, \tag{5}$$

where $W^{(n)}$ is the potential of mean force for the n particle set.

When each of $1 \cdots n$ is microscopically far from the double layer region, $g^{(n)}$ assumes a value $g^{(n,b)}$ typical only of the bulk structure of the electrolytic fluid, and hence completely independent of the nature (shape, charge distribution) of the surface of the system. In particular, the pair correlation function $g^{(2,b)}$ depends only on the radial distance r separating a pair of particles.

The quantities of dominant interest for the double layer development are the singlet distributions, $g_\alpha^{(1)}(\mathbf{r})$. In the interior of the fluid they are unity, but deviations occur near the electrode on account of non-vanishing average force acting on a single particle there. For a position $\mathbf{r}$ within the Gouy double layer, the mean electrostatic charge density ρ_{el} may be expressed trivially in terms of the several $g_\alpha^{(1)}$,

$$\rho_{el}(\mathbf{r}) = \sum_{\alpha=1}^{\eta} c_\alpha \xi_\alpha e g_\alpha^{(1)}(\mathbf{r}). \tag{6}$$

c_α is the bulk concentration of the αth species, and does not differ significantly from the reciprocal volume per α particle computed for the entire system volume v. This charge density ρ_{el} vanishes when $\mathbf{r}$ is within the bulk fluid; here, then, one has a bulk electroneutrality condition

$$\sum_{\alpha=1}^{\eta} c_\alpha \xi_\alpha = 0. \tag{7}$$

If our system includes the uniformly charged planar electrode giving rise to the potential (3), a second electroneutrality condition may be formulated. The average charge residing in the double layer must precisely neutralize the charge density σ

$$-\sigma = \int_l^u \rho_{el}(x)dx. \tag{8}$$

The limits of integration on x, the normal distance to the electrode, must span the region over which excess space charge attributable to the ionic fluid is sensibly different from zero. These limits will be, respectively, just within the electrode (l), and well inside the electrolyte bulk (u).

The distribution of charge both on the electrode and induced within the electrolyte as the diffuse double layer produces an average electric field. On account of the complete and exact shielding of the electrode charge, as illustrated by condition (8), this mean field will be nonzero only within the Gouy layer. By integration, the field defines an average potential $\psi(\mathbf{r})$ at a point $\mathbf{r}$ in the double layer relative to the bulk liquid. The value of $\psi(\mathbf{r})$ for the present situation (planar, uniformly charged electrode) will depend only on the coordinate x. Simple electrostatics suffices to provide the result

$$\psi(x) = (4\pi/D)\int_x^u (x - y)\rho_{el}(y)dy. \tag{9}$$

Once again the upper integration limit u on y must be sufficiently large that ρ_{el} is substantially zero. The value of ψ at the electrode surface defines the ζ potential.

The correlation function definitions (5) may be manipulated to yield finally a power series expansion of each $W^{(n)}$ in the charging parameter ξ_j for one of the set $1\cdots n$ (we shall choose ξ_1). In order to do so, first rewrite the total potential V_N in the form,

$$V_N(1\cdots N;\xi_1)$$

$$= \xi_1[V^{(1,e)}(1) + \sum_{j=2}^{n} \xi_j V^{(2,e)}(1j) + V_{1,N-n}{}^{(2,e)}] + V_N(1\cdots N;\xi_1 = 0),$$

$$V_{1,N-n}{}^{(2,e)} = \sum_{k=n+1}^{N} \xi_k V^{(2,e)}(1k), \tag{10}$$

which specifically emphasizes the dependence of this quantity on the charge of particle 1. If (10) is inserted in (5), the correlation functions may be transformed to

$$g_{\alpha\cdots\nu}{}^{(n)}(1\cdots n;\xi_1) = \exp\{-\beta W_{\alpha\cdots\nu}{}^{(n)}(1\cdots n;\xi_1 = 0)$$

$$-\beta\xi_1[V^{(1,e)}(1) + \sum_{j=2}^{n} \xi_j V^{(2,e)}(1j)]\}$$

$$\times \frac{\langle \exp\{-\beta\xi_1 V_{1,N-n}{}^{(2,e)}\}\rangle_{\xi_1=0}{}^{(n)}}{\langle \exp\{-\beta\xi_1[V^{(1,e)}(1) + V_{1,N-1}{}^{(2,e)}]\}\rangle_{\xi_1=0}{}^{(0)}}. \tag{11}$$

The angular brackets denote averages in a canonical ensemble in which particle 1 has been discharged (i.e., $\xi_1 = 0$),

$$\langle f\rangle_{\xi_1=0}{}^{(j)}$$

$$= \frac{\int_v\cdots\int_v f\exp[-\beta V_N(\xi_1 = 0)]dv_{j+1}\cdots dv_N}{\int_v\cdots\int_v \exp[-\beta V_N(\xi_1 = 0)]dv_{j+1}\cdots dv_N}. \tag{12}$$

The process of removing, as in Eq. (12), the electrostatic charge from a single ion in an electrolyte has no physically operational meaning. From the standpoint of the correlation functions $g^{(n)}$, it is often convenient to regard a discharged ion as corresponding qualitatively to a noble gas atom (isoelectronic with the original ion) dissolved in the electrolyte. Since a discharged ion can interact with the electrode and other ions only through the short-range functions $V^{(1,s)}(\mathbf{r}_1)$ and $V^{(2,s)}(r_{12})$, the correlation functions $g_\alpha{}^{(1)}(\mathbf{r}_1;\xi_1 = 0)$ and $g_{\alpha\beta}{}^{(2)}(\mathbf{r}_1, \mathbf{r}_2;\xi_1 = 0)$ can differ significantly from unity only when x_1 and r_{12} are small enough to bring these potentials into play. This behavior contrasts sharply with the correlations acting between fully charged ions, which extend over many molecular diameters on account of the long-range nature of electrostatic forces.

By taking logarithms in (11), and expanding the averaged exponential functions, the nth order potential of mean force becomes expressed as a contribution remaining when ion 1 is discharged, plus correction terms, which may be exhibited as the desired power series,

$$W_{\alpha\ldots\nu}{}^{(n)}(1\cdots n;\xi_1)$$

$$= W_{\alpha\ldots\nu}{}^{(n)}(1\cdots n;\xi_1=0)+\xi_1[V^{(1,e)}(1)+\sum_{j=2}^{n}\xi_j V^{(2,e)}(1j)]$$

$$-\beta^{-1}\log\left[\sum_{s=0}^{\infty}\frac{(-\beta\xi_1)^s}{s!}M_s\right]+\beta^{-1}\log\left[\sum_{s=1}^{\infty}\frac{(-\beta\xi_1)^s}{s!}\bar{M}_s\right]$$

$$= W_{\alpha\ldots\nu}{}^{(n)}(1\cdots n;\xi_1=0)+\xi_1[V^{(1,e)}(1)+\sum_{j=2}^{n}\xi_j V^{(2,e)}(1j)]$$

$$+\sum_{s=1}^{\infty}\frac{(-\beta)^{s-1}}{s!}[\Lambda_s(1\cdots n)-\bar{\Lambda}_s]\xi_1^s. \qquad (13)$$

M_s and $\bar{M}_s$ are moments of the electrostatic interactions involving particle 1

$$M_s = \langle[V_{1,N-n}{}^{(2,e)}]^s\rangle_{\xi_1=0}{}^{(n)},$$

$$\bar{M}_s = \langle[V_{1,N-1}{}^{(2,e)}+V^{(1,e)}(1)]^s\rangle_{\xi_1=0}{}^{(0)}, \qquad (14)$$

and are related to the cumulants Λ_s, $\bar{\Lambda}_s$ by the relations[10]

$$M_s=\sum_{r=1}^{s}\binom{s-1}{r-1}\Lambda_r M_{s-r},$$

$$\bar{M}_s=\sum_{r=1}^{s}\binom{s-1}{r-1}\bar{\Lambda}_r \bar{M}_{s-r},$$

$$M_0=\bar{M}_0=1. \qquad (15)$$

On solving for the cumulants, one easily finds:

$$\Lambda_1 = M_1,$$

$$\Lambda_2 = M_2-(M_1)^2,$$

$$\Lambda_3 = M_3-3M_2M_1+2(M_1)^3,$$

$$\Lambda_4 = M_4-4M_3M_1-3(M_2)^2+12M_2(M_1)^2-6(M_1)^4; \qquad (16)$$

precisely the same relations (16) hold for the barred quantities.

The power series (13) allows one, at least in principle, to compute each nth order potential of mean force in ascending orders of ionic charge. In practice, the integral equations arising in this task require knowledge of higher order W's, and so in this sense are coupled to each other in complicated fashion. The following section proposes a scheme for circumventing some of these difficulties.

---

[10] H. Cramér, *Mathematical Methods of Statistics* (Princeton University Press, Princeton, New Jersey, 1946), p. 185.

III. APPROXIMATE DOUBLE-LAYER IONIC DISTRIBUTIONS

Having outlined the general moment method for ionic correlations, we now proceed to apply these ideas specifically to the diffuse double layer region. The terms of increasing ξ_1 order in the complete expansion (13) rapidly become more and more complicated to evaluate, even for the single-particle distributions. We shall adopt the viewpoint, for the present, that retention of only those terms linear in ξ_1 will yield a sufficiently accurate description of the double layer.[11] In the interests of concreteness, furthermore, the electrolyte (chosen to be a single component salt solution) will be described as consisting of uniformly charged, spherically symmetric particles which are suspended in a dielectric continuum. The ions (anions and cations may have different short-range forces) can penetrate neither one another extensively on account of strong core repulsions, nor can they penetrate the planar electrode appreciably. The latter will act essentially as a rigid charged "wall", and for convenience the coordinate system may be chosen to locate it near $x = 0$.[12]

It is a fairly simple matter to include the molecular nature of the solvent medium in the following development if these latter particles interact with central forces. However, the results of this generalization differ only slightly from those to be obtained with the dielectric continuum, and hence do not seem to merit the extra notational complication. Attention, then, will be focused only on particles of ionic nature, and since we wish to consider only a single electrolyte, the relevant charge parameters ξ_1 can assume only two values, ξ_+ (cations) and ξ_- (anions).

In the linear ξ_1 approximation, the singlet potentials of mean force are written

$$W_\alpha^{(1)}(\mathbf{r}_1; \xi_1) = W_\alpha^{(1)}(\mathbf{r}_1; \xi_1 = 0) + \xi_1[V^{(1,e)}(x_1) + \langle V_{1,N-1}{}^{(2,e)}\rangle_{\xi_1=0}{}^{(1)} - \langle V_{1,N-1}{}^{(2,e)} + V^{(1,e)}(1)\rangle_{\xi_1=0}{}^{(0)}], \quad \alpha = +, -. \tag{17}$$

As anticipated earlier, the additive constant A has no effect on these expressions for the $W_\alpha^{(1)}$; it cancels in the combination

$$V^{(1,e)}(x_1) - \langle V^{(1,e)}(1)\rangle_{\xi_1=0}{}^{(0)}. \tag{18}$$

One may immediately make certain simplifying observations concerning relations (17). Because of the symmetry of our problem about the electrode normal direction, the singlet mean-force potentials $W_\alpha^{(1)}$ will depend only on the x_1 coordinate, as do $V^{(1,e)}$ and $V^{(1,s)}$. In addition, the second of the two average value quantities in (17) is just a constant, independent of $\mathbf{r}_1$. In view of the fact that the electrostatic potential $V^{(1,e)}$ is a simple linear function of x_1, a considerable reduction in complexity is achieved by performing a twofold x_1 differentiation on both members of (17)

$$d^2\phi_\alpha(x_1)/dx_1{}^2 = (D/2\pi e\sigma)(d^2/dx_1{}^2)\langle V_{1,N-1}{}^{(2,e)}\rangle_{\xi_1=0}{}^{(1)}. \tag{19}$$

[11] Reference to Eqs. (13) shows immediately that this approximation is equivalent to replacing the moments M_s and $\bar{M}_s$ by $(M_1)^s$ and $(\bar{M}_1)^s$.

[12] The exact position of the electrode is not critical; we wish only to imply here that for x decreasing through zero, the short-range electrode potential $V^{(1,s)}(x)$ becomes rapidly very large (strong repulsion).

ϕ_α is a reduced electrostatic single-particle average potential for the species α,

$$W_\alpha^{(1)}(x_1; \xi_1) - W_\alpha^{(1)}(x_1; 0) = (2\pi e\sigma\xi_\alpha/D)\phi_\alpha(x_1). \tag{20}$$

The quantities ϕ_α therefore carry the long-range electrostatic correlation of the diffuse double layer.

By utilizing the definitions (5), the averaged potential remaining in Eq. (19) may be expressed in terms of the singlet and pair correlation functions for the discharged particle 1

$$\frac{d^2\phi_\alpha(x_1)}{dx_1^2} = \frac{e}{2\pi\sigma}\frac{d^2}{dx_1^2}\int_v \frac{d\mathbf{r}_2}{r_{12}}\left[c_+\xi_+\frac{g_{\alpha+}^{(2)}(\mathbf{r}_1, \mathbf{r}_2; 0)}{g_\alpha^{(1)}(x_1; 0)} + c_-\xi_-\frac{g_{\alpha-}^{(2)}(\mathbf{r}_1, \mathbf{r}_2; 0)}{g_\alpha^{(1)}(x_1; 0)}\right]. \tag{21}$$

The integration in this last expression is over all configurations $\mathbf{r}_2$ of a second ion inside the containing volume v.

When x_1 is sufficiently large, the $g_\alpha^{(1)}(\mathbf{r}_1; 0)$ do not differ sensibly from unity, and the pair correlations $g_{\alpha\beta}^{(2)}(\mathbf{r}_1, \mathbf{r}_2; 0)$ may be replaced by the product of a bulk pair correlation, and the long-range singlet correlation for charged ion 2,

$$g_{\alpha\beta}^{(2)}(\mathbf{r}_1, \mathbf{r}_2; 0) \to g_{\alpha\beta}^{(2,b)}(r_{12}; 0)g_\beta^{(1)}(x_2). \tag{22}$$

This replacement is the analog, for the double-layer theory, of the superposition approximation used extensively in the molecular theory of bulk liquids. For the present purposes, it should be noted we find it necessary to use (22) only for large x_1, rather than over the entire range of values for this variable.

In view of the reduction (22), one is led to the integrodifferential equation, valid if x_1 is not too small,

$$d^2\phi_\alpha(x_1)/dx_1^2 = (e/2\pi\sigma)[d^2I(x_1)/dx_1^2],$$

$$I(x_1) = \int_v (d\mathbf{r}_2/r_{12})[c_+\xi_+g_{\alpha+}^{(2,b)}(r_{12}; 0)g_+^{(1)}(x_2) + c_-\xi_-g_{\alpha-}^{(2,b)}(r_{12}; 0)g_-^{(1)}(x_2)]. \tag{23}$$

Three contributions to $I(x_1)$ may be distinguished:

$$I(x_1) = I_1(x_1) + I_2(x_1) + I_3(x_1),$$

$$I_1(x_1) = \int_v (d\mathbf{r}_2/r_{12})\{c_+\xi_+g_{\alpha+}^{(2,b)}(r_{12}; 0) \times [g_+^{(1)}(x_2) - 1 + (2\pi\sigma e\xi_+/DkT)\phi_+(x_2)] + c_-\xi_-g_{\alpha-}^{(2,b)}(r_{12}; 0) \times [g_-^{(1)}(x_2) - 1 + (2\pi\sigma e\xi_-/DkT)\phi_-(x_2)]\},$$

$$I_2(x_1) = \int_v (d\mathbf{r}_2/r_{12})[c_+\xi_+g_{\alpha+}^{(2,b)}(r_{12}; 0) + c_-\xi_-g_{\alpha-}^{(2,b)}(r_{12}; 0)],$$

$$I_3(x_1) = -(2\pi\sigma e/DkT)\int_v (d\mathbf{r}_2/r_{12}) \times [c_+\xi_+^2g_{\alpha+}^{(2,b)}(r_{12}; 0)\phi_+(x_2) + c_-\xi_-^2g_{\alpha-}^{(2,b)}(r_{12}; 0)\phi_-(x_2)]. \tag{24}$$

The square-bracketed quantities in I_1 represent the nonlinear (in the ϕ_α)

portions of the singlet correlations in the double layer, as well as the non-electrostatic ($\xi_2 = 0$) correlation; these differ significantly from zero only in the immediate vicinity of the electrode. When x_1 is large, therefore, the only contribution to the integral I_1 occurs when r_{12} is large, so that each $g_{\alpha\beta}{}^{(2,b)}(r_{12}; 0)$ is essentially just unity. As a result, then, $I_1(x_1)$ represents (for x_1 large) the potential energy of a uniform and somewhat diffuse sheet of charge density $\rho^*(\mathbf{r}_2)$,

$$\rho^*(\mathbf{r}_2) = c_+\xi_+[g_+{}^{(1)}(x_2) - 1 + (2\pi\sigma e\xi_+/DkT)\phi_+(x_2)] + c_-\xi_-[g_-{}^{(1)}(x_2) - 1 + (2\pi\sigma e\xi_-/DkT)\phi_-(x_2)]. \quad (25)$$

This amounts to concluding that $I_1(x_1)$ is asymptotically a linear function of x_1 similar to (3).

Since the pair correlations $g_{\alpha\beta}{}^{(2,b)}(r_{12}; 0)$ settle down rapidly to unity, the integrand of $I_2(x_1)$ differs from zero only when particle 2 is near 1. As a result, again valid for large x_1, the $\mathbf{r}_2$ integration may be extended over all space. It is established therefore that $I_2(x_1)$ is asymptotically constant.

On account of the double x_1 differentiation in Eq. (23), only $I_3(x_1)$ will survive in the large x_1 limit. After performing the requisite differentiations, and carrying out integrations parallel to the electrode surface, the ϕ_α are found asymptotically to satisfy linear homogeneous integrodifferential equations

$$d^2\phi_\alpha(x_1)/dx_1{}^2 = \tfrac{1}{2}\int_0^\infty [\kappa_+{}^2 k_{\alpha+}(x_1 - x_2)\phi_+(x_2) + \kappa_-{}^2 k_{\alpha-}(x_1 - x_2)\phi_-(x_2)]$$

$$k_{\alpha\beta}(x_1 - x_2) = (d/dx_1)g_{\alpha\beta}{}^{(2,b)}(x_1 - x_2; 0),$$

$$\kappa_\alpha{}^2 = 4\pi c_\alpha(\xi_\alpha e)^2/DkT. \quad (26)$$

In the large x_1 region, (26) is entirely independent of the lower x_2 integration limit, since the $k_{\alpha\beta}$ decay rapidly to zero. The origin has been chosen as this lower limit, since it has been made roughly to coincide with the electrode surface. The pair correlation functions $g_{\alpha\beta}{}^{(2,b)}$ have been defined in (26) as odd functions of their distance variable, so that the kernels $k_{\alpha\beta}$ are even. The well-known Debye-Hückel parameter κ, appropriate to our electrolytic fluid, is related to κ_+ and κ_- by

$$\kappa^2 = \kappa_+{}^2 + \kappa_-{}^2. \quad (27)$$

Since Eqs. (26) were derived under the supposition that x_1 was not small, the ϕ_α can be given exactly over the entire range $0 \leq x_1 < \infty$ by adding suitable inhomogeneous functions h_α to (26),

$$d^2\phi_\alpha(x_1)/dx_1{}^2 = h_\alpha(x_1) + \tfrac{1}{2}\int_0^\infty [\kappa_+{}^2 k_{\alpha+}(x_1 - x_2)\phi_+(x_2) + \kappa_-{}^2 k_{\alpha-}(x_1 - x_2)\phi_-(x_2)]dx_2. \quad (28)$$

The h_α are essentially designed to correct for the fact that the local density of β ions, in the environment of a discharged α ion at $\mathbf{r}_1$ near the electrode, is not precisely given by the expression

$$c_\beta g_{\alpha\beta}{}^{(2,b)}(r_{12}; 0)[1 - (2\pi\sigma e\xi_\beta/DkT)\phi_\beta(x_2)]. \quad (29)$$

It is of course necessary only that each h_α differ from zero near $x_1 = 0$, since outside this small region (26) and (28) are identical. These inhomogeneous functions contain contributions arising through short-range force electrode interface correlations, through deviations from superposability of the actual pair function $g_{\alpha\beta}^{(2)}$ near the electrode [in terms of the approximation $g_{\alpha\beta}^{(2,b)}(r_{12})g_\alpha^{(1)}(x_1)g_\beta^{(1)}(x_2)$], and finally through the nonlinear ϕ_α terms neglected in the integral $I_1(x_1)$.

It is rather instructive to examine the form of Eqs. (28) under a simplifying assumption regarding the bulk correlations $g_{\alpha\beta}^{(2,b)}(r_{12};\, 0)$. In particular, suppose that each pair of ions, one of which is discharged, will be correlated only to the extent of exhibiting a sphere of exclusion, or impenetrability, of radius a (the same for all pairs). Accordingly,

$$\begin{aligned} g_{\alpha\beta}^{(2,b)}(r_{12};\, 0) &= 0 \qquad 0 \leq r_{12} \leq a, \\ &= 1 \qquad r_{12} > a. \end{aligned} \tag{30}$$

Since the derivative of this unit step is a Dirac delta action, the kernels all have the common form

$$k_{\alpha\beta}(x) - \delta(x + a) + \delta(x - a). \tag{31}$$

Now when $x_1 > a$, the integral in (28) is trivial, and leads to a differential-difference equation satisfied by ϕ_α,

$$\begin{aligned} \phi_\alpha(x_1)/dx_1^2 = h_\alpha(x_1) + \tfrac{1}{2}\{\kappa_+^2[\phi_+(x_1 + a) + \phi_+(x_1 - a)] \\ + \kappa_-^2[\phi_-(x_1 + a) + \phi_-(x_1 - a)]\}. \end{aligned} \tag{32}$$

If the ionic diameter a is allowed now to vanish, ϕ_+ and ϕ_- satisfy the same second-order differential equation for x_1 sufficiently large. Since the difference $\phi_+ - \phi_-$ tends to zero as x_1 increases, both ϕ_+ and ϕ_- must asymptotically be equal to $\exp(-\kappa x_1)$ times a common constant. These rather naive assumptions therefore lead to the exponential decay solutions characteristic of the Poisson-Boltzmann theory. It will become apparent in the following section that retention of a finite ion size, even by means of the rather crude postulate (30), gives rise to solutions ϕ_α, and hence singlet correlations, which are qualitatively different from this monotonic decay function.

The pair of linear coupled Eqs. (28) may be formally solved by standard integral transform methods. It is desirable for this purpose to extend the definition of $\phi_\alpha(x_1)$ to negative x_1, as the solution of (28) for these values of the variable; we set $h_\alpha(x_1)$ identically equal to zero on the negative axis. The functions $\phi_\alpha(x_1)$ may now be separated into two parts, $\phi_\alpha^{(n)}(x_1)$ and $\phi_\alpha^{(p)}(x_1)$, which are the negative axis, and positive axis parts of ϕ_α, respectively,

$$\begin{aligned} \phi_\alpha(x_1) &= \phi_\alpha^{(n)}(x_1) + \phi_\alpha^{(p)}(x_1), \\ \phi_\alpha^{(p)}(x_1) &= 0 \qquad x_1 < 0, \\ \phi_\alpha^{(n)}(x_1) &= 0 \qquad x_1 > 0. \end{aligned} \tag{33}$$

As a consequence, (28) is equivalent to

$$\begin{aligned} &(d^2/dx_1^2)[\phi_\alpha^{(n)}(x_1) + \phi_\alpha^{(p)}(x_1)] \\ &= h_\alpha(x_1) + \tfrac{1}{2}\int_{-\infty}^{+\infty} [\kappa_+^2 k_{\alpha+}(x_1 - x_2)\phi_+^{(p)}(x_2) \\ &\qquad + \kappa_-^2 k_{\alpha-}(x_1 - x_2)\phi_-^{(p)}(x_2)]\,dx_2. \end{aligned} \tag{34}$$

In Fourier transform space, the integral equations (34) become a pair of simultaneous linear algebraic equations whose solution is elementary:

$$\Phi_+^{(p)}(z) = 1/D(z)\begin{vmatrix} -H_+(z) - z^2\Phi_+^{(n)}(z) & \tfrac{1}{2}\kappa_-^2 K_{+-}(z) \\ -H_-(z) - z^2\Phi_-^{(n)}(z) & z^2 + \tfrac{1}{2}\kappa_-^2 K_{--}(z) \end{vmatrix},$$

$$\Phi_-^{(p)}(z) = 1/D(z)\begin{vmatrix} z^2 + \tfrac{1}{2}\kappa_+^2 K_{++}(z) & -H_+(z) - z^2\Phi_+^{(n)}(z) \\ \tfrac{1}{2}\kappa_+^2 K_{-+}(z) & -H_-(z) - z^2\Phi_-^{(n)}(z) \end{vmatrix}; \qquad (35)$$

$$D(z) = \begin{vmatrix} z^2 + \tfrac{1}{2}\kappa_+^2 K_{++}(z) & \tfrac{1}{2}\kappa_-^2 K_{+-}(z) \\ \tfrac{1}{2}\kappa_+^2 K_{-+}(z) & z^2 + \tfrac{1}{2}\kappa_-^2 K_{--}(z) \end{vmatrix}; \qquad (36)$$

$$[\Phi_\alpha^{(\mu)}(z), H_\alpha(z), K_{\alpha\beta}(z)] = \int_{-\infty}^{+\infty} \exp(izx)[\phi_\alpha^{(\mu)}(x), h_\alpha(x), k_{\alpha\beta}(x)]dx,$$

$$\alpha, \beta = +, -, \qquad \mu = n, p.$$

The inversion integrals are

$$\phi_\alpha^{(p)}(x_1) = (1/2\pi)\int_{-\infty}^{+\infty} \exp(-ix_1 z)\Phi_\alpha^{(p)}(z)dz, \qquad (37)$$

where the results (35) are to be inserted for $\Phi_\alpha^{(p)}(z)$. The contour of integration for (37), when x_1 is positive, may be closed along the infinite, lower half-plane semicircle; subsequently, $\phi_\alpha(x_1)$ may be evaluated in terms of the poles z_j of the transform $\Phi_\alpha^{(p)}(z)$, lying below the real axis

$$\phi_\alpha(x_1) = \sum_{j=1}^{\infty} A_{j,\alpha} \exp(-iz_j x_1). \qquad (38)$$

The multiplicative constants $A_{j,\alpha}$ are related in the usual way to the residues at these poles

$$A_{j,\alpha} = i \lim_{z \to z_j} [(z - z_j)\Phi_\alpha^{(p)}(z)]. \qquad (39)$$

These constants must naturally be such to make ϕ_+ and ϕ_- real functions of the real variable x_1.

Computation of the $A_{j,\alpha}$ by (39) clearly requires knowledge of $\Phi_\alpha^{(n)}(z)$. This transform must have the property of making the inversion integral (37) vanish identically for every negative x_1. In practical cases, this condition may be met in either of two ways. If only a finite number m of terms in the entire series (38) would suffice to provide an adequate description of the double layer structure, each of the two integrals (37) could be equated to zero for m

distinct negative values of x_1, to provide a sufficient number of conditions for unique determination of the coefficients. Alternatively, (37) may be cast in the role of a pair of coupled integral equations on the negative axis for complete determination of the $\phi_\alpha^{(n)}(x_1)$; these solutions in turn would provide the entire set of $A_{j,\alpha}$ through (35) and (39).[13]

It should be remarked that the poles z_j may in general arise either as roots of the denominator $D(z)$, or as poles of the $K_{\alpha\beta}(z)$ or $H_\alpha(z)$ occurring in the determinental numerators of (35). Since $\phi_\alpha^{(n)}(x_1)$ decays rapidly to zero with decreasing x_1 on the negative axis, the transforms $\Phi_\alpha^{(n)}(z)$ cannot have poles in the lower-half z plane; therefore, these two functions are effective only in determining the exact values of the multiplicative constants $A_{j,\alpha}$, rather than in providing z_j's for the solution (38). Furthermore, it should be noted at this juncture that since the $h_\alpha(x_1)$ decay rapidly to zero on the positive axis, the set of z_j contributed as poles of the $H_\alpha(z)$ lie well below the real axis; the corresponding terms in $\phi_\alpha(x_1)$ therefore themselves decay very rapidly with increasing x_1.

If all of the kernels $k_{\alpha\beta}(x_1)$ as well as the inhomogeneous functions $h_\alpha(x_1)$ were zero for all x_1 greater than some fixed positive constant, then the transforms $K_{\alpha\beta}$ and H_α would be analytic in the entire z plane. As a result, each z_j would necessarily be a root,

$$D(z_j) = 0. \tag{40}$$

The series expressions (38) for ϕ_+ and ϕ_- under these circumstances would differ only insofar as the exact numerical values of the coefficients $A_{j,\alpha}$ are concerned, since the same exponential functions must appear for both anions and cations.

IV. SIMPLIFIED RIGID-SPHERE MODEL

To clarify the way in which the formalism of the preceding sections leads to predictions concerning the detailed nature of the double layer, we are now in a position to deduce the properties of a simple, though informative, model. We choose to investigate that system of equal-sized rigid spherical ions which led to the differential-difference Eqs. (32). For the sake of simplicity also, we shall wish to disregard the effect of the inhomogeneous functions $h_\alpha(x_1)$; it has already been noted in this connection that such an assumption can have no effect on the asymptotic (large x_1) equations determining the ionic distributions. The nonelectrostatic effect of the planar electrode may be taken as that of a completely impenetrable "wall". By locating the surface of this wall at $x_1 = -a/2$ (a distance from the origin equal to the ion radii), the single particle potentials $V_\alpha^{(1,s)}$ are just

$$\begin{aligned} V_\alpha^{(1,s)}(x_1) &= +\infty \qquad x_1 \leq 0, \\ &= 0 \qquad x_1 > 0. \end{aligned} \tag{41}$$

On account of the pair correlations (30) being identical for any species pair, we have already emphasized that the kernels $k_{\alpha\beta}$ are identical, as indicated by Eq. (31). As a result of the foregoing idealizations, one has to deal with only

[13] The use of these integral equations actually corresponds to allowing m to increase to infinity.

a single homogeneous integro-differential equation,

$$d^2\phi(x_1)/dx_1{}^2 = \tfrac{1}{2}\kappa^2\int_0^\infty k(x_1 - x_2)\phi(x_2)dx_2,$$

$$\phi_+(x_1) = \phi_-(x_1) = \phi(x_1), \qquad k_{\alpha\beta}(x) = k(x). \tag{42}$$

The unpretentious double-layer picture described by the solution of (42) is probably a reasonable approximation to the actual physical state of affairs if the density of ion spheres is not too near the close-packed density; i.e.,

$$c_+ + c_- \ll 2^{\frac{1}{2}}a^{-3}. \tag{43}$$

The inversion integral for the solution to (42) may now be written down with the help of Eqs. (35)–(37)

$$\phi(x_1) = -(1/2\pi)\int_{-\infty}^{+\infty}\frac{z^2\exp(-\,ix_1z)\Phi^{(n)}(z)}{z^2 + \kappa^2\cos(az)}\,dz \quad (x_1 > 0)$$

$$= \sum_{j=1}^{\infty} A_j \exp(-\,iz_jx). \tag{44}$$

In accordance with previous remarks, the z_j are precisely the roots of the transcendental equation

$$z^2 + \kappa^2\cos(az) = 0. \tag{45}$$

Consequently, the constants A_j may be displayed as

$$A_j = -\frac{iz_j{}^2\Phi^{(n)}(z_j)}{2z_j - \kappa^2 a\sin(az_j)}\,\cdot \tag{46}$$

For small values of the dimensionless parameter κa, the transcendental Eq. (45) has two roots $\pm\, z_1$, which may be expanded about $\kappa a = 0$

$$y_j = iaz_j,$$

$$y_1 = \kappa a[1 + \tfrac{1}{4}(\kappa a)^2 + \tfrac{11}{96}(\kappa a)^4 + \tfrac{25}{192}(\kappa a)^6 + \cdots]. \tag{47}$$

The leading term in the series (44) corresponding to the root $+\, z_1$ produces a $\phi(x_1)$ of the form

$$\phi(x_1) \sim \exp(-\,\kappa x_1) \tag{48}$$

in the limit of zero electrolyte concentration. It is in this manner that the predictions of the linear Poisson-Boltzmann equation of the Debye-Hückel electrolyte theory are verified, even for finite ion sizes. It is possible to show that this result is in no way dependent upon the special form of the short-range ion-ion forces chosen for our simple model.

There is a second pair of pure imaginary roots $\pm\, z_2$ which, again for κa sufficiently small, may be represented by an asymptotic series

$$y_2 = \log[2/(\kappa a)^2] + 2\log\log[2/(\kappa a)^2] + \cdots. \tag{49}$$

It is evident that in dilute solutions, the z_2 contribution to $\phi(x_1)$ damps to zero extremely fast.

The remaining roots of (45) in the small κa region are all complex, and occur in quadruples

$$y_j = \pm\, \alpha_j \pm i\beta_j. \tag{50}$$

Numerical analysis shows that as κa increases from zero, the roots z_1 and z_2 move toward each other on the negative imaginary axis. They finally merge at $\kappa a = 1.03$, and thereupon move away from the imaginary axis as complex conjugates. The values of the roots nearest the origin $z = 0$ are exhibited in Table I for selected values of κa.

Even if only the first two terms in the complete sum (44) corresponding to z_1 and z_2 are retained as an approximation to the actual statistical state, it is clear that the ion size, or excluded volume, is capable of exerting a profound influence upon the charge density in the double layer. Although for small κa, in this two-term approximation, ϕ is a sum of damped exponentials,

$$\phi(x_1) = A_1 \exp[-\, y_1(x_1/a)] + A_2 \exp[-\, y_2(x_1/a)], \tag{51}$$

this sum becomes a damped sinusoid when $\kappa a > 1.03$, and y_1 and y_2 are complex conjugates. On account of the resultant sign changes in ϕ, the average double-layer charge density likewise alternates in sign. This behavior denotes, in an average sense, that planar layers of anions and cations are held against, and parallel to, the electrode surface. This local structure is somewhat similar to the situation in ionic crystals where also alternate planes of positive and negative ions are encountered.

A detailed study of even the two roots z_1 and z_2 alone therefore provides insight into the transition from very dilute solutions, where the distribution of ions may be deduced from consideration of electrostatic forces alone, to concentrated solutions in which short-range forces are important. These latter begin to cause interference between the ions at moderate density, and to relieve this situation, the ions must begin to settle into locally ordered arrangements, the extreme case of which would be the long-range regularity of the ionic crystal. Only for very low electrolyte concentrations, therefore, is it reasonable to neglect exclusion volumes in deducing double layer structures.

The special kernel (31) gives the functional Eq. (42) for $\phi(x_1)$ three distinct forms in three different intervals

$$\begin{aligned} d^2\phi(x_1)/dx_1^2 &= 0 && x_1 < -\, a, \\ &= \tfrac{1}{2}\kappa^2\phi(x_1 + a) && -a < x_1 < a, \\ &= \tfrac{1}{2}\kappa^2[\phi(x_1 - a) + \phi(x_1 + a)] && x_1 > a. \end{aligned} \tag{52}$$

In the first of these intervals, ϕ obviously must be the linear function

$$\phi(x_1) = B_1 x_1 + B_0 \qquad x_1 < -\, a, \tag{53}$$

with the constants B_1 and B_0 having values to provide a smooth fit onto $\phi(x_1)$ for $x_1 > -a$. Repeated use of (52) shows that ϕ has simple discontinuities in its second derivative at $-a$ and $+a$, in its fourth derivative at 0 and $2a$, and in the $2n$th derivative ($n > 2$) at na. This series of discontinuities propagated down the x_1 axis arises solely by use of singular short-range ion interactions, and has no fundamental physical basis. It is of course possible to eliminate them by using differentiable functions $V_\alpha^{(1,s)}$ and $V_\alpha^{(2,s)}$.

A single restriction to which the constants A_j must conform is provided by the double layer electronentrality condition (8). One might attempt further to determine the A_j for the present model by substitution into the integrodifferential equation (42), or equivalently, into the relations (52). When $x_1 > a$, no information is provided since each member of the sum (44) separately satisfies the condition imposed. However, the set of admissible values A_j is restricted by insisting that (44) satisfy (42) or (52) in the interval $-a < x_1 < a$. Demanding that $\phi(x_1)$ be a solution for this entire finite interval provides sufficient constraint to fix all the A_j. This finite interval procedure has a distinct advantage over the more general integral equation subsidiary problem of Sec. III, in which case the function $\phi_\alpha^{(n)}$ would have to be determined over the entire negative axis, $x_1 < 0$.[14]

TABLE I. Roots of the transcendental equation $y^2 - (\kappa a)^2 \cosh y = 0$ near $y = 0$ in the complex plane; $y_j = \alpha_j + i\beta_j$.

κa	α_1	β_1	α_2	β_2	α_3, α_4	$\beta_3, -\beta_4$
0.100	0.100	0	9.88	0	11.11	14.42
0.500	0.536	0	5.48	0	7.70	14.75
0.900	1.22	0	3.28	0	6.48	14.89
1.00	1.62	0	2.56	0	6.26	14.90
1.03	2.07	0	2.07	0	6.19	14.91
1.06	2.03	0.45	2.03	−0.45	6.14	14.93
1.15	1.92	0.89	1.92	−0.89	5.97	14.95
1.50	1.53	1.62	1.53	−1.62	5.43	15.02
2.00	1.06	2.08	1.06	−2.08	4.84	15.07

For the purposes of numerical computation, the two term representation (51) of $\phi(x_1)$ discussed previously, will suffice. Since the terms to be neglected correspond to z_j's with large negative imaginary parts, the predicted ion distributions will be in error only very near the electrode.

If the electrode surface charge is not too large, the double-layer electroneutrality condition adapted to the present example may be linearized with respect to ϕ to yield

$$2/\kappa^2 = \int_0^\infty \phi(x_1)dx_1. \tag{54}$$

The corresponding linearized result for the ζ potential, as expressed in (9) for $x = 0$, becomes

$$\zeta(\sigma) = (2\pi\kappa^2\sigma/D) \int_0^\infty x_1\phi(x_1)dx_1. \tag{55}$$

The second condition on A_1 and A_2 in (51) to be utilized simultaneously with condition (54) results from the demand that the second of Eqs. (52) be satisfied at $x_1 = 0$,

$$d^2\phi(x_1 = 0)/dx_1^2 = \tfrac{1}{2}\kappa^2\phi(x_1 = a); \tag{56}$$

[14] Such simplification was inherent in the rigid-sphere model by using step-function pair correlations.

this is precisely the center of the interval over which the second form in (52) is valid.

When the two term approximation (51) is inserted in each of (54) and (56), there is obtained a pair of independent linear equations in A_1 and A_2. One thus readily finds

$$A_1 = [2a/(\kappa a)^2]y_1y_2\left[\frac{\exp y_2}{y_2 \exp y_2 - y_1 \exp y_1}\right],$$

$$A_2 = [2a/(\kappa a)^2]y_1y_2\left[-\frac{\exp y_1}{y_2 \exp y_2 - y_1 \exp y_1}\right]. \tag{57}$$

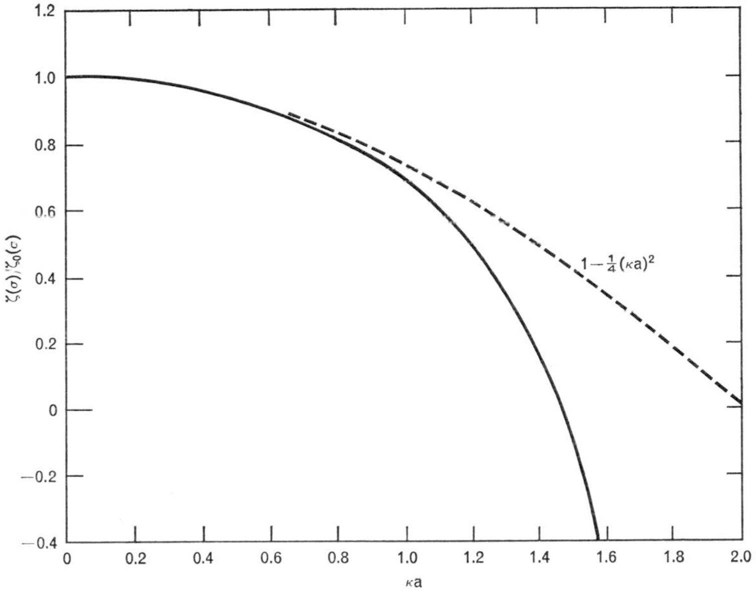

FIG. 1. Computed values of the ζ potential ratio (solid line), with the limiting parabolic behavior (dotted line) shown explicitly.

The results (57) reduce to

$$A_1 = 2/\kappa, \qquad A_2 = 0, \tag{58}$$

as κa approaches zero, to yield the correct Debye-Hückel result anticipated earlier:

$$\phi_0(x_1) = (2/\kappa)\exp(-\kappa x_1). \tag{59}$$

The ζ potential predicted on the basis of (59) follows from (55)

$$\zeta_0(\sigma) = 4\pi\sigma/\kappa D, \tag{60}$$

a well-known result.

The ζ potential for finite κa may be exhibited in the following reduced form:

$$\zeta(\sigma)/\zeta_0(\sigma) = (\kappa a/y_1)\left[\frac{1 - (y_1/y_2)^2 \exp(y_1 - y_2)}{1 - (y_1/y_2)\exp(y_1 - y_2)}\right]. \tag{61}$$

Reference to the asymptotes (47) and (49) for y_1 and y_2 show that the lowest order deviation (in κa) from ζ_0 is in the direction of decreasing ζ potential. In particular,

$$\zeta(\sigma)/\zeta_0(\sigma) = 1 - \tfrac{1}{4}(\kappa a)^2, \qquad \kappa a \ll 1. \tag{62}$$

As noted earlier, y_1 and y_2 have a common value when $\kappa a = 1.03$. At this point, both A_1 and A_2 diverge, but ϕ in fact remains finite

$$\phi(x_1) = (c_1 x_1 + c_0) \exp[-y_1(x_1/a)], \qquad \kappa a = 1.03. \tag{63}$$

Likewise, the ζ potential ratio as written in (61) is indeterminate, but may be properly evaluated as a limiting value as κa approaches 1.03 from either side.

When $\kappa a > 1.03$, the complex conjugates $y_1 = \alpha + i\beta$ and $y_2 = \alpha - i\beta$ yield the ratio,

$$\zeta(\sigma)/\zeta_0(\sigma) = \kappa a/(\alpha^2 + \beta^2)\left[\frac{(\alpha^2 - \beta^2)\sin\beta + 2\alpha\beta\cos\beta}{\alpha\sin\beta + \beta\cos\beta}\right]. \tag{64}$$

The ζ potential ratio has been computed on the basis of Eqs. (61) and (64) using the tabulated y_1 and y_2 values. The results are shown in Fig. 1. The low κa behavior is a parabolic decrease from unity in accord with (62). The ratio then decreases at an even more rapid rate, finally changing sign near $\kappa a =$ 1.46.[15] Since ζ_0 is always positive, therefore, we find that at a certain finite concentration, the ζ potential due to the diffuse Guoy layer (and, therefore, the Gouy layer reciprocal capacitance) becomes precisely zero. It is of interest to observe in addition that there is no break in the ζ potential curve at the singular value $\kappa a = 1.03$, although the nature of the mean charge density, ρ_{el}, changes rapidly there.

[15] In water, at room temperature, this corresponds to about 0.8 moles/liter for a univalent electrolyte with a equal to 5×10^{-8} cm.